FIFTH EDITION

The Skills of Helping Individuals, Families, Groups, and Communities

LAWRENCE SHULMAN

University at Buffalo
The State University of New York

THOMSON

BROOKS/COLE

Australia • Canada • Mexico • Singapore
Spain • United Kingdom • United States

THOMSON

BROOKS/COLE

*The Skills of Helping Individuals, Families,
Groups, and Communities,* Fifth Edition
Lawrence Shulman

Executive Editor: Lisa Gebo
Development Editor: Julie Martinez
Assistant Editor: Alma Dea Michelena
Editorial Assistant: Sheila Walsh
Technology Project Manager: Barry Connolly
Senior Marketing Manager: Caroline Concilla
Marketing Assistant: Rebecca Weisman
Marketing Communications Manager: Tami Strang
Project Manager, Editorial Production: Candace Chen
Art Director: Vernon Boes

Print Buyer: Karen Hunt
Permissions Editor: Sarah Harkrader
Production Service: Melanie Field, Strawberry Field
 Publishing
Text Designer: Carolyn Deacy
Copy Editor: Molly Roth
Cover Designer: Paula Goldstein
Cover Image: © Tracy Walker/i2iart.com
Cover/Text Printer: Thomson West
Compositor: Interactive Composition Corporation

For more information about our products, contact us at:
Thomson Learning Academic Resource Center
1-800-423-0563
For permission to use material from this text or product,
submit a request online at
http://www.thomsonrights.com.
Any additional questions about permissions can be
submitted by email to **thomsonrights@thomson.com.**

Library of Congress Control Number: 2005922208

Student Edition: ISBN 0-534-51413-8

Thomson Higher Education
10 Davis Drive
Belmont, CA 94002-3098
USA

Asia (including India)
Thomson Learning
5 Shenton Way
#01-01 UIC Building
Singapore 068808

Australia/New Zealand
Thomson Learning Australia
102 Dodds Street
Southbank, Victoria 3006
Australia

Canada
Thomson Nelson
1120 Birchmount Road
Toronto, Ontario M1K 5G4
Canada

UK/Europe/Middle East/Africa
Thomson Learning
High Holborn House
50/51 Bedford Row
London WC1R 4LR
United Kingdom

Latin America
Thomson Learning
Seneca, 53
Colonia Polanco
11560 Mexico
D.F. Mexico

Spain (including Portugal)
Thomson Paraninfo
Calle Magallanes, 25
28015 Madrid, Spain

To my wife, Sheila, with love

Brief Contents

Contents

CHAPTER 4

Skills in the Work Phase 113

CHAPTER 5

Endings and Transitions 178

Preface

This book is designed to be used in a first-year introductory course on social work practice. The focus is on method—what social workers do as their part of the helping process. I believe that the dynamics of giving and taking help are not mysterious processes that defy efforts at explanation. Helping skills can be defined, illustrated, and taught. The helping process is complex; it must be presented clearly and broken down into manageable segments. Theories and simple models need to be developed to provide tools for understanding.

The book is built on the assumption that we can identify an underlying process in all social work helping relationships. This process and its associated set of core skills can be observed whenever one person attempts to help another. These are the constant elements of the helping process. Elements of the process may vary according to the setting for the engagement (such as school, hospital, welfare agency), the age and stage of life of the client, the particular life problems the client brings to the encounter, and whether the client is participating voluntarily or involuntarily. The social worker will also introduce variant elements to the process related to factors such as education and experience, life events, and effectiveness of the support available to the worker.

In spite of the varying aspects of practice, when we examine interactions closely, the similar aspects become apparent. This book addresses a range of helping situations in the belief that each social worker can incorporate the models into his or her own work context. In addition, findings drawn from my studies of social work practice, supervision, management and medical practice, as well as the research of others, provide empirical support for the importance of the core skills that make up the constant elements of practice. The book reviews "evidenced-based" practice models, when available, but also draws on practice wisdom that is still waiting for research support.

An additional assumption in this text is the existence of common elements in work with individuals, families, groups, communities, and significant others in the systems (teachers, doctors, other social workers). A range of encounters illustrates the skill model developed in this book. The core processes and skills identified in the chapters on work with individuals reappear as the focus shifts to work with families, groups, communities, and organizational systems. For example, the contracting skills discussed in the beginning phase of work with individuals are also applied in first group sessions, family meetings, and community organizing efforts. In addition, the unique dynamics of, for example, first sessions with groups illustrate the variant elements.

In a like manner, the book presents common elements of beginning work with different populations, such as children, people with AIDS, survivors of sexual abuse, psychiatric patients, residential living groups, and community action groups. Unique aspects introduced by the setting and the purpose of the work are also considered.

This book represents an effort to conceptualize and illustrate a generalist practice model without losing the detail of the specific ways social workers practice. The term *generalist* has been used in different ways over the years, sometimes referring to practice models so abstract that one can hardly find the social worker or client in the description. The focus here is not just on what is common about what we know, value, and aspire to, nor on our common models for describing clients (as in systems theory), but rather on the common elements and skills of the helping person in action.

Another underlying assumption of this book is that social workers need to be prepared to offer clients service in the modality (individual, group, family, community) most suitable to the client, rather than the one most comfortable for the worker.

What's New in This Edition

Readers familiar with the fourth edition of this book will immediately notice a major difference: Although there is a good deal of new and updated material, the book has been streamlined. The first edition, published in 1969, focused on working with individuals and groups and was 369 printed pages. Later editions added sections on work with families and communities; with other additional content, the fourth edition reached over 800 pages. Detailed surveys of users by the new publisher, Wadsworth, indicated that for most courses it would be more useful if shortened. The change to Wadsworth with its extensive online web support for textbooks provided a way of reducing the book's size while still making much of the former content available to the reader. For example, links to two different codes of ethics are now available online.

Readers have always noted that one of the strengths of the book lies in its many detailed examples of process recordings illustrating social workers in action. These directly connect the theory and research to the realities of working with clients. I have made a systematic effort to update the examples and illustrations used in this edition. The fourth edition was published in 1999. Since that time social workers have deepened their understanding and skill in many emerging practice areas. The AIDS epidemic, homelessness, problems of addiction to crack cocaine and other substances, and sexual violence remain at the forefront of practice. Work in each of these areas has also changed at a rapid pace as new understanding of the issues has led to new strategies for intervention. In addition, social workers have progressed in the implementation of significant social policies, such as managed care and welfare reform, and these continue to profoundly affect the lives of clients and the nature of practice. Illustrations drawn from these areas bring the practice theory closer to the realities of today's students and practitioners.

As in the fourth edition, this book shares theories and constructs about human behavior—some supported by research, others drawn from experience in practice—when relevant to specific practice issues. In this way, what is known about the dynamics of helping, oppression and vulnerability, resilience, group process, substance abuse, family interaction, and so on is directly linked to the worker's interactions with the client and with relevant systems. My research and theory building work (Shulman, 1991), designed to develop a holistic theory of practice, is more thoroughly integrated into this edition. This theory recognizes the complexity of social work practice. Focusing solely on the social worker-client interaction ignores many factors such as supervision, availability of resources, client motivation and capacity, the impact of cost-containment efforts, and the effects of client-related traumatic experiences (such as the death of a client) on both worker and client. This book systematically addresses these and other elements of practice.

The book also builds more on a strengths and resiliency perspective when considering practice with oppressed and vulnerable populations. Workers need to understand the socioeconomic factors that contribute to individual, family, and community problems, yet they also must recognize, understand, and respect the existing strengths and resiliencies that have helped people cope. The major ideas of this socially oriented framework for understanding individual, family, group, and community behavior are presented in the first chapter of the book and then illustrated with appropriate examples throughout the text. This concept of working with clients' strengths is expanded in this edition and now incorporates promising new models such as solution-focused practice. While the adoption of any one model is not advocated, concepts and interventions that can be added to one's basic framework are discussed and illustrated.

Finally, the sections dealing with the historical roots of the social work profession and the values and ethics that guide our work have been updated. Illustrations of the impact of legislation and court decisions in areas such as confidentiality, mandated reporting laws (such as those regarding child abuse), informed consent, and duty to warn a client or third party in danger, as well as the new HIPPA regulations, help the reader become more attuned to the ways in which society, government, courts, and professional associations influence practice. The ethical dilemmas associated with the impact of private practice, managed care, and other changes are also addressed. Following recommendations of reviewers, many of these sections have been moved to a last chapter in the book in order to facilitate the flow of skill-based material in earlier chapters.

New: CD Supplements to the Fifth Edition

Two significant additions to this edition are the packaged CDs designed to provide the reader with illustrations of the identified skills as well as excerpts from a workshop I have conducted. The first CD, entitled *The Interactive Skills of Helping* (ISH), was produced by two of my colleagues, Mark Cameron and Denise Krause, with the production assistance of Steven Sturman. The CD contains role-play excerpts that illustrate the core skills such as tuning in and contracting. For each skill there are three segments on the CD. The first demonstrates the skill in a role-play graciously acted out by University at Buffalo colleagues and students. A variety of worker-client situations provide the substance of the practice. By way of contrast, the second excerpt, called "the blooper," demonstrates lack of the skill. The third element is a brief discussion and debriefing between the "worker" and me, exploring her or his thinking and feelings during the previous two segments.

A second CD, entitled *Engaging and Working With the Hard-to-Reach Client* (EWHRC), consists of video excerpts from an interactive workshop I conducted with a volunteer group of child welfare workers. Although the examples come from child welfare, the principles discussed can easily be applied to other populations. The workshop is organized using the phases-of-work framework that provides structure for this text. The workshop segments combine a presentation by me, discussion, detailed case examples, and an illustration of the mutual-aid process as participants support one another. In many ways the workshop is an example of an educational mutual-aid support group, with the workshop leader attempting to demonstrate many of the dynamics and skills of the interactional model in his role as teacher.

There are icons inserted throughout the book that refer the reader to the specific CD and the section of the CD associated with that particular section of the book. The icon for the *Interactive Skills of Helping* (ISH) CD is

The icon for the *Engaging and Working With the Hard-to-Reach Client* (EWHRC) CD is

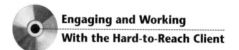

Associated with the icon in the text is the specific section of the referenced CD as well as a brief description of the content. The reader should view the welcome section of the ISH CD and the introduction section of the EWHRC CD, as well as the table of contents of both, to gain familiarity with the contents.

Engaging and Working

With the Hard-to-Reach Client

WORKSHOP INTRODUCTION The author provides introductory comments that clarify the purpose of the workshop as well as identifying assumptions about how the workshop will be conducted.

PROBLEM SWAPPING—IDENTIFYING EXAMPLES The author shares "handles for work" by identifying common practice problems. Participants in the workshop then share examples from their own practice. These examples are then used in the later parts of the workshop as illustrations of the application of the underlying model.

These two sections of the CD also provide a demonstration by the author of the contracting process with an educational group.

Organization of the Book

To simplify the complex task of describing methodology, a single frame of reference described as the interactional model is presented. Introductory comments in Chapter 1 help to place this point of view in context with other models. Included is a description of a theory of the helping process, several models (middle-range descriptions) connecting theory and practice, the identification of skills needed to put the framework into action, and empirical data that support major elements of the framework.

The interactional model was developed by William Schwartz. This colleague's original thinking helped to focus my early curiosity about method. Published and unpublished works, conversations about practice, and other collaborative efforts have all contributed to Schwartz's influence on the contents of this book. I alone, however, must take responsibility for the final shape of the book. While a single framework provides the unifying structure for the book, many of the skills and models can fit comfortably within other frameworks. Also, concepts from other helpful models (cognitive-behavioral, self-in-relation, feminist, psychodynamic, brief treatment, solution-focused, and so on) are incorporated wherever they can help the reader understand and practice more effectively.

Part I of the book consists of a chapter introducing the major theoretical constructs of the interactional model as well as other models and frameworks that set the stage for the text. Part II focuses on work with individuals, examining this process against the backdrop of the phases of work: preliminary, beginning, work, and ending phases. As the helping model is developed, illustrations from a range of settings help point out the common as well as variant elements of the work. Parts III and IV move into the more-complex issues of working with more than one client at a time. They focus on social work with families and groups, respectively. The common elements of the model established in Part I are reintroduced in the family and group contexts. The special dynamics of working with more than one client are also introduced. Part V moves from the microlevel or clinical level to the macrolevel by exploring the skills involved in working with communities and with people in the larger systems and organizations important to the client. Examples show social workers helping members of a community (such as a neighborhood, a housing project, a ward group in a psychiatric hospital) to empower themselves by focusing on community issues related to their personal concerns. Conversations with teachers, doctors, and politicians help illustrate effective impact with other professionals. The final chapter explores a range of issues important to practice, including values and ethics, licensing, legislation, guidelines for practice, the impact of managed care, and evaluation.

The reader is also provided with a reference list and glossary at the end of the book. A glossary organized by chapter can be accessed on the book's web page. In addition, subject, author, and case example indexes are provided. This will allow for quick access to specific material. For example, the subject index will direct readers interested in adolescents to all the places in the book that address that age group. Readers could also go to the case example index and find references to the case material that involves adolescents, whether individual, family, group, or community work.

The book is intended to address the practice needs of the foundation-year social work student whether in a BSW or MSW program. In addition, the depth of discussion and the large number of examples in the book and online also makes it useful for advanced courses such as one on group work. The more experienced practitioner will also find it helpful for continued learning. The book provides models that help articulate concepts that the practitioner has already developed through experience in practice. Using these models, any practitioner can become more systematic and effective. A clearly developed framework will increase consistency and help explain more quickly why some sessions go well and others do not.

Research Findings

Many of my research studies have contributed to the insights shared in this book. Starting with Schwartz's framework, I developed instruments to measure social work practice skills and to relate the use of these skills to effective helping. The findings were then used to analyze the practice approach critically, to confirm some hypotheses while also generating new assumptions for future research. Each successive study built on the preceding ones as well as on the knowledge base developed in social work and related professions and disciplines. Appendix A on the web page provides a summary of the methodology of this author's studies that are discussed in this book. The reader is referred to my other publications (1970, 1978, 1979a, 1979b, 1981, 1991) for more-detailed descriptions of the methodology of each study and their findings. While all findings reported in this text are still tentative and should be considered in light of the limitations of each study, some findings have been repeated in my studies and the studies of other researchers. Confidence in these findings increases with each replication.

While the reader is urged to read the more complete discussion of methodology in the publications just cited, a brief summary of the author's study most often quoted in this text follows.

Study Design

This study was conducted in a government child welfare agency in British Columbia, Canada. Project staff reviewed family files that had been recently opened in 68 district offices. Of the 1,056 families identified as potential subjects, 348 (33 percent) agreed to participate. The final sample consisted of 305 families with 449 children served by 171 social workers in 68 district offices.

Most of the data were gathered during the first 3 months of the project. Home interviews were conducted with the parent(s). A mail survey of staff at all levels (workers, supervisors, managers, and so forth) was carried out at the same time. Project staff also read the participating clients' files. Much of the analysis is based on the data obtained during this time. Follow-up data were obtained through surveys mailed to clients and staff at intervals over the subsequent 15-month period. Project staff also reviewed the family files every 3 months. Twenty-three questionnaires and interview guides were developed and tested for this study.

Description of Study Participants

The five executive directors had MSW degrees; however, only 60 percent of the regional managers, 44 percent of the district supervisors, and 20 percent of the social workers held that degree. When MSWs, BSWs, and other professional degrees were included, 90 percent of the managers, 60 percent of the supervisors, and 68 percent of the social workers held professional degrees.

Two thirds of the families were headed by a single parent. One third of the families also reported "some" or "severe" disability with respect to physical and emotional health, learning problems, or drug and alcohol problems. Fourteen percent reported some or severe alcohol or drug problems for themselves. Eight percent reported that their spouses had similar problems. Unemployment was present for one third of the families. Forty-seven percent of the families were living on welfare or unemployment insurance benefits. Finally, in 10 percent of the families at least one family member was a Native American (of Canadian origin).

Family problems included periodic and severe neglect of children, inability of parents to care for children (because of illness, addictions, and so forth), and physical and sexual abuse. By the end of the study, 28 percent of the families had been listed on the child abuse registry. Forty-nine percent of the families had at least one child in care during the study period.

Limitations

The study is limited by the self-selection of the families involved. We compared the participating and nonparticipating groups on several variables and found no significant differences between the groups. An additional limitation was added when the Province of British Columbia cut back funding and services to the provincewide child welfare program. In particular, these cutbacks led to the nonrenewal of over 600 family support workers. Because the cutbacks were implemented differentially in regions, we could gather data on the impact over time. Thus, we could incorporate the impact of these cutbacks into the study design. The findings of this aspect of the study take on added meaning today, as social workers face an increasingly conservative climate that encourages politicians to compete in their efforts to demonstrate their ability to shred the safety net developed over the years to protect our most vulnerable populations. These findings are reviewed in the current sociopolitical context, and the call for social workers to become more actively involved in policy and political efforts is clearly articulated. My own experiences as a politically active social worker are used as illustrations.

Acknowledgments

I would like to acknowledge the many people who contributed to this book. William Schwartz developed the interactionist perspective on which much of my work has been based. Bill's substantial body of work initiated a paradigm shift for our profession and was the first to introduce to social work the ideas of mutual aid, contracting, the demand for work, and other concepts. He died in 1982 and is still missed; however, he remains very much alive in this text.

I would also like to thank my wife, Sheila, who has always been supportive of my work in more ways than I can say.

Early research of mine reported in this book was supported by the Edna McConnell Clark Foundation; the Welfare Grants Directorate of Health and Welfare, Canada; and the P. A. Woodward Foundation of Vancouver, British Columbia.

Various colleagues have helped along the way. Several faculty members at the School of Social Work of the University of British Columbia and at Boston University have offered valuable advice. More recently, collaboration with colleagues at the University at Buffalo School of Social Work has also been helpful; thanks in particular to Denise Krause, Mark Cameron, and Steve Sturman, who developed the *Interactive Skills of Helping,* one of the video teaching CDs that enhance this book.

Alex Gitterman, of Columbia University, is a colleague who has been a sounding board for my ideas about practice. Our joint editorial work and coleadership of workshops have also enriched my understanding. I am especially grateful to several social work faculty members who responded to a request for suggestions for revisions. Many of their suggestions have been carried forward in this edition. An additional group of faculty reviewers made many excellent suggestions after reading the fifth edition draft:

James Bembry, University of Maryland–Baltimore County

Toby Berman-Rossi, Barry University

Elizabeth P. Cramer, Virginia Commonwealth University

Virginia David, Nazareth College of Rochester

William E. Powell, University of Wisconsin–Whitewater

Deborah Valentine, Colorado State University

David Woody, III, University of Texas–Arlington

Their suggestions have resulted in reorganizing of chapter content to make the material flow more easily for the reader.

In addition to peer reviewers of the developing revision, I wish to thank all of my colleagues who took the time to respond to Brooks/Cole's preliminary online survey. Your invaluable input gave me much insight into the directions this book should take.

Lisa Gebo and the editorial staff at Thomson Brooks/Cole were particularly helpful in the production of this book but also in convincing me that it was perfectly OK to cut material as well as to add. Their suggestion that I move into the information age by placing some of my material on their web page as well as their creative idea of moving some of the extensive group work chapters to a separate book on group practice was very helpful and much-needed advice. Barry Connolly worked with us on the technical issues related to the development of the two CDs packaged with new copies of this book. Other members of the production team included Alma Dea Michelena and Candace Chen. Final editing and formatting was overseen by Melanie Field of Strawberry Field Publishing. I also need to express my special appreciation for the work of Molly Roth, who served as copy editor of this edition. Her editing skills as well as her understanding of the content of the book helped significantly to enhance this edition.

Finally, I want to thank the staff and clients who participated in the cited studies, the workers and students who shared examples of their practice, and my own clients who allowed me to share their experiences in the interest of helping others. These illustrations of the joint efforts of workers and clients give life to the theory and stand as a tribute to their courage and determination.

A Model of the
Helping Process

P art I consists of a single, major chapter that introduces and
illustrates the major themes of the interactional approach
to social work. Chapter 1 sets the stage for the rest of the
book with a discussion of the underlying assumptions of the model,
the history of the profession, underlying theories of oppression and
resilience, and the importance of integrating the personal and professional selves. A brief summary of other theoretical approaches—
elements of which can be integrated into the interactional
model—provides a wider perspective.

An Interactional Approach to Helping

This chapter introduces some of the central ideas of the interactional social work practice theory. A discussion of theory building in social work will place this effort in context. The client will be viewed in a dynamic interaction with many important social systems, such as the family, school, and hospital. The chapter also presents the underlying assumptions about the nature of the relationships between people and their social surroundings.

Our discussion of the assessment process will center on a strengths perspective rather than on client pathology (the medical model). The role of the social work profession as mediating the individual-social engagement will be traced to the roots of the profession, which has historically been concerned with both "private troubles" and "public issues."

Social work practice skill will then be described as the method by which the social worker strives to develop a positive working relationship with the client, a relationship that allows the social worker to help the client. The impact of the social worker's personal self—that is, the effect of his or her feelings, ethics, or values—on her or his professional practice will be examined. Finally, the chapter presents alternative views of social work practice.

Social Work Practice Theory

This book centers on the **interactional model** of social work practice, which we shall explore shortly. This model has developed from many diverse theories guiding the helping professions. By the late 1980s the helping professions were in what Kuhn described as a "pre-scientific stage" (1962). The social work profession had just begun to use theories to translate empirical research into practice. In a scientific stage, by contrast, the results of research are used to modify theories, which are then used to guide new research. In the 1990s the profession was moving toward a scientific stage and beginning to follow an **empirically based practice theory.** Today, I believe that the helping professions have made the transition and are now in the early phase of a scientific stage. As such, this book integrates recent research results from both quantitative and qualitative methods.

Because social work professionals are just beginning this crucial theory-building process, there is room in the profession for a wide range of views. In recent years social work has seen a significant expansion of efforts to strengthen theory building by employing empirical approaches. I have completed my own effort to develop a holistic, empirically based theory of social work practice, which has at its center the interactional approach to helping (Shulman, 1991). Ideas from that model have been included in this book, as have findings from the study associated with that effort. In particular, I emphasize resilience theory and the strengths perspective as models for understanding human behavior.

All practitioners eventually develop their own practice frameworks, some more and some less explicit, and judge them by how well they explain their practice. The framework for social work described in this book has been most helpful to me in my practice, my theory building, and my research. It is not engraved in stone, however. Having evolved for over 30 years, it will continue to be used as a framework just as long as it appears to do the job. You should test its ideas against your own sense of reality and use those portions that seem helpful. Many of the skills and intermediate models are not bound by one approach and can easily fit into other theoretical frameworks. Ideas from other models, some of which are identified and briefly summarized in this chapter, are integrated whenever they help to enrich the core framework. For example, strategies and interventions from solution-focused models join the list of available practitioner tools.

Because I refer to practice theory, models, and skills throughout the text, a brief explanation of how I use these terms may be helpful. In developing his framework, Schwartz (1961) defined a *practice theory* as

> a system of concepts integrating three conceptual subsystems: one which organizes the appropriate aspects of social reality, as drawn from the findings of science; one which defines and conceptualizes specific values and goals, which we might call the problems of policy; and one which deals with the formulation of interrelated principles of action. (p. 27)

A practice theory, then, first describes what we know about human behavior and social organizations. The social worker then establishes a set of specific goals or outcomes based on these underlying assumptions. Finally, a description of the worker's actions to achieve these specific goals completes the practice theory. This approach to theorizing about practice is used throughout the text. For example, when we examine the beginning phase of work, assumptions about how people behave in new situations are related to outcomes the worker wishes to achieve in first sessions. These outcomes, in turn, are linked to specific activities of the worker, described as *contracting*.

The term **model** is used to describe a representation of reality. One would construct a model to help simplify the explanation or description of a complex process or object. In this text, models are used to describe helping processes (such as the dynamics and skills required in a beginning, middle, or ending phase session), individual and social psychologies (such as resiliency theory), and the entities with which professionals work (such as families, groups, communities, or organizations).

The term **skill** refers to a specific behavior that the worker uses in the helping process. Many of the skills described in this text are core relationship skills, useful in the performance of professional as well as personal tasks. For example, empathic skills are needed by parents, spouses, and friends. The focus here will be on their use in relation to social work helping functions.

Finally, although I have been conducting empirical testing of the hypotheses contained in the practice theory, this work should be seen as an ongoing process. The **grounded theory** approach to theory building, first described by Glaser and Strauss (1967) in the field of sociology, guides this work. Formal and informal observations from practice are used to develop constructs of the theory. Formal research is conducted both to test propositions and to generate new ones. Some of the most interesting findings of my earlier study did not support my initial hypotheses. These helped me to expand the theoretical constructs, leading to the development of the more general and **holistic theory** presented in the text that complements this book (Shulman, 1991).

Many of the core findings about skill from my earlier research have been supported by research in social work and related fields. Some propositions have begun to reach the stage at which they may be described, in Rosenberg's term (1978), as **theoretical generalizations.** These propositions have received repeated support from many research efforts. As these ideas are presented, I shall provide citations to the supportive literature. However, even these propositions must be open to modification as further empirical efforts direct. It is in this spirit of evolution that the ideas in this book are shared.

The Client-System Interaction

A critical factor in the helping process is the way one views the client. In early attempts to conceptualize this process, the helping professions borrowed the medical model developed by physicians. The term *medical model* has also been used in recent years to characterize a view of the client that focuses on illness and pathology; however, I use it here in another sense. The **medical model** is defined here as the four-step process of thinking about practice commonly described as study, diagnosis, treatment, and evaluation. In this framework, the knowing professional studies the client, attempts to make an accurate diagnosis, develops a treatment plan, and then evaluates the outcome.

It is entirely possible that practitioners who are preoccupied with illness or pathology and those who use other models of viewing clients (such as systems or ecological approaches or a strengths perspective) may still be employing a medical model in the way they conceptualize their practice. Even practitioners who reject what they call "Band-Aid" help, and who advocate social action and advocacy, often employ the medical model in their thinking. The only difference, in their case, is that it is the "system" that is studied, diagnosed, and treated.

One of several problems with this model has been the heavy emphasis on the study phase, in which the social worker attempted to obtain a great deal of information about the client (such as family history, work history, medical history), in order to develop what was called the psychosocial study on which the diagnosis and resulting treatment plan were developed. Obtaining such information in the early stage was important and, in some settings, essential for reimbursement of the service, yet the question-and-answer format could lead workers to ignore the equally important processes required to engage the client and to begin to develop the working relationship.

The following example illustrates how a social work student begins to connect with her new client during their first session, loses the client as she switches to taking the family history, and then catches herself as she reconnects with her client on an emotional level.

WORKER: Come on in and sit down. If you get too cold, just tell me and I'll close the window.

CLIENT: No, that's fine, it's very nice outside. So, what is your experience, your specialization? They tell me this is an important question to ask.

WORKER: Well, I'm a second-year graduate student at the School of Social Work. This is my second internship. My first one was at a child welfare office. I could tell you all of the theories I have learned and books I have read, but I think it is more important for you to see how comfortable you are with me.

CLIENT: I never had therapy before so I guess we'll make a good team.

WORKER: What brought you here today?

CLIENT: I felt like driving my car into the canal. I left my husband in Florida, and I came home. I feel like this is where I belong. Basically, I feel like I'm drowning. (Tears fill her eyes.)

WORKER: Sounds like this is a very painful time for you. (Client is silent, head down.) When did you leave Florida?

CLIENT: Two and a half weeks ago. I went to Florida a year ago to save my marriage. I gave up everything for him—my friends, family, job—and I realize the sacrifice is not worth it. I'm going through the empty-nest syndrome without the children. I had to adjust to his family, his way of living. There was no communication between us. I got scared! I felt more like his roommate. I always have to take care of everyone!

WORKER: You sound angry.

CLIENT: Yes, and I'm tired of it!

WORKER: Because this is an intake I need to ask you some questions in order to complete the paperwork portion of our meeting.

CLIENT: Oh, I'm sorry. Go ahead.

WORKER: Don't be sorry. I just wanted you to know we needed to shift gears for awhile.

CLIENT: Go ahead; that's fine.

WORKER: Tell me about your family.

CLIENT: I have five grown children: Pam, Jane, John, Cathy, and Tina. She's my baby. She recently had a baby and (tears fill her eyes). That's another subject.

WORKER: Seems like babies are a tough subject for you to talk about.

CLIENT: (Beginning to cry) It's OK. Go ahead, ask your questions.

WORKER: They are not as important as your feelings are right now. We'll have plenty of time later to complete the forms.

When the example was discussed in class, the student worker recognized that she had switched to the questioning format just when the client expressed strong feelings of anger. Other students in the class acknowledged that having a structured first interview in which they could focus on asking a series of questions made them feel more comfortable, while possibly making the client feel less comfortable. They could also see how important it was to stay close to the feelings of the client. Many of the questions would be answered in the course of the interview, and the social worker could always leave some time at the end to obtain the missing data.

Because assessment schemes are usually integrated into the practices of social agencies, I try to help my students develop a workable approach while recognizing its limitations. We develop creative approaches for obtaining the required information and skillfully engaging the client in the first interview. Involving the client actively in the process, discussing the reasons for the information gathering, and making sure that the study phase does not substitute for contracting work are essential elements. Students are also encouraged to find ways of relating to the team when discussing specific clients, such as in a case conference, which may affect a shift in attitude toward clients from pathology to strengths. In later chapters we examine assessment models and systems work in more detail.

Another problem with the medical model is that it has tended to present clients in static terms. The model emphasizes attributing descriptive characteristics to the client (such as resistant, hard to reach). In extreme cases, workers refer to clients as diagnoses, as in "I'm working with a borderline" rather than "a client with a borderline diagnosis." Even the term *therapy,* often used by social workers to describe work with individuals, families, and groups (such as family therapy) implies that something is wrong with the client that requires fixing. For many years now, dynamic systems theory has profoundly influenced the way helping professionals view their clients. One central idea has been the emphasis on viewing a client in interaction with others. Instead of seeing a client as the object of analysis, workers began to focus on the way in which the client and the client's important systems were interacting. In fact, according to this viewpoint, one can never understand the movements of the client except as affected by the movements of others.

This shift in thinking can be illustrated using the example of a depressed middle-aged woman admitted to the psychiatric ward of a hospital. One could choose to focus only on her depression and other symptoms. In fact, current knowledge about the biological sources of some forms of depression requires that professionals be aware of treatment possibilities that can include the use of psychotropic drugs.

An alternative framework would also seek to identify those important systems in her life that she has had to deal with: her husband, her children, her job, her peer group, her parents or siblings, her society and its many sexist attitudes, and so on. In addition, one could include the hospital, her doctor, ward staff, and other patients. A diagrammatic way of viewing this is shown in Figure 1.1.

This important change in perspective alters the kind of questions the worker mentally asks. Instead of simply focusing on the state of the patient's mental health,

FIGURE 1.1

Relationship of Client and Systems

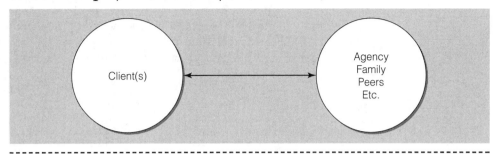

the degree of the depression, and its possible cause (such as early childhood trauma or substance abuse), the worker is equally curious about the state of the interactions between the patient and each of the relevant systems. What is the nature of the relationship between the woman and her husband? Can they talk to and listen to each other? Is the relationship emotionally or physically abusive? The worker would also be interested in the relationship between the patient and the hospital. How well is the patient integrating into the ward? Is she reaching out to other patients, creating an informal support group, or is she cut off and isolated?

These are not questions the worker will be asking the client in the early interviews (the structure of first sessions will be discussed later). Rather, they are examples of the potential areas of work on which the helping process may focus. Furthermore, the worker will not focus only on the client's part in the interaction. As stated earlier, the client's movements can only be understood in relation to the movements of those around her. How well do the family, friends, and the other clients reach out to her? Part of the outcome of these interactions will be determined by the client's input, but other parts will be a result of the system's responses. In fact, the relationship will be reciprocal, with the movements of each constantly affecting the movements of the others.

The self-in-relation theory emerged from efforts to rethink women's psychology initiated by Miller (J. B. Miller 1987, 1988; J. B. Miller & Stiver, 1991, 1993) and Gilligan, Lyons, and Hammer (1990) as part of the Harvard Project on Women's Psychology and Girls' Development, as well as by others at the Stone Center in Wellesley, Massachusetts (for example, Fedele, 1994; Jordan, 1991, 1993). If we were to apply some of this theory, we might rethink this client's situation in terms of paradoxes. For example, in an article on the use of relational theory in group work practice, Fedele describes a central paradox first identified by Miller as follows:

> This paradox states that during the course of our lifetime, in the desire to make connections and be emotionally accessible, we all experience harm or violation that leads to a need to develop strategies to keep large parts of ourselves out of connection. In the face of intense yearning for connection and in order to remain in the only relationships available, we develop strategies that keep more and more of ourselves out of connection. Simply put, the paradox is that in order to stay in connection, we keep parts of ourselves out of connection.
> (J. B. Miller, 1988)

The paradox of maintaining connection through disconnecting offers some additional insights into the potential causes of a client's depression, rooted in current and possibly past experiences. It also suggests how to help clients find ways of making new connections (with family members, the hospital, other women in a mutual aid support group) without the need for maintaining the disconnection defenses. (The relational model will be discussed in more detail in Chapter 12.)

In addition, to truly understand clients, workers need to understand clients' interactions in the context within which they take place. We are much clearer now about how our society's stereotypes of women and men affect relationships. In many examples, when one looks beneath the depression of some middle-aged women, one finds an understandable anger, even rage, related to sex-role stereotyping and oppression by a male-dominated society. Does the woman experience herself as able to influence her social environment, or does she feel powerless (Weick & Vandiver, 1982)? Has she experienced significant victimization in her life (Berlin & Kravetz, 1981)? Is this a situation where it is important to empower the client (Smith & Siegal, 1985)? Does the view of her situation change if workers apply one of the many feminist models more recently summarized by Saulnier (1996, 2000), such as "liberal feminism," "radical feminism," or "postmodern feminism"?

If the client is also a person of color and economically disadvantaged, then we have the classic triple oppressions related to gender, race, and class. A severe depression may well represent an understandable defensive reaction in response to the oppressive conditions imposed by the increasing "feminization of poverty" or the impact of welfare reform efforts that require recipients to find work when jobs are unavailable and resources are limited.

Oppression psychology, as described by Fanon and elaborated by Bulhan (1985) is discussed in more detail later in this chapter. Fanon suggested that prolonged exposure to oppression could lead clients to internalize the "oppressor without," adopting negative self-attitudes and self-images. Internalized rage, often masked by depression, can lead clients to behavior that is maladaptive and destructive to themselves and others. "The oppressor without becomes an introppressor—an oppressor within" (p. 126). Such a person, according to Fanon, becomes an "autopressor" by participating in her or his own oppression. Ironically, and conveniently, the maladaptive behavior that results from prolonged experience of oppression is then used by the majority group to justify continued stereotyping and oppression, maintaining a vicious cycle.

If the client is also a **vulnerable client**—for example, lacking a strong social support system of family or friends—then the essentially maladaptive responses of the client become all the more understandable. In addition, given the client's situation, one has to be impressed by the strength the client has shown in simply surviving and continuing to struggle. By viewing the client from a strength perspective and a resiliency model as well as incorporating solution-focused strategies, discussed later in this chapter, the social worker can focus on the part of the client that has demonstrated a capacity to deal effectively with life.

A worker starting from this perspective will be more interested in identifying what is right than what is wrong about clients. The worker will want to help them identify times in their lives when they effectively coped and the resources they needed then. For example, rather than focusing only on the causes of relapses in substance abuse recovery, the worker will want to help clients focus on how they maintained their recovery between relapses. The subtle signs of life and strength are what the worker will reach for in trying to help clients overcome the effects of oppression.

To return to our earlier example, as the client-system interactions are identified, the woman's depression may take on new meaning. The sadness and passivity are not the problems; rather, they are the symptoms of the breakdown in these important interactions and the result of the experienced oppression. The depression is not the illness to be cured, but rather a signal that important areas of interaction in the life of this woman have broken down. The worker will not try to "cure" the client, but rather to affect the client's capacity for coping and change, the way she thinks about her feelings and problems, and how she and these important systems interact. The cure for the "problem" will emerge not from the professional's treatment plan, but rather from the client's increasing understanding of her situation and her own efforts to find new ways to interact with the systems that matter to her—either reaching out to them or cutting herself off from them and finding new sources of support. Similarly, the systems (such as the family) may have to find new ways to reach out to this client in order to reengage her. Both the client and the systems may find implementation of this process difficult. Here, the job of the social worker plays a crucial role.

At this point, you may have many questions and possibly some objections. What if the client is too weak to deal with the system, doesn't want help, and refuses to work on the interaction? Perhaps the problem is with the system. As mentioned earlier, what happens if the depression is related to biological factors for which pharmaceutical treatment is needed, perhaps in conjunction with counseling? These and other objections are pursued in some detail in the discussions that follow. For the moment, try to set them aside. At this point, the most important concept to grasp is that the client to be helped is viewed as an interactive entity, often ambivalent, acting and reacting to the various demands of the systems she must negotiate. The systems will be viewed in this way as well.

Each client is a special case within this general model. The unwed pregnant teen in a child welfare agency might be dealing with the systems of the agency, the child's father, family, friends, societal attitudes as reflected in recent welfare legislation, prejudices towards women and sexuality in general, and so on. Of equal concern to her may be issues of income (welfare or work), housing, child care, and the medical system. If she lives in a group care home, the house parents and other residents become part of the active systems in her life. Her feelings about herself as a woman, her reactions to society's norms, and her own, often harsh, judgments of herself (the oppressor within) may all be part of her agenda, but always in relation to the way in which she deals with those systems that matter to her. Whatever the category of client discussed in this book—the child in the residential center, the husband in marital counseling, the student who is failing, the client with a terminal illness, the client learning to live with AIDS, the client in the early stages of recovery from substance abuse, or the member of a citizens' community action group—all will be viewed in the context of the interaction with their social surroundings and an understanding of their potential strengths.

Underlying Assumptions in the Interactional Model

All models of social work practice are based on underlying assumptions about people and their social surroundings. These are the starting points for theory building, and they need to be made explicit. While many assumptions about people and the helping process will be examined throughout this book, three core ideas underlying the interactional model are presented here. The first is the **symbiotic assumption:** a belief in the essential symbiotic relationship between people and their social surroundings. The second is the assumption that this mutual need is systematically blocked by obstacles, some raised by the client and others by the systems the client must negotiate. The third basic assumption is that the social worker must always assume and reach for the client's (and system's) strengths for change. These assumptions are explored in the sections that follow.

Assumption of Symbiosis

Now that we have placed clients in interaction with the various systems that impinge on them, we need to examine the nature of this relationship. If we return to the example in the previous section of a depressed, middle-aged woman, our view of how to help this client will depend on our assumptions about the individual-social engagement. If we examine her interactions with her environment, we can perceive a certain amount of ambivalence. Some part of her will seem to be reaching out, however faintly, toward life and the people around her. On the other hand, her withdrawal, depression, and general communications appear to signal a retreat from life. She may have experienced life as being too difficult, her feelings too painful to face, and the demands seemingly impossible to meet.

A part of her seems to be giving up and saying that the very struggle seems useless. She can be observed placing barriers between herself and these systems, including that part of the system (the worker) that is reaching out to help her. She is simultaneously reaching out for life, growth, and the important systems around her and moving away from each.

The assumption that a part of us is always striving toward health lies at the core of the practice theory formulated by Schwartz. Borrowing a "symbiotic" model of human relationships, he views the individual-social interaction as

> a relationship between the individual and his nurturing group which we would describe as "symbiotic"—each needing the other for its own life and growth, and each reaching out to the other with all the strength it can command at a given moment. (Schwartz, 1961, p. 15)

The term *symbiotic* is used to describe the mutual need of individuals and the systems that matter to them. This woman's needs can best be met in interaction with the world around her, not through complete withdrawal from it. Similarly, society has a stake in maintaining this client as an active, involved, unique, integrated individual. The idea of symbiotic striving fits comfortably with the constructs of the relational model described earlier.

Unfortunately, the term *symbiotic* has taken on a professional connotation of unhealthy mutual overdependency, as between a mother and child. In the world of biology, symbiosis actually describes two organisms living in a mutually beneficial relationship. The exploitation of one organism by another would be described as a parasitic relationship.

Schwartz uses the term to underline our mutual dependency and our essential interest in each other. It is a statement of the interdependence that is fundamental to a belief in social responsibility for the welfare of each individual. It also recognizes that each individual finds life's needs best satisfied in positive relationships with others.

You may be wondering at this point how this assumption of a symbiotic model relates to experiences where individual-social interaction appears to be far from symbiotic and, in fact, has been defined as often oppressive. Schwartz points out that

> in a complex and often distorted society, the individual-social symbiosis grows diffuse and obscure in varying degrees, ranging from the normal developmental

problems of children growing into their culture to the severe pathology involved in situations where the symbiotic attachment appears to be all but severed. (1961, p. 15)

The very fact that the mutual self-interest of people and their surrounding systems is often obscured creates the working ground for the helping professional. The observation that people and their systems often appear to be acting against each other's self-interest is not an argument against the symbiotic model; rather, it is an argument for some helping person to help both system and client regain their sense of mutuality.

Following this model, the worker will search not only for the part of the client that is reaching out toward systems, but also for the part of the family, friends, peer group, and hospital system that is reaching out toward the patient. For instance, if the husband appears to turn away from his wife during the family session, closing off his feelings, then the worker might reach for the underlying sense of loss and hurt that he attempts to hide even from himself. When the hospital rules, procedures, and services seem to work against the best interests of a patient, the helping person will attempt to influence the part of the system that cares about the people it serves; in doing so, the worker will employ several strategies such as mediation, brokering, or advocacy.

In example after example throughout this book, you will observe that the helping person's movements with the client, the moment-by-moment interventions, are affected by the worker's view of the individual-social relationship. At critical moments in the interactions, connections will be discovered between husbands and wives, parents and children, students and teachers, community groups and politicians, individual group members and the group, and so forth, because the helping person was searching for them. This idea will be termed the **two-clients construct,** in which the social worker will always be seen as having two clients. The second client will change in each situation. In the current example, it may be the woman's family, the hospital system, friends, and so on.

The practical implications of this philosophical assumption are important. For example, in the case of our female client, the worker's belief in the importance of helping her find her connections to people around her and the belief in this woman's partial striving for this connection will cause the worker to search for faint clues that the client is still emotionally alive and trying. The worker will not be fooled by the defenses thrown up by the client but will concentrate instead on the spark of life that still exists, often associated with the anger, even rage, buried under the depression and apathy. The work of the helping person is not to remotivate the client, but rather to discover and develop the motivation already there. Helping the client understand the nature of her internalized oppressor is an important step in helping her take control over her life and begin dealing with the oppressor without.

Belief in this symbiotic model does not necessarily exclude the existence of important tensions and real conflicts of interest between the individual and the systems. Interactions in life involve conflict and confrontation. Not all interests are mutual. Oppression happens for a reason. The effective helping person brings these underlying differences into the open so that the engagement is a real human process invested with a range of feelings. Examples abound in which the skilled helper challenges the illusion of agreement between the parties in conflict by reaching for and demanding real work. What the model does is provide the worker with a sense of the potential common ground on which both the client and the important life systems can build.

For workers to be effective in this role, they need to recognize that oppression clearly has some psychological and concrete payoffs for the majority group in any situation. For example, when a man uses battering and intimidation to attempt to control a woman in his life, he receives psychological and concrete benefits from the interaction. If we consider the "master-slave" paradigm developed by Hegel in 1807 (1966), elements of which underlie oppression theory, the insecure "master" seeks to "recognize" or define himself through the unreciprocated recognition by the "slave" (Bulhan, 1985). In effect, the male batterer uses the subjugation of his female partner to bolster his sense of self by his partner "recognizing" him without his having to "recognize" her.

In considering such relationships, social workers' first concern should be protecting oppressed clients and holding the oppressors accountable for their actions. Battering is a criminal offense and must be treated as such. Work with a battered woman often involves helping her find her own strength and the social resources needed to leave the abusive relationship safely. However, when also working with the male batterer, workers would need to recognize that this use of violence for control can have significant negative effects on him, including legal consequences, emotional damage to the self, and precluding of an intimate relationship based on mutuality and equality—a relationship of mutual recognition.

We can extend this individual psychology to a social psychology if we recognize that the wider sexist attitudes that support this brutal form of oppression can be explained by the same psychological dynamics. The payoffs for sexism are not only psychological but concrete and financial as well. When women are consistently paid less than men for the same jobs, profits are higher, even in nonprofit organizations. When a "glass ceiling" stops women (and other minority groups) from advancing in business or government agencies, more senior positions are available for men and members of the majority groups. Even these gains, however, are offset by the long-term social, moral, and economic prices paid as a result of such shortsighted practices.

On a broader scale, oppression by all majority groups against all minority groups—such as people of color, women, immigrants, Jews, gays and lesbians, or people with mental illness, mental retardation, or significant physical disabilities—results in specific economic and psychological benefits for the majority group. However, the significant personal, social, and even economic costs are often ignored. For example, when the AIDS epidemic was viewed as a problem affecting only gays, Haitians, and intravenous drug users, many of whom live in inner-city ghettos, the U.S. government largely ignored it. Some groups actually pointed to this disease as retribution for "immoral" behavior and saw the growing numbers of deaths as a "cleansing" of society. Although these views were extreme, they may have represented a more general undercurrent of racism and homophobia that fostered lethargy and inaction by the larger community. One has only to imagine the difference in the response if such an epidemic had initially struck middle-class, heterosexual whites instead of these minority populations.

The differential provision of medical research and support to minority populations represents a deadly form of oppression. Only now is the majority group coming to grips with the incredible social and health-related costs associated with the increase in this epidemic and its spread to the majority population. The same is true if one considers the true costs of the inadequate health care services provided in the United States to the poor and the oppressed. Lack of a universal health care system in this country stands in stark contrast to programs developed in Canada and Europe. These examples can be added to the list of the many documented incidents of racism in medicine, including the "shocking and scandalous recently halted Tuskegee experiment on syphilis among blacks in Macon County, Alabama" (Bulhan, 1985, p. 87), in which the effects of the untreated disease on 400 black men and their families were observed for more than 40 years without the knowledge of the study participants or the provision of available treatments. It was only in 1997 that President Clinton publicly acknowledged and apologized for these actions on behalf of the American people.

The existence of the many powerful examples of oppression and exploitation of vulnerable populations in U.S. history does not change the essential, symbiotic nature of the relationship between people and their social surroundings. These instances instead reveal how much we have lost sight of these connections. They also provide a rationale for the unique functional role of the social work profession described later in this chapter.

Assumption of Obstacles in the Engagement

Thus far we have focused on the client's interactions with important environmental systems. Both the individual and the systems are vitally linked through mutual need. Each is seen as reaching out to the other with all the strength available at the moment and with the capacity to reach out more effectively. The next logical question is this: What goes wrong? The mutual dependence can be blocked or obscured by any number of obstacles. We now briefly examine three potential obstacles to interaction between the individual and the social system: changing social systems, conflicts between self-interest and mutual interest, and the dynamics of interpersonal communication.

The Increasing Complexity of Human Social Systems One problem is the increasing complexity of human social systems, such as the family. The relationships between parents and children and husbands and wives (or same-sex partners) have become increasingly difficult. Important sources of social support across generations have diminished as modern nuclear families tend to live apart from grandparents and other relatives. As society's norms and values change more rapidly than they did in past generations, parents are forced to reconcile their own beliefs with the newer values of their children. Further, the world of work absorbs more time and energy, often leaving parents less opportunity to foster family stability.

Middle-aged parents find themselves attempting to provide support for their adolescent (and often young adult) children, while simultaneously feeling responsible for the well-being of their aged parents. Called by some the "sandwich generation," they often ask, "When will I have time for me?" Is it any wonder that family members at times find dealing with one other quite complicated?

Our definition of *family* has changed dramatically. The typical two-parent family of a generation ago has been replaced by an ever-higher percentage of single-parent families. These families, as well as low-income two-parent families, face increasing stress because of the breakdown of the formal support network—the government "safety net"—as a result of budget cuts. The full impact of the 1996 Welfare Reform Act has just begun to be known, but early indications suggest that at least some of the families cut off from welfare have not been able to make the predicted transition to work and independence and are now far worse off than they were before.

The availability of day care, low-cost housing, financial subsidies, and adequate health care has decreased almost in proportion to the increase in need. Some political and economic leadership has stressed a "me-first" ethic that has encouraged the majority to ignore the needs of disenfranchised populations. We were at first shocked by the appearance of the homeless on our urban streets, then encouraged to be angry at them by political leaders who suggested that shelter was available for anyone who really wanted it.

Periodically, we have experienced severe problems in the economy that have undermined employment stability. Employment patterns relying on temporary workers and corporate restructuring that lay off midlevel managers are more common now than before. The increased globalization of the economy and the ability of corporations to "outsource," move jobs to other counties to increase profits, has led to fears that unemployment in the United States may be an ongoing problem even when the economy appears to be robust. When higher-paying jobs are lost and replaced by lower-paying ones, often without benefits, a larger portion of our population moves into poverty and vulnerability rather than into economic and social security. The high levels of unemployment and uncertainty have led to increased family tension. In one of my early research projects (Shulman, 1991), Canadian workers in British Columbia reported significant increases in the number and severity of child abuse cases, which appear to be linked to economic stress—either loss of a job or fear of such a loss. Normal family tensions, such as parent-teen conflicts, become exacerbated when parents face economic stress or must cope with the "earthquake" of unemployment.

Even during stable economic conditions, a politically divided federal government, debates over a balanced budget, pressures to provide tax breaks (which mostly benefit the wealthy), the rising costs of health care in general and prescription drugs in particular, demands for "smaller government," and the abandonment of federal responsibility to be replaced by state control over health and social welfare programs—all have led to an increasing gap between the rich and the poor, the healthy and the sick, the fully participating members of our communities and those who are left out.

More generally, as the poor collect in cities, and as the institutions (welfare, medical, educational) designed to serve them grow more complex, the basic relationship between people and these important systems is bound to become obstructed. One need only think of one's reactions to the first day at a new school or to entering a busy hospital in order to remember how strange, overwhelming, and impersonal the system can seem. The obstacles related to complexity are inherent, and they often emerge inadvertently from the realities of the system.

Divergence in Self-Interest and Social Interest A second set of obstacles is associated with the divergent interests of people and the systems that matter to them. Life does not consist only of mutual interest and interdependence. There are times when self-interest directly conflicts with the interests of others. In fact, each individual, as part of the growth process, must learn to set aside his or her own immediate needs in order to integrate into the social order.

For example, in marriage or partnerships, the man may believe he has some stake in maintaining a traditional and privileged gender role. The rules of behavior, norms, and the traditional structures in such relationships provide some payoffs for the male partner. A confident woman who is able to develop a sense of her self differentiated from her husband and her family may be a more interesting person, but she may also intimidate a partner who is struggling with his own sense of worth. Obstacles to the symbiotic relationship can be generated by the ambivalence family members feel toward change. Rapid changes produce anxiety for all in our society, so we often attempt to maintain the status quo and preserve continuity.

Complex systems are also ambivalent toward the people they serve. For example, politicians may view community action pressure groups as thorns in their sides. As these groups expose important unmet needs, they also reveal problems that are difficult to handle. Government bodies face demands from many sources for a share of the economic pie, and to have this pressure heightened by citizen groups creates new difficulties.

While society has a fundamental stake in strengthening and incorporating its most vulnerable populations, it also has an element of economic self-interest in maintaining the poor and in fostering a stereotype that blames them for their own problems. It is easy to see how the need for strong, active, community pressure groups as sources of feedback for our society can be obscured by the immediate need for peace and quiet. Similarly, large institutions such as schools and hospitals find it easier to deal with students and patients who conform, make no trouble, and go along with the present order. They often fail to realize the price they pay in terms of effective teaching and healing.

Problems of Interpersonal Communication A third major set of obstacles involves problems of interpersonal communication. Sharing and understanding painful or taboo thoughts and feelings is hard. People find it difficult to speak of feelings about sex, authority, intimacy, dependency, loss, sexual orientation, and so on. The powerful norms of our society are brought to bear in each interpersonal relationship, often making achievement of mutual understanding difficult. Most important conversations between people take place through the use of indirect communications that can be extremely hard to decipher.

For example, the husband who feels hurt and rejected by his wife's apparent lack of interest in sexual relations may express this through hostile or sarcastic comments in a totally unrelated area. The wife, in turn, may be expressing her own reactions to the husband's continual criticism through lack of interest in sexual contact. Each may be feeling a powerful and important need for the other that is obscured by the built-up resentment developed by their immature means of communication.

Students who feel the teacher is always on their back, or is racist, or does not like them, respond with failure, lack of preparation, and cutting classes. The teacher, out of frustration at not being able to reach the children, responds with increased exhortation or punishment, or in some cases by developing stereotypes based on race, class, ethnicity, or gender. To the children, the message is that the teacher does not care. To the teacher, the message is that the children (or their parents) do not care.

In most cases, they are both wrong. The children's stake in the successful completion of their education and the teacher's stake in helping students through a difficult learning process may be overwhelmed by their mutual misconceptions. Instead of strengthening the relationship, the student and the teacher turn away from each other. The difficulty of overcoming these obstacles is heightened when reduced financial support for education results in larger classes, diminished support services, and reduced resources for children with special needs. The teacher might not recognize the community and family issues that are profoundly affecting the student. Substance abuse, physical and sexual abuse, vicarious trauma from witnessing community violence, and so forth can severely impact the healthiest people. Often, behavior problems in school are a cry for help.

The gay man previously rejected by his family for being gay but who has been diagnosed as HIV-positive may feel a strong need to repair a fractured family-of-origin relationship. Having been hurt deeply by his family, he may be reluctant to contact his parents and inform them of his illness. For the family, the crisis of their son's illness may be the very catalyst needed to break the cycle of rejection and allow for some form of family reunification and healing. An understandable fear of another painful rejection may cut a client off from his ability to communicate his need for renewed family relationships.

In the relationships between parent and child, hospital ward and patient, student and school, the person with AIDS and his family, individual and group—that is, in each special case of the individual-social engagement—the essential mutual need is fragile and easily obscured by the complexity of the situation, by divergent needs, or by the difficulty involved in communication.

Out of this ever-present possibility of **symbiotic diffusion**, the loss of a clear sense of the symbiotic striving, the need for the social work profession emerged (Schwartz, 1961). The profession's tasks relate directly to the fact that obstacles can easily obscure the mutual dependence between the individual and important systems. When both sides have lost sight of this important connection, a third force is needed to help them regain this understanding. According to Schwartz, the social work profession, with its historical roots firmly planted in two streams—concern for individual well-being and social justice—is uniquely suited to play this role. This idea of the third force leads to the mediating function of the social work professional described later in the chapter.

Assumption of Strength for Change

Belief in the existence of symbiotic striving is closely linked to another assumption about the individual-social engagement: that both the individual and the system contain within them the strength to implement this mutuality. This assumption depends on a view of people (and complex systems) as being able to act in their own interest without being bound by their past experiences. An alternative approach considers that people fundamentally act according to the sum of the strengths and skills accumulated by past experiences. Causal links can be drawn between a person's present apparent immobility and earlier traumatic events.

While it seems logical that past experiences affect the way in which an individual attempts to negotiate new surroundings, the danger exists, with this view, of prejudging and underestimating a client's (or the system's) resiliency, strength, and capacity for change. Within the framework presented here, the individual is best described by actions and is as strong or as weak as he or she acts in the present moment. The practice implication of this attitude is that the worker must believe that the individual or the system has the capacity to move in its own self-interest, even if only by small steps, and that this movement will lead to increased strength and more change. These strengths and resiliency perspectives will be discussed more fully later in this chapter.

With this basic assumption in mind, the interactional perspective calls for the helping person always to place a "demand for work" before the client. The **demand for work** occurs when the worker exhorts the client to work effectively on her or his tasks and to invest that work with energy and affect. The work itself, the goals of the process (even with mandated clients), must be shared by the client, not merely imposed by the worker. Also, this demand must be integrated with support in what could be called an empathic demand for work. A similar demand will be placed on the system.

A familiar expression in this connection is "reach for the client's strength," suggesting that the very act of reaching for strength—that is, believing in the potential of the work and refusing to accept even the client's own self-description of weakness—is a central part of what helps a client to act. Possibly the client has reached the present impasse precisely because all the signals received from important "others" have reinforced belief in the client's own impotence. The social worker, by contrast, will operate on a basic principle: No matter how hopeless it seems, there is always a next step.

In an example from my own practice, I confront a group of people with AIDS in early recovery who have apparently given up on their ability to have nonexploitive and drug- and alcohol-free intimate relationships with others; I tell them that they must set aside their own concerns and issues and become a mutual support group for each other. This demand for work is rooted in the belief that even these clients, who have experienced years of polysubstance abuse, prison sentences, prostitution, and traumatic childhood experiences, still have the strength to reach out for each other within the group, which serves as a microcosm of larger society. The group members' ability to care for others is a tribute to themselves and an affirmation of the strengths perspective.

The assumptions just demonstrated will interact in important ways in the models and examples shared in this book. Workers will always search for subtle connections and will always demand that clients and systems act on their potential for change. This view of practice is built on a deep investment in the concept of interdependence; a view of the client as the source of energy for change, healing, and growth; a belief in client strength; and a preoccupation with health rather than sickness.

This stance does not negate the fact that some clients and some systems, for many complex reasons, will not be able to use the worker's help at a given moment. The helping process is interactional, with workers carrying out their parts as best they can. As such, clients have a part to play, and their strength helps to determine the outcome. For example, no matter how skillful the worker, he or she may not be able to reach a substance-abusing client until the client enters detox and stops using cocaine. Using findings from my own research and that of others, we shall throughout this book explore the ways in which stress, acceptance of a problem, and motivation affect the client's ability to receive and use help at any given moment.

Socioeconomic factors, such as income, housing, and employment trends, also profoundly affect social work outcomes. Social workers must therefore be concerned with social policies that affect the human situation. Becoming aware of and working for changes in social policies is part of the task of helping. Recognizing that a particular client may be unable to use help at that time, the worker will nevertheless always attempt to reach for the client's strength because this is the way in which help is given.

The Social Work Profession: A Historical Perspective

Thus far in the discussion, we have tried to view each client as a special case of the more general individual-social interaction in our society. The issue we explore in this section is the role that the social work profession plays in this process. Although providing a detailed discussion of the complex history of the development of the profession lies beyond the scope of this book, a general understanding of its unique historical roots will place the helping role in perspective.

The Roots of the Profession

The profession, as we know it now, was created through the merger over the years of two basic streams of thought about the helping process. One was rooted in the work of those interested in issues of social change. An example was the early settlement house movement, most often associated with the work of Jane Addams at Hull House, founded in 1889 (Addams, 1961). This movement, which began in England, was one of the many established at the turn of the century to cope with the stresses created by urbanization, industrialization, and the large-scale influx of immigrants to North America. The mission of these early, community-oriented social agencies included attempting to help immigrant and other poor families integrate into U.S. society more effectively. At the same time, the leadership of these movements, mostly middle and upper-class liberals of the day, waged a fight against the social conditions facing these populations. Poor housing and health services, child labor, sweat-shop conditions in urban factories—all became targets for social change.

While Jane Addams was known for her relatively radical approach to working with and involving actively oppressed people, many in the settlement house movement incorporated a "doing for" approach to the populations with which they worked. Little effort was directed at actually organizing the poor, through an empowerment process, to fight effectively against the forces of oppression related to class, gender, race, ethnicity, and the like. An **empowerment process** involves engaging the client (individual, family, group, or community) in developing strengths to personally and politically cope more effectively with those systems that are important to them. It is likely that if the leaders of these early social movements had attempted to mobilize client groups in this way, they would have been viewed as too radical and would have themselves faced political repression.

In addition, this early movement saw as one of its major roles the acculturation of the poor to the values and beliefs of their own upper-middle-class society. Developing an appreciation of the arts, such as classical music and literature, and participating in other "refined" activities were seen as paths for self-improvement and "building character." Workers often lived with clients in the settlement houses; helping was seen as practical in nature. For example, if cities were overcrowded and unhealthy, then children needed to be removed to camps in the country during the summer. Not until the 1930s did this social-change orientation join the mainstream of the emerging social work profession. This early driving concern for social justice for vulnerable populations gave the social work profession an important element of its current identity. The early roots of the group work and community organization methods can be traced to these professional pioneers.

The other major stream of professional development was rooted in a focus on fulfilling individual needs. The founder of this stream is often identified as Mary Richmond, whose work at the Charities Organization Society made a major contribution toward the professionalizing of social work (1918). Her efforts were directed at moving social work beyond the notion of "friendly visitors" who were charitable to the poor toward a systematic, professional approach to helping. Richmond was interested in the helping process and wanted it to be recorded, analyzed, and then taught.

By the 1930s, two new specializations in social work had developed: group work and community organization. Group work was closely associated with the informal education and socialization movements. Early leaders included Grace Coyle (1948) and Gertrude Wilson and Gladys Ryland (1949). The work focused on using the peer group to help people cope with the normative tasks of life. A typical group might consist of teenagers forming a social club in a community center, with the group worker assigned to help them learn to work effectively together. Activities such as games, singing, crafts, or bowling provided ways through which group members could enjoy recreation and work on appropriate individual and group developmental tasks.

The early community organization activity was designed to coordinate social services through, for example, councils of social agencies. A second function was to raise funds for private social welfare activities through organizations such as community chests, the forerunners of today's United Way campaigns. It would not be until the late 1950s and early 1960s, reflecting the social activist themes of the times and the civil rights movement, as well as borrowing from community action and organizer models developed by activists such as Saul Alinsky (Reitzes & Reitzes, 1986), that community organization practice would shift to an approach that emphasized organizing and empowering clients and other members of the community to achieve social changes.

Specht and Courtney (1993) describe the convergence of the three streams of casework, group work, and community organization in the mid-1930s as creating the social work trinity:

> Social work practice had evolved into specializations: social casework, social group work, and community organization. Each drew on different theories. Community organization was related clearly enough to the organizational frameworks within which social casework was practiced to make the relationship practical even though it was not compatible philosophically and theoretically. Social group work began with a philosophical concern for social improvement and moral uplift of disadvantaged people. However, social casework focused on individual causes of problems, while social group work concentrated on citizen education for social action and social development. (p. 36)

Thus, these three major modalities of practice, each defined by the targeted client (individual, family, group, and community), merged to become the modern-day social work profession.

This creation of a unified profession was consummated in 1955, when seven separate social work organizations—the American Association of Group Workers, the American Association of Medical Social Workers, the American Association of Psychiatric Social Workers, the American Association of Social Workers, the National Association of School Social Workers, the Social Work Research Group, and the Association for the Study of Community Organizations—united to form a common professional organization, the National Association of Social Workers (NASW). While sharing a code of ethics, a value system, knowledge, and skills, social workers still differentiated themselves into groups by methodology, describing themselves as caseworkers, group workers, or community organizers.

For the caseworkers, the "friendship" of the friendly visitors became the "relationship" of the clinician with the client. The strong influence of psychoanalytic theory was evident at schools of social work, and with few exceptions, the diagnostic model of medicine—the three-phase process of study, diagnosis, and treatment—was seen as a model of professionalism worthy of emulation.

In more recent years, the three modalities of practice have been subsumed under two more general categories. Casework, family work, and group work are often combined into "micro-" or "clinical" practice. Community organization practice has become more closely linked to policy and management-oriented social work in a "macro" subgrouping. A trend toward the deemphasis of specialization has led to the wider use of the term **generalist practice**, which has come to describe a social work practitioner whose knowledge and skills encompass a broad spectrum and who assesses problems and their solutions comprehensively. The term **generic social work** is often used interchangeably with *generalist practice*, although the former refers more specifically to the social work orientation that emphasizes a common core of knowledge and skills associated with social service provision.

This historical review presents an oversimplified description of the development of the social work profession. For our purposes, the main point is that the profession is the product of a unique merger of interest in individual healing and social change for social justice. This is the basis for what will be presented as the "two-client" idea, which is central to the interactional model of social work. In the complex interaction between the individual and her or his social surroundings (such as society, community, family, small group), the social work professional will always be identifiable because of her or his attention to both clients. While common values, knowledge, beliefs, skills, professional associations, codes of ethics, and so on help to unify the profession, it is the shared sense of social workers' function in society that makes their profession unique.

The Function of the Social Work Profession

In developing his view of the social work profession's function in society, Schwartz (1961) did not accept the broadly held idea that the profession was defined solely by a base of shared knowledge, values, and skills. He also rejected the notion that one could describe the profession's function solely in terms of aspirations for positive general outcomes, such as "enhancing social functioning" or "facilitating individual growth and development." He understood that a profession required a general and yet unique functional statement that would direct the actions of all social workers regardless of the setting in which they practiced. While many variant elements of practice would be introduced by the particular problems facing the client, the mission of the agency or host setting, the modality of service (such as individual, group, or family counseling), the age and stage of life of the client, and so forth, Schwartz viewed professional function as a core element of any social work practice theory.

Function is defined here as the specific part the profession that each social work professional plays in the helping process. To understand the term better, consider how an automobile engine might work if all the parts were like people. If we defined the function of the carburetor as "helping to make the car move," we would be defining function in terms of outcome. This would not provide specific direction to the carburetor, which would be left on its own to figure out how to play its part in the process. On the other hand, if we specifically defined the carburetor's function as mixing air and gasoline to create a vapor that could then be ignited by a spark plug, our anthropomorphic carburetor would have a clear idea of how to do its part. If all parts of the engine understood clearly their functional roles, and if all parts implemented that role effectively, the car would start to move.

This kind of functional preciseness is what Schwartz felt every social worker needed in order to understand his or her role in the many complex situations faced in everyday practice. This professional role would travel with the social worker to any agency or host setting and would, in part, define the social worker's interventions at any given moment. We would be able to recognize a social worker in action, and distinguish him or her from other professionals with similar knowledge, values, and skills, because we would see the functional role in action. Schwartz's definition of the function of the social work profession was based on the earlier described underlying assumptions about the essentially symbiotic nature of the individual-social relationship. He examined the history of the profession and tried to identify the essential functional assignment that might define a unique role for social work.

His definition of the professional function is "to mediate the process through which the individual and his society reach out for each other through a mutual need for self-fulfillment." To the earlier diagram of a hypothetical client attempting to deal with several important systems, a third force is introduced (see Figure 1.2).

With the addition of the worker, the basic triangular model is complete. On the left is the client reaching out with all available strength, attempting to negotiate important systems while often simultaneously throwing up defenses that cut him or her off from the needed systems. On the right are the systems reaching out to incorporate the client but often reaching ambivalently. At the bottom is the social worker, whose sense of function and skills are mobilized in an effort to help client and system overcome the obstacles that block their engagement.

One could argue that this functional statement is too limited. I have already indicated that the term *mediation* is used in a broad sense and can include other activities such as confrontation and advocacy. There are times when the crucial work in the area between the helping person and the system requires conflict and social pressure. In one example, the social worker helps a tenant group confront the political system because of the unresponsiveness of the housing project administrator (see Chapter 16).

Even with a broad interpretation of mediation, one might still argue that this functional statement is too limited. However, if the helping person is clear about the helping function and that function is specifically defined, then the chance of consistently

FIGURE 1.2

Relationship of Client, Systems, and Worker

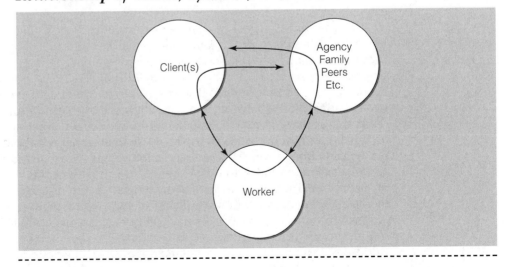

performing it improves. Jessie Taft (1942), one of the early leaders of the functional school of social work practice, stressed this view. In addition, the client who understands what the helping person does—the way in which help is given—will be better able to use the worker's services.

Couple's counseling provides a good illustration. The division between the given couple has caused most people they know (family, friends, coworkers) to take sides with one or the other. An early, often unstated question on the minds of both partners as they enter the counseling process is "Whose side will the social worker be on?" Only through explanation and demonstration can the skillful worker help the couple understand that the worker must be on both sides at the same time in order to help them. Practice experience has taught most workers that the moment they identify with one side versus the other, they have lost their usefulness to the client who feels cut off.

Clarity about one's professional function and role in the helping process is essential for effective practice. When a social worker is clear about his or her part in the interaction, the worker will be less likely to take over the client's part—for example, doing things for the client instead of with the client. Once a social worker has integrated a sense of professional function, then the communications, relationship, and problem-solving skills become the tools through which the social worker puts her or his function into action. I have long believed that most students and new practitioners already have many of the basic human relations skills needed to be helpful. Once they have integrated a clear sense of their general function as social workers, and the specific way it emerges in a particular setting with a particular client, in a particular modality of practice, then developing more sophisticated skills will follow. Clearly knowing one's role, then, matters a great deal; beginning workers can do well from the start with a clear purpose in mind.

Again, a profession is differentiated from other professions by its functional role, not by its knowledge, values, and skills. For example, in a hospital, empathy skills are important for the social worker, the doctor, and the nurse. Each professional must harness these skills in pursuit of his or her separate functions. In the scores of examples included in this book, you will see that social workers often get in trouble in their practice when they lose their sense of functional clarity. For example, you will see incidents in family work in which the social worker identifies with the children and loses the parents. Such a worker can no longer help the family work on its issues. In another example, a new worker who claims he has "solved" the client's problem by taking him to church on Sunday may once again be unclear about the role. One might see ongoing professional development as a continual deepening of the social worker's understanding of the helping function as well as a developing understanding of those situations that may lead to functional confusion and diffusion. *Functional diffusion* occurs when the social worker tries to be everything for everyone, losing sight of the core job. This is not a terminal illness, however, and is usually cured by a dose of functional clarity.

At this point, you may be wondering how generally applicable this mediation assignment can be. In the rest of the book, we shall work toward the answer, drawing illustrations from a range of settings with varying types of individuals, families, groups, and communities. In each example, you should mentally step into the shoes of the worker. The argument is that the worker's sense of the next step at specific moments of interaction will be vitally affected by an internalized sense of function.

These introductory comments have laid out the general model applied in each step of analysis throughout the book. A further elaboration of this function and worker tasks will be shared in the context of practice illustrations.

Social Work Skill and the Working Relationship

At the core of the interactional theory of social work practice is a model of the helping process in which the skill of the worker helps to create a positive working relationship. In turn, this relationship is the medium through which the worker influences the outcomes of practice. This simple model can be visualized as in Figure 1.3.

While the model suggests that applied skill leads to relationship, which then influences outcomes, the double-pointed arrows imply that the model is dynamic. For example, a change in the working relationship will affect the worker's use of skill. A worker may be influenced in her or his interaction with a client by the changing nature of the relationship (for example, a positive relationship leading to more empathy on the worker's part). Similarly, positive or negative outcomes for the client may influence his or her sense of the relationship.

Another model incorporated into this theory has to do with the relationship between clients' ability to manage their feelings and their ability to manage their problems. These ideas were developed as part of the theory-building effort I have described in other publications (Shulman, 1978, 1981, 1991). The construct is based on the assumption that how we feel powerfully affects how we act. The relationship between feelings and action is reciprocal: How we act also influences how we feel.

To this feeling-behavioral connection we can add a third element: cognition. *Cognition* refers to the way clients think about themselves and their environment. The contributions of cognitive-behavioral theory (Berlin, 1983) have helped us to broaden our understanding of how a client's perception of reality can have a powerful impact on self-image, identification of the nature of a problem, and self-assessment of the ability to cope. I argue throughout this book that how clients think affects how they feel, which affects how they act, in a circular and reciprocal manner. The model presented could be termed a cognitive-affective-behavioral framework without confusing it with other models that incorporate cognitive-behavioral approaches.

For example, some female survivors of childhood sexual abuse describe themselves as "damaged goods" as they enter their teenage years. These clients may respond to the oppression they have experienced by internalizing a negative self-image and assuming some form of responsibility for what was done to them. They may express feelings of guilt and concern that they may have been seductive toward the offending adult, thus shifting responsibility for the problem to themselves—a form of self-blaming the victim. This is an example of the internalized oppressor at work. Symptoms of depression and personal apathy often cover an underlying rage that the child learned to suppress in order to survive. The use of alcohol and drugs provides an escape, a flight from the pain associated with the abuse, and is an

FIGURE 1.3

Worker Skill and the Working Relationship

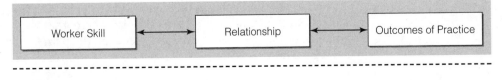

example of the self-destructive behavior, described earlier, in which oppressed clients become autopressors.

The association between these perceptions of low self-image and the feelings (such as shame) that they can generate may lead these teenage survivors to enter into relationships and life patterns that perpetuate their exploitation. For example, a low sense of self-esteem may lead to relationships with exploitive men who use physical, emotional, and sexual violence to maintain control over the lives of women. The use of drugs and involvement in the street culture may lead to prostitution. These actions on the client's part, related to the client's feelings, may in turn deepen the sense of being "damaged." Thus, negative reciprocal relationships among how the client feels, thinks, and acts result in a deepening of the problems in living. Of course for many survivors, protective factors, described later in this chapter, may mitigate the impact of the abuse on their lives.

An intervention is needed to disrupt this vicious cycle. In the example of the survivor, as the worker helps the client to examine the underlying pain and rage, and to face the oppressor within, the client can begin to take control of the emotions and more effectively manage them rather than being managed by them. Effective practice can help the client reframe the source of the problem and begin to perceive herself as a survivor rather than a victim. Techniques associated with solution-focused practice, also described later in this chapter, can also help the client see his or her strengths and begin the healing process. The principle of dealing with feelings in pursuit of purpose, discussed further in later chapters, will cause the worker to help the client connect her feelings and perceptions with her actions. Being aware of the connections between how we think, feel, and act is an early step in taking control over these thoughts and feelings and over our resultant behaviors. As the client better manages these feelings and develops a more accurate assessment of herself and her situation, she can begin to manage her life problems more effectively. Success with her life's problems, in turn, will influence her thoughts and feelings.

For example, the teenage survivor in this illustration may begin to change her self-destructive behavior by taking some first step on her own behalf. Obtaining help with her addiction, leaving the streets for a shelter, or attempting to break off from an abusive and exploitive relationship may be the first step in breaking out of her trap. Each step that she takes in her own self-interest, however small, can contribute to a more positive feeling about her self and strengthen her to take the next step. Thus, managing her feelings helps her to manage her problems, and managing her problems helps her to manage her feelings.

As this model is explored, we shall see that if the worker is to help clients manage their feelings, the worker must be able to manage his or her own emotions. For example, feeling the client's pain, a worker who is helping a survivor of sexual abuse may prematurely attempt to reassure her that she is not damaged. Or the worker may take on the woman's anger against the men who have exploited her, which may preempt the client's essential work in facing her own anger. Both of these understandable emotional reactions by the worker may block the client's ability to manage her own feelings. The worker would need to share his or her sense of the client's pain without trying to relieve it. For example,

> As I listen to you I'm feeling how much pain you are in, how damaged you must feel. A big part of me wants to say, "Don't feel that way! You are a person of value." But I know that no matter what I say the pain is there, and I can't make it go away.

The anger against the exploitive men—for example, a sexually abusive father—can also be shared, but in a manner that helps the client face her own anger rather than doing the work for her. For example,

It makes me angry when I think of what was done to you by people you expected to take care of you and to protect you. But from what you are saying to me, it seems that your feelings are mixed right now. It sounds like a big part of you wishes your family could be different, could change, and that you could still be like a real family.

Sharing the worker's feelings, in an integration of personal and professional selves, is a crucial element in this model.

The eight skills examined in my study (Shulman, 1991) were drawn from those that proved to be most important in my prior research (1979b, 1978). Twenty-two specific skills were examined in the earlier research, with 10 of the 22 associating at a significant level with developing a positive relationship and worker helpfulness. While all of these skills and others are discussed in the chapters that follow, a particular emphasis is placed on the eight skills examined in the more recent work. (For a clearer understanding of methodology, findings, and limitations, review a more detailed outline of this research in Appendix A on the book's companion page on the Wadsworth website.) These eight skills have been organized into two groupings. The following list summarizes the two sets of skills:

Workers' Skills for Helping Clients Manage Their Feelings

Reaching inside of silences

Putting the client's feelings into words

Displaying understanding of the client's feelings

Sharing the worker's feelings

Workers' Skills for Helping Clients Manage Their Problems

Clarifying the worker's purpose and role

Reaching for client feedback

Partializing concerns

Supporting clients in taboo areas

All of these skills are important in all phases of practice. However, each skill may have various meanings or impacts at different stages in the relationship. Because the helping process is so complex, it helps to analyze it against the backdrop of the phases of work. The four phases of work described in this book are as follows:

- Preliminary (or Preparatory) Phase
- Beginning (or Contracting) Phase
- Middle (or Work) Phase
- Ending and Transition Phase

Each phase of work—preliminary, beginning, middle, and ending-transition—has unique dynamics and requires specific skills. Jessie Taft (1949), referring to the beginning, middle, and ending phases, was one of the first to draw attention to the effect of time on social work practice. Schwartz (1971) incorporated this dimension into his work, adding the preliminary phase and modifying the ending phase to the "ending and transition" phase. The **preliminary (or preparatory) phase** is the period prior to the first encounter with the client. The **beginning (or contracting) phase** refers to the first sessions in which the worker develops a working contract with the client and begins developing the working relationship. The **middle (or work) phase** is the period in which the work is done. Finally, in the **ending and transition phase**, the worker prepares the client to bring the relationship to an end and to make transitions to new experiences.

Another way of thinking about these phases is that the client (individual, family, group, or community) must make a first decision in the beginning phase about whether or not to face the problems and engage with the worker. Even mandatory clients (such as child welfare or probation) must make that decision in order for the work to be effective. The second decision comes as the client makes the transition to the middle phase and decides to deal with the more difficult and often painful issues. The third decision is made by the client as she or he prepares for the termination of the relationship and, in a manner often described as "doorknob therapy," raises the most powerful and difficult issues of the work. These processes are identified in the balance of this book using examples of micro- (clinical) and macropractice.

We begin the exploration of these constructs in Chapter 2, which focuses on the preliminary phase of practice in work with individuals. The phases of work serve as an organizing principle for the rest of the book as well.

The Integration of Personal and Professional Selves

In the history of social work, another carryover from the medical model was the importance placed on maintaining one's professional self. Most helping professions stressed the professional role and the need to suppress personal feelings and reactions. For example, in order to work with stressful patients, one might have to keep one's real reactions in check so as to avoid appearing judgmental. A professional worker was described as one who maintained control of emotions and would not become angry or too emotionally involved, would not cry in the presence of a client, and so forth. The injunction to the worker appeared to be "Take your professional self to work and leave your personal self at home." This image of professionalism was (and still is) widely held, with many of my social work students starting their careers wondering if they would have problems becoming a social worker because they "felt too much."

The practice model presented in this text will suggest that we are faced with a false dichotomy when we believe we must choose between our personal self and our professional self. In fact, I will argue that we are at our best in our work when we are able to synthesize the two by integrating our personal self into our professional role.

The conflict of views about what defines the professional self was brought home dramatically in a workshop I led on direct practice. One pediatric oncology social worker described an incident in which a mother appeared at her door after being referred by the attending physician. The mother had just been told that her 7-year-old daughter had a terminal illness. After explaining this to the social worker, the mother broke down and cried.

When I asked the worker what she did, she described how overwhelmed she felt by the mother's grief. All that the worker could do was sit and hold the mother's hand, softly crying with her. I maintain that while there would be much work to be done in this case (such as helping the mother to deal with the dying daughter and her family over the next few months), at this point what the mother needed most was not advice but someone to be with her. In fact, as the worker partially experienced the mother's pain, and shared it with her through her own tears, she was giving that client an important gift of her own feelings. The worker was being professional in the best sense of that word. Other workers, who might not cry with a client, might make the same gift in other ways—through facial expressions, a respectful silence, or a hand on the shoulder—each worker responding in a way consistent with his or her own personality. The crucial factor would be the worker's willingness to be honest and to share his or her own feelings.

In my example, the worker continued her story by telling us that her supervisor passed the open door, called her out, and berated her for unprofessional behavior. The supervisor said, "How could you let yourself break down that way? You can't help your clients if you become overwhelmed yourself." When I asked the worker what she took from the experience, she replied, "I learned to keep my door closed."

While many who hear that story are upset with the supervisor, I am not. I realize that she may have been trained, as I was, in a time when personal expressions of emotion were considered to be unprofessional. I encouraged the social worker to talk to her supervisor, because I felt it was crucial for her to obtain support from her supervisor and colleagues if she was to continue to provide this kind of help to clients. My research (Shulman, 1979b) has emphasized the importance of formal and informal sources of social support for social workers. This worker was making a gift to the client of her willingness to "be with" her at a terrible moment in her life. The worker's capacity to continue to be there for the client depends somewhat on her having someone—supervisor, colleague, or both—there for her.

This artificial split between personal and professional selves was created because of the profession's understandable concerns over the inappropriate use of self by helping professionals. For example, concern arose about *countertransference,* a process in which workers might project onto clients their own unfinished family business (relating to a father in a family as if he were one's own parent, for instance). The profession was troubled by workers who used the argument of spontaneity to justify acting out with clients, such as getting inappropriately angry or judgmental or sharing personal problems ("If you think you have troubles with your kids, let me tell you about my family"). Unethical behavior with clients, such as abusing the powerful forces of the helping bond to sexually exploit a vulnerable client, is another example. Each of these examples illustrates a lack of integration of personal and professional selves. The concerns about the use of the personal self were and continue to be well founded. Unfortunately, the solution to separate personal from professional led to more problems than it resolved.

The argument advanced throughout this text will be that each of us brings our own personal style, artistry, background, feelings, values, and beliefs to our professional practice. Rather than denying or suppressing these, we need to learn more about ourselves in the context of our practice, and find ways to use our self in pursuit of our professional functions. We will make many mistakes along the way, saying things we will later regret, having to apologize to clients, then learning from these mistakes, correcting them, and then making what I call more sophisticated mistakes.

In other words, we will be real people carrying out difficult jobs as best we can, rather than paragons of virtue who present an image of perfection.

As we demonstrate to our clients our humanness, vulnerability, willingness to risk, spontaneity, honesty, and lack of defensiveness (or defensiveness for which we later apologize), we shall be modeling the very behaviors we hope to see in our clients. Thus, when workers or students ask me, "Should I be professional or should I be myself?" I reply that the dualism implied in the question does not exist. They must be themselves if they are going to be professional. Fortunately, we have the whole of our professional lives to learn how to affect the synthesis.

Oppression Psychology

Social workers need to draw on the social sciences and the large theory and knowledge base about human development, behavior, and the impact of the social environment. This theory base can help the practitioner understand the client in new ways and to hear underlying client communication that might otherwise be missed.

As one example of a theory that can guide social work practice, I have selected the **oppression psychology** of Frantz Fanon. A brief introduction to the life, views, and psychology of Fanon will help to set the stage for the use of his central ideas and those of others who have built on his work. Fanon, an early exponent of the psychology of oppression, was a black, West Indian revolutionary psychiatrist who was born on the French-colonized island of Martinique in 1925 and who died at age 36. His short life was chronicled by Bulhan (1985). At age 17, Fanon enlisted in the French army to fight against the Nazis in World War II. He later became interested in and studied psychiatry. While working as a chief of service at a psychiatric hospital in Algeria, he secretly provided support and medical services to the national liberation front (FLN) fighting against the French colonial government. When he resigned his position, he became a spokesperson for the FLN and was based in Tunisia. These experiences and others shaped his views of psychology, which challenged many of the constructs of the widely held, European American, white, male-dominated psychology of the day. Bulhan states,

> In the first chapter of his classic *The Wretched of the Earth* (Fanon, 1968), Fanon elaborated the dynamics of violence and the human drama that unfolds in situations of oppression. He boldly analyzed violence in its structural, institutional, and personal dimensions.
>
> Fanon analyzed the psycho-existential aspects of life in a racist society. He emphasized the experiential features and hidden psycho-affective injuries of blacks and the various defensive maneuvers they adopted. Another unstated objective was quite personal: He himself had experienced these injuries, and writing about them was a way of coming to terms with himself. (p. 138)

While Fanon's psychology emerged from his analysis of race oppression, particularly oppression associated with white, European colonial repression of people of color, many of the key concepts apply to any oppressed population. In such an application, workers need to recognize the significant differences in degree and types of oppression experienced by clients. The results of the oppression of African

Americans, for example, rooted in the unique experience of slavery, must be seen as one of the most critical, major social problems still facing urban areas in the United States.

In addition, we must be cautious in how we think about the impact of oppression, because we might inadvertently ignore the significant strengths and resiliency demonstrated by oppressed clients and communities. Such a one-sided view can lead to a practice that does not recognize or work with existing sources of support (such as the extended family, the church, community leadership). The next section of this chapter complements this oppression model with a summary of a resiliency model that helps uncover clients' strengths for coping.

If social workers think about issues of oppression, vulnerability, and resiliency broadly, then they can use such a model in understanding many of their clients. People with mental illness, female survivors of sexual abuse, people with AIDS, people with significant physical or mental disabilities, long-term unemployed people, people of color, the homeless, aged nursing home residents, neglected and abused children, clients addicted to substances or in recovery—all of these clients and others can be understood using a framework that takes oppression, vulnerability, and resiliency into account.

These concepts will be illustrated in the examples of practice explored in this book. Strategies for social worker intervention, based on understanding emerging from this psychology, will be directed toward helping clients deal with both the oppressor within and the oppressor without. In fact, it will be argued that unless they broaden their understanding of many of their clients' problems by seeing them as dynamic and systematic in nature and related to oppression, then the social agencies, social work departments, and helping professionals who are trying to help these clients can themselves inadvertently become part of the system of oppression.

The Master-Slave Paradigm

We have already noted the influence of Hegel's (Hegel, 1966) formulation of the master-slave dialectic, which described relationships in which two people, each depending on recognition of the self by the other, struggle to determine a hierarchy. The winner of the struggle (the master) is recognized by the loser (the slave) without having to reciprocate the recognition. While the complete exposition of the dialectic is more complex than presented here, the central idea of gaining one's sense of self through exploitation of others can be seen in many different oppressive relationships. The abusing parent and the abused child, the battering husband and his wife, societal male-female sexism, the scapegoating of religious groups (such as Muslims and Jews) and ethnic and racial groups (such as Southeast Asian immigrants, Hispanics, African Americans, Native Americans), the treatment of people with physical or mentally disabilities, the "normal" population and people who are mentally ill, and the straight society's repression of homosexuals—all are examples in which one group (usually the majority) uses another group for enhancing a sense of self.

Repeated exposure to oppression, subtle or direct, may lead vulnerable members of the oppressed group to internalize the negative self-images projected by the external oppressor—the "oppressor without." The external oppressor may be an individual (such as the sexual abuser of a child) or an aspect of society (such as the racial stereotypes perpetuated against people of color). Internalization of this image and repression of the rage associated with oppression may lead to destructive behaviors toward oneself and others as oppressed people become autopressors participating in their own oppression. Thus, the oppressor without becomes the oppressor within. Evidence of this process can be found in the maladaptive use of addictive substances and the growing internal violence in communities of oppressed people, such as city ghettos populated by people of color.

Oppressed people may develop a victim complex, "viewing all actions and communications as further assaults or simply other indications of their victim status. This is an example of 'adaptive paranoia' seen among the oppressed" (Bulhan, 1985, p. 126). The paranoia is adaptive because oppression is so omnipresent that it would be maladaptive not to be constantly alert to its presence. For the white worker with a client of color, the male worker with a female client, the straight worker with a gay or lesbian client, and so forth, this notion raises important implications for the establishment of an effective and trusting working relationship. These implications are explored in later chapters dealing with the dynamics and skills involved in developing a positive working relationship between worker and client.

Indicators of Oppression

Bulhan (1985) identifies several key indicators for objectively assessing oppression. He suggests that "all situations of oppression violate one's space, time, energy, mobility, bonding, and identity" (p. 124). He illustrates these indicators using the example of the slave:

> The male slave was allowed no physical space which he could call his own. The female slave had even less claim to space than the male slave. Even her body was someone else's property. Commonly ignored is how this expropriation of one's body entailed even more dire consequences for female slaves. The waking hours of the slave were also expropriated for life without his or her consent. The slave labored in the field and in the kitchen for the gain and comfort of the master. The slave's mobility was curbed and he or she was never permitted to venture beyond a designated perimeter without a "pass." The slave's bonding with others, even the natural relation between mother and child, was violated and eroded. The same violation of space, time, energy, mobility, bonding and identity prevailed under apartheid, which in effect, is modern-day slavery." (p. 124)

The model of a slave is an extreme example of the violation of space, time, energy, mobility, bonding, and identity as indicators of oppression. One can find current examples of these restrictions. Institutionalized racism in North America toward people of color (for example, African Americans, Native Americans) currently offers examples of restrictions on all six indicators. Not long ago, as Bulhan's comments attest, an oppressive, white government dominated South Africa through apartheid.

While the slavery experience of African Americans in North America must be considered as a unique example of oppression, the indicators may be used to assess degrees of oppression for other populations as well. In this way, a universal psychological model can help us to understand the common elements that exist in any oppressive relationship. Consider these six indicators as you read the following excerpt of a discussion among battered women in a shelter, as they describe their lives:

> Candy said one thing that she didn't like was that her husband had to be number one all the time. He felt he should come first even before the children. She said, "The man's got to be number one. Just like the president.

He's a man and he's number one. You don't see no female presidents, do you?" I said, "Are you saying that a man has the right to abuse his partner?" She said no and then turned to the women to say, "But, who's the one who always gives in in the family? The woman does." All the women nodded to this remark. Linda said, "To keep peace in the family." Candy said, "In the long run, we're the ones who are wrong for not leaving the abusive situations." She said she finally came to the realization that her man was never going to be of any help to her. In the long run, she felt that her children would help her out if she gave them a good life now. She feels very strongly about her responsibilities to her children.

Another woman, Tina, said that when she called the police for help, they thought it was a big joke. She said when she had to fill out a report at the police station, the officer laughed about the incident. The women in the group talked about their own experiences with the police which were not very good. One woman had to wait 35 minutes for the police to respond to her call after her husband had thrown a brick through her bedroom window. I said, "Dealing with the police must have been a humiliating situation for all of you. Here you are in need of help and they laugh at you. It's just not right."

Joyce said that she wanted to kill her husband. This desire had been expressed by an abused woman in a previous group session. Other women in the group said it wouldn't be worth it for her. "All he does is yell at me all the time. He makes me go down to where he works every day at lunch time. The kids and I have to sit and watch him eat. He never buys us anything to eat. Plus, he wants to know where I am every minute of the day. He implies that I sit around the house all day long doing nothing." Marie said her ex-husband used to say that to her all the time. She said, "But now I'm collecting back pay from my divorce settlement for all the work I never did around the house."

Then Joyce said she was going to tell us something that she had only told two other people in her life. Joyce said that she had been molested from the ages of 5 to 7 by her next-door neighbor, Pat. She said that Pat was friendly with her parents. Her mother would say, "Bring a glass of lemonade over to Pat." The first time she did this, he molested her. After that incident, when her mother told her to bring something over to Pat, Joyce would try to get out of it, but her mother insisted that she go over. Pat had told Joyce not to tell anyone what went on. At this point in the session, Joyce began to cry. I said that I understood this was a difficult situation for her to talk about. Candy said, "Joyce, it wasn't your fault." Joyce said she had kept this incident to herself for approximately 25 years. Finally, when she told her husband, he said, "You probably deserved it." Joyce said she felt like killing him for saying that.

Candy said she watched while her father beat her mother. She said she used to ask her mother why she put up with it. She said now she sees that it's easier to say you want to get out of a relationship than it is to actually do it. Candy said that leaving was better in the long run. By staying, the children will see their father abusing their mother. "What kind of example is that going to set for the children?" She felt her children would be happier by their leaving. Joyce said her children were happy to leave their father. She said, "They're tired of listening to him yell all the time." She said her son was more upset about leaving the dog behind than he was about leaving his father. Linda said another good reason for leaving is self-love. She said, "It comes to a point where you know he's going to kill you if you stay around."

Careful reading of the preceding excerpt provides examples of the violation of these women's space, time, energy, mobility, bonding, and identity—the six identified indicators of oppression. Other examples with differing numbers of indicators violated, and different degrees of violation, could include an inpatient in a rigidly structured psychiatric setting; a wheelchair-bound person constantly facing buildings that are not accessible; an African American woman who is the only person of her race in an organization and who is held back from advancement by the "glass ceiling" and excluded from the "old boys' network"; an unemployed, 55-year-old man who cannot get a job interview because of his age; an elderly person in a home for the aged who is tied to a chair or tranquilized all day because of staff shortages; a large, poor family, forced to live in inadequate housing, a homeless shelter, or on the street. To one degree or another, space, time, energy, mobility, bonding, and identity may be violated for each of these clients.

Alienation and Psychopathology

Bulhan believes that Fanon's complete work suggests five aspects of alienation associated with the development of "psychopathology." *Alienation* is a term commonly used in psychology and sociology to describe a state of withdrawal or estrangement. Fanon's five aspects of alienation are

- Alienation from the self
- Alienation from the significant other
- Alienation from the general other
- Alienation from one's culture
- Alienation from creative social praxis

Fanon's work emphasized alienation from the self and from one's culture. These were the inevitable results of prolonged oppression and the "deracination" (uprooting) of people of color by the oppressor. The destruction of the culture, such as the forced use of another language, is an assault on the oppressed person's sense of self, which is already alienated by the internalization of the negative self-image. Alienation from the general other refers to the estrangement between the oppressed group and the oppressor, such as the majority group. Significant others include family, friends, neighbors, and so forth. The creative social praxis refers to organized activities of society, such as employment.

An example illustrating wide-scale oppression and these five aspects of alienation can be found in the experience of Native American groups in the United States and Canada. These "first peoples" were displaced by the immigration of European, white settlers; eventually forced off their traditional lands; resettled on reservations; and cut off from their traditional forms of activity, such as hunting and fishing. Efforts on the part of Native people to fight back were met with brutal repression. During one period in U.S. history, their children were removed from their families and sent to white boarding schools. Native children in many of these boarding schools report being told to "speak white" and punished for using their native language. More recent shocking revelations have indicated that in some schools many of these children suffered physical and sexual abuse by staff and administrators.

Even social welfare services, such as those designed to protect children, participated in the alienation process by removing Native children whom they saw as neglected or abused (by certain white, middle-class, cultural standards) and then placing these children in white foster or adoptive homes. This was often done without first making a serious effort to use the formal and informal support system that existed in the Native American community. The results of these assaults on a whole people, and the resultant alienation, can be seen in high levels of family violence, alcohol addiction, and suicide among some groups of Native Americans. The alienation is reversible, however, and significant progress has been made by Native people in opposing and changing many of the oppressive influences on their culture. For example, in British Columbia, Canada, several bands (tribal subgroups) take full responsibility for child welfare services and have maximized the use of native resources for children in need. An emphasis on traditional values and a reintroduction of traditional ceremonies and events, such as the potlatch, a large-scale meeting and celebration that is attended by different bands within a tribe and that includes healing circles, have served as important vehicles for reversing the alienation process.

In working with clients who are members of groups that have experienced long-term oppression, workers must understand the potential impact of alienation as an underlying cause of and contributor to the current problems. Cultural awareness on the part of the social worker can make a major difference in developing intervention approaches that use the strengths of the culture to decrease the alienation. Examples of this approach to practice can be found in the chapters that follow.

Methods of Defense Against Oppression

A final element of the oppression psychology theory concerns methods of defense used by oppressed people. Bulhan (1985) summarizes these as follows:

> In brief, under conditions of prolonged oppression, there are three major modes of psychological defense and identity development among the oppressed. The first involves a pattern of compromise, the second flight, and the third fight. Each mode has profound implications for the development of identity, experience of psychopathology, reconstituting of the self, and relationship to other people. Each represents a mode of existence and of action in a world in which a hostile other elicits organic reactions and responses. Each also entails its own distinct risks of alienation and social rewards under conditions of oppression. (p. 193)

Bulhan sees these modes of defense as implemented in stages, although it is possible for individuals and whole groups to be stuck in a stage or take decades for a transition to take place to a new stage. The first stage involves capitulation, in which the oppressed people identify with the oppressor without and assimilate into the majority culture. This is associated with a rejection of one's own culture—the alienation mentioned earlier. The second stage, which he calls revitalization, involves a rejection of the dominant culture and a "defensive romanticism of the indigenous culture" (1985, p. 193). The third stage, in which a clear commitment toward radical change is made, is termed the radicalization stage. Individuals and whole populations can move with a different timing through these stages, and some may become fixed in one or the other. For an individual or a group, whatever stage is in effect will have a profound effect on all aspects of alienation as well as on the mode of reaction of the dominant culture.

While the model just described is most directly related to issues of cultural identity, a wider model of defensive reactions to oppression can be understood when one applies certain elements to cases. Examples in the chapters that follow will illustrate how oppression can lead to capitulation, resulting in symptoms that are then viewed as pathological. In one illustration, a group of survivors of childhood sexual abuse describes the pattern of capitulation that led to their loss of self-identity and their identity as women. The resultant internalizing of the belief that they are "damaged goods," as well as their willingness to feel guilty about what was done to them, profoundly affects their current lives and relationships. A revitalization of their selves and their sense of their identity as women can be seen developing, enhanced by the social support of the group. Finally, a form of radicalization is noted when the group decides to join a "Take Back the Night" march in the community, protesting actively against violence toward women. This leads to their making a commitment to work toward changing community understanding and attitudes toward children who have been sexually abused.

This brief summary of some central ideas in oppression psychology theory sets the stage for the use of these constructs in later chapters. Although there are many other models that can help workers understand their clients and develop effective intervention strategies, it is a very useful model for thinking about work with oppressed and vulnerable populations, which makes up a large part of the social worker's practice. As we consider the impact of oppression, we must also understand the elements of resilience that help individuals, families, communities, and entire population groups survive and often thrive in the face of adversity.

Resilience Theory

During the 1970s and 1980s, developmental research focused on risk factors that appeared to be associated with negative outcomes for clients. A child growing up in an inner-city neighborhood besieged by drugs and violence faced a degree of risk in attempting to negotiate the passage to young adulthood and beyond. If the same child also had experienced childhood trauma (physical or sexual abuse, abandonment, and so on) and had parents and family members who were active abusers of drugs and alcohol, research indicated that the degree of risk for the child's negative developmental outcome increased exponentially.

Yet, a recurring anomaly in social work practice experience and literature indicated that not all children exposed to high degrees of risk and trauma had negative developmental outcomes. As Butler (1997), examining the "anatomy of resilience," pointed out,

> A growing number of clinicians and researchers were arguing that the risk-factor model burdens at-risk children with the expectation that they will fail, and ignores those who beat the odds. Broad epidemiological studies, they say, don't explain why one girl, sexually abused by a relative, becomes an unwed mother or a prostitute while another becomes an Oprah Winfrey or a Maya Angelou. Retrospective studies can't explain why one man, raised in a harsh, crowded household in impoverished Richmond, California, becomes addicted to crack cocaine and dies of AIDS, while his younger brother—Christopher Darden—graduates from law school, and goes on to prosecute O. J. Simpson. It's time, they say, to see what the Dardens and Winfreys of the world have to teach. (p. 25)

Given the widespread nature of substance abuse, the evidence of substantial emotional, physical, and sexual abuse, the increase in the nature and degree of violence in many communities, and the growing numbers of children living in poverty, it is little wonder that research shifted toward understanding why some children, families, and communities can still thrive under these conditions, given the risks that they face. This focus lends itself to the development of both preventative and curative approaches to clients at risk.

Rak and Patterson (1996, p. 369) identified four major groupings of protective factors associated with the "buffering hypothesis": that is, variables that may provide a buffer of protection against life events that affect at-risk children:

1. The personal characteristics of the children (e.g., an ability from infancy on to gain others' positive attention)
2. Family conditions (e.g., focused nurturing during the first year of life and little prolonged separation from the preliminary caretaker)
3. Supports in the environment (e.g., role models, such as teachers, school counselors, mental health workers, neighbors, and clergy)
4. Self-concept factors (e.g., the capacity to understand self and self-boundaries in relation to long-term family stressors such as psychological illness)

Garmezy, Masten, and Tellegen (1984) suggested three models for understanding the relationship among risk, vulnerability, and resilience. These were the compensatory model, in which protective factors simply outweigh risk factors; a challenge model suggesting that limited risk factors enhance competency; and the conditional model, which focuses on personal factors that increase or decrease the impact of the risk factors.

Masten (2001) reviewed the existing resilience models and research and identified two major streams of thought. One is the variable-focused study, which suggests that parenting qualities, intellectual functioning, socioeconomic class, and so forth correlate with positive adaptive behavior. The second line of inquiry is the person-focused study, which tries to understand the whole individual rather than specific variables. Researchers using this latter approach seek to identify groups of individuals with patterns of good versus poor adaptive functioning in life contexts of high versus low risks and then compare outcomes. After reviewing studies using both approaches, Masten drew the following conclusions:

> The accumulated data on resilience in development suggest that this class of phenomena is more ordinary than one was led to expect by extraordinary case histories that often inspired the study. Resilience appears to be a common phenomenon arising from ordinary human adaptive processes. The great threats to human development are those that jeopardize the systems underlying these adaptive processes, including brain development and cognition, caregiver-child relationships, regulation of emotion and behavior, and the motivation for learning and engaging the environment. (p. 238)

Developmental Psychology Theory and Research

A landmark study in this area involved 698 infants on the Hawaiian Island of Kauai who, in 1955, became participants in a 30-year, longitudinal study of "how some individuals triumph over physical disadvantages and deprived childhoods" (Werner, 1989, p. 106). Werner described the goals that she and her collaborators shared as follows: "to assess the long-term consequences of prenatal and perinatal stress and to document the effects of adverse early rearing conditions on children's physical, cognitive, and psychosocial development" (p. 106). She described their growing interest in resilience as follows:

> But as our study progressed we began to take a special interest in certain "high risk" children who, in spite of exposure to reproductive stress, discordant and impoverished home lives and uneducated, alcoholic, or mentally disturbed parents, went on to develop healthy personalities, stable careers, and strong interpersonal relations. We decided to try to identify the protective factors that contributed to the resilience of these children. (p. 106)

The researchers identified 201 "vulnerable" children (30 percent of the surviving children) as high-risk if they encountered four or more risk factors by the age of 2 (severe perinatal stress, chronic poverty, uneducated parents, or troubled family environments marked by discord, divorce, parental alcoholism, or mental illness). Two-thirds of this group (129) developed serious learning or behavior problems by the age of 10 or had delinquency records, mental health problems, or pregnancies by the time they were 18.

It was the other third (72) of these high-risk children, who "grew into competent young adults who loved well, worked well, and played well" who attracted the researchers' attention (Werner, 1989, p. 108). They identified several constitutional factors as sources of resilience (high activity level, low degree of excitability and distress, high degrees of sociability, ability to concentrate at school, problem-solving and reading skills, and effective use of their talents, for example). They also identified environmental factors (coming from families with four or fewer children, spaces of two or more years between themselves and their next siblings, the opportunity to establish a close bond with at least one caretaker who provided positive attention during the first years of life, and so forth). These resilient children were found to be "particularly adept at recruiting such surrogate parents when a biological parent was unavailable or incapacitated" (p. 108). These children were also able to use their network of neighbors, school friends and teachers, church groups, and so forth to provide emotional support in order to succeed "against the odds" (p. 110).

The researchers concluded on a hopeful note:

> As long as the balance between stressful life events and protective factors is favorable, successful adaptation is possible. When stressful events outweigh the protective factors, however, even the most resilient child can have problems. It may be possible to shift the balance from vulnerability to resilience through intervention, either by decreasing exposure to risk factors or stressful events or by increasing the number of protective factors and sources of support that are available. (Werner, 1989, p. 111)

Researchers and theorists have built on this basic set of ideas: Life stressors can lead to negative outcomes for people at high risk; however, personal and environmental factors can buffer the individual, providing the resilience to overcome adversity.

For example, Fonagy, Steele, Steele, and Higgitt (1994) examined attachment theory, which focuses on the impact of early infant-caregiver attachments on a child's development and the security of such attachments. They examined the intergenerational transmission of insecure attachments, focusing on factors that might disrupt a negative cycle: in other words, ways to help mothers who had themselves experienced insecure attachments avoid transmitting these to their own children.

Other researchers have applied the basic model to specific populations (as defined by race, ethnicity, and so forth) or economic status (poverty), or community variables (inner-city, level of violence). For example, Daly, Jennings, Beckett, and Leashore (1995) make use an "Africentric paradigm" to describe an emphasis on collectivity, expressed as shared concern and responsibility for others: "Scholarship using this perspective identifies positive aspects of African American life richly embedded in spirituality and a world-view that incorporates African traits and commitment to common causes" (p. 241)

As an example on the individual level, referring to the resilience of successful African American men, the authors cite research findings (Gary & Leashore, 1982; Hacker, 1992) that suggest the following:

> Much of their success can be attributed to individual and family resilience, the ability to "bounce back" after defeat or near defeat, and the mobilization of limited resources while simultaneously protecting the ego against a constant array of social and economic assaults. To varying degrees, success results from a strong value system that includes belief in self, industrious efforts, desire and motivation to achieve, religious beliefs, self-respect and respect for others, responsibility toward one's family and community, and cooperation. (Daly et al., 1995, p. 242)

In another example, researchers examined age, race, and setting by focusing on risk and resilience for African American youths in school settings (Connell, Spencer, & Aber, 1994). They developed a theoretical model that they tested with data from two large samples in two cities: New York and Atlanta. Their findings confirm that family involvement is an important target for these interventions. This study's results also support efforts to develop intervention strategies for increasing poor African American youths' belief in their own abilities and capacities to affect their academic outcomes and for improving their relationship with peers in the school context. Further,

> perhaps the most intriguing and disturbing implication of this study for our understanding of risk and resilience is that disaffected behavior in low-income African-American youth can lessen parental involvement, which in turn contributes to negative appraisals of self that exacerbate disaffected patterns of action and contribute to negative educational outcomes. (p. 504)

Christian and Barbarin (2001) also examined the importance of parental involvement on the adjustment of low-income African American children. They found that children of parents attending church at least weekly had fewer behavior problems than did those that attended less frequently. This supported the importance of religiosity as a sociocultural resource in African American families with children potentially at risk for behavioral and emotional maladjustments related to growing up in poor families and communities. In a second and related line of inquiry, the researchers hypothesized that parents who reported a positive racial identity, as well those who tended to externalize by attributing the causes of negative African American life outcomes to external forces, would have children with fewer behavioral problems. While these two variables might be related to parental self-esteem, they did not directly affect the children's incidence of behavioral problems. In fact, parents who tended to internalize explanations of poor outcomes (such as not working hard enough, lack of persistence) had children with fewer behavioral problems. The authors concede that the limitations of the study do not allow wider generalizations; nonetheless, this finding was both unexpected and intriguing.

Richters and Martinez (1993) offer an example of resilience research that examines the impact of community violence on childhood development. They examined factors contributing to resilience on the part of 72 children attending their first year of elementary school in a violent neighborhood of Washington, D.C. Their findings indicate the following:

> Despite the fact that these children were being raised in violent neighborhoods, had been exposed to relatively high levels of violence in the community, and were experiencing associated distress symptoms, community violence exposure levels were not predictive of adaptational failure or success. Instead, adaptational status was systematically related to characteristics of the children's homes. (p. 609)

The authors point out that only when the environmental adversities contaminated the safety and stability of children's homes did their odds of adaptational failure increase.

In a study of the risk and protective factors associated with gang involvement among urban African American adolescents, the researchers found that youths with current or past gang membership documented higher levels of risk involvement, lower levels of resilience, higher exposure to violence, and higher distress symptoms than did youths with no gang affiliations (Li et al., 2002). The findings persisted when controlled for age, gender, and risk involvement. The authors suggest that gang membership itself is associated with increased risk and ill effects on psychological well-being. They also found that strong family involvement and resiliency protects against gang involvement.

Garmezy (1991) focused on the resilience and vulnerability of children in relation to the impact of poverty. He states,

> The evidence is sturdy that many children and adults do overcome life's difficulties. Since good outcomes are frequently present in a large number of life histories, it is critical to identify those "protective" factors that seemingly enable individuals to circumvent life stressors. (p. 421)

The author points to a core of variables. These include "warmth, cohesion, and the presence of some caring adults (such as a grandparent) in the absence of responsive parents or in the presence of marked marital discord" (p. 421). Similar findings in studies examining the resiliency of children exposed to poverty and other traumas have identified emotional responsivity in the parent-child relationship as a buffering factor (Egeland, Carlson, & Sroufe, 1993).

In one example of a study focusing on children from maltreating homes, Herrenkohl, Herrenkohl and Egolf (1994) report on a longitudinal study of the effects of abuse and neglect on 457 children. The study began in 1976 and continued with follow-up studies of 345 of the children in 1980–1982 (elementary school age) and again, in 1990–1992 (late adolescence). The 1980 phase included children receiving services from the local child welfare agencies for abuse ($N = 105$) or neglect ($N = 86$), as well as a control group of children in day care ($N = 52$), Head Start programs ($N = 52$), and private nursery schools ($N = 50$). All of the children were rated on several variables and then grouped into high-functioning, low-functioning, and middle-functioning categories. School success (as in attendance, graduation) was one of the key outcome measures for determining success.

The authors suggest that their findings, although based on a limited final sample, indicate that "at least average intellectual capacity is a necessary, though not sufficient, condition for minimal success for abused and neglected children" (Herrenkohl et al., 1994, p. 304). Chronic physical abuse by one parent, without intervention or protection from another parent, created "insuperable obstacles to academic success" for children who remained in such an environment (p. 304). Their data also suggested that "the presence of at least one caretaker throughout childhood appeared to be a necessary, although not sufficient, condition for school achievement" (p. 304). Finally, positive parental expectations for self-sufficiency on the part of parents with children who experienced severe physical health problems appeared to "stimulate the child's goal-setting and determination, with good effect on their academic work" (p. 304). Unger and Wandersman (1985) explored the importance of neighbors and neighboring as sources of both informal support and social networks that helped children cope with stress.

In a more recent study examining resilience among abused and neglected children (who reported the information as adults), McGloin & Widom (2001) matched 676 abused and neglected children (substantiated cases between 1967 and 1971) with a control group of 520 non-abused and non-neglected children. The two groups were matched by gender, age, race, and approximate family social class. Both groups were administered a 2-hour in-person interview, including a psychiatric assessment, between 1989 and 1995. Of the original group, 1,307 (83 percent) were located and 1,196 (76 percent) interviewed. The authors' definition of resilience required success in eight domains of functioning: employment, education, and social activity; lack of homelessness, psychiatric disorder, and substance abuse; and two domains assessing criminal behavior. Significant differences in favor of the control group were found for the domains of employment, no homelessness, education (high school graduation), no psychiatric disorder, no arrest, and no self-reported violence. Only in the domains of no substance abuse and social activity were the results similar for both groups. When the sample was analyzed by gender, the only difference was that the control group of men had significantly less substance abuse.

In a review of the literature on resilience and poverty, Garmezy (1993) suggests that

> these findings provide new questions and new avenues for research. What factors are involved in the seeming diminution over time of resilience in some hitherto adaptive children and adults? Prolonged and cumulated stress would appear to be a prime candidate for examination. Another factor worthy of consideration would be the absence of a support structure and its availability over time. Other candidates for effecting change may be critical modifications in the child's environment such as the physical dissolution of the family. (p. 130)

Other examples of resilience studies that are population specific include research on youths with high incidence disabilities (Murray, 2003), homeless students (Reed-Victor & Stronge, 2002), and adolescents who experience marital transitions (Rodgers & Rose, 2002).

Resilience and Life-Span Theory

Resilience theory does not apply only to children and families. Staudinger, Marsiske, and Baltes (1993), working in the area of aging, have attempted to integrate the notion of resilience with work concerning developmental reserve capacity emerging from the field of life-span psychology. Life-span theory suggests that development throughout life is characterized by joint occurrence of increases (gains), decreases (losses), and maintenance (stability) in adaptive capacity (p. 542).

They suggest this theory challenges a one-dimensional model in which aging, for example, might be seen as simply the loss of capacity. Plasticity, which can be positive or negative, is another central notion of life-span theory. *Plasticity* can be defined as the individual's ability to be flexible in response to stress. This idea suggests that variable components of change can be attributed to individuals or populations and may be associated with cross-cultural or historical differences. The degree of an individual's plasticity may depend on the individual's reserve capacity, which is constituted by the internal and external resources available to the individual at a given point in time. Cognitive capacity and physical health are examples of internal resources; one's social network and financial status are external ones. Note that an individual's resources need not be fixed but may change over time (p. 542).

The authors describe two types of reserve capacity. *Baseline reserve capacity* is the individual's current "maximum performance potential" with existing internal and external resources. *Developmental reserve capacity* refers to resources that can be activated or increased. The life-span theory argues that as reserve capacity increases, so does the potential for positive plasticity.

Social work intervention activities, such as case management, may be seen as focusing on helping elderly clients, for example, to use their baseline reserves while intervening to activate their clients' developmental reserves. For example, increasing the client's social network (external reserves) through involvement in a senior citizens' program could directly improve the internal reserve capacity (health, emotional state, cognitive capacity), which in turn strengthens the client's capacity for developing stronger social networks. This client would have demonstrated positive plasticity in the area of social relationship.

Staudinger et al. (1993) attempt to merge these two streams—resilience theory and life-span theory—as follows:

> Mapping definitions of resilience onto the concepts of reserve capacity and plasticity suggests that resilience can be conceptualized as one type of plasticity. While plasticity, in principle, can be seen as encompassing the potential for any change in adaptive capacity (including increase, maintenance and decrease), resilience refers to the potential for the maintenance and regaining of levels of normal adaptation; that is, resilience is a subtype of the broader range of changes in adaptive capacity encompassed by plasticity. Like reserve capacity, resilience implies the presence of latent resources that can be activated. Unlike resilience, however, reserve capacity is not only relevant to maintaining or regaining normal levels of adaptation. Reserve capacity also refers to factors and resources that promote growth beyond the normal level of functioning. (pp. 543–544)

More recently, researchers have examined the concept of "cognitive hardiness" and coping style as buffering or moderating variables between life stress events and trauma and psychological and somatic distress (Beasley, Thompson, & Davidson, 2003). The study involved analysis of questionnaires completed by 187 students who had returned to the university as mature adults. In general, findings supported a direct effect on outcomes of life stress and psychological health. Cognitive hardiness, coping style, and negative life events also impacted outcomes. Several cases supported the concept that cognitive hardiness moderated the impact of emotional coping styles and adverse life events on psychological distress. The researchers used Kobasa and Pucetti's (1983) definition of cognitive hardiness as a personality variable; specifically, the quality of hardy individuals who

> (1) believe that they can *control* or influence events, (2) have a *commitment* to activities and their interpersonal relationships and to self, in that they recognize their own distinct values, goals and priorities in life, and (3) view change as a *challenge* rather than a threat. In the latter regard, they are predisposed to be cognitively flexible. (p. 841)

Implications for Social Work Practice

This growing interest in resilience theory and research, along with the concepts of life-span theory, fits nicely with evolving theory and practice in social work and with the interactional model. For social workers who have long held a psychosocial approach to understanding and working with clients and who have more recently embraced ecological models and a strengths perspective, these theoretical models and research findings tend to confirm what their practice wisdom and research has told them. These models also reinforce the first practice principle I was taught in graduate school: "Always reach for the client's strength!"

The strong emergence of a resilience model, with its concepts of reserve capacities and plasticity, together with the life-span idea of cognitive hardiness, can influence social work practice on many levels. For example, we have just seen in this chapter, through our own exploration of theory development, how theories provide underlying propositions about people and their behavior that can guide our interventions. Gilgun (1996) provides one example of an effort to integrate resilience theory with social work practice theory—what has been commonly described as **systems or ecological approach** or framework. She suggests that this framework leads to social work interventions that are "wide-ranging, covering research, program development, direct practice, and policy formulation, implementation, and evaluation" (p. 399). She points out that developmental psychopathology introduces social work to a language full of generative concepts and theory, while social work provides the ecological framework, strengths-based focus, and phenomenological perspectives. In combination, social work and developmental psychopathology can greatly advance knowledge to inform research, program development, practice, and policy.

We can find one example of the use of resilience theory and research in its implications for child welfare practice with African American families. Scannapieco and Jackson (1996) review the historical response of African American families to separation and loss, starting with slavery and continuing through the reconstruction period, World War II, the civil rights years, the 1970s and 1980s, and on to the 1990s. In each stage, they describe the resilience of the African American family and the ways in which it coped with life stresses brought about by racism in U.S. society. Current stresses associated with poverty, AIDS, child abuse and neglect, and reductions in services have elevated childhood risks to crisis proportions. These authors point to "kinship care" placements where the resources of the extended African American families are used to provide some of the resilience factors described in the previous discussion of the research. The authors suggest that all members of the extended family should be involved in case planning, because any of them may need to take over as full- or part-time caregivers:

> Social work practice within kinship care programs must recognize the resilient nature of the African-American family and work with the "kinship triad," made up of the children, the biological parents, and the caregiver relatives. A system of services should be directed at this union of three to ensure a permanent living arrangement for the children. (p. 194)

This same example could be conceptualized in life-span theory terminology as focusing on resources (internal and external, baseline and developmental) that have increased the positive plasticity of the African American family, thus allowing not only for recovery from trauma but also for the optimizing of individual, family, and community growth and development.

For the purposes of this chapter, I suggest that resilience and life-span theory and their related research provide an important framework for understanding and engaging any client. If we understand that clients—even those who appear to be totally overwhelmed—have the potential for overcoming adversity, we will always be looking for what is right with them rather than what is wrong. By doing so—and by representing to the client a professional who believes in the client's capacities for growth, change, and adaptation—the social worker becomes a source of resilience for the client. This strengths perspective also provides a rationale for the integration of solution-focused interventions, discussed later in this chapter.

Additional Social Work Perspectives

The social work profession is still in a stage of development with many emerging theoretical frameworks to draw on. Many professionals are engaging in theory building and empirical testing of constructs about practice to develop evidenced-based practice. While this book offers one perspective on the role of the profession and the processes of helping, other perspectives compete for attention. This is healthy. The approach taken in this book will be to borrow practice concepts and ideas from all of the models described in this chapter and to integrate them into the general framework of the interactional approach. The emphasis will be on finding "what works" rather than on maintaining ideological purity. The sections that follow briefly summarize some of the models that have made major contributions or are under active consideration by the profession. They were also selected because of elements that have been integrated into the interactionist approach. Constructs from these models will be referenced in the chapters that follow.

Solution-Focused Practice

A more recently developed model of practice that has elements that fit nicely within the interactional framework is called solution-focused practice. While not advocating the practice of the model itself, I suggest that several of its underlying assumptions and intervention techniques can be useful, particularly in the beginning phase of work. Further, these interventions may not be appropriate for all clients and in all situations. The practitioner needs to discern when they might be suitable or not. This section provides a brief introduction to the model and identifies core techniques.

Major Assumptions on the Nature of the Helping Relationship The solution-focused model is built on the strengths perspective, described earlier. As a form of "existential" practice, it focuses on the client's current issues and assumes that, with the help of the social worker, the client can identify and make use of inherent strengths that might be overlooked in a pathology-oriented practice. Put in simple terms, the social worker is thinking about what is right with the client rather than what is wrong. The social worker also believes that the source and methods of change will come from the client. This model emerged from an integration of the strengths perspective with interest in short-term treatment (deShazer, 1988; deShazer & Berg, 1992).

Some of the specific assumptions in the model that are clearly compatible with the approach advanced in this book include the following:

- Intervention should focus on the present and what clients bring with them to the process.
- Achieving behavioral changes takes place in and affects the present, rather than resolving problems of the past.
- While focusing on the present, the model recognizes that longer-term treatment may require examination and resolving of issues in the past (as for survivors of sexual abuse).
- When engaging the client, workers might acknowledge the person's discomfort but they do not engage in a prolonged discussion of etiology and pathology.
- Individuals have within themselves the resources and abilities to solve their own problems.
- Clients are often caught in feelings of powerlessness regarding their problems in living.
- Clients need to be helped to imagine what their future would look like without the problem, that is, if they were unstuck.
- When working with mandated clients, the involuntary nature of the relationship must be acknowledged and becomes the starting point for the work.

Prior to the engagement the worker will make minimal use of history and agency records, preferring to let the client tell the story. This can help the worker avoid stereotyping the client from the judgments of previous workers. In the classic example, a new worker's colleagues chime in, "They gave you the Jones family!" The worker's perception that this will be a difficult family helps to create the conditions that can lead to a self-fulfilling prophecy.

With mandated clients, the worker typically asks the clients to share their views about the mandating agency's expectations and requirements. The worker recognizes that while the agency or court can demand certain changes, clients serve as the final "authority" on what they want or need to change in their lives. When the worker asks what the client wants and the response is "Get the god-dammed agency off my back!" the worker can respond, "OK, let's start with what you have to do to get the agency off of your back." Essentially, the client is invited to be the "expert" who informs the worker about her or his situation.

Defining Techniques Several specific techniques have been identified as associated with this model. All of them share a common focus on the client's strengths and capacity for coping with adversity.

- *Asking about presession changes:* The worker recognizes that change may have occurred even before the first session. The fact that a client has made an appointment, voluntarily or not, may begin a change process. The worker will be curious and inquire about how the client made these changes and who was responsible for them.

- *Asking about between-session changes:* The worker recognizes that the client has a life between sessions. Many factors will have influenced the client's life, and the worker will want to explore these at the beginning of the session. For example, the worker may ask, "What's better this week, compared with last week?"

- *Asking about exceptions:* This technique asks the client to begin to examine when the problem did not occur in the past and what the conditions were that created these exceptions. For example, "You've relapsed and started drinking again at least three times over the past five years, but you've also been able to maintain your recovery for longer and longer periods. What was going on during the time you maintained your recovery, and how were you able to do that?" A variation on this question would be to ask about times when the problem was not that serious or severe, was less frequent, or lasted a shorter time. The goal would be to search for and reinforce factors that made a difference. This is a subtle yet important shift from focusing on the problem to identifying potential solutions.

- *The miracle question:* While there are different forms of the "miracle question," the most common is this: "Imagine you were to wake up tomorrow and a miracle had happened." The miracle would be that the client's life had changed for the better and the "problem" had been resolved. Questions such as "How would you first know that things were different?" or "What would others notice that would indicate the problem was gone?" are designed to help the client conceptualize the desired change. A variation includes "Imagine this isn't so much of a problem" or "This appointment has helped you in just the way you thought it would" or "It is 6 months in the future and we have been working together and problems have been resolved. How would you know this? What would be different?" The one caveat that the worker has to include in asking the question is that the client cannot answer that the problem itself did not exist. For example, a grieving widow cannot wake up the next day and find that her husband had not died.

- *Scaling questions:* This technique asks clients to identify the degree of the problem by thinking about zero representing the worst end of a continuum and some other number being the ideal. The worker can then ask clients what number represents where they are in respect to this problem at a certain point in the work. In this way, clients may be able to identify incremental changes rather than seeing a problem as "solved" or "not solved."

- *Coping questions:* Another technique that emphasizes the clients' strengths and helps clients see themselves in new way is to ask "coping" questions. For example, after acknowledging the problem, the worker might ask, "How have you managed to cope?" Another question might be "Given how bad things are, how come they are not worse? How have you kept things from getting worse?"

Radical Social Work Practice

In a second model, there are social work theorists who call for a more radical social work approach. This model emerged with some force and impact during the 1960s and 1970s when movements for social change, such as the civil rights movement, were active. Advocates for radical social work practice rightly point to persistent social problems and the lack of social justice, particularly for oppressed and vulnerable populations. These challenges to the profession were and still are healthy in that they have reminded us of our historical concern with social change as well as individual adaptation. This "social" aspect of social work can easily be lost as the profession moves to become more "clinical," taking on models of practice used by other professions—such as psychotherapy or psychology. They have also provided a needed reminder of our unique professional role, which can easily be lost if we allow our function to be solely defined by the job description written by our agency or host setting.

For a segment of this group of radical social work theorists, at times identified with what might be called "critical theory," direct practice with clients, by definition, is ineffective. For example, Galper (1967) views social services as failing to be effective because they derive from the existing social order, and play a role in maintaining it. Problems are defined in terms of economic, political, or social contexts. These theoreticians point to the very real problems in approaches to practice that seemed to ignore social realities and issues of oppression. The reason they have had such a powerful impact on faculty, students, and workers is that they focused on aspects of our practice about which we were already feeling defensive. Workers who feel oppressed by their own agencies and somewhat overwhelmed by their clients' life situations are responsive to the charge that they are involved in "band-aid" work rather than bringing about real social change.

However, practitioners know that when they work with real clients, employing a critical analysis of the clients' problems is often just a first step. Such an analysis can lead to new and more helpful ways to intervene in the process with clients who need help now—today—in this interview, family session, or group meeting. However, the client often cannot wait for the major changes in our society that will be needed to modify institutionalized oppression. Thus, while we need a conceptualization of practice that reframes our way of viewing client troubles and requires us to act on injustices in our society (and agencies and institutions), we simultaneously must provide services to the victims of these injustices. The real task is technical in nature. How can we integrate radical views of society, psychology, and interpersonal relationships into our ongoing practice, and how can we develop the skills to have an impact on systems as well as clients? The use of oppression psychology in this book is one example of an effort toward integration.

While one is free to differ with the particular interventions, these "radical" approaches contribute to the general professional development by providing models that can be applied to practice with oppressed and vulnerable clients. In fact, many of the intervention constructs of the model would constitute good practice principles for any worker-client intervention. The important point is that these theory builders have not given up on the idea of social workers playing an influential role with individual clients as well as dealing with issues of social justice.

Feminist Practice

A third group of models influencing our professional development is the emergence of a body of literature related to what is termed "feminist practice." While this view can also be considered a form of radical practice, and it draws heavily on social and political issues related to gender oppression, its proponents tend to translate their ideas into specific method theory that helps to connect ideas to the realities of day-to-day practice.

Feminist approaches to practice have diverged into identifiable streams. As I mentioned earlier, Saulnier (1996, 2000) has attempted to identify these various viewpoints. Her typology includes the following models: liberal feminism, radical feminism, socialist feminism, lesbian feminism, cultural and ecofeminism, womanism, African American women's feminism, postmodern feminism, and global feminism. While some may disagree with the specific categorization of the models and the associated descriptions, analysis, and critiques, Saulnier's contribution highlights this important area of theory development and identifies implications for social policy and social work practice.

Sands and Nuccio (1992) specifically address the emergence of postmodern feminist theory and its implications for social work. The authors describe how the feminist literature has identified three general categories of philosophical and political feminist orientations: liberal, socialist, and radical feminism. *Liberal feminism* emphasizes the attainment of political rights, opportunities, and equality within the existing political system. *Socialist feminism* attributes women's oppression to the interaction among sexism, racism, and class divisions, which are produced by patriarchal capitalism. *Radical feminism* finds patriarchy an omnipresent influence that needs to be dismantled (p. 490).

They then trace the emergence of postmodern feminism from its postmodern philosophical and French feminist theoretical roots. While identifying differences in the roots and the emergent thinking of this model, they point to a shared political agenda with American feminism:

> Regardless of whether a feminist has a liberal, socialist, radical or other perspective, she has a desire to change the social and political order so that women will no longer be oppressed. Thus, organizing and taking political action to redress injustices are significant dimensions of postmodern feminism. (Sands & Nuccio, 1992, p. 492)

An example of the specific application of this shared principle can be found in Chapter 13, in which a social worker approaches the ending phase of work with a group of survivors of sexual abuse. After many months of difficult and powerful work on the impact of the abuse on their lives, the worker suggests that they consider attending a local march against sexual violence directed toward women.

> Then group members asked me to review information about the local "Take Back the Night" march with them. We had told them about the march against sexual violence against women a few weeks before and, after some exploration of their fears about participating in a public demonstration, they decided to march as a group. I supported the group's readiness to act independently and support each other in new experiences. I shared with them how good I felt that they wanted to march together and gave them the information they needed.

At the Next Session

We supported the group's growing independence and shared our feelings with them. As the group processed how the march had felt for them, Jane and I shared how powerful it had felt for us to see them there, marching, chanting, and singing. We also shared that it was hard for us to see them and know that the group was ending. The group was special for us and it would be hard to let it go.

After their experience with the march, the group members decided to contribute samples of their poetry and art to an exhibit dealing with issues of violence toward women. They also decided to contribute proceeds from the sale of their art to a fund devoted to support groups for survivors like themselves. This represents an example of combining the personal and political, and choosing which part of their work was more "therapeutic" would be difficult. The cake they shared in their last session had written on it, "Survivors—Striving and Thriving!"

Another model that brings a feminist perspective to social work practice emerged from efforts to develop a new psychology of women. Much of the rapidly evolving work in this area is rooted in the publications and a series of working papers from the Stone Center in Wellesley, Massachusetts. This framework is often referred to under the general rubric of self-in-relation theory, mentioned earlier. In one application of this theory, Collins (1994) "reconstructs" the concept of codependency using a feminist social work perspective to analyze the concept and its underlying assumptions about recovery and relationships.

Many of the core constructs of this theory and, in particular, the group work implications of the model fit well with the interactional framework presented in this book. For example, Schiller (1993) uses the self-in-relation framework to rethink a classic theory of group development known as the Boston Model (Garland, Jones, & Kolodny, 1965) and adapts it to a feminist perspective.

In another example of an application of feminist theory to practice, Holmes and Lundy (1990) present what they term a feminist perspective on work with men who batter. They provide specific prescriptions for intervention that are based on feminist theoretical and ideological assumptions. Other examples that draw on feminist perspectives include Berman-Rossi and Cohen (1989), focusing on work with homeless, mentally ill women, and Breton (1988), providing an example of a "sistering" approach in a drop-in shelter for homeless women. O'Brien (1995) identifies the self-empowerment of a group of African American women, who were long-term public-housing residents and activists, as contributing to their resilience and effective mothering.

In an effort to merge a feminist perspective with a cognitive-behavioral approach (discussed later in this chapter), Srebnik and Saltzberg (1994) describe how internalized cultural messages negatively affect a woman's body image. The authors then propose interventions to influence thought patterns and dysfunctional behaviors.

In another example, Collins (1994) uses feminist theory to challenge the concept of codependency in substance abuse practice. The author refutes the view that women need to view their relational strengths as pathology. Instead, she argues that they can get well by naming and discussing the injustices in their relational context.

In more recent work in this area, Wood draws on feminist and social constructionist positions, anthropology, and narrative ideas to describe and illustrate a framework for social work with groups of women who are being battered and raped by husbands and boyfriends. She emphasizes the role of resistance and protest in developing self-representation and proclaiming it in definitional ceremonies (Wood & Roche, 2001).

In another example, Westbury and Tutty (1999) conducted a small, quasi-experimental study comparing women who were sexually abused as children and who were receiving individual and group treatment that included feminist techniques with women on a wait list who were receiving only individual counseling. They found that the treatment group had significantly improved depression and anxiety scores, when compared with the wait list group, as well as a near significant improvement in self-image.

Social Work as Psychotherapy

A fourth model, associated with the growth of private practice and the certification of social workers as eligible to receive third-party insurance payments, has intensified another influence on the profession—the "social worker as therapist" model. While many social workers applaud this recognition of the competency of the profession, some have raised a serious concern about social work's continued commitment to oppressed and vulnerable populations. Many social work clients are economically disadvantaged and do not have the medical insurance required to use private services. Social workers have traditionally found their place working in social agencies or social work departments in host institutions (such as hospitals, schools, and residential centers). A real fear exists that the profession may abandon its important and unique roles in these settings in the search for increased status, income, and professional autonomy.

As ever more social workers describe themselves as therapists or psychotherapists, sometimes even avoiding the use of their social work title, they blur the distinctions between their profession and others engaged in private-practice counseling. The very existence of a unique profession of social work could be jeopardized if we do not keep clear what it is that makes social work different. Because this private-practice movement is growing, one solution may be for the profession to identify and research the elements in the work of private-practice colleagues that maintain their unique identity as social workers. Identifying themselves as social workers and affiliating with certain professional associations are examples. A willingness to intervene with other professionals and systems, on behalf of a client, might be another.

Cognitive-Behavioral Therapy

A fifth emerging and promising model is related to interest in constructs borrowed from cognitive-behavioral psychology and therapy. In cognitive-behavioral therapy, the therapist uses strategies and techniques designed to help clients correct their negative, distorted views about themselves, the world, and the future, as well as the underlying maladaptive beliefs that gave rise to these cognitions (Beck, Rush, Shaw, & Emery, 1979; Elkin, Parloff, Hadley, & Autry, 1985).

Earlier in this chapter, I pointed out the powerful interaction between how we feel and how we act. Essentially, cognitive-behavioral approaches, building on social-learning theories, suggest that how one thinks also interacts with one's behavior. When feelings and cognitive distortions combine, they can result in maladaptive behaviors, which in turn strengthen the distortions, which then continue to affect the behavior. In cognitive-behavioral treatment models, the therapist would help the client identify and modify cognitive distortions and would reinforce behaviors that were more adaptive for the client.

Concepts drawn from a widely recognized and researched cognitive therapy model based on the work of Beck, who explored the causes and treatment of depression

(Beck et al., 1979), can be usefully incorporated into the interactional model of practice. Oei and Shuttlewood (1996) summarize the three dimensions of Beck's theory.

First, life experiences lead people to form assumptions about themselves and the world ("schemata" or "underlying predispositions") that are then used to interpret new experiences and to govern and evaluate behavior. "Some assumptions reached on the basis of past negative experience may become rigid, extreme, and resistant to change and, hence, are termed dysfunctional or counterproductive." (p. 93)

Second, Beck posed the existence of "automatic thoughts," short pieces of "internal dialogue" that are associated with negative emotions and can lead to self-statements such as "I am a failure." According to Beck, a pattern of frequent and "highly negative automatic thoughts" can develop into a vicious cycle leading to depression, which then leads to more depressive cognitions.

Third, automatic thoughts are seen as containing "errors of logic," which Beck termed "cognitive distortions." These could include overgeneralizing, disqualifying the positive, catastrophizing, minimization, and personalization.

Beck's treatment approach "disrupts the vicious cycle of depression by teaching the patients to question negative automatic thoughts and then to challenge the assumptions (schemata) on which they are based" (Oei & Shuttlewood, 1996, p. 94).

There are many examples of how one can incorporate constructs from the cognitive-behavioral model into the interactional framework. Albert (1994) writes about a mutual aid support group for chronic mental patients using a cognitive approach. He describes a patient in a day treatment center, which had so many groups that patients often felt "grouped out," surprising staff by suggesting another group:

She said, "We need to talk just about being mental patients, what it means, what it feels like." One patient after another seconded the motion. They wanted to address the mental patient identity. How were they thought of in their families and neighborhoods? How should they think of themselves? Was the mental patient stigma justified? Where did it come from? What were its effects? Although their "patienthood" was at the heart of what the patients had in common, it seemed to have remained an oppressive presence, at once too obvious and too painful to mention. (p. 109)

In one example from the group, patients are dealing with the ideation of permanent thinking—that when they are depressed, for example, treatment can seem "interminable and futile." This sense of failure and permanency, in turn, affects their ability to continue to cope.

Sharon said, "I had the leaves raked into piles. Then the wind blew them all around the yard again. I thought, 'What's the use? They'll never get done. There will always be leaves.' Then I went back to bed. My body started feeling heavy. I couldn't get out of bed." I (the worker) pointed out that Sharon had used the word "always" when speaking about her hospitalization, too. ["I'll always go back to the hospital."] I asked, "Is it true that there will always be leaves? Is the job never done?" Sharon said, "That's one way of looking at it." I asked the group for other ways. Members suggested that Sharon think about other tasks she has completed. [Disputation] Nick said, "Maybe you would have to redo the raking once or twice; maybe even three times—But not forever. [Disputation] I mean, you do what you can, then it snows and you're done." [laughter] I repeated, "You do what you can." (Albert, 1994, p. 110)

Cognitive-behavioral approaches represent good examples of how related disciplines can provide powerful ideas that can be integrated into a social work practice model. In addition, the emphasis by the cognitive-behavioral social work theoreticians on a **practitioner-researcher** model, in which the social worker is continuously evaluating his or her own practice, is also healthy for the field as it accelerates the movement toward development of a more empirically based practice.

While contributing to professional theoretical and research growth, the expansion of cognitive, behavioral, or cognitive-behavioral models in social work practice raises two concerns. The first is evident in efforts by some theoreticians to propose such models as a unified social work practice theory (Thyer, 1987). Such an effort would substitute a model borrowed from a foreign discipline, one that is not rooted in the same history as the social work profession, for its unique sense of professional function.

Examination of the literature of this approach, for example, indicates it has been applied most often to very specific populations and problems (such as anxiety disorders, anger management, parenting training, and depression), while social work has developed a broader constituency, including specific attention to oppressed and vulnerable populations.

In addition, the model is generally built on a base of individual psychology. This is evident in its lack of attention to the social change aspects of practice that have been central to the social work profession. In an example of an exception to this criticism, Stern and Smith (1995) report on a study of family processes and delinquency in an ecological context. They tested a model "hypothesizing that family content influences parenting, which in turn influences adolescent behavior" (p. 703). Their results for 804 adolescents and their families showed that "the family's disadvantaged neighborhood, life distress, social isolation, and lack of partner support were associated with dysfunctional parenting that increases delinquency" (p. 703).

Stern and Smith (1995) reviewed the literature and identified several behaviorally focused interventions that have proved helpful in, for example, providing tools for parents to identify the sources of stress from their children's behavior and to find parenting methods for coping with that stress. However, as they also point out,

> Our research supports the growing recognition of the importance of multidimensional approaches to intervention with delinquents and their families. It seems clear that intervention focused solely on the micro-processes in families will generally be inadequate to address the complex problems that juvenile delinquency presents. If we look at parents without considering the complex contexts in which they operate and the multiple stresses operating in them, we are likely to promote ineffective intervention models and high levels of treatment dropout. We also run the risk of blaming and re-victimizing families struggling with considerable adversity who are already victimized by a society that does not adequately support disadvantaged and distressed children and families. (p. 722)

In my view, if social work can hold on to the core of its unique role, which always recognizes the two-client concept, then workers can incorporate ideas from a wide range of models and theories. The task for the profession is to treat frameworks from foreign disciplines with appropriate respect and to borrow constructs that can enhance the work, while guarding against substituting these constructs for the profession's own model-building efforts.

A second issue related to the growth of this model is the apparent co-optation of the term *empirically based practice* by some proponents of this specific framework. This has occurred somewhat by default as social work as a profession was slow in developing a solid body of research focused on practice method—what it is the social worker actually did with clients. While many outcome studies existed, they were usually weak in defining the independent (predictor) variables. For example, in Fischer's (1973) well-known article on the effectiveness of social work practice, out of more than 40 studies reviewed, not one described what it was the social worker actually did while spending time with the client. Operational definition of the worker's intervention is one of the strongest points of cognitive-behavioral practice models, allowing this framework to move quickly to attempt to fill this research vacuum.

Empirical work can be undertaken from a range of theoretical perspectives, including some that could be termed interactional. The early work of the psychotherapy researchers associated with the client-centered approach of Carl Rogers (Truax, 1966) broke ground in this area. More recently, empirical work that involves specifying worker interventions has been more evident in the field, with a wide range of research approaches and methodology emerging. The work reported in this book is one example of the use of quantitative and qualitative research methods for building social work practice theory (for example, statistical analysis and content analysis of interviews, respectively). One contribution of the feminist practice movement has been to focus our attention on qualitative models of practice research that are useful for exploring worker-client interactions in ways that enhance the practice knowledge base.

Finally, the profession must guard against the tendency of proponents to oversell a particular framework or model, often by first attacking the efficacy of models currently in use. In reality, as pointed out by Oei and Shuttlewood (1996), there are many unanswered questions about what makes any form of therapy effective. Their review of the literature indicates that the evidence does not yet support the superiority of any particular form of therapy, and the debate still rages over whether specific therapy-related factors or else nonspecific or more general factors produce the positive results of therapy when compared with no treatment at all. They point to the most researched nonspecific factor, the therapeutic alliance, as an example of a variable that, while defined variously, may nevertheless cross models of treatment and account for some measure of effectiveness. This concept closely parallels the idea of the working relationship at the core of the approach described in this book.

In summary, developing a model of social work practice involves incorporating as many ideas as are helpful while still holding onto a unique professional identification. Many emerging theoretical models compete for social workers' attention. We are far from being ready to vote, as a profession, on which one will best suit us in the years to come. More likely, an integration of many of the universal constructs developed from differing points of departure will provide us with a unified practice theory. The interactional model discussed in this book may provide some of these constructs.

The framework described in this book will allow you to view relationships between clients and their important systems in an ecological context. Real conflicts between clients and systems will be identified; however, emphasis will be placed on attempting to identify areas of common ground. Practitioners will be described as trying to deal directly with clients, as well as trying to influence families, agencies, political systems, and so on. These practitioners will at times function in different roles, mediating where appropriate, confronting and advocating when necessary. In whichever role they play, however, they will keep in mind the essential common ground between the individual and society. This is the basis from which change can be brought about, and it is the real challenge for developing a radical social work practice.

● Chapter Summary

The interactional theory of social work practice views the client as being in a symbiotic relationship with his or her social surroundings. The mutual need between the individual and the social surroundings is blocked by obstacles that often obscure it from view.

A historical perspective of social work shows the profession rooted in the twin streams of concern for individual well-being and for social change. As such, the functional assignment for the social work profession is that of mediating the engagement between the client and the systems important to that client. Practice methods and communication and relationship skills are the tools that enable the social worker to put his or her function into action. Practice skills are the instruments for developing a positive working relationship that serves as the medium through which the social worker influences the client.

Central to the effectiveness of the worker is her or his ability to integrate the personal self with the professional self. The social worker's practice is guided as well by a set of professional and personal values and by a well-defined professional code of ethics.

An oppression and vulnerability psychology model, as well as a resilience framework, can be helpful for understanding clients. This model assumes that the strength for change is always present although not always possible to engage.

Many other social work practice perspectives—such as solution-focused practice, radical social work practice, feminist practice, social work as psychotherapy, and cognitive-behavioral therapy—help place the interactional perspective in context.

Related Online Content and Activities

Visit *The Skills of Helping* Book Companion Website at www.socialwork.wadsworth .com/Shulman06/ for learning tools such as glossary terms, InfoTrac College Edition keywords, links to related websites, and chapter practice quizzes.

The website for this chapter also features additional notes from the author.

Social Work
With Individuals

Part II of this book consists of four chapters that elaborate and illustrate the interactional approach to social work in the context of work with individuals. Chapters 2 through 5 use the model of the four phases of work—preliminary, beginning, middle, and ending/transition—as the organizing framework. In Chapter 2, on the preliminary phase, we examine the skills required to prepare for a new contact with a client. In Chapter 3, on the beginning phase, we focus on the contracting skills for creating a clear structure for work. In Chapter 4 we examine the middle (work) phase of practice, providing a model of the stages of an individual session. Finally, in Chapter 5 we explore the ending and transition phase of practice, in which the worker and client bring their relationship to an end and prepare the client to move on to new experiences.

Each chapter describes the specific dynamics and skills associated with the particular phase. Research findings are cited to provide an empirical basis for the work. Detailed illustrations of social workers interacting with clients help to connect the theory to day-to-day realities that are familiar to the reader. These examples illustrate the constant or core elements of practice while demonstrating the many variations introduced by the nature of the client population, each client's particular problems, and the impact of the practice setting.

The Preliminary Phase of Work

In Chapter 1 we outlined four phases of work: the preliminary, beginning, middle, and ending/transition phases. In this chapter, we begin to explore the constructs introduced earlier, starting with the preliminary phase of practice. The indirect nature of the communication process is examined, with suggestions provided for ways in which the worker can respond directly to indirect cues. We then look at an approach for developing a preliminary empathy, prior to the first interview, with potential client feelings and concerns related to the worker, the agency or setting, and the client's problems. The importance of a social worker "tuning in" to his or her own feelings is also stressed.

The rationale for the preliminary phase of practice is based on the idea that preparing for social work interactions can increase the likelihood of establishing a positive worker-client relationship and of hearing and understanding what the client has to say. We start this chapter by looking at the complexity of the human communication process in general, and then we move on to explore issues specific to social work practice.

Communications in Practice

Human communications can be complex under any circumstances. Let us examine the nature of a single communication. We start with a sender—an individual who has an idea to transmit. This idea must first be encoded—that is, translated from ideas into symbols. Then it is transmitted to the intended receiver through spoken or written words, touch, or nonverbal means (such as facial expression or posture). The message must next be received. This involves hearing, reading, seeing, or feeling by the recipient. Next, the message must be decoded—that is, translated by the recipient from symbols to the ideas that they represent. The recipient must then acknowledge the message through some form of feedback to the sender, thus completing the cyclical process.

Obstacles to Direct Communication

Considering how complicated even the most simple communications can be and how many points in the process there are where meanings can be distorted, we might wonder why any communication is ever completed. In the helping relationship, additional factors can complicate the process. These obstacles to open communication often cause a client to employ indirect methods of expressing thoughts and feelings.

One obstacle may be the feeling of **ambivalence** associated with accepting help. Our society responds negatively to almost all forms of dependency, stressing instead the norm of independence—being able to handle things on one's own. For the client, however, the urgency of the task at hand counters society's pressure. The resulting vector from these conflicting forces is often an ambiguous call for help. Particularly in early sessions, before a working relationship has been established, clients may present concerns in an indirect manner; they may also else present "near problems," that is, real issues that are not the ones they really need to talk about.

A second potential block to direct communication, **societal taboos**, reflect a general consensus to block or prohibit discussion in areas of sensitivity and deep concern. The client enters the helping relationship with a conscious or unconscious internalization of these taboos, hindering free speaking. Major taboos in our society discourage "real" talk about topics such as sex, dependency, substance abuse, authority, and money. The discomfort clients experience when talking about issues and feelings in certain areas may cause them to use indirect methods of communication.

A third obstacle is associated with the feelings that accompany concerns. Clients may find certain feelings painful and frightening. The raising of a concern may be blocked by conscious or unconscious defenses that clients use to avoid moving into areas that produce these feelings. This can lead to clients sharing the facts of an issue while ignoring their own feelings. Because all issues of concern are invested with both facts and feelings, this represents only a partial communication. In one example, a client with a chronically ill child was able to share her anger but was less in touch with the pain that contributed to her rage. She was using a form of **flight-fight** that served as a defense from her own distress. Because it cut her off from the support she desperately needed, it was a maladaptive defense.

Finally, the context of the contract with the helping person may contribute factors that block real talk. For example, in a child welfare agency, workers carry dual functions and in some cases may have to act for the state in apprehending (removing) a child. Parents are quite aware of the worker's authority and power and thus will be wary of sharing information or feelings that can be used against them. An officer who can revoke parole, a nurse who can make a hospital stay unpleasant, a psychiatrist who can decide when a patient can go home, an adoption worker who can decide if a person gets a child, a worker in a mandatory group for male batterers—all these helping people have power over the lives of their clients, and this power may become an obstacle to real talk.

Examples of Indirect Communication in Practice

Because of the obstacles that block the direct expression of feelings, clients may use indirect means to present them, as in the classic case of the client who has "a friend with a problem." Hinting is an important indirect cue; the client makes a comment or asks a question that contains a portion of the message. The mother who asks the worker if she has children, for example, may be using a question to raise, very tentatively, a more complex and threatening issue: "Will this worker understand what it is like for me?" Clients may also raise their concerns through their behavior. For example, a child in a residential setting who has not been asked to go home for a family visit over a holiday may let his child care worker know how upset he is by "acting out" more. Adults in counseling sessions who "come on" negatively may be doing the same thing.

Another illustration can be drawn from the child welfare setting. A social worker was visiting a young, single-parent mother who had three children under the age of 4. The worker had been called in to investigate an abuse complaint. As the worker spoke to the harried mother, the youngest child pulled at her mother's leg until the mother said, "Leave me alone, I'm talking now." The child continued to try to engage the mother, who finally grabbed the little girl by the shoulders and shouted, "Leave me alone!"

The worker was stunned and immediately, responding to that part of her function that called for the protection of children, began to counsel the mother: "Mrs. Jones, don't you think there might be other ways in which you can tell your child you wish to be left alone?" The mother understood the implied criticism and immediately began to feel more tense and defensive with this worker.

If the worker were in touch with her own feelings and those of the mother, and if it had been clear to the worker that the mother was a client in her own right and not just an instrument for providing service to the child, then she might have recognized the indirect cues of the negative behavior and responded as follows: "Is this what it's like for you all the time—no chance to be alone, to talk to other people without the kids pestering you?" If said with genuine understanding of the plight of a single mother who is young, trying to raise kids on her own, probably struggling with an inadequate income, and so on, then this direct response to indirect cues would likely strengthen the working relationship.

In one of my studies, the use of this skill contributed directly to the client's perception that the worker was there both to protect the child and to help the mother (Shulman, 1991). The worker might also acknowledge how hard it must be on the mother to have a social worker come and talk to her about these things. It might still be necessary for the worker to intervene by offering respite care to give the mother a break. Because protecting the child matters most, the worker might also have to remove the child, with or without the mother's agreement. Nonetheless, the impact of exercising this authority would be somewhat moderated by the worker's caring for the mother as a client in her own right.

Clients sometimes use metaphor and allegory as means of indirect communication. As in literature, the intent is to send a message without necessarily expressing its content directly. This is illustrated by an interview with a depressed adolescent foster child who has recently lost his parents. The youngster is getting ready to leave the care of the agency because he is 18, and he is worried about where he will live. He has had eight changes of residence during the past year. Note both the indirect communications and the means by which the worker uses her preparatory empathy to reach for the underlying message:

> Frank asked me if I ever thought of the fact that space never ended. I said I hadn't really. I wondered if he had, and if it worried him somehow. He said it did, because sometimes he felt like a little ball, floating in space, all alone. A little bit higher and more to the right, and bye, bye world—just like a wee birdie. I said he really has been floating in space, moving from place to place, and that he must be feeling all alone. Frank's eyes filled with tears and he said, emphatically, "I am all alone!"

While the worker skillfully responded to one part of the indirect communication, she did not pick up on the second, more difficult and disturbing, part, in which he says, "Bye, bye world." The client might have suicidal fears and the worker should explore what he meant by this part of his statement.

Nonverbal forms of communication can also be used to send important indirect messages. The client who always arrives late or early or who misses sessions after promising to attend may be commenting on his reactions to the process of helping. The children in the family session who arrive looking tense and angry and refuse to take off their coats may be saying something about their feelings about being there. The client who sits back looking angry, with arms firmly folded across his chest, may be saying, "Go ahead, try and change me." These are all important messages; however, the common element is that the clients are not using words.

The crucial point here is that indirect communications often make it hard to understand what clients are trying to say. In particular, negative behavior is difficult to understand, particularly for new workers, because it throws them off balance. The capacity to reach behind negative behavior for the client's real message comes with the growth of the worker's sense of professional competency.

With communications so complex, how can the worker ever hear what the client is trying to say? This is where developing a preliminary empathy prior to a session through the use of the "tuning in" skill can be helpful. It can substantially increase the odds in favor of understanding, particularly in the beginning stage of work, when the conversation tends to be indirect. In the next section we examine tuning in more closely.

The Preliminary Phase: Tuning In to Self and to the Client

A major skill in the preliminary phase of work is development of the worker's sense of empathy. This technique can be employed before contact with the client has begun. Schwartz termed this process **tuning in**. It involves the worker's effort to get in touch with potential feelings and concerns that the client may bring to the helping encounter. The purpose of the exercise is to help the worker become a more sensitive receiver of the client's indirect communications in the first sessions. For reasons discussed earlier, some of the most important client communications are not spoken directly. By tuning in, the worker may be able to hear the client's indirect cues and then respond directly. A direct response to an indirect communication is one of the skills a worker can use to help clients manage their feelings. It is called **putting the client's feelings into words.**

In the sections that follow, we explore the importance of tuning in to issues related to the worker's authority, the differences between affective and intellectual tuning in, tuning in to the worker's own feelings, and different levels of tuning in.

Tuning In to the Authority Theme

All levels of tuning in will be illustrated in this book. I believe, however, that the first question on the client's mind is "Who is this worker, and what kind of a person will she or he be?" For that reason, I will begin with what I call the **authority theme,** focusing on issues related to the relationship between the client and the social worker. An example from practice will illustrate the general issues involved. This particular experience has been shared by workers in consultation sessions so often, with only slight variations, that it probably represents an archetype. The presenter was a social worker in a child welfare agency. She was 22, unmarried, and new to the job.

Her first interview was with a 38-year-old mother of seven children who had come to the agency's attention because of a neighbor's complaint about her care of her children. Another worker had met with her for four months but was leaving the agency. The new worker was the replacement, making her first visit. After introductions, the worker and client had been sitting in the living room chatting for a few minutes when the client suddenly turned to the worker and said, "By the way, do you have any children?" There was a brief silence after this embarrassing question. Recovering quickly, and hiding her feelings, the worker said to the client, "No, I don't have any children. However, I have taken a number of courses in child psychology." Discussing this incident in a consultation session, the worker reported her internal feelings and her thoughts: "I panicked! I thought, 'Oh my God, she knows I don't have any children—how am I supposed to help her?'"

This is just one example. Many variations exist on the same theme: the recovering alcoholic who wonders if the worker has "walked the walk" (been an alcoholic) or "talked the talk" (been a member of Alcoholics Anonymous), the gay man with AIDS who inquires if the worker is straight, or the person of color who describes prior white workers who "didn't understand our people." These variations and others will be explored throughout the book. For now, however, let us return to our first example.

The conversation in the interview with the mother shifted back to the worker's agenda of agency business and never returned to this area. An important issue had been raised indirectly, however, and an unprepared worker had responded defensively. If we were to analyze the more subtle, indirect communications involved in this incident, we could interpret the client's question in the following manner:

CLIENT: By the way, do you have any children? (The client is thinking: I wonder if this one will be like the other worker. They have all kinds of ideas about how I should raise children and have never changed a dirty diaper themselves. How can they understand what it's like for me?)

Other interpretations are possible; however, I believe that this question is central for all clients in first sessions. The crucial part of the message left unsaid was the client's concern that she would not be understood. The worker's response, a product of her own concern about her capacity to help, only confirmed the client's apprehension. It is quite normal for clients to wonder if a new worker will be like other helping professionals whom they have met—in this case, the stereotypical cold, unfeeling "expert" who thinks she has all the answers. This thought was too dangerous to express openly, so it was only hinted at. The worker's reaction was also quite normal, especially for a new worker who had not anticipated the question.

If the worker had been tuned in to the client's potential concern, not intellectually but by actually trying to get in touch with the way this or any client might feel, she might have been able to read the real question behind the question. If she had been given some help in understanding her own feelings, either by a supervisor or by colleagues, she might have been able to consider in advance how to respond directly to an indirect cue in this important area. Each worker develops his or her own unique responses, but one way to deal with this situation might be to say:

WORKER: No, I don't have any children. Why do you ask? Are you wondering if I'm going to be able to understand what it's like for you having to raise so many? I'm concerned about that as well. If I'm to help you, I'm going to have to understand, and you are going to have to help me to understand.

Such a response might have opened up a discussion of the woman's past experiences with other workers, some helpful and some not. The response also allows the worker to share her own feelings of concern without overdoing them. She says, "I'm concerned about that as well." If the worker withholds his or her own affect, then the energy invested in suppressing the worker's feelings will not be available for investing into the affect of the client. Of course, integrating personal and professional selves requires some restraint on the worker's part. It would not have been appropriate for the worker to have said, however truthfully, "You're absolutely right! What are they doing sending me out to work with you when I've never changed a diaper or heated a bottle?" The client does not want to hear that level of concern. These feelings need to be shared with supervisors and colleagues before the interview.

As the client begins the worker's education, the work gets underway. Instead of the working relationship being closed, the potential exists for this one to begin to grow. If nothing else, the client might end the interview thinking, as one client in an earlier study of mine said, "This worker is different. Perhaps I can train her."

Although the empathic skills will be discussed in more detail in Chapter 4, we should focus a moment here on the issue of genuineness. One of the key reasons for tuning in is to combat the ease with which helping professionals can learn to say the words related to affect without really experiencing the feelings. For example, a popular technique advocated in some texts on practice involves the use of reflection. That is, the worker reflects back to the client the affective words. If a client says, "I'm really angry at my kids," the worker might repeat, "You're really angry at your kids." If I were the client in that situation, I probably would feel like saying, "Dummy, I just told you I was angry at my kids."

The problem with a reflective response is that it is often mechanical and artificial. The worker is not really feeling the client's anger. When I press practitioners on this question, they usually admit that they reflected because they did not know what else to say. Unfortunately, the client perceives the response as uncaring. The workers would have been better off being honest and admitting not knowing what to say.

An even better response might be to remain silent for a few moments—the skill of **containment**—and to try to feel how angry parents can get with their children, and then to respond with reactions that might deepen the conversation. For example, instead of being slightly behind the client, as illustrated in the reflective response, one approach might be to try to be one half step ahead of the client by putting the client's unstated feelings into words: "That's the thing, isn't it—how can you be so angry at the kids but at the same time love them so much?"

The exact words one uses are not crucial, because each of us develops our own personal style and way of expressing our feelings and those of clients. What is crucial is that the worker should be feeling something. My students have pointed out that this is easy for me to say and hard for them to do. The fact is, most of us have not learned how to deal well with our feelings, let alone those of others, in most areas of our lives. As one mature student put it, "I have trouble dealing with my kids' feelings; how am I going to help this client deal with hers?"

Fortunately, helping professionals have their whole practice lives in which to develop their ability to be genuinely empathic. As they listen to clients, trying to tune in, they will discover feelings within themselves that may have been earlier ignored. In the beginning, they will borrow the words of others. It is not uncommon for my students to bring the audiotape of an interview into an early class, with the students using my words in their efforts to empathize. With some, you can even pick up traces of my New York City accent. When this was pointed out by a fellow student once, the mimicking student replied, with some feeling, "I know, and I don't want to be a little Shulman." I try to reassure my students and suggest that they can borrow whatever words they need in the beginning. With continued work at developing their skills, they soon become more comfortable and find their own voice. This point is elaborated in Chapter 4.

In describing the situation with the young mother and the new worker, I mentioned the term **working relationship.** This is similar to the concept of therapeutic alliance. A generally accepted concept contained in most practice theories suggests that the activities of the helping person can help him or her develop a positive working relationship with the client. Something about the way the worker and client talk to and listen to each other, the flow of both positive and negative feelings between them, can affect the outcome. I believe that the development of a working relationship is a precondition for helping.

Note the use of the word *working* to differentiate this relationship from those that may be personal in nature, such as a parent-child relationship or a friend. This is a simple yet crucial idea. The relationship is based on the work to be done together. The purpose of the encounter will affect the relationship directly, and the relationship will be the vehicle through which this purpose is achieved. A common misconception about practice is that the worker must establish a relationship first and then begin to work. This leads to a practice of "chatting" with a client during the first contact, discussing the weather or other superficial matters, supposedly to set the client at ease. Actually, the reverse is often true, with the worker feeling more at ease and the client more uncomfortable. I suggest in Chapter 3 that the relationship grows out of the work itself and that a worker needs to get down to business quickly. The relationship is not separate from the work, but rather, it is part of the work. The very act of defining the nature of the work together (contracting) helps to develop the working relationship.

The Impact of Diversity

Of course, the worker must also be aware of cultural diversity issues that may moderate the just-stated rule of getting to the work quickly. In some cultures, directness might be perceived as offensive; this is true, for example, for some Asians and Native Americans. Cultural awareness would help a worker distinguish those situations where small talk about families or appropriate discussion of life experiences might be exactly what is needed to set the stage for the development of a working relationship.

Lum (1996) addresses this issue directly. The author identifies the many barriers that may exist in the beginning stage in cross-cultural, or what I term *interethnic*, practice. The author provides an example:

> A common question asked by Native Americans in formal helping situations is: "How can I tell you about my personal life, which I share with my lifelong friends, when I have just met you only a half hour ago?" Mistrust and reservation are typical responses of ethnic clients until the social worker moves out of the category of stranger. Taking the first step of professional self-disclosure sets the stage for openness and relationship-building. (p. 145)

Lum also provides the following "practical suggestions for professional self-disclosure":

> Introduce yourself.
>
> Share pertinent background about your work, family, and helping philosophy.
>
> Find a common point of interest with the client. (p. 145)

Sensitivity to issues of race, gender, ethnicity, sexual orientation, physical and mental ability, and so on, can be just as important in *intraethnic* practice—that is, working with someone with whom you share some important characteristic. For instance, an African American male student presented an example during a video-taped discussion of diversity issues and practice (Shulman & Clay, 1994). He was working intraethnically with an African American female client. The student recognized, however, that gender and class (he was from an upper-middle-class, suburban background, and she was poor and living in the inner city) meant he was also working interethnically and would have to deal with these potential barriers. Tuning in to his own feelings about working with people of color as a part of the "system" would also be essential to his development as a social worker and his ability to deal with the authority theme.

Proctor and Davis (1994) identify three concerns that that clients experience in working with practitioners of different races: whether the practitioner is a person of goodwill, whether she or he is trained and skilled, and whether the help offered is valid and meaningful to the client. While these questions are common for all helping relationships, they take on a special meaning when interethnic factors are involved. In this book, the term *interethnic* will be used broadly to include a range of differences not limited to ethnicity, for example, a male worker with a female client or straight worker with a gay client.

A study of the differences between the culturally sensitive practice of white and Latino clinicians with Latino immigrant clients found that Latinos responded with more culturally relevant interpretations while non-Latinos were more directive and instrumental (Lu et al., 2001). Reinforcing the notion that there is diversity within diversity, Castex (1994) suggests that factors that need to be taken into account in working with the U.S. Hispanic/Latino population include national origin, language, family names, religion, racial ascription, and immigration or citizenship issues. Mendez-Negrete (2000) suggests that practitioners need to begin with a broad understanding of what constitutes the idea of "family" and to recognize the "myriad" of forms that families can take. Congress (1994) proposes the use of culture-grams to assess and empower ethnic families. Chung and Bemak (2002) focus on the relationship between culture and empathy when working with diverse populations and suggest guidelines for establishing "cultural empathy."

These findings reinforce the importance of cultural education. Yet, in a study of undergraduate social work students, researchers found that most students indicated only partial support for multicultural goals (Swank, Asada, & Lott, 2002). While agreeing that multicultural information should be used and that more minority faculty and staff should be hired, their acceptance was conditional in that they were reluctant to make classes on this content conditional for graduation. In addition, only one fourth felt personally compelled to learn more about cultural diversity. The study also found that these attitudes changed as students initiated interracial exchanges and completed social diversity classes. Boyle and Springer (2001) point out that while cultural competence is crucial to social work practice, there are gaps in the ability to measure the achievement of competency as well as the gap between social work education and implementation in practice.

Elements of the Working Relationship

Many elements make up the working relationship. Three included in one of my studies (Shulman, 1991) are rapport, trust, and caring. **Rapport** refers to the client's general sense of getting along well with the worker. By **trust**, I mean the client's willingness to risk sharing thoughts, feelings, mistakes, and failures with the worker. By **caring**, I mean that clients sense that the worker is concerned about them as clients in their own right and that the worker wishes to help them with concerns that they feel are important. For example, a middle-aged son of an aging parent would experience the elder care worker as being concerned about him as a stressed caretaker, as well as being concerned about the well-being of his aged parent. In another example, a parent who has been reported as neglectful of her child would experience the child welfare worker as attempting to help her cope with stresses that may cause the neglect, as well as attempting to investigate the child's situation for protective purposes. In later chapters, I show how these themes of rapport, trust, and caring are affected by issues of confidentiality, the fact that the worker may be a **mandated reporter**, who is required by law to report certain abuses, and so on. For now, I simply wish to put into operation the construct of the working relationship.

I believe that many elements of a working relationship, such as trust and a sense of caring, also matter greatly in other areas of our lives. This is sometimes the source of confusion about the differences between relationships in general and the working relationship. As numerous examples in later chapters show, these elements take on special meaning in the context of social work.

I have defined the working relationship at this point in the discussion because my research suggests that the ability of the worker to be tuned in to and articulating the client's unspoken feelings and concerns in the preliminary phase of work contributes to the establishment of a positive working relationship (Shulman, 1991, 1978). In fact, all of the skills for helping clients manage their feelings, when used in the beginning phase of practice, have been found to affect the working relationship positively (Shulman, 1991). This underlines the importance of preparatory empathy and the worker's ability to respond directly to indirect cues.

When I present these ideas in classes or workshops, the eyes of the participants often indicate that they have begun to free-associate to their own caseloads. This may be happening right now to you as well. When I ask them what is happening, they share that they are feeling guilty for passing over the indirect cues of their clients, particularly in taboo and sensitive areas. I try to reassure them with the following advice.

If they still have a client active on their caseload, they can always go back and reopen what they may feel is unfinished business. For example, the worker in the earlier example who responded defensively could return and say, "I was thinking about your question last week about whether or not I had children. I think you were really wondering if I could understand what it was like for you." Three months later, it might sound like this: "I think I ducked your question when we first met, about whether or not I had children. It made me feel uncomfortable. I suspect you were really wondering whether or not I would understand what it was like for you raising seven children. I wondered if during our three months together I had come across as not understanding." I believe clients love it when a worker shares a mistake and can be perceived as "more like a real human being."

Skillful practice involves learning how to shorten the distance between when a worker makes a mistake and when he or she catches it. Very skillful workers catch their mistakes in the same session that they make them. Further, becoming an effective practitioner involves learning from **active mistakes** (as opposed to inactivity resulting from fear of making a mistake), developing better intervention skills, and then making more-sophisticated mistakes.

For example, a second-year student was preparing to take over as a new group leader for an ongoing group of mothers with children who had a chronic disease. The group met in a hospital. This student had read my book and had done his tuning in. His field instructor had helped him explore his feelings about being a young, unmarried man working with an all-female group of mothers. He had role-played how he would respond to the questions "Are you married?" and "Do you have any children?" He had prepared for everything except what actually happened.

Before he could make his prepared opening statement, one group member said, "Before you start, I want to let you know what we think of this damned hospital!" The force of the anger in her voice stunned him. She continued, "We have doctors who patronize us, nurses who push us around, and we keep getting young social workers like you who don't even have kids!" You can probably imagine what happened to all of his tuning in. As he put it later, "It went right out the window." When I asked him what he had felt like saying, he replied, "I may be in the wrong room!" Fortunately, he was so thrown by the comment that he did not switch to what I call a "counseling voice"; that is, he did not suppress the feelings churning away inside of him and respond mechanically by saying, "I'm glad you could share that with me," or "Go with that feeling, Mrs. Smith." He was so thrown that he responded spontaneously, saying, "I may not have any children, but I have a mother just like you!"

He was shocked, and the group members were shocked. The angry Mrs. Smith looked again at this new worker and probably saw him for the first time. Up to that moment, he had been seen as a stereotype. He was most likely concerned about what he was going to put in his process recording for his field instructor. The group was an ongoing one, so other members moved in and shifted the conversation to a more general discussion. The remainder of the meeting could be characterized as an *illusion of work,* an idea to be more fully defined later in this text. In this case, it meant conversation without real focus, meaning, or feelings.

He returned the following week after further discussion and tuning in with his supervisor. He began as follows:

> Mrs. Smith, I would like to discuss last week for a moment. I was unready for so much anger from you, and as a result, I think I missed the pain that must be under that anger for you and for all of the group members. You must have run into a lot of professionals who simply did not understand how much it hurts to have a child who is always ill and who never gets better. You saw me, a young worker, and felt, "Here comes another one."

His comment was greeted with silence in the room. Silences will be discussed in detail later in the text. For now, I suggest that they are full of meaning, but they are sometimes hard to interpret. Most people guess that inside the silence some of the members might be getting in touch with their pain or some positive response to the human quality of this young worker.

Mrs. Smith, who had been so angry, started to cry and said to the other women in the group, "You are all married. You have someone to help you. I'm a single parent. Who helps me cope? I never have time for myself!" Another woman responded to her, "I'm married, but big deal!" She went on to describe her husband working 12 hours a day, 6 days a week, since the birth of the ill child (his form of flight from pain). The group took off as the worker listened and began his education.

I do not believe he would have been able to reach for the underlying pain the first week. I am not sure he could have done it the second week if he had not risked his spontaneous response the first week. He would have still been struggling with suppressing his own feelings. Some might argue it is possible to get to the empathy of the second week without having to risk the spontaneous expression of feelings the first week. That has not been my experience, however. You will have to explore that question in your own practice. In any case, this young worker now is probably better able to share some of his feelings when faced with anger in a first session and then more quickly move to reach for the client's underlying pain. He now makes more sophisticated mistakes.

A second line of reassurance I give to workers is that they are usually more effective than they think they have been. More than two thirds of the clients in one of my studies found their workers to be helpful (Shulman, 1991). This is similar to the findings in my earlier work (Shulman, 1979b). Workers tend to underestimate their positive impact on clients. They eventually communicate their caring and concern for the client. In some cases it just may take longer, with a period of testing that might not have been necessary if the worker had tuned in and responded directly.

Finally, regarding those clients whom they did not reach and who are no longer on their caseload, I suggest that they realize that they did the best they could, given the training and level of support that they had at the time. Somewhat like an artist who must hang up an early painting that reflects limited skill and knowledge, learn from it, and begin a new painting, the worker must start anew with the next client. I suggest that a little guilt is helpful, because it keeps the worker in a self-discovery and learning mode of practice. A lot of guilt would be overwhelming and counterproductive. Workers who are overly judgmental of their own work will find it hard to help clients manage their feelings of guilt.

The practice described in the preceding examples raises the following three areas for further discussion: affective versus intellectual tuning in, tuning in to the worker's own feelings, and the different levels of tuning in. Each of these is explored now in more detail.

Affective Versus Intellectual Tuning In

To tune in effectively, a worker must try to experience the client's feelings. One way to do this is to recall personal experiences that are similar to the client's. For example, the client is having a first contact with a person in authority. This is true even if the client is there voluntarily and the helping person has no specific control functions (such as protection of children or maintenance of parole). The first encounter is also a new situation, filled with unknown elements. What new experiences or first encounters with people in authority has the worker had? Can the worker remember how it felt, what his or her concerns were? A new school, a new teacher, the first experience of hospitalization—any of these might serve to remind workers and put them in touch with feelings related to those of the client. The important point is that workers need actually to experience these feelings.

Engaging and Working
With the Hard-to-Reach Client

THE PHASES OF WORK: THE PRELIMINARY PHASE OF PRACTICE The author presents a model for the preliminary phase of practice and uses as an illustration the example of a young unmarried social worker's first session with a mother who asks the dreaded question "And how many children do you have?"

Supervision in practice, or field instruction in social work education, can provide important assistance to the worker or student in developing genuine empathy in the tuning-in process (Shulman, 1993a, 1993b). For instance, in a preparatory consultation session with a social worker who is working with AIDS patients, their family members, friends, and lovers, the supervisor attempts to help the worker get in touch with issues facing all of the parties concerned. In this excerpt, the tuning in is to a gay man whose lover has recently been diagnosed with ARC (AIDS-related complex), which is a precursor to an AIDS diagnosis.

SUPERVISOR: What do you think John must be feeling right now?
WORKER: Devastated! It must be as if an earthquake has hit him and his lover.
SUPERVISOR: Are you really feeling devastated right now?
WORKER: Really feeling it? Well no, but I can imagine how it must feel.
SUPERVISOR: Try to take it further. Can you remember a time in your life when you felt devastated by a family earthquake? I'm not asking for the details of your personal life. I'm just trying to help you get in touch. For me, it was a breast cancer diagnosis for my sister. I can still remember the feelings well.
WORKER: The closest I can remember was when my grandfather had a heart attack. We were close to each other. He was old, but I still couldn't believe it, and it took a long time until I really faced it.

SUPERVISOR: Now you're closer. So tell me, what would you be feeling right now if you were John?

WORKER: Oh my God, this can't be happening. It must be a mistake. Maybe the diagnosis was wrong. I can't believe I'm going to lose him. What am I going to do?

SUPERVISOR: What do you mean—going to do?

WORKER: We have been sleeping together for over a year. What if I have it? Am I going to stay with him? I must stay with him; he needs me now more than ever. What about my life? I've seen so many friends in these relationships. I want to help him—I must help him—but what about my own life?

SUPERVISOR: As John, how are you really feeling right now?

WORKER: I'm overwhelmed, depressed, and I think I'm even angry at him for having AIDS. But how can I be angry at him when I love him?

SUPERVISOR: I think you are getting closer to possible themes. We have to remember to be prepared for a totally different response from John. Each person may be quite different. What are your feelings right now about working with John and with his lover, Rod?

WORKER: I'm not sure how I feel about anything right now. I know I'm a little scared. A part of me is not sure I want to get close to this pain. I'm not sure what it will do to me. If I get close to Rod, I'm going to lose him as well.

SUPERVISOR: I'll try to help you through this. It is going to be tough, in part, because it's the first time around for you. My problem is that I have gone through it so often, with so many clients, that I sometimes forget what it was like the first time. (silence) No, to be honest, I don't forget—I just feel like closing it off myself. We should both monitor this process and help each other if our defenses get in the way. Also, raise it at the next staff meeting. I think others can offer some support.

TUNING IN TO SELF AND THE CLIENT In this example the supervisor helps a worker in a residential center tune in to a teenaged client who feels overwhelmed and hopeless. In tuning in to the worker's feelings the supervisor explores the worker's sense of failing with the client and how that affects her practice.

Perhaps the most important contribution made by the supervisor to the worker's growth was her willingness to admit that the struggle to deal with one's own feelings persists throughout one's professional life. The supervisor provided a model for the worker to emulate. She could not ask the worker to tune in to the feelings of the client unless she was simultaneously tuning in to the worker's emotional response. The suggestion that the worker reach out for additional support from colleagues was also helpful. In one of my studies, workers who reported access to support from supervisors and colleagues were more effective at providing that same support to their clients than were those who did not have such support (Shulman, 1991, 1993a). The study also indicated that the supervisor would need access to support as well.

Tuning In to One's Own Feelings

The AIDS example emphasizes how important it is for workers to get in touch with their own feelings. How we feel can have a great deal to do with how we think (cognition) and how we act. Because of their preoccupation with their own feelings of inadequacy, the young, unmarried workers in the earlier examples could not immediately respond to the clients' concerns. The worker in the AIDS example, as he explores his own reactions to working with the terminally ill, will discover many of the same feelings of helplessness and impotency often felt by friends, lovers, and family members of a person with AIDS. Health professionals often feel quite deeply their inability to save a dying patient. Precisely because the helping person's feelings are similar to the client's, it may be difficult to listen and respond. In a recent experience coleading a group for people with AIDS in early substance abuse recovery, I commented to my coleader, a full-time, experienced staff person at the AIDS agency, that I would need his help in dealing with the serious decline in health of one of our clients. He responded, "And what makes you think it ever gets any easier for me?"

By tuning in to one's own feelings and experiencing them before the engagement, their power to block the worker can be lessened. In many ways, the helping process is one in which workers learn a great deal about their own feelings as they relate to their professional function. One's capacity to understand others and oneself can grow while one engages in this continual process. In fact, I believe this is one of the reasons many workers have entered the social work profession.

This stress on the importance of the worker's own feelings runs counter to many conceptions of professionalism. As pointed out in Chapter 1, a central construct of the medical model stresses the hiding of real feelings, which are seen as interfering with one's professional role. In a study of the effects of family physicians' communications and relationship skills, the strongest predictor of positive outcomes—such as patient satisfaction and comprehension—was whether the doctor felt positively or negatively toward the patient (Shulman & Buchan, 1982). Also, patients were very good perceivers of their doctors' attitudes toward them. The crucial point is that we need to learn to understand and use our feelings, instead of pretending to deny their existence. This core issue will be explored in many different ways throughout the rest of the book.

Different Levels of Tuning In

Tuning in can be done at many different levels. Take, for example, the task of a social worker at a residential center for delinquent adolescent boys. A first level of tuning in would be to the general category of adolescents. The literature on stages of development and the worker's own recollections can help in this process. The adolescent is going through a time of normative crisis in which he must begin to define himself in a new role. Several central questions dominate his thinking. He is trying to sort out conflicting messages in our society about the qualities that make a "real man."

Sensitivity to underlying currents of feelings, to the ways in which clients struggle to deal with the normative crises of life, can also be enriched through reading works of fiction. The adolescent's efforts to develop his sense of differentiation from his family, to further his independence while at the same time trying to maintain some sort of relationship, has been explored with great perceptiveness by various authors.

Workers must tap into their own adolescent experiences in an effort to remember the feelings associated with this stage of life. Here are some examples from a training session in which workers, using a first person voice, attempted to express some of the problems of adolescence.

There are so many things I need to know about sex and girls. When I talk to adults about these things, they make me feel dirty or try to scare me with AIDS. It's important to me that I get accepted by the guys—be one of the gang. It feels great when we hang out together, kid around, talk about girls, gripe about parents and other adults. I'd be willing to do almost anything, even things I don't feel comfortable about, to be in and not left out.

I'm feeling a bit trapped by the drugs at school. I'm under a lot of pressure to use—and I've tried to resist—but it's hard not to go along. I'm worried about my friend. He's gone over the edge and could get himself in trouble. Who can I talk to? I don't want to be a fink. If I talk to a teacher, all I will get is a lecture, and my friend could get thrown out of school. I can't talk my parents. My mother would have a fit, and Dad is so drunk himself most evenings I can't talk to him.

The second level of tuning in is the specific client: in this case, youngsters who are in trouble with the law. Information on the background of the boys, the nature of the delinquent acts, their relationships with their families, and so forth can all prove useful in attempting to orient oneself to the thoughts and feelings of a specific group of adolescents.

They probably feel that society is starting to define them as outcasts who can't fit in. Their feelings must be mixed. They must be thinking, The hell with them; who wants to be part of all of that crap anyway! Parents, teachers, social workers—they are always pushing you around, telling you what to do. I don't give a damn. What the hell is happening to me? I'm getting deeper and deeper in trouble. People are taking control over my life. Maybe I am a loser—how in the hell am I going to end up?

The third level of tuning in relates to the specific phase of work. For instance, an adolescent has been judged delinquent and is about to enter a new residential setting. What are the feelings, questions, and concerns on his mind about this new experience, and what are some of the indirect ways they may be communicated?

I'm scared stiff but I'm going to act cool—I won't show it. I wonder about the workers, what kind of people are they? How do they treat kids like me? And the other kids, what will they be like? Is it going to be hard to break in? I've got to watch my ass.

Many of the general fears people bring to new situations will be present. For example, the client may be apprehensive about the new demands placed on him and concerned as to whether he will be able to meet them. At the same time, his feelings may include a sense of hope.

Maybe this place will be OK. Maybe these workers and the kids will accept me, make me feel at home. Maybe I can get some help here. Anything is better than going back home.

The key element in all tuning in is the recognition of ambivalence. A part of the client is moving toward the service, hopeful but guarded. Another part is using past experiences or hearsay about the service, workers, and so on and defensively holding back.

Finally, what happens if we add race and class to the example? Consider an African American teenager from a poor, inner-city neighborhood who has been mandated by a judge to a residential program for "delinquent boys" in a rural, middle-class, white community. The core focus of the program is on anger management skills.

Not only is he in a new and potentially frightening situation, he is also in a community where he will be an outsider. For teens of color, finding themselves in a white neighborhood is threatening. If the staff of the center are also white, he will probably begin (and possibly end) the experience wondering what any of it will have to do with what he faces when he returns to the streets of the city.

In the tuning-in exercise of workers preparing to meet new clients, I have usually observed that the first efforts at tuning in always pick up the resistance, the defensive side of the ambivalence. This often reflects the worker's frustrating past experiences. It also embodies the worker's concerns that the client will not want help. This can be a self-fulfilling prophecy unless the worker has a sense of the client's potential for resilience and change, as well as a belief that part of the client is reaching out to the worker. Otherwise, the worker's pessimistic stereotype of the client will meet head on with the client's pessimistic stereotype of the worker. The tuning-in process is a first step in trying to break this self-defeating cycle.

An important objection often raised to the tuning-in skill is that the worker may develop a view of the client that is far removed from what the client actually feels and thinks. The worker may then proceed to make sure the client fits the preconceived picture. This is a real danger if the tuning in is not tentative. In a sense, the key to the successful use of tuning in rests in the worker putting all hunches aside when beginning the engagement. What the worker responds to in the first contacts are the actual "productions" of the client, that is, the direct and indirect cues that emerge in conversation with the client.

For example, if the worker in the residential setting has tuned in to the front a tough kid might put up on the first day as well as the concerns that may underlie the client's attitude, the worker will have to see evidence of this behavior before acting. The worker reaches only tentatively for indirect messages and remains prepared to have the client share totally unexpected responses. Each client is different. Tuning in is an exercise designed to sensitize the worker to potential concerns and feelings. It does not dictate what the client's feelings must be. The assumption is that, after tuning in both to the client's feelings and the worker's own, there is a better chance that the worker's spontaneous reactions to the client's productions will be more helpful. If it simply produces a new stereotype of the client, it will be self-defeating.

I remember one example in which a worker tuned in to what he believed would be the client's anger at having to come to counseling. Appropriately, the worker reached for these feelings. The client indicated that he was not angry, and the worker provided a second chance by suggesting that other clients had felt angry under the same circumstances. The client, with some exasperation in his voice, answered a second time, indicating he was not angry. When the worker, on automatic pilot, then said: "Well, I can't understand why you are not angry!" the red-faced client responded, "Well, damn it, now I am angry!" The lack of tentativeness on the part of the worker had led to a self-fulfilling prophecy.

This section of the chapter has highlighted the importance of preparatory empathy in the beginning phase of practice. In later chapters, we shall return to tuning in as we explore different phases of work, different modalities of practice (such as family and group), and even the importance of tuning in when working with other professionals. In the next section, we focus on the skill of responding directly to indirect cues.

Responding Directly to Indirect Cues

The importance of tuning in during the preliminary phase lies in preparing the worker to hear indirect cues in the first contacts and to respond directly to these cues. In the first example given in this chapter, the new worker would have demonstrated this skill if she had said in response to the client's question, "Do you have any children?" something like, "No. Why do you ask? Are you wondering if I'm going to be able to understand what it is like to raise kids?"

A direct response to the indirect cue would have been just as important if the worker did have children. In one example, a worker in an agency dealing with physically challenged children was asked by a new client if she had children. When the worker responded positively, the client asked, "Teenage children?" The worker shared that her children were teenagers. After a brief silence, the mother inquired, "A handicapped teenaged child?" The worker in this case was able to respond, "As a matter of fact, the reason I was attracted to work in this agency was that my own teenager does have a physical handicap." After a long pause, the client responded, "But not like mine!"

The client was not satisfied with the responses, because the real question was not related to the worker's family situation. I believe this worker would have been better off answering, "I do have a handicapped teenaged child; however, the experience is different for each of us. You'll have to let me know what it has been like for you."

The advantage of a direct response in this example is that it opens up an important area of conversation that can then deepen the working relationship. A common objection is that the worker may "lead" the client by putting words into his or her mouth that are not really there. In addition, the argument goes, even if the worker guesses correctly, the client may not be ready to deal with that particular feeling or concern and may react defensively, be overwhelmed, and not come back. Because of this fear, the worker may be cautioned to withhold hunches and to wait for clients to raise a concern or feeling when they are ready to do so.

Nonetheless, I argue in favor of risking direct responses early in the first contacts. As the working relationship develops, the client is watching the worker, trying to sense what kind of a helping person she or he is. If the relationship includes diversity (as in a Latino family and a white worker), the question carries even more potency. Indirect communications are employed because the client is reluctant to risk communicating directly some of the more difficult and taboo feelings. Let us consider what happens when the worker responds directly to the indirect cues by using the skill of articulating the client's feelings. If the worker's guess misses the mark, the client will usually let it be known. Even if the client goes along reluctantly, hesitation in the voice and lack of affective response will tip the worker off to the artificial agreement. The worker can then respond directly to that cue. This is an example of how the worker can learn and grow from an active mistake.

In one common example of indirect communication, the client, early in the interview with a new worker, says, "I'm glad to see you. My last worker was really terrible!" There are few comments that can strike more fear into the heart of a new worker. The usual response is to change the subject immediately. Workers claim to be uncomfortable discussing another professional. In my experience, they are particularly quick to change the subject if they secretly agree that the other worker is terrible.

The mistake they make is to think the client is really talking about the previous worker. When in early contacts clients refer to other people, such as social workers and doctors who have not helped, it is usually the new worker they are really talking about, only indirectly. A direct response to this indirect cue might be "It sounds like you experienced a hard time with John. Can you tell me what went wrong so that I can understand what you are expecting from me? I'd like to try to make our relationship a positive one." The discussion of the past relationship is cast in the context of the beginning of this new relationship. The worker is not making a judgment about the previous worker—rather, the intent is simply to acknowledge what the client has experienced.

Another early client statement, even harder for the new worker to hear, often sounds like this: "My last worker was really terrific! My kids used to look forward to his visits." Once again, if the new worker can handle his or her own feelings, then a direct response to the indirect cue might be the following: "It sounds like you and your children really got close to John. You must really miss him. Can you tell me why you felt he was terrific? I may not be able to be just like him, because I'm a different person, but it would help to know what you are looking for in a worker." Once again, the ensuing discussion moves the worker and the client quickly into the authority theme—the relationship between the giver and taker of help. The worker both acknowledges the feelings of loss and reaches for the client's concern about how well the new worker will replace the previous worker. In effect, the new worker is starting to answer the client's implied question.

Students and workers have said to me, "That sounds great, but how do you say that when you are scared spitless?" I point out that workers usually do not say it the first time, but with practice they catch themselves before the end of the interview or during the next contact. For example, one might say, "I was thinking about our last conversation, and I wondered if, when you were talking about your problems with John, you might also have been thinking about what kind of a worker I'm going to be?"

A second objection raised by workers, particularly those with some elements of mandated authority (such as financial aid workers, probation officers), is that they fear the client who is positive about the last worker might say something like this: "Well, John, he didn't hassle me. When I needed something extra, he came up with the money." Or they might say, "John wasn't all uptight about every beer I had." If the comment about the last worker is an indirect communication related to how the worker is going to enforce his or her authority, then a direct response opens up the discussion for the worker to be clear about how he or she will operate—what the client can expect from the worker, and what the worker will expect from the client.

If a child welfare client is angry at the last worker for "always trying to prove I was a bad mother and trying to take away my kids," a direct response about this worker's perspective on the use of authority would be helpful. For example, the worker might say,

> Mrs. Smith, my agency is not trying to take away children. There are too many in care already. I would like to try to help you keep your family together. I would only recommend removing your children if I felt they were in danger

through abuse or neglect. And even if that ever happened, I would still want to try to help you get them back. I hope I can convince you that I really mean this.

This is an important part of the contracting process, and getting the issue on the table early can speed up the work. The issue of authority and contracting is discussed in more detail in Chapter 3.

In early sessions, clients not only respond to workers as symbols of authority and stereotypes based on prior experiences, they sometimes operate on the basis of specific information about the particular worker (or agency) provided through the grapevine. For example, one parole officer reported a first session with a recently released ex-con in which they got into a battle of wills over whether or not the client's last worker had been too tough. The new parole officer tuned in, between sessions, and inquired during the next session, "Were you really asking what kind of a parole officer I'm going to be?" After a long pause, the ex-con said, "The word back at the pen is that you're a real dink." The parole officer asked what that meant, and the ex -con revealed that he had left the penitentiary with a dossier on the parole officer at least as long as the one the worker had on him. The parolee was beginning with a stereotype of the worker that needed to be dealt with early in the work. Even if the parolee had not possessed any information on this particular parole officer, there would have been a general stereotype of parole officers to contend with. In reverse, the worker has to be careful not to be so worried about being "conned" that he or she relates to the client as a stereotype rather than a person.

If the client is not ready to pick up on the worker's direct response to an indirect cue, particularly in taboo areas, because of lack of trust or lack of readiness to share the concern or feelings, the client can choose not to respond. The worker must give the client that room. The most important outcome of the worker's direct responses is not that the client will always immediately deal with the concern. The crucial message to the client is that the worker is prepared to discuss taboos, tough issues (such as authority), or painful concerns when the client is ready. In effect, these interventions give the client permission to deal with these issues, while simultaneously showing the worker to be a feeling, caring, direct person who can see the world through the client's eyes and not judge harshly.

My research findings have repeatedly supported the importance of using the tuning-in and direct-response skills. Specifically, my study in a Canadian provincial child welfare program (Shulman, 1991) replicated earlier findings (Shulman, 1978) supporting this view. Although findings in any study are always tentative, even when replicated, these shed some interesting light on this issue. I was able to examine whether a specific skill, or group of skills, contributed to strengthening the worker-client relationship. The working relationship construct consisted of the two elements described earlier as trust and caring. This working relationship, in turn, provided the medium for effective helping and positive outcomes.

Clients in the study were asked to rate their workers' use of eight specific skills. The scores for the four skills most related to this discussion were averaged to create a scale called Skills for Helping Clients to Manage Their Feelings. These skills were

- *Reaching inside of silences:* Exploring the meaning of a silence by putting the client's possible feelings into words (for instance, "Are you angry right now?").

- *Putting the client's feelings into words:* Articulating the client's feelings, in response to tuning in or perceiving the client's indirect communications, prior to the client's direct expression of affect.
- *Displaying understanding of the client's feelings:* Acknowledging to the client, through words or nonverbal means, that the worker has understood how the client feels after the affect has been expressed by the client (for example, a response to crying).
- *Sharing worker's feelings:* Appropriately sharing with the client the worker's own affect. These feelings should be shared in pursuit of professional purposes as the worker implements the professional function.

In one explanation, employing a technique called **causal path analysis**, I determined the path of influence and strength of influence of these skills on the development of the working relationship and a number of outcome measures.[1] Findings indicated that the use of this group of skills positively affected the client's perception of the worker's caring; in turn, the caring dimension of the working relationship had a moderately positive impact on the client's perception that the worker was helpful. In addition, caring had a small but statistically significant impact on two other outcome measures: the final court status of the child (such as permanent custody) and the number of days children spent in care. These findings provide further support for the central construct of this practice model—that worker skills affect outcomes through their influence on the working relationship.

The average scores achieved for each skill by workers also revealed an interesting pattern. While clients reported that their workers acknowledged their feelings "fairly often," their rating of the workers' articulating their feelings for them was between "seldom" and "fairly often." Exploring silences was rated closer to "seldom" and sharing the worker's feelings was rated "seldom" by study clients. This pattern, repeated in several of my studies, provides some sense of the degree of difficulty in developing these skills as well as support for my argument of the dominance of the medical paradigm in the profession (see Chapter 1).

Because 81 families out of the 305 in the study provided us with ratings of their workers' use of skills at the time my team and I interviewed them, as well as a retrospective rating of skill use when they first met their workers, I could do some tentative analysis of the impact of time on the model. Employing a statistical method called **regression analysis**, I found that the use of these skills for helping clients manage their feelings in the beginning phase of practice had a moderately strong predictive ability for both the caring and trust elements of the working relationship. When the use of these skills in the middle phase of practice was examined, they still had a moderate impact on the relationship, although less than in the beginning phase. Both of these findings are consistent with the constructs of the practice theory.

---

1. The analytical technique of causal path analysis and the cited study is discussed in more detail in Appendix A, the research supplement to this book available on the text's companion web page. Essentially, the statistical technique allows a researcher to construct a model of the process under examination and to estimate the influence of variables along a defined causal path. For example, the model of worker skill (the independent or predictor variable) influencing the development of a working relationship (an intervening or mediating variable), which in turn influences the outcome of the client's perception of the worker's helpfulness (the outcome or dependant variable), was examined in the cited study.

Finally, I examined each specific skill in the study, when used in both the beginning and middle phases, and analyzed their simple correlations with the elements of trust and caring as well as the client's perception of the worker's helpfulness. All four skills for helping clients manage their feelings were found to have moderate positive correlations with relationship and outcome measures, increasing to moderately strong correlations in the middle phase of practice. In general, the positive impact of the use of these skills appears to be supported by research findings.

Consider this additional example, in which a white, high school social worker is talking to Dean, an African American teen, about his expressed desire to return the following year to a public school in his inner-city community. He had been part of a special program that bused volunteer teens of color from the inner city to white, suburban private schools for enriched educational programs. Because the worker had already acknowledged and explored their racial difference early in their work together, the stage was set for the worker to reach for the underlying reasons motivating the desire to change. After tuning in to the possible reasons, the worker reached for underlying issues, although still reluctant to name race as one of them.

WORKER: I remember a couple of weeks ago you mentioned you wanted to go to the public school next year. I'm curious why you would want to do that if you like getting away from the city to come to school.

DEAN: I do like it here, but my brother and cousin go to public schools in the city.

WORKER: Is that why you want to go to the public school?

DEAN: Sort of. I don't think they get as good of an education as I do, though.

WORKER: I see. I guess I'm still a little confused why you would want to go the public school. Maybe you're not sure yourself? I'm thinking that it may be difficult to come to school out here where you have a totally different atmosphere from what your brother and cousin experience in the public schools. Then you have to go back home and fit into the routine there, which is very different from what your friends at this school experience.

DEAN: It really is different.

WORKER: Tell me how it is different.

DEAN: Well, it's like I have to act different when I am at school than when I am home.

WORKER: Like you're struggling with two different identities? You are expected to act a certain way at this school, and that way doesn't fit in with how you are supposed to act at home?

DEAN: Right! Here, I'm supposed to act "white," and at home I have to act "black" or people will accuse me of being too "white." I have to be mean at home, but I can be nice here.

This conversation, aided by the worker's tuning in, created the opportunity for the young man to explore with the social worker his ambivalent feelings about making the change. Of course, because social workers have experienced the same set of taboos and have observed the same set of norms of behavior as their clients, it will take training and support, from supervisors and/or peers, for the workers to feel comfortable enough to give clients permission to explore these areas of work.

I would argue that for most clients, their difficulty in articulating their own feelings at the beginning of a new relationship, perhaps even being conscious of what they feel, requires workers to take the risks represented by tuning in and responding directly to indirect cues. I believe the client is often ready early in the contacts to discuss tough issues, explore taboo subjects, and even deal with the worker-client relationship if only the worker will give the invitation. Workers have said in consultation sessions that they often hesitate because they are not sure if they are ready. Thus, the worker's own ambivalence about exploring an area of work can produce the block. In the guise of protecting the client, workers are actually protecting themselves. As one worker put it, "I don't reach directly for those cues early in the work, because I'm afraid the client may take up my invitation. What will I do with all that feeling if I get it?" This excellent question is explored in more detail in later chapters. For more examples of responding directly to indirect communications, see *Additional Process Recordings—Chapter 2* on the book's companion website.

Chapter Summary

The complexity of human communications often makes it difficult, particularly in a relation to taboo subjects (such as authority and dependency), for the worker to hear and to understand what a client is thinking and feeling. A worker can increase his or her sensitivity to indirect communications by employing a skill called tuning in, or putting oneself in the emotional shoes of the client, prior to the first contact. The worker must also tune in to his or her own feelings first, particularly those related to anxiety about the first meetings. A set of four skills can particularly assist workers in helping their clients manage their feelings: reaching inside of silences, putting the client's feelings into words, displaying understanding of the client's feelings, and sharing worker's feelings. Many research results suggest the importance of using these skills in the beginning phase of practice to develop a positive working relationship and to be helpful.

Related Online Content and Activities

Visit *The Skills of Helping* Book Companion Website at www.socialwork.wadsworth .com/Shulman06/ for learning tools such as glossary terms, InfoTrac College Edition keywords, links to related websites, and chapter practice quizzes.

The website for this chapter also features additional notes from the author and additional process recordings:

- Interview With a Single Parent Just Returned from the Hospital: Responding Directly to an Indirect Communication
- School Counselor With a Sixth-Grade Child: Responding Directly to an Indirect Communication
- Worker in a School Setting With a Depressed Teenager With the Possibility of Sexual Abuse: Reaching for Indirect Communications in a Taboo Area

Beginnings and the Contracting Skills

I n this chapter, we explore the dynamics of new relationships in general and new helping relationships in particular. A model for contracting with the client in the first sessions is presented and illustrated. I then describe specific skills for helping clients manage their problems, including clarifying the worker's purpose and role, reaching for client feedback, and dealing with issues of authority. The contracting process is presented as flexible and changing over time. We also discuss the special concerns involved in contracting with resistant clients.

Next, we explore several models for assessment that can be useful at times in helping the social worker obtain a clearer picture of the client in relation to the environment. Issues of diversity and culturally competent assessment and practice are addressed, and research on the intervention process is shared.

During a first interview, a 25-year-old client put his social worker through an indirect test to see if she would be honest with him. The worker, responding directly to the indirect cues, asked, "Did I pass?" After acknowledging that she had passed, the client said, "I had to see where we stand. The first meeting is really important, you know."

First meetings in all helping relationships are important. If handled well, they can lay a foundation for productive work and begin the process of strengthening the working relationship between client and worker. If handled badly, they can turn the client away from the service offered. In this chapter, we explore the special dynamics associated with new relationships.

In Chapter 2, we focused on skills designed to help clients to manage their feelings. This chapter explores an associated set of skills called *worker's skills for helping clients manage their problems.* These skills are described in detail later in this chapter. They include

- ***Clarifying the worker's purpose and role:*** A simple, nonjargonized statement by the social worker usually incorporated into the opening statement to a client, describing the general purpose of the encounter (and/or services of the agency) and providing some idea of how the social worker can help.

- ***Reaching for the client's feedback:*** An effort by the worker to determine the client's perception of his or her needs. The working contract includes the common ground between the services of the setting and the felt needs of the client.

- ***Partializing the client's concerns:*** Helping a client break large and often overwhelming problems into manageable parts.

- ***Supporting clients in taboo areas:*** Helping clients talk about issues and concerns that are normally treated as taboo (for example, sex, death, authority, dependency).

- ***Dealing with issues of authority:*** The worker's efforts to clarify mutual expectations, confidentiality issues, and the authority theme.

The following sections discuss each of these skills and others. Because not all clients are pleased to have the social worker and the agency involved in their lives, this chapter also explores the special dynamics of working with involuntary (mandated) or semivoluntary clients. While I cautioned in Chapter 1 against using the study process in a manner that interfered with the engagement process, social workers nonetheless need to obtain an accurate picture of the relationship between the client and the environment. We shall look at several models for developing this framework. Issues in the beginning phase related to ethnic-sensitive practice and assessment will also be explored. In this book, *ethnic-sensitive practice* refers to the ways we shape our assessment and interventions in order to be respectful of the particular culture of the population with which we work. For example, the importance of respect for elders may shape our intervention with a Native American family, determining in part who needs to be present in family counseling and even to whom we address our interventions.

Now let us begin our exploration of the beginning phase of work by examining what we know about the dynamics of new relationships.

The Dynamics of New Relationships

All new relationships, particularly those with people in authority, begin tentatively. Clients perceive workers as symbols of authority with power to influence their lives. Clients often bring with them a fund of past experiences with professionals or stereotypes of them passed on by friends or family. So the first sessions are partly an effort to explore the realities of the situation. Encounters with people in authority usually involve risks, and clients will be careful to test the new situation before they expose themselves.

Ambivalent feelings will occur in any new situation. The client's doubts about adequacy and competency increase, as do fears concerning the worker's expectations. The other side of ambivalence is hope of receiving help. Depending on the individual and the helping context, one side of the ambivalence may be stronger than the other.

The two main questions on the client's mind in individual work, rarely spoken, are "What is this going to be all about?" and "What kind of worker is this going to be?" The urgency of these questions stems from the client's fear of the demands to be made. People in authority often have hidden agendas, and the client may fear that the worker will try to change him or her. This suspicion will affect the client's actions until the two questions are answered. Fear of feelings of dependency will be present until the client can see the helping person, not in the imagined role as the all-powerful authority doing things *to* the client, but as someone with skills who will do things *with* the client. Even in situations where social workers deal with mandated clients, acknowledging that the client will be the one who is really in control is crucial. The worker must be viewed, in the final analysis, as helping the client to work on the client's own concerns.

Another way to consider this early process is to realize that the client is making what I call the first decision. The **first decision** is essentially whether or not the client will engage with the worker in a meaningful way and begin to develop what has been called the therapeutic alliance. Without a client's real commitment to the work and the worker, the relationship is doomed to failure. Clients can drop out by not returning, or they can continue to come and engage in the "illusion of work," in which they go through the motions but no real work or change is occurring. With a mandated client, this illusion can be a form of conning the worker, whereby the client says what she or he thinks the worker wants to hear, not what the client really feels.

The **second decision** is made as the worker and the client make the transition to the middle or work phase. In the beginning phase, clients may not be aware of the hard work they face, the painful issues they must address, and their own responsibilities to address their problems. As they become more aware of these things, they have to decide, once again, whether to continue the engagement.

The **third decision** comes as the client approaches the ending and transition phase and realizes there is little time left in the working relationship. At this point, in a process that has been termed "doorknob therapy," the client must decide whether or not to face the most difficult and yet important issues in the work.

In the illustrative interview that follows, some of the concerns of the beginning phase arise in the client's indirect communication. The worker heightens the client's feeling of concern by not addressing her questions about the purpose of the session and the role of the worker. The setting is a hospital, and the patient a 43-year-old woman with three young children. Although laboratory tests have been negative, persistent symptoms have necessitated exploratory surgery and raised the specter of cervical disk disease. Referral to the social worker was made because a long convalescence would be required, during which household duties and child care would be impossible. In his written introduction to the recording of the interview, the worker describes his purpose as exploring aftercare possibilities and determining whether homemaker or alternative services might be necessary.

WORKER: Good day, Mrs. Tunney. I'm Mr. Franks from the social service department. Your doctor asked me to visit you and to see in what way we could be of help.
PATIENT: Is this a habit? Do you visit all the patients or only me? (She was smiling, but seemed anxious.)
WORKER: We interview patients whenever it seems to be indicated, when there is such a medical request.

The patient is asking, "What's this all about?" and expressing a natural anxiety. She might be wondering but not saying, "Oh my God! It must be more serious than they told me." The worker's response does not answer this question and does little to address the concern. Instead of clarifying the reasons for the referral, such as concern over a possible need for homemaking services, the patient is left in the dark. She responds with an unusually direct demand.

PATIENT: All right, in what way do you think you can help me? I am in the hospital for the second day. My children are being looked after by their father. Most probably I will be operated on in the near future. You know this started because I felt I had arthritis. I had difficulty in moving my hands and fingers, so I decided to come here and see what I really have. (Occasionally she works on her crocheting while she speaks.)
WORKER: I would like to ask a few questions, Mrs. Tunney. But first, tell me, do you feel more comfortable talking while you are working?
PATIENT: Perhaps. I always do something with my hands. I have to.

Once again the worker has not responded to a direct question. The worker is proceeding according to his agenda, conducting a fact-gathering interview. The client is left out of the process. As long as the patient is unclear why this worker is talking to her and what his purpose and role as a social worker are, she will be unable to use him effectively. The client will experience the interview as being "acted on" by the worker. Her sense of dependency and her fears of intrusion into her personal life will increase. She will remain uncertain of what to say because she has no framework for weighing her responses. The interview continues:

WORKER: You said, Mrs. Tunney, that your husband is taking care of the children. If I am correct, you have three. Is that right?
PATIENT: Yes, but the 8-year-old is a very hard one. He cannot be left alone. Fortunately, my husband's superiors are understanding people, and he can take off time whenever he needs to, and now he needs it. Usually, he is away on trips, and sometimes he is gone for weeks.
WORKER: I understand your husband is in the army. In what capacity does he serve?

The client might understandably be thinking at this point, "Why do you want to know about my husband?" The worker's questions are designed to elicit family information for the worker's study, but the client must wonder how disclosing this information is meant to help her.

Clients do not usually ask why the worker wants to know. That is not polite in our society. They may even cooperate, providing answers to all of the social worker's questions. As long as the doubt persists, however, suspicion and tension will remain. The interview continues with the worker asking questions about how the pain began, how the husband helps out at home, where the patient was born, and if she has family in this country. The patient's responses become shorter and consist of direct answers to the worker's questions. When the worker suggests meeting with the husband and the children "to get a clearer picture of how we can be helpful," the client agrees and says, "Jeez! Do you do this for all of the patients?"

In his summary of the first interview, the worker reports, "Inappropriate, almost childish, smiling and expressions of distress. Distress is covered by rigid attitudes and a compulsive personality. There are rules and consequently a role distribution which for some reason she would not negotiate."

Alternatively, one might interpret the "childish smiling and expressions of distress" as signals of her feelings about the interview. These feelings can be expressed in many indirect forms. The new boy at the residential institution who acts out his anxiety by immediately breaking rules and picking fights is one example. The adolescent whose total vocabulary during a first interview consists of the words *yes* and *no* and the parent who responds to the child welfare worker with open hostility are others. When the worker interprets the behaviors as reflecting the client's personality or resistance, the worker is viewing the client as an object rather than as someone in **dynamic interaction** with the worker, that is, an interaction in which both parties affect each other reciprocally, moment to moment. As a result, the initial client behavior often becomes part of a stereotyped view of the client initiating an endless cycle. The interactional framework alternative, incorporating the notion of reciprocity in relationships, would require that the social worker understand the client's behavior as, in part, responsive to the worker's interventions. The worker's interventions are also dynamically affected by the client's responses.

Many factors can lead workers into first contacts such as the one just described. First, the medical paradigm itself, borrowed from physicians, suggests a four-stage approach to conceptualizing practice. Recall that in this model, one studies the client, develops a diagnosis, plans treatment, and then evaluates the results. The emphasis on a first stage of study encourages some workers to see the initial interview as a fact-gathering exercise in which the client's function is to provide information. This can lead to an interview somewhat like our earlier extreme example.

This discussion of the medical model always leads to some anxiety from students who may be placed in fieldwork agencies that require this format for a first interview. In some situations, workers must complete a detailed intake form that requires them to obtain a **psychosocial history**, the client's psychological and social life story, elements of which may have some bearing on the current problems. The worker must then provide an initial diagnosis or assessment. In some settings, a checklist is provided to guide the worker's responses. Students often ask me, "How can I conduct a first interview in the way you described if I'm expected to complete this form?"

Examination of these forms and detailed analyses of such first sessions often reveal the following. First, while protesting the rigidity of the structure, the worker often feels much more comfortable having the form to guide the first interview. Use of the form allows the worker to maintain control, makes the first session more predictable, and gives the worker time to become comfortable. Of course, the opposite may be true for the client, who may feel more and more uncomfortable as the interview goes on.

Second, one can design the first interview so the worker can, without undue effort, simultaneously contract with the client, try to help the client feel more at ease, and still obtain the required information. For example, a worker could say, "There are several questions I need to ask you for us to be able to obtain insurance reimbursement, but before I do so, I thought I would explain how I might help, and find out what's on your mind."

In example after example, students discovered that this preliminary discussion often yielded much of the information they needed to obtain for the form, but it followed an order that fit the client's sense of urgency instead of the worker's. Time could be set aside in the second half of the interview for covering missing information by going through the form. The client was often ready to provide the data at that point, especially if the worker explained why it was required (for medical insurance, obtaining a more complete understanding of the family's health experiences, and so forth).

An explanation of how the information would be used is important not just to help build trust, but also to maintain the worker's ethical responsibility regarding informed consent from the client. The client has a right to know how his or her personal information will be used by the worker and the agency. The client also has a right not to share such information as a condition of service, unless the worker shows that the information is essential for the client to receive service. The National Association of Social Workers' Code of Ethics provides direction for a social worker on this question. (See the link on the book's companion website for the link to the Code.)

Although students can structure the interview to work within the framework provided by their setting, they still have to face assessment and diagnosis. Even this can be dealt with if one thinks of diagnosis as a description of the state of the relationship between the client and the various systems to be negotiated, as well as an assessment of the client's sense of strength and readiness to cope with the problem. The discussion of the resilience research in Chapter 1 provided more than enough evidence of factors that could be included in the assessment, thus focusing on what is right with clients rather than what is wrong.

Diagnosis could be seen dynamically as something that changes and shifts, often moment to moment, as opposed to a fixed description of a client's "problems." Thus, in most settings, students and new workers could adopt more flexible structures for first interviews while still working within the framework of the setting. Even in those situations where a worker must make a specific assessment, such as a medical insurance requirement to provide a specific diagnosis, the worker needs to incorporate elements of contracting in the first session. Simply recognizing the difficulty of actually listening to a client and empathizing with him or her, while trying simultaneously to "categorize" the client, will often free the worker to respond more, with greater affect.

After the medical paradigm, a second factor that can contribute to the worker's reluctance to be direct about purpose is the notion that one must "build a relationship" before the work begins. In the model described thus far, the term *working relationship* has been used. The hypothesis advanced now is that the working relationship will develop only after the purpose of the encounter has been clarified and the worker's role explicitly described. In effect, the relationship emerges from the work, rather than preceding it.

Of course, the nature of the relationship can change over time. A client may be less likely to share a particularly difficult or embarrassing problem in the beginning, before a "fund" of positive working relationship has been developed. This is one of the reasons for the common phenomenon of clients raising **near problems**—defined as real issues in their lives that are close to the most difficult concerns—at the start of the work. The contracting skills described here are designed to build up this fund from which both the worker and the client can then draw. As the working relationship strengthens, clients may move on to more powerful themes of concern. I referred to this process earlier as making the "second decision," which allows the transition to the middle phase and the discussion of more difficult and often painful material. The skills of clarifying purpose and role, used in the beginning phase of practice, provide the groundwork for this transition by helping develop a positive relationship, in particular the element of trust, between worker and client (Shulman, 1982, 1991). Again, the worker's initial directness enables the relationship building, not the other way around.

A third factor preventing directness is the worker's tendency to be embarrassed about either the client's problem or the worker's intentions. In our society, having a problem has become identified with weakness and dependency. Workers therefore sometimes feel uncomfortable talking about a client's problems. Some of the client's difficulties, such as a physical or mental ability that some people judge negatively, are considered so difficult to discuss directly that workers have invented euphemisms to describe them. One group for teenage unwed mothers met for four sessions during which no mention was made of their pregnancy, while their midsections grew with each passing week. Children having great difficulty in school have been brought together by school counselors in "activity groups" for after-school fun activities with no mention of why they were selected. They are not usually fooled, because they all know they are considered to be the "dummies" or the "problem kids." The worker is embarrassed about mentioning the problem, and so the client gets a message that reinforces reluctance to discuss painful areas.

When workers begin their sessions with hidden agendas, they are equally ill at ease about making a direct statement of purpose. If a worker believes the client's problem is all figured out and the task is now to proceed to change the client's behavior, then reluctance to be direct is understandable.

A final factor leading to difficulty in being direct is the use of professional jargon. When I graduated with a professional degree in social work, my mother asked me at a dinner in my honor, "Now that you're a social worker, tell me, what do you do?" I replied, "I work with people to enhance their social functioning, to facilitate their growth, and to strengthen their egos." She smiled at me and said, "But what do you do?"

In fact, I was unclear about how to articulate my professional function. What made it worse was that the other social work graduates appeared to be clear about theirs. I thought, desperately, that perhaps I had missed a key lecture or had not completed a key reading. In reality, all the helping professions, not just social work, have had trouble with direct statements of purpose and role and have tended to obscure this confusion with jargon. Key words such as "enhance," "facilitate," and "enable," followed with a statement of hopes and aspirations (such as "enable clients to be empowered"), avoid the functional question. If, in training sessions with professionals, I restrict their use of jargon and insist that they describe what they have to offer me as a client in simple, clear sentences, they usually find it difficult to do so. The more ingenious try to avoid the difficulty by asking me, the client, "What is it that you want?" I point out at such moments that they are answering a question with a question. While it is a good question, in that it reaches for client feedback, I do not think I can really answer it without some structure from the worker. In effect, the structure provided by the worker through a clear opening statement will potentially free the client to respond. This is another example of a false dichotomy—structure versus freedom. In effect, freedom emerges from structure.

There are situations in which the client has come to the worker for service—for example, a voluntary client coming to a family counseling service. In such a case, the worker may well begin by explaining the purpose of the first visit as one in which the client can tell the worker what brought him or her to the agency so that the worker can see whether she or he can be of any help. The worker listens for the client's sense of urgency; when that is clear, the worker can explain how she or he can help.

In the section that follows, I present a model that depicts how to use a first session to clarify the worker's purpose and professional role directly and simply, without jargon or embarrassment.

Contracting in First Sessions

The first sessions described in this book take place in the context of an agency or a host setting, such as a hospital, school, or residential institution. Many of these concepts of helping apply equally to social work in individual private practice, group practice, or fee-for-service managed care clinics in which workers are reimbursed for the number of counseling hours provided. However, the issues involved in private practice, and the profound implications for private practice from changes in managed care in our country, mostly go beyond the scope of this text, which focuses on social work that takes place in more traditional and formal settings.

Because the effect of the context of practice is particularly important in the contracting phase, we explore it here. Social workers usually work for an agency or institution (the host setting). The setting is more than a convenient place for sessions to take place. It has a function in society, which means it has a stake in the proceedings. In the societal distribution of tasks, each setting deals with a particular area of concern. The hospital is concerned with the health of patients, the school with the education of students, the family agency with family functioning, the parole agency with monitoring released prisoners and helping them function in the outside world, and so on. The mission of the setting significantly affects the helping person's actions.

In the first chapter, I identified some of the pressing life tasks that face clients: dealing with school, family, work, the welfare or medical systems, and so on. The client sees successfully accomplishing these tasks as the immediate need. In each illustrative example, I described some life tasks that might be important to the client.

The tasks of the agency and of the client, as well as their possible convergence, are what Schwartz considered in developing the contracting concept (1971). Writing in the context of group work practice, he said,

> The convergence of these two sets of tasks—those of the clients and those of the agency—creates the terms of the contract that is made between the client group and the agency. This contract, openly reflecting both stakes, provides the frame of reference for the work that follows, and for understanding when the work is in process, when it is being evaded, and when it is finished. (p. 8)

In the beginning phase of work, the worker's function can be considered as mediating the initial engagement between the client and the service, searching for the connection between these two sets of tasks. Although many obstacles—such as the authority of the worker, an involuntary client, an insensitive doctor in the hospital—might block the mutual interests of the setting and the client, the worker searches for the often elusive **common ground,** the overlap between the specific services of the setting and the felt needs of the client.

Schwartz describes three critical skills in this phase of work: clarifying purpose, clarifying role, and reaching for client feedback (the client's perception of his or her stake in the process). Although these skills are central to all beginning engagements, many variations in their implementation exist. For example, the setting introduces variant elements. The issue of authority, whether the client is voluntary or the worker makes the first contact, can also introduce variations. The rest of this section details these three skills, illustrates them in different contexts, and describes the results of my research on their effects.

Contracting Example

Given the dynamics of new relationships described earlier in this chapter, the worker must attempt to clarify the purpose of the meeting with a simple, nonjargonized, and direct **opening statement.** This statement should openly reflect both the stake of the setting and the possible stake of the client. For example, in the hospital interview described earlier, the worker might have begun in the following way, among many:

> My name is Mr. Franks, and I am a social worker from the social services department. Your doctor asked me to see you to determine if there was any way I could help with some of the difficulties you might be facing in taking care of your children or your home while you're recovering from the operation. I know that can be a difficult time, and I would like to help, if you wish. I would like to discuss this with you to see if you want some help with these problems or with any other worries you might have about the operation or your hospital stay.

Such a simple statement of purpose sets the stage for the discussion that is to follow. The purpose of the visit is to discuss the service and to see how that service fits with what the client feels she needs. With this simple framework in place, the client's energy can be involved in examining areas of possible work. With a clear boundary in place, the client does not have to worry about why the worker is there. Conversation and the worker's subsequent questions should be related to this task, a mutual exploration of areas of potential service.

The worker also needs to be prepared for the client's inevitable question about how the worker can help. In this example, clarifying the worker's role might consist of spelling out several possible forms of assistance. For example, "I can help you examine what you may be facing when you return home, and if you think you need some help, I can connect you with some homemaking resources in the community." Another form of assistance could be presented in relation to the family: "If you're worried about your husband's ability to help at this time, I can meet with the two of you and try to sort this out." Still another could be offered in relation to the hospital and the illness:

> When you're in a big, busy hospital like this, you sometimes have questions and concerns about your illness, medication, and the operation that are not always answered; if you do, you can share these with me and I can see if I can get the staff's attention so that they can help out, or perhaps I can do so myself.

Each of these simple statements defines a potential service the client may wish to use immediately or at some future date. They may seem overly simple, but for a worried patient on the ward, these statements provide an orientation to services that she may simply not know about. They can be described as **handles for work** that provide a way for the client to "grab onto" the offer. The specific examples shared by a worker reflect his or her tuning in to the particular situation faced by the client (see Chapter 2). Previous clients may have taught the worker about the themes of concern that are most common in the particular situation. Thus, the worker not only speaks directly to the heart and mind of the specific client but also normalizes the problems because they have been shared by so many clients in similar situations.

Contracting is a negotiating period involving both the client and the worker. The skill of reaching for client feedback is essential. In the latest example, this skill might sound like this: "Are any of these issues of concern to you, and would you like to discuss how I might help?" It is quite possible that in the feedback stage the client may raise issues that were not part of the worker's tuning-in process. The agenda for work can expand. The only limitations are the tasks of the setting: The worker cannot offer services that are not relevant to those tasks. For example, the acute care hospital social worker in this example would not get involved in long-term marital counseling with this woman and her husband, even if early contacts indicated that this was needed. Instead, he would focus on the marital issues associated with the illness and hospitalization. He might also make a referral to an appropriate family counseling agency or hospital service.

The boundaries to the work created by the agency service and the needs of the client help the worker focus; they also relieve the client's anxiety that private areas may be intruded on. Contracts are negotiated continuously and can be openly changed as the work proceeds. Often a client, not fully trusting the worker, will risk discussing only the near problems in the early interviews. When the working relationship strengthens, areas of concern that were not part of the initial agreement may enter the working contract.

Here I want to distinguish between my use of the term *contracting* and some other uses in the field. Sometimes, the term refers to a specific written document, or "service plan," that the client literally signs and agrees to fulfill. In the case of an involuntary client, or perhaps a teenager in a residential setting, the contract specifies the agreed-on goals and the way they will be achieved; for example, a substance-abusing child welfare client might agree to attend meetings of Alcoholics Anonymous or some other self-help group. In many cases, such documents represent the agency's or the worker's perception of what needs to be done, which the client will go along with to obtain the service or to create the illusion of cooperation. While a genuine, mutually agreed-on contract may be put into writing in appropriate settings, this is not required in my broader use of the term.

Engaging and Working

With the Hard-to-Reach Client

BEGINNING PHASE: CONTRACTING The author presents the elements of contracting.

Some Variant Elements in Contracting

The contracting procedure is not mechanistic; variations in the first sessions are often required. As pointed out earlier in this chapter, the helping person who is contacted by a client for assistance may begin the first interview by indicating a wish to understand what brought the client to the agency—to know what is on the client's mind. As the client shares concerns, the worker tries to connect these to potential service areas and to explain available help. The important point is not the order of skills used, but rather that the contracting is started, that it is an open process, and that both parties are involved. Some illustrations of statements of purpose and role from various settings might help at this point.

MARRIAGE COUNSELOR: Living together over a long period can be tough, with many ups and downs. You have been describing a crisis in your marriage, which I am sure is a frightening time. It's also an opportunity for change, perhaps to make a new marriage out of the one you already have. One of the ways I may be able to help is by helping both of you talk and listen to each other about the problems you are having. I can help you tell each other how you are feeling, try to help you figure out how you get into trouble, and help you do some thinking about what each of you can do to strengthen the relationship. As we work, I'll throw in some of my own ideas about living together, and some of these may be helpful.

SCHOOL SOCIAL WORKER: Your teacher told me that you were having trouble in her class and that she thought school was not much fun for you. My job at the school is to meet with kids like you to see if we can figure out, together, what's going wrong for you at school and to see if there are things we can do to make it better. How about it—how is school for you right now? (After some discussion of the problems, the worker tries to define her role.) If you really feel Mrs. T. (the teacher) is down on you, maybe I could talk to her a bit about how you feel and help her understand that it makes it harder for you to work. With so many kids, she may just not understand that you feel that way.

RESIDENTIAL TREATMENT SOCIAL WORKER: (First contact with new resident) I thought I should tell you what I do around here so if there is any way I can help, you can let me know. My job includes being interested in how you guys are making out. For example, right now, you're new to the house and that can be a scary time; if there is some way I can help you get connected with the other staff or the kids, or if you want me to answer any of your questions about the place, I'd be happy to. (In the course of the conversation, other functions can be clarified.)

Sometimes you may have troubles on your mind and need someone to talk to about them. For example, if it's not going well at school, or you're having problems with the guys in the house or your family when you visit, or you're mad at the staff or the rules, I'll be around to listen to your troubles, if you want me to, and to try to help you figure out how you might handle them.

CHILD WELFARE WORKER: (With a young, unmarried mother who is rejected by her family) I know it's tough when you're young, pregnant, and feeling very alone. We could meet each week and talk about some of the things on your mind right now. Perhaps I can help you think them through and figure out some answers to some of your concerns, such as trouble with your parents or your boyfriend, or uncertainty about whether you can make it if you keep the baby or if you need to give the baby up. How about it, are some of these things on your mind right now?

Workers may well need to tailor the opening statement to the specific capabilities of the client population. Young children need to be addressed at a level of language that they can understand. In a sexual abuse investigation, for example, purpose might be explained in terms of adults touching children in places that make them feel uncomfortable. Realistic dolls are often used to help the child understand the areas of the body involved.

In a back ward of a psychiatric hospital, to a group of patients described as catatonic (appearing to be completely out of contact with their environment) an opening statement describing a discussion group to provide mutual support would have little meaning. A worker who says, in a loud voice, "I'm going to try to get all of you to talk to each other" might be closer to the mark. In just such a group, one worker met with the patients each day for months, showing them magazine pictures. Initially, there was little response. Just before Christmas, while looking at a picture of a family around a Christmas tree, one patient began to cry. Another patient next to him began to cry as well. The purpose of this group—to establish contact of any kind between patients—was appropriate to the population.

CONTRACTING IN FIRST SESSIONS This example demonstrates the single-session work done by a hospital social worker interviewing a mother and her teenage daughter who are facing medical expenses without having health coverage. Issues of privacy are raised when the worker receives a telephone call about another client.

These illustrations show how one can fashion contracting to reflect the particular service of the setting and possible needs of specific clients. This is where the tuning-in process can help. Later in this chapter, an example of contracting with a voluntary yet resistant client, as well as another with a mandated client, will provide an opportunity to discuss the importance of clarifying issues of authority, such as confidentiality and the worker's potential use of authority, which are also essential elements in the contracting process.

Research Findings on Contracting

In my research studies (Shulman, 1978, 1991), the skill of reaching for client feedback about purpose was significantly associated with a worker's ability to be helpful. This supports the concept that the areas in which the worker can be most effective are those in which the client perceives some stake. Garvin (1969) found the same principle to be true for group work practice.

Recall that the four skills for helping clients to manage their problems are (1) clarifying the worker's purpose and role, (2) reaching for client feedback, (3) partializing the client's concerns, and (4) supporting clients in taboo areas (Shulman, 1979b, 1991). The scale that included these skills was predictive of the development of trust in the working relationship. Trust, in turn, was the medium through which the worker influenced outcomes of service. These findings supported the idea that contracting creates a structure that is freeing to the client.

The skill of exploring taboo areas is included in this grouping, because some of the most important client issues are taboo in nature. This skill helps a client to move from the near problems to the real problems.

Partializing is included in this grouping because it also serves a contracting purpose. By listing the specific issues, the worker is providing potential handles for work for the client. The worker is also breaking down big problems into more manageable components and suggesting that some next steps are possible. Even if a client faces a terminal illness, there is still some work that can be done during the remaining time in relation to friends, family, lovers, and the general quality of life.

Contracting Over Time

Our discussion thus far has focused on the initial contact with the client and the beginning of the contracting process. In practice, the **contracting process** takes place over time, with both the worker and client deepening their understanding of the content to be covered and of the expectations each can have of the other. For example, as pointed out earlier, clients often share near problems in the early sessions as a way of testing a worker. If the worker deals with these in a way that helps the client lower defenses, then more serious (and often frightening) themes may emerge. For the worker's part, even a clearly stated description of purpose and role might not be heard or remembered by a client overwhelmed with anxiety on a first session. Thus, contracting should be understood as a process that, in some ways, may continue throughout the life of the relationship.

The worker can also feel overwhelmed in a first session and, as a result, miss or skip over clues to crucial issues related to contracting. In the following example, a client uses the device described earlier of referring to a former helping professional who was not helpful, as an indirect cue to her concerns about this new worker. The strength of her feelings frightens the worker, a student with some counseling experience, who ducks the issue. The client also raises her past suicide attempts, further upsetting the student. The student starts to catch her mistakes at the end of the first session and then continues to clarify the contracting at the start of their second meeting.

> Right at the beginning of our first session, Mary indicated that she had been to see a psychiatrist over a year ago, shortly after her husband had left her. When I asked if that experience had been helpful, she described at length how terrible it had been. She stated laughingly that if she was violent she would like to go and punch him out right now. I failed to respond to this message—failed to relate it to me—and instead, asked her to elaborate.

MARY: He told me more or less that I was just feeling sorry for myself and that the relationship had ended, and that I had to accept it and get on with my life. I knew I was feeling sorry for myself, but I couldn't help it. I didn't need him to tell me what I already knew. I just wanted an assist—not for him to solve my problems. He wanted to give me pills but I wouldn't take them. I was afraid enough of myself that I would do something stupid—like I have.

WORKER: Like you have?

MARY: Yeah, I've tried to commit suicide a few times—a number of times—lots of times (pause—a strange laugh)—and one of these days I'm going to succeed.

WORKER: Have you been thinking of suicide lately?

MARY: (Silence) Yeah, that's a good question. I think I hit the age of 12 and I really felt like I was 95 in my mind.

The client continued to talk about suicide, describing how she was not afraid to die, how nobody would miss her, and so on. The worker changed the subject by picking up on the problems the client faced. The worker described her feelings as follows:

I felt that Mary was trying to manipulate me into feeling sorry for her and I was angry at her for doing this. I also felt a little bit nervous at what I'd gotten myself into—this was my first client at field placement number three (my first two did not work out). All I needed was someone to commit suicide on me. I wasn't able to empathize with Mary since I was caught up with my own feelings.

I had heard her message loud and clear that she was desperate for help; however, I didn't let her know that I'd heard or that I was prepared to help. I didn't realize at the time this was her way of saying: "Hey, are you sure you can handle me?" Although I didn't reassure her at the beginning that I was prepared to take her on, because I was feeling ambivalent myself, I had my opportunity at the end of the interview. As we were leaving at the end of the session, Mary suddenly stated, "You know, I once called a crisis center and told the person I felt like killing myself. They told me I might as well go ahead and do it."

WORKER: I'm wondering if you are worried that I might tell you something like that. I guess you're worried about if I'm going to be able to help you. You know, I can't decide for you if you want to live or die—that's something only you can decide. But if you want to live, I can help you to begin sorting through some of your problems, one step at a time. I don't have any magic cures to help you feel better—I wish I did, because I know you're feeling pretty low right now. It'll take lots of hard work for both of us. I'll try my hardest if you want to continue. (Long silence)

MARY: Yeah, I guess that's fair. At least I can talk to you.

I had some anxieties about whether or not Mary would show up the following week. She was 10 minutes late, and I was on pins and needles thinking the worst had happened. I couldn't believe how relieved I felt when she finally arrived. I tried to own up to my mistake, declare myself as human, and return to some of Mary's concerns I had missed last week.

WORKER: Mary, you know I was going over the tape of last week's session and I think a lot of what you were trying to tell me went right over my head. It seems like you were quite worried that you wouldn't be able to get the kind of help you needed. Who wouldn't be after the experience you had with the psychiatrist? I guess I first want to let you know that I am going to make mistakes too and I'm probably going to say things that you don't agree with, so you're going to have to let me know if you feel I've screwed up. It'll be hard, but please don't keep it in.

MARY: Well, at least you seem real and I'm glad you're not a guy. I didn't trust him. It was all a big game of verbal semantics, with him trying to guess what I was thinking and feeling and me going along with him because I wanted to give the right answers. I wanted him to like me. I didn't realize it at the time.

WORKER: Do you find it hard to say things sometimes because you're afraid the person won't like you?

MARY: Yeah, I think I do that, especially with men.

When I asked her to elaborate, she described her relationships with men, her fear of making demands, how she gets angry and "starts acting like a bitch." When I asked if that was what was happening with her current boyfriend right now, she elaborated in some detail, and we spent the remainder of the session on this theme.

The contracting process is not completed in this example. Both worker and client will have to come back to discussions of their way of working, as well as expansions of the content (themes of concern) of their work. The worker has laid the groundwork for the discussion of their process by letting the client know that she will make mistakes and that it is the client's job to help keep her honest. The worker's job will be to create the conditions that will help the client do just that. This would be one example of the skill referred to earlier as helping the client deal with authority in the relationship to the worker. The goal is to help the client deal with the worker as a real person, not just as a symbol of authority.

The discussion thus far has described contracting work with clients who appear open to help or who have sought it out. What about work with clients who are resistant? How can you find common ground when the client appears defensive and not open to your intervention? How can you contract with a client when your function includes authority over the client's life (as in parole supervision or child welfare protection)? In the next section we explore this variation on the contract theme, stressing the importance of dealing directly with the issue of authority. The analysis of first sessions expands to include discussion of the skills required to begin to strengthen the working relationship.

Contracting With Resistant Clients

All clients bring into the first interview some ambivalence toward the idea of taking help. Resistance to the worker may be strong for some clients because of their past experiences with professionals, their particular concerns, or the problems created by the authority of the helping person. It may be expressed passively, as by an apathetic response during the interview, or actively, as by open hostility. Although students and inexperienced workers often indicate they prefer apathy over anger, they soon come to realize that an angry client who is openly resistant can be much easier to work with than one who sits quietly, nodding and agreeing with the worker, while inside feeling exactly the same as the openly resistant client.

Consider the following example of a mandated client, a young mother who was on probation for substance abuse offenses. She was required to meet regularly with her probation officer, attend a group program, see a social worker at a court clinic, and stay free of drugs and alcohol. The social worker, a first-year student, tried to be understanding and to engage with the client but never made clear her expectations. After repeated appointment cancellations, the worker finally decided to confront the client and set limits.

> (Session 4) In keeping with the client's pattern of canceling and rescheduling her appointments, it was no surprise that she called the Court Clinic at 12:05 today. I answered the phone and spoke to her briefly. She asked if she could change her 12:30 appointment to 1:30 because her "kid was sick" and she was at home taking care of him. I asked her if it would be possible for her mother to watch over him while she came to the clinic, but she told me that her mom "wasn't up yet because she takes medication."
>
> I told Deedee that this recurring problem with her appointments cannot continue. She admitted that she realized that this was a problem and offered a variety of excuses. Yesterday, the problem was that she went into work early; today, it is her son. I told Deedee that, if she would like, she could "come in at 2:30 today." "2:30 is no good," she replied, because of her work. I explained to

Deedee that I was busy until then, as other clients were scheduled to come into the clinic. I was not prepared to change their appointments or to keep others waiting because of this problem. Consequently, Deedee became very abrupt and angry. She raised her voice and said, "Fuck it all. I'll try to get in. What time is it now?"

This confirmed for me that she had no idea of the exact time. She was just trying to get out of today's meeting. "My kid's sick" was the last I heard before she hung up. Deedee had tried to get me to let her off the hook for her appointment by employing her manipulative techniques, including guilt. (She told me that she didn't want to have to take "Stevie" out in the heat with a fever.) She asked if she could just see her probation officer next week as she was already scheduled to see him on Tuesday. I explained to Deedee that, regardless, she had to see me on a weekly basis.

At 12:45, and still no sign of Deedee, the telephone rang. Obviously, after some rethinking, Deedee had called the court clinic to apologize for her behavior. She began immediately by apologizing. "I'm sorry, Lois. I'm so sorry. I'm disgusted with myself. I have split personalities, you know. That wasn't me. I had to cool down." I excused Deedee and asked her when she would be coming in. She told me that she would be able to make it in at 2:30 today, as I requested. She arranged with her coworker to fill in for her, as she would be a few minutes late (according to Deedee, "work" now starts at 3:00). I told Deedee that her schedule was something that we were going to have to review again, as this seems to be a recurring problem. She explained that "I wouldn't want someone to do it to me" (i.e., hang up), and that she wasn't brought up that way. She told me that she hangs up on her mother, too. I told Deedee that I appreciated her apology. She thanked me once again.

The worker's beginning efforts to confront the client and to set limits opens up a discussion of the authority theme and the client's difficulty in responding to demands placed on her by people in authority. It is not uncommon for clients who begin serious substance abuse to appear stuck developmentally at the stage of the life cycle associated with the start of the addiction. If the client sounds like a teenager in the interviews, it may well be because she is still stuck in that stage of her growth. In part, the helping process involves beginning to work through these developmental issues.

Deedee arrived promptly at 2:30. As soon as I greeted her she apologized. We were unable to sit in our usual meeting place as hearings were being held, so we sat in the hall at a table. I began by explaining to Deedee that I was concerned about her difficulties arriving at the clinic each week. I asked her what the problem was. She explained that it was nothing personal; however, she hated feeling "trapped by the court." I asked Deedee if she felt that the terms of her probation were unfair. Deedee recognized that she was the cause of these terms and admitted that they exist because of her actions. (Too bad that next week she'll forget that she admitted this.) Deedee explained that she "wished all of this didn't happen." She "hates to see her friends lead a normal life"—they didn't have to comply with the terms of the court, could "go shopping when they want," and "don't have to worry about their appointments." Deedee expressed a sense of feeling overwhelmed by having to "go to a special group program, the Court Clinic, see her probation officer, and go to work" while managing her own responsibilities.

I tried to help Deedee with this feeling by partializing her responsibilities. I focused on our task of meeting weekly. I explained to Deedee that I think picking a firm meeting time that we would adhere to strictly would best serve us. We agreed on Fridays at 12:30. I suggested that by having a permanent appointment, it would make it easier for her to organize her other meetings and priorities. This way, she would not have to think about or try to remember when we were scheduled to meet, thereby increasing her anxiety and frustration, and resulting in her changing or canceling our appointment.

Further, I told Deedee that she should use these meetings for her benefit, as that was their purpose. It was her chance to outline her goals and discuss any pressing issues. Deedee told me that she "loves to talk and could do so." She explained that, once her job is finished in two weeks, that she will have more time. However, she likes working, as it gives her money, which she plans to use for Christmas gifts. She told me that she loves to buy gifts for everyone, especially her son. I asked her how he was doing (aside from feeling sick today). She said he is "doing great" and that he knew that she is supposed to be seeing me weekly. It was "Stevie," Deedee explained, who told her to call me back and to come in today.

I asked Deedee if she hangs up on everyone, not just her mother. She said she does it all the time, to everyone, when she gets mad. I asked her how she feels once she's hung up, whether or not she's still mad. Deedee told me that she felt "like running away, escaping to a far-off place." These are the same feelings she was having prior to her encounter at Burger King that led to her arrest. Clearly, Deedee was feeling overwhelmed and tried to escape today rather than confronting her anger. I told her that her hanging up is "not acceptable," while at the same time, I appreciated her apology. I told her that next time she should tell me what the matter is instead, if possible. (I realize that Deedee has certain limitations that I and others do not.)

I reminded Deedee that she had told me over the phone that she "didn't care if I was going to give her a bad report when she hung up," and wanted to "fuck it all." She said that she was ashamed of her previous behavior and that coming to the court is all just a "bad reminder" for her. However, she recalled what I had just said to her, that she "must take everything one step at a time." She mustn't look at everything that she has to do as one task, but as many smaller ones. "Stevie" had helped her today by making her realize that she has to go the clinic. Deedee asked me if I'd ever met him, and recalled that he used to come in for a group last year. I told her that we would arrange a time for him to come in. She told me that she was excited by that idea.

I reviewed briefly with her how the rest of her week had been otherwise. No drug or alcohol problems. She asked what Dr. Simms had said about her taking the Valium last week. I explained that, because it was not condoned, she must focus on not taking any more and remain drug-free. I asked her what her plans were for the long weekend. She was planning to pick up groceries, as she had just received her check yesterday.

We then chatted briefly about what else she had to do, and Deedee asked if she could go. I reminded her that I would see her next week, and to have a good weekend and week. She said one last time that "it wasn't me before." I explained to her that over the phone it was her voice, and that's "all I have to go on." She said she understood and said I must have thought she was "crazy." I told her that today's conversation was forgotten and that from now on, this shouldn't be

FIGURE 3.1

Obstacles in the Worker-Client Relationship

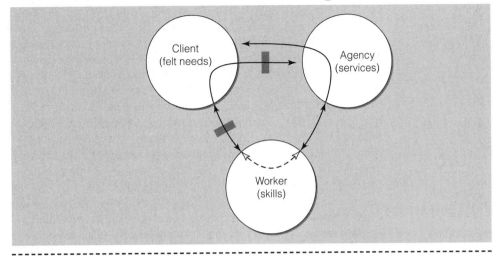

a problem as we have contracted an agreement and are beginning to formulate goals (who am I kidding?).

The question of how long these meetings would continue resurfaced again. At the beginning of the meeting I had told her that, unless I hear otherwise from her probation officer, she would go to the group program for two months and remain at the clinic for the duration of her probation. I feel, though, that this issue was dealt with by telling her the meetings are permanent. While I realize that today Deedee agreed with these terms, chances are that our next meeting will reflect a lack of compliance to these terms. Finally, when Deedee left she seemed to be in brighter spirits. As she said good-bye, she said, "Have a good weekend, Hon. See you Friday."

When the client has not made the first decision (to engage the worker), whatever the specific reasons or the form of expression, an obstacle sits squarely on the line between worker and client (see Figure 3.1). Therefore, the worker's efforts to turn the client toward the service must be integrated with efforts to deal with this obstacle.

Engaging and Working

With the Hard-to-Reach Client

CONTRACTING WITH A DRUG-ABUSING FEMALE CLIENT The social worker has difficulty just getting a time for an interview with a client who is court ordered to meet with the worker. The client is denying that she has a problem with drugs.

The first step in this process begins with the worker honestly facing his or her own feelings about the engagement. Workers are human, and a new client who appears not to want help or who seems volatile or hostile can cause the worker to hold back on efforts to reach for the client. Workers experience difficulty in offering help in the face of possible rejection. In the example just described, the student shared that this was her only client at the time (the start of the school year at the school of social work) and she was afraid of losing her. This fear caused the student to wait three sessions to confront the client. I had pointed out to her that she really couldn't "lose" the client because, at this point, she didn't "have" the client.

When a worker feels relief whenever the client misses appointments, the worker's offer of service may contain the same elements of ambivalence the client is feeling. This can easily lead to a self-fulfilling prophecy of the first engagement breaking down.

Social work professionals have debated whether one can work effectively with mandated clients. Some believe that the use of authority to require engagement so profoundly distorts the helping relationship that it can only be an illusion of work. In some cases, it is clearly true that no matter what the worker says or does, the client refuses to accept the service. In some situations, the client may not yet be ready; in others, the client may never be so. This is one of the reasons children must be removed permanently from some abusive homes, some men need to go to prison for battering their partners, and some heroin addicts end their lives overdosing on the street. The worker can only do her or his best to maximize the possibility that the client will use the help, leaving the final decision to the client.

For some categories of clients, however, the requirement that forces them to seek help serves as the beginning of a process of change. Writing about his development as a professional in working with men who batter, Trimble (1994) describes his own understanding of this process:

> I was idealistic when I started this work. I wanted men to come to the service because they realized they had a problem which had hurt another person physically and psychologically and had hurt themselves. I hoped they would come to realize that they needed to change themselves even if their wives would never return. In reality, few of us face our problems unless we have to. It has been my experience that most violent men who come to our group and stay long enough to make a change are there because they have to be. That "have to" is either a court order or their wives saying they won't return unless the men get some help. This does not mean that most men want to be violent but rather that most of them cannot tolerate for very long the pain and fear I mentioned earlier. Their inability to tolerate pain, fear, and loneliness forms a part of the foundation for both their violence and for the impulsivity which carries them out of the group. Because of this impulsivity an outside pressure is needed to keep them in the group past their usual tolerance level for self-confrontation. (p. 261)

The skills of beginning discussion with a resistant client are the same as those described earlier: clarifying purpose, clarifying role, and reaching for feedback. A negotiating process is taking place, but this time the potential obstacles to a working relationship must be part of discussion. In effect, the worker is asking the client if they can work together in spite of the barriers that may block their efforts. Often, when an obstacle has been identified and explored, it loses its power, and the client and the worker are free to move past it into a deepening relationship.

To see how this might work, consider an example of a first session with a voluntary but resistant client in a child welfare agency. The client, Mr. Gregory, is 25 years old. He has recently separated from his wife. She has applied to place their three children in temporary care of the agency. Mr. Gregory has a long record with the agency in which different workers have consistently characterized him as hostile and defensive. In fact, when the worker told her colleagues she was going to see him, their comment to her was "Good luck!"

This worker described the purpose of her first interview as informing him of his legal rights, describing the meaning of the agency's intervention, having him sign consent forms, and seeing if some help could be offered to him for his own concerns. The interview began with the worker's efforts to clarify purpose.

WORKER: You know that your wife has signed forms to place your children under the care of this agency. I wanted to meet with you to have you sign agreements, but before that, to discuss what this means for you and your children. I know it can be an upsetting time, and I thought you might also have things on your mind you want to discuss.

MR. GREGORY: For how long are my kids going to be in care?

The worker's opening statement clarified the purpose of the interview, placing a strong emphasis on the offer of service to the client. The client is not just someone called in to sign forms, but someone with feelings and concerns as a client in his own right. In a sense, her direct reaching for him represents a form of skill called making a demand for work (see Chapter 4). In the present context it means the worker is gently attempting to involve the client actively in the engagement. The demand is synthesized with the worker's ability to express some genuine empathy with the client's situation. This is demonstrated in the sentence, "I know it can be an upsetting time." In the client's response, "For how long are my kids going to be in care?" we see a shift back to the children—a polite way for him to refuse her offer. The interview continued with the worker responding to the direct question but also refusing to be put off by the client's first refusal.

WORKER: Your wife has signed forms for 6 months. That means that we are responsible to look after your children for that time, but with 24-hours' notice you or your wife can have your children home at any time. If you wish, after 6 months, the time can be extended.

MR. GREGORY: It's a long time for the kids.

WORKER: Yes, it is, and for you also.

MR. GREGORY: Yeah, I haven't seen them yet, but I hear they're doing fine.

WORKER: Would you like to see them?

MR. GREGORY: I thought I wasn't allowed to.

WORKER: Sure you are. You have the right to see your children whenever you wish.

MR. GREGORY: I was told that it would upset the kids, especially Alan, to see me, so it would be better not to.

WORKER: Sure it will upset him. It will upset you, too. It's hard to see someone you love and can't be with.

The worker's continued "empathic demand" is contained in the phrase "and for you also." In response, the client began to explore the visiting issue. The issue of visiting is important to the client and is an example of feedback on the contracting. The worker continued her emphasis on his feelings with the comment, "It will upset you, too. It's hard to see someone you love and can't be with." This persistence resulted in his beginning to explore the difficult feelings surrounding visiting. In the next segment, the worker opened up this area by using the skill of putting the client's feelings into words. She used her tuning-in preparation to articulate the underlying difficulty clients face in visiting children who have been placed in care.

MR. GREGORY: Yeah, Alan has been in care before, and he's confused and sad.

WORKER: Yes, that must make it hard on you to see him.

MR. GREGORY: Yeah. Like what do I say to him?

WORKER: Like when he asks, "When do I come home?"

MR. GREGORY: Well, yeah.

WORKER: What do you say?

MR. GREGORY: Oh, I change the subject and cheer him up.

WORKER: Does it work?

MR. GREGORY: Not really.

WORKER: What do you want to say?

MR. GREGORY: Well, I don't know when he's coming home.

WORKER: I guess that hurts you.

MR. GREGORY: Well, kids don't understand.

WORKER: Have you tried telling him?

MR. GREGORY: No, not really.

WORKER: I think it's hard to tell your child you don't know when he's coming home, but clearing that up might make it easier for you both once it's discussed.

MR. GREGORY: Yeah, I won't feel like I'm holding out. But I won't be seeing him until he comes to my wife on the weekend. Can I do that?

The worker's persistent and genuine concern with his feelings caused the client to begin to open up and deal with a real concern. When she responded to his comment, "Like what do I say to him?" by saying, "Like when he asks, 'When do I come home?'" she effectively opened the door for him to explore one of the roughest issues facing parents who place children in care—the guilt they feel, which often results in difficulty in visiting. Even in these first few minutes, the relationship has opened up, disturbing the client. Before he can allow himself to go further, he has to clarify how things stand between them. The next excerpt demonstrates how this discussion of the authority theme emerged.

WORKER: Whatever visiting arrangements you want to make will be done. I have to know in advance to help plan and to know where he is, since he's our responsibility. Seeing him at your wife's place is fine if your wife wants that.

MR. GREGORY (IN A LOUDER VOICE): I want to know something. Are you going to be my social worker? I know you see my wife and you help her. So how does it work? Are you on her side or mine, or do I get another social worker?

The directness of the client, which workers in the past may have confused with aggressiveness, is apparent. Consider the effect of this question on the worker. When asked about her reactions to the client's question, the worker admitted to being taken aback and feeling put on the spot by his assertiveness. Clients often ask questions or make statements that throw a worker off balance. This worker responded to her own feelings of defensiveness by delivering a substantial lecture that contrasts with her earlier terse reactions.

This type of response is not uncommon when workers feel put on the spot. Rather than responding with their gut reaction—their honest feeling at the moment—they try to control the situation with the use of words. Compare the following speech, delivered quickly, with the worker's previously terse, focused, and on-target responses.

WORKER: I'm on no one's side. I try to help your wife with what's on her mind. I'm here to help you with whatever you want. I do this so you can both come to the point of finally making a decision about your children—do you want them home? If yes, when and how many of them? Whatever we discuss is confidential, and the same goes for your wife and me. When the two of you make decisions that will affect each other, we'll do it together. Then I won't take sides but try to help the two of you talk to each other and work together on arriving at a decision. (Quiet)

The silence that followed this speech was important, because it contained a message for the worker. Several possibilities existed. It could simply have been that the client was confused by the words ("What did she say?"). He may have felt that he was not getting a direct answer to his question ("She must be on my wife's side"). In the next segment, the worker is seen demonstrating the important skill called reaching inside of silences (see Chapter 2). Recall that this is the worker's effort to explore the meaning of the silence to understand better what the client is thinking or feeling.

In an earlier research project of mine, we viewed more than 120 hours of videotaped social work practice and rated sessions according to an observation system we developed (Shulman, 1979a, 1981). Often, silences occurred just after the worker appeared to misunderstand the client's concern. Silence was often, but not always, a message that the client felt cut off. Other times, silence was not a signal that the worker was off base, but rather that the worker had hit home. In this study, workers responded to silences most often by changing the topic of discussion. Workers often experience silences as uncomfortable because they sense negative feedback. Silences can, of course, mean other things as well. For example, the client may be reflecting on the worker's comments, or he may be experiencing strong emotions. (The different meanings of silence will be discussed further in the next chapter.)

As illustrated in the next segment, by reaching inside the silence, this worker demonstrated skill in catching her error at the same time she was making it. Workers often have the mistaken notion that in good practice one never makes errors. In reality, good practice involves spontaneity on the worker's part, and so mistakes will be a natural part of the work. If workers always wait for exactly the right thing to say, they will always be thinking and analyzing while the client is working well ahead of them. This was a key moment in the interview, and this skilled and experienced worker proved herself up to the challenge.

(Silence)
WORKER: Why did you ask? It sounds like you may have had trouble with social workers before.
MR. GREGORY: I did. All the other social workers seemed to be with my wife and against me. I was always the bad one.
WORKER: And you're worried that I might do the same thing?
MR. GREGORY: Well, yeah, you might.
WORKER: I try to help the two of you decide to do what's best for you and the children. If you feel I'm siding or if you don't like how things are going with me, I want you to tell me because I want to help you both.
MR. GREGORY: Don't worry, you'll know. Are you new at this job?

As a result of her tuning in, the worker correctly guessed the meaning of his earlier question, "Are you on her side or mine?" She knew that his past experiences might well have led to the development of a stereotype about social workers and that at some point she would have to deal with this. By reaching directly for this in her comment, "It sounds like you may have had trouble with social workers before," she gave him permission to talk directly about what some clients would consider a taboo subject.

Workers sometimes express concern about exploring such a question. They feel it would be unprofessional to discuss other workers or other professionals. They say that they might be perceived as not identifying with the agency or as simply trying to get on the client's side. If one views most discussion of other helping professionals as the client's way of indirectly exploring the present working relationship, then the problem does not exist. This worker picked up the indirect cue and reached for his present concerns with her comment, "And you're worried I might do the same thing?"

This client responded directly and acknowledged that this was what he meant. Many clients who lack this strength and ability to be direct hold back at this point. Because the obstacles are powerful, they needed to be explored openly in first sessions. The worker needs to push, gently, a bit harder for such concerns. For example, in response to a client who says, "Oh no, I wasn't worried about you," the worker might continue, "It would be easy to understand how you might be concerned about me. After all, I'm a social worker, too, and you have had some tough experiences. How about it—perhaps you are just slightly concerned?"

The client will often sense, in this second invitation, that the worker really means that it is all right to talk about their relationship. If not, the worker can let things be and try to return to this topic at another time when the client's trust has grown. Meanwhile, the client knows that this issue can be discussed when he or she feels ready. (Other examples in this book demonstrate the process of accepting a second invitation.)

Returning to the interview, we have the interesting question posed by the client, "Are you new at this job?" When students discussed the possible meaning of the client's question, they considered several alternatives: "Maybe he was trying to figure out what kind of worker she is, because she doesn't talk like a social worker." "Maybe he was thinking that after she have been around for a while, she'll change." This time, in contrast to her reactions to the earlier direct question, the worker tried to explore its meaning. This involved the skill of elaboration, inviting the client to expand on the meaning of his comment or question.

WORKER: No, I've been here for a while. Why do you ask?

MR. GREGORY: Well, the last worker I had was really green. She knew nothing. She took me to court—didn't get anywhere, but what a mess.

WORKER: Are you wondering if I'll take you to court?

MR. GREGORY: Oh, no. And if you did, I'd go and fight.

Once again, the worker reached into his description of past experiences in order to find the implications for their current relationship. In the next excerpt, she tries to clarify some of the terms of their working relationship in the context of the agency and her dual responsibility of trying to offer him a service while still carrying statutory responsibility for the protection of his children. This is part of the contracting process. The terms of the relationship must be defined openly. The client may be able to overcome the obstacle posed by the worker's dual function if there is an honest discussion of it and a clear definition of the worker's responsibilities.

This is just as true with the elder care worker during a first visit who must deal with the elderly client's fears of being "put in a home" or the adoption social worker who must make a report on the suitability of the prospective parents. When these realities are openly discussed in the first sessions, when the responsibilities and mutual expectations are clearly defined for both the client and the worker, the client often can overcome the obstacles they pose. The worker in this illustration attempted to define this part of the contract.

WORKER: I think it's important for me to let you know under what conditions I'd go to court. Children can be in care of the agency either by court custody or voluntary agreement. In your case, it's voluntary, so there is no court involvement. But if I see the kids harmed when they're with your wife or you while visiting—by harmed, I mean beaten, black and blue, bones broken, or not fed or supervised for the whole weekend home, then I go to court. But only under those circumstances—beaten or neglected.

MR. GREGORY: What if I want to take my kids home? Can you stop me, go to court and stop me?

WORKER: No. You can take your children whenever you want.

MR. GREGORY: That can't be. What if I'm not working, can't care for them, you won't let them come home.

WORKER: I can't stop them. If, however, once they're home and they don't get fed, clothed, taken care of, then I can go to court and bring them back.

MR. GREGORY: (Smiling) I really knew the answers to this, but I was misinformed by other people in the past. I used to sort of test my last worker to see if she would tell the truth.

WORKER: Did I pass?

MR. GREGORY: Not you, her. (Quiet) Yeah, you passed [he smiled]. I had to do it to see where we stand. The first meeting is really important, you know.

WORKER: Yes, it is. And it is also scary, since you don't know what to expect.

MR. GREGORY: Yeah, but it looks OK.

They talked some more about procedures, rules, and regulations; arranged a next meeting; and then summed up. The worker asked if Mr. Gregory would like to meet again to discuss his children and their care. Mr. Gregory declined this invitation. He indicated he was too overwhelmed just then trying to find a new job. I contacted this worker several months after I obtained the process of this interview. Because so many people had asked me about Mr. Gregory, I asked if she had seen him again. The worker told me that, a few months after this interview, Mr. Gregory had called the agency and asked for her by name. When they met, he told her he now had a job and an apartment of his own, and felt he could take his children home. He indicated that he could not handle this by himself and that he would need her help. She agreed and discussed possible support services. Soon afterward, the children returned to their father. He may not have been ready to use her help after the first interview; however, she had laid the groundwork in the first session so that when he was ready he saw her as a source of real help.

Engaging and Working With the Hard-to-Reach Client

CONTRACTING WITH A RESISTANT MALE CLIENT The author and workshop participants discuss the previous interview in depth.

After reviewing this interview, many students and workers comment on the client's directness. They even ask, with a touch of hopefulness in their voices, whether clients like this come into agencies often. The key point is that he seems like such a good client only because the worker responded to him with skill. Another worker, and even this worker in her early student days, would have been put off by an assertive client such as this. The interview might have had a much different ring to it if the worker had not tuned in and prepared herself to reach for the part of this client who, in spite of his ambivalence, was still reaching out to the agency, the worker, and his children. The directness and anger is actually a sign of his caring.

We could make a similar analysis of a social worker in a residential setting dealing with a new resident and reaching past the false bravado put up by the "tough" teenager. Even if the teenager does not immediately accept the worker's offer to help with the fear and stress associated with suddenly finding oneself in a strange setting with potentially threatening peers, it is important that the worker acknowledge these feelings.

Another example might be an alcohol addiction counselor facing a client whose arms are tightly folded across his chest, thus expressing physically his feelings about being referred to the program by his boss. The worker needs to make clear her or his recognition that the client is present on an involuntary basis and that the worker is powerless to help the client without his active involvement. Trimble (1994) was quoted earlier as learning to understand the value of mandated attendance to his group. In a first session with a group for men referred for battering their wives, Trimble also told the men he recognized that they could continue to attend and meet the requirements of the group without ever changing, thus acknowledging that control—a crucial issue for male batterers—remained in their hands. Trimble incorporated this reality into his opening statement:

> I'm sure it is possible to follow all these rules and not change, not open up to facing yourself or to the other men here. You can probably get through this group and really not change. That's up to you. The judge may order you to be here or your wife may be saying that she won't come back unless you get help. And as I have just said, we require your anger diary and regular attendance in order for you to stay here, but no one can reach into your mind and heart and order a change. That's where you have complete control. (p. 262)

In each case, the worker must tune in to prepare for indirect cues and to get in touch with his or her own feelings about the engagement. A clear statement of purpose and role, incorporating the client's potential sense of urgency, is needed. An opportunity for client feedback about purpose must be given in addition to the exploration of the potential obstacles to developing a working relationship.

As with any client, the worker begins in the first session to use skills to start developing a positive working relationship while the contracting process is taking place. These skills include elaboration, reaching inside of silence, empathizing with expressed feelings, and articulating unexpressed feelings slightly ahead of the client.

The worker attempts to carry out the helper role as well as her or his abilities permit, making mistakes along the way but correcting them as soon as possible. The client also has a part in the proceedings: the decision to use this worker, to trust, to take some responsibility for part of the problems. If worker and client are both up to their interdependent tasks, then in the first sessions they can lay a foundation for movement into the work phase. This phase is examined in the next chapter, with a more complete discussion of many of the skills mentioned in this one.

Models for Assessment in the Beginning Phase

As mentioned before, the medical paradigm (study, diagnosis, treatment, and evaluation) is one model that has guided our profession's practice, theory development, and research. The individual elements contained in this model can be useful tools for the practitioner. Thus, within the interactional paradigm described in this book, obtaining relevant information (study), using models to guide our understanding of our client's circumstances (diagnosis), developing intervention strategies (treatment), and assessing our impact on the process and outcome (evaluation) all play important roles. However, several specific characteristics of this model have led me to reject it as a useful paradigm for my teaching, research, and practice: (1) the fact that it is a four-stage, linear model, in which each stage appears to follow the other; (2) the associated trappings borrowed from medicine; (3) the focus on pathology; and (4) the assumption that change comes from the worker rather than the client. With these reservations in mind, we should explore some of the questions associated with assessment and to examine some innovative models for determining "where the client is."

Kirk, Siporin, and Kutchins (1989) reviewed the history of social work and diagnosis in an article focusing on the profession's apparent ambivalence toward a formal classification system and the impact of the Diagnostic and Statistical Manual of Mental Disorders (DSM). The DSMs are a series of psychiatric manuals used to describe and classify mental disorders for the purpose of developing responsive treatment plans. (These researchers cited the DSM-IIIR, but the most recent version is the DSM-V.) Referring back to the publication of *Social Diagnosis* by Mary Richmond (1918) as the beginning of social work's "distinctive model of assessment, on which a distinctive approach to treatment was based" (Kirk et al., 1989, p. 296), they point out the following:

> The conception of "social diagnosis," as Richmond named this process, was a complex one. It consisted of analysis of three interacting elements: the social situation, the personality of the client or client group, and the problem. This process of diagnosis did not result in the affixing of a label, but rather in an accurate assessment of the dynamics of the problem in its life context. Richmond further contributed to this change by leading a movement within the social work profession to adopt a medical model for assessment and intervention and to view charity/social workers as "social physicians" who provide "social therapeutics." (p. 296)

The authors trace the evolution of social work's unique approach to assessment through several models leading up to the "person in situation" perspective, more recently reframed as the ecological approach, which has been widely adopted in the field. While their analysis raises many important questions about the suitability of the DSM system for social work assessment, and they call for work in developing a unique social work system rather than borrowing from psychiatry, they do not challenge the core of the medical paradigm in terms of the stages of the process.

Mailick (1991) calls for "re-assessing" assessment in clinical social work practice, according to changes in client populations, agency services, and treatment technologies (p. 3). For example, she highlights emerging controversies that influence assessment; this approach is associated with the "social constructivism" of postmodern theory:

> Customary ways of thinking about how information is obtained and how it can be confirmed are being re-examined. Social workers are debating whether it is the context in which information is sought, the purpose for seeking it, and the theoretical framework that shapes the investigator's search that critically influences the meaning of what is obtained. Social constructivism suggests just such an argument. For social work clinicians, it both raises the question of whether facts exist and can be discovered and challenges the usefulness of a monolithic model of assessment. (p. 4)

Her proposal for a new approach to differential assessment calls for acknowledging three major determinants that contribute to assessment: the nature and scope of agency service (such as goals of the service, identified population, time frame of service); the theoretical and value orientation of the practice (psychodynamic, behavioral); and the unit of attention (individual, family, small group). Thus, an assessment of an individual client might read quite differently (or be constructed differently) depending on the setting, the practice orientation, whether the service was individual or family oriented, and the time limits placed on the service.

Several authors have developed assessment frameworks or instruments that ask the social worker to pay attention to variables that might otherwise be overlooked. For example, Gutheil (1992) points out the importance of understanding the physical environment and its impact on behavior in the home, the family, the agency, and the interview. For example, the placement of the worker's chair behind a desk or the type and arrangement of furniture in a waiting room can convey a message to clients about the formality or informality of the practice. In the client's home, issues associated with personal space, crowding, privacy, and territory can influence family functioning and individual behavior. The author argues for training to help social workers be more observant and skillful in assessing physical space and its impact on clients.

Tracy and Whittaker (1990) propose using a "social network map" as a means of assessing a client's sources of social support. This instrument, which has been developed and tested by the authors, allows both clinicians and clients to evaluate several aspects of informal support: (1) existing informal resources, (2) potential informal resources not currently used by the client, (3) barriers to involving social network resources, and (4) factors to be considered in the decision to incorporate informal resources in the formal service plan (p. 462).

The social network map provides a tool for a client to identify both the number of significant people in different domains (such as household, friends, and neighbors) and the nature of the interaction (such as concrete support, emotional support, information, and advice). Given the contributions of social support networks to resilience (see Chapter 2), identification of these actual and potential resources could play an important role in helping the client develop strategies to buffer stress.

Finally, an example of the use of a "culturagram" to assess and empower culturally diverse families is described by Congress (1994) as a means for strengthening ethnic-sensitive practice, particularly in relation to immigrant families. The author created an assessment model that allowed social workers to move past generalizations about ethnic groups and to recognize significant levels of diversity within diversity, as well as unique cultural factors that may be client or family specific. As the author points out,

> A Puerto Rican family that has lived in the United States for 30 years may be very different from a Mexican family that came to the United States without legal documentation in the past year. An African-American family that relocated from a small southern town to a northern city will be unlike a Haitian family. Use of the culturagram helps the social worker clarify differences among individuals and families from similar racial and ethnic backgrounds. (p. 533)

Topics included in the culturagram include reasons for immigration, length of time in the community, legal or undocumented status, age at time of immigration, language spoken at home and in the community, contact with cultural institutions, health benefits, holidays and special events, and values about family, education, and work. The author provides examples of information that workers gained through the assessment and that helped them understand values, attitudes, and behaviors that would have been differently and incorrectly assessed in the absence of cultural sensitivity. Such examples include the following two: a 2-year-old Mexican child brought to a hospital by a mother who had not previously sought medical care—not because of neglect, but rather because of fear of deportation as an undocumented alien; a 7-year-old Haitian schoolchild whose increasing depression was connected to his family's emigration from Haiti for political reasons and the family's increasing sense of hopelessness about returning to their homeland.

Other assessment instruments will be described in later chapters dealing with family practice, child welfare, and substance abuse. I want to end this section with some suggestions for how a worker can judge the assessment process before deciding whether use a particular instrument in the beginning phase of practice. If an instrument is appropriate, a worker should be able to answer yes to each of the following questions:

- Will the information gained through this process provide specific understanding that will directly help me and the client in our work together?
- Is the client fully aware of the reason for using the assessment tool?
- Has the client provided informed consent for the use of the tool and is the client in control of the process?
- Can the assessment process be used in a manner that does not interfere with the crucial contracting and engaging process of the beginning phase?
- Is the use of the assessment tool critical to the work, as opposed to providing a structure that makes the social worker feel more comfortable?

If the answer to each is yes, then I believe use of the instrument early in the development of the working relationship can enhance the process.

Culturally Diverse Practice

Lum (1996) defines *culturally diverse practice* as follows:

> Culturally diverse social work practice recognizes and respects the importance of difference and variety in people and the crucial role of culture in the helping relationship. Its primary group focus is on people of color—particularly African

Americans, Latino Americans, Asian Americans and Native Americans—who have suffered historical oppression and continue to endure subtle forms of racism, prejudice, and discrimination. In working with an individual, family, group, and/or community, the practitioner draws upon the positive strengths of diverse cultural beliefs and practices and is concerned about discriminatory experiences that require approaches sensitive to ethnic and cultural environments. (p. 12)

Rapid changes in demographics in the United States and Canada have been brought about by a surge of immigration over the past two decades. Social workers often find themselves working with clients of different races and ethnicities whose cultures are foreign to them. Differences can also be related to gender, sexual orientation, class, physical ability, and so on, with distinct cultures associated with each population group.

Significant differences also exist within general population groups. For example, when one refers to a Native American client, one would also need to know which tribe or nation the client comes from. An Asian American client can be Chinese American, Japanese American, or a recent immigrant from Southeast Asia. While there are many shared experiences and cultures, an African American client from the rural South may seem very different from one raised in Chicago. A black immigrant from the West Indies will bring a perspective that is quite different from one from Haiti. Among Latin American clients, one would expect to find differences between Puerto Rican Americans in New York City and Mexican Americans in southern California, or Hispanics from Central America living in Boston. Cultural "sensitivity" that leads to stereotyping of clients according to general population groups, which does not allow for diversity within diversity, is actually a form of cultural insensitivity.

I remember working with white child welfare workers in British Columbia, Canada, who described their Native Canadian clients as very "passive" and tending to be "silent." They would interpret this behavior as a cultural trait when they worked with Native Canadian clients on the reserves or in the cities. There is some truth to this notion in that thoughtful pauses before responding often characterize such conversations. When I conducted workshops for Native counselors, however, they had another interpretation of this behavior. One counselor told me that a Native client had noted, "When you stay very quiet long enough, the white workers get so nervous, they go 'natter, natter, natter'." The white social workers in this example were explaining the silence as a cultural trait instead of understanding it as a form of indirect communication from this particular Native Canadian client, in this particular interview, with this particular white child welfare worker.

A lack of understanding of cultural differences can create barriers between the social worker and the client, particularly in the beginning phase of practice. As described earlier in this chapter, a social worker risks misinterpreting client behaviors, values, and attitudes if he or she cannot see through the cultural eyes of the client. As Weaver and Wodarski (1995) point out,

> Clearly, professionals cannot be expected to know everything about every cultural group; however, rather than judging a client by dominant society standards, it is the practitioner's responsibility to seek out relevant information, just as a social worker must seek out information when a client is referred to them with an unfamiliar case situation; for example, a particular disability, a need for advocacy, a question of eligibility for an entitlement program. Often one of the best sources of information about clients' culture are the clients themselves. (pp. 219–220)

In those settings and geographic locations where a particular population group is regularly a part of the caseload, the additional responsibility for learning about the group and appropriate culturally sensitive practices rests with the individual social workers and the social work department or agency.

It is beyond the scope of this book to explore fully the wide range of diversity issues and populations and how they affect practice. Note that several excellent social work texts have addressed these areas, including books by Davis and Proctor (1989), Devore and Schlesinger (1996), and Lum (1996). In this section, I instead set the stage for how one might address diversity issues, providing some illustrative examples of research and practice with different populations. Discussions in later chapters—for example, on work with families, treatment of substance abuse, group work, and community practice—will expand on this initial discussion by addressing other important populations (such as Asian Americans, immigrants) and by identifying diversity issues as they emerge from the work.

Working With Mexican Americans

In one study, Lum (1996) discusses how Mexican Americans value the family as a "source of identity and support in times of crisis" (p. 51). The author further points out,

> Mexican American "familism," or concept of family identity, extends beyond the immediate family unit (la casa) to include two other similar but distinguishable systems—la familia (extended family) and los compadres (godparents). In times of crisis, Mexican Americans are inclined to seek the family first for support. . . .
>
> Mexican Americans frequently extend the definition of family membership beyond la casa to include individuals labeled compadre and familia. Las compadres are important individuals who are often, but not always, related in some manner. Familia is variably defined in the literature. Generally, it connotes a social network resembling a modified nuclear structure. Elder males in the community may hold positions of respect and authority, and other members may or may not be related, but have some sort of significant interaction with the family. (pp. 51–52)

Lum (1996) points out that each of the three systems have a sense of responsibility that leads to a "volunteerism," with *la casa* as "the center of Chicano identity and commitment" (p. 52). Lum uses this understanding to develop guidelines for practice with Mexican American families; these guidelines take into account and work through this "triad of systems" that can provide support for the family members involved. Once again, this example emphasizes the importance of the worker respecting and involving the social support system, which has been shown to be an important element of resilience in the face of adversity.

Working With African Americans

Lum (1996) suggests that, from a historical perspective,

> The African American family has long existed within a well-defined, close-knit system of relationships. Authority and responsibility have been clearly assigned, and complex rules of behavior have embedded them in village and regional

linkages. Family life in the United States was impaired by slavery, but the African American community has survived as an active unit to meet the needs of its members. The church is still a central community institution. (p. 95)

Lum identifies underlying themes of the African American community to include "strong bonds of household kinship, an orientation to work for the support of family, flexible family roles, occupational and educational achievement, commitment to religious values, and church participation" (p. 95).

This description of the essential values of the African American community often clashes with perceptions of social workers who deal with clients who do not appear to fit this general model. For example, the frequency and problems associated with adolescent pregnancy in inner-city communities suggests a breakdown of this value system. Stevens (1994) studied adolescent development and pregnancy among African American women. She suggests that current paradigms of adolescent pregnancy "tend to view the female adolescent's behavior as disordered, diseased or as an intergenerational transmission of psychological dysfunction" (p. 435). She argues that nonpathologic analysis of problematic behaviors is required to better understand and respond to this pattern. Her findings support the following theoretical perspectives: (1) Pregnancy can serve as a primary way of confirming existence and providing a sense of identity rather than the result of sexual acting-out behavior; (2) parenthood is perceived as a viable route to an adult social identity when opportunities for alternate routes of negotiating an adulthood status are blocked; (3) the adolescent does not have to disconnect or individuate from familiar relationships for the development of self (p. 434).

In comparing a group of 20 pregnant teens with 16 nonpregnant teens, she found that the

> non pregnant females manifested a sense of care and responsibility to others in varied relationships and articulated more frequent self-expectancies for social mobility. They were actively engaged in church, work and school environments. They demonstrated civic competency by being registered voters. Non pregnant females were less restrictive in their dating and mating behaviors and experienced multiple dating partners. (Stevens, 1994, p. 449)

Stevens suggests that the findings supported the view that both pregnant and nonpregnant participants viewed pregnancy as a way of "managing concerns for personal and social maturation," providing a maturational experience and an indicator of adult status, and felt that their age group was mature enough to deal with parenting (p. 449). In summary, Stevens suggests that adolescent pregnancy, rather than being viewed as a sign of pathology, may be better explained as an alternate lifestyle choice. With this understanding, the social worker might well be advised to engage such a client with a nonpathologic orientation, focusing instead on both the adaptive and maladaptive aspects of this behavior. Stevens advocates for early intervention with troubled populations before sexual decisions are made (for example, primary and middle school prevention programs). She also suggests that social workers emphasize mother-daughter dyads, the adolescent peer group, mentor-apprenticeship programs, and collaborative programs with inner-city institutions.

While nonpathologic approaches to troubled clients are crucial in developing the working alliance in the early stages of engagement, the impact of long-term and persistent racism and discrimination have influenced many members of the African American community in their perception of social workers and others from the dominant society. Davis and Proctor (1989) suggest that "persons of African descent are especially reluctant to disclose themselves to whites, due to the hardships they and their forebears experienced in the United States" (p. 23). They suggest that this represents a special case of their unwillingness to disclose themselves to any representatives of the white world.

As the authors further suggest,

> Practice with black families may also be facilitated by the employment of certain practitioner styles. Practitioners should keep in mind that blacks in the United States have historically received less respect from this society than perhaps any other ethnic group. Hence, a style that indicates respect for them by the therapist will be positively received. As an example of demonstrating respect, the adult members of these families should be referred to, upon introduction, by their last names. The practitioner should not supplant the family's desire to be respected with his or her desire to be informal or even to establish a positive therapeutic rapport. Specifically, in the interest of establishing rapport, informality does not automatically facilitate the establishment of a sincere relationship. (Davis & Proctor, 1989, p. 82)

The importance of showing respect by the use of the last name was brought home by a participant in a workshop of mine when, referring to her work with African Americans in the South, she emphasized the relatively recent history of slavery during which slaves had their last names ignored and were referred to by first names in a manner that was demeaning. Thus, efforts by young white workers to establish informality with elderly clients by using their first names were actually perceived as insulting.

Working With American Indians

Williams and Ellison (1996) address issues of culturally informed health and mental health practice with American Indian clients, providing guidelines for non-Indian social workers. For example,

> American Indian clients will involve themselves in interventions they perceive to be appropriate. Involving a traditional healer may increase the desirability of an intervention. Social workers should use ceremony and ritual—two important aspects of healing—in an intervention. Giving gifts, serving food, and involving family and friends emphasize the importance of an intervention. The inclusion of family members underscores that the family is a supportive and protective unit whose help is valued. (p. 148)

Weaver and White (1997) raise the issue of the impact of historical trauma on Native families:

> In order to work effectively with Native families, social workers must first acquire an understanding of the historical influences on contemporary issues and problems. The root of many current social and health problems among Native people lies in the past. Specific and deliberate attempts were made to destroy Native people both physically and culturally. The impact of these actions cannot be minimized. Although Native people have survived, tremendous damage

was done to individuals, families, and communities. The trauma experienced by Native families has never healed. Social workers must be prepared to acknowledge and confront the historical trauma and grief experienced by Native people if they are to successfully assist contemporary Native families. (p. 67)

Weaver and White's injunction was brought home to me personally when I met with a group of Native leaders, homemakers, counselors, friendship center workers, and clients to conduct a group key informant interview in preparation for my child welfare research project. In the early part of the meeting, I listened to stories of recent abuses experienced by Native families and communities as, one by one, participants shared with great anger and frustration their experiences with child welfare services. As I attempted to listen and understand, without defensiveness, their stories moderated and began to reflect the anguish that seemed to lie just beneath the surface of their anger. Although I was in the role of researcher attempting to enlist their aid in designing and implementing my study, many of the practice principles for effective cross-cultural social work proved important.

Weaver and White (1997) point out that a "deep respect for people is a basic value for even many non-traditional Native people and Native children. In particular, a strong respect for elders is common among Native people" (p. 69). They point out that sharing and giving are highly valued and that even families in poverty will express generosity through "giveaways" that earn respect. This culturally appropriate behavior can create problems if the social worker does not understand its meaning and importance.

> Resources expected to last over a period of weeks may be gone within a day or two because they have been shared with other relatives. From the point of view of many Native people, it is inconceivable not to share resources with needy family members. However, from the point of view of the social worker, limited resources designated for a nuclear family in need have been squandered on people that may not be deserving and in any event were not part of the case plan. (p. 70)

Weaver and White (1997) point to the importance of humor, which Native people often use to teach norms and values, as well as the Native sense of connection to land and the environment. Time is measured "in terms of natural phenomena, not the movements of a clock" (p. 70). Additional strong Native values include privacy, the primacy of the group over the individual, decision by consensus, cooperation, and decentralization of power.

These researchers also illustrate differences between Native family structure and the dominant culture's extended and nuclear family models. They point out that the Lakota Indian word for family, *tiospaye,* includes a variety of people. In the dominant culture, this grouping would be called an extended family, while in most Indian cultures the word itself means "family." In the dominant society a common question when meeting someone for the first time might be "What do you do?" while among Native people it might be "Who are your relations?" (Weaver & White, 1997, p. 72). The Native community also emphasizes the importance and influence of tribal elders and grandparents.

Weaver and White (1997) offer specific suggestions for practice interventions to provide culturally competent services to Native people:

- Seek the sanction and support of people in gatekeeping roles.
- Include Native people in a variety of supportive roles.

- Maintain a positive, objective approach to each Native American family assessment.

- Advocacy around the issues of tribal sovereignty and treaty rights by the client should not be considered a threat to the service plan for the family.

- Members of tribes/Nations may be able to get services or funding for services through their Nations. (pp. 77–78)

Working With Canadian Indians

Much of the discussion of the American Indian culture can be applied as well to Canadian Indians. In fact, some of the tribes and nations extend across the border, with the Indian identity viewed as primary. In the Canadian Indian community in western Canada, I found similar extensions of support, starting with the family and including extended family members, neighbors, and the leadership of the band. My own child welfare research (Shulman, 1991) indicates that workers whom Native clients perceived as understanding and respecting the Native Canadian culture were more effective in establishing positive working relationships and influencing positive outcomes for the children involved. On a macrolevel, those regional offices of the provincewide child welfare agency who involved and worked cooperatively with the band leadership, Native Canadian friendship workers, homemakers, or court workers, and who involved this Native Canadian social support system in deliberations on how to help the family, had a better record than others of maintaining children in their own homes, finding kinship placements in the Native Canadian community, or being able to return children to their own families.

Issues in Cross-Racial Practice

Proctor and Davis (1994) address their perception of the reasons for "the sustainment of race as a salient issue for practice" (p. 314) and the roots of the lack of understanding in cross-racial practice. They suggest that the higher rates of growth of populations of color when compared with white populations, the fact that nonwhites continue to be segregated from whites and the mainstream of America, and the negative connotation associated with race issues "leaves both groups uncomfortable discussing race" (p. 315). They continue,

> The combination of these social forces may be quite ominous for personal and professional cross-racial interactions. Although economic problems are likely to increase the numbers of minority group members who need social work services, the white professionals who will be asked to help them may have little prior contact with these groups and hence little substantive knowledge of them. At the same time, minorities are apt to be increasingly distrustful of representatives from "the system." As a worst-case scenario, society may confront increasing numbers of minority clients who must be helped by white practitioners who understand too little about them and for whom their clients have too little trust. (p. 315)

The authors state that one of the questions on the mind of a minority client with a majority worker (actually, on the minds of all clients) is whether the helper is a person of goodwill. This is the equivalent of the "Who is this worker, and what kind of person will she or he be?" questions I posed in the previous chapter. Proctor and Davis (1994) point out that "respect and professional courtesy are particularly important with minority clients, to whom society frequently gives less" (p. 317). They go on to suggest how to show that respect:

> Signals of respect and goodwill may be conveyed in several ways. Social workers are advised to extend a warm greeting to the clients, to move physical barriers that inhibit communication out of the client's way, and to address the client by his or her last name. The client should be given an opportunity to get settled before the worker begins to talk. Privacy should be maximized, and the worker should appear unhurried with the client and refer to the shortage of time only in the final minutes of the session. (p. 317)

If you are thinking that these are good principles for practice with all clients, you are right. However, social workers must also understand the differential perceptions based on race, culture, ethnicity, and so forth that the client may bring to an experience. The ease with which majority workers can miss these crucial differences was brought home to me in a workshop I was leading for county child welfare investigators in Florida. An African American worker was describing his experiences making an investigation call to an upper-middle-class, white family living in a gated, almost all-white community. He described his feelings as the guard at the community entrance gate scrutinized his identification card and seemed reluctant to admit him to the property. His white colleague, sitting next to him at the workshop, said, "But they wanted to see my ID as well." I pointed out that I suspected the first worker experienced the examination differently because he was black. He agreed, adding, "I always wear a suit, even on dress-down day, because I know I will need to be wearing one to be treated seriously if I get a call from that community."

Davis and Proctor (1989) offer specific suggestions on managing early treatment interactions in which race is a salient factor:

> First, racial difference and its potential salience should be acknowledged. Acknowledgment, by the worker, of worker-client dissimilarity will convey to the client the worker's sensitivity and awareness of the potential significance of race to the helping relationship. It will also convey to the client that the worker probably has the ability to handle the client's feelings regarding race. It is probably best to introduce this topic by asking if the client has racial concerns and issues, rather than problems. Obviously the most likely answer to the question, "Do you have problems with my race?" is "No"! Thus we suggest a question such as, "How do you think my being white and your being nonwhite might affect our working together?" Or the practitioner might ask, "If during the course of our meetings you have concerns or issues pertaining to race, please feel free to discuss them." If the client hastens to assure the worker that race is not an issue, the worker can reply, "I don't think it will be a barrier either. But if at any time you feel that I don't understand something you say or mean because our backgrounds are different, I hope you will feel free to tell me. I want to help and I will work hard at understanding you and your situation." (pp. 120–121)

These types of comments, when used in appropriate situations, convey openness to the client and sensitivity to the impact of the difference. Variations on this theme can apply to early sessions in which the differences involve gender, sexual orientation, age, religion, physical or mental ability, or any other factor that could create a barrier if not addressed.

Education and Training for Culturally Sensitive Practice

Today, the social work education field and agency training programs show increased attention to cultural sensitivity. There are many obstacles to culturally sensitive training, such as the structure and organization of the school (for example, the absence or underrepresentation of black faculty and students) (Hardy & Laszloffy, 1992). New strategies for teaching clinical practice with specialized populations are emerging (for instance, working with Asian and Pacific Island Elders) (Richards, Browne, & Broderick, 1994). Proposals have been advanced for using ethnographic research methods to encourage practitioners to become sensitive observers of cultures and to learn how to form assessments within culturally relevant frameworks (Thornton & Garrett, 1995).

For many students and practitioners, peers can enrich the common learning process by sharing their experiences in life and practice. Unfortunately, it is difficult in our society to hold conversations that allow for honest self-reflection on attitudes, values, and stereotypes in areas such as race, gender, sexual orientation, and ethnicity. Supervisors or teachers must create an atmosphere in the class or work group that allows for such discourse while maintaining mutual respect and openness to hear.

I once worked with an African American colleague to create videotapes that would demonstrate this process for faculty and students (Clay & Shulman, 1993). The key element in setting the stage for a frank and constructive conversation was a preliminary exercise that asked participants to identify factors that made this kind of conversation hard. Participants were also asked about conditions that might make the effort easier. As the discussion on the process of talking about taboo subjects began, the social work students found themselves actually talking about taboo subjects. It was also important for the two faculty members to disclose their own struggles with these issues through the presentation of brief examples.

Issues of interethnic and intraethnic practice and culturally sensitive practice will follow throughout the remainder of the book as they relate to other stages in the social work process as well as working with clients other than individuals. Clearly, these issues and others speak of the many challenges workers must face in first sessions with a client.

Chapter Summary

All new relationships, particularly those with people in authority, begin somewhat tentatively. Clients perceive workers as symbols of authority with power to influence their lives. Clients often bring with them a fund of past experiences with professionals or stereotypes of helping professionals passed on by friends or family. Thus, the first sessions are partly efforts to explore the realities of the situation.

A structure is needed to free the client to accept the offer of help. The crucial skills involved in the beginning phase of practice include clarifying the purpose of the interview, clarifying the worker's role, reaching for the client's feedback, and exploring issues of authority. Contracting is never completed in the first session. It is an ongoing process, with the common ground between the client's felt needs and the agency's services evolving and changing over time. With resistant clients and clients who are mandated to be involved, it is important that the worker bring up the obstacles that may block the client's ability to take help. Mutual expectations need to be defined and are part of the contracting process.

Social workers must also take into account how the diversity of client populations affects practice. Models of practice need to be adapted to ethnically sensitive variations introduced by knowledgeable and responsive social workers.

Related Online Content and Activities

 Visit *The Skills of Helping* Book Companion Website at www.socialwork.wadsworth .com/Shulman06/ for learning tools such as glossary terms, InfoTrac College Edition keywords, links to related websites, and chapter practice quizzes.

Skills in the Work Phase

In the course of a training workshop, one participant expressed her feelings about the work phase in a manner that sums up the experiences of many helping professionals: "I'm good at the beginning phase, and I can even deal with the endings, but I'm at a loss when it comes to what happens in the middle." After a session of discussion with social workers about the problems of contracting clearly with children in a group home, one of the participants echoed this sentiment, saying, "I'm afraid that if I make a direct and clear offer to help the kids with their problems, they might take me up on it, and I would be in the middle phase. What do I do then?"

This chapter explores the answer to the question, "What do I do then?" That is, what is done after tentative clarity about the working contract has been achieved in the beginning phase? We shall examine the processes of the middle phase by using the phases of work: tuning in, beginning, work, and ending and transitions. In this chapter, these phases are applied to each session with a client. Each interview, family session, or group meeting can also be analyzed using the model of the phases of work.

First, however, we look at a simplified, general model of a work phase interview. Then we move on to a detailed analysis of each segment of a typical interview. Specific skills are identified and illustrated using examples from a variety of practice situations. Findings from research projects are discussed where relevant.

A Model of the Work Phase Interview

In Chapter 1 the idea of the phases of work—preliminary, beginning, middle, and ending/transition—was introduced as a model for understanding the dynamics of practice with clients over time. These four phases are revisited in this chapter, but this time we use them to understand each individual worker-client encounter. Every interview, family, or group session can be understood as having certain unique dynamics associated with its beginning, middle, and ending. Specific practice skills are useful in each of the phases of a session. Some of these general skills, such as tuning in, have been discussed in previous chapters, but we now examine them in a more specific context. For example, instead of discussing general tuning in to prepare to meet a new client, we look at sessional tuning in, referring to the preliminary phase preparation undertaken by the worker prior to each encounter.

The second decision, defined in the previous chapter, is associated with the middle phase of work. After clients understand that emotional pain might be involved and that they might have to take some responsibility for their own part in their problems, they have to decide if they will continue the work. This decision marks the transition from the beginning to the middle phase of practice.

In earlier chapters, eight of the core skills of helping were combined into two groupings: skills to help clients manage their feelings and skills to help clients manage their problems. Some of these skills are discussed in more detail in this chapter, and additional skills are also examined. To simplify the description of this phase, the skills of the work phase have been reorganized into general categories called skill factors. A **skill factor** consists of a set of closely related skills. The general intent of the worker using the skill is the element common to a given set of skills. For example, in this model all behaviors associated with the efforts of the worker to deal with client affect are grouped together under the title "empathic skills."

Table 4.1 lists the skill factors included in this middle phase model.

TABLE 4.1

The Work Phase Model

1. Preliminary (Sessional)

Sessional Tuning-In Skills

2. Beginning (Sessional)

Sessional Contracting Skills

Elaborating Skills

3. Middle (Sessional)

Empathic Skills

Sharing Worker's Feelings

Exploring Taboo Subjects

Making a Demand for Work

Pointing Out Obstacles

Identifying Content and Process Connections

Sharing Data

Helping the Client See Life in New Ways

4. Ending and Transition (Sessional)

Sessional Ending/Transition Skills

Work Phase Summary

This section summarizes the work phase model. The sections that follow elaborate and illustrate each skill factor in that model.

In the preliminary phase, the worker attempts to sensitize herself or himself, before each session, to themes that could emerge during the work. A review of the previous session, information passed on by the client or others, or the identification of subtle patterns emerging in the work can alert the worker to the client's potential current concerns. The worker also develops some preliminary strategies for responding directly to the indirect cues. This involves the use of the skill described earlier as putting the client's feelings into words.

In the beginning phase of each session, the central task of the worker is to find out what the client is concerned about at the moment. **Sessional contracting skills** are used to clarify the immediate work at hand. In some cases, the worker may bring up issues that need to be addressed, and these will then be included in the contracting discussion. Because clients often use indirect communication to indicate their concerns, workers must take care to determine the client's agenda before moving quickly into the work. Elaborating skills are also important in this phase to help the client tell his or her story.

When the sessional contract has been tentatively identified, the process shifts into the middle or work phase of the session. A priority in this phase is the worker's use of empathy to help the client share the affective part of the message. The worker must also be ready to share the worker's feelings as spontaneously as possible. Because many concerns touch on taboo areas, the worker must be ready to help clients to overcome social norms that often block free discussion and to explore taboo feelings.

As the work progresses, it is not unusual to encounter some resistance from the client, who is often of two minds about proceeding. A part of the person is always reaching out for growth and change, but another part is pulling back and holding on to what is comfortable and known. This ambivalence often emerges just as the work in the session starts to go well. It can be seen in evasive reactions (such as jumping from one concern to another), defensiveness, expressions of hopelessness, or other forms. A premium is placed on **exploring client resistance**, or the ability of the worker to identify and discuss this resistance with the client, including making a demand for work that can help the client prepare to take the important next steps. The worker needs to realize that resistance is a normal part of the work. Workers often assume that client resistance is a sign that they have done something wrong. Ironically, just the opposite is often true. Lack of resistance many mean the worker has not pushed hard enough. Resistance is often a sign that the worker is doing something right.

As the work phase proceeds, obstacles may emerge that frustrate the client's efforts on his or her own behalf. For example, the flow of feeling between the client and the worker may itself become an obstacle. As the worker makes demands for work, the client may react to the worker, and this reaction in turn will affect the working relationship. Workers and clients must pay attention such obstacles as they emerge. Because the worker-client relationship resembles the client's other relationships, discussion of sessional obstacles can contribute to the client's understanding of his or her larger concerns. These obstacles are usually brought to light when the worker notices patterns in the work.

Another skill grouping is called **identifying process and content connections.** The central idea underlying this category of skills is that the process, or way of interacting between the worker and the client, often offers clues as to the content of the work. In effect, the client may (consciously or not) use the working relationship as a medium for raising and working on issues central to the substantive issues under discussion. For example, a client working on developing independence of thought and action may demonstrate extreme dependence on the worker. It is as if the client were saying, "Do you want to see what my problem around dependence and independence is all about? Watch me!"

There are two worker skills associated with identifying content and process connections: (1) identifying these connections and (2) pointing them out to the client. Clients who are aware of the way in which they use process to deal with content may be able to learn from that awareness and take control over their interactions with others. For example, recognition of the meaning of the dependency on the worker may free a client to become more independent in the helping relationship by taking more responsibility for the work. In turn, this serves as a training medium for the client to practice new skills of independence—skills that can later be transferred to other significant relationships.

Another example was cited in Chapter 2, when the angry mother in a mutual aid support group for mothers with chronically ill children in a hospital attacked a new worker at the first meeting. I suggested then that the mother was actually showing the worker how she used anger to avoid dealing with her painful feelings and how she pushed helpful people away when she needed them the most. This demonstrated how addressing the process (the authority theme) was directly connected to the work of the group.

The client must also be allowed to have access to the worker's own relevant data. Contrary to some views, which require a form of neutrality on the part of the worker, one can argue that worker sharing of data such as facts, opinions, and value judgments are an important part of the helping process. The worker, though, needs to consider when sharing data is appropriate and how that data is shared. For example, the worker must take care to share only data that would otherwise be unavailable to the client and is relevant to the client's work. Such data needs to be shared openly and in such a way that the client is left free to accept or reject the worker's views.

Another skill grouping is called **helping the client see life in new ways.** It could also be called "reframing," "helping clients see systems people in new ways," or any of several other terms based on the idea that clients' thoughts (cognitions) have contributed to their difficulty. Many of the solution-focused practice techniques described in Chapter 1 could be included in this skill group. These skills involve helping the client to revisit cognitions—about themselves, their problems, other people, and so forth—and then examine them, with the goal of developing a more accurate picture. For example, a chronically mentally ill client may see himself as a failure in life. Reviewing events of his life where he has succeeded, including those he had not conceived of as successes, may help him to change his self-image. This process can affect his feelings and his behaviors, helping him to cope with current issues in his life.

Endings and transitions of sessions present important dynamics and require the worker's attention. In addition, issues that have been raised indirectly throughout the session may emerge with some force when the client is about to leave (the classic "doorknob therapy" phenomenon, discussed later). Finally, transitions need to be made to next sessions and future actions. **Sessional ending and transition skills** are used by the worker to bring a session to a close and to make the connections between a single session and future work or issues in the life of the client.

In an effort to describe this complex process in simple terms, I have had to over-simplify the central ideas. The work session does not proceed as neatly as I have outlined here. Further, the skill categories are not mutually exclusive. For example, as the sessional contracting proceeds, the worker will use elaborating, empathic, and demand-for-work skills. The advantage of describing this complex process in an over-simplified form is that it gives us a model with which to orient ourselves as we explore each phase and each skill factor in further detail.

Engaging and Working

With the Hard-to-Reach Client

THE MIDDLE OR WORK PHASE OF PRACTICE The author presents each of the elements for the framework for analyzing a work phase session with illustrations drawn from practice.

Sessional Tuning-In Skills

All the principles of tuning in described in Chapter 2 apply equally to each encounter with the client. This process involves efforts by workers to sensitize them-selves to potential concerns and feelings that may emerge during the session. The worker must also tune in to her or his own feelings about the encounter. This is also a time when workers can draw on personal memories, the literature on human behavior, or input from colleagues and supervisors to deepen understanding of the client's struggle and, especially, of the symbiotic connection between the client and the people and systems that matter. Each of these types of preparatory work, or **sessional tuning-in skills**, is now explored.

Tuning In to the Client's Sense of Urgency

Because of the client's ambivalence or lack of conscious awareness of concerns, client communications are often indirect. For example, a client may begin a conversation by describing "how great the weekend was compared with the week before." The client may continue to describe in positive tones the details of the "great" weekend. In the midst of all of the words is the phrase "compared with the week before." This comment is a red flag for the worker—a signal to the worker of the real work of the session. The client may be ambivalent about raising painful feelings and unsure that the worker really wants to hear them. Thus, the client has opened the session by expressing emotions that are the opposite of what he or she feels underneath. The client waits to see if the worker will notice the **first offering**, the initial hint of a con-cern, and respond to it in a direct fashion. The worker significantly increases the chances of catching the crucial issue early in the work by being prepared to "hear" it. For example, in this case, the worker might be aware of events in the client's life that have taken place between sessions and may affect the client's sense of urgency.

In another example, a worker was preparing for a conversation with an ongoing client who was being seen because of an HIV-positive diagnosis, a signal of the possible onset of AIDS. The client had called the worker for an appointment and informed the worker that his doctor had now indicated that he had developed ARC (AIDS-related complex), a set of mild symptoms indicating the next step in the progression to full-scale AIDS. The worker in this case attempted to tune in, once again, to the shock, pain, and fear associated with this change in diagnosis. First, however, the worker needed to tune in to his own feelings about another of his clients becoming progressively sicker and, even with the new drug treatments, possibly facing death. This triggered many feelings about other clients and friends who had already died. The worker found it helpful to share some of his own distress with a colleague prior to the session.

In another illustration, a social worker in a residential institution might be informed by child care staff of an incident in the house that had been difficult for a resident or told that the resident's parent had not shown up for a visit on the weekend. The worker would prepare by tuning in to the sense of rejection and hurt that the client might be feeling. The worker would also anticipate from past experiences in general or observed patterns with this resident in particular, some of the indirect ways in which the feelings might be raised. For example, a pattern of flight or fight when faced with pain is not unusual. Various residents might demonstrate "flight" from the pain through hyperactivity, or passivity and withdrawal, or the use of drugs or alcohol. Others might respond with "fight" by provoking a confrontation with peers, child care workers, or even the social worker.

In one example from a residential setting, a worker was told that a teenager had just heard about the death of his father and that he had to leave the residence the next day to return home for the funeral. The youngster had appeared to take the news badly but handled it by withdrawing. The worker tuned in to the effect this had on the resident. He did this by getting in touch with his own feelings about the death of a close relative. He thought of the mixed feelings that must exist: on the one hand, wanting to be alone and not talk about the hurt and, on the other, desperately wanting to share the feelings with another person. He thought about the boy's need to cry, despite the societal injunction that crying is supposedly not "manly." He worked hard to be in touch with his own sense of sadness so that he would be sure not to run from the sadness of this youngster.

He guessed that the cues would be indirect. In this case the youngster was hanging around in the lounge, looking sad but not saying anything. As such, the worker prepared to reach for the feelings and make an offer to talk while still respecting the boy's right to be left alone. Even if the boy did not respond immediately or at all, at least he would know the worker cared. At an appropriate time, he made his offer:

> I heard about your father's death, and I wanted you to know how sorry I am. I think I can understand how much it must hurt. If you want to talk with me about it, or just spend some time together this evening, I'd be glad to. If you just feel like being alone for a while, I'd understand that as well.

In this case, the youngster said he wanted to be left alone. He had heard the message, however, and at bedtime when the worker stopped by to say goodnight, he began to cry. The worker sat for a while, sharing some of the hurt and then listening as the boy spoke of his father.

When an incident is traumatic, the worker can strategize to reach for it directly in the sessional contracting stage. If other, less urgent themes might arise, the worker can be alert to their potential emergence. When the session starts, the worker will clear all these potential themes from her or his mind and listen to and watch the client. Tuning in is tentative, and the worker must be open to the possible emergence of feelings, issues, and responses that are completely different from those emerging from the tuning-in process.

Tuning In to the Worker's Own Feelings

The worker's feelings can facilitate or block the work to be done. For example, when thinking about an interview, a worker may believe that she or he has "blown it" by not listening to the client, by attempting to impose an agenda, and by preaching at the client. The worker can easily tune in to the client's frustration and anger, then plan to begin again by apologizing, pointing out how the worker had "missed" the client, and inviting the client to discuss his or her reactions.

It would be important in this case for the worker to tune in to his or her own feelings about receiving this negative feedback. For inexperienced workers, reaching for negative feedback is one of the hardest skills to develop. How will it feel if the client accepts the invitation and provides negative feedback? If the worker can get in touch with his or her own feelings of doubt, insecurity about the work, and possible panic if the client were actually to get angry, that worker will have a better chance of avoiding defensiveness. This can then be the start of a new idea about what makes a professional. Specifically, instead of believing that a professional is always right and never makes mistakes, as often portrayed in the practice literature, the worker can begin to be more comfortable with the notion of a professional as someone who can own up to mistakes. The worker's honesty and lack of defensiveness provides a model for the client to develop the same ability.

Another illustration might be an interview wherein the helping person anticipates having to set limits or carry out the part of the helping function that involves control over the client's access to resources. For example, a social worker in an agency working with recent immigrants from Eastern European countries may find out a client has lied about available family resources in order to obtain certain benefits from the agency. If the worker has developed a good relationship with the client, the worker will likely feel hurt and disappointed by the client's actions. The worker may grow angry wondering if the client has "conned" him or her all along.

Client behavior often serves as an indirect signal of an important work issue, as a sign of some difficulty in the helping relationship, or as a way of testing limits. In this example, the deceptive behavior was related to the client's perceptions of how to deal with authority—views that had been firmly developed while the client was living under an oppressive, Eastern European government. Social workers were seen as agents of the government with significant power to control the client's life. The client was also extremely anxious about protecting whatever family resources he had been able to bring with him from his former country. Once the behavior had been confronted, the social worker could both set limits on the client in terms of the benefits and use the incident as a way of helping the client develop a new perspective on the role of social agencies and government—an important shift in thinking required for a successful adaptation to the client's new country. I remember a group of workers in an immigrant assistance agency describing, with good humor, their first reactions when they began to work with some Russian immigrants who offered bribes in the first interviews. They were shocked at first, until they began to understand that this was the only way one received services in the country the clients had just left. Rather than responding with anger, the social workers could use such incidents to help the immigrants with their transition.

Helping professionals are just as vulnerable as clients and often refuse to take risks, because of their fear of being emotionally taken for a ride. If the social workers in these examples can get in touch with their feelings, then they stand a better chance of using the incident as a critical turning point in the relationship, rather than feeling that it signals an end to the work.

The line of argument pursued here is that, like the client, the worker is a human being with a special function and skills to put that function into action. The worker's feelings can affect actions as profoundly as the client's feelings can. For example, a child welfare worker who has developed a beginning relationship with a mother will often dread the interview following a neighbor's report of neglect of her child. As one worker put it, "I feel like a rat. I have encouraged this woman to open up to me, to share her feelings, and now I may have to take her kid away." At a time in the work when the most help is needed, this feeling can lead workers to harden themselves, put up a front, and cut themselves off from the very feelings they need in order to be helpful.

Engaging and Working With the Hard-to-Reach Client

MIDDLE PHASE WORK WITH A 15-YEAR-OLD SURVIVOR OF SEXUAL ABUSE This excerpt demonstrates the difficulty involved in helping a client discuss a taboo area such as sexual abuse.

Tuning In to the Meaning of the Client's Struggle

As patterns emerge in work with a client, the worker must often step back and attempt to understand the client's struggles in a new way. For example, consider the worker meeting with a father who is attempting to deal with his 17-year-old son's efforts to break away. The battle is a classic one, but the worker must consider what the special meaning of the struggle might be for this father. Understanding the stage of life development that the father may be going through can be helpful in getting at the unique qualities of this particular father-son engagement. The literature on midlife crisis tells us something of the struggle people face in their late thirties to work on their own sense of differentiation as individuals in their marriage. The father may be seeing signs of rebellion in his son that mirror feelings in himself that he is still trying to deal with.

The worker who sensitizes him- or herself to the father's potential conflict will be better able to "hear" this theme if it emerges in discussion. Helping the father face his own crisis may be the best way to help him understand and deal with his son's experience. The worker's understanding can be gained through life experience, work experience, professional literature, and fiction. In many ways the work experience is an education about life, and the worker is an eager learner. Each client will teach the worker something new. If the worker is listening and feeling, then every encounter with a client will result in some change in the worker. In fact, if the worker has not been moved, or educated in some way, something is probably wrong with the worker's approach.

One particularly important aspect of the tuning-in process in the interactional practice approach is the worker's ability to find the threads of common ground when obstacles frustrate the parties. In developing his practice approach, Schwartz described *method* as the means by which the worker implements the helping function. He then identified five general tasks of the worker that constitute social work method (Schwartz, 1961). The first of these is "the task of searching out the common ground between the client's perception of his own need and the aspect of social demand with which he is faced" (p. 17).

The worker can carry out this task in many and various ways; in our current example, the connection between the father and the son would need to be explored. I have already pointed out one possible connection: The son's struggle may not be so different from that of the father. Let us explore others. For example, as a young man pursues independence, some part of him will also want to hold on to the security of home and people who care about him. The connection between the son's need for security as he moves into adulthood and the father's concern about his son's budding independence may be only partial, and thus difficult for the father or the son to perceive, but present nevertheless.

On the other side of the coin are the father's hopes and aspirations for his son's growth into adulthood. What connections exist between these aspirations and the son's effort to find some form of independence? Clearly, these connections are subtle and can easily be lost by both parties as they become overwhelmed by the obstacles related to their ambivalent feelings. This is why the worker must tune in to the common ground to be sensitive to it when it emerges. Under the anger and recriminations of father and son is a fund of feelings for each other that needs to be identified and nurtured. It will not make the son's struggle for independence or the father's struggle to let go easy, for both are always difficult. It may, however, allow the parties to hang on to what matters most between them.

Tuning In and the Worker's Realities of Time and Stress

Workers often say to me, "It sounds great, but who can take the time?" Having time to prepare for a session is often prevented by large caseloads or the speed with which events happen. In fact, many social workers, particularly those in the public services, face overwhelming caseloads. In developing the Interactional Social Work Practice Theory research design (Shulman, 1991), I included job stress and job manageability as elements of the final model. The findings of the associated research, in a large, public, child welfare agency, indicated that 84 percent of the frontline workers felt that their jobs were stressful ("strongly agree" and "agree" combined). Only 25 percent of the workers felt that their jobs were manageable (p. 140). More recently, restrictions imposed by managed care have added to these stresses.

Given these realities, workers with heavy caseloads need to tune in whenever possible and to recognize the limits of their ability to provide service for all their clients. Workers will often admit they have time to connect emotionally with some of their clients while they drive home or as they review the work of the week. In addition, many examples can be identified where lack of a few moments of tuning in resulted in the worker missing early cues to a problem (the client's first offering), resulting in escalation of the problem until it became much more difficult to deal with. For example, when cues of stress in a foster home are ignored, the amount of time required for a worker to transfer a foster child to a new setting can easily become a major contributor to job stress and unmanageability. Thus, workers get caught in a vicious cycle of reacting to crisis rather than providing ongoing preventative services.

A pattern often emerges in high-stress agencies, which deal with difficult problems such as sexual abuse or terminal illness. Workers and managers engage in what I call agency hyperactivity. The heavy demands of their jobs indeed require them to work hard. However, some element of the "busy-ness" appears to be a maladaptive way in which staff members run from the pain of their work. They are simply too busy to tune in. Workers who continue to connect affectively with their clients but lacking their own sources of support often experience **burnout**. Closing off feelings is not a solution, because that can also lead to burnout. In one of my studies, I found that the availability of support for the worker from the supervisor and/or colleagues, as well as the worker's willingness to use this support, were predictive of the worker's ability to tune in to the client (Shulman, 1991).

Tuning In to the Worker's Own Life Experiences

In my view, a worker's capacity for **empathy** expands with use. This exciting part of the worker's growth comes from engagement with clients. Within limits, the worker gradually can feel more often, more accurately, and more deeply what the clients are experiencing. Life and work experiences contribute to understanding, and this understanding can be drawn on when needed. Workers may discover their own feelings about many of the issues their clients deal with, some of which may touch on unresolved concerns in their own lives. This is one of the payoffs in the field that motivates many to enter it. Social workers rarely come into the field because they look forward to the working hours or the financial compensation. The motivation to help others is there, but so is an understanding that they help themselves when they help others.

This is one sense in which the work is interactive, with the feelings of the client affecting the feelings of the worker. This idea is easier to understand when one views the professional worker not as someone who has found all of the answers to life's problems and is now prepared to share them with the client but rather as a fellow learner with a special functional role and skills for implementing that function.

Because of the close parallels between the social worker's life experiences and those of the clients, the worker must guard against a process called **countertransference**, defined as the complex of feelings of a worker toward a client. For example, young workers still close to the battle for independence from their own families may discover that their own feelings lead them to identify with the child in the struggle with the parent. The worker may start to relate to a parent in the family as if she or he were his or her own parent.

A supervisor can be very helpful to the worker in the lifelong educational process of discovering oneself through practice. A common danger, however, is that the supervisor may lose her or his sense of function and begin to relate to the social worker as a client rather than as a student or employee. Supervision can turn into an inappropriate form of personal therapy as the conference explores the worker's unresolved issues with his or her own family of origin, rather than focusing on the impact of personal experiences on practice with clients.

Sessional Contracting Skills

In one subdesign of one of my early research projects, I videotaped and analyzed client interviews, with their permission (Shulman, 1991). The clients knew that these tapes would be analyzed at the university by researchers unknown to them; however, during the interview, the client and the worker were alone in the room with the camera.

One videotape illustrated dramatically the issues related to sessional contracting. As the session began, the client touched on a concern she was feeling about her child, hinting at it instead of raising it directly. The worker listened to the concern, but it soon became obvious that she had her own agenda for the session as her questions attempted to lead the client to other issues. After a few minutes the client hinted again, making a second offering of her concern, this time a little more strongly and clearly. The worker still did not "hear," because she was preoccupied with her own agenda. The client made a third attempt a few minutes later, which the worker once again missed. At this point, with a look of complete frustration, the client turned to the video camera and said, "Do you understand?"

This interview illustrates the problems that occur when the client and the worker are operating on two different agendas. It also raises the larger issue of control over the interview. This, in turn, stems directly from the paradigm that guides the helping professional in thinking about his or her work. The sessional contracting skill provides us with a good opportunity to elaborate on this general issue.

In an interactional approach, clients are seen as attempting to work, as best they can, on issues that matter to them. Clients find that their sense of urgency about problems shifts from week to week, depending on the realities of their lives. A major assumption of the interactional practice theory is that clients will only invest in those areas of concern that they feel are important. The worker's task is not to decide what the client should be working on. Instead, using sessional contracting skills, the worker attempts to discover what the client actually *is* working on.

I have already discussed some of the difficulties clients experience in communicating their thoughts and feelings directly, especially at the beginning of each session. Clients often raise their concerns ambivalently and express this ambivalence in indirect forms of communication. For example, a client may begin a session describing how great things have been that week, while actually facing a difficult problem. An example from a couples' group illustrates this situation:

WORKER: Does anyone have anything they would like to be discussed?

FRAN: We've had no problems this week; it has been really great. We have been communicating with each other better than ever before. (Silence) We had a problem last week that I used to get really angry about, but I think I was more helpful to Ted this time (looking over to her husband).

WORKER: Can you tell us a bit about it?

FRAN: It was a problem that had to do with our sexual relations (looking nervously over at Ted now), but I'm not sure Ted wants to discuss it.

Further discussion revealed that the concern was over Ted's premature ejaculations, a major concern for this couple. This client offered her concern this first time by emphasizing something opposite to the true state of affairs.

In another example (touched on in Chapter 2), an 18-year-old foster child, who is about to leave the care of the child welfare agency, used a metaphor to introduce a discussion of his feelings of lacking roots and terrible loneliness:

CLIENT: Have you ever thought about space, about space never ending?

WORKER: Yes, I have. Have you thought about it, and does it bother you?

CLIENT: Sometimes I imagine that I'm a little bird and that I'm floating up into never-ending space. A little bit higher and a little bit to the right, and it's "bye, bye world."

WORKER: You have been floating in space this year, with all of the changes you've made.

The client responded by detailing with great feeling all of the places he had stayed during the year (eight of them), the deaths of his mother and an uncle, and his feelings of being alone in the world. The discussion continued with a poignant description of what it was like to spend important family holidays, such as Christmas, alone in a movie theater. The worker noted, but did not respond to, the client's hinting of suicidal ideation in the comment "bye, bye world." In her next session, she listened carefully for additional hints of how deep his desperation was and asked him directly if he had considered suicide. He indicated that he had felt "low" enough but that he wanted too much out of life not to keep fighting.

Examples of indirect first offerings of concerns are almost endless. A parent, who is dreadfully worried about how her child is doing and who feels guilty about her own parenting, raises the concern by attacking the worker's competency to help her child. A child in the residential treatment center, who found out his parents were not taking him home for a visit over Christmas, acts out his feelings by fighting with other residents and staff. A mother of a young man who has just died from AIDS begins her first session with a worker by talking nonstop about all of the things she did that week to keep busy, thus demonstrating to the worker her use of flight to run from her pain. The adult child of an elderly patient in a nursing home, still feeling guilty for not taking her mother into her own home, questions the quality of care provided by the nursing staff. An attractive, female teenage survivor of sexual abuse wears provocative clothing and "comes on" to her young male social worker in a residential setting, which turns out to be her way of signaling her need to work on issues of relationships with men and her own sense of self-worth as a woman.

In each case, the clients are working on important issues. Sometimes they are aware of the concern but have difficulty expressing it. Other times the feelings are there, just below the surface, but the clients themselves are unaware of the central theme. Whatever the circumstances, the clients' offerings are present, but they are hard to understand in their early forms. Because of the complexity of communication, a worker often feels that the client is not working and so decides to take over the task of determining the client's agenda. As in the example that opened this chapter, the worker can rarely understand the client's agenda without actively attempting to determine what it is.

One of the findings of a subdesign of another one of my research projects concerned the question of sessional contracting (Shulman, 1981). It centered on the practice of 11 workers, out of the 118 in the major study, who agreed to have their practice videotaped and analyzed. It would be a mistake to generalize the findings beyond this sample. In my experience as a consultant in various settings, however, I have found this pattern to be persistent.

Each videotape was analyzed by a trained rater who assigned a number representing a category of behavior (such as clarifying purpose, encouraging elaboration, dealing with feelings) every three seconds. A numerical record of the session was available for computer analysis. More than 120 hours of individual, family, and group practice were analyzed in this manner.

It was possible to judge whether workers were relating to the client's concerns, as judged by the raters, or working on their own agendas. According to this analysis, workers related to the client's concerns only 60 percent of the time. We further analyzed separately each third of every session. This roughly approximated the beginning, middle, and ending phases of work. Workers began by relating to client concerns 65 percent of the time but dropped to 58 percent in the middle and ending phases. This finding was interpreted as suggesting a high incidence of unsuccessful sessional contracting in the beginning phase.

In a more recent study (Shulman, 1991), the overall score for all of the workers on the skill called reaching for feedback (asking for the client's perception of his or her sense of urgency) was between "seldom" and "fairly often." This skill was ranked sixth out of the eight skills studied. When time was introduced as a factor, we found that the **correlation** (a nondirectional measure of association between two variables) of this skill on the development of the working relationship was stronger when used in the middle phase than in the beginning phase. This finding could be interpreted as supporting the continued and increased importance of sessional contracting.

Earlier, I suggested that the question of sessional contracting was related to the larger concerns of control of the interview and which paradigm of the helping process is guiding the worker. I believe that some of the workers in the study operated from a paradigm of helping that gave them the central responsibility for determining the agenda. They saw a good worker as one who controlled the interview so as to reach selected goals for the clients. Case conferences with supervisors and colleagues might even develop an agenda for the session, with specific goals to be accomplished by the worker. Unfortunately, clients, not having been involved in the conference, would remain unaware of the plan. Workers operating from this model would find it impossible to hear the clients' indirect efforts to communicate their own sense of urgency.

Clearly, there are times when the worker must bring an agenda to the conference. Agency issues, information to be shared or obtained, and other topics may have to be part of a session. Sessional contracting suggests that the worker can openly and directly raise these issues with the client while simultaneously attempting to determine the client's perception of the sense of urgency. The sessional contract emerges from the convergence of the worker's agenda items and the acuteness of the client's felt needs. Either client or worker may have to set their own issues aside for a moment.

It becomes clear that, even as we discuss specific skills such as sessional contracting, we need to consider the worker's sense of function. If one believes that the worker's tasks include selecting the agenda for the work, then sessional contracting, as discussed here, is impossible. If one believes that this is the task of the client, however, and one has faith in the client's ability to do this with help from the worker, then all beginnings are tentative. The worker begins each session by listening for the client's concern, and the question of control of the interview is settled. The important point is that this is a joint process, because, no matter what the worker's view, the client will "own" the session.

Elaborating Skills

When a client begins to share a particular concern, the first presentations of the problem are usually fragmentary. These initial offerings provide a tool that the worker can use to deepen the work. The **elaborating** skills are important in this stage, because they help clients tell their own story. The worker's questions and comments focus on helping the client elaborate and clarify specific concerns. The examples of elaborating skills explored in this section include containment, moving from the general to the specific, focused listening, questioning, and reaching inside of silences.

Containment

As clients begin to tell their story, workers too often attempt to "help" before the whole story is told. This is especially true for people who are new to helping. The desire to help is so strong that they will often rush in with unhelpful suggestions that are not directed at the client's actual concerns. The elaborating skill of containment is an interesting one, because it suggests that not acting—that is, a worker's ability to contain himself or herself—is an active skill (see Chapter 2).

In the following example, we see a new worker in a public welfare setting failing to contain herself in response to a mother whose children have grown up and who is thinking of pursuing a career.

CLIENT: I've been thinking that now that the kids are older, perhaps I can find a job. But you know, finding jobs is difficult these days.
WORKER: I think that's a great idea. You know we have a job-finding service, and I bet if you speak to one of the workers, he could come up with something for you.
CLIENT: (Hesitantly) That sounds like a good idea.
WORKER: Let's set up an appointment. How about next Wednesday at three?

Although the client agreed to the appointment, she did not show up.

When we explore the worker's feelings in interviews such as this, they often exemplify what I call the "heart-soaring" sensation. The worker is pleased at the client's interest in doing something about the problem and is feeling like a very successful worker indeed. If job referral is one of the ways in which practice is evaluated, we can imagine the worker mentally checking off one more successful referral for the month. Containment in response to the client's interest in a job, and further exploration of the client's feelings and concerns about return to the workforce, would be much more helpful. Specifically, picking up the hesitancy in the client's voice as a signal of unexplored issues would be helpful. Even when the client enthusiastically says she will go to the appointment, using the containment skill of **looking for trouble when everything is going the worker's way** would be important. For example:

WORKER: You sound excited about the appointment and I'm happy for you. However, you have not been in the workforce for quite a while, and you have not had to deal with an employment interview, either. I wonder if after you leave the office you might have some second thoughts.

By reaching for the concerns, the worker gives the client an opportunity to explore them with the worker, rather than having to face them on her own the night before the interview. However, the worker can always go back and catch a mistake. At the next interview, the disappointed worker asked the client why she missed the appointment. The client said that she forgot, and this time the worker contained herself and did not schedule a new appointment. Instead, she attempted to explore further the client's perception of what was involved in taking a job.

WORKER: I was thinking about this business of taking a job, and it struck me that it might not be so easy for you after so many years at home.
CLIENT: That's what I'm worried about; I'm not sure I can handle work again—you know, I've been away so long. I'm even nervous about what to say at a job interview.

Feelings of fear and ambivalence are usually associated with most concerns. Workers who attempt to find simple solutions often discover that if the solutions were indeed that simple, then the client could have found them without the help of the worker.

Moving From the General to the Specific

Clients often raise a general concern that is related to a specific event. The general statement can be seen as a first offering by the client to the worker. It may be presented in universal terms because the client experiences it that way at the moment. The general nature of its expression may also reflect the ambivalence the client feels about dealing with it in depth.

In one example, at the beginning of an interview a mother stated, "It's impossible to raise teenagers these days." Responding to the general theme, the worker might have engaged in a discussion of changing mores, peer group pressure, drug availability, and so on. An example of **moving from the general to the specific** would be to ask, "Did you have a tough time with Sue this week?" The client's response in this case was to describe a fight she had with her 15-year-old daughter, who had returned home after two A.M. and refused to say where she had been. This second offering of the concern was a more specific and manageable piece of work. By this, I mean that the general problem of raising teenagers is pressing in our society, but this client and this worker could not do much about it. However, this mother's relationship with her daughter was open to change.

Behind most early general statements is a specific hurt. If the worker does not encourage elaboration, the concern might emerge at the end of the session as a "doorknob" communication (offered as the client is leaving the office). The teenager in the living room of the group home who casually comments during a general discussion that "parents just don't understand" may be reacting to a letter or phone call received that morning. The patient on the ward who mentions to the nurse that "doctors must work hard because they always seem so busy" may still be reacting to terse comments overheard during rounds, which the patient was too frightened or overwhelmed to inquire about. In each case, the skill would involve reaching for more specific information.

Helping professionals have suggested to me two major reasons why they might refrain from reaching for the specifics behind general comments. First, they have not been aware of how specific work must be; that is, they did not realize that they can only give help in terms of the details of a problem. One cannot help a parent with the problems of dealing with teenagers through general discussion alone. The learning will take place through the discussion of the specific interactions between parent and child. The worker can help the parent develop general principles about her relationship with her daughter, but these principles must emerge from the discussions of the specific events. Without the specific discussion, the worker's attempts to generalize may be perceived by the mother as theoretical advice.

For example, the parent in the earlier encounter might describe a conversation with her daughter in which she did not level about her distress and hurt but instead gave way to the surface feelings of anger. After a while, the worker may be able to help the client see how, in incident after incident, she finds it hard to be open with her daughter about certain feelings. The client may be able to understand this point because of the discussion of specific incidents. The discussion should develop an experiential base on which the client can build the new understanding and a reframing of her perceptions about the problem and possible solutions. The client may not be able to do much about changing mores in our society, but she can conduct her next conversation with her daughter in a different way. Lack of understanding of the power of specific discussion may lead the worker to overlook the usefulness of this elaboration skill.

The second reason why workers do not reach for the specifics, even when they sense the concrete problem connected to the client's general offering, is that they are not sure they want to deal with it. Hospital social workers, for example, suggest they do not reach for a patient's comment about busy doctors because they are not sure what they can do about it. As one put it, "I find the doctors too busy to answer my questions, so how can I help the patient?" The source of the worker's ambivalence may vary, but feelings of ambivalence are common. I believe that when workers feel more confident about offering help, they reach more easily for specifics.

I propose a third, and less obvious, reason for failure to reach for elaboration. It has to do with the parallel process between workers and supervisors described earlier. Often, a worker or student raises a question with a supervisor such as "Do you have any thoughts about techniques for handling angry clients?" Unless the supervisor inquires, "Did you have a tough interview?" the remainder of the conversation may stay at a general level. If the modeling is sound, the supervisor will always be moving from the general to the specific, thus teaching by modeling the skill. In turn, the supervisor is aided by having an administrator reach for her or his specific concerns behind the general offerings. My research on supervision of supervisors has indicated that this is rarely done (Shulman, 1994).

Focused Listening

Listening is something we do all the time; however, **focused listening** involves attempting to concentrate on a specific part of the client's message. I discussed earlier how complex even the simplest interchange of communication can be. In complex communications at the beginning of sessions, the worker must focus on whatever the client is working on at that particular moment. By listening to the early communications with this purpose in mind, the worker has a better chance of hearing the message.

A simple analogy is the difficulty of hearing two simultaneous conversations at a crowded social event. If one listens in a general way, all one hears is a loud buzz. If one attempts to focus on one particular conversation, however, it begins to stand out clearly, and the buzzing noise recedes. Similarly, when one is driving at night in a rural area, sometimes two radio stations are heard at once. The driver must tune in one station and tune out the other in order to really "hear" anything. In the same way, the "noise" of the client's early communications may make it difficult for the worker to understand the single strand representing the basic concern. Focused listening, directed to determining the concern, often makes the theme stand out clearly.

A common mistake is for the worker to take control of the interview when the worker does not immediately understand the meaning of the communication. Focused listening would involve attempting to hear the communication as the client's effort to work, and to search for the connections when they are not apparent. The worker can ask for the client's help. For example, "Could you help me connect this discussion with the concern you raised abut your daughter at the start of the session?" Clients will often be able to do so, either immediately or after some reflection. They do not get the opportunity if the worker has already decided they are simply not working and more worker activity is needed. If there is no real connection, and the client is simply evading work by changing the subject, then focused listening will clarify that as well. The client is signaling resistance to a topic, and the resistance is what the worker should hear and deal with.

Questioning

Questioning in the elaboration process involves requests for more information as to the nature of the problem. As a fledgling high school journalist, I was encouraged to make sure to answer the "five w's" early in my articles: the who, what, when, where, and why of the story. These are useful areas for exploring the details of a client's concern. For example, in the earlier illustration of working with the mother and daughter, we left the process at the point where the client responded to the worker's effort to move from the general to the specific by describing a fight with her daughter. In the next part of the session, we can see that the worker's questions are designed to elicit more detail about what happened in the encounter.

CLIENT: We had some row last night when Sue came home at two A.M.
WORKER: What happened?
CLIENT: She had told me she was going to a movie with a friend, but when she didn't get home by eleven, I was really worried.
WORKER: You were afraid something might have happened to her?
CLIENT: Well, you know we have had some problems in the neighborhood with men.
WORKER: What did you say to Sue when she came home?
CLIENT: I let her have it good. I told her she was irresponsible and that I was going to keep her home for two weeks.
WORKER: What did she say back to you?

As the conversation proceeded, the worker helped the client elaborate on the details of the interaction. A term to describe this process between worker and client would be *memory work,* in which the client reaches back into her memory to recall the incident. In other situations the worker may aim questions at getting a fuller picture of the client's concern. In the earlier example of the woman considering a return to the workforce, the questions would be designed to elicit the "what" and "why" of the concerns she might have about returning to work.

Reaching Inside of Silences

Recall from Chapter 2 that silence during a helping interview may be an important form of communication. The difficulty with silences is that it is often hard to understand exactly what the client is "saying." In one situation the client may be thinking and reflecting on the implications of the conversation. In another, a discussion may have released powerful emotions that are struggling to surface in the client. The client may be at the critical point of experiencing suppressed and painful feelings. Silence can indicate a moment of ambivalence as the client pauses in trying to decide whether or not to plunge headlong into a difficult area of work. This is not uncommon when the conversation deals with an area generally experienced as taboo. Silence may also signal that the worker's preceding response was "off base" in relation to the client's expressed concern. The worker has "missed" the client, and the silence is the client's polite way of saying so. Finally, the client may be angry at the worker. Frequent silence in an interview may reflect a systematic attempt to express this anger passively by withholding involvement.

Because silences carry a variety of meanings, the worker's response must vary accordingly. An important aid is the worker's own set of feelings during the silence. For example, if the silence represents the emergence of difficult feelings, the worker may have anticipated this reaction from the content of the conversation or from the nonverbal communications sent by the client. Posture, facial expressions and bodily tension—all speak loudly to the observing worker and can trigger empathic responses. As such, the worker may experience the same emergence of feeling as the client. At moments like this, the worker can respond to silence with silence or with nonverbal expressions of support. All these responses offer some support to the client while still allowing time to experience the feelings.

If the worker senses that the client is thinking about an important point of the discussion or considering a related problem, then to respond with silence allows the client room to think. Silence demonstrates respect for the client's work. However, a problem can be created if the worker maintains the silence too long. Silence can also be particularly troublesome if the worker does not understand it or if it is used to communicate either a negative reaction or passive resistance. In such cases, the client may experience the silence as a battle of wills. What started as one form of communication may quickly change to a situation in which the client is saying, "I won't speak unless you speak first." In this battle, both worker and client always lose. The skill of reaching inside the silence matters most during these kinds of silences.

This skill involves attempts to explore the meaning of the silence. For example, the worker who responds to a silence by saying, "You've grown quiet in the last few moments. What are you thinking about?" is encouraging the client to share the thoughts. In another case, the worker could try to articulate what the silence may be saying. For example, the client who hesitates as he describes a particularly difficult experience might be offered this response: "I can see this is hard for you to talk about." Once again, the worker's own feelings guide her or his attempts to explore or acknowledge the silence. The worker must be open to the fact that the guess may be wrong and must encourage the client to feel free to say so.

Workers often find silences in interviews to be difficult moments. They have been affected by societal norms that create the feeling that a silence in a conversation is embarrassing, and they may feel that the most helpful thing to do is fill the gap. When one works with clients from different cultures, one is struck by the differences in these social norms. For example, American Indian clients describe how talking to non-Indian workers is hard because they never keep quiet. As one Native worker said to me, "The problem with white workers is that they never stop 'nattering.'" She pointed out that Indian culture respects silence as a time to reflect, but non-Indian workers continue to talk because of their own anxiety, without giving the Native person a chance to think. In some cases, the Indian client might simply be trying to translate the non-Indian worker's English into the Indian language and then trying to translate back to English.

In my early research project on practice, the skill of reaching inside silences was one of the 5 skills used least often of the 27 skills studied (Shulman, 1978). But another analysis showed it to be the one of the most significant. The 15 workers (out of 155 total) with the most positive overall skill scores were compared with those workers with the most negative ones. The former were found to have more positive working relationships and were more helpful than were the latter. The practice skill profiles of the workers were compared according to their scores on 27 specific skills. The skill of reaching inside silences was one of the three most important in which the positive skill group of workers differed from the negative skill group (p. 281).

In my more recent study, reaching inside of silences was one of the four skills included in the skills for helping clients manage their feelings (Shulman, 1991). This grouping was related to the client's sense that the worker cared, one element of the working relationship. When the skill was examined by itself, workers were perceived by their clients to use it seldom. In fact, out of the eight skills examined, it was almost the least-used skill, only slightly ahead of the skill of the worker sharing his or her own feelings (p. 61).

The particular impact of each of the four skills on the development of the working relationship (caring and trust) as well as the client's perception of the worker's helpfulness was also examined (Shulman, 1993b). The striking results, replicating the general findings of the 1978 study, indicated that this skill, when used in the beginning phase of practice, showed the highest correlation with the client's perception of the worker's caring (.56) and trust in the worker (.68). It was fifth in importance in terms of helpfulness (.51). The findings of both studies support the notion that the worker needs to actively explore the hidden meaning of silences in interviews.

Another finding from a separate design of the 1978 study yielded additional evidence that this important skill may often be lacking. In this part of the study, the individual interviews and group sessions of 11 volunteer workers were videotaped and then analyzed by trained raters using a system I developed. In an analysis of 32 individual interviews, raters scored the worker's or the client's behavior by entering a number describing the interaction at least every 3 seconds. A total of 40,248 individual observations of group sessions were scored and then analyzed by computer. In one analysis, we were able to determine which behaviors of the workers most often followed silences of 3 seconds or longer.

The findings were striking. Of all the entries scored, only 1,742 (4 percent) indicated that a silence of 3 seconds or more had taken place. Raters found that client comments followed silences only 38 percent of the time. A 3-second silence was followed by another 3-second silence 26 percent of the time. Workers' active comments in response to silences occurred 36 percent of the time. When these ratings were examined more closely, they revealed the following results:

- When workers actively intervened after a silence, they attempted to encourage elaboration 31 percent of the time.
- Their efforts to deal with the client's feelings or share their own feelings were noted in only 4 percent of their responses.
- The most common active action in response to silence was to direct the client away from the client's presented theme of concern. This occurred 49 percent of the time.

Remember, however, that the subdesign involved only 11 workers in one child welfare agency, each of whom faced the unusual pressure of being videotaped as part of a research project. My attempt to generalize from these findings to other settings or workers is tentative; even so, my observations as a training consultant and the findings of the more recent study support these conclusions (Shulman, 1991).

I share these tentative findings with you because they reflect statistically my own observations that workers often seem reluctant to explore silences. In addition to the reasons already advanced, workers have suggested that they often perceive silences as representing a problem in the interview. If there is silence, then the worker must have done something wrong. The irony in the situation is that silence results more often from a worker doing something right. The worker often sees silence as negative feedback, even in those cases when it may stand for other things. A worker's willingness to reach inside the silence when there is a possible negative response is directly related to feelings of comfort in the work and willingness to deal with negative feedback. (This aspect of the process will be discussed more fully under the skill factor called pointing out obstacles.) Understandably, a worker may be unsure about what to do with the feelings and concerns that may live within the silence, and she or he may choose to change the subject rather than reach inside the silence. At this point, after the worker has successfully helped the client elaborate concerns, the discussion needs to move to the question of feelings and how to deal with them.

When these findings are shared with workers in training sessions, their reactions provide further clues as to the apparent low frequency of use of this important skill. Many indicate that their skill training specifically cautioned them not to put a client's thoughts or feelings into words. They report having been encouraged to ask questions but avoid "putting words into the client's mouth" or "doing the clients' work for them." One worker reported being told by a supervisor that it was "like tying a client's shoelaces for him." While these are legitimate concerns, these repeated findings suggest that workers make more errors of omission (failing to articulate the feelings) than errors of commission (articulating the wrong feelings).

ELABORATING This is an interview in a college counseling center with a graduate student feeling stress from trying to manage her relationship with her partner and the demands of school. This example may hit close to home for many readers in similar situations.

Empathic Skills

As clients tell their stories, workers use many skills designed to keep the discussion meaningful by having clients invest it with feelings. Clients often share difficult experiences while seeming to deny the affect associated with them. For some, the experience may be so painful that they have suppressed the emotion to the point that their own feelings are not clear to themselves. For others, the emotions may seem strange or unacceptable, and they are fearful of discussing them with the worker.

Whatever the reason, the affect is there, and it will exert a powerful force on the client until it can be acknowledged and dealt with. Clients can deal with affect in three different ways. Clients' sharing of feelings with the worker can release an important source of energy. Clients can also learn how emotions directly affect their thoughts and actions. Finally, they can develop skills that allow them to understand the sensations, accept them without harsh self-judgment, and disclose them to those who matter. This can be described as the **feeling-thinking-doing connection.** How we feel affects how we think and act, and how we act affects how we think and feel. This interaction among feeling, thinking, and doing leads to the model described in this book, in which a worker's skills for helping clients manage their feelings takes on such importance in helping clients to manage their problems.

Taft (1933) was one of the first social work theorists to discuss the power of feelings:

> There is no factor of personality which is so expressive of individuality as emotion. The personality is impoverished as feeling is denied, and the penalty for sitting on the lid of angry feelings or feelings of fear is the inevitable blunting of capacity to feel love and desire. For to feel is to live, but to reject feeling through fear is to reject the life process itself. (p. 10)

Rogers (1961) stressed the importance of the helping person listening for the affective component of the communication:

> Real communication occurs when the evaluative tendency is avoided, when we listen with understanding. It means to see the expressed idea and attitude from the other person's point of view, to sense how it feels to him, to achieve his frame of reference in regard to the thing he is talking about. (pp. 331–332)

As workers allow themselves to get closer to clients, to experience clients realistically and not necessarily as clients have presented themselves, workers also give their clients permission to be natural. The acceptance and understanding of emotions and the worker's willingness to share them by experiencing them frees a client to drop some defenses and to allow the worker and the client more access to the real person. The worker also serves as a model of an adult with empathic ability. The client can learn to develop powers of empathy to be used in turn with those who need support. On the other hand, a worker might so identify with a child in a family conflict situation that the worker pushes the parent to understand the child's feelings while expressing little understanding of the parent's feelings. Providing genuine empathy for the parent's dilemma is often the key to helping the parent understand the struggles of the child.

Expressing empathy with the client can prove difficult for the worker in many ways. The capacity to be in touch with the client's feelings is related to the worker's ability to acknowledge his or her own. Before workers can understand the power of emotion in the life of clients, they must discover its importance in their own experience. Workers often find it hard to express empathy in specific personal areas. Workers are human, facing all the stresses and difficulties associated with daily living, including crises. When workers hear their own difficult feelings being expressed by clients, the capacity for empathy can be blunted. Another major block to empathy can be the worker's authority over the client. For example, a child welfare worker who has apprehended (removed) a child in an abuse situation may find empathic responses to the client blocked at the time when they may be most needed.

The following example effectively illustrates this difficulty and shows how it can lead to a relationship devoid of feeling—where the worker seems cold and uncaring. The excerpt is from a recorded interview with a mother who had undergone psychiatric treatment for a time and was separated from her husband. Her 9-year-old adopted and only daughter had come into care of the agency one year before this interview because the mother had found her unmanageable. A short time into the interview, there was a pause followed by this comment:

CLIENT: You know I'm afraid of you.

WORKER: Why?

CLIENT: Because you are sitting in judgment of me. You're only human—you might make a mistake.

WORKER: I'm only judging how we can help you—help you to improve.

CLIENT: No, you are judging whether or not I can be a mother to Fran—whether I can have my child back. (Silence) I feel at the moment I am not capable of caring for Fran on a full-time basis—I know that. Don't you understand—I'm grieving— I'm grieving for Fran. Wouldn't you be upset and worried and confused?

WORKER: I'm worried about other things as well.

The worker was not in tune with the client's feelings. She regarded the child as her client and did not respond to the mother as a client in her own right. After further discussion in which the worker indicated that the client was not working hard enough in her contacts with her psychiatrist, the worker asked how long she had been seeing the doctor.

CLIENT: I'm not sure—I don't remember—(with tremendous feeling)—It's absolutely terrible not to be able to remember. It makes me feel incompetent, incapable— (silence)—There are some things in my head I know can't be real—(silence)— but I feel I can be competent and capable of looking after Fran—or I wouldn't want to—because I know she is a problem to look after. But I love her even with her faults.

WORKER: When you think of Fran, what do you think of most—her faults?

CLIENT: No! Fran wants to laugh—enjoy people—not to analyze them. She's a baby bird, full of life, receptive, loving people. I may seem aloof, but I'm really just shy.

WORKER: You say Fran is sociable, but before, you told me she had no friends.

The worker ignored the client's productions of sensitive subjects for discussion, including her self-depreciation and her expression of loss and guilt. Her capacity to help this mother was minimal, because she saw her intellectually, not affectively. Smalley (1967) described this process as follows:

The self of another cannot be known through intellectual assessment alone. Within a human, compassionate, and caring relationship, selves "open up," dare to become what they may be, so that the self which is known by a worker, a worker at once human, caring, and skillful, is a different self from that diagnosed by one who removes himself in feeling from the relationship in an attempt to be a dispassionate observer and problem solver. As an adolescent girl once said to her new social worker, in referring to a former worker, "She knew all about me, but she didn't know me." (p. 86)

Because of the difficulty of this area of skills, workers must develop over time their ability to empathize. The capacity for empathy grows with experience. Workers open to this development can learn more about life from each client, which will help them better understanding the next client. Workers also learn more about their own feelings and true reactions to the plight of others. Awareness of the sensitive areas in one's own emotional armor will help one avoid denying or intellectualizing difficult emotions when they are presented. The worker will more readily allow a client to share more difficult emotions as the worker becomes comfortable with their effects, particularly those of negative feelings, both worker's and client's, which form a natural part of any helping relationship.

Supervision can play an important part in a worker's emotional development. The concept of the **parallel process** suggests that the helping relationship between a supervisor and a worker, or a field instructor and a student, parallels the relationship between the worker (student) and the client. Thus, a supervisor must model effective empathic skills in the supervisory relationship.

For illustration, consider the supervision session between the field instructor and the student involved in the verbatim interview, just described, with the mother who was fearful of losing her child. If, as they listened to the tape together, the supervisor simply criticized the student for her lack of affective response to the client, then the student might remain stuck, showing little growth. The supervisor's words might be teaching empathy for the client, but his or her actions would be repeating the student's mistake. In effect, she would be asking the student to "be with" the mother, but at exactly the same moment, the supervisor would not be with the student. In contrast, if the supervisor asked the student, "What were you feeling when she was describing her relationship with her daughter?" the crucial affective work would begin. If the supervisor could genuinely acknowledge the student's struggle to be emotionally with the parent and the child at the same time, a powerful lesson would be taught. The supervisor would be modeling by demonstrating her ability to be with the student as a social worker and a client at exactly the same time.

In my most recent supervision study, we found that the worker's perception of the effectiveness of supervision was a powerful predictor of the worker's morale (Shulman, 1993a). Supervisory skill also contributed to the development of a positive working relationship with staff and to their sense of the supervisor's helpfulness. When I share these findings with supervisors, a short period of silence usually follows. When I reach inside of the silence, one supervisor will often say, "But who listens to me?" The appropriateness of that question was suggested by other findings in the supervision study. The skill of articulating the supervisee's feelings, the skill parallel to articulating the client's feelings, was positively associated with relationship and helpfulness on every level of the study (supervisors-workers; managers-supervisors, executives-managers).

The three empathic skills described in the rest of this section—reaching for feelings, displaying understanding of the client's feelings, and putting the client's feelings into words—will be illustrated by excerpts from practice with a mother whose child is about to be apprehended because of parental abuse. This example provides a contrast to the earlier one and demonstrates how the functions of protecting a child and caring for the parent can be integrated. That is, it will illustrate how a worker can "be with" the parent and the child at exactly the same time.

Reaching for Feelings

Reaching for feelings is the skill of asking the client to share the affective portion of the message. Before proceeding, however, I should clarify one point. This process is sometimes handled superficially, in a ritualistic manner, thus negating its usefulness. The worker who routinely asks a client, "How do you feel?" while not really being open to experiencing the feeling, may be perceived by the client as not really caring. Experienced clients have been known to say at that moment, "Stop social-working me." Of course, what they are reacting to is the worker's intellectualizing, which is not effective social work. Genuine empathy involves stepping into the client's shoes and summoning an affective response that comes as close as possible to the experience of the other.

With the emergence of technique-centered training programs focusing on developing a patterned response by the worker, the danger of expressing an artificial response increases. One worker described how she had been taught by one program to reflect back the clients' feelings with the phrase, "I hear you saying . . ." When she used this technique in one interview, her client looked surprised and replied, "You heard me saying that!" The reaching for feelings must be genuine.

In the illustration that follows, a worker talks with a mother about her reactions to one of her five children being taken into the care of the agency after being admitted to the hospital with bruises. In discussions with the hospital social worker, the mother had admitted having beaten the child. The child welfare social worker discussed the placement with the mother.

WORKER: We have to be honest with you, Mrs. Green. Did the hospital social worker talk to you about the possibility of your child being placed?
CLIENT: Yes, but not with my mother; anywhere else but there.
WORKER: I guess your mother has enough kids already.
CLIENT: It's not that; it's that we don't get along.
WORKER: Can you think of anyone else your son can live with?
CLIENT: I have a friend, Sara, who helped me when my husband died and when I had my baby.
WORKER: This must be a hard time. How are you feeling about the possibility of your son being placed?
CLIENT: I can't stand the idea. I don't want the other children with me if John is placed. I have often said this to the kids when I was angry at them—I told them I would place them all, and the kids remember that.

Displaying Understanding of the Client's Feelings

The skill of displaying understanding of the client's feelings (introduced in Chapter 2) involves indicating through words, gestures, expression, physical posture, or touch (when appropriate) the worker's comprehension of the expressed affect. The worker attempts to understand how the client experiences the feelings even if the worker believes that the reality of the situation does not warrant the reaction. The worker may believe that the client is being too self-punishing or taking too much responsibility for a particular problem. Even so, the client may not agree at that moment, and the worker must respond to the client's sense of reality. Further, the worker needs to resist the natural urge to rush in with reassurances and attempts to help the client feel better.

Efforts at reassurance are often interpreted by the client as the worker's failure to understand. As one client put it, "If you really understood how bad I felt, you wouldn't be trying to cheer me up."

We return to the interview with the mother at the point where she commented that "I told them [the children] I would place them all, and the kids remember that."

Worker: We often say things when we are hurt or angry that we regret later.

Client: I told the hospital social worker that if John was placed, all of the kids might have to be placed. I feel very strongly about this. It will hurt me to lose my kids, but I can't bear to think about getting up in the morning and only counting four heads instead of five.

Worker: You mean that together you are a family, and if one is missing, you're not? (She nodded when I said this and began to cry softly.)

The worker's gentle restatement of the client's feelings has communicated to the client the worker's understanding and compassion. The client expresses her emotions by crying. This is an important form of communication between worker and client. Part of the healing process includes the client's sharing of feelings with a caring person. Workers often express their fear of strong emotions. They are concerned that a client might become too depressed and that the worker's effort to bring the emotions to the fore could result in more problems. Some workers worry that the client's feelings will overwhelm them to the point where they feel equally depressed and hopeless. They would then lose their ability to be effective. For many workers, the ultimate fear is triggering such deep feelings in the client that the client feels overwhelmed and commits suicide.

Note that the emotions themselves do not create the problems; rather, clients' inability to face their feelings or to share them with someone important does. The power that feelings can have over clients may be dissipated when these feelings are expressed and dealt with. The greater danger is not in the facing of feelings but in their denial. The only thing worse than living with strong emotions is the feeling that one is alone and that no one can understand.

As for the worker's fear of being overwhelmed by emotions, this can be alleviated somewhat if the worker is clear about the function and purpose of the engagement. The worker's sense of function requires placing a demand for work on the client (as discussed in the next section). No matter how strong the client's feelings of hopelessness, some next step can always be taken. The worker needs to experience the client's feelings of being overwhelmed (the empathy) while still indicating a clear expectation (the demand) that the client will do something about the situation, even in those cases where doing something means coming to grips with the reality (such as the death of someone close) and picking up and beginning again (as in searching out new significant relationships). Belief in the strength and resilience of the client enables a worker to make this demand.

With clarity of purpose in mind, the worker can help the client find the connections between the emotions and the purpose of the discussion. Significant work with clients in painful areas can be done only after the expression and acknowledgment of feelings. The flow of affect and understanding between worker and client is a necessary precondition for further work. Workers who attempt to make demands on clients without first having experienced the affect with them will be perceived as "not understanding," and their demands will be experienced as harsh and uncaring. Empathic responses build a fund of positive work that the worker can draw on later. This fund is a buffer that helps the client experience a worker's later confrontation as a caring gesture.

Putting the Client's Feelings Into Words

Thus far, I have described how a worker might reach for feelings and acknowledge those that have already been stated. There are times, however, when a client comes close to expressing an emotion but stops just short. The client might not fully understand the feeling and thus be unable to articulate it. In other cases, the client might not be sure it is all right to have such a feeling or to share it with the worker. Putting the client's feelings into words is the skill of articulating the client's affect a half step ahead of the client. This occurs when the worker's tuning in and intense efforts to empathize during the session result in emotional associations as the client elaborates a concern.

In our previous example, the worker had said, "You mean that together you are a family, and if one is missing, you're not?" and the client had responded by crying softly. The worker gave the client a tissue and waited a few minutes. The client was just sitting and looking at the floor.

WORKER: You must be feeling like a terrible mother right now. (The client nodded.) It must be really rough with all of the problems with the house, everything breaking down on you, having these hassles every day, and five kids also must make it pretty rough some times.

The client had not said anything about her parenting or about feelings of guilt, but by articulating this emotion, the worker gives permission to the client to discuss her own feelings about herself. Often, as in the first illustration in this section, the worker is so busy trying to consciously or unconsciously communicate disapproval of the client's actions that she cannot hear the client's own harsh judgment of herself. The assumption here is that how we feel about ourselves has a great deal of influence on how we think about ourselves and how we act. The way to begin to help this mother is to break a vicious cycle where her own guilt leads to feelings of helplessness and hopelessness and a negative self-image, which in turn leads to poor parenting, and so on. The ability to articulate and face her feelings, sharing them with a caring and yet demanding worker, can be a beginning. The worker's acceptance of the client, including her feelings, can be the starting point for the client's acceptance of herself.

EMPATHIC SKILLS A social worker meets with an elderly client who is in a wheelchair and has great difficulty in speaking. The empathic skills are demonstrated in the practice excerpt under difficult circumstances. In the "blooper," the worker ignores the feelings of the client and tries to rush the interview because he is having difficulty understanding her words.

Research on Empathy

The empathic skills have consistently been identified as important in helping relationships. Working in the field of psychotherapy, Truax (1966) found a relationship between personality change and therapist empathy, warmth, and genuineness. Rogers (1969) points to several studies that found empathy to be central to the worker's effectiveness. In the field of educational research, Flanders (1970) found empathy to be an important skill for teachers in improving student performance. A growing body of evidence suggests this is one of the core skills that is important for all helping functions.

My own research supports these findings. The skill of acknowledging the client's feelings appears to contribute substantially to the development of a good working relationship between worker and client as well as contributing to the worker's ability to be helpful (Shulman, 1978). It was the second most powerful skill, ranking only behind the skill of sharing worker's feelings, which is discussed in a later section. This finding was replicated in both the study of supervision skill (Shulman, 1981, 1984) and the study of the practice of family physicians (Shulman & Buchan, 1982).

Videotape analysis data indicated less concern with affect on the part of workers than the overall study suggested. Workers shared their own feelings or dealt with client feelings in only 2.3 percent of their interventions in the individual sessions and in 5.3 percent of their interventions in the group sessions. When total interactions in the session were analyzed, including the times when the client was speaking and the worker listening, the total interventions dealing with the affect in the group sessions dropped to 1.4 percent. This figure is very close to Flanders' results from analyzing teaching behaviors (Flanders, 1970).

When examining the skill profile of the average worker, I found that clients perceived their workers as acknowledging their feelings "fairly often" and as articulating their feelings without their having to share them between "seldom" and "fairly often" (Shulman, 1993b). When the correlation between this skill and the development of the caring dimension of the working relationship was examined, it was the second strongest associating skill when used in the beginning phase of practice ($r = .54$) and the strongest associating skill when used in the middle phase ($r = .77$). Similar patterns were found in relation to trust and worker helpfulness.

In a recent qualitative study of empathy as an interpersonal phenomenon, Hakansson and Montgomery (2002, 2003) examined the experiences of 28 empathizers and 28 targets through analysis of their narrative accounts of situations in which they experienced empathy. Their subjects were 20 to 64 years old. The researchers focused on the constituents of both the empathizers' and the targets' experience of empathy. They examined four constituents:

> (1) The empathizer understands the target's situation and emotions, (2) the target experiences one or more emotions, (3) the empathizer perceives a similarity between what the target is experiencing and something the empathizer has experienced, and (4) the empathizer is concerned for the target's well-being. The data suggested that the actions associated with the fourth constituent—concern—make empathy an interpersonal phenomenon. (p. 267)

The researchers' definition of the dimension of concern included such acts as "giving time, paying attention, giving the target advice, doing something for the target, being concerned for the target, being respectful towards the target, and performing coordinated acts demonstrating concern" (p. 279).

This finding offers additional support for my construct describing how skill, including empathy, develops a working relationship with the client. The expression of "concern" for the client corresponds to the term "caring" in my own research. All of the behaviors associated with concern could be perceived as contributing to the client's perception of the worker as "caring as much about me as my children" and "here to help me not just investigate me" (Shulman, 1978, 1991).

While there exists a consensus that the skills of empathy are important in the helping relationship or "therapeutic alliance," some researchers have suggested that some clients, such as unmotivated and volatile ones, would be better served by "therapeutic detachment" (Galloway & Brodsky, 2003). This view suggests the need for research that further defines and differentiates the mechanics of the process through which empathy affects a working relationship and outcomes. Addressing questions such as "Under what circumstances does empathy help?" "With which clients?" and "For what kind of problems?" can help determine whether detachment would be more appropriate.

Sharing the Worker's Feelings

An essential skill is related to the worker's ability to present himself or herself to the client as a "real" human being. Theories of the helping process that follow the medical paradigm have presented the ideal worker as an objective, clinical, detached, and knowledgeable professional. In these models, direct expression of the worker's real feelings is considered "unprofessional." This has resulted in a concept of professionalism that asks the worker to choose between the personal and the professional self.

In an example described earlier, one worker illustrated the effect of this attempt to dichotomize the personal and the professional during a training workshop. She described her work with a woman who had just discovered her child was dying of cancer. As the woman spoke, grief overcame her and she began to cry. The worker felt compassion and found herself holding the woman's hand and crying with her. Recall that a supervisor, passing by the open door, criticized the worker for her "unprofessional" behavior.

My view is that the worker was helping at that moment in one of the most important and meaningful ways we know. She was sharing the pain with the client, and in expressing her own sorrow she was making a gift of her feelings to the client. This worker was responding in a deeply personal way yet at the same time was carrying out her helping function. The interactional practice theory suggests that the helping person is effective only when able to synthesize real feelings with professional function. Without such a synthesis of personal and professional, the worker appears as an unspontaneous, guarded professional, unwilling to allow clients access to the worker's feelings. The irony is apparent, for the social worker asks clients to take risks and be open, honest, and vulnerable in sharing feelings, while in the name of professionalism he or she is doing just the opposite. The result is often the "mechanical" worker who always maintains self-control, who has everything worked out, and who is never at a loss for words or flustered—in short, a person impossible to relate to in any helpful way.

Clients do not need a perfect, unruffled worker who has worked out all of life's problems. They require someone who cares deeply about the clients' success, expresses the clients' own sense of urgency, and openly acknowledges feelings. When clients experience the worker as a "real" person rather than mechanical, they can use the worker and the helping function more effectively. If the worker shows no signs of any humanity, the client will either be constantly testing to find the flaws in the facade or idealizing the worker as the answer to all problems. The client who does not know at all times where the worker stands will have trouble trusting that worker. If the worker is angry at the client, then it is much better for the client to get the anger out in the open where it can be dealt with honestly. Workers who fear the expression of angry feelings as signs of their own "aggressiveness" often suppress them, only to have them emerge indirectly in ways to which the client finds it harder to respond. Professional expressions of anger, for example, through an unfeeling interpretation of a client's behavior, can be more hurtful than an honest statement of the feeling.

Direct expression of feelings is as important for the worker as it is for the client. A worker who suppresses feelings must use energy to do so. This energy can be an important source of help to the client if it can be freed for empathic responses. The worker cannot both withhold feelings and experience those of the client at the same time. The worker may also become cut off from important forms of indirect communication in which the client uses the worker's feelings to express his or her own. Consider the following example of this process. A worker in a residential center for children was confronted by an angry parent after an incident on an excursion in which the child was left on a bus during a field trip and lost for a time. This child had been apprehended by the agency because of numerous complaints of neglect and abuse. During a visit to the center, the client began a loud, angry tirade directed at the worker.

CLIENT: What kind of a place do you run here anyway? He's only been here three weeks, and already he's sick, had a bump on his head, and you jerks lost him on a bus.

WORKER: (Obviously upset but trying to control himself) Look, Mr. Frank, we do the best we can. You know with 15 kids on the bus, we just lost track.

CLIENT: Lost track! For God's sake (his voice getting louder), you mothers are paid to keep track, not lose track of my kid. Do you realize what could have happened to him on that bus alone? (The client screamed the last question. The worker felt embarrassed, overwhelmed, backed against the wall, conscious of the other workers and the kids watching, and angry at the client.)

WORKER: (With great control in his voice) You know, we simply can't tolerate this behavior in the house. You're upsetting all of the children, and if you don't calm down, I'm going to have to stop your visiting.

The truth of the matter is that the client was upsetting the worker, who did not know what to do about it. His anger was expressed in a controlled fashion, turning it into an attempt to exert his authority on the client. He tried to tame the client by using his ability to influence access to the child. The calmer and more controlled the worker seemed, the angrier the client became. With his own feelings racing away in all directions, the worker's efforts to put up a calm front actually cut him off from a professional response. He had no way of understanding, at this point, that parents who have had children apprehended also often feel guilty, embarrassed, overwhelmed, backed against the wall, and quite conscious of the reactions of their children. The client was unconsciously using the incident to make the worker feel exactly how he himself had felt for the past three weeks. In this sense, the client's feelings were projected onto the worker and the attack was a form of indirect communication. Unfortunately, the worker expended his energy on defending himself and suppressing his anger. He could not work with this client in a meaningful way as long as he blocked expression of his own feelings. The client needed to keep pushing him until he got some reaction. Returning to the interview, we see that the worker's attempt to "read the riot act" to the client resulted in an escalation on the client's part.

CLIENT: You can't stop me from seeing my kid. I'm going to call my lawyer and bring charges against you and the agency for incompetency.

WORKER: (Finally losing his temper) Well, go ahead and call. I'm tired of hearing you complaining all the time. Do you think it's easy to deal with your kid? Frankly, I'm tired of your telling me what a lousy worker I am.

CLIENT: (With equal intensity) How the hell do you think I feel? (Silence)

WORKER: (A deep sigh as the worker seems to be catching his breath) I guess as frustrated, angry, and guilty as I do. You've been feeling this way ever since they took Jim away from you, haven't you?

CLIENT: (Subdued, but still angry) It's no picnic having your kid taken out of your house and then being told you're an unfit parent.

WORKER: Look, we can start all over. I felt angry, guilty, and very defensive when you put me on the spot, and that's why I threatened you about the visiting business. I guess I just didn't know how else to handle you. You know, we really need to get along better in spite of your being angry at the agency, for your sake, for mine, and especially for Jimmy's. How about it? (Silence)

CLIENT: I guess I was a little rough on you, but you know, I worry about the kid a lot and when he's not with me, I feel (struggling for the right word)

WORKER: Powerless to help him, isn't that it?

The worker's expression of his own feeling freed his energy to respond to the client's question, "Well, how the hell do you think I feel?" The results of this important step were threefold. First, the worker began to strengthen the working relationship between himself and the child's parent. This parent cared, and his anger and assertiveness could make him an excellent client to work with. Second, it allowed the worker to begin to respond empathically to the client, a crucial skill in the helping process. Finally, it demonstrated openness on the part of the worker to admitting feelings and mistakes. The client perceived an adult, a helping professional, who understood the connection between his own feelings and his actions. It is precisely this kind of openness to self-examination that the father will need to develop if the family relationship is to be strengthened.

In the two illustrations thus far, we have seen how the worker's feelings of caring and anger, when expressed openly, can be helpful to clients. This honest and spontaneous expression of feelings extends to a broad range of worker responses. Another example is the feeling of investment a worker can have in a client's progress. For some reason, the idea of self-determination has been interpreted to mean that the helping person cannot share a stake in the client's progress and growth. At points in the struggle toward change when clients feel most hopeless and ready to quit, workers sometimes suppress their own feelings of disappointment. This is a misguided attempt not to unduly influence the client's choices.

The following example illustrates the importance of direct expression of a worker's hope and expectations. A professional is working with a paraplegic young adult in a rehabilitation center. A relationship has developed over months as the worker has helped the patient deal with his feelings about this sudden change in his life. The exercise program to help the patient develop some limited functioning in his limbs has gone slowly and painfully, and with no signs of a quick recovery. Disappointed by the pace of his progress, the patient becomes depressed and apathetic, refusing to continue. It is at this point the following dialogue begins. Keep in mind that this excerpt follows months of development of the working relationship. The professional has a fund of positive feelings to draw on as she makes this

facilitative confrontation, or confrontation designed to make the work of the patient easier.

PATIENT: It's no use continuing—I quit!

WORKER: Look, I know it's been terribly frustrating and damn painful—and that you don't feel you're getting anywhere—but I think you are improving and you have to keep it up.

PATIENT: (With anger) What the hell do you know about it? It's easy for you to say, but I have to do it. I'm not going to get anywhere, so that's that.

WORKER: (With rising emotion) It's not the same for me. I'm not sitting in that wheelchair, but you know, working with you for the past three months has not been a picnic. Half the time you're feeling sorry for yourself and just not willing to work. I've invested a lot of time, energy, and caring in my work with you because I thought you could do it—and I'm not about to see you quit on me. It would hurt me like hell to see you quit because the going gets rough.

The patient did not respond immediately to the "demand for work" expressed in the worker's affective response. However, the next day, after some time to work through the feelings, he appeared for physiotherapy without a word about the previous conversation. Once again, we see how a worker's statement of feeling can integrate a highly personal and at the same time highly professional response. The worker's feelings are the most important tool in the professional kit, and any efforts to blunt them results in a working relationship that lacks substance.

Another way in which sharing the worker's feelings can be helpful in a relationship is when the affect is directly related to the content of the work, as when the worker has had a life experience similar to that of the client. Self-disclosure of personal experiences and feelings, when handled in pursuit of purpose and when integrated with the professional function, can promote client growth.

In one dramatic example, a student social worker was describing in my practice class her work in a residential setting with a group of young men who were mildly mentally challenged. All of these clients had recently lost a significant family member. They had been brought together to discuss their losses because they had been exhibiting ongoing depression and denial. The group was to help them face their feelings and to accept, or at least learn to live with, their sadness. Two weeks into the group, the student's father died, and she had to return home to take care of her own grieving. The clients were aware of her loss.

When she returned, she picked up with the group but did not mention the reason she had been away, even though she knew the members had been informed. One of the members said to her, "Jane, your father died, didn't he?" The worker later described feeling overwhelmed by his comment and struggling to maintain her "professional composure." She reported that the group members must have sensed her emotions, because another member said, "It's OK to cry, Jane, God loves you too!" In response to his comment she began to cry and was joined by most of the group members. After a few moments, she commented to the members that she had been encouraging them to share their pain over their losses, and then she had been trying to hide her own. The group members began their first serious and emotion-filled discussion of their own losses and why they tried to hide their feelings, even from themselves. As the student described the incident in class, she cried again and was joined by many other students and this instructor as well.

Even as I write about this incident, I can remember the many objections raised by workers when I advance the argument in favor of sharing the worker's feelings. Let us take some time to examine these.

Issues in Sharing the Worker's Feelings

The first concern relates to the boundaries within which personal feelings can be shared. I believe that if a worker is clear about the contract (the purpose of the work with the client) and the particular professional function, then these will offer important direction and protection. For example, if a client begins an interview by describing a problem with his mother-in-law, the worker should not respond by saying, "You think you have problems with your mother-in-law? Let me tell you about mine!" The client and worker have not come together to discuss the worker's problems, and an attempt by the worker to introduce personal concerns, even those related to the contract area, is an outright subversion of the contract. If the student in the previous example had started to discuss the death of her father and her own loss, rather than using the moment to return to the clients' issues and to deepen their work on their losses, she would not have been synthesizing the personal and professional, she would simply have been unprofessional.

The client seeks help from the worker, and the worker's feelings about personal relationships can be shared only in ways that relate directly to the client's immediate concerns. For example, take a situation where a worker feels the client is misinterpreting someone's response because of the client's feelings. The worker who has experienced that kind of miscommunication might briefly describe the experience as a way of providing the client with a new way of understanding an important interaction.

A second area of major concern for workers is that in sharing their feelings spontaneously—that is, without first monitoring all their reactions to see if they are "correct"—they risk making inappropriate responses. They worry that they will make a mistake, **act out** their own concerns, and perhaps hurt a client irretrievably. This fear has some basis, because workers do, at times, respond to the client out of their own needs. A young worker gets angry at an adolescent client's mother because this mother seems as overprotective as the young worker's own. Another worker experiences great frustration with a client who does not respond immediately to an offer of help but moves slowly through the process of change. Although the client makes progress at a reasonable pace, it still makes the worker feel ineffective. Still another worker misses several indirect cues from a group home resident about a serious problem with his family, whom he is about to visit over the holidays. The worker then responds to the resident's acting out of the feelings by imposing angry punishment instead of hearing the hidden message.

Spontaneous expression of feeling leads to all these mistakes and others. In fact, a helping professional's entire working experience will inevitably consist of making such mistakes, catching them as soon as possible, and then rectifying them. In these cases, a good worker will learn something about his or her personal feelings and reactions to people and situations. As this learning deepens, these early mistakes diminish. The worker then becomes conscious of new, more sophisticated mistakes.

When teachers, supervisors, theorists, and colleagues convey the idea that the worker should try during interviews to monitor her or his feelings continuously, to think clearly before acting, and to conduct the perfect interview, they are setting up blocks to the worker's growth. Only through continuous analysis of some portion of their own work after the interview has taken place can workers develop the ability to learn from their mistakes. The more skilled workers, who are spontaneous, can catch their mistakes during the interviews—not by withdrawing and thinking, but by using their own feelings and by reaching for the cues in the client's responses.

What is often overlooked is that clients can forgive a mistake more easily than they can deal with the image of a perfect worker. They are truly relieved by a worker owning up to having "blown" an interview, not having understood what the client was saying or feeling, or overreacting and being angry with a client. An admission of a mistake both humanizes the worker and indirectly gives the client permission to do the same. Workers who feel clients will lose respect for their expertise if they reveal human flaws simply misunderstand the nature of helping. Workers are not "experts" with the "solutions" for clients' problems, as suggested by the medical paradigm. Instead, workers possess skills that can help clients work on developing their own solutions to their problems. One of the most important of these skills is the ability to be personally and professionally honest.

Finally, some worker feelings are seen as potentially too harmful to be expressed. This is true; however, there are few such feelings. For example, many feelings of warmth and caring may flow between a worker and a client. These positive feelings constitute a key dynamic that helps to power the helping process. Under certain circumstances, feelings of intimacy are associated with strong sexual attraction. These mutual attractions are often understandable and normal. However, a client would find it difficult to handle a worker who honestly shared a sexual attraction.

Because of the authority of the worker, as well as the process of transference, sharing feelings of sexual attraction—and even worse, acting on them—constitutes a form of unethical sexual exploitation. Clients are vulnerable in the helping relationship and need to be protected. It is especially tragic and harmful when clients who are seeking help to heal their wounds from exploitive relationships find themselves in yet another one. Again, the problem is not that the worker is sexually attracted to a client. This can be understandable, and the worker should be able to discuss these emotions with a supervisor and/or colleagues. The unethical part is acting on feelings with the client.

Workers sometimes feel in a bind if clients begin to act seductively toward them and even directly request some response from the worker. For example, a young and attractive female worker described her reactions to the "come-on" of the paraplegic male client in a rehabilitation setting as "stimulating." She felt somewhat ashamed of her feelings, because she thought they revealed a lack of professionalism. Most workers in the consultation group where this illustration was presented reported that they, too, had experienced these feelings at times. They had not discussed them with colleagues, supervisors, or teachers because they felt a professional taboo against doing so.

When the discussion returned to the interaction in the interview with the paraplegic, I asked them to tune in to the meaning of the sexual "come-on" in the context of the contract. They speculated that the young client feared he could not be sexually attractive as a paraplegic. With a new handle for approaching the issue, it was clear to the worker that the client's feelings and fears about his sexual attractiveness might be a central issue for work that the worker would miss if overwhelmed by her own feelings. This illustrates how the worker can use the process (interaction with the client) as a tool for exploring the content (the substantive content of the working contract). In this example, the worker confronted the client directly about his comments to her, clarified her professional and ethical responsibilities, and then reached directly for his issues with regard to relationships to the opposite sex. The work proceeded to explore this painful, yet crucial area of content. (A later section discusses process and content connections in greater detail.)

Engaging and Working

With the Hard-to-Reach Client

MIDDLE PHASE CONTINUES Integrating False Dichotomies: The author addresses the apparent dualisms or dichotomies that can negatively influence practice. These include the suggested dichotomies between personal and professional, structure and freedom, support and confrontation, and content and process.

Research on Sharing Feelings

Several helping professions have produced research on sharing workers' feelings. The findings indicate that this skill plays as important a part in the helping process as the empathic skills described earlier. The skill has been called "self-disclosure" or "genuineness," among other labels. In my 1978 study, the worker's ability to "share personal thoughts and feelings" ranked first as a powerful correlate to developing working relationships and to being helpful. Further analysis of the research data suggested that the use of this skill contributed equally to the work of developing the working relationship and the ability of the worker to be helpful.

The importance of this skill was replicated in the more recent practice study (Shulman, 1991). It was one of the four skills in the grouping called skills to help clients manage their feelings. These skills had a strong impact on the development of the caring element of the working relationship, and through caring a strong impact on the client's perception of the worker's helpfulness. In addition, there was a low but significant influence on hard outcome measures (final court status of the children and days spent in care).

When examined by itself, the skill was found to correlate significantly with caring, trust, and helpfulness when used in the beginning and middle phases of practice, but it was usually at the low end of the list of eight skills. The difference in the importance of this skill in this study, compared with the 1978 study, may be related to a change in study design.

What inferences can we take from these findings? It may be that, in sharing personal thoughts and feelings, the worker breaks down the barriers that clients experience when they face the feelings of dependency evoked by taking help. As the worker becomes more multidimensional—more than just a professional helping person—there is more "person" available for a client to relate to. In addition, thoughts and feelings of a personal nature appear to provide substantive data for the client's tasks and therefore increase the worker's helpfulness. Perhaps the personal nature of the data is what makes it appear more relevant to the client, easier to use and to incorporate into a sense of reality. This skill, like many others, may simultaneously serve two functions. By sharing feelings freely, a worker effectively strengthens the working relationship (the process) while contributing important ideas for the client's work (the contract).

When the skill-use profiles of the average worker in the 1978 and 1991 studies were examined, I found that clients perceived their workers as seldom sharing their personal thoughts and feelings. When these findings were later shared with workers in various training groups, they always provoked important discussions in which workers explored the reasons why they found it difficult to reveal themselves to clients. The group's first response was to cite a supervisor, book, or former teacher who had made it clear that sharing feelings was unprofessional. As one worker put it, "I was told I had to be a stone-faced social worker."

After a discussion of these injunctions and their impact on the workers, I would say, "Based on my research, my practice experience, my expertise, I am now telling you that it is no longer 'unprofessional' to be honest with clients and to make your feelings part of your work." I would then inquire how this new freedom would affect their work the next day. After a long silence, a typical response from a worker would be "You have just made things a lot tougher. Now I'm going to have to face the fact that it's my own feelings that make it hard for me to be honest. I'm not really sure how much of myself I want to share." At this point in the workshop discussion, the work would deepen.

Developing the ability to be honest in sharing feelings is difficult, but workers ask clients to do it all the time. It is an essential skill for providing effective helping. As one client said of her worker, "I like Mrs. Tracy. She's not like a social worker. She's like a real person." This model suggests that Mrs. Tracy was both a real person and a real social worker.

Making a Demand for Work

In constructing this model of the helping process, we have seen the importance of five components: establishing a clear contract, identifying the client's agenda, helping the client to elaborate concerns, making certain the client invests the work with feeling, and sharing the worker's feelings. At this point in the model-building process, we should examine the question of ambivalence and resistance. Clients will be of two minds about proceeding with their work. A part of them, representing their strength, will move toward understanding and growth. Another part of them, representing the resistance, will pull back from what is perceived as a difficult process.

Work often requires lowering long-established defenses, discussing painful subjects, experiencing difficult feelings, recognizing one's own contribution to the problem, taking responsibility for one's actions, giving up long-held cognitive frameworks about life, and confronting significant people and systems. Whatever the difficulty involved, a client will show some degree of ambivalence.

Perlman (1957) describes client ambivalence as follows:

> To know one's feelings is to know that they are often many-sided and mixed and that they may pull in two directions at once. Everyone has experienced this duality of wanting something strongly yet drawing back from it, making up one's mind but somehow not carrying out the planned action. This is part of what is meant by ambivalence. A person may be subject to two opposing forces within himself at the same moment—one that says, "Yes, I will," and the other that says, "No, I won't"; one that says, "I want," and the other, "Not really"; one affirming and the other negating. (p. 121)

Relating client ambivalence to the relationship with the worker and the process of taking help, Strean (1978) describes **resistance** as follows:

Recognizing that every client has some resistance to the idea and process of being helped should alert the social-work interviewer to the fact that not every part of every interview can flow smoothly. Most clients at one time or another will find participation difficult or may even refuse to talk at all; others will habitually come late and some may be quite negative toward the agency, the social-work profession, and the social worker. (p. 193)

An example of this ambivalence at work is found in the following excerpt from a videotaped interview with an adolescent foster boy. Early in the interview, the 18-year-old indirectly hinted at his feelings about leaving a group home and particularly about the warm feelings he had established for the head child care worker. The worker missed the first cues, because she was preoccupied with her written agenda resting on the table between them. Catching her mistake during the session, the worker moved her agenda aside and began to listen systematically to this theme, encouraging the client to elaborate, and reaching for and articulating his feelings. The following excerpt picks up the interview at the point where the worker responded to the client's second offering of this concern.

Worker: Is it going to be hard to say good-bye to Tom (the head child care worker)?
Client: It's not going to be hard to say good-bye to Tom, but I'll miss the little kittens that sleep with me. Last night one dug his claws into me and I screamed and screamed and yelled to Tom—"Come and get this goddamn kitten—do you think I'm going to go around ruptured all my life?" (At this point the client had told the story with such exuberance that the worker was laughing along with him. The client quickly reached over to the table for the worker's written agenda and said, "OK, what's next?")

When the worker was distracted by the agenda, the client continually offered indirect cues related to this important theme. As the worker began to deal seriously with the theme, the part of the client that feared the discussion and the accompanying feelings found a way to put the worker off by using the worker's own agenda. The client might also be testing to see if the worker is ready for the discussion. By allowing herself to be put off, the worker sent the message, "I'm not ready, either." When this was explored with the worker, her reflections on the process led her to recognize that she was also about to end with this client—an ending she was avoiding. Once again, the ability of the worker to manage her own feelings influenced her ability to help the client manage his. (The ending phase of practice is discussed in detail in Chapter 5.)

The important thing to remember is that resistance is quite normal. In fact, a lack of resistance may mean the progress of the work is an illusion, with the real issues still unexplored. If this client could have easily dealt with his feelings about terminating his relationship with Tom, he would not have needed the worker's help. Termination feelings form the core of the work for foster children who must struggle to find ways of investing in new, meaningful relationships in spite of deep feelings of rejection. When the worker approached the core area of feeling, it would be surprising if resistance did not appear.

A crucial concept is that resistance is a part of the work. Less experienced workers who do not understand this may back off from an important area. Their own confidence in what they are doing is fragile, and so when the client shows signs of defensiveness or unwillingness to deal with a tough problem, they allow themselves to be put off. This is especially true if workers experience their own ambivalence about the area. Communication of ambivalence in tough areas can be seen as the client's way of saying, "This is tough for me to talk about." It can also be a question to the worker: "Are you really prepared to talk with me about this?" It is one of those life situations in which the other person says he is reluctant to enter the taboo area, hoping you will not really believe him. The surface message is "Leave me alone in this area," while the real one is "Don't let me put you off." These are the moments in interviews when the skills of making a demand for work are crucial.

The notion of a demand for work is one of Schwartz's (1961) most important contributions to our understanding of the helping process. He describes it as follows:

> The worker also represents what might be called the demand for work, in which role he tries to enforce not only the substantive aspects of the contract—what we are here for—but the conditions of work as well. This demand is, in fact, the only one the worker makes—not for certain perceived results, or approved attitudes, or learned behaviors, but for the work itself. That is, he is continually challenging the client to address himself resolutely and with energy to what he came to do. (p. 11)

The demand for work is not limited to a single action or even a single group of skills; rather, it pervades all the work. For example, the process of open and direct contracting in the beginning phase of work represents a form of demand for work. The attempt of the worker to bring the client and feelings into the process is another form of a demand for work. The illustration of the first interview with the angry father in which the worker kept coming back to his feelings in the situation is a good example. The father said, "It's a long time for the kids." The worker responded, "And for you too." Similarly, in the interview with the foster child, the youngster was discussing, at one point, the feeling that had grown between Tom (the child care worker) and himself, and he said to the worker, "How does it hit people like him?" The worker's response was "How does it hit you?" This is another illustration of the demand for work. Note that this demand can be gentle and coupled with support. It is not necessarily confrontational. I underline this point because of a tendency for people to see confrontation as negative and uncaring. Some models of practice, particularly in the substance abuse area, have been designed to use confrontation to "break down" defenses. It is quite possible for the worker to make an empathic demand for work—and, as emphasized earlier, confrontation is experienced as caring if carried out in the context of a positive working relationship.

Several specific skills can be categorized as demand-for-work skills: partializing client concerns, holding to focus, checking for underlying ambivalence, challenging the illusion of work, and pointing out obstacles. Each is related to specific dynamics in interview situations that could be interpreted as forms of resistance. Note that the consistent use of demand-for-work skills can only be effective when they are accompanied by the empathic skills described earlier. As the workers express their genuine caring for the clients through their ability to empathize, they build up a fund of positive affect that is part of the working relationship. It is almost like a bank account that the worker can draw on when needed. Only when clients perceive that their worker does understand, and is not judging them harshly, can they respond to the demands.

A balance of empathy and demand for work is called for. On the one hand, workers who have the capacity to empathize with clients can develop a positive working relationship but not necessarily be helpful. On the other hand, workers who only make demands on their clients, without the empathy and working relationship, will be experienced by clients as harsh, judgmental, and unhelpful. The most effective help will be offered by workers who can synthesize, each in their own way, caring and demand. This is not easy to do either in the helping relationship or in life. There is a general tendency to dichotomize these two aspects of relationship. Workers might see themselves as going back and forth between the two. For example, caring about someone, expressing it through empathy, but getting nowhere leads to anger and demands, with an associated hardening of empathic response. However, it is precisely at this point, when crucial demands are made on the client, that the capacity for empathy is most important. With this stipulation clearly in mind, in the next section we will explore four demand-for-work skills.

Partializing Client Concerns

Clients often experience their concerns as overwhelming. A worker may find that a client's response to an offer of help in the contracting phase consists of the recitation of a flood of problems, each having some impact on the other. The feeling of helplessness experienced by the client is as much related to the difficulty of tackling so many problems as it is to the nature of the problems themselves. The client feels immobilized and does not know how or where to begin. In addition, maintaining problems in this form can represent resistance. If the problems are overwhelming, the client can justify the impossibility of doing anything about them.

Partializing is essentially a problem-managing skill. The only way to tackle complex problems is to break them down into their parts and address these parts one at a time. The way to move past perceptions of helplessness and feelings of being immobilized is to begin by taking one small step on one part of the problem. This is one way the worker can make a demand for work. While listening to the concerns of the client, while attempting to understand and acknowledge the client's feelings of being overwhelmed, the worker simultaneously begins the task of helping the client to reduce the problem to smaller, more manageable proportions. This skill is illustrated in the following excerpt of an interview with a single parent.

WORKER: You seem really upset by your son's fight yesterday. Can you tell me more about what's upsetting you?

CLIENT: All hell broke loose after that fight. Mrs. Lewis is furious because he gave her son a black eye, and she is threatening to call the police on me. She complained to the landlord, and he's threatening to throw me out if the kids don't straighten up. I tried to talk to Frankie about it, but I got nowhere. He just screamed at me and ran out of the house. I'm really afraid he has done it this time, and I'm feeling sick about the whole thing. Where will I go if they kick me out? I can't afford another place. And you know the cops gave Frankie a warning last time. I'm scared about what will happen if Mrs. Lewis does complain. I just don't know what to do.

WORKER: It really does sound like quite a mess; no wonder you feel up against the wall. Look, maybe it would help if we looked at one problem at a time. Mrs. Lewis is very angry, and you need to deal with her. Your landlord is important, too, and we should think about what you might be able to say to him to get him to back off while you try to deal with Frankie on this. And I guess that's the big question, what can you say to Frankie since this has made things rougher for the two of you? Mrs. Lewis, the landlord, and Frankie—where should we start?

The demand implied in the worker's statement is gentle and yet firm. The worker can sense the client's feelings of being overwhelmed, but she will not allow the work to stop there. In this example, one can see clearly two sets of tasks: those of the worker and those of the client. The client raises the concerns, and the worker helps her to partialize her problems. The client must begin to work on them according to her sense of urgency. This is the sense in which work is interactional, with the worker's tasks and those of the client interacting with each other.

When a worker partializes an overwhelming problem and asks a client to begin to address the issues, she or he is also acting on a crucial principle of the helping process: There is always a next step. The next step is whatever the worker and client can do, together, to begin to cope with the problem. Even when a client is dealing with a terminal illness, the next steps may mean developing a way of coping with the illness, getting one's life in order, taking control of the quality of one's remaining time, and so on. When social supports, such as adequate housing, are not available for a client, the next steps may involve advocacy and confrontation of the system or, if all else fails, attempting to figure out how to minimize the impact of the poor housing. While the worker may not be able to offer hope of "solving" the problem, the worker needs to help the client find the next step. When a client feels overwhelmed and hopeless, the last thing he or she needs is a worker who feels exactly the same way.

In my more recent practice study, partializing was one of the four skills for helping clients manage their problems that contributed to the development of the trust element in the working relationship (Shulman, 1991). The other skills in the managing problems grouping included clarifying purpose and role, reaching for client feedback, and supporting clients in taboo areas. The trust element of the relationship, in turn, contributed to the client's perception of the worker as being helpful. This is a logical finding, because workers who help their clients to deal with complex problems are going to be seen as more helpful.

Further, when used in the beginning phase of practice, the partializing skill ranked fifth out of eight skills in the strength of its correlation with the caring element of the working relationship. It moved to second place in relation to the trust element of the relationship, and to first in importance in terms of its impact on helpfulness. This association between partializing and the working relationship replicated a finding in my earlier study, in which the skill appeared to contribute to the outcome of helpfulness though its impact on relationship (Shulman, 1978).

Why, then, does use of the partializing skill positively affect relationship building? One explanation may be that the worker's use of the partializing skill conveys several important ideas to the client. First, the worker believes the tasks facing the client are manageable. Second, the worker conveys the belief that the client can take some next step: that is, that the client has the strength to deal with the problem when properly broken down into manageable pieces. Third, because partializing also serves to focus the work clearly, it may be another form of clarifying role and purpose. In any case, the findings on the partializing skill suggest that workers might do well, especially early on, to help clients identify clearly the component parts of the concerns they bring to the worker.

Holding to Focus

As a client begins to deal with a specific concern, associations with other related issues often result in a form of rambling, with great difficulty in concentrating on one issue at a time. **Holding to focus**—asking the client to stay on one question—is a second problem-solving skill incorporating a demand for work. Moving from concern to concern can be an evasion of work—that is, if the client will not stay with one issue, then he or she does not have to deal with the associated feelings. Holding to focus sends the message to the client that the worker means to discuss the tougher feelings and concerns. This skill is illustrated in the interview with the single parent, discussed earlier. After the client decided, because of her fear of police involvement, to deal with Mrs. Lewis first, the discussion continued:

CLIENT: When Mrs. Lewis came to the door, all she did was scream at me about how my Frankie was a criminal and that she would not let him beat up her son again.

WORKER: You must have been frightened and upset. What did you say to her?

CLIENT: I just screamed back at her and told her that her son was no bargain and that he probably asked for it. I was really upset because I could see the landlord's door opening, and I knew he must be listening. You know he warned me that he wouldn't stand for all of this commotion any more. What can I do if he really kicks me out on the street?

WORKER: Can we stay with Mrs. Lewis for a minute and then get back to the landlord? I can see how angry and frightened you must have felt. Do you have any ideas about how Mrs. Lewis was feeling?

By acknowledging the distress (support) and then returning to the issue of dealing with Mrs. Lewis (demand), the worker helped the client stay focused on this issue instead of allowing the client's anxiety to overwhelm her.

Checking for Underlying Ambivalence

One of the dangers in a helping situation is that a client may choose to go along with the worker, expressing an artificial consensus or agreement, while really feeling ambivalent about a point of view or a decision to take a next step. **Checking for underlying ambivalence** is thus another important task of the worker.

Clients may go along with the worker in this way for several reasons. A client who feels that the worker has an investment in the "solution" may not want to upset the worker by voicing doubts. The client may also be unaware at this moment of his or her current doubts or the ones that might appear later on, when implementation of the difficult action is attempted. Finally, the client may also withhold concerns as a means of putting off dealing with the core of the issue. In this sense, the client shows another form of resistance that is subtle because it is expressed passively. In these circumstances, when words are being spoken but nothing real is happening, we have the **illusion of work**, which is the single most dangerous threat to effective practice. Workers and clients develop marvelous ways of maintaining the illusion, each for their own reasons.

Sometimes workers are aware of clients' underlying doubts, fears, and concerns but simply pass over them. As one worker put it, "I knew we were just spinning our wheels, but I was afraid to confront the client." Workers believe that raising these issues may cause the client to decide not to take the next step. They believe that positive thinking is required, and they do not wish to heighten the client's ambivalence by discussing it. The reverse is true. It is exactly at moments such as these that the worker should check for the underlying ambivalence. When a client has an opportunity to express ambivalence, the worker has access to the client's real feelings and can be of help. When discussed with the worker, negative feelings usually lose their power. Perhaps the client is overestimating the difficulties involved, and the worker can help clarify the reality of the situation. In other cases, the next step will indeed be difficult. The worker's help consists of empathic understanding of the difficulty and expression of faith in the client's strength and resilience in the face of these feelings. Whatever the reasons for hesitation, they must be explored so that they do not block the client's work outside the session.

Workers need to struggle against a sense of elation when they hear clients agreeing to take an important next step. Schwartz (1961) describes the need for workers to "look for trouble when everything is going your way." For example, in working with a client with a substance abuse problem, an enthusiastic worker might accept the client's agreement to enter a treatment program and then be disappointed when the client does not show up for the intake appointment. Careful examination of the session reveals that the client sent signals that he was still in the "contemplative" stage and not yet ready to move into the "action" stage of seeking help. Workers often admit sensing a client's hesitancy but believing that it can be overcome through positive encouragement. This mistake comes back to haunt the worker when the ambivalence and fears emerge after the session.

All is not lost if in the next session the worker can admit to having moved too quickly and encourage the client to explore his mixed feelings, which are normal at this stage of the process. This example provides a good opportunity to elaborate on the earlier comment that resistance is part of the work. It would be a mistake simply to think of client resistance as an obstacle to progress; rather, there are important "handles for work" within the resistance itself. In this example, as the worker explores the client's resistance, important work themes may emerge: concerns regarding acceptance of a problem with substances, how employers would view him, feelings of shame, memories of traumatic events that serve as "triggers," and so on.

In another example, a young university student, who had been admitted to a psychiatric unit after a suicide attempt, announced early in the first interview that she would not discuss her boyfriend or her family because that would be blaming them. She simultaneously expressed resistance and one of her central concerns related to her guilt over her anger and resentment. Exploring why she does not want to discuss them could lead directly into a central theme of concern.

Challenging the Illusion of Work

As mentioned earlier, perhaps the greatest threat to effective helping is the illusion of work. Although helping can be achieved through nonverbal means such as touch or activity, much of the helping process takes place through an exchange of words. We have all developed the capacity to engage in conversations that are empty of real meaning. It is easy to see how this ability to talk a great deal without saying much can be integrated into the helping interaction. This represents a subtle form of resistance, because by creating the illusion of work, the client can avoid the pain of struggle and growth while still appearing to work. For the illusion to take place, however, two must engage in the ritual. The worker must be willing to allow the illusion to be created, thus participating actively in its maintenance. Workers have reported helping relationships with clients that have spanned months, even years, in which the worker always knew, deep inside, that it was all illusion.

Schwartz (1971) describes the illusion of work in this passage about group work:

Not only must the worker be able to help people talk but he must help them talk to each other; the talk must be purposeful, related to the contract that holds them together; it must have feeling in it, for without affect there is no investment; and it must be about real things, not a charade, or a false consensus, or a game designed to produce the illusion of work without raising anything in the process. (p. 11)

The skill involves detecting the pattern of illusion, perhaps over a period of time, and confronting the client with it. An example from marriage counseling illustrates this process. The couple had requested help for problems in their marriage. As the sessions proceeded, the worker noted that most of the conversation involved problems they were having at work, with their parents, and with their children. Some connection was made to the impact on their marriage; however, they seemed to have created an unspoken alliance not to deal with the details of their relationship. No matter how hard the worker tried to find the connections to how they got along, they always seemed to evade him. Finally, the worker said,

You know, when we started out, you both felt you wanted help with the problems in your marriage, how you got along with each other. It seems to me, however, that all we ever talk about is how you get along with other people. You seem to be avoiding the tough stuff. How come? Are you worried it might be too tough to handle?

The worker's challenge to the illusion brought a quick response as the couple explored some of their fears about what would happen if they really began to work. This challenge to the illusion was needed to help the couple begin the difficult, risky process of change. In addition, their resistance itself revealed a great deal about their underlying problems. They were demonstrating to the worker how they avoided talking to each other about their real problems.

DEMAND FOR WORK: PART I Here is a private practice interview with a gay man who has been coming for counseling after being assaulted. The example demonstrates demand-for-work skills and the skills involved in challenging the illusion of work.

Pointing Out Obstacles

When developing his theory of the mediation function for social work, Schwartz (1961) broke down the function into five general sets of tasks. One of these was the task of searching out the common ground between the client and the systems to be negotiated. This task is evident when workers attempt to contract with clients—to find the connections between the felt needs of the client and the services of the agency. It is also apparent when the workers attempt to alert themselves, for example, to the subtle connections between a teenager's need for independence and the parents' desire to see their youngster grow.

Because the common ground between the individual and the system may appear to each to be diffused, unclear, even totally absent, Schwartz elaborates his mediation function with a second set of important activities, the task of **detecting and challenging the obstacles to work** as these obstacles arise. Like all of Schwartz's tasks, this one is repeated, moment by moment, in every helping encounter. Two major obstacles that tend to frustrate people as they work on their own self-interest are the blocking effects of social taboos and the effect of the authority theme, the relationship between the person who gives help and the one who takes it.

Supporting Clients in Taboo Areas

In moving into a helping relationship, the client brings along a sense of society's culture, which includes taboos against open discussion in certain sensitive areas. For example, we are taught early in life that direct questions and discussions about sex are frowned on. Other areas in which we are subtly encouraged not to acknowledge our true feelings include dependency, authority, loss, and financial issues.

To feel dependent is to be weak. The unrealistic image of a "real man" or a "real woman" presents one who is independent, who can stand on his or her own feet, and who deals with life's problems without help. In the real world, however, life is so complex that we are always dependent on others in some way. Most people experience the bind of feeling one way, consciously or not, but thinking they should feel another way. The norms of our culture include clear taboos that make real talk about dependency difficult.

Money is considered a taboo subject as well. Many families deeply resent questions related to their financial affairs. Having enough money is equated with competency in our society, and poverty is embarrassing. Reluctance to discuss fees with professionals is one example of the effect of the taboo in social work practice. Clients sometimes contract for services without asking about the fee, feeling that it would be embarrassing to inquire.

One of the most powerful taboos involves feelings toward authority. Parents, teachers, and other authority figures do not generally encourage feedback from children on the nature of the relationship. We learn early on that commenting on this relationship, especially negatively, is fraught with danger. People in authority have power to hurt us, so we can only, at best, hint at our feelings and reactions. Revealing positive feelings to people in authority is almost as hard, because it is considered demeaning. The authority taboo creates an important problem in the working relationship between the worker and the client, as I shall demonstrate in the next section.

Loss represents another taboo—one that takes many forms, affecting various types of clients and areas of work. For example, the loss of a relationship because of death or separation may be considered too difficult to discuss directly. A parent whose child has been born with a physical or mental problem may secretly mourn the loss of the perfect child he or she had wished to have. A survivor of sexual abuse or of emotional or physical abuse may mourn the loss of childhood and innocence. The adult child of an alcoholic may mourn the loss of the family once hoped for, but he or she may not feel free to discuss this because the family taught that the "problem" must be kept secret. Many of the messages of our society indicate that direct discussion of loss is not acceptable.

To help a client discuss taboo feelings and concerns, the worker has to create a unique "culture" in the helping interview. In this culture it will become acceptable to discuss feelings and concerns that the client may experience as taboo elsewhere. The taboo is not going to be removed for all situations. There are some good reasons for us not to talk freely and intimately on all occasions about our feelings in taboo areas, as the discussion on sharing worker feelings showed. Discussing taboos in the interview is meant not to change the client's attitudes forever, but rather to allow work in the immediate situation. The worker enables such discussion by monitoring the interaction of the work with the client and listening for clues that may reveal a taboo-related block in the process. Past experiences with clients and the tuning-in process may heighten the worker's sensitivity to a taboo that lies just beneath the surface of the interview. On recognizing the taboo, the worker brings it out in the open and begins the negotiation of a new norm of behavior for the interview situation. The following illustration concerning taboos is from an interview between a helping professional and a 48-year-old male patient:

PATIENT: I've been feeling lousy for a long time. It's been especially bad since my wife and I have been arguing so much.

WORKER: Tell me more about the arguments.

PATIENT: They've been about lots of things—she complains I drink too much, I'm not home often enough, and that I always seem too tired to spend time with her. (At this point, the worker senses the patient's difficulty in talking. His hesitation and an inability to look directly at her are the cues.)

WORKER: Often when there is a lot of difficulty like this, it spills over into the sexual area.

PATIENT: (After a long pause) There have been some problems around sex as well.

WORKER: You know I realize that it's tough to talk about something as intimate as sex, particularly for a man to discuss it with a woman. It's really not something one can do easily.

PATIENT: It is a bit embarrassing.

WORKER: Perhaps you can speak about it in spite of your embarrassment. You know there is not much I haven't heard already, and I won't mind hearing what you have to say. Anyway, we can't do much about the problems if we can't discuss them.

PATIENT: I've been tired lately with a lot of worries. Sometimes I have too much to drink as well. Anyway, I've been having trouble getting it up for the past few months.

WORKER: Is this the first time this had happened?

PATIENT: The first time. I usually have no trouble at all.

WORKER: It must have come as quite a shock to you. I guess this has hit you and your wife hard.

The discussion continued as the client went into more detail about the nature of the problem. Other symptoms were described, and the worker suggested that a complete physical was in order. She pointed out that it was not at all unusual for these things to happen to men of this age and that often there were physiological reasons. At the end of the interview the worker reinforced the development of the new norm in their working relationship by commenting, "I know how hard it was for you to speak to me about this. It was important, however, and I hope this discussion will help you feel free to talk about whatever is on your mind." The patient answered that he felt better now that he had been able to get it off his chest.

While this conversation would still be difficult for most men in our society, changes in the culture may have made it a bit easier. It's hard to turn on the TV without seeing a commercial for Viagra or other impotency treatments. At first these featured a former U.S. senator who took the first step toward challenging the taboo. These commercials now include athletes, a former football coach with a reputation for being "tough," and young men. Clearly the pharmaceutical companies are trying to make the discussion and treatment of erectile problems acceptable and to change the norm of what makes a "real man."

It is important to see that identifying the taboo or any other obstacle is done to free the client's energy to work on the mutually agreed-on contract. Sometimes simply naming an obstacle will release the client from its power. In other situations, some exploration of the obstacle may be needed before its impact abates. For example, a client might need to talk briefly about the difficulty he feels in discussing issues related to sex. His family norms might have added to the pressure against such open discussion. Once again, as the client discusses the difficulties in talking about sex, he is actually beginning to talk about sex.

The worker needs to guard against a subtle subversion of the contract that can easily occur if the discussion of the obstacle becomes the focus of the work. The purpose of the helping encounter is neither to examine the reasons why the taboo exists nor to free the client from its power in all situations. Clarity of purpose and function can assist the worker in avoiding the trap of becoming so engrossed in the analysis of the process that the original task becomes lost.

In my early study, the skill of supporting clients in taboo areas was one of four skills that distinguished the most effective workers from the least effective, from their clients' perspective (Shulman, 1978). In the more recent study, this skill was only the sixth most used out of the eight skills examined (Shulman, 1991). Clients reported that their workers used this skill between "seldom" and "fairly often." This is not unexpected, because workers face the taboos that clients do. Workers need experience and supervision to find the courage to speak directly about many of these issues.

The introduction of time to the analysis for this skill yielded some interesting findings. Supporting clients in taboo areas, when used in the beginning phase of work, was the third strongest skill (out of eight) correlating with the client's perception of the worker's caring ($r = .52$). The correlation for the use of the skill in the middle phase of work was slightly higher ($r = .58$). These findings were expected, because support of any kind, particularly in sensitive and painful areas of work, could contribute to the client's perception that the worker was concerned about him or her.

When the association between the beginning phase use of this skill and trust was examined, however, it was significant but smaller ($r = .37$). The correlation was higher when the skill was used in the middle phase ($r = .57$). A similar pattern was found when the skill use was correlated with client perception of the worker's helpfulness ($r = .39$ in the beginning phase and $r = .50$ in the middle phase). One inference from these findings might be that the use of this skill in the early phases of work, before a solid working relationship has been established, primarily contributes to the working relationship through the development of a client's sense of the worker's caring. This provides some justification for the argument that it is better for the worker to risk and be too far ahead of the client than to be overly cautious.

The use of the skill may have less of an impact on trust and helpfulness early in the work because of the lower levels of trust in the beginning phase of any relationship. In short, the client needs to trust the worker somewhat before the worker's efforts to explore taboo areas have their largest impact on trust.

Dealing With the Authority Theme

Schwartz (1971) describes the *authority theme* as referring to "the familiar struggle to resolve the relationship with a nurturing and demanding figure who is both a personal symbol and a representative of a powerful institution" (p. 11). As the client uses the worker's help to deal with this task, positive and negative feelings will arise. There will be times when the client thinks fondly of this caring and supportive figure. There will be other times when the client feels anger toward a worker who demands that the client take responsibility for the client's own part in the events of her or his life. Workers are not perfect individuals who never make mistakes. Even the most skilled worker will sometimes miss a client's communications, lose track of the real function and begin to sermonize, or judge the client harshly without compassion for real struggles. Reactions and feelings on the part of the client will result. As one enters a helping relationship, problems with the authority theme should be anticipated as a normal part of the work. In fact, the energy flow between worker and client, both positive and negative, can provide the drive powering the work.

Two processes central to the authority theme are transference and countertransference. Drawing on Freud's psychoanalytic theory, Strean (1978) describes their effects on the worker-client relationship:

> This relationship has many facets: subtle and overt, conscious and unconscious, progressive and regressive, positive and negative. Both client and worker experience themselves and each other not only in terms of objective reality, but in terms of how each wishes the other to be and fears he might be. The phenomena of "transference" and "counter-transference" exist in every relationship between two or more people, professional or nonprofessional, and must be taken into account in every social-worker-client encounter. By "transference" is meant the feelings, wishes, fears, and defenses of the client deriving from reactions to significant persons in the past (parents, siblings, extended family, teachers), that influence his current perceptions of the social worker. "Countertransference" similarly refer to aspects of the social worker's history of feelings, wishes, fears, and so on, all of which influence his perceptions of the client. (p. 193)

Unfortunately, the authority theme is one of the most powerfully taboo areas in our society. Clients have as much difficulty talking about their reactions and feelings toward their workers as they do discussing subjects such as sex. When these feelings and reactions remain undiscussed, the helping relationship suffers. These strong feelings operate just below the surface and emerge in many indirect forms. The client becomes apathetic or is late for appointments or does not follow up on commitments. The worker searches for answers to the questions raised by the client's behavior. In Strean's view, workers attempt to understand this behavior in terms of the client's "personality." However, the answers to the worker's questions are often much closer to home and more accessible than the intangible notion of personality. The answers often may be found in the interactional process between the worker and client.

The skill of dealing with the authority theme involves continual monitoring of the relationship. A worker who senses that the work is unreal or blocked can call attention to the obstacle and respond directly to it if she or he thinks it centers on the authority theme. Once again, as with other taboo subjects, the worker is trying to create a culture in this situation in which the client perceives a new norm: "It is all right to treat the worker like a real person and to say what you think about how the worker deals with you." The worker can begin this process in the contracting stages, in responding directly to the early cues that the client wants some discussion about what kind of worker this will be (see Chapter 3). The new culture will develop slowly as the client tests this strange kind of authority who seems to invite direct feedback, even the negative kind. As the client learns that the worker will not punish, the feedback will arise more often and more quickly than before. Also importantly, the client gets to see a nondefensive worker demonstrating the capacity to examine his or her own behavior and to be open to change—exactly what the worker will be asking the client to do. This is another example of integrating content and process.

The following illustration demonstrates the skill in action. It describes a brief interaction between a worker and John, a 14-year-old resident in a group home. The resident had been disciplined by the worker that afternoon for a fight he appeared to have provoked with another resident, Jerry. The worker's one-sided intervention had shifted the fight to a battle of wills between John and himself, which then escalated until he finally imposed strict consequences. John had been quiet and sullen throughout dinner and the early evening. The worker approached him in the lounge.

WORKER: John, you have been looking mad all evening, ever since the fight. Let's talk about it.

CLIENT: F—k off!

WORKER: Look, I know you're mad as hell at me, but it won't help to just sit there and keep it in. It will be miserable for both of us if you do. If you think I wasn't fair to you, I want to hear about it. You know I'm human, and I can make a mistake, too. So how about it, what's bugging you?

CLIENT: You're just like all the rest. The minute I get into trouble, you blame me. It's always my fault, never the other kids'. You took Jerry's side in that fight without ever asking me why I was beating up on him.

WORKER: (Short silence) I guess I did come down hard on you quickly. You know you're probably right about my figuring it was your fault when you get in trouble—probably because you get into trouble so often. I think I was also a little tired this afternoon and maybe not up to handling a fight on my shift. Look, let's start again. OK? I think I can listen now. What happened?

The discussion carried on about the fight and the issues that led up to it. It became clear that there were some ongoing questions between John and Jerry that needed to be argued out. The worker suggested another meeting with Jerry present, at which time he would try not to take sides and try to help both John and Jerry work this out. John seemed willing but showed a great deal of skepticism. The interview continued, and the worker returned to the authority theme.

WORKER: You know, I really wasn't helpful to you this afternoon, and I'm sorry about that. But you know, I'm only human, and that is going to happen sometimes. What I'd like you to do, if it happens again, is not just sit around upset but to call me on it. If you do, I may catch myself sooner. Do you think you can do that?

CLIENT: Don't worry—I'll let you know if you get out of line.

WORKER: I guess this kind of thing happens a lot to you, I mean with the other staff here and maybe even the teachers at school.

CLIENT: You bet it does! Mr. Fredericks is always on my back, the minute I turn around in my seat.

In this illustration the worker caught his mistake, and he had an important discussion with his client about how they worked together. His willingness to own up to his mistake and to take negative feedback contributed to a change in the subtle rules that have governed John's reaction to adults in authority. The worker was very conscious that one of the most important outcomes of the young man's stay in the group home may be his development of greater skill in dealing with people of authority, who are not always skillful about dealing with him. In many ways, the helping relationship itself is a training ground in which the client develops new skills at dealing with authority. For some clients, particularly children in alternative care facilities, the ability to trust adults and to risk themselves is so limited that learning to relate in a new way to the worker represents a profound change. It becomes a first step in developing their skills at dealing with the outside world.

The worker also demonstrated an advanced level of skill when he deftly integrated process and task, toward the end of the illustration. Part of his work involved helping John deal with the other systems of his life, such as his school. By generalizing to another situation, the worker found the work element related to their contract that was contained in the process. Dealing with the authority theme is not only a requirement for maintaining a positive working relationship, but it may also provide important material for helping clients to work on the substance of the contract. The process-content integration issue is discussed in more detail in the next section.

Identifying Process and Content Connections

Process refers to the interaction that takes place between the worker and the client (the authority theme) and the client and other clients, such as family or group members (the intimacy theme, discussed in Chapters 11 and 12). Another way to describe process is that it refers more to the way of working than the substance or content of the work. **Content** is defined here as the substantive issues or themes that have been identified as part of the working contract.

At any one time, the work in an interview (or family or group session) is related to either process or content. However, because of the indirect nature of client communications, it is often hard to know which is really under discussion. For example, a single parent may have contracted to work on issues related to dealing with her children, employment, and relationships with friends and family. She may begin a session apparently talking about content—how none of her friends or relatives understood her pain. The issue is real to her, but she has also been angry at the worker since the previous session, when the worker missed her signals of distress. This example emphasizes the importance of sessional turning in and worker tentativeness in the sessional contracting phase of a session, discussed earlier in this chapter. The worker who is tuned in to the client's pattern of indirect communications around issues of authority may be better prepared to hear that the discussion is really about process (the worker's ability to understand) rather than about content (friends and relatives). If the worker prematurely assumes it is only content related, the session may turn into the illusion of work, with the process issues buried under the surface.

Thus far, the terms *content* and *process* have been described and illustrated; however, the concept of the integration of the two requires further elaboration. One major, common mistake made by workers is to fail to see the possible connections between process and content that allow for a synthesizing of the two. Workers often describe being torn between process and content. Group leaders will describe trying to "balance" the two, spending some time on process (how the group is working) and some time on content. What they do not realize is that they have fallen into the trap of accepting the false dichotomy of process versus content. When workers embrace this false dualism, they cannot avoid getting stuck. Instead, the worker must search out the connections between process and content so that the discussion of process deepens the work on the content, and vice versa.

Returning to our single-parent example, the worker who looks for this synthesis may recognize (usually between sessions, rarely during a session) that the way in which the client indirectly raised her anger and hurt feelings at the worker's lack of compassion is a good example of the way this client deals with friends and other important people in her life. When her needs are not met, she gets angry because she expects other people to intuitively sense her feelings. She does not take responsibility for being direct about her pain and thereby helping others to understand. In this case, if the worker opens up a discussion of the authority theme, the client can gain a deeper understanding of the skills she must develop to create and maintain a social support system. The client can be held accountable for her own responsibility in the relationship with the worker as well as relationships with other significant people in her life. Thus, we see in this example that the content of the work can be synthesized with process issues, and the process issues can be integrated into the content.

In another illustration, a social worker used her discussion with a foster teenager about the termination of service to open up a discussion of the difficulty the youth encountered in making new relationships after so many had ended badly. They were able to explore this pain over the ending with the worker as well as the many other losses he had experienced in his life. The teenager was able to see how difficult it was for him to invest in new relationships that might also end and therefore cause pain. The worker used a review of their relationship (the authority theme) to help the client understand and take some control over the feelings that affected him and his life. The importance of being willing to risk by getting close to other people was a central theme of the ending discussions, helping in the transition work. Their own ending provided an important opportunity for substantive work on how he could deal with new relationships now that he was leaving the care of the agency.

In a final example, one worker explored the difficulty a married client was having in allowing himself to feel dependent on the female worker and the discomfort he felt at expressing his need for help. The difficulty seemed related to many of his notions of what a "real man" should feel. The work on the authority theme led directly to discussions of how hard it was for him to let his wife know how much he needed her.

In each of these examples, dealing with the authority theme served two distinct functions. It freed the working relationship from a potential obstacle and led directly to important substantive work on the contract. But this can only happen if the worker rejects the process-content dichotomy and instead searches for the potential connections between the two.

At times, the difficulty for the worker in being able to see and make use of the process-content connection is related to the emotions engendered in the worker by the manner in which the client uses process to communicate. In one example from the first session of a married couples' group I led and videotaped, all five men indicated on arrival that they were there to do whatever they could to help "straighten out" their wives. All of the wives indicated they were depressed and seemed to accept the role of *identified patient,* the client in a family system who is identified as having the problem. When clients accept the designation, the family cannot address the problems of the whole family and its dynamics. Two women in the group indicated that they were being seen by psychiatrists (all male in this example) who had prescribed drugs for their depression.

When I show this tape in my classes, many students express anger at one of the men, a 69-year-old who talks at great length about his wife's depression while she sits passively and silently. They become angry at me for not confronting this man at the start of the session, not demanding that he not speak for his wife. Some want me to "tell him to use 'I' statements!" The students are understandably upset about the sexist attitudes and myths that allow the male partner to deny his responsibility in the problem and to project all the difficulty onto his wife. I try to point out that the couples are letting me know in the first few minutes of the session exactly what the core of their problem is. This husband is saying to me:

> Social worker, if you want to see how we mishandle our marital relationship, just watch. I defend myself by taking no responsibility and defining my wife as the problem, while my wife accepts the blame outwardly, covering her rage with apathy and depression. Most helping professionals we have seen have colluded in accepting this maladaptive pattern of behavior as the definition of the problem.

I explain to my students that it is hard for me to get angry in a first session at clients who are acting out the very problem that brought them to the group for help. Understanding the connection between process and content reframes the interaction into a positive call for help. The process is the content.

In the detailed discussion of this example in Chapter 10, as I kept coming back to the male partner and reaching for his feelings while he was trying to talk about his wife, a noticeable lowering of his defenses took place. For example, he said, "My wife has been an inpatient for six weeks, and it has been a long time for her." I responded, "And it hasn't been easy for you either." After a short while, in a dramatic moment, he accepted some responsibility for his part in the problem when he revealed an incident of verbal abuse of his wife, which caused him to cry in the session. As is often the case, during the group meetings that followed this first session, the women who were defined as the problem emerged as strong partners in the relationship and internal group leaders. In effect, the depression was their call for help—a signal of their strength rather than their weakness. During later sessions, for some of the men, a confrontation by the worker was needed as they continued to defend themselves and minimize their own part in the problem.

Once again, workers' ability to manage their own emotions powerfully affects their ability to help clients manage their own feelings and problems. As a male group worker in the previous example, I found it fairly easy to tolerate the men's denial in the first session, to reframe the process as a call for help, and to reach for the related content. For a female worker, the struggle might be greater, as she would have experienced the oppression associated with sexism firsthand.

This important understanding was reinforced for me by an incident that occurred when I was teaching a class on group social work. By chance, the class consisted of all female students and myself, the only male and a symbol of authority. I commented on this class composition issue and pointed out that we all might want to monitor this to see if it affected our work. There was no immediate response.

A turning point came in the sixth class when Jane, a student working in the criminal justice system, was presenting her work with a client who had been convicted of assaults. She related his story, in which he told how he had assaulted and raped his wife. She had experienced the manner in which he told the story as threatening to herself. It was as if he were trying to intimidate her in the telling of the story. The class discussion proceeded as follows:

> I asked Jane and the class to take a few minutes and explore what it felt like to work with clients who had done things that were very upsetting to them. In this case it was rape of a woman; in another situation it might be an adult who had sexually abused a child. We were discussing examples of male oppression of women and children. I wondered what Jane and the other students experienced as they heard this client's story. There was a brief silence, followed by Jane saying, "I was furious at him!" The class members began to tell stories of clients who had engendered similar feelings in them. Some indicated that their feelings were so strong that they didn't think they could ever work with a client like this.
>
> After several minutes, I intervened and said, "I think this is going to be the hard part for you, trying to examine the feelings provoked by clients like this and deciding whether or not you can work with them as clients in their own right." There was a momentary silence, following which one student said to me, with great feeling and anger, "You could never understand what this means to us!" I was stunned by the force of her comment. The other students stared at me to see how I would respond. I remained silent for a moment and realized that as I was giving them my sage advice about examining their own feelings, I had not been feeling a thing.
>
> I broke the silence by saying, "You are absolutely right! I gave an intellectual response just then. It was easy to do, since I have not experienced the kind of gender oppression you have. What you said just now, about my never being able to understand, hit me very hard. I guess on this issue, you are going to have to help each other."

After I spoke, I could sense the tension lifting. I remained silent as they began to talk with one other about how they have tried to handle these situations. One student with work experience in shelters for battered women said she had felt she could never work with batterers, because she so strongly identified with the women. She went on to describe how she had taken a risk and co-led a group for male batterers with a male colleague. She had been amazed to find that she could retain her anger at the men but still start to overcome the stereotype of them she had developed. She found she had been able to hold the men accountable for their actions and take steps needed to protect the women still in their lives. Further, she could see the men as clients in their own right. She said she felt she now did a better job with women after having worked with the men. Discussion continued along these lines, with some students feeling they would be able to do it and others sure they could not:

> As we neared the end of the class, I pointed out that Jane was going to be seeing this client again this week. I wondered if we could help her think through how she might handle the next interview. Last time she had sat on her feelings because she needed to be "professional." What advice did [the students] have for her now? Jane indicated the discussion had helped already. She realized that she wanted to work with this client in spite of her feelings. If she didn't reach him, he eventually would abuse other women. She felt she should confront him with his behavior toward her the previous week. Others in the class supported this. I asked her what she might say. She tried to role-play how she could get back to the issue. Other students provided suggestions and feedback. I pointed out that she could also view his behavior toward her as demonstrating how he related to women—how he tried to exercise control through intimidation. Perhaps she could use the process in their work together and generalize to his relationship with other women. She agreed that it was worth a try, saying that at least she now felt she had a next step with him.
>
> I credited Jane and the class with their fine work. I thanked the student who had confronted me. I asked them all to keep an eye on this issue and said that if they ever felt in future classes that I was not really understanding their struggle they should say so as soon as possible.

This example is another illustration of process and task integration. The process in this class in relation to the authority theme (the relationship of the students to me) and issues of gender (a male teacher with female students) provided a medium for an important learning experience for the class. As the instructor I had to model in the class a way of using process to deepen the work on the content, especially at a time when my own feelings were influencing me in a powerful way. This was exactly what I was attempting to help them do with their clients. As is often the case in teaching and learning, more is "caught" than "taught."

Sharing Data

In a social work setting, we define *worker data* as facts, ideas, values, and beliefs that workers have accumulated from their own experiences and can make available to clients. Further, as Schwartz (1961) argues,

> The worker's grasp of social reality is one of the important attributes that fit him to his functions. While his life experiences cannot be transferred intact to other human beings, the products of these experiences can be immensely valuable to those who are moving through their own struggles and stages of mastery. (p. 23)

Sharing worker data is not only important because of the potential usefulness to the client, but the process of sharing the data also helps build a working relationship. The client looks to the worker as a source of help in difficult areas. If the client senses that the worker is withholding data, for whatever reason, the withholding can be experienced as a form of rejection. As a client might put it, "If you really cared about me, you would share what you know."

During my social work training, a student who was majoring in group work described his work with a group of teenage boys in a residential institution. They were planning their first party and were obviously underestimating the quantities of food and drink required. When I asked if he had pointed this out to them, he replied that he had not interfered, feeling that they would learn something important about planning. I was shocked and felt that if they ever found out he knew their supplies would fall short and had not told them, their significant learning would be about him.

While the skills of sharing data may sound simple, several misconceptions about how people learn, as well as a lack of clarity about the helping function, have served to make a simple act complex. The problems can be seen in the actions of workers who have important information for the client but withhold it, thinking that the client must "learn it for himself." These problems are also apparent in the actions of workers who claim to be allowing clients to learn for themselves while they indirectly "slip in" their ideas. This is most easily recognizable in interviews wherein the worker leads a client to the answer that the worker already has in mind. The belief is that learning takes place if the client speaks the words the worker wants to hear. In the balance of this section I shall identify some of the skills involved in sharing data and discuss some of the issues that often lead workers to be less than direct.

Providing Relevant Data

The skill of *providing relevant data* is the direct sharing of the worker's facts, ideas, values, and beliefs that are related to the client's immediate task at hand. The two key requirements are that the data be related to the working contract and that it be needed by the client for the immediate work.

Regarding the first requirement, if the worker is clear about the purpose of the encounter and that purpose has been openly negotiated with the client, then the worker has a guideline as to what data to share. A problem is created when the worker wants to teach something indirectly to the client and uses the interchange to subtly introduce personal ideas. This mistaken sense of function on the worker's part is rooted in a model in which the worker attempts to change the client by skillfully presenting "good" ideas. The problem is that the client soon senses that the worker has a hidden agenda, and instead of using the worker as a resource for the client's own agenda, he or she must begin to weigh the worker's words to see what is "up her sleeve." This hidden purpose often creates a dilemma for the worker in sharing data directly. On the one hand, sharing may help the client. On the other, imposing an ideology on the client treats the client as an object to be molded. This worker's ambivalence comes out in the indirectness with which the ideas are shared. If data are related to an openly agreed-on purpose, however, then the worker is free to share them directly.

The second requirement for directly sharing data is that the data be connected to the client's immediate sense of concern. Clients will not learn something simply because the worker feels it may be of use to them at some future date, even if it is related to the working contract. The attraction people feel toward ideas, values, and so forth is related to their sense of their usefulness at the time. One reason for the importance of sessional contracting is that the worker needs to determine the client's current sense of urgency and must share data that the client perceives as helpful.

From my observations of work with preadoptive couples in child welfare agencies, I can offer an example of sharing data that are not immediately relevant.

Individual or group work is often employed for the dual purpose of evaluating the couples' suitability as adoptive parents and helping them to discuss the adoption. Workers will often prepare a well-developed agenda for group meetings touching on all the issues that they feel the couples will need to face as adoptive parents. Unfortunately, such an agenda can miss the immediate concerns preadoptive parents have about adoption and about agency procedures for accepting and rejecting potential parents. In the following illustration, preadoptive couples in a second group session respond to the worker's query, "Should one tell adopted children they were adopted and when and how should I do this?" The important point to remember is that these couples are still waiting to hear if they are going to get children, and all are expecting infants. The issue of whether to tell will not present itself until a few years after the child has been adopted.

MR. FRANKS: I think you have to tell the child or you won't be honest.

MR. BECK: But if you tell him then he probably will always wonder about his real parents and that may make him feel less like you are his parents. (This comment starts a vigorous discussion between the men about how a child feels toward his adoptive parents. The worker uses this opportunity to contribute her own views indirectly; she already has in mind an "acceptable" answer to her question.)

WORKER: I wonder, Mr. Beck, how you think the child might feel if you didn't tell him and he found out later.

MR. BECK: (Recognizing that he may have given the wrong answer to the worker, who will also judge his suitability to be an adoptive parent) I hadn't really looked at it that way. I guess you're right—it would be easier to tell right away.

When the group had apparently reached the consensus that the worker had intended from the start, she shifted the discussion to the question of when and how to tell. Unfortunately, the urgency of the issue of "telling" was not an immediate one. Preadoptive couples are more concerned with how they will feel toward their adoptive child. This is a sensitive subject, particularly because preadoptive couples are not sure about the agency's criteria for acceptance. They worry that they will be rejected if they don't express the "right" attitudes and feelings. This cuts them off from a supportive experience in which they might discover that most preadoptive parents face the same issues, that it is normal for them to have doubts, and that the agency will not hold this against them. In fact, parents who are in touch with their feelings, including such feelings as these, are often the ones who make excellent adoptive parents. Because the worker was so occupied by "teaching" ideas for future use, she missed the most important issue. Compare the earlier example with the following excerpt. In this case, the parents raised the question of "Should one tell?" and the worker listened for cues to the present concern.

MR. FRIEDMAN: (Responding to a group member's argument that the kids would not feel they were their real parents) I can't agree with that. I think the real parent is the one that raises you, and the kids will know that's you even if they are adopted.

WORKER: You have all been working quite hard on this question of how your adopted child will feel toward you, but I wonder if you aren't also concerned about how you will feel toward the child? (Silence.)

MR. FRIEDMAN: I don't understand what you mean.

WORKER: Each of you is getting ready to adopt a child who was born to another set of parents. In my experience it is quite normal and usual for a couple at this stage to wonder sometimes about how they will feel toward the child. "Will I be able to love this child as if it were my own?" is not an uncommon question and a perfectly reasonable one, in my view.

MRS. REID: My husband and I have talked about that at home—and we feel we can love our child as if he were our own.

WORKER: You know we would like the group to be a place where you can talk about your real concerns. Frankly, if you're wondering and have doubts and concerns such as this, that doesn't eliminate you from consideration as an adoptive parent. Being able to face your real concerns and feelings is very much in your favor. You folks wouldn't be in this group if we hadn't already felt you would make good adoptive parents. It would be the rare situation in which we would have to reconsider.

The worker shared some important data with these clients that was relevant both to the general contract of the group and to their immediate sense of urgency. They learned that their feelings, doubts, and concerns were not unusual, that the agency did not reject prospective adoptive parents for being human and having normal worries, that the group was a place to discuss these feelings, and finally, that their presence in the group indicated that they were all considered good applicants. This comment was followed by a deeper discussion of their feelings toward their prospective child and the adoption. These included their concern over possibly getting a child from a "bad seed," their fears regarding the reactions of friends and family, and their anger about the delays and procedures involved in dealing with the agency. The data shared by the worker in these areas were more meaningful to these parents than was information about future problems. Agencies often offer follow-up groups for adoptive parents at key moments along the child's developmental path; these can focus more clearly on issues that are only theoretical in the preadoptive stage.

Providing Data in a Way That Is Open to Examination

Workers are sometimes fearful of sharing their own fears, values, and so forth because of a genuine concern over influencing clients who need to make a difficult decision. The unwed mother, for example, trying to decide whether to abort her child, to have it and keep it, or to have it and give it up for adoption faces some agonizing decisions—none of which will be easy. Each case holds important implications for her future. The skillful worker will help such a client explore in detail these implications and her underlying feelings of ambivalence. During this work, the client may turn to the worker at some point and say, "If you were me, what would you do?" Workers often have opinions about questions such as these but hold them back, usually responding to the question with a question of their own. I believe it is better for workers to share their feelings about revealing their opinions and then to allow the client access to their views as representing one source of reality. For example,

When you ask me that question, you really put me on the spot. I'm not you, and no matter how hard I try, I can't be you, since I won't have to live with the consequences. For what it's worth, I think the way you have spelled it out, it's going to be an awfully tough go for you if you keep the baby. I probably would place the child for adoption. Now, having said that, you know it's still possible that you can pull it off, and only you know what you're ready for right now. So I guess my answer doesn't solve a thing for you, does it?

Workers who withhold their opinion do so because they fear that the client would adopt it as the only source of reality. Rather than holding back, however, a worker can simultaneously allow the client access to his or her opinions while guarding against the client's tendency to use them to avoid difficult work. Schwartz (1961) describes this consideration that guides the worker's movements as follows:

> The first (consideration) is his awareness that his offering represents only a fragment of available social experience. If he comes to be regarded as the fountainhead of social reality, he will then have fallen into the error of presenting himself as the object of learning rather than as an accessory to it. Thus, there is an important distinction to be made between lending his knowledge to those who can use it in the performance of their own tasks and projecting himself as a text to be learned. (p. 11)

Thus far I have described how a worker can provide data to clients in a way that is open to examination by making sure that the client uses the data as just one source of reality. An additional consideration is to make sure that what is shared is presented as the worker's own opinion, belief, values, and so forth, rather than as fact. This is one of the most difficult ideas for many workers to comprehend, because it contradicts the normal pattern in society for exchanging ideas. Workers have an investment in their own views and will often attempt to convince the client of their validity. We are used to arguing our viewpoint by using every means possible to substantiate it as fact. New workers in particular feel they must present their credentials to clients in order to convince them that they know what they are talking about. In reality, however, our ideas about life, our values, and even our "facts" are constantly changing and evolving. A cursory reading of child-rearing manuals would convince anyone that the hard-and-fast rules of yesterday are often reversed by the theories of today. I have found that inexperienced workers are often most dogmatic in relation to areas where they feel most uncertain.

The skill of sharing data in a way that is open for examination means that the worker must qualify statements in order to help clients sort out the difference between their reality and the worker's sense of reality. Rather than being a salesperson for an idea, the worker should present it with all of its limitations. A confident and honest use of expressions such as "This is the way I see it" or "This is what I believe, which doesn't mean it's true" or "Many people believe this" will convey the tentativeness of the worker's beliefs. The worker must encourage the client to challenge these ideas when they do not ring true to the client. Any nonverbal signals of disagreement mean that the worker needs to reach for the underlying questions. For example, "You don't look like you agree with what I just said. How do you see it?" The client's different opinions need to be respected and valued. Even if all the experts support the idea, fact, or value at issue, it will only have meaning for the client if and when the client finds it useful. In many ways, the worker is a model of someone who is still involved in a search for reality. Every idea, no matter how strongly held, needs to be open to challenge by the evidence of the senses. The worker is asking the client to do the same in relation to life, and the client should not expect any less of the worker. Schwartz (1961) sums this up:

> As he (the worker) helps them to evaluate the evidence they derive from other sources—their own experiences, the experiences of others, and their collaboration in ideas—so must he submit his own evidence to the process of critical examination. When the worker understands that he is but a single element in the totality of the [group] member's experience, and when he is able to use this truth rather than attempt to conquer it, he has taken the first

step toward helping the member to free himself from authority without rejecting it. (p. 25)

Ethical Dilemmas in Withholding Data

The question of providing data has taken on increased complexity as governments and other funding agencies have introduced economic and political issues into the equation. For example, cost-containment efforts in the health care system have led government and private third-party payers to develop a standard of care that dictates how long, on average, a patient should remain hospitalized after a specific procedure. Reimbursement to the hospital is a fixed amount, which means patients who leave the hospital early earn money for the hospital, while those who stay longer lose money for it. Social workers often feel pressured to help "empty the bed" as quickly as possible. In some settings, the social work department has defined this as one of its major roles and may even be viewed as a "revenue-generating center" if it does its work effectively.

The ethical dilemma emerges when a patient, family members, or even the social worker feels that a patient may not be ready for discharge for any of various reasons, perhaps related to psychosocial issues or the availability of suitable community resources. The social worker has a responsibility to help the client to negotiate the system, which includes working to advocate for the client's interest (see Chapter 17). The question here is whether the social worker should inform the patient of his or her right to appeal a decision to discharge the patient early, even if the patient does not ask. What if the medical or administrative staff specifically ask frontline staff not to share such information unless it is requested?

Another, even more striking example comes from the political controversy surrounding a decision by the U.S. Supreme Court in May 1991, which supported the right of the government to cut off funding for family planning centers that informed pregnant clients of the option of abortion. Many of these clients were young, poor, people of color. Even if clients requested information on this option for dealing with an unwanted pregnancy, or even if the client's health and safety might be in danger, any center that provided such information or referred a client to an alternative source of counseling, where such information might be available, would lose its funding. Many centers indicated an unwillingness to accept such a restriction on free speech and a client's right to be fully informed so that they could make a sound, personal decision on the issue. However, what if a center decided that continuing to provide family planning services to poor women was so important that they would accept this restriction rather than closing down for lack of money? For many social workers, regardless of their views on the issue of abortion, denying access to this information to women dependent on public social services is sexist, racist, and classist. Should a social worker try to subvert the policy? Should a social worker refuse to work in such a setting?

The NASW Code of Ethics (National Association of Social Workers, 1996) makes clear the social worker's responsibility to the client in both of these examples. The ethical worker would need to make available to the client all information required by the client to make a sound personal decision about her health care or her options in the face of unwanted pregnancy. Acting ethically, however, might require courage and might well involve personal risk. This represents another example of how practice may be affected as much by ideological, financial, and political issues as by theories of human behavior.

Helping the Client See Life in New Ways

A specific form of data is important enough to be included as a separate skill category. These are the skills by which the worker helps clients re-examine perceptions (cognitions) about themselves, their life situations, or important people or systems in the client's life (such as husband, parent, school). Recall the discussion of cognitive-behavioral therapy from Chapter 1. To summarize briefly, clients have developed their views of life subjectively. Given the difficulties involved in communications, they quite possibly distort other people's actions or have internalized perceptions of themselves and their life experiences that lead to negative feelings and self-defeating behaviors. By exploring alternative views in collaboration with the client, the worker attempts to help a client rethink his or her life situation and correct negative and inaccurate "automatic thoughts" and perceptions. This approach is consistent with some of the solution-focused techniques and strategies discussed earlier.

One way the worker can do this is by identifying the person or part of the system that may still be reaching out to the client. In a way, the worker plays the role of the missing person, articulating during the interview the thoughts and feelings that might be lying beneath the surface. For example, here is an excerpt from an interview between a school social worker and an adolescent who is having trouble in a class.

CLIENT: Mr. Brown is always after me, always putting me down when I'm late with my work. I think he hates me.

WORKER: You know, it could be that Mr. Brown knows that you're having trouble keeping up and is really worried about your failing. He may be keeping after you to try to get you going again.

CLIENT: Well, it doesn't help. All it makes me do is want to miss his class.

WORKER: He might not realize that what he says makes you feel so bad. Maybe it would help if I could let him know that you feel he is really mad at you.

The work continued with a discussion of the student's fears of what might happen if the counselor talked to the teacher and the counselor's reassurance about how he would handle it. Mr. Brown was surprised at the student's feelings. He had been frustrated because he felt the student did not care about school. A joint meeting was held to begin to discuss what each really felt in relation to the child's schoolwork. This started to open doors for collaboration.

After a period of bad experiences, the blocks in the reality of the relationship become the client's (and sometimes the system's) only view of reality itself. The worker needs to help the client explore this maladaptive pattern and to break the cycle that prevents the client from connecting to people and systems important for success. At these moments a worker offers the possibility of hope and a next step by being able to share a view of others in the system that allows the client to glimpse some possibility of mutual attraction. This is only possible when workers themselves see these possibilities, described earlier as the areas of common ground. For example, when a worker helps a teenager see that his parents' setting of curfew limits may show that they care for him and recognize that he is growing up, the worker has not solved the problem, but at least he has put a new light on the interaction. The child care worker who helps a resident see that a parent who misses visits may not be saying that he does not care for the child, but rather that he really cares too much, also holds out the possibility of reconciliation.

The finding of my earlier research on this particular skill was not strong; however, the skill correlated with helping to develop a working relationship, perhaps indicating that the importance of sharing new ways of perceiving other people lies not in its content but rather in its impact on the relationship with the worker (Shulman, 1978). The client will have to use personal experiences to revise some thinking about people and systems during the time between sessions. It takes many years to build up stereotypes of oneself, parents, systems, and people in authority, and it will take more than the worker's words to change them. In expressing these alternative views, which can help the client see strengths and mutual attraction, the worker is making an important statement about views of life. The willingness to see the positive side in people's behavior and not to judge people's weaknesses may say a great deal to clients about how the worker might view them. This could contribute to strengthening the working relationship.

Sessional Ending and Transition Skills

As with beginnings and middles, endings contain unique dynamics and special requirements for worker skills. I call this phase the **resolution stage.** It is not unusual to find workers carrying out their sessional contracting, demonstrating sensitive work with clients regarding their concerns, but then ending a session without a resolution of the work. By resolution of the work, I am not suggesting that each session end neatly, with all issues fully discussed, ambivalence gone, and next steps carefully planned. A sign of advanced skill is a worker's tolerance for ambiguity and uncertainty, which may accompany the end of a session dealing with difficult work. If uncertainty is present for a client at the end of a session, then the resolution stage might consist of identifying the status of the discussion. The five skills discussed in the balance of this section include summarizing, generalizing, identifying next steps, rehearsal, and identifying "doorknob" communications.

SESSIONAL ENDINGS AND TRANSITIONS In an interview with a young lesbian woman who is anxious about "coming out" with her family, the client shares an important issue as the session comes to a close.

Before we examine these skills, a word on client activity between sessions is in order. Workers sometimes act as if clients have no life between sessions. They review an individual counseling session or a group meeting and then prepare to pick up the next session "where we left off." The worker needs to realize that the client has had life experiences, contacts with other helping systems, new problems that may have emerged during the week, and time to think about problems discussed in the previous session. After having given much consideration as to how to help a client with a particular problem, a worker may be surprised to discover that the client has resolved the issue between sessions. It would be a mistake not to recognize and legitimate these between-session activities. That is one reason why the sessional contracting skill, described at the beginning of this chapter, is so important.

Summarizing

In many ways, the client is learning about life and trying to develop new skills for managing it in more satisfying ways. It can be important to use the last moments of a session to help the client identify what has been learned. How does the client add up the experiences? What new insights does the client have in understanding relationships to others? What has the client identified as the next, most urgent set of tasks? What areas does the client feel hopeless about and need more discussion on? I believe the process of **summarizing** can help a client secure what he or she has learned. Sometimes the client summarizes the work, other times the worker does it, and sometimes they do it together. Note that summarizing is not required in all sessions. This is not an automatic ritual, but rather, a skill to be employed at key moments.

The skill is illustrated in the following excerpt from an interview with a mildly mentally challenged 16-year-old boy. He was discussing his relationship with his mother, who he feels is overprotective. After a painful session in which the worker asked the youngster to examine his own part in maintaining the problem, the resolution stage began.

(John paused and seemed thoughtful.)
WORKER: This hasn't been easy, John; it's never easy to take a look at your own actions this way. Tell me, what do you think about this now? (Silence)
JOHN: I guess you're right. As long as I act like a baby, my mother is going to treat me like a baby. I know I shouldn't feel like such a dummy, that I can do some things real well—but you know that's hard to do.
WORKER: What makes it hard, John?
JOHN: I have felt like a dummy for so long, it's hard to change now. I think what was important to me was when you said I have to take responsibility for myself now. I think that's right.
WORKER: If you did, John, then maybe your mother might see how much you have grown up.

The worker's request for summarizing the work constitutes a demand for work. Her silence allows time for the response, and her support ("This hasn't been easy") helps the client face a painful realization.

Generalizing

Earlier discussion underlined the importance of **generalizing**: moving from the specific to the general as a way of facilitating the immediate work of the client. The worker must often move from the general to the specific first, however, then move back to the general from the client's details. For example, one worker responded to a general comment by a mother about the difficulty of raising teenagers by requesting specific information on conflicts that week. As the mother gave details, problem by problem and system by system, the worker helped her generalize from the experiences to recognize how her learning applied to a whole category of experiences. This is a key skill of living, because it equips the client to continue without the worker and to use the newfound skills to deal with novel and unexpected experiences.

This skill is demonstrated in the continuation of the interview with the adolescent, started in the previous section. The discussion has moved to the importance of talking more honestly with his mother about his feelings. He balks and expresses doubts about being able to do this.

JOHN: I could never tell her how I felt, I just couldn't.

WORKER: Why not? What would make it hard?

JOHN: I don't know why, I just couldn't.

WORKER: Is it anything like what you felt when we discussed talking to your teacher, Mr. Tracy, about how dumb he sometimes makes you feel in class?

JOHN: I guess so, I guess I'm afraid of what she would say.

WORKER: You were afraid then that he would get angry at you or laugh at you, do you remember?

JOHN: Yeah, I remember. He didn't get mad. He told me he hadn't realized I felt that way. He has been nicer to me since then.

WORKER: Maybe it's also like that with other people, even your mother. If you could find a way to tell her how you felt, she could understand better. Do you remember how proud you were of yourself after you did it, even though you were scared?

Generalizing from the experience with the teacher is an important learning tool. Any life skill, such as the importance of being direct with one's feelings, becomes clearer as clients observe its power in different situations and then learn to generalize it to others.

Identifying the Next Steps

We have all experienced at one time or another the frustration of participating in some form of work that goes for naught because of lack of follow-up. A good example is a committee or staff meeting in which decisions are made but the division of labor for implementing the decisions is overlooked, and no action follows. The worker must make a conscious effort to help the client in **identifying the next steps** involved in the work. No matter what the situation, no matter how impossible it may seem, some next step is possible, and the worker will ask the client to discuss it. Next steps must be specific; that is, the general goal the client wishes to achieve must be broken down into manageable parts. In the example used earlier in this section, next steps included helping the young man plan to spend time thinking of some of the things he can do differently to help his mother see another side of him, identifying what he felt about the relationship, and deciding to confront his mother with his true feelings.

The next steps for an unemployed mother on welfare needing to find a job might include exploring day care centers for her child and meeting with an employment counselor. The next step for a couple in marital counseling who feel their relationship is worsening might be to identify specific areas of difficulty for discussion the following week. In essence, the identification of next steps represents another demand on the client for work.

Lack of planning by the client does not always represent poor life-management skills. It may also be another form of resistance. Talking about a tough subject may be difficult, but doing something about it may be even harder. By demanding attention to future, specific actions, the worker may surface another level of fear, ambivalence, and resistance that needs to be dealt with.

Sometimes the expression of understanding, support, and expectation by the worker is all the client needs to mobilize resources. There may be no easy way for the client to undertake the task, no simple solution, no easy resolution when two genuinely conflicting needs arise. For the client, verbalizing the dilemma to an understanding and yet demanding worker may be the key to movement. At other times, the client needs help figuring out the specifics of how to carry out the act. For example, the client may need some information about community resources.

Rehearsal

In the example of our adolescent, where the next step involved implementing some difficult interpersonal strategy, the skill of **rehearsal** was crucial; that is, he practiced what to say. Talking about confronting another person around difficult, interpersonal material is one thing, but actually doing it is quite another. A client who protests, "I don't know what to say" may be identifying an important source of blockage. A worker can help by offering the safe confines of the interview situation as a place for the client to rehearse. The worker takes on the role of the other person (boss, teacher, husband, mother, doctor, and so forth) and feeds back to the client possible reactions to the client's efforts. All too often, the worker skips this simple and yet powerful device for aiding a client by saying, "When the time comes, you will know what to say." Words do not come easily for most people, especially in relation to their most difficult feelings. With the help of a worker, clients may be able to find a way of saying what must be said, and with some successful rehearsal under their belts, may feel a bit more confident about doing it. We return to the illustration at the point the teenager said that he did not know what to say.

WORKER: Look, John, perhaps it would be easier for you if you practiced what you would say to your mother. I'll be your mother, and you say it to me. I can tell you how it sounds.

JOHN: You will be my mother? That's crazy! (Laughing)

WORKER: (Also laughing) It's not so crazy. I'll pretend I'm your mother. Come on, give it a try.

JOHN: (With a lot of anger) "You have to stop treating me like a baby!" Is that what you mean, is that what I should say?

WORKER: Yes, that's what I mean. Now if I were your mother I could tell you were really angry at me, but I'm not sure I would understand why. I might think to myself, "That's just like John, he always runs around hollering like that." Maybe you could begin a bit calmer and tell me what you want to talk about.

JOHN: I don't understand.

WORKER: Let me try. I'll be you for a minute. "Mom, there is something I want to talk to you about—about the way we get along. It's something that really bothers me, makes me sad and sometimes angry." Now I don't know, perhaps that's not so good either. What do you think?

JOHN: I see what you mean. Tell her I want to talk to her about how we get along. That's good, but I don't like the part about being sad.

WORKER: Why not? It's true, isn't it?

JOHN: I don't like to admit that to her.

WORKER: You mean you don't want to let her know how much it hurts? (John nods.) How will she ever understand if you don't tell her? Maybe there are things she would like to tell you, but she feels the same way.

As the conversation continued, the worker and John explored the difficult problem of real communication between a teenager and his mother, with this case a special variation on the theme because of the mental challenge. John tried to formulate what he would say, using some of the worker's ideas and incorporating some of his own. The worker offered to speak to John's mother or to be there during the discussion if John wished. The illustration underlines the value of rehearsal, as well as the way in which role play can reveal additional blocks to the client's ability to deal with important people in his life. A worker who thinks she has done a marvelous job in helping a client learn to deal effectively with an important person may find that additional work needs to be done when the client formulates the words to be used. In this case, the difficulty in sharing the client's sense of hurt with his mother was important, unfinished business.

Identifying "Doorknob" Communications

A **"doorknob" communication** is shared as the client leaves the office, often with his or her hand on the doorknob, or during the last session or sessions. This commonly observed phenomenon, described in the literature of psychotherapy, refers to any comments of significance raised by the client toward the end of a session when there is too little time to deal with them. We have all experienced a session with a client, or a conversation with a friend, when after a relatively innocuous discussion he says, "There is just one thing that happened this week." Then we hear that he lost his job or found out that his girlfriend was pregnant or received an eviction notice or noticed a strange lump in his groin. When reflecting on the session, the worker may see where the first clues to the concern were presented indirectly in the beginning phase. There may have been no clues at all.

A doorknob comment signals to the worker the client's ambivalence about discussing an area of work. The concern is raised at a time when it cannot be fully discussed. It may be a taboo area or one experienced as too painful to talk about. Whatever the reason, the desire to deal with the concern finally overwhelms the forces of resistance. The urgency of the concern, coupled with the pressures created by the lack of time left in the interview, finally results in the expression of the issue. This kind of comment is actually a special case of obstacles blocking the client's ability to work. As with all forms of resistance, it is a natural part of the process and provides the worker with an opportunity to educate the client about the client's way of working.

The skill involves identifying the process for the client. For example, in a session with a young woman concerned about her marriage, at the end of the second session the client directly revealed a difficult sexual problem between her husband and herself. The worker responded directly:

WORKER: You know you have just raised a really important issue, which we will not have time to talk about. You raised it at the end of a session. Were you feeling it was too tough to talk about, too uncomfortable?

CLIENT: (Brief silence) It is embarrassing to talk like this to a stranger.

WORKER: I can understand how it would be hard to discuss sex, I mean really talk about it, with anyone. You know, it's quite common for people to be reluctant to discuss this subject directly, and they often raise these kinds of difficult areas right at the end of the session, just like you did. (The client smiles at this.) Would it help if we started next session talking a bit about what makes it so hard for you to talk about sex? That might make it easier for us to discuss this important area. What do you think?

CLIENT: That sounds OK to me. This is a hard one for me, and I would like to discuss it.

WORKER: I think you are making a good start even raising it at the end.

The worker did not blame the client for her difficulty but instead offered support for the strength she had shown in raising the issue. By identifying the lateness of the comment, she started to build into the interview comments on the way in which the two of them work. The client's sophistication about how she works will increase, and after more such incidents, she can begin to understand and control how she introduces material into the interviews. In addition, the discussion of the source of the embarrassment in the interview will open up related feelings about the difficulty of discussing sex in our society, as well as the couple's problems with open communication in this area. The discussion of the process in the interview will lead directly into work on the content—another illustration of the process-content connection.

This discussion of sessional ending skills brings to a close our analysis of the work phase. The purpose of this analysis has been to identify some of the key dynamics in giving and taking help that follow the negotiation of a joint working contract. The discussing of doorknob comments is an appropriate one to serve as a transition to the next chapter on the skills of the ending and transition phase. In many ways, the last portion of the work with a client may have a "doorknob" quality in that some of the most important and hard-to-discuss issues may make their appearance at this time. This phase of work provides an opportunity for the most powerful learning of the entire encounter. It does not always happen that way, however, and in the next chapter we discuss why the ending phase can create problems if not handled well, or solve others if the worker is skillful.

Chapter Summary

A session in the middle phase of practice can be understood as having four stages: preliminary (sessional tuning in); beginning (sessional contracting); middle (work); and sessional ending and transition. The indirect nature of client communications at the start of a session, often related to client ambivalence, means that the worker must tune in to potential themes of concern prior to the session and remain tentative in the beginning phase, listening for cues of underlying issues. As a middle-phase session proceeds, the worker uses several groups of skills, called skill factors. These are designed to help the client tell his or her story and to do so with affect. They are also important for the worker to be able to challenge the illusion of work and to be able to find the connections between the process (way of working) and the content (substantive areas of work) in a session. These skill factors include elaboration, empathy, sharing worker's feelings, making a demand for work, pointing out obstacles to work, identifying process and content connections, sharing worker data, and helping the client see life in a new way. Several skills were also identified for bringing a session to a close and helping the client to make the transition to postsession activities or the next session.

Related Online Content and Activities

 Visit *The Skills of Helping* Book Companion Website at www.socialwork.wadsworth .com/Shulman06/ for learning tools such as glossary terms, InfoTrac College Edition keywords, links to related websites, and chapter practice quizzes.

The website for this chapter also features additional notes from the author and an additional process recording:

- Geriatric Psychiatric Ward Interview for Long-Term Placement: Sessional Tuning In

Endings and Transitions

B y examining the ending and transition phase of practice, this chapter completes our look at the phases of work for individuals. The chapter explores the unique dynamics and skills associated with bringing the helping process to a close and helping the client make appropriate transitions. Practice examples will illustrate how this phase can be the most powerful and meaningful phase of work as the client makes the third decision—the decision to deal with core issues that may have only been hinted at in the earlier phases. In this chapter we also examine the danger of this phase becoming a moratorium on work, in which both the client and the worker participate in an illusion. Specific skills for increasing the possibility of positive endings and transitions will be described and illustrated.

Recall that in the beginning phase, clients face a first decision. They must decide if they are prepared to engage with the worker—to lower defenses if needed and to begin to work. In the second decision, clients agree to take some responsibility for their part in problems and agree to face the emotional pain involved in work. In the third decision, clients must decide whether to deal with the most difficult issues as they approach the end of the working relationship.

The ending phase offers the greatest potential for powerful and important work. Clients feel a sense of urgency as they realize there is little time left, and this can lead to the introduction of some of the most difficult and important themes of concern. The emotional dynamics between worker and client are also heightened in this phase as each prepares to move away from the other. Termination of the relationship can evoke powerful feelings in both client and worker, and the worker can often connect discussion of these to the client's general concerns and tasks. The ending phase holds tremendous potential for work, yet ironically this phase is often the least effective. Missed appointments, lateness, apathy, acting out, and regressions to earlier, less mature patterns of behavior often characterize this phase of work. Moreover, the worker as well as the client show these behaviors at times.

In many ways the ending sessions are the most difficult ones for both worker and client. The source of the strain stems from the general difficulty we have in dealing with ending important relationships. Our society has done little to train us how to handle a separation; in fact, the general norm is to deny feelings associated with it. For example, when a valued colleague leaves an agency, the farewell party is often an attempt, usually unsuccessful, to cover the sadness with fun. The laughter at such parties is usually a bit forced. Similarly, children and counselors who have developed a close relationship in summer camps usually end by resolving to meet again at a winter reunion, which often does not take place. When someone moves to another city, leaving a close and valued friend behind, the two may occupy themselves with elaborate plans for keeping in touch by mail, phone calls, and visits, rather than mutually acknowledging the fact that the relationship will never be quite the same.

The worker-client association is a specific example of this larger problem. It can be painful to terminate a close relationship; when you have invested yourself meaningfully in a relationship, have shared some of your most important feelings, and have given and taken help from another human being, the bond that develops is strong. Strean (1978) has described the difficulties involved in terminating a close working relationship:

> Whether a social worker-client relationship consists of five interviews or a hundred, if the worker has truly related to the client's expectations, perceptions of himself, and transactions with his social orbit, the client will experience the encounter as meaningful and the worker as someone significant; therefore, separation from this "significant other" will inevitably arouse complex and ambivalent feelings. Still, a long-term relationship with a social worker will probably include more intense emotions at termination than a short-term one. A prolonged relationship has usually stimulated dependency needs and wishes, transference reactions, revelation of secrets, embarrassing moments, exhilaration, sadness, and gladness. The encounter has become part of the client's weekly life, so that ending it can seem like saying good-bye to a valued family member or friend. (pp. 227–228)

The ending process in a helping relationship can trigger the deepest feelings in both worker and client. As such, they can do powerful work during this phase, as well as ineffective work if the feelings are not dealt with. In this chapter, we explore the dynamics of the ending phase, identify some of the central skills required to make effective endings, and discuss how workers can help clients make transitions to new experiences.

The Dynamics and Skills of Endings

Schwartz (1971) described the ending phase in the group context:

> In the final phase of work—that which I have called "transitions and endings"—the worker's skills are needed to help the members use him and each other to deal with the problem of moving from one experience to another. For the worker it means moving off the track of the members' experience and life process, as he has, in the beginning, moved onto it. The point is that beginnings and endings are hard for people to manage; they often call out deep feeling in both worker and members; and much skill is needed to help people to help each other through these times. (pp. 17–18)

One of the dynamics that makes endings hard has already been mentioned. This is the pain associated with ending a relationship into which one has invested a great deal. In addition to the pain, a form of guilt comes up. Clients may feel that if they had worked harder in the relationship, played their parts more effectively, and risked more, then perhaps they could have done a better job. This guilt sometimes emerges indirectly with their saying, "Can't I have more time?" As with many of the feelings in the ending phase, this sense of guilt is often shared by the worker, who may feel that he or she should have been more helpful to the client. Perhaps if the worker had been more experienced, more capable, he or she could have been more helpful about some of the unresolved issues. Instead of understanding that the client will need to work continually on life's problems, the worker feels guilty at not having "solved" them all. Social work students often articulate this feeling as follows: "If only the client had a real worker!" Usually, they are underestimating the help that they have given.

The flow of affect between worker and client often increases during the ending phase. Because of the general difficulty of talking about negative and positive feedback, both worker and client may have many unstated feelings that need to be dealt with in the final phase. Things may have been left unsaid because of taboos against honest talk about the role of authority. This theme needs to be discussed before the relationship can properly end. For example, the worker may have said and done things that made the client angry. The reverse might also be true, with the worker somewhat frustrated over the client's inability to take risks and to open up to the worker. Providing this feedback, if it is related to the worker's real caring for the client, can serve to clear the air. Even if a client and worker have not been able to get along together and both face the impending separation with a sense of relief, the discussion at the end should be real. What was it about the worker that the client could not relate to? In turn, the client should know what made it difficult for the worker. There may have been misconceptions on the part of either or both parties, and discussing these can help clear them up. This could be quite helpful to the client, who may choose to enter another helping relationship at another time. The importance of feedback to the worker is also obvious. In addition, if the negative feelings are not dealt with, a client might transfer them to his next worker in the way that some of the examples on beginning showed in Chapter 3.

Even more difficult for worker and client to handle than the negative feelings may be the positive ones. It is not easy for any of us to tell those close to us, particularly people in authority, that they have meant a great deal to us. Moreover, many workers find accepting positive feelings with grace extremely hard to do. I have repeatedly observed workers responding to a client's genuine expression of thanks for all that the worker has done by protesting, "It wasn't really me, I didn't do that much, it was really all your work." One student in a social work training program asked during a class if it was all right for her to accept a fruitcake offered to her by an elderly client at the end of their work together. This was not a case in which a client was trying to pay a worker for her services, which were normally free. It was simply this woman's way of saying thank you to a worker who cared. I asked the student if the fruitcake looked good and suggested that if it did, the student ought to take it.

When I press workers as to the cause of their embarrassment in such cases, they usually point to the general cultural barriers against appearing immodest, as well as their belief that they could not have really given that much help. The second response reflects an underestimation of the effect of the help given. Clients respond with great feeling to a caring, honest worker. They are not usually as critical as the worker about what the worker might have done. Cultural barriers notwithstanding, mutual sharing of positive feelings at the end of a relationship matters a great deal because it enables both client and worker to value what has taken place between them and to bring it properly to an end. Both client and worker can carry feelings of regret for unspoken words long after they have stopped seeing each other, thus making the actual ending process protracted and more difficult. The problem with delaying endings is that it ties up energy that both parties need to invest in new relationships.

The timing of this phase depends on the length of the relationship. For example, in weekly counseling over a one year, the last 8 weeks or so constitute the ending process. In short-term work—for example six sessions—evidence of feelings about endings may emerge in the fourth or fifth session as the worker receives subtle cues to the client's reactions. While these cues mark the beginning of the ending phase, thoughts about the end are present even in the beginning. Often, a client will inquire early in the process, even after a first session that was helpful, how long the sessions will continue. Time is an important factor, and clients will orient themselves accordingly. A long break in the work phase, whether caused by the worker's illness, a vacation, or perhaps a holiday season, can provoke ending feelings as the client associates the break in the work with the ending to come. It is not uncommon to observe apathy, withdrawal, and other premature ending symptoms immediately after such a break.

Schwartz has outlined the stages of the ending process as follows: denial, indirect and direct expressions of anger, mourning, trying it on for size, and finally, the farewell-party syndrome. Each of these is discussed now in more detail, and the required worker skills, as suggested by Schwartz, are identified and illustrated.

Denial

Because of the general difficulty of facing feelings associated with the ending of important relationships, the first stage often reflects denial. The client neither admits to the impending ending nor acknowledges her feelings about it. During this first phase, the client may refuse to discuss the ending, insist on a nonexistent agreement with the worker to continue the sessions long past the ending date, "forget" that an ending date has been set, or request that sessions be prolonged because the client feels "unready." Unless the worker raises the ending issue, the client may simply ignore it right up until the last session. Workers as well may handle their feelings toward endings through denial and avoidance as, for example, when they leave a job. Many clients have greeted a new worker with stories of how their former workers had simply told them during their last session that they were leaving the agency. These clients are often left feeling that their workers did not care about them. In reality, these workers' denials are often rooted in the fact that they cared very much but could not face their own feelings.

If workers are to help their clients manage their feelings at this stage, then the workers must be able to manage their own feelings. They must address feelings about ending with the client as well as about ending with the setting, supervisors, and colleagues. In my workshops, often enough a field instructor will present his or her problem with a student worker who is having trouble ending with clients at the end of the school year. When I inquire if the supervisor has begun to discuss endings with the student, the supervisor is shocked to recognize that she or he is also avoiding dealing with endings. Once again, more is being caught by the student than taught by the field instructor.

The ending process must provide enough time for the worker and client to sort out their feelings and use this phase productively. A sudden ending will be difficult for both worker and client and will cut necessary work short. Because the worker wants the ending to be experienced as a process rather than as a sharp closure, the skill of **pointing out endings early** should be employed far enough ahead of time for this to happen. At the appropriate time, which depends in part on the length of the relationship, the worker reminds the client of the impending ending.

An example from a child welfare setting will help illustrate this skill. The client was a young man who had been a ward of the agency for 8 years. The worker had been in contact with him for the past 2 years. In 2 months, the client would be 18 years old, at which time he would leave the care of the agency. The worker set the ending process in motion by reminding the client of the ending date.

WORKER: Before we start to talk about that job interview next week, I wanted to remind you that we only have eight more weeks before you leave the agency. You have been with the "Aid" [the term used by clients to describe the Children's Aid Society] for a long time, and I thought you might want to talk about the change.

CLIENT: Only eight weeks? I hadn't realized it was coming so soon. That's great! After eight years I'm finally on my own; no more checking in, no more "Aid" on my back. You know, I'm going to really need that job now, and I'm worried about the interview.

WORKER: What's worrying you?

By commenting on the limited time left, the worker set the process in motion. The client's reaction reflected both denial of the impact and recognition of its importance. Schwartz describes the "graduation quality" of endings, when clients feel excited and ready to test their ability to make it on their own. The quick switch from the ending topic to the job interview represented resistance. The client did not want to talk about it right then. The worker was also reluctant to discuss it and thus allowed it to be dropped easily. In addition, he had identified the issue of ending only in terms of the agency, not in relation to their work together. This evasion by the worker signals his own ambivalence. Nevertheless, the statement of the impending ending is enough to set the process in motion.

In the following example, the worker presses for the ending feelings, but the client resists. Jane is the worker, and Thelma the client.

JANE: I will be leaving the office at the beginning of May, which gives us four more times together. I thought we might want to talk about this.

THELMA: I don't understand—why are you leaving?

JANE: I'm not sure if you remember, Thelma, but I mentioned to you last October that I was a student, which means I will be leaving my placement in early May. (Silence)

JANE: Thelma, you have turned quiet. What are you thinking about?

THELMA: (After a pause) I don't know what I am going to do now. I don't understand why you have to go.

JANE: Are you worried about what is going to happen with you after I leave? (Silence)

THELMA: Yes, but you are not leaving for a month, right?

JANE: Yes. I know that we have been seeing each other for many months now, and talking about my leaving is hard—it is hard for me too—but we both need to share our feelings and thoughts about this. (Silence)

JANE: I know that I am feeling a little sad. We have been through some tough times together. It's tough letting go.

THELMA: (Looking down; picked up a piece of her child's schoolwork) Hey, did you know that Gladys will be going into grade two next year? Ivan and I went up to the parent-teacher meeting last Friday and the teacher told us then. She even showed us some of her schoolwork. She is doing so well. (I tried to have Thelma elaborate on her feelings about the ending of our sessions, but she denied and avoided the opportunities, and the remainder of the session covered some superficial topics and how her children were doing.)

Although the client moved away from the painful work, the worker's strong message through the demand for work has sent a signal that this topic must be addressed. The worker understands and accepts the client's reluctance to continue, demonstrating a respect for the client's defenses. The stage has been set, and the worker will return to the ending theme in the weeks to come.

Indirect and Direct Expressions of Anger

The denial stage of ending is often followed by the client's indirect or direct expression of anger toward the worker. The circumstances of endings may vary; for example, the worker may be leaving the agency, as opposed to the client ending contact. While these circumstances may affect the intensity of the angry feelings, they are usually present even in those situations in which the ending seems perfectly reasonable. The anger may be expressed directly, by the client challenging the worker who has changed jobs: "How could you leave if you really cared for me?" The ending is perceived as a form of rejection, and the worker must be careful to face these feelings directly and not try to avoid them.

Alternatively, the cues to the underlying feelings may be communicated indirectly—for example, by lateness or missed sessions. Conversations with clients may take on an element of antagonism, and the worker may sense the hostility.

Sarcasm, battles over minor issues, or indications that the client is glad to see the relationship finally end may also be evidence of this reaction. However, under the angry feelings are often sad ones. It is therefore important to allow the expression of anger and to acknowledge it even though the worker's instincts make it hard to do so.

As with all stages of the ending process, the skill involved here calls for the worker to respond directly to the indirect cues. On perceiving these signals, the worker should point out the dynamics of the stage to the client. In the case of anger, the worker should reach past the indirect cue and encourage the client to express any angry feelings directly. The worker should also acknowledge the validity of the feelings and not attempt to talk the client into feeling differently. This direct acknowledgment is important even if the client does not take up the worker's invitation to discuss the anger but instead denies its existence. By **identifying the stage of the ending process**, the worker allows the client to increase her or his understanding of the experience. This can then free energies for productive participation in the ending-phase work. The worker must be honest in sharing any personal reactions to the client's anger.

The following illustration involves a worker in a residential setting who was leaving the home to attend graduate school. The day after she announced she was leaving, a young female client had a blowup at home with her mother and her mother's girlfriend and had to be brought to the center to be "in-house." The example illustrates clearly the struggle for the worker, who must deal with her own guilt and pain at leaving a client with whom she has become very close and a setting in which she has enjoyed working.

> I was sitting with Jane, ready to check in, and I knew by the look on her face that last night was a hard one. I felt two things: first, "This is such bull—it is so easy for her to do well at home, especially since her brother is gone" and second, "I just don't want to have to deal with her being in-house." I had just announced the day before that I was leaving the program, and I was exhausted. She gave me her book, and as I was reading it she started to cry and yell, "I hate your stupid system, I hate this program, I hate you!" As I sat there reading about her night, listening to her yell at me, I thought, "This child will never change." I was ready to give up from my own exhaustion, but I couldn't let her know that.
>
> Jane's mom wrote that Jane had a really hard night. She refused to clean her room, started throwing things, and called her mom and her lover bitches and homos. When her mom told her to get in the time-out area, Jane hit her. When her mom's lover tried to intervene, Jane kicked her. Jane's mom and her lover eventually left her alone (she's too big for them to restrain) and she calmed down after a while and went to sleep.
>
> I knew she was going to have an in-house suspension, and she knew too. I just didn't want to deal with it. She was still crying and saying, "I hate you! I'm glad you're leaving!" All of this process took about two minutes and then I knew I had to speak. I tried really hard to get my tone of voice to be supportive, yet confronting, and I said, "What do you think made you have such a hard time last night?" She kept crying and yelling, "I don't know!" I thought back to my announcement yesterday and remembered her reaction. "Are you mad at me for leaving?" I asked. She said, "No! I don't care! I hate you! You're a bitch!"
>
> At this point, I was thinking, "Oh yeah! Well you're a brat!" but instead I said, "I understand that you are having feelings about me leaving and that's OK.

What's not OK is that you swore at me. You have a reminder for that." (We use reminders for behavior management. When a kid gets a third reminder, they get a time out.)

"I know that my leaving is hard for you. Good-byes are always hard. You and I have worked together for a long time and we've had a lot of fun together. It's going to be hard for me to say good-bye to you, too. The important thing is that you tell me you're mad or whatever feelings you have. It's OK to feel that. It's not OK to swear and it's not OK to hit your mother."

She just continued saying over and over again, "I hate you." I felt irritated again. I said, "We have a choice: we can make the best of the next four weeks and really talk about what's going to be hard about saying good-bye to each other, or we can struggle and try to hate each other so it won't hurt. You know you're in in-house today because of last night, and we're going to use that time to do a little work around my leaving." With that, she cried louder and yelled, "No!" I could see how upset she was about this. She once told me I was the only person that she felt she could depend on, and here I was leaving her. I felt like saying, "OK, I won't go back to school, I'll stay here with you." She really pulls at me. So, knowing I had to say something else, I said, "This isn't easy for me either," and then I talked with her about how I felt about leaving her and saying good-bye to her.

We talked about fun things we had done together and looked at pictures, and all through it I kept assuring her that no matter what, I would never forget her. I was trying to keep good boundaries, but I started to really feel the sadness over my leaving. I was leaving a job I love, kids I love, and a team that had become my second family. I felt myself getting too emotional, so I cut the conversation short by saying, "We are going to be able to talk about this a lot before I leave." I was torn about what to do. I thought about continuing the conversation so she could understand that someone really did care about her and that her feelings about my leaving are all very normal. But on the other hand, I felt that if I had kept talking about it, I would've cried. When I said we'd be able to talk more about it, she said OK, got up, hugged me, cried, and said, "I'm going to miss everything about you." Well, that did it. I felt myself wanting to cry and my eyes were getting watery. I walked her over to the in-house area, got her settled, and then composed myself.

I wish that I could've let go of my own sadness. I am usually really good at sticking with hard feelings even though I can relate it to my own life. I sat through a check-in with a kid who was my absolute favorite kid I've ever worked with, and I had to tell him his mother was in the hospital. She went in while he was in school. I was his age when I found out my mother had cancer. He looked at me with tears in his eyes and said, "Is she gonna die?" I could sit with that. I was kind of annoyed that I couldn't stick with the conversation [with Jane]. I think this was different because it was so emotionally charged for me, the team and most of the kids. I also wish I could've addressed her behaviors more directly, too.

This excerpt illustrates the importance of supportive supervision. The worker's instincts were on target; however, she was afraid of showing her emotions too directly and was concerned about crying. At the same time, the worker demonstrated good professional work as she analyzed her own struggle with this most difficult ending. It is important that she did this, so that the process of her ending could be directly synthesized with the content of the work. Most children in residential settings are dealing with profound losses; and yet, the staff and the system often have great difficulty in dealing with losses themselves.

Mourning

Under the anger expressed by the client, there often lie feelings of sadness. When these emerge, the client begins the mourning stage of the ending process. During this stage, the client experiences fully the feelings he or she may have been struggling hard to suppress. When this happens, some clients express their feelings directly to the worker, while others do this indirectly. A normally active and involved client suddenly seems apathetic and lethargic. Interviews are marked by long periods of silence, slow starts followed by minimal activity, and conversations that trail off rather than end. One worker described arriving at a woman's home to find the blinds drawn at midday and a general feeling of gloom pervading the usually bright room. In part, the difficulty in working reflects the client's unwillingness to open up new areas just when the work seems about to end. In addition, the work left to the end is often the most difficult for the client, adding to the ambivalence. Essentially, the feeling is one of sadness over the ending of a meaningful relationship. The denial and anger are past, and the ending must now be faced.

Two important skills in this phase involve acknowledging the client's ending feelings and sharing the worker's ending feelings. As we have seen, the skill of acknowledging and sharing worker's feelings is both crucial to the helping process and difficult for workers to employ. In the ending phase, this difficulty is compounded by the intensity of feelings and our society's taboos against their direct expression. Workers have suggested that even when they did pick up cues to the sadness, they did not acknowledge the feelings, because they felt somewhat embarrassed. "How can I tell clients I think they are sad because we won't be seeing each other anymore? It sounds like I'm taking my impact on the client and blowing it out of proportion. And anyway, how will it feel if the client says I'm all wet?" The worker feels vulnerable to the risks of commenting on the importance of the relationship. This also holds the worker back from expressing personal feelings toward the client. As one worker said, "It doesn't sound professional for me to tell a client I will miss him. He will think I'm just putting him on. Won't that be encouraging dependency?"

In most cases the reluctance to share feelings stems from the difficulty the worker has in coming to grips with his or her own sadness when separating from a valued client. The flow of affect between the two has first created and then strengthened a bond that the worker values. The significance of this relationship needs to be recognized as it comes to an end. Often, workers must take the risk of expressing their own feelings before clients will feel free to do the same. Both may feel vulnerable, but it is part of the worker's function, and a measure of professional skill, to be able to take this first, hard step. Let us look at an illustration of an 18-year-old foster child about to leave the care of the agency:

WORKER: You seem quiet and reserved today. You don't seem to have much to say.
CLIENT: I guess I'm just tired.
WORKER: And then again, this is almost our last session together. I've been thinking a lot about that, and I have mixed feelings. I'm glad to see you getting ready to go out on your own, but I'm really going to miss you. We've been through an awful lot together in the past two years. (Silence) How about you? Are you a little down about our ending too?

CLIENT: (Long silence) I guess we have gotten close. You've been my best worker—although sometimes you were a real pain.

WORKER: Why do you feel I was your best worker? It can be important to talk about this.

After the mutual acknowledgment of feelings, the worker took another step by asking the client to reflect on the relationship. The client had experienced the breakup of many important close relationships and had sharply felt the resulting rejection and pain. Many people develop armor against such vulnerability, an unwillingness to risk getting close again only to experience another loss. Once again, an important synthesis between process and content is possible. Understanding this worker-client relationship can be an important aid to the client in his future efforts to make close contacts, that is, his transitions (discussed later in the chapter).

In the following discussion and process recording, a social work student describes the difficulty of sharing her own feelings as she and her client approached the end of the field placement:

Beginning termination was a difficult and emotional process for both me and my client, Joan. As I attempted to discuss the ending of our relationship, Joan stated that she wanted her next income assistance check mailed to her home address. I asked her why. Joan replied that by doing so, she would no longer have to go into the office for her check.

WORKER: Joan, I don't really understand that. You've always picked your checks up. In fact, you preferred it that way, didn't you?

JOAN: Well, yeah, but I'm getting tired of seeing the same people, and I think they're tired of seeing me every month. (Silence; Joan looking away)

WORKER: Joan, is it that you don't want to see me at the end of this month? (Silence) Check days have been our "hi/keep in touch days." I feel like you want to avoid seeing me on my last check day here.

JOAN: Maria, what am I going to do without you?

WORKER: Joan, do you feel you really need me?

JOAN: I need somebody to talk to. Well, sometimes I feel like I don't. Other times I feel like I'm going to fall apart. I don't know what I'm going to do without you.

WORKER: Joan, I know we've been through a lot and shared a lot together, but to be honest, I feel you're much stronger now than you were in the beginning, and I feel you can make it without me. That's not to say I think things will be easy for you, but I've seen a growth in your own self-confidence. You're beginning to take more risks, make your own decisions.

JOAN: Yeah, my self-confidence has increased slightly, hasn't it?

WORKER: It really has, Joan. I know it's going to feel weird and empty without me, but you know you've made a lot of new friends in the past few months at the center, at your new place. Sherri has been a real support and a good friend for you, hasn't she?

JOAN: Yeah, she has, she really has. But it won't be the same. I just know it.

WORKER: It won't be the same for me either, Joan. You know I've never had an ongoing involvement with any client before. It feels weird to think that I won't be your worker after May. Right now I can't describe exactly how I feel, but I know it's going to feel weird without you. I know I'm going to keep thinking about you, about how you're doing. I know I'm going to miss you and Don (her son). (Joan silent; looking down) I feel you'll make your goal (to be self-dependent and off of income assistance). It'll be slow and you'll have to take a lot of steps, but I really feel you'll do it. I wish I could be there to see that.

JOAN: Yeah, I'm going to make it!

WORKER: You sound determined. That's another change I've noticed.

JOAN: Yeah, I am more determined. I have to get off I.A. (income assistance). The changes in me have been because of you.

WORKER: Well, I may have helped you, but the changes came from you. (Joan shrugged her shoulders.) Joan, what kind of a worker have I been for you?

Joan stated: (1) that I was the first worker that ever shared personal feelings with her. She felt that this made it easier for her to discuss problems and to relate to me; (2) that I expressed a great deal of concern for her, but at times Joan felt I was overly concerned; (3) that in the first term I seemed to think I was always right, whereas in the second term I was easier to talk to, more relaxed, more open; (4) that whenever I was late, Joan felt I was treating her like "scum," even though I did apologize to her each time. As Joan began to know me better, she realized that my apologies were genuine, that I really did care for her.

I also relayed my feelings to her regarding our relationship. For example: (1) I struggled with her resistance; (2) as I noticed more strength and confidence in herself, I felt threatened—I wanted to keep "protecting" her; (3) I've learned a great deal about single parenthood, the hardships and difficulties associated with sole child-rearing, with no outside support. Near the end of the session, we began to discuss Joan's feelings regarding new beginnings with a new worker in a new office. Joan stated that prior to myself, she had had two good workers. Both these workers were older and had children of their own. Joan hoped that her new worker would also be older; she felt this would help in the new beginnings. This issue was tabled for our next session. As I was leaving, Joan stated that she would see me on check issue day.

The discussion about what the work has meant is interactional in nature: Both the client and the worker have been affected by the relationship and the evaluation of how things have gone, and what has been learned is important for both parties. The client needs to see the worker as being involved in a process of continual growth and learning—not, as many clients fantasize, as a "finished product." The worker exemplifies the value of reflection, analysis, learning, and growth. When the worker shares that at times she felt "threatened" by the client's growth, she forces the client to begin to see this worker (and possibly future workers) as human and vulnerable.

Trying It On for Size

Earlier I referred to the graduation quality of the ending. As the client moves to the final sessions, the worker often senses an effort to test out new skills and the ability to do things independently. It is not unusual to have a client report having tackled a tough problem or dealt with an issue that earlier on she or he would have first discussed with the worker. The worker senses the client's positive feelings of accomplishment and employs the skill of crediting the client. This consists of a direct acknowledgment of the client's ability to "go it alone."

When the client remains with the service and the worker leaves, discussion of the new worker often begins to dominate the conversation: "Who will the new worker be, and what will he or she be like?" This can represent "trying the change on for size" as well as being an expression of anger toward the worker.

I have experienced this process during my classes when I have worked with students during a year-long course. The way we interact is, in some ways, a model of the process we study, although both the content and my function differ from that found in social work practice. Nevertheless, I can remember times during the last classes when I found it impossible to get into the class conversation. When I would comment on the work under discussion, the students would look at me briefly and then continue to talk as if I were not there. After a few such attempts to enter the conversation, I would comment that it felt like I was not in the classroom, but again, the students would merely look at me and then return to their conversation. As I sat back and listened, I could hear the students carrying on important discussion and analysis of practice within the peer group and without my help. This was a part of our ending process.

The Farewell-Party Syndrome

Schwartz uses the term **farewell-party syndrome** to refer to the tendency to "pad" ending discussions by concentrating only on the positive aspects of the relationship or even by planning a celebration. All working relationships have both positive and negative aspects to them. The worker must not allow the ending discussion to get so caught up in the positive feelings that an honest analysis of the content and process is bypassed. The worker should reach for negative evaluation to encourage the client not to hold a "farewell party."

Thus far I have detailed some dynamics and skills involved in the ending process with individuals. Parts III and IV examine further illustrations in the family and group context and address some of the differences in the dynamics. In addition to the process of ending, the worker must pay attention to the substantive content that can make the ending important for the client's learning. In the next section, I review those skills of the ending phase that help the client to use the experience with the worker to make an effective transition to new situations that she or he may face alone.

The Skills of Transitions

A new beginning is always inherent in the ending of a working relationship. As the former foster child, now a young adult, leaves the care of the agency, she begins a new phase of her life and faces a new set of demands. Some of these are similar to those faced by any young person of the same age, but others are unique to someone who has been the ward of an agency. The ex-con who is completing the term of parole begins to function in society without the supervision and support offered by the parole officer. The patient who is leaving the rehabilitation center must face negotiating the outside world, even though she is still limited by the effects of the accident or illness. The former narcotics addict who leaves the treatment center must deal with many of the same pressures and demands on the street that had helped lead to the addiction. This time, the ex-addict needs to make it without the support of either the worker or the drugs. The adolescent delinquent leaving the protection of the wilderness camp may be facing again a family that has changed little during his time away. For each of these clients, the time of ending is also the time of a powerful beginning.

The worker needs to pay attention to this process of transition during the ending phase by focusing on the substance of the work together as well as on the process of ending. In work that has gone well, clients may have discovered new things about themselves, their strengths and weaknesses, their patterns of behavior under pressure, and their abilities to handle problems. They may also have learned new ways to view some of the important people and systems they must deal with. Ending should be a time for adding up what has been learned.

Because the client's work is never really finished, clients end with some new ideas about how to deal with issues in their lives, as well as ending with an agenda for future work. By asking the client to identify the specific areas he or she needs to work on, the worker communicates that the learning process does not end with the end of their relationship. The worker also sends a message that he or she feels the client will be capable of continuing the work.

Next, workers can help clients synthesize the process and content of the ending phase. As with all phases of the relationship, the interaction between workers and clients offers fertile areas of learning related to the contract. Workers can use the dynamics of the ending process to help clients generalize from their learning to new experiences.

Finally, workers can help clients make direct transitions to new experiences and to other workers and alternative sources of support that may be available for their use. These tasks of the ending phase are examined in the next three sections.

Identification of Major Learning

Endings are a time for systematically evaluating the helping experience. The worker asks the client to reflect on their work together and to identify some of the things that have been learned. One week before the final session, for example, the worker could ask the client to prepare to share these important ideas during the last week. In the very first session, the worker asked the client for feedback on the issues that seemed to be of concern. Now that the sessions are ending, the worker and client need to review jointly where things stand on these issues and others that may have emerged during their work together. The worker must demand specifics; a general summing up is not enough. When the client says that the sessions with the worker were valuable because the client has learned so much about himself or herself, the worker might respond, "Exactly what was it you learned that was important to you?" This process helps the client consolidate the learning. A second benefit accrues from the client's recognition of newly developed abilities. This can strengthen the client in preparing to end. The worker can participate in this process as well, because in any real interactive experience, the worker will learn from the client. What does the worker now understand differently about the client's problems and about the worker's personal and professional self? The summing up should include discussion of what both worker and client are taking away from the experience. The following example illustrates this adding-up process.

> Christine came in because she felt so bad that she hit her oldest daughter whenever she became angry. It was established that she wanted techniques of parenting that would prevent her from hitting her child. We openly discussed her lack of bonding with this oldest daughter, and the poor marital situation Christine found herself in. Christine tried but could not get her family to participate. This was to be the second-to-last session (fourth) with a follow-up in February (2 months).

Worker: Let's review a little where we started and where we are now.

Chris: The reason I came was because I had been hitting Raphaelle, much more than I felt good about. But things have been going very well. In the beginning I thought that if I could stop hitting her altogether, I would feel really happy about it. Well, I haven't struck her once, and I don't even feel like it. It is going very well.

Worker: And it's been about three months.

Chris: It almost seems so far away now.

Worker: You mean from the time we started?

Chris: Yes, it seems almost a little unreal—do you know what I mean?—a little embarrassing.

Worker: Well, it has been some time since October, but it was all very real then.

Chris: No kidding. But it feels good to end, because I don't feel I need it anymore—things are going well. But it does feel good that I can come back in February.

Worker: Why did you say it is embarrassing?

Chris: It was embarrassing to even come in and state that I was hitting my children. I had to talk to my family doctor and explain it all to him. I wish I could have solved it within the family without outside help.

Worker: I guess it seems easier to solve this hitting now, eh?

Chris: Well, this is it, but I am glad I came because I might still be hitting Raphaelle. You know, just the commitment of getting help was the biggest factor.

Worker: Asking for help makes you vulnerable, but ironically it also makes you stronger. Is there anything else that's different for you and Raphaelle?

Chris: For some reason I look at her a little different. I see her having some problems, but I see her also as older. Remember how you said that she is becoming a teenager and won't take hitting anymore. I also think like she could be gone in five years. Where have all the years gone? (Showing sadness)

Worker: What is happening for you right now? (Some discussion followed about Raphaelle.)

Chris: I guess I also feel that things aren't going so well between my husband and me. I suppose that will always be there.

Worker: Well, you know I always did feel it was a shame that you couldn't get him to participate in these sessions. But maybe that's for another time and under different circumstances. Have things deteriorated between you two? I guess I am asking if you need to spend some time on this issue even though he won't come in?

Chris: No, not really. I guess I don't really want to dwell on the negative. I am glad for me and as you said, that's what counts.

Worker: Sure, but the door is open. I don't know how aware you were but a couple of times I really pushed hard for you to bring your husband into these sessions.

Chris: (Laughing) Oh, I felt it! (This was followed with some discussion about this issue.)

Worker: You seem to have consolidated some strengths and determination. You seem to put your foot down. I guess it will take some adjustment for your relationship (with husband). Somehow you have to find a way to support each other. You do tend, it seems to me, to walk a bit of a tightrope sometimes and as a result, you end up having to give quite a bit, even when you need to get your own needs met.

CHRIS: You know how you said, last time, that I am a giving person. My husband just thinks I am a selfish manipulator. I think he is more right. But it sure is nice to hear.

WORKER: You mean that you are a giving person?

CHRIS: Yes. (A little teary)

WORKER: It's hard to hear, isn't it?

CHRIS: It's just not something I heard before. My husband says I do some nice things but doesn't say I am a nice person. I don't think of myself as a nice person.

WORKER: It can be your secret that you are a nice person.

CHRIS: (Laughing) What do you mean?

WORKER: Well, we'll say good-bye and we'll see each other only one more time in the end of February, but you'll remain a nice person, even though I won't say it anymore.

CHRIS: It's nice of you to say so and it's funny but you have to hear it to believe it, but I have also thought about it as well and that makes a difference. (We reviewed some of the main themes of the sessions and discussed what was help-ful and what wasn't. We contracted to see each other at the end of February. We planned to have a short session in February to see if things are still OK with her and Raphaelle.)

The following is the end of our follow-up session in February, a short half-hour session in which Christine brought in a little book as a gift.

WORKER: Well, maybe we can just say good-bye?

CHRIS: Good-bye, John, and thank you.

WORKER: You're welcome; good-bye, Christine, good luck to you and your family. It's funny, but I feel a little sad about saying good-bye.

CHRIS: I feel a little bit sad as well. Just a little sad but I am also happy that I came and now I don't feel I need to come anymore. I felt good about having this six weeks to see if I could keep it up.

WORKER: In retrospect, that does seem like it was good. Anyway, you have our tele-phone number, and don't hesitate to call even if it is to say hello.

CHRIS: Yes, thanks a lot for that. Bye, John, and good luck with your studies. You're not a bad social worker (laughing).

WORKER: Thanks, good-bye, Christine and of course thanks for that beautiful little book.

Identification of Areas for Future Work

The worker should convey to the client that the work will continue after the ending. It is all right for the client to have unanswered questions, to be faced with unsolved problems, and not to have life all figured out. The client began the experience with certain problems or life tasks and has learned how to handle some of these more effectively than at the beginning. The experience ends with other problems or life tasks ahead. The difference now is that the client has learned how to deal better with these concerns. If some of the uncertainties and accompanying ambiguity are detailed, the worker must resist the temptation to "jump in" and try to "solve" these last-minute concerns. Part of the learning experience involves being able to live with some uncertainties. The worker's task is to help the client inventory these unresolved issues, create an agenda for future work, and use their experience together to determine how the client can continue to work on these concerns. The worker must also resist the temptation to reassure the client who expresses doubts about competency. Acknowledging and understanding these fears of not being able to continue alone is more helpful. The worker needs to convey a belief in the client's potential to tackle future tasks without in any way attempting to minimize the feeling that the going may be rough.

To illustrate this point, we return to the ending sessions of the 18-year-old who was about to leave the care of the child welfare agency. The worker had asked the client to identify those things he had learned as well as those areas he still felt he needed to consider. This excerpt from the last session begins as they review what the client has learned.

WORKER: What ideas hit you hard during our discussions together? What will stay with you?

CLIENT: I learned that I have to be more responsible for myself. That was important to me.

WORKER: Exactly what do you mean by that?

CLIENT: Well, I used to walk around with a chip on my shoulder. All my problems were someone else's fault. I was angry at my mother for giving up on me, it was always my foster parents who were the cause of my fights, and the "Aid" (Children's Aid Society)—well, I hated the place.

WORKER: And how do you see it now?

CLIENT: Well, I did have it tough. It wasn't easy moving from home to home, never having the kinds of things normal kids had. But I think I understand better that what happens to me from now on is pretty much up to me. I can't blame everyone else anymore. And the "Aid," well, for all my complaining, with all the changes in foster homes, the "Aid" has been the only place I can call home.

WORKER: I guess you have a lot of mixed feelings about this place, but now that you're leaving, a part of you is going to miss it.

CLIENT: (Silence) Even with all the complaining and all the crap I had to take, I'm still going to miss it. You know, I'm scared about being on my own.

WORKER: Sure it's scary. What exactly are you afraid of?

CLIENT: I'm going to have to make it on my own now. I'm starting this new job, and I'm worried about how I'm going to do. And what if I don't make any friends in the rooming house? There are other people my age there, but it's hard to get to know them. It's not like a group home where you spend a lot of time together and you always have the house parents to talk with.

WORKER: So you have two questions to work on: how to make it on the job and how to make some new friends.

The two critical tasks identified in this discussion are major ones for any young adult and quite appropriate to this client's phase of life. As he moves into adulthood, he must tackle issues related to how he will fit into the world of work, and he must also begin to shift his relationships from parental figures to his peer group. Having moved through the child welfare system makes these tasks more difficult for him than for others. His life has been marked by so many broken relationships that he has become reluctant to risk being hurt again. In the next segment, we continue this illustration to demonstrate how the worker-client ending process can be directly related to the content of the work.

Synthesizing the Ending Process and Content

If we keep in mind that the worker-client relationship is one of many the client deals with in life and is in fact just a special case among all relationships, then the experience can be used to illustrate important themes. The relationship can be viewed as a training ground for the client. Skills that have been developed in dealing with the worker are transferable to other situations. The astute worker can tune in to identify connections between the worker's own interactions with the client at the ending. For example, to return to our illustration, this client had to overcome his guardedness and establish a close relationship with the worker. It was a long time before the client allowed himself to be vulnerable, to risk being hurt. In effect, the client needed to learn what we must all learn: For our life to have meaning, we must risk getting close to people, even though this may mean getting hurt sometimes. If we go through life remembering only the hurt, then we may build a wall between ourselves and people who could provide comfort and support. The typical "graduate" of the child welfare system has been hurt so often that he or she often begins a new relationship with the expectation that it will not work out. Such children may seek out close ties (for example, marry early) but will hold back on really investing themselves. This worker recognized that intimacy is a central issue for clients who must now risk themselves with their peers in the rooming house and elsewhere. Eventually they will face the same problem as they consider marriage.

Let us return to the interview as the worker tries to help the client learn from their experience together.

WORKER: You know, I think what we have gone through together might offer you some ideas about how to handle this friendship question. Do you remember how it was with us when we first met?

CLIENT: Yeah, I thought you would be just another worker. I wondered how long you would stick around.

WORKER: As I remember it, you made it pretty tough on me at the beginning. I had the feeling you wouldn't let me get close to you, because you figured it wouldn't last too long anyway.

CLIENT: That's right! I didn't build it too high 'cause I knew it was only temporary.

WORKER: It was frustrating for me at first because I couldn't seem to get anywhere with you. You seemed determined not to let anything get going between us. Somehow, it worked out. Because I feel real close to you, it's going to hurt now not to be seeing you all the time. I knew from the first day that someday we would have to say good-bye and it would be painful. No matter how much it hurts now, I wouldn't want to have missed knowing you this way. It was something special for me, and I will remember you.

CLIENT: (Silence—obviously struggling with emotion) I'm glad you stuck with me. You're the only worker who really did.

WORKER: What can you take out of our experience that relates to you and the people at the rooming house, or wherever you meet friends—at work, the Y?

CLIENT: You mean the same thing could happen there? If I build the walls too high, they might not get through?

WORKER: You said before that you had discovered how responsible you are for a lot of what happens. I think that's true in this case as well. If you're afraid of risking yourself, of being rejected, of getting close to these people and then losing them, then you will be alone. Maybe the most important thing you have learned is that you can get close if you want to, that it does hurt when you say good-bye, but that's life. You pick yourself up and find new people to get close to again.

CLIENT: You mean like the kids at the rooming house?

WORKER: Right! And on the job and maybe at the Y, or other places where you can meet people your own age.

CLIENT: So it's up to me.

WORKER: It usually is.

In many ways the worker is sharing his own learning with the client. Every time the worker starts with a new client and finds himself investing feeling, he must do so with the knowledge that it will hurt to say good-bye. This is the gift a worker can give to a client. The best way for workers to handle their own feelings of loss is to share them in the ending and then begin with a new client.

Transitions to New Experiences and Support Systems

As the worker brings the relationship to a close, it helps to identify what it is about their work together that the client valued and to discuss how the client can continue to receive this support. In the previous illustration, a worker helped a client think about how he might shift his need for support to a peer group. This suggestion made sense for his stage of development. In another case, a worker might help the client identify family or friends who could offer help if the client will use them, employing the skills developed while using the worker. In cases where a transfer is made to a new worker, some discussion of the strengths and weaknesses of the present working relationship can help a client develop a strategy for using the new worker more effectively. Community resources for social, vocational, and counseling needs can also be identified.

In addition, workers can convey to the client that the counseling process is not necessarily a one-time experience that leaves the client capable of facing all of life's crises. It is helpful for getting through a particular period of life and may be needed again at different points in life and at different stages in the life cycle. For example, a young child who is a survivor of sexual abuse may need immediate help to cope with the trauma and the resulting disruption of her family. New issues will emerge as she enters her teen years, and a mutual-aid support group may be helpful to her, and to her nonoffending parent as well, during this normally difficult transition stage. As a young adult, when she is getting ready to enter into partnerships of her own, and again later, as a new parent, she may need support in coping with the normative issues of the transitions in age and status that are compounded by the unique issues facing survivors. An ending at any one stage should help the client realize she has not "solved" her problems but instead has learned how to use social support to cope with them. She should not see it as a sign of failure if she needs help again.

Finally, a physical transition to the new situation can also be made. For example, a joint session with the new worker can ease the change, or a worker from a residential center might accompany a resident on visits to a new foster home. In many circumstances, concrete steps can be taken, in addition to conversation about endings and transitions.

The following recorded material provides a complete illustration of a session in which a social worker in a psychiatric residential setting tells a teenage client that she is leaving the agency. Their relationship has been very positive, using dance therapy as a medium for helping the client express her thoughts and feelings. Even as the worker begins to deal with her own feelings and those of the client, she incorporates first steps for affecting a transfer of the work to other support staff.

Sandra arrived in a good mood and with a bouncy step and said, "I've been looking forward to this. I'm glad to get back." She was talkative and indicated she hadn't had enough activity or exercise over Christmas, felt sluggish—and had difficulty with her feelings. She said Christmas was hard for her—she missed me while I was on holidays, and she tried not to get into anything too heavy.

As we were talking, I began to put on the videotape, and Sandra noticed the video equipment. I asked whether she was really energetic, saying, "We've been away for a while. Was it difficult to start again?" Sandra said it was a bit scary. She not sure how deep she wanted to get in—we were working on some very frightening things—she wanted to get into it but felt safer if she avoided it, too. I said, "Sounds right on—you've been taking lots of risks with me, and our dance work has been getting deeper and deeper." I pointed out that safety was a must if she was to go on with it, and we must build and establish that important trust. I said, "This was really important, Sandra, and we have to be honest with each other and not take things for granted."

I stopped working on the equipment and said, "Before we go on, I've got something to tell you first—we have to talk about it—I'm going to be leaving in two months, on April 2." I choked a little as I said this and revealed feeling in my voice, and a tear ran down my face. I stopped for a moment, and Sandra stepped forward to me and put her arms around me in a hug, and I put my arms around her. We held each other for several moments. She stepped back and looked me directly in the eyes and said, "But why are you going? Why?" I answered, "Sometimes that's a hard question to answer." I said that we'd have six weeks together to complete our work and to say good-bye, but stopped talking when I saw Sandra's feelings were still back at the sense of loss. She said, "Just like that—you're walking out just like that!" I said, "It's been very hard for me to come and tell you. I knew it would hurt. It just seems when things start going for you, somebody important leaves. I want you to know it's not you, what we've been doing together was very important, and you're doing very well—I know it's a bad time for me to have to go. We're not finished, and we're at a critical point in your treatment. I feel terrible." She, as if in a trance, said, "Then why are you going? I don't understand. Are you going to a new job? Did you get fired?" The questions came like a barrage demanding to be answered, insisting on a response as her anger mounted. She became more direct, and her contact and communication became more personal and intimate.

My own feelings were stirred, and I grasped in my mind for an answer that would sound "right." I replied, "I am tired, my job has been demanding, and I feel I need a change. My husband and I will be having his family to visit us this summer, and we're thinking we might want a family of our own. I would like to be at home for a while."

Sandra said brightly, "That's nice that you want your own family—you're the same age as my mother." To which I replied, "But I'll be leaving you and that will be hard—I'll really miss you—we've become very close and you've shared a very private and special part of yourself with me." Sandra visibly appeared to sag—at which I took her by the arm and said, "Let's sit down together." She sat down, and tears formed in her eyes. I gave her a handkerchief from my purse, and she wiped her eyes and began twisting the cloth. I asked, "What are you feeling now—can you get it out?" She replied initially as if not hearing me, "Why? How can you do this to me? It's like I'm losing my best friend, or my dog. You're just like my mother and now you're leaving." I said, "Like your real mother or your adoptive mother?" She said, "Like the real mother I never had—you're what I would like my real mother to be like, as I imagine her." I said, "You've been very special to me, too, Sandra. I'd be proud to have a daughter like you." She said, "Not one as mixed up as me." I said, "You're putting yourself down again, Didn't you hear what I said? You've given me a lot, to—but you are not my daughter, and I am not your mother, and we must not lie about that. We must look each other in the eye and treasure the real things between us." Sandra looked up and said, "I don't know if I can, it's too hard and it hurts too much. You're the person I've really cared about here. I've never told you that. What will happen to me when you go?" I replied, "That's very honest, Sandy—I believe you can make it, but we'll have to work on it. There was lots to do yet. Do you think we can use the next five sessions to do that?" She weakly replied, "Only five left—they're disappearing already. It's all happening too fast." So she added, "We'd better get busy. I want to get as much as I can before you go. I do want to get through my fears." I hugged her and said, "You're a very determined young lady when you make up your mind, aren't you!" She replied, "That's what you've taught me, to say what I want and I'm determined toward that!"

I cautioned her, "But we probably won't finish everything—and in a couple of weeks you may need to close down, you may want to stop, but as long as you can and as long as it is safe to keep going—we'll keep working—but you must keep me informed on how you're doing and how much you can handle—you must take some control of the safety, and I'll watch closely—that must be our bargain. I want to leave you with support and with staff who can understand, but we will have to bring our work together to a safe finish."

Sandy agreed, saying, "Let's get started—I don't want to lose a day." I said, "And as if that's not enough, I have one other thing to say. You've asked me to be confidential on some of the really scary things until you felt safer to talk about it. Well, we've got to begin sharing the material with cottage staff." Sandra said, "Not yet, don't ask me this now, this was too much." I replied, "I must. I want to show your videotape to staff from your cottage. We can't keep secrets. They won't understand, and you'll need them. I'd like your permission to show the tape, and I want you to know that this material must be shared." Sandra became quite vulnerable and said, "They'll think the tapes ugly. I'm scared of what they'll think about me, I'll feel like something inside has been violated!" I paused and said, "I know—I'm asking a lot, maybe too much of you all at once, but I'm asking you to keep your trust in our work, that I'll treat the material as we have in these sessions with love, with care and with dignity, as something beautiful and a part of your inner world." Sandy shrugged her shoulders and said, "Now you're determined, aren't you?" to which I replied, "I am, and this sharing was part of our work. It would be wrong and hurtful to both of us to keep it to ourselves. You know I've talked to your cottage staff about what we're doing, but they have not seen the videotapes." (Long pause) Sandy said, "Oh, go ahead, you'll do it anyway, I don't feel very good about it, but you can show them if you want to." I replied, "If I would do it anyway, I wouldn't be talking to you now—we must be together on these things—that's our bargain—I would like your permission." She said, "I agree, but I don't have to like it." We both looked at each other, and I laughed, saying, "That's a deal, but I promise I'll give you time to get mad at me." Sandy replied, "I won't get mad—I like you," to which I replied, "It [the anger] will come, but we'll work on it when it comes."

As we cleaned up at the end of the session, Sandy claimed, "If I'd only known what was waiting for me when I came today!" I said, "It has been a really hard session for me, too. Are you feeling OK to go back to the cottage?" She replied, "I'm feeling OK now, but I feel a bit low." I said, "You've really struggled with hard things today. I don't expect you to be singing, but if you start to feel bad, talk to Fran or Rhonda. They'll be available for you." I walked her back to the cottage arm in arm and said good-bye. She replied, "It sounds so final." I said, "It does, but we've got to start—and I'll see you next week."

The tapes referred to by the worker were videotapes created by the client with the worker's help. They involved the client's use of singing and dancing to break out of her shell and to speak of very difficult experiences and emotions. The singing and dancing itself represented an assertion by the client of her own competency and willingness to risk herself and be vulnerable. This was a side of her that the worker felt needed to be shared with other workers in the system. However, the worker's own anxiety about connecting the client with social support systems may have led the worker to press too hard in insisting on the sharing. Even though they had agreed, as part of their initial contracting, on an eventual sharing of information with other professionals in the system, the client's rights to confidentiality regarding material that the worker was not required to share would take precedence. Along with the strong assertion by the worker of the importance of the sharing, the worker needed to also stress the client's right to say no.

Variations on Endings

When I discuss these sorts of emotional endings with students and workers, usually at least one group member will courageously say, "These endings sound great, but what if you and the client really don't feel so bad about endings?" When I credit the commentator for being honest, another participant sometimes follows up by commenting, "What if you don't like the client and are actually glad to see the relationship come to an end?" In this section, we explore several variations on the ending model: endings of relationships that the workers feels never really got started, endings when the worker is angry rather than sad about ending, endings associated with the worker's job loss, and endings associated with the death of a client—in one case, a suicide, and in another, a client in the last stages of AIDS.

Ending a Relationship That Never Really Began

When students review examples of powerful and emotion-laden endings with clients, they often feel guilty if their own experiences have not been similar. They share examples in which the working relationship never got off the ground. Intellectually, the student understands that the client may have played some part in the creation and maintenance of the illusion of work. Emotionally, however, the student often takes full responsibility for the "failure" because of feelings of guilt and incompetence. These feelings, in turn, may block the student from moving fully into the ending/transition phase of work, causing her or him to avoid the process of evaluating the experience with the client.

First, students need to gain a clear perspective on the interactional nature of their practice. No matter how effective and skillful they become, they will never be able to reach all clients. Second, social workers can only do the best they can at any particular moment in their professional careers. They cannot hold themselves responsible for not being able to give a client more than they had. Instead, they should guard against allowing their feelings to cause them to underplay the help they have given—just as big a mistake as overplaying their contribution. Once workers have developed perspective and received support from their supervisor and/or colleagues, then the ability to manage these feelings can help workers mobilize themselves to use the ending period as a time in which to provide additional help to the client. Support is crucial to the success of this process, because students and inexperienced workers are vulnerable at this stage in their careers, experiencing negative feedback as particularly painful.

In many cases, discussing the endings is even more important when the work has gone poorly than when it has gone well. The ending process centers on an honest evaluation of the working relationship. The worker needs not only to own up to his or her part in the process, but also to help the client examine the part she or he played in keeping the work superficial. If handled in a nonaccusatory and constructive manner, this discussion can constitute the worker's most important contribution to the client's growth. Significant professional growth for the worker can also emerge from this conversation.

In the following example, a worker levels with the client as the ending phase work begins, making the demand for work that the worker failed to make during the beginning or middle phases of practice. In this example, the client is an African American, inner-city teenager who has been in a residential setting in a rural area of the state. The original referral was from the court system and the state child welfare agency. Problems with the law, drug use, and family members are part of the teenager's history. While the client has superficially conformed to the program, the worker, who is white, has always felt "conned" by the client but has failed to confront the issue. The dialogue has been modified a bit, because the original transcript contains a street jargon that the worker said was like a "foreign language" he had to learn. The jargon and the worker's feeling like an "outsider" were key signals of the core of the problem.

WORKER: We only have two more weeks left, and I think it is important that we discuss our time together. I realize that you are probably looking forward to finishing, because I don't believe you have found the program very helpful. I have to admit to feeling the same way. I think it is important that we discuss why it didn't work out. I'd like to know what you think I could have done to be more helpful, and I'd like to let you know what I think you could have done.

CLIENT: Man, I don't think you understood what it is like for me. This place is OK, no hassles, no problems. But when I get back home, it starts all over. The pressure is on to use when I'm on street, and who's going to help me then? You don't have any idea at all. I mean, my ass is on the line back home, every day.

WORKER: I think you're right about that; I don't have any idea. I was hoping I could help you anyway, fix you up so when you went back home, you could handle it differently. Why didn't you level with me from the beginning—why did you just play along with me?

CLIENT: Are you kidding? You're the "Man"—I'm not going to level with you.

WORKER: I think I knew it was bull all along; I should have been more honest with you. I'm white, and you're black. I have a job and a safe place to live, while you're just scratching to survive. I pretended that didn't matter.

CLIENT: Look, don't get me wrong. You're not so bad for a white dude. You just don't have a clue.

WORKER: You know, it would have helped if you had taken a risk, been a bit more honest and let me know what it was really like. I understand why you didn't, why you just conned me, said the right words, and I realize I could have pushed you harder, right from the beginning. But you had a part to play as well. You can keep on playing the game when you get back home, but it seems to me, that's when you are going to need some real help the most. You are going to have to trust someone sometime.

CLIENT: What good is that going to do me? Talk isn't going to help no one. I'm stuck in that hole and I'm not getting out. So I just gotta work on survival.

WORKER: It's like you're up against a stone wall, isn't? No future, no hope—like you're trapped.

The conversation continued, with the worker listening and acknowledging feelings that were present for the client but had been only hinted at earlier. Even though it was the ending of their work together, this conversation was real and might begin to lay the groundwork for the client's future use of a helping professional. The focus turned to what resources the client might be able to tap back home when the pressure started again. The conversation also helped this worker to tune in better to the realities of oppression related to race, class, and gender, which most of his inner-city clients faced. This would increase the chance that the worker could make a quicker start with the next client, pushing for honesty earlier, while integrating support with a demand for work. The worker could also focus more on the realities of life back in the city instead of thinking that the client's "personality" could be changed in the country. By acknowledging that their time together had mostly been an illusion of work, the worker turned the ending phase into a positive experience—perhaps some of his best work with this client.

In another example, where an angry and openly resistant client responded to the worker's request for some honest evaluation of their work together, the client said, with feeling: "The problem was that you were one hell of a real asshole." The worker responded, with feeling:

> Well, you know, you weren't much of a bargain to work with either! The fact is, you never gave me a chance, right from square one. I made my mistakes, I'll own up to that. But you should realize that as long as you keep your wall up, and won't let anyone inside, you are going to be all alone with this stuff. And that's a shame, because I think you're really hurting and could use some help.

It is quite possible that the client did not take in a word the worker said. Even so, the worker needed to level with the client. The hard part for this worker was to tune in to the source of his anger and frustration. If rooted in a sense of failure and incompetence, the disclosure may not help. If the worker can see past the client's defenses, and the emotions are coming from concern for the client, then it may be the most helpful gift the worker can make. This is where supervision and peer support can help a worker ending with a difficult client.

Endings Caused by the Termination of the Worker's Job

With severe cutbacks in federal and state funding of social services over the past decade, as well as the impact of managed care in health settings, endings caused by the professional's job loss are raised more frequently in my workshops with workers, supervisors, and managers. Supervisors describe workers who are depressed, cynical, and apathetic as they enter the final phase of work. Anger over the restriction of services and the job loss often leads the worker to want to ignore the ending phase issues, sometimes withholding disclosure of the termination of work until the last session with a client or even avoiding it completely. This lack of closure serves neither clients nor workers.

Clients are disempowered in such interactions and are denied the chance to deal with their ending feelings, to take some control over the endings, and to make an effective transition to life without their workers. The abruptness of the ending can negatively affect the transition to the new worker or service, or make the client reluctant to become emotionally invested with any other helping professionals. Clients are also denied the opportunity to challenge the loss of the services. In some situations, when clients have been made aware of what is happening, they have mobilized resources (other clients, family members, and so forth) to object to the loss, and they have even been able to reverse or moderate the decisions leading up to it.

Workers pay a price for abrupt endings as well, as they lose out on the opportunity to end professionally, which is one way to deal with some of their guilt over "abandoning" their clients. In addition, on later reflection, workers often report how helpful it was that their supervisor held them to a professional level of practice in the ending phase, rather than allowing them to withdraw out of anger and depression. Of course, a crucial element in the process is the work done to create a supportive atmosphere in which workers know they can get assistance in managing their feelings. In workshops I have led for frontline workers facing the potential or actual loss of their jobs, I have focused first on their anger and then on the pain and sadness that is usually also present. The guilt of remaining workers (survivors) needs to be dealt with so that their anxiety does not cause a flight-fight response. After some supportive work, staff can respond to my request to tune in to the impact of the cutbacks on their clients and to strategize how best to help clients to cope with loss, while the workers struggle with their own feelings.

In the following excerpt, a worker announces that she has lost her job and will be ending her work with the client, a single parent involved in family support work focusing on problems with her teenager.

WORKER: I'm afraid I have some bad news for you. You may know that the state was considering cutting the funds available for support agencies like ours. Well, the cuts have come through, and because of seniority, I will be one of the first workers to lose my job. I'm afraid this means we only have four weeks left, and we are going to have to start to discuss how to end our work and connect you up to other sources of help.

CLIENT: Oh my God, you must feel terrible. You mean they're letting you go, just like that?

WORKER: Actually, we have known there might be cuts for a few months. I didn't want to worry you because we just were not sure what would happen. But now we know, and you and I have to start to face it. I am feeling terrible about losing my job, and part of the reason for that is that I am going to have to say good-bye to clients I have gotten close to—and that includes you. (Silence) How about you, what are you feeling right now?

CLIENT: I'm furious at your agency. Just when I find a worker I can really like, they take you away. Does this mean I will get another worker? What will happen to me now?

WORKER: I want you to know I have really felt close to you and it means a lot to me to hear that you will miss me too. I'm also angry, but underneath that I'm feeling a lot of sadness and loss. We need to talk about that over the next few weeks as well as where do you go from here. I must be honest. I don't think the agency really has had time to consider what we are going to do for clients like yourself. We never felt the cuts would be this bad, with so many positions lost. I will try to find out what may be available to you, and if you wish, I will put you in touch with my supervisor, who is staying on. That way you can ask some of the questions yourself. If it turns out that you cannot get the help you need here, we are going to have to see what else may be available in the community. Also, we better discuss where you can get help from other sources—your family and friends, for example. I can't make any guarantees about services because every other agency is also getting clobbered, but I will make sure we spend time on how you can cope no matter what we find out. You have grown a lot in the last few months, and I think you have more strengths than even you realize.

CLIENT: Those bastards! (Starting to cry) Don't they realize it's going to be hard on me to cope on my own? (Silence—the worker also starts to fill with emotion—the two sit quietly for a while, the client crying softly and the worker with tears in her eyes.)

WORKER: (After a short while) I'm not sure they do realize the impact of all of this on clients. If you want to discuss ways in which you can let them know, tell me. I'll be glad to help you communicate your views. Your needs are important, and they have to realize these decisions have serious impact on real people. In the meantime, let's start to talk about our work together, what you have learned, your strengths, areas where you still feel vulnerable, and what other sources of help you have available. I want to make sure we work hard right up to the end.

There were many points in this dialogue at which the worker could have lost her sense of professional function. When the client asked the worker how she felt about the job loss, the rest of the conversation could have revolved around the worker's reactions. It did not, because the worker came right back to the impact on the client. When the client expressed anger at the agency, the worker might have joined in the anger, focusing on her own sense of the unfairness of the situation. Instead, she shared her own feelings of loss and reached for those of the client. When the client asked, "What will happen to me now?" the worker could have expressed her resentment and bitterness by reflecting back the client's sense of hopelessness. Instead, the worker empowered the client, suggesting that she begin actively to make some demands on the system. The worker did not try to falsely reassure the client, but she did focus on next steps available to the client if the formal systems failed her. Also, when the client focused on her anger at the political neglect and lack of understanding, the worker offered to empower the client in finding ways to communicate her feelings, rather than reflecting her own sense of hopelessness by saying, "What's the use—you can't fight city hall." Finally, instead of focusing just on the social action possibilities open to the client, the worker came back to the immediate issues, leaving the door open for further discussion. All in all, this worker should feel good about her efforts to help the client cope, her maintenance of a professional role, and her commitment to the client. It was all the more admirable given her understandable anger toward the political system and the community, which lacked the will to meet their commitments to vulnerable clients.

Endings Caused by the Death of the Client

Coping with the death of a client on a caseload, or working with a dying client, can be extremely traumatic for a worker. While workers have always had to deal with the issue of death and dying as a normal part of their caseload (as in accidental deaths, suicide, terminal illness), the epidemic growth of health and social problems such as AIDS and crack cocaine addiction has increased the likelihood of such traumas. In the next sections, we explore the impact of a sudden death (a suicide) on the caseload as well as the implications of working with a client dying of AIDS. First, a word on the effect of traumatic events on workers may help you understand these more specific traumatic circumstances.

Traumatic Events and Their Impact on a Worker's Practice The impact of a trauma on a specific worker, or on his or her colleagues, can be significant and often subtle. A trauma, in the sense it is used here, causes a deeply felt negative emotional reaction. This may be experienced immediately or, as is often the case, at a later date when the impact of the experiences reemerges. For example, one study examined the impact of a traumatic event, such as the death of a child on caseload while in foster care or left at home with the biological parents (Shulman, 1991). Analysis of the data indicated that the trauma not only affected the practice of the caseworker, it may also have affected the practice of other workers in the same office and region. The incidence of traumatic events in a region was positively associated with more children going into care, being less likely to return home, and staying in care longer. A traumatic event on a specific worker's caseload also suggested such negative consequences as negative morale and decreased practice skill with clients. Other examples of traumatic events included a physical attack or threat of attack by a client on a worker, cutbacks in budget that lead to layoffs, and the death of a colleague.

A social support system can buffer the impact of trauma; this system would need to aid not only the particular worker involved but all of the other workers in the office or agency as well. My work with such an affected office revealed a tendency by the staff to avoid the pain associated with the traumatic event through the flight-fight syndrome. The stress often increased when the administration responded (from their own anxiety) with the question, "Who is at fault?" Workers consistently report that, at such a time, what they desperately needed was for supervisors and administrators to be asking, "How are you doing?"

Interestingly, under the direction of a social worker, a large Canadian bank developed a program to provide support to bank branch staff immediately following a traumatic armed robbery. The branch would be closed for a day, with the social worker flown in to meet individually and in groups with all staff for trauma counseling. The bank discovered that it experienced fewer sick leaves, less absenteeism, less staff turnover, and even a lowering of the level of mistakes if it paid attention to the needs of its staff after a trauma. It is ironic that a corporate entity was able to recognize the benefits of support for its employees, while social and health services often seem not to understand.

An ending of a working relationship brought on by the sudden and traumatic death of a client should immediately mobilize the resources of the agency to attend to the needs of workers involved. In the next section, I outline some steps to help workers not only deal with their own feelings but also work effectively with the feelings of clients. (For a more complete discussion of the impact of trauma and the importance of social support, see Shulman, 1991, 1984.)

Suicide on a Caseload The suicide of a client can powerfully affect a worker, as well as other workers and clients in the system. A sudden and permanent ending to a working relationship can evoke guilt in the worker. Even if he or she logically understands that such a decision was made by the client and was not the responsibility of the worker, self-doubt often remains. This doubt can affect a worker's current and future practice. In one example, a social worker in a veterans' hospital reported having difficulty ending his work with a Vietnam veteran even after 5 years. When the issue was examined closely, it became apparent that the suicide of another, similar client on his caseload, shortly after they had ended their work together, had made the worker overly cautious about ending before all of a client's problems had been "solved."

Further discussion revealed that the worker had received little help with his own emotions at the time of the suicide, with most of the administrative responses geared to an investigation of the circumstances (for example, whether the recording was up to date and all of the proper procedures had been followed). Even colleagues seemed to shun him, turning away in a form of flight from his pain. Some simply may not have known what to say. In addition, the suicide may have raised anxiety about their own clients. Lacking a defined protocol for dealing with staff in traumatic situations, and lacking leadership from supervisors and managers, the system's reaction to the suicide left the worker feeling abandoned. Unable to manage his feelings, he became less able to manage his practice-related problems—particularly, ending with clients.

The impact of such an event on an entire staff system was brought home to me dramatically during a 2-day workshop I led for the staff of a psychiatric ward for inpatient teenagers. During the first day, staff presented problems with one Native American patient who was emotionally isolated from other patients, resistant to work, hard to reach, and in general considered to be the ward's **deviant member.** In this role, the client acts significantly differently from other clients in the system but may actually be sending an indirect message on behalf of the other clients. (The concept of the role of deviant member will be discussed more fully in the chapters on family and group work.) In discussing this patient, I tried to help the staff see him in a new way—as a patient who could be sending a signal to staff of issues and feelings related to the ward as a **dynamic system**, in which the behavior of each participant in the system (staff and clients) affects and is affected by the behaviors of all other members of the system. Staff moved quickly to integrate this new view of his behavior and to strategize about how to intervene differently with him and the other teens on the ward.

When I arrived to start the second day of the workshop, I noticed staff speaking in hushed tones at the coffee urn. When I asked about what had happened, they told me the client they had presented had been home on a pass the previous evening and that he had shot himself and was dead. I felt stunned at the news. I knew the staff was also in shock. When the session started, I acknowledged the impact of this traumatic event. I then suggested that, in order to deal with this event, we abandon the other examples we had scheduled for discussion. I told them I thought we could connect the discussion to the purpose of our workshop. I was conscious of the fact that I would be modeling for the staff a way of dealing with the group of patients they would be meeting that evening. I believed the patients would be experiencing many of the emotions that staff would be feeling in reaction to the suicide. How I handled the staff discussion should somewhat parallel the work they would need to do with the teens on the ward.

The morning's work that followed could be divided into three related phases. The first phase of this work involved expressions of grief, loss, and guilt. The second phase involved discussion of how to provide support to staff in these circumstances. In the third and final phase, we examined the impact on other clients and the implications for practice.

> I began by telling them that even though I did not know this child, except for their brief description of him the day before, I felt stunned and tremendously sad about his loss of life. I asked if we could take some time, with each person having a chance to share what she or he was experiencing. Staff began to speak slowly and in quiet tones as they shared how upset they were by the event. One staff member, the patient's **key worker**, who had particular responsibility for providing continuity of service, began to cry. She felt guilty about not having reached him sooner—she wondered how alone he must have felt on the ward, cut off from the other patients and staff. A colleague next to her offered support by putting her arm around her. Other colleagues cried as well. She went on to wonder if she had made a mistake in agreeing to allow him home on a pass. She said that if she had not let him go home, he might be alive today. I acknowledged her feelings and asked if the other staff could be helpful to her. I suggested helping her might also be helpful to them, because I thought they all felt some of her emotions and doubts.
>
> One staff member pointed out that they had all participated in the decision to allow weekend passes—it was a joint responsibility. Another pointed out that the patient had done well on his previous passes and that they had had no way of predicting this suicide. A third pointed out that while they might want to review their procedures for assessing a client's readiness for passes, he thought it would be a mistake to stop the leave program suddenly or become overly cautious and restrictive. Weekend passes worked well for most kids most of the time. Another staff member pointed out that this teen had brought his pain with him to the hospital—staff had not caused it. He might well have committed suicide no matter what staff had done. One staff member noted that he was a Native patient, and wondered if he had felt even more isolated on the ward with "white workers, white patients, even white walls." (I had raised issues of race and culture during the workshop the previous day.) A supervisor suggested that they put on their future agenda some discussion of the issue of race—a topic they usually ducked. He said he often felt cut off from the Native patients and had to think about how to reach them more effectively. Some suggested the need to recruit Native staff, who might be able to relate more effectively.

The conversation continued along these lines. There were long periods of silence and many moments when each staff member seemed to be lost in his or her own feelings and thoughts, as well as other moments when they seemed to be able to come together. As the conversation continued, I felt a deepening of the staff's feelings of depression and sadness. Allowing time for these emotions to emerge and taking time to accept them were important. The initial instinct to reassure or move too quickly into next steps can preempt the space needed for the emotions to be felt and acknowledged. As is discussed in more detail in Part IV, powerful healing can occur with group support that allows people to feel that they are "all in the same boat." Given the brief time we had left, I decided to help the staff focus on where they could go from here as a way of coping with the loss.

> I shared my own feelings about the depth of sadness we were experiencing and then wondered if it might not be helpful at this point to discuss how to help the key worker and all of the staff over the next few weeks. I thought this might be a way of developing a protocol of how to handle such traumatic events in the future. A number of suggestions emerged, including the acknowledgment that it was useful just to have some time together to share in the grieving. One worker asked the key worker if she felt up to meeting with the teen's family; if not, she would do it for her. The key worker thanked her but said that she felt she should do it herself. Another worker revealed a similar incident he had experienced a number of years before in another setting. He said he still felt the pain, and this incident had brought it all back. He told of having been given time off to attend the funeral and said that this had been important to him and to the family. The supervisor indicated that this could be arranged if the key worker wished. She indicated that she would like the opportunity. Further discussion focused on their concerns about how the hospital administration might react. The whole group shared with their supervisor some suggestions about how he might handle the issue so that administration was tuned in to the needs of the staff over the next few weeks.

From my perspective, focusing on the needs of the staff must receive the highest priority. If those needs are ignored, then staff may not be able to focus on the needs of current and future clients. It is also important, however, to reach for the professionalism of staff and not let them get lost in dealing with their own pain. Focusing on the clients they can still help offers an important way in which workers can heal themselves and lessen their guilt over the client they feel they did not help. In the next excerpt, I asked staff to shift their focus from self to other—the remaining clients on the ward.

> As this discussion proceeded, one could almost sense a lifting of the pall over the room. Staff seemed energized by a focus on what they could do as next steps. I summarized the suggestions that had emerged thus far and then asked if they could give some consideration to the teens still on the ward. If staff was reacting so strongly, how would the patients—many of whom may have had similar feelings as the patient who had committed suicide—how would they be reacting? One participant pointed out how in the past, when there had been a suicide attempt, staff had tried to hide it from the patients. They were afraid that it might trigger other attempts. He indicated he thought that this was probably a mistake, because patients knew something was wrong and soon found out what had happened through the grapevine. By trying to hide it, they closed off the possibility of helping the teens with their reactions. He recognized that it was his own fears he was running from. He proposed that they raise it at this evening's community meeting.

The remainder of the session was devoted to tuning in to the potential reactions of the patients and developing strategies for helping them cope. I pointed out the parallels between their experience during the workshop and the group experience they were about to lead. They recognized the importance of sharing their own feelings, allowing time for grieving, shifting to the impact of this death on each of the remaining patients, and discussing the mutual responsibility each patient and staff member had for the others. They decided to involve the patients in a discussion of what they could do if they ever felt so cut off and alone and how they could try to be more supportive of each other.

At the end of the session, I congratulated the staff on their work and their professionalism. I told them they had had a rough shock to their systems but I saw a lot of strength in their ability to help each other and to stay focused on their professional tasks with their clients. I wished them luck, and the session ended.

The three-step model discussed in this section—grieving, the need for support for the worker, and then moving to focusing on clients—can be helpful in conceptualizing the stages of coping with trauma of any kind.

Working With a Dying Client With the exception of settings associated with terminal illness, such as a **hospice**—a residential setting for people who are in the final stage of a terminal illness—or a medical setting, such as an oncology (cancer) ward, most social workers traditionally do not deal with dying clients. Unfortunately, with the continuing AIDS epidemic, this has changed. Participants in my workshops have increasingly raised examples of clients who are in some stage of this illness. While the success of the triple-drug treatment has significantly affected survival rates, many clients with AIDS cannot take advantage of this new treatment, because they have other medical problems that prevent the use of these drugs.

Others have detailed the stages of death and dying (Kubler-Ross, 1969) and the worker skills required to help a client take some control over the process. Our discussion here focuses on how having a dying client affects the working relationship and how the worker can integrate process and content in this sort of case. The illustrative example comes from a worker who discussed in a workshop the stress involved in working with a male client with AIDS in the final stages of the illness. The client was living at home with the support of his lover, some friends, and family members. The worker introduced the example by asking, "How do you work with a client when you don't know from week to week if you will ever see him again?"

When the example was explored in detail, one of the client's major issues became clear: None of the people who mattered to him were willing to talk to him about his impending death. He felt he had come to grips with this ending of his life, but his efforts to raise the issue with his lover, friends, and family members had all hit a wall of denial. He was angry at them for not being willing to talk with him and for trying to "cheer him up." He was afraid he might die before he could complete some work with each of these important people.

I asked the worker if she had discussed with the client her feelings about not knowing if the client would be there for the next interview; she had not. It became clear that the worker, too, was distressed about this client's impending death. She was also having difficulty with her own ending work with him, thereby mirroring the client's problem with the other significant people in his life. With support from other workshop members, she developed a strategy for confronting the issue with her client and using the conversation about their relationship (the process) to help him with his concerns about family and others (the content). Here is her report of her next conversation with the client.

I began our conversation by telling him there was something I needed to talk to him about that was very difficult for me to raise. I told him I had been trying to help him deal with a number of people who were denying that he was facing death, when I now realized I was doing exactly the same thing. I told him it was very difficult for me coming to see him each week, not knowing if he would be around for our next session. I had come to care a great deal about him and it was hard for me to face his impending death. I was going to miss him.

He was quiet for a few moments, and then smiled. He told me he had been aware that I was avoiding the issue and had wondered if I was ever going to raise it. He said I had been very important to him, this past year, and that he wanted to make sure I knew how much he had appreciated my help. At this point I began to cry, unable to maintain my "professional" composure. After a while, I told him that I wondered if the other people in his life he wanted to talk with had similar feelings. Perhaps they too cared so much for him that it was hard for them to face losing him. I wondered if they were afraid they might upset him and were holding back their real feelings. I wondered if they were like me, and were simply afraid of the pain of losing him.

He was thoughtful for a while, and said that was probably it. But what could he do about it, because at this point it was more painful for him not to talk about his death? I suggested that perhaps he needed to tell them that he understood why they kept avoiding the issue. Perhaps, if they knew how important this was to him and that he was really ready to face his death and wanted them to face it with him they might find the strength to stop avoiding it. At this point, he started to cry and I sat quietly. I asked him if he thought he might have some mixed feelings himself about having this conversation with these people. I noted that he was aware we were ducking the issue between us, but he had not raised it with me. I had to raise it with him. Was he sending mixed signals to these people who were so important to him? Could they be sensing his ambivalence? He indicated that he probably was not being as direct as he could be and was simply blaming them for changing the subject. I suggested we might discuss ways he could initiate this conversation more directly and how he could refuse to be put off by their initial denials. We worked on this for some time.

At the end of the conversation, I told him that I wanted to be sure that we discussed our own work together and made sure we said all that we needed to, just in case. We agreed that we would focus on our work together next week as well as how well he did with his family members. As I left, I told him I was glad we had spoken so honestly and I would see him next week. He smiled and said, "God willing."

For the ending work to continue, the worker in this example needed to deal with her own ambivalence and start the process of expressing her real feelings. This signaled to the client that the worker was ready to face the client's real feelings about ending with others in his life.

ENDING AND TRANSITION SKILLS This presents a white worker with a middle-aged African American client dealing with divorce discussing the ending of their working relationship. Discussion of the early difficulty in establishing an interethnic working relationship is explored.

Chapter Summary

The ending and transition phase of practice can be the most important part of the work, during which clients deal with some of their most significant issues. Because of the feelings involved in the loss of a relationship, this phase may become a moratorium on work unless the worker helps the client identify the stages of the process (denial, anger, mourning, trying it on for size, and the farewell-party syndrome) so that the client can maintain some control. Specific worker skills involved in the ending phase include pointing out endings early, identifying the stages of the process, asking for a mutual exchange of the feelings related to ending, pointing out process and content connections, and asking for an honest evaluation and summary of the work together. Skills of transition include identification of major learning and areas for future work, synthesizing process and content, and helping the client move on to new experiences and support systems. Variations on the ending themes include situations in which the work has gone badly, the worker is fired, the work ends because of a traumatic event such as suicide, or the client is dying.

Related Online Content and Activities

Visit *The Skills of Helping* Book Companion Website at www.socialwork.wadsworth .com/Shulman06/ for learning tools such as glossary terms, InfoTrac College Edition keywords, links to related websites, and chapter practice quizzes.

The website for this chapter also features an additional process recording:
*   Transition of a Single Parent to a New Worker: Dealing With Indirect Anger

Social Work With Families

Part III of this book consists of two chapters that elaborate and illustrate the interactional approach to social work in the context of work with families. The chapters distinguish between social work with families and family therapy.

Chapter 6 sets out the basic model of family practice in the social work context. A brief summary of constructs from family therapy theory is presented. These constructs are illustrated in the context of social work with families, focusing on the family counseling and family support functions.

In Chapter 7, the agency services (rooted in agency mandate) and specific client problems come to the foreground. Illustrations demonstrate how the boundaries of this working contract give focus and direction to family work in a child resources agency, a child welfare setting, and a school.

Family Practice in the Social Work Context

In this chapter, we build on the concepts explored in Parts I and II by applying the helping model to working with families and family problems. While the core elements of the model are the same—the phases of work, the importance of contracting, the skills required to build a positive working relationship, and so on—significant variations arise when one attempts to provide help to families and family members. The chapter addresses such variations to help you make the transition from work with one client to work with more than one client at a time.

Note that this chapter is not meant as an introduction to family therapy. Although we draw on ideas from a limited number of family therapy models, we harness these constructs to the family support and family counseling functions. These models fit comfortably in the framework described in this book, whereas the larger field of family therapy involves more than we can discuss here.

Social Work With Families

Social workers have a long history of working with families that predates the emergence of family therapy as a practice modality. In this chapter, the term *family* includes a wide range of associations, many of which do not fit the traditional two-parent-family image. (A formal definition will follow.) The increasing number of single-parent families, as well as families headed by gay or lesbian partners, has broadened our understanding of the concept of family. The discussion in Chapter 3 of culturally competent practice also introduced the idea that even the word for family in some population groups refers to what the dominant culture would call the extended family.

Social work with families falls into two general categories. In the first, examined in this chapter, the practice is often called **family support** work or family counseling. This activity is usually short-term and is designed to help families facing normative crises, such as the first child reaching the teen years or a crisis provoked by the birth of a new baby. An environmental crisis, such as the loss of a job by one parent, may also require professional intervention. The work centers on helping a relatively healthy family get through a difficult time, using the experience to strengthen rather than erode the family system. Services may also be provided to couples without children. This general type of social work with families is often provided by voluntary family service agencies or private practice.

Child welfare agencies also provide family support services. Most child welfare agencies deal with families facing problems ranging from the normative problems just described to more serious issues of abuse and neglect requiring court involvement and protection of the children (as in foster care placement). In addition to the ongoing child protection social worker, a family support worker might be assigned to a family.

For example, a social worker might work with a family by helping the parents strengthen their child-rearing skills and find more effective ways to cope with aspects of their life that are making parenting more difficult. Just as the worker would make referrals to other agencies for alcohol counseling, job counseling, and so on, he or she would also make a referral for ongoing marital counseling or intensive family therapy if needed. The work would be directed by the agency's mandate to work with families with children at some level of risk.

Many of the concepts and theories introduced in the earlier chapters can be applied to understanding the family. For example, from the life-span framework the social worker would attempt to help the family members identify the available baseline reserve capacity, both internal (within the family) and external, that could increase the family's ability to cope with the sources of stress. If, for example, the family crisis involves an elderly parent who can no longer cope independently because of physical deterioration, then the work might involve identifying the developmental reserve capacity potentially available through interventions such as the services of a home-care aide or housekeeper.

Other practice models introduced in Chapter 1 provide constructs that are useful in this work. For example, cognitive practice interventions can help family members identify automatic thinking processes that cause them to misinterpret the reality of their family interactions, thereby allowing the family members to break maladaptive cycles of blaming and conflict and to identify individual and family strengths and sources of support. Feminist practice frameworks can help members of the family identify gender-stereotypical behavior that has led to the internalization of anger and frustration and the generation of interactional-related depression on the part of parents or children. Solution-focused approaches that help family members identify their strengths and how they have coped in the past can also be used.

Resilience theory and research would offer suggestions to the worker and the family on interventions, such as the involvement of extended family members or elders, or other resources in the community (such as a Big Brother or Big Sister) designed to buffer the impact of a trauma, such as physical abuse, on the children or one of the parents. In this sense, the work is essentially restorative, designed to strengthen the family and to lead to more normal or positive growth and development.

Social workers often confront two kinds of family work: one that focuses on helping the family work as a family and another that focuses on a specific problem. First, in some families, the crisis leads to the revelation of deeper, more long-term problems. In these cases, short-term family support work will often involve (1) helping the family identify the real problems, (2) creating a working relationship so that the family can begin to see helping professionals in a positive way, and (3) referring the family for more traditional forms of long-term family therapy. The professional providing this more intensive help may well be a social worker, because many serve in family therapy practice within agencies or in group or private practices as managed care providers. The family support worker, as defined here, does not undertake the long-term, intensive family therapy task.

The second major set of circumstances in which most family support workers find themselves involves providing families with forms of assistance that are directly connected to the specific services offered by their agency or host setting. For example, a hospital social worker in a medical setting might work with family members on their adjustment to a patient's illness or other medical condition. A school social worker might undertake family work in helping parents and a teenager deal with serious school failure problems. A social worker in an elder care agency may work with the adult children of an elderly client preparing to make the transition to a nursing home. This type of work centers on a particular problem or life crisis that both guides and limits the nature of the work. This second type of social work practice, centering on specific problems, will be explored more fully in Chapter 7. By contrast, in the first type of family work, the emphasis is on the family itself with the life crisis as perhaps one of several issues affecting family dynamics.

In this chapter, then, we focus on ways of helping families through normative crises, creating the conditions for effective referrals to long-term, intensive family services for more troubled families, and working with families and family-related problems in the context of child welfare services. This focus is intended to help you see how the ideas of the first five chapters can be useful in the family modality. It is also meant to help workers in many different settings understand how work with families can be an extension of their ongoing tasks, rather than the introduction of a completely different practice. As you will see, the chapter draws on many ideas and techniques borrowed from family therapy approaches; however, no one model of family therapy has been adopted as the sole working approach.

Selected Concepts From Family Therapy Theory

When working with families, one should take several factors into account. First, families have a history that goes back many generations. Family members beyond the nuclear family, both dead and alive, often affect the present. That is, the nuclear family's relationship—or lack of relationship—to the extended family or the community may play a large part in its functioning. Next, different family members exert different amounts of power in relation to one another. For example, children (or a spouse) may face serious threats of retribution, including physical violence, when family members return to their lives between counseling sessions. Finally, the fact that the stereotypes, roles, communication patterns—the whole family structure—has developed and been reinforced on a daily basis, 24 hours a day, over many years, can create strong resistances to the "unfreezing" process needed for change. The family has had years to develop a **family facade**—a false front it presents to outsiders—and each family member has also had time to create the external role that he or she presents to the other family members. One of the major advantages of seeing whole families, as opposed to working with one member of a family at a time, is that it allows the worker to observe many of these factors in the family interaction (for example, who sits where, who speaks for the family).

Family therapy theory can help us better understand family dynamics and choose effective interventions. There are many different views about how families function and what workers should do to help. One text on the subject describes 17 different models (Horne & Passmore, 1991). We shall identify and briefly describe key concepts from a few of these models.

One early contributor to family therapy theory, whose work has influenced many of the current theories, was Nathan Ackerman (1958). Our discussion will draw on his framework for viewing a family and explore many of his practice strategies for describing the role of the worker in carrying out family work, while also integrating concepts from other theorists. Ackerman viewed family work as a special method of treatment of emotional disorders based on dynamically oriented interviews with the whole family. He sees the **family** as a natural living unit including all those persons who share identity with the family and are influenced by it in a circular exchange of emotions. The family has a potential for mutual support that can be blocked by communication problems and anxieties of individual members. This leads to family disorders and the family's inability to carry out its tasks.

Although Ackerman does not specifically define the function of the helping person as mediation, many of his treatment skills can be explained as implementing this function in action. For example, he recognizes that treatment usually begins at a time of crisis, when the emotional equilibrium of the family has been upset. In the beginning stages of work, after contracting to help the family members work together to improve their communications and deal with the family problems troubling them, the worker employs the skill of observation to identify the idiosyncratic language of the family. Using personal emotions stirred by the feelings of the family members toward each other and the worker, he or she tests hunches about the family and its feelings by sharing them with family members. In this way, the worker helps the family move past the facade presented in the first stage toward a more honest disclosure of their interpersonal conflicts. For example, the worker might help the family move beyond viewing the family problem as concerning a single child, who serves as the family scapegoat. The child in this case is called the **identified patient (IP)**, or the client in a family system who is identified as having the problem. This process of moving past the facade has been described by other family theorists as **reframing the problem** to help the family see it in a new way.

The worker would identify unhelpful patterns and roles and point them out to the family members. Roles might include scapegoat, victim, persecutor, and so on. Facilitative confrontation (similar to the demand for work) is used to break the vicious cycle of blame and punishment that usually characterizes disordered family relationships. The worker challenges the illusion of work using the "here and now" of the family session to bring out the central issues. Because the family acts out its dysfunctional patterns in front of the therapist, the process of the family session is directly synthesized with the content of the work. In Ackerman's model, the therapist controls interpersonal danger, selectively supports family members, and attempts at all times to present a model of positive interpersonal functioning.

Another theorist whose ideas are helpful in understanding and working with families is Murray Bowen (1961, 1978). Bowen also views the family as guided in its activities by an emotional system that may have developed over years. He stresses the importance of understanding and exploring the intergenerational contribution made to the development of this family emotional system. Key concepts in Bowen's model include the importance of each individual being able to differentiate between emotional and thinking systems so that control can be maintained over behavior. (This is somewhat similar to one of the key concepts of the interactional model, in which clients are helped to manage their feelings in order to be able to manage their problems.) Bowen also stresses the impact of anxiety on the family system. Increased anxiety, resulting from a perceived threat, can lead to efforts toward "togetherness" in the family as a maladaptive means of coping. One example is the process of **triangulation**, in which one party attempts to gain the allegiance of a second party in the struggle with a third party as a means of coping with anxiety. Each parent might try to pull in the child for support against the other parent, for instance. This is a maladaptive way of coping with a problem and can result in significant negative consequences, as in the case of the child forced to choose between parents.

Without needing to adopt a particular model whole, we can borrow concepts and techniques that can be integrated into effective family work at any level. Freeman's work has been useful in explicating Bowen's theoretical model and describing and illustrating the method for its implementation (Freeman, 1981). In particular, his use of time in organizing his discussion of family work (beginning family therapy, the family therapy process, and the terminating stage) makes it easy to fit useful concepts within the model presented in this book.

Freeman points out that the family therapy process begins before the first interview as the helping professional responds to the call to set an appointment. Rather than rigidly requiring all members of the family to attend a first session, the therapist can conduct a skillful and sensitive telephone discussion with the caller, usually the person who most often takes responsibility for dealing with the family's problems, and thereby discover important information about who is involved in the problem and gain clues as to whom should be asked to attend the first sessions. Instead of challenging the caller's definition of who should attend, the therapist respects the feelings of the caller and agrees, for example, to see the parents alone at first. In this case the worker does this to develop a working relationship that will encourage the parents to allow the therapist entry into the family. Freeman points out how the discussion of whom the caller sees as involved can be the beginning of helping the family members redefine who is involved in the problem and who should attend the sessions.

Freeman describes four phases in the first interview: warming up, defining the problem, reframing the family's thinking about the problem, and obtaining the commitment to work as a family. The warming-up phase helps reduce the family's anxiety. Defining the problem involves a form of contracting, trying to understand how all family members perceive the problem. The reframing phase involves helping the family see the problem in new ways (for example, as a family problem, not just as a result of the behaviors of the identified patient). Finally, the commitment-to-work phase lays the groundwork for future sessions.

The middle phase of practice is where Bowen's theory adds its special emphasis on intergenerational work. As individuals take more responsibility for their own actions, and the sessions are thereby marked by less blaming and reactive behavior, the relative calm allows for identification of subsystems within the intrafamilial and extrafamilial networks to which the family can direct its attention. It is at these points in particular that the multigenerational concepts are used to help families expand their boundaries. The worker tries to help the family understand the impact of the family history and use the extended family as a source of support.

Another family therapy theory, termed the person-centered approach, builds on the ideas developed from the early work of Rogers (1961). In this approach, as described by Thayer (1982),

> The therapist works on establishing a healthy psychological climate which the family members can use to establish realness in family relationships, express true feelings, remain separate and yet identify with the family, develop effective two-way communication, start a healthy process for family development and problem-solving, and clarify societal effects on the family as well as clarify conflicts, seek solutions, explore values, make decisions, experiment with new behaviors, and develop a family model/direction unique to its needs and wants. (p. 192)

The followers of this approach focus on the core helping skills that have been demonstrated repeatedly to facilitate change. These components of a healthy psychological climate include the therapist's genuineness (being real as a person); the therapist's caring and prizing of family members (unconditional positive regard for family members); and the therapist's willingness to listen carefully to what family members have to say (hearing and understanding family members' needs, wants, conflicts, fears, joys, loves, goals, values, hates, disappointment, dreams, sorrows, and worlds or realities). These core conditions will be familiar to the reader from Parts I and II of this book.

Many of the core ideas in family therapy cut across theories. For example, multigenerational issues are important in most models, with Satir (1967) interested in "family fact chronology" and Keith and Whitaker (1982) referring to a "longitudinally integrated, intra-psychic family of three generations." The core issue of integration and differentiation—how to be part of a family and at the same time a separate individual—appears in most formulations, although the terms used may differ (for example, Keith and Whitaker refer to unification and separation).

Most theorists refer to the problem of triangulation, discussed earlier. Where they tend to differ is in their views of how to avoid the trap, change the pattern, or make strategic use of being the third party in the situation. The importance of developing a safe atmosphere is also stressed, although theories differ sharply in their timing and methods of confrontation for upsetting the dysfunctional patterns.

In the sections that follow, we discuss several constructs borrowed from family therapy theorists. Examples of family work drawn from a variety of social work settings will illustrate these concepts as well.

The Two-Client Concept and the Worker's Role

One of the major differences in working with families rather than individual clients is that the worker is dealing with more than one person at a time. Even though the model called for conceptualizing the client in interaction with important systems, the worker usually had only one person to deal with at a time in most of the examples in Part II. As soon as the helping unit expands to more than two, it becomes more complex, introducing new problems, new possibilities, and new demands on the worker's skills. One of the most common problems observed in family work results from worker identification with a subunit of the family system.

Perhaps the best way to describe the problem is to give an example of how it typically emerges in workshops I conduct for helping professionals. The workshop participant in this case was presenting an example of a general problem: "How do you work with a family if the father is unmotivated and very defensive?" In response to my request, the worker described the family as containing middle-aged parents (the father was an immigrant from Europe), a 15-year-old daughter (the identified patient, or IP, whom the parents viewed as the problem), and an 11-year-old son whom the parents described as no problem at all. The parents had called, indicating they could not control the daughter, and wanted the child welfare agency to "straighten her out or get her out." While the particulars may differ, this type of situation and the conversation that follows is typical of hundreds of workshops.

After the description of the family and the circumstances of the worker's involvement, I asked for the details of the first session (word for word) to the best of the worker's ability to recall. He described the father angrily taking the lead and confronting the daughter with accusations of misbehavior. These were addressed to the worker almost as a prosecuting attorney might speak to a judge. When I inquired what the daughter was doing, the worker said, "She was just sitting there, her head hanging down, very close to tears." When I asked for the worker's feelings at the moment, he replied, "I felt badly for her and could easily understand why she had trouble dealing with that father. He didn't seem to have any sense of how upset she was." I replied, "You must have also felt angry at him for his insensitivity. You were feeling her hurt and pain, and he seemed closed off from her." The worker agreed.

At one point the worker described the father berating his daughter for running around with girls who "came in late, dressed like sluts, smoked dope, and didn't listen to their parents." I asked how the worker responded, and he said, "I asked Maria [the daughter] if it hurt her to hear her father say those things, and she just nodded. I asked if she could tell her father that, and she just sat there, unable to speak and about to start crying." I said to the worker, "You wanted the father to understand her hurt. Did it seem to get through to him?" The worker replied that the father was so dense, he couldn't hear a thing. The father simply escalated the anger, saying, "In Europe children listen to their parents and respect them." I continued, "Which made you even angrier. What did you say to him?" The worker replied, "I told him that I thought he had to understand that he was in the United States now, and that teenagers here were quite different in many ways from the old country. I don't think it helped much, because he just sat there and glared at me. How do you get through to a guy like that?"

It is at moments such as these that it is possible to help workers see the problem in a new way. Using a diagram with three circles—one for the daughter, one for the family, and one for the worker—I asked if the worker could put himself back into that moment and tell us where he was with respect to his emotional identification. Pointing to the daughter's circle, I said, "It would be quite understandable if you were really with the daughter." The worker replied that I was right. I then asked the workshop group, "Who was with the father?" After a few moments of silence, someone said, "He was all alone."

This is the moment when the two-client idea, proposed by Schwartz (1961) in the context of group work, becomes helpful in understanding the worker's function in work with families. To mediate the individual-social engagement effectively, in the special case of the family, the worker must understand the importance of conceptualizing and identifying with two clients simultaneously: the individual and the family system. Thus, in the conflict just described, for the worker to be helpful, he must find a way to emotionally identify with (be with) both the daughter and the parents in the family system. By identifying with the daughter, however understandable his reaction might have been, the worker cut himself off from the parents, particularly the father, just at the moment when the father needed him the most. His response to the daughter was helpful in that he recognized her pain and articulated her feelings. If, at the same moment, he could have understood the father's feelings and responded with genuine empathy, the conversation might have sounded as follows:

FATHER: In Europe, children listen to their parents and respect them.
WORKER: So it makes it hard for you to understand what's going on now—why it doesn't seem to work the same way here in the United States.

In this moment, the worker needs to feel genuine empathy along with saying these words. The worker must be feeling something of the father's struggle to figure out how to be a good parent when the world seems upside down from the way in which he was raised. As indicated in the previous section, the worker will work in this first session to reframe the family's thinking about the problem, trying to help the parents as well as the children shift from blaming and confronting the daughter to seeing the problem as one facing the whole family system. At this moment, however, the worker needs to be able to develop his working relationship with the parents, particularly the father. The worker must resist the pull toward triangulation, in which the family members may attempt to align the worker with their side. Instead, the worker must align himself with both clients—each individual family member and the family as a whole.

In fact, as the first full example described next will show, the father's behavior is in part an effort to find out just what kind of worker this is going to be. Since he was already likely feeling guilty about his parenting (something he may not admit even to himself), he probably began the session assuming that the worker would be on his daughter's side. When the father saw the worker's informal dress and guessed at the worker's age, a part of him said, "He's not much older than she is. How is he going to understand?" When the worker responded with the lecture on American culture, the father knew he had been right.

The worker was suffering from an advanced case of **functional diffusion**, or a loss of functional clarity that causes workers to diffuse their activity and implement a role or roles inappropriate for the moment. That is, the worker ends up trying to take on several different roles (such as teacher, cop, or preacher). Fortunately, this is not a terminal illness and can be overcome with a dose of functional clarity. If the worker is there to mediate the individual-social engagement, and the worker can understand his responsibility to be with, at one and the same time, each individual family member (including the father) and the family as a whole. The importance of this can be seen clearly if one realizes that in the example presented by the worker, at precisely the moment he was trying to get the father to understand the daughter's feelings, he was demonstrating his complete inability to feel with the father. Because the worker demonstrates a model of personal functioning, he said more to that father by his actions than through his words. He wanted the father to understand the daughter's behaviors, even those the father experienced as "deviant," but he himself was having difficulty reaching behind the father's deviant behavior to understand the message he was sending.

In reality, even with functional clarity, workers continuously find themselves overidentifying with one part of the family system and cutting themselves off from another. The countertransference process (discussed in Chapter 4) is never stronger than in work with families. Younger workers, some not far removed from situations similar to those experienced by the teenager in the family, must work hard to deal with their own feelings toward authoritative fathers or mothers if they are ever to begin to relate to these parental types as individuals instead of as cardboard caricatures.

This is a lifelong task, with workers using their professional experiences to understand their own personal lives better and using their personal experiences to understand their professional practice more. In this sense, each family one works with represents an opportunity to learn more about one's own family of origin. Some family therapy theorists, such as Bowen (1978), incorporate family-of-origin work as a central part of the training for family therapists. As the therapist comes to grips with personal issues in relation to the family of origin, his or her insights can have a profound impact on work with clients.

Although it seems a truism that work on a social worker's own family issues (or any form of therapy) may add to her or his ability to work with families, this idea raises a controversial issue in social work training. Students have reported supervision sessions that apparently abandoned work on the actual practice problems, focusing instead on the student's own family history, life issues, and problems. Take, for example, a student who grew up in an alcoholic family. Instead of reflecting on the specific ways this life experience may be affecting the student in moment-by-moment interactions with an alcoholic client-parent, the supervisor might focus on the student's history itself, thereby trading the educational focus of supervision for therapy. This is an example of functional diffusion on the part of the field supervisor.

In the balance of this chapter, and in Chapter 7, several examples will illustrate the key concepts outlined in Parts I and II of this book and the first half of this chapter.

The Beginning Phase

The concepts introduced in Chapters 2 and 3 dealing with the importance of tuning in and contracting apply to family work as well. A major difference, however, is that the worker must now also tune in to the entity called the *family as a whole*. This requires the worker to consider each member of the family but also to step back and view and understand the family as a dynamic system in which the behavior of each member affects and is affected by the behavior of the others as well as by the family culture. A family culture consists of the norms of behavior, rules of interaction, taboo subjects, roles played by individual members (such as the family scapegoat), and so forth. Much of the work done with families involves attempting to influence a change toward a more constructive family culture that meets the common needs of all members while respecting the individual needs of each member.

The contracting process is also influenced by the fact that the worker is dealing with more than one client at a time. Being clear about purpose in the contracting remains important, as does obtaining feedback from the clients. However, each client may start with a different idea of the work to be done. A teenager may want to have more freedom, while a parent may want the worker to "change" the child so that she conforms more to the rules of behavior. The worker must be able to identify common ground as well as important differences between family members.

Because family members often attempt to treat the worker as a judge and jury trying to get the worker to identify with their views and issues, the worker must also clearly define his or her role. This is where the two-client concept comes in. The worker must make clear that he or she is identified with each individual but also with the family as a whole. In the illustrations that follow, we shall see how important explaining and maintaining this two-client role really is.

First Family Session With an Angry Father

In the example that follows, we see a worker dealing with a family not unlike the one described earlier in this chapter. In this example, we have an angry, volatile father and a 14-year-old son. It illustrates how a worker can catch a mistake and correct it during the session. This worker was a social work student in a family support worker role in a large child welfare agency. Because of a complaint of physical abuse of the teenager, the social worker with the protection responsibility had made the first contact. The family support worker was called in to provide family counseling to see if the family could be helped to deal with the problem while keeping the child at home. The material that follows is from the worker's report of the first contact.

Description of the Curakis Family

Father: A Greek store owner. He was described to me as an angry, volatile, and violent man. Those who had tried to work with him described him as "a write-off," unworkable. He held very definite ideas of family life, including roles, expectations, etc. He came from a family where his father hit him often when disciplining. Obedience was valued.

Mother: A German teacher. She was a quiet, soft-spoken woman from an upper-middle-class background.

Son: A 14-year-old who was defiant toward his father. He smoked in front of him, in direct contravention of the father's orders. He performed well in school and had no apparent peer problems.

Precipitating Incident

Mother sought help after husband repeatedly hit her son with his fist and once with a board. (Mother was not present during this incident. The story was shared by the son.) Father denies he hit the boy with anything other than an open hand.

History

During the family's previous contacts with professionals and family friends, they scolded—in one form or another—the father for his behavior and showed sympathy for the boy. The most recent contact with a social worker was similar, with the additional threat to remove the boy from the house. The mother was planning to remove the child at the time of this meeting, and did so the following day against the father's wishes. The father believed the family and its functioning were his responsibility.

Both the husband and wife said that their marriage prior to the birth of their son had been fine, though Mrs. Curakis's voice was tentative. Discord arose shortly after the child's birth. From Mr. Curakis's point of view his wife was too soft; from her point of view he was too hard. Throughout the child's life they could not agree on parenting procedures.

Mr. Curakis was the boss in the house. What he said was done. His wife was able to modify these edicts to a moderate degree in regard to herself, but only to a minor degree in regard to her son. At times of discipline the father took command—often in a physical way. While this was happening, Mrs. Curakis would not become involved unless she felt that her son would be seriously hurt. However, after Mr. Curakis finished, she would take her son aside (in Mr. Curakis's absence), calm him, cuddle him, and in most instances contradict or modify what Mr. Curakis had said.

These actions on Mrs. Curakis's part were a constant irritant to the couple's relationship. She felt it was necessary to her son's development. He felt it was undermining his authority and was the reason the boy was acting the way he was. I gave the above history to indicate how—from the father's point of view and in reality—he had been undermined, excluded, and put down, and at the same time how his son was "sided with" (coalition)—against him—by family friends, social workers, his family doctor, and his wife.

It would be easy to see how the social worker in this example, after reading the agency records and making the initial assessment, might begin the interview already identifying with the family members versus the father. It would also be natural for the father to assume that this worker would be like all the rest. As the interview began the father, son, and mother acted out their issues in a conflict over smoking. The worker skillfully responded to the process by recognizing it as a communication to him and used it to focus on the content. During the early part of the session, the worker failed to pick up on the escalating clues of the father's anger and concern about the worker siding against him. In a skillful example of catching one's mistake while one is making it, as well as trusting one's feelings, the worker finally reached for the issue of the authority theme.

The Interview

The family had just been introduced to me by the social worker. The boy walked into the interview room smoking a cigarette.

I introduced myself and began to give a brief introduction of myself and my role in the agency. As I was about two minutes into the introduction, the father began admonishing the boy for smoking. The boy said nothing at first. The father kept shouting. His statements became more derogatory and turned into a general attack on the boy's attitude. Mrs. Curakis, under her breath, said her husband's name, thereby asking him to stop.

I asked her if this is how the fights between her husband and her son often began. Mr. Curakis glared at me, at his wife, and then continued attacking his son (verbally).

Throughout the next 10 or 15 minutes, I made numerous attempts at connecting with individual family members by empathizing, understanding, etc. I connected easily with Mrs. Curakis and her son, but was unable to do so with Mr. Curakis. In fact, he was becoming more and more angry each time I spoke, regardless of whom I spoke to. But he was most hostile while I was speaking with the boy. Each time I began speaking to the boy, the father would, in a voice louder than mine, accuse the boy of some transgression. They would then get into a loud argument.

After a while, this pattern changed. Now each time I spoke to the boy, Mr. Curakis would start arguing with the boy, but ended up shouting at me. At first I did not realize this change; I only realized that I was beginning to understand what my colleague had warned me about. I was becoming impatient and angry with this "jerk." Almost mechanically, I said, "You are angry with me?" There was little or no concern in my voice.

The nonverbal cues did not seem to matter. The quality of anger changed. He was now focused on me, but he was not angry with me. For the next 15 minutes he angrily related the years of no one understanding him, the sincere attempts he had made and was making to help his son grow up properly, the repeated incidents of "people" siding with his son against him after he had disciplined his son and how that had created the present situation, and how his wife and he could not get close because of it. I said something like, "And that makes it even more difficult, doesn't it?" in a sincere manner.

But he just continued letting it out. There was a pregnant silence—a very pregnant silence. I began to get uncomfortable and wanted to find something appropriate to say. Something that would summarize what he was trying to say. But I couldn't think of anything. Then a sentence came to mind: "And you think I'm going to be like all the rest."

"That's right!" he shouted, almost coming out of his seat. He went on for a few minutes about his concern that when I talked to his son I was acting just like the others.

There was a long silence. I was nodding, admitting to both of us that he was right. I apologized and told him that what I had done was not what I was trying to do. I went on to say that it was my job to be helpful to both of them, and if I wasn't then I wasn't doing my job the way I wanted to. I asked him to do me a favor. If he noticed me doing that again—to anyone in the family—to please let me know. I would appreciate it.

The remaining 10 to 15 minutes of the meeting were spent, to a large degree, discussing "old" parenting issues (between Mr. and Mrs. Curakis)—nothing significant. What was significant was that they were talking on a topic that they had avoided—except in argument—for many years. I asked them if they wanted another appointment. After a few moments' discussion they decided they did— as a family.

As they were on their way out, I said goodbye to the boy. He was a little less "cocky," but not very different. Mrs. Curakis seemed quiet, not quite at ease, but it looked like the universe she had been carrying around on her shoulders was reduced to a solar system. The biggest change was in Mr. Curakis. He shook my hand with both hands, looked me in the eyes and said, "Thank you, thank you, thank you very much." There were tears in his eyes. I put my other hand on his and said, "You're welcome." Tears welled up in my eyes.

When I walked into the front office after they left, some of the office staff shook their heads, thereby referring to what I must have gone through and what a "jerk" he was. (It seems that he had been quite gruff to the receptionist on the way in.) I told them that he was really quite a nice guy. (Pregnant silence.)

Discussion of This First Family Session

In a first session with a family, as with an individual counseling session, contracting is crucial. The key questions on the minds of all the family members are "Who is this worker, what kind of worker will he or she be, and what will happen here?" Because of the family's prior experiences with other helpers, they begin with a stereotype of the worker that must be dealt with head-on. The worker in this example had tuned in to the potential feelings and concerns of the family members and was sensitive to the past experiences described in the brief history. Even so, when the father exploded at the son, all of the worker's best plans, opening statements, strategies, and so forth went up in smoke. His first reactions were quite normal for a new worker. His skill was revealed in the quickness with which he caught the mistake in the same session and began to address the real issues raised by the boy who entered with a cigarette, the mother who displayed her passivity, and the father who said through his actions: "If you want to see what it's like around this family, just watch."

The worker had been set up by previous workers (even the office staff) to see the father as the stereotype he presented. The father was ready to see the worker as a stereotype as well. By responding directly to the anger and the implied question about how he was going to help, the worker broke the pattern. Previous workers had found this father hard to work with because of his anger. As the worker reached past the cardboard caricature presented by the father and responded to the process of the session rather than just the content, he began to develop a working relationship with one of the most important family members, revealing a side of the father previously hidden from other workers and the family members. In fact, the father's open expression of anger made him an easier client to work with, in some ways, than if he had hidden his real reactions and participated in an illusion of work, while all the time really feeling, "He's just like all of the rest of those workers; against me, and with the kid."

Because of the urgency of dealing with the father, and the "which side are you on?" issue, other steps remained undone. For example, the worker still needs to be clearer about the purpose of these meetings and the specific role he will play. He started this process by trying to say that he wants to help all of them and not take sides. At a next session, he might want to say something about helping the family members talk to each other about how they operate as a family, and helping them to understand how the other family members really feel. In addition, he will need to make sure that, in his effort to be with the father, he does not lose sight of the mother and the son.

The worker will need to help the family reframe the problem as well. At first they met to discuss their "problem" teenager. Even in the first session, however, the problem with the son quickly led to the problem between the parents. A family needing help will often use a teenage child as a "ticket of admission" to the helping agency. In this case, the struggle over authority and the role of the father in the family was just as much an issue for the husband and wife, but the wife found it easier, and perhaps safer, to deal with that struggle through the child. The pattern of relationship in the family is oppressive, because the father attempts to use emotional and physical intimidation to retain control over the family members. Some of this may be closely related to family and cultural background. This pattern will need to be confronted by the worker; however, such a confrontation may be more fruitful after he develops a relationship with the family.

The worker needs to stay focused on how the parental struggle relates to the couple's ability to parent effectively, helping them to see the connections to their general relationship, but not embarking on a course of general marital counseling (which would be outside of the agency-family working contract). Reassurance on this point may make it safer for both the husband and wife to drop the family facade—the false front discussed earlier.

Another issue that was not dealt with directly in this interview was confidentiality. A child welfare agency was involved, and a threat to apprehend (take into care) the teenage son had already been expressed. The worker will need to deal honestly with this issue; he has to report any information related to child abuse to the child protection social worker. This issue lay just under the surface of the first interview and must be raised and clarified. Under what conditions might the family support worker have to report child abuse to the social worker in this case? Avoiding such a discussion will not make the authority issue go away—rather, it will invest it with more power to block the work.

In summary, the worker made a start toward developing a working relationship with the family, especially its most potentially resistant member. Much work remains, and the outcome depends somewhat on how the worker handles his part and how ready the family members are to tackle their responsibilities.

The Middle Phase

As in the beginning phase, the dynamics and skills described in the earlier chapters in work with individuals can be applied to work with a family in the middle phase of work. The importance of sessional tuning in and sessional contracting is heightened by the fact that the family members have likely interacted intensively for a period of time. No matter what agenda was planned, a new and more urgent agenda may emerge. The worker needs to stay tentative at the start of the session and use elaborating, empathic, and demand-for-work skills to avoid participating in an illusion of work. Depending on the family's history and how long the family has been together, members may be practiced in creating and maintaining the illusion while the real issues remain a "family secret."

In the example that follows, a child welfare social worker brings in a family support worker to help a family in which the 12-year-old son is having trouble staying in school. The family had a 2½-year history of difficult times with the agency staff and is seen as "hard to work with." As the worker's tuning-in comments indicate, he is aware of the past history and of the need to deal with it at the beginning of the relationship. In this case, a 15-year-old daughter raises the question for the family. He is also aware of the family's concern that the session will turn into marital counseling between the mother and her common-law husband of 5 years.

The example demonstrates how the worker tried to develop a working contract that respected the family's concerns, and then redefined the contract as it became clear that the parents wanted help in sorting out how they dealt with the children. A central issue, not uncommon in families with stepparents, is how involved the nonbiological parent shall be. Often, the stepparent is wary about "butting in," while the biological parent wants to avoid burdening the other parent. In the early sessions, the mother indirectly chooses to exclude the stepfather. After confidence grows in the new family support worker, the mother and father are more open to including their relationship in the working contract.

To describe this practice, I use what is called a **record of service** (Garfield & Irizary, 1971). This is a written record that describes the client system, identifies the central problem area, describes and illustrates the practice over time, assesses the status of the problem after a period of work, and then identifies next worker interventions to continue the work. I use it as an assignment with social work students to help them assess a particular problem faced by a client (individual, family, or group) and then to describe their efforts to address the problem over time. A full description of the record of service instrument as well as a discussion of how it may be used in a practice class or field work can be found in the *Instructor's Guide to the Skills of Helping* on the instructor's web page for this course.

The record of service begins with the worker's description of the client and the time frame under discussion. A brief statement of the problem, as seen by the worker, is followed by examples of how this particular issue came to the worker's attention. Next comes a summary of the work using excerpts from process recordings to illustrate the worker's efforts to address the problem. The record of service concludes with an assessment of the current status of the problem (identified at the start of the record) and the worker's strategies for further intervention.

The worker's analysis of what she or he could have done differently is included in the description. The reader will be able to note how a careful self-analysis of practice can lead to significant, positive change in both the worker's interventions and the client's responses. The device provides a means for a worker to incorporate an ongoing analysis of his or her practice.

RECORD OF SERVICE *The Smith Family*

Client Description and Time Frame

Composition: Natural mother, Linda, 35; common-law husband of 5 years, Brian, 29; Marie, 15; Mike, 12; and foster child, Sally, 15. The time period covered is from November through April. The setting is a child welfare agency.

History: Linda, 35, natural mother of Mike and Marie, was from a very unhappy background, having an alcoholic father, being abused by him, and living in fear. School was a bad experience, and she prides herself on being very financially successful with only a grade 6 education. She believes that Mike can do just as well if he can learn the basic "three R's." Brian, 29, has lived with Linda for the past 5 years as her common-law husband. He was born and raised in Europe, immigrated to the United States when he was 15 years old, and works successfully with a small business. He only gets involved with the children if Linda is desperate. His family, which lives in town, feels that Linda has led him into a sinful life, and he visits them on his own. He cannot accept the fact that Mike has a severe learning disability and [Brian] feels that he must be made to sit down and learn. Brian had not spoken to the previous worker in 2½ years except to exchange hellos.

Marie, 15, was in the process of dropping out of school and trying to get into an accelerated program in order to get school finished quickly. Sally, 15, joined the household in January, had been Marie's best friend previously and couldn't manage living with her own family. Mike, 12, had been at numerous resources and was expelled from school as he'd threatened several teachers and beaten up different children at the school. The special teacher later supplied had threatened to resign if she was required to tutor Mike. When I contacted the last resource he'd been in, I was informed that the family and Mike were "unworkable." With this and the information at the office, I was more than a little wary about being involved.

Description of the Problem

Linda (the mother) was in a bind; she had turned to the agency for assistance but was very hesitant to work with an agency that she felt wasn't responsive to her needs. Both Linda and her previous worker of years had seen each other as adversaries, each trying to do what they thought was best for Mike. My record will follow how I worked to develop a culture in which Linda and the agency could identify their common ground of getting Mike back into school.

How the Problem Came to the Attention of the Worker(s)

The Smith family was my first chance to get working with a family, and Jane, the previous worker, went over the file with me. It soon became clear that the agency and Linda went through a definite pattern whenever the social worker found a facility that would consider taking Mike. The worker would find a facility, set up intake interviews, inform Linda; she'd agree to attend the interviews but always ended up by saying it wouldn't work. Mike would initially attend the program but after about a month, he wouldn't show up. In frustration, the worker would tell Linda that Mike had been missing, and she'd confirm that she knew this. Mike would always stop attending the facility close to the times that there were to be "family sessions" and Linda's perception of these was a time when her relationship with Brian would be examined and the two of them would be blamed for Mike's problems.

Summary of the Work

In preparation, I did some resource hunting and came up with some possible placements from the description of what Linda wanted from conversations we'd had by telephone. I also did some preliminary tuning in. In considering the work to follow, I came up with several taboo areas:

- Telling Linda about parenting techniques.
- Trying to probe Linda and Brian's relationship.
- Trying to do a sales pitch for a resource.
- Trying to steer Linda where I though she should go.

I realized that things must be getting desperate for Linda to call for help. Linda had been through the routine many times and knew the ropes much better than I. I knew I had to level about my agenda. In addition, I had to do a lot of work on the negatives before we could move. I had to let the family know that there might be nothing available for Mike.

January (The First Meeting; I Was Nervous)

I was let in the door by Linda, who seemed tired, flustered, and looked as if she were in pain. They'd just finished supper and another social worker who was seeing Sally had left about 20 minutes previously. Linda offered me a seat in the living room, turned off the TV, and called Mike, who sat next to me on the couch. To my amazement Mike was a pleasant-looking 12-year-old who spoke as I'd expect a fellow his age would. I relaxed a bit, figuring he must either have been well drilled beforehand or a top-blower. Marie sat about 6 feet away looking at a book but was all ears. Brian sat at the far end of the dining room reading and looked up occasionally. I opened the meeting by establishing role and purpose.

> WORKER: Linda, you and I have spoken on the telephone and I'm wondering if the others know why I'm here tonight. What have you told them?
> LINDA: Well, I told these guys that we're having a new social worker to find a place for Mike to go to school. He's 12 now and needs to get something—anything—so that he'll know how to read, do some math, and get a job. We need someone to find out where he can go and still be able to stay at home.

Linda continued speaking, and Brian had stopped his reading and looked interested, so I asked him what he thought about plans for Mike. He agreed that Mike needed to be in school and hoped that I could find a place. Linda jumped in suddenly, "Brian works really hard and I do all the kids' schoolwork planning, you know." It seemed like Linda was trying to shut me off from talking with Brian, but I fought the urge to try to override her. Linda said, "Brian, why don't you make us some coffee?" He slowly disappeared into the kitchen and only appeared to deliver coffee, then returned to the kitchen. I wondered why Linda wanted Brian out of the discussion but didn't feel comfortable asking, so I turned to Mike and asked him what he'd like.

> MIKE: The same things you've been talking about.
> WORKER: Some regular schoolwork and some things to do with your hands like mechanics and carpentry?
> MIKE: Yeah, I'd really like that. I fix my bike all the time and I've made things, you know. Would you like to see something?
> LINDA: Show Frank your blue vase.

Mike got a blue ceramic vase from the knick-knack shelf and proudly showed it. It was a good job, and I told him that I liked it. Marie was getting fidgety and I thought she wanted to get in so I asked her what she thought about plans for Mike. She spoke angrily.

> MARIE: I don't want to talk about that. I want to talk about social workers and how they don't care about people. All they care about is making money and themselves.

She gave a rundown on all the things that had been tried, failed, and a list of social workers' faults. I was glad for our class work on checking out previous experiences and felt Marie's strength in speaking out.

> WORKER: (Moving from the general to the specific) Boy (I sighed), from what you've said I'm sure you must be wondering if I'll be just like all the rest. I do want to find out exactly what Mike wants, as I know that there's no point in trying to force something on Mike that he doesn't want and that everyone doesn't agree to try. I hope that Mike and Linda will tell me, like you have, when I've missed the point or am not listening.
> MARIE: Well, you are different. You're the first person who's asked Mike what he wants and not just come here and told us what to do.

I thanked Marie, felt like she'd done a lot of work for me as everyone agreed to let me know if I was missing their point. I told them that I'd let them know if I thought they were missing my point or assuming without checking. This led into a discussion about years of misunderstandings and the frustrations involved.

February

As the weeks passed, no facility was available for Mike. Our first meeting in February started with Mike meeting me at the door; he had two friends with him and was eager to talk and leave. I'd been looking for a tutor for Mike and had been unsuccessful.

MIKE: Have you found a tutor for me yet? It's getting to be a long time, you know, everyone says they're going to do something and then nothing ever happens.

WORKER: No, I haven't found anyone yet. Right now it looks like it could be several weeks before there'll be someone. Bet you're angry waiting to see who'll come.

MIKE: Yeah, you know the longer things go, the worse they'll get; sometimes I just get mad and say to Mom—just tell him to stuff it if he can't get someone to help.

WORKER: I get really frustrated too. Sometimes it seems like forever before there's a tutor available.

In the kitchen Linda was tallying her day's receipts, so I sat down and helped sort them out.

LINDA: No news, it sounds like, from your call.

WORKER: That's right. You sound like you've been through this before, Linda—fed up with the whole waiting business.

With that we got into a discussion about hassles she's had with the agency, the school system, and other agencies. She asked if I'd go with her to find out exactly what had happened when Mike had got suspended, and I agreed. Brian, who so often barely said two words, came in and sat opposite me at the table and looked as if he wanted to join the conversation.

I tried to include Brian and needed to recontract if he were to be included.

WORKER: Do you know what we've been talking about so far, Brian?

BRIAN: Yes, I could hear from the living room and want you to know that it's no good if you get someone for two hours a day. If Mike can get into doing something he wants, then he'll leave the schoolwork and never learn.

Brian went on to explain how he'd learned English, etc., when he arrived from Europe by studying 8 hours a day, and he began to attack Linda's parenting skills and blame her for Mike's failure. I could see Linda freeze up and referred to our contract.

WORKER: Linda, Brian is talking now about your differences, and we've agreed that you will decide if I'm to be involved in those discussions.

I could see the smoke inside Linda, didn't want to lose Brian's impetus, but wasn't going to break my agreement with Linda.

LINDA: Brian, you know I don't want to talk about this in front of others, it always leads to trouble.

BRIAN: We've got to talk about it or it'll always be the same, nothing's going to change if we don't try something different.

Brian was visibly shaken; he motioned to his chest indicating that he could hardly breathe and stuttered badly while he told me of an old injury that causes this condition when he's angry. I still wanted Linda to have the say as to my participation.

WORKER: I still want you to ask me to wait in the living room, Linda, if you want to talk with Brian privately. I am willing to stay if you want; I might be able to help sort out some of the things both you and Brian are saying. This conversation sounds like it's been talked through a number of times without any solutions, just going around in circles with both of you getting really mad at each other.

LINDA: You can stay.

They talked about the differences in their upbringings and their expectations for their own family. They seemed to exaggerate their differences and I pointed out many similarities such as the belief that you have to be tough to survive and at the same time they both wanted warmth and affection. Brian's gasping for breath made it almost impossible to get his words out. At that point it seemed like they both wanted each other's support so badly but couldn't say it.

WORKER: You both sound so frustrated and both really want things to be good here. Linda, you sound like you could use some support from Brian. (I missed "vice versa.")

Linda looked startled and said, "Yes, I could." Brian was done in, but heard, and excused himself from the room. Linda talked more about how hard it'd been for her and how she felt the kids were biologically hers so she should take all the responsibility for them. I told her we could talk more about that and thanked Brian on the way out for telling his part.

Because conversations between the husband and wife had broken down and turned to blaming and recriminations, Linda had feared opening up the "taboo" area. And yet, if the family system was going to work effectively, she would need all the help she could get from the whole family to tackle their problems—Brian included. By creating a positive and safe working relationship, and by focusing on the part of their relationship dealing with the children, this worker helped set the stage for Linda's agreement to open the door on this important area of work. When Linda and Brian explore their different cultural backgrounds and family histories, they may find they can better understand both their commonalities and differences. It is only a beginning, but a rather important one in reframing the problem.

Another interesting observation is that the worker sat down with Linda and helped her sort her receipts. Workers often complain of the difficulty of getting a family's attention with so much going on. This worker did not ask Linda to stop what she was doing but instead sat with her and helped. In another case, this worker carried out an excellent interview with a single-parent mom while helping her fold laundry. These ongoing family activities are often a signal to the worker of the stress the family feels about the session, and sometimes it may be easier to work within the activity than to try to bring it to a formal stop.

In the excerpt that follows, the worker brings a tutor into the situation and meets with her, Linda, and Mike to discuss their working contract. When the tutor mentions the possibility of a family meeting to discuss Mike's school progress, both Mike and his mother go off into "flight" to escape the uncomfortable subject. The worker responds to the process of the session and calls everyone's attention to what happened. This allows the concerns about family sessions to be aired and the contract clarified. In the second excerpt, we see the worker beginning the phase of transitions and endings, getting ready to connect the family members to new sources of help after he leaves.

March

By March, I was able to get a tutor for Mike—Betty, who had worked with him 2 years before and was the only tutor the Smiths had identified as having been helpful. We met together to draw up Betty's contract. Mike was eager to have Betty work with him.

> WORKER: Now, what do you two want Betty to work on during her time with Mike?

There was silence, many shrugs, looks at the ceiling, and "I don't knows"; then Linda asked me, "What do you think should go down there?" referring to the contract.

> BETTY: No, no, no—it's not up to Frank [the worker] to say what you want, it's up to you and Mike. There's no way I can work with you unless we agree on the contract. We can change as we go along, but you have to say what you want.

After more silence, Linda listed what she wanted. Betty added a weekly family meeting to discuss how things were going at school and at home for Mike and Linda. Suddenly Mike started talking about the paint on the ceiling, and he and Linda spoke at full speed about the ceiling paint.

> WORKER: Wait a minute—what's going on here? All of a sudden you two took off and I don't know what's happening. What just happened here? (Responding to indirect cues)
> LINDA: Oh, nothing, I'm sorry.
> WORKER: Mike, do you know what happened to you, you started looking at the ceiling all of a sudden?
> MIKE: It's the family meetings—she doesn't like them, that's what happened before, she didn't want to go to them. (Linda looked shell-shocked.)
> WORKER: What happened when you didn't have the sessions, Mike?
> MIKE: I got kicked out.
> WORKER: Are you worried that the same thing might happen again? (Supporting Mike in a taboo area)

Mike went on to say that he wanted to have the school work out for him. Linda explained to him what she'd disliked about previous family meetings. After some clarification of Betty's role and purpose in the meetings, Mike thought it would work and was first to sign the agreement, looking proud of playing his part. Betty and I told them that they'd both taken big steps in leveling with us and each other. (Crediting work done)

April

At a regular evening meeting in early April we'd been talking about endings, and Linda had been shocked at first that the time was so short and then angry at me for leaving and frustrated about having to start all over again with another worker.

> WORKER: I remember our first meetings, Linda. I wasn't sure if we'd be able to work together at all. I feel that we've come through a great deal together and it's been pretty shaky at times—you know the times we've both got pissed off. You've all made me feel welcome in your home, I've come to like you very much, and I'm going to miss you.

LINDA: Then why are you leaving? I know you have to leave. Who will be my new worker?

WORKER: That's something I've been checking out. You've said that you've had a hard time whenever a new worker is involved. (Linda agreed and said that she wouldn't fool around and be nice to a new worker she didn't like.) That's one of the things I really like about working with you, you give it to me straight. I was always confident when I felt like I'd blown it that you'd tell me. That's a feeling I enjoy. Also I was honored last week when you told me that you trusted me—I knew that was hard for you to say—that's when you added "almost."

LINDA: Well, I do trust you. (She laughed and added "almost.")

I explained that I'd talked to my supervisor to find out who'd be getting the Smiths after I left, and we talked about getting together in order to clarify what would be happening. The conversation continued around some of the snags we'd hit, how things were resolved, and what obstacles might come up. It hadn't occurred to me until that evening how much I'd become involved with the family, and the conversation about leaving really hit me.

Current Status of the Problem

Where It Stands Now

Linda has begun to see the agency as an ally and took the opportunity to suggest a joint meeting with Debbie, who'll be the new worker, in order to establish a working contract. Brian has joined in the last four out of five meetings and has said that he's willing to help with Mike when Linda asks. She's agreed to include Brian in the weekly family sessions.

Strategies for Intervention

- Betty will continue working with Mike until the end of June and will be available in September for schoolwork and family sessions.
- Debbie and I will follow up on our meeting to discuss future plans, and she'll be available to the Smiths and Betty.
- Linda, Mike, Betty, and I will visit another possible resource this week and discuss future plans.

Note that the worker's analysis of the current status of the problem does not consider it to be "solved." Very rarely are problems solved; in fact, I encourage workers to remove that word from their vocabulary. What the worker does instead is identify important changes in the state of the relationship between the family and the agency and among the family members themselves. The worker has helped to build a platform for ongoing work. In the lives of these clients, he has been only an incident—but an important one. Keeping this perspective helps workers avoid two common types of mistakes in analyzing practice: overestimating or underestimating the impact on a client.

Two Special Circumstances

In dealing with families, social workers face many issues, some specific to the kind of family they serve. Before looking at the ending and transition phase, we take a moment to discuss the issues that arise from working with a single-parent family. We also look at a case in which support from the larger culture and community play a key role. As we have seen in the chapters on work with individuals, sensitivity to such issues can greatly increase the worker's effectiveness.

Working With a Single-Parent Family

Our old view of the average family as consisting of a working father, a mother at home and two to three children has become more myth than reality. The rate of growth of single-parent families is increasing. At one of my speaking engagements on the subject of working with single parents, I asked the audience—all helping professionals—how many of them were single parents, had been children in homes of single parents, or had close relations who were involved in single parenting. Almost two thirds of the five hundred people in the audience raised their hands.

Although single-parent and two-parent families have much in common, they differ in several ways that helping professionals should note. Single parents have to face many of the same normative crises faced by other families, but they have to face them alone. Most single parents are women, and a large percentage of these must either work (often in low-pay, low-status, dead-end jobs) or depend on welfare. Further, welfare reform law set a 5-year limit for receiving welfare, so that many families face the possibility of losing or have already lost welfare payments. For many, the lack of affordable day care facilities makes working, and therefore improving their financial situation, impossible. Between low pay and welfare, most single-parent mothers must try to live on income levels below the accepted poverty level—a factor that significantly increases the stress of raising a family alone. This, combined with the limited availability of decent-paying jobs, does not augur well for single-parent families.

Housing is another major area of distress for single parents. Many housing options are not open to them, and as a result, they need to pay more of their income for housing than the general population does. A female single parent quickly discovers that her credit rating left with her husband, even if she had a positive relationship with her local bank while she was married. She may suddenly find herself in a catch-22—needing a positive credit record to get credit, but needing credit to obtain a positive credit record. Thus, if she wishes to purchase a home, she may run into discrimination that keeps her from improving her housing situation.

Single parents also face special problems in dealing with friends. Many single parents report that, after their divorce, former close friends change their attitudes toward them and take sides. Another common factor is the "Noah's ark syndrome," in which friends seem to be operating under the general belief that people should come "two by two." Old friends slip away, and new friends are harder to find. This problem, often compounded by the single parent's depression and lack of effort to create new support groups, leads to further isolation and loneliness. With these added pressures, a single parent often has difficulty finding time to meet her personal needs while still taking care of the needs of the children. Dealing with school meetings, dental appointments, homework, and so on is difficult enough for two parents.

In addition, dealing with the feelings of one's children when one is so vulnerable can be too hard to do alone. As a result, barriers start to grow in a family, and certain areas become taboo. One crucial taboo area may be the feelings of the children about the absent parent and the rejection they feel. As one woman said in a group I led for single parents, "It's hard for me to help my kids face their rejection, because I still haven't been able to face mine." The guilt felt by the remaining parent often makes an honest discussion with the children difficult. The children may show signs of distress through behavior cues appropriate to their age. For example, young children regress and wet the bed; latency-age children cut themselves off from friends, have school trouble, and get into fights; and teenagers get into trouble with the law. In such cases, the parent often senses the cause; however, the parent's guilt can create a significant communication blockage that prevents work on the problem.

Ongoing relations with the ex-spouse can also take a toll on the parent and the children. Often, the battles of the marriage or feelings concerning the split emerge around custody issues, financial support issues, and struggles over loyalty. Children already hurt by a split between their parents, for which they may feel responsible, are further distressed by feeling they must take sides and cannot be loyal to both parents at the same time. (For a detailed example of work with a single parent—one that illustrates many of these issues—see the Chapter 6 process excerpts on this book's companion web page.)

The Impact of Culture and Community: A White Worker and an American Indian Family

One of the greatest tragedies in North America has been the impact of the white society on its "first peoples," the Indians or Native Americans. A strong family and community tradition, a whole culture, and a way of life, were systematically stripped from a people in what has been described as cultural genocide. This problem is a special case of the struggle each minority group faces, whether aboriginals or immigrants. Each must find a way to preserve what is of value to its own culture and still come to grips with a surrounding and dominating culture. When the group is of another race—Indian, black, Chicano, Asian—the struggle is usually intensified by a persistent racism, sometimes subtle, other times open and direct.

In the Native community, from which the family in this example is drawn, years of neglect, discrimination, and exploitation have often led to a breakdown in individual, family, and community functioning. Once-proud cultural traditions have been lost for many of the community's members. In particular, teenagers must go through a crucial step in their normative development in which they struggle to understand who they are and how they shall be. The separation and integration issue is just as important in relation to one's culture and community as it is in relation to the immediate family. In fact, the two struggles become intertwined in important ways. Ambivalent feelings increase when the subculture, the peer group for a teenager, encourages and supports deviant behavior (the extensive use of alcohol, criminal activity, and so on) and the future appears to be bleak. When a teenager looks around and sees members of the adult community who appear to have given up, her or his internal struggle can lead to complete alienation from the larger society, or in a shockingly large number of cases, teenage suicide. Facing the problems, finding the strength to cope, and accepting the role model of many of the adult members of the community who have refused to surrender to years of oppression represent another choice. For the teenagers in this situation to make this transition, they will need all the help they can get from family, community (the local band), and their cultural heritage.

In the example that follows, culture and community are key issues as Jim, a 14-year-old Native teenager, struggles with this crucial, transitional crisis. The worker must also deal with the fact that she is white. No matter what her attitudes and feelings may be with respect to people of color, she is an outsider—a member of the oppressor group. White workers must be alert to the fact that, as one African American social work supervisor described it in a training workshop, "For a person of color, the antennae are always up on the lookout for racism."

In a study cited throughout this book (Shulman, 1991), the issue of race and practice in relation to Native clients was explored. Two variables included in the analysis were the worker's understanding of the Native culture (as perceived by clients) and of the impact of race on the relationship (as perceived by the worker). Both of these variables showed strong positive associations with the client's perceptions of a positive working relationship with the worker and the worker's helpfulness. These variables, as well as those that measured the attitude of the regional staff as a whole toward Native clients, also affected other outcome measures. A first step in dealing with racism in practice is for helping professionals to face and accept the existence of their own internalized racism and sexism, which is a product of centuries of white, male, Euro-centered history, philosophy, medicine, psychology, and so on (Bulhan, 1985; Fanon, 1968). Only then can workers begin the task of monitoring and purging its impact on their practice. Each new client who is different from the worker can be part of the worker's education. Workers also have a responsibility to work on their own education.

With a clearer sense of the impact of oppression on the psychology and sociology of people of color, coupled with an understanding of the resilience factors that have helped people cope with oppression, the worker may be able to perceive problems in living in new ways. The focus shifts from personal pathology and a reinforcement of oppressive stereotyping to a practice that helps the client to perceive the devastating impact on self that can occur for any member of an oppressed group. In addition, the identification of baseline and developmental reserve capacity in individuals, the family, and the community offers opportunities to break the cycles that block growth and development. Techniques drawn from solution-focused therapy can help clients identify how they have coped.

This perspective is important for work not only with people of color but also with other oppressed and vulnerable populations (such as women, the mentally ill, survivors of the Nazi Holocaust and their descendants, gays and lesbians). Such a shift in perspective by the helping professional opens up the possibility of finding important areas of strength in the client, the community, and the culture. It also more clearly defines a professional responsibility for social workers to influence their own agencies, the community, and society away from oppressive practices.

Examples of adoption of self-destructive behavior and self-denigrating attitudes painfully emerge in the following example as the parents refer to their son's "crazy Indian" and "dirty Indian" behavior. The worker's recognition of culturally based strengths appear in her attention to the importance to the son of his dancing and carving skills.

RECORD OF SERVICE

Client Description and Time Frame

Father is 40; stepmother is 29; and son, Jim, is 14. The family is being seen as part of a probation program ordered by a judge because of Jim's arrests for breaking and entering.

Description of the Problem

Jim, in the throes of puberty, is searching very hard to establish his identity. Most of all, he wants to feel and be proud of his Native heritage, but the conflicting messages he has internalized about "being Indian" do not allow him to do so positively. His anger and confusion manifest themselves by his acting out: he has committed seven B&Es (Breaking and Entering) on the reserve, two of them specifically focusing on the Indian Band office. He has developed an alcohol problem. His acting out has alienated him from the elders of the band, who refuse to be involved in helping him with the court process, as is usually the case for juvenile delinquents of this band. I perceive his B&Es as cries for help with his home situation.

Jim's parents are disheartened and upset. They feel they have tried their best and have failed. They are considering sending him away to a residential school. Their medium of communication and major stumbling block between Jim and themselves is discussion of Native identity: all emotions, conflict, and disagreement are discussed under the heading "Indian." In my efforts to help this family, I must also deal with their feelings about me—a white, female probation officer. I realize I will have to become more than just a symbol of white authority.

How the Problem Came to the Attention of the Worker(s)

My first meeting with Jim and his parents was to discuss the B&E charges in the hope of sparing Jim court appearances. I had great difficulty keeping the session on focus: it was too painful a topic for everyone to discuss directly. Actually, Jim and his parents reenacted their communication pattern in front of me: The war was on. Jim's mother said angrily that these B&Es were "crazy Indian stuff." I tried to reach for the feelings of pain and disappointment behind the anger and said, "Jim's B&Es are hard on the family right now; they would be for any family, Indian or not." Jim's father said, "I knew nothing about them Indians." Jim didn't give me a chance to say anything and counterattacked by angrily saying that his parents are Honkies in disguise but he is an Indian, he is a super dancer and carver and can drink and fight with the bigger guys on the reserve any day. I said that his parents might be proud about his dancing and carving. Jim's mother said, "Honkies or not Honkies, we know that Jim is a no-good Indian." The energy they put out fighting made me believe that there was a lot of concern and care hidden behind the anger. Their faces indicated they were clearly in pain.

Summary of the Work

Second Session

I tuned in to Jim's feelings and tried to put his feelings into words. Jim had a tough look on his face. He slid himself into a chair, his knees up close to his chest as if to protect himself. I said, "You look angry as hell today." No response. I waited out his silence. He said with a tone devoid of affect that he had a big fight last night after Indian dancing and that it lasted until 4 in the morning. I asked him if he'd got hurt (empathizing). He said no, he never gets hurt. He was drunk anyway. I was lucky he was sober this afternoon. I said, "Alcohol dims the pain. A 14-year-old drunk is a sad story to me." He said he knew. Jim said he had also siphoned gas out of a car last night. I said, "It is a lot for one night. Are you trying to tell me how bad you can be?" Jim looked at me intently. I said that behind his tough facade I thought there was a lot of pain. His voice changed. With a defensive tone he said "Pain about what?" I said, "Maybe it is painful to feel you have to act like a hellion to get attention." He giggled and said it wasn't funny. I said, "I agree, it's not funny, it hurts." He cocked his head down. I waited out his silence. He said suddenly, "Nothing ever hurts anymore. Nobody cares about me anymore." I said, "Are you talking about home?" (recognizing his indirect communication) He said simply, "Yeah."

I recognized his indirect communication and tried to help him go from general to specific concerns. Jim had done a rerun of the above two weeks in a row; that is, enumerating all the "bad" behaviors he had gotten into. I said it was the third weekend that he had asked me to give him hell. He said that if I didn't, nobody would. I asked him if that's what he wanted his parents to do. He said, "No, I want them to understand me." I said that I knew things were rough for everyone at home right now; could he tell me what had taken place at home that hurt? He looked away and said in a low voice, "They called me a rotten Indian." The affect of pain was so strong that he could not elaborate on his feelings or the specific circumstances. I said, "It hurts a lot doesn't it? I wish I could take the pain away from you."

I tried to share my feelings openly. Jim said that he was sick and tired of being called a dirty Indian at home. The affect was anger. I tried to reach for the specific feeling but got nowhere. He said that all his parents talked about was "dirty Indians this, silly Indians that. Who do they think they are, anyway?" I said, "It may hurt to hear the word *Indian* coming from your own parents as a curse word." He asked me if I though he was a dirty Indian. I said no, he was Indian all right, "but the two words together are a terrible combination." He said, "What about a silly Indian?" I reached for his indirect communication and said, "You're checking out if I'm prejudiced, aren't you?" He said, "Yup." I said it was for him to judge. He said I would be on probation for awhile. I said I knew. He said in a low voice that he didn't think I could understand. I said gently, "Do you feel you can't win: You can't be right and you can't be Indian?" (Putting the client's feelings into words) He said suddenly, "I don't know what 'Indian' means. How am I supposed to grow up okay?" I put my arms around him and said that he was right. I wasn't sure I could understand fully what it means to grow up as an Indian. I said that his hurt was choking me up right now.

I tried to help Jim view his parents in new ways. Jim said that his parents put him through a grinder whenever he is home. I said that it sounds horrible, what does it mean? (Reaching for elaboration) He said that his parents hassle him about every little detail about what he does at night. I jokingly said, "It's not such a horrible grinder after all!" He laughed. He said that really they don't care about him, they just want him on a leash. I said, "And you want to be more independent, don't you?" (Recognizing the metaphor) He said, "Yup."

I asked him to give me an example of the grinder. He said that last night he came home at midnight. They just had to know who he was with, where he had been. I said, "That sounds to me like they care about you. They worry about you, and frankly at midnight I would worry too." Jim pouted. I waited out his silence. He said, "I don't think they care. They're just angry." I said that maybe they felt both fear and anger. Did he think that they had any reason to be angry last night? He said, "Maybe so. Midnight is kind of late." I agreed. I asked him if he knew what his parents felt waiting for him. He said, "They always assume the worst. That's dumb." I said, "We all do that when we're worried." He said, "I guess I give them reasons to be angry and I don't like it." I said sadly, "and they don't, either. I bet they feel just as bad as you do about yesterday."

I supported him in a taboo area and tried to stay close to his feelings of anger and rejection. Jim said that he was going to kill his mother one of these days. She isn't his real mom anyway. I asked him if he was angry about something she had done or angry because she isn't his real mom. (Trying to partialize his concern) He said, "Both." I asked him what his mom had done for him to be so upset. He said, "She is really unreal; she phoned the school to insist that she be warned if

I skipped out. It's none of her business. My dad's, sure, but not hers." I kept the issue in focus and said, "Not hers because she is your stepmom?" He said, "Yup, I'm not her son. She's got no rights on me." I said sadly, "No right to care? She can't win, can she?" Jim said, "No, she can't win. She's the one who made us move from the reserve." I said I knew about that, that she wanted to make a better home for him and his dad. Jim nervously twisted his hair around his fingers and said that he would rather have his mom around than "her" care. I said that he had expressed real and deep feelings. (Crediting his work) "It's real hard to get over one's Mom's death."

I tried to help Jim identify the affect obstacle and offered to mediate with his parents. Jim said that he doesn't know how to tell his parents to stop calling him names when he does something wrong—names like "silly Indian." When they do, his blood boils and he goes out and gets drunk. He can't say anything. He just walks out. And he does start acting silly. I asked him to tell me exactly what he would like to tell his parents. He said that he just wants them to stop calling him names. But he can't say it to them. I said, "That's their way of criticizing you, isn't it?" He said, "Yeah. It's bad enough being told off when you do something wrong, but then calling me names like that, it's below the belt." I said, "It's like you're nobody all of a sudden." He said, "Yup." He had tears in his eyes.

I said, "Do you want me to help you talk to your parents?" He said, "Yeah." He couldn't do it alone. I said that I'd phone his parents, and if they agreed we'd try to talk about the name-calling and try to understand what is behind it from their side. Jim said that he didn't want to talk about the things he does wrong. I said that he forgets he does a lot of things real well too. We have to take the bad with the good. He said, "Yeah, but I'm far from perfect." I said that perfection is like a rainbow— nobody can reach it, we can only try. He said his parent didn't know that. I said I was sure they did, they just had high expectations for him. He said he didn't believe in high expectations. I laughed and said, "Baloney—you want to be the best about everything." He said, "How do you know?" I said that I had seen some of his carvings. They're beautiful. It was obvious to me that he was trying to be the best. (Emphasizing the positive) Jim had a long drawn-out "oh." I brought the conversation back on focus and said, "So if your parents are willing, we'll talk about both sides." He said he was willing to try but that I was going to get myself into a lot of trouble with his parents. I said, "Because I'm white?" He said, "Yeah." I said I could only try, that things should go easier if I didn't take sides. (Emphasizing the contract)

Third Session

I tried to tune in to the feelings of ambivalence of the one (Jim) and the many (the family), tried to include everyone in the commonality of the experience, and clarified the contract. At the first meeting I said that they must feel a bit uncomfortable about having a white probation officer coming into their home. Mr. Jones smiled and said, "You bet, you're the first one we managed to get in here." Mrs. Jones said that she didn't mind, today she'd had to clean her home for the health nurse anyway. I recognized her ambivalence and said that I know how it feels, it's a hassle to clean house because a stranger is coming in. She nodded hesitantly. I said I felt a bit like an intruder today (putting my personal feelings into words) but that I hoped we would feel more comfortable once we knew each other better.

Jim's eyes were covered by his cap and his arms crossed at his chest. I asked him what he was angry about. He said, "Nothing, leave me alone." Mrs. Jones firmly said that he couldn't talk to me like that. I said it was okay to be angry. Did they

(Jim's parents) know what was making Jim so angry? (Beginning to partialize and trying to help the family members help each other) Mr. Jones said that Jim is like that around home, not to worry. I said that maybe Jim is afraid that we might all gang up on him. (Putting client's feelings into words) "It's certainly not my intention." I said that I was here to have them talk about a real painful issue: Jim can't stand being called a dirty Indian and it hurts so much that he can't talk about it usually.

I got a nasty look from Mr. Jones. Mrs. Jones said she thought it was simple: I should forbid Jim from doing any of that crazy Indian stuff then she'd stop calling him a crazy Indian. Mr. Jones agreed with her. I said that I know they often worry about Jim, but I can't do that. That's not my role, and it wouldn't work anyway. Jim nodded sullenly. I said that I felt uncomfortable about the words "crazy Indian stuff." (Acknowledging feelings) I asked Jim if he knows what his parents mean by that. He lifted his cap from his eyes and said that he knew for sure that "all Indians are dirty, crazy, violent, and lazy drunks." Mr. Jones said, "Here he goes again, acting crazy. Everyone knows that Indians aren't violent and drunk." Jim giggled, and Mr. Jones cracked his knuckles. I said that perhaps Jim was hitting something very painful. That was the prejudice they had to live with day in and day out. Mr. Jones said I was damn right. Mrs. Jones said that's what she worried about, that Jim would become like the rest of them Indians. I said, "You are Indian and you aren't violent, lazy, and crazy. Neither is Jim." (Gentle demand for work) Mrs. Jones said no, but that's because they'd moved away from the reserve. I said that maybe it was time to look at the positive things of the present rather than the bad things of the past. (Emphasizing the positive and the potential to work)

I tried to reach their feelings in their way, to establish contact, and to help the family members help each other. Jim said, "You can't help but act on impulse, that's what my B&Es are all about." I said, "You forget to pray to the spirit of the bear, don't you?" Mr. Jones nodded and said I was right. He told us an Indian story about a little boy becoming a man becoming a bear. It was the opposite of Jim's progress at this point, but it emphasized his potential. Jim said that the story was OK, but that the elders had better ones. I said to Jim that maybe the story hit home a bit hard. (Demand for work) I got nowhere.

Jim said that he had been kicked out of English today and that he wasn't much more disruptive than some of the white kids. I said that a little more disruption is all it takes to make a difference. (Silence) Mr. Jones said that white teachers are racist. Mr. Jones [also] said that females are more racist than men. He would fight with a white man any day, but you can't fight with a white woman. I acknowledged my feelings and said that I was afraid the arrows might start flying toward me. We all laughed at the relief of tension. Jim said that the Indians only scalp white people who have no honor. Mr. Jones grinned. I recognized their offering and said that it felt good to hear I have honor. Their feelings for me are important to me, because I respect them.

I tried to put the client's feelings into words for the benefit of the other family members so that they would gain a new understanding of each other. Mrs. Jones asked me what I intended to do about Jim's alcoholism. I said Jim was doing his best to stay away from alcohol and the reserve, but sometimes he got so depressed about feeling bad about himself that he couldn't help it. Jim said I was right. He can't control himself when his parents call him a crazy Indian. Mr. Jones said that he and his wife mean well. They just don't know what else to say. I said, "I know, when you're worried words don't come easily." Jim said gently, "When I'm rotten, why don't you just say I let you down, Dad?" Mr. Jones put his arms around his son.

Mrs. Jones said that Jim was wasting his time carving; you can't make a living out of it. I said that I was really impressed by Jim's carvings. They are really beautiful. Mrs. Jones said that Jim spends too much time doing that. I said that it takes a lot of time to create a piece of art. Mr. Jones said he knew, because he tried when he was younger and couldn't do half as well as Jim. Jim was beaming. He asked his dad how good an Indian dancer he was when he was younger.

I offered to mediate between the family and a system that made it harder to communicate between Jim and his parents as a result of his delinquencies. Everyone was silent. Mrs. Jones, especially, looked grim. I asked if I had offended them in any way. (Silence) I said, "Anything I have done or said in relation to Jim?" "No," said Mr. Jones, "I guess we are taking it out on you." Jim says that he knows what it's all about. It's about the band. I recognized the indirect communication. "You wish you were on good terms with the band, don't you?" Mrs. Jones said it wasn't possible. There was so much politics going on. Mr. Jones said they were arrogant. Jim continued rocking in his chair and looked hurt. I said, noting his eyes, "You feel guilty about it; you want to cry. Your B&Es stand in the way, don't they?" (Demand for work) He nodded. I said that I would talk to the band office. Maybe they would agree to supervise Jim's probation once I'm gone. Mr. Jones said, "They refused in the past; why would they accept now?" I said that they had had time to get over the shock, just as Jim had had time to do a lot of growing. Jim nodded. (Crediting client's work)

Current Status of the Problem

Where It Stands Now

The problem has shifted in urgency. Jim and his parents are starting to be able to discuss the problem of Indian identity with less anger and pain and are starting to be able to discuss other issues without approaching them from a perspective of ethnic origin. Jim's parents are beginning to be able to give positive strokes to Jim for his "Native Indian–oriented" achievements (e.g., his beautiful carvings and his proficiency in Indian dancing). They are striving to live together under the same roof without feeling that it is a battlefield of "good Indians" versus "bad Indians." Jim's anger has lessened, largely because he has regained the support of the elders in the band. He has stayed away from committing further delinquencies.

Specific Next Steps

- For the next white worker, do not shy away from discussing the racial element of the interaction, because it is a central element for Jim and his family and permeates all their lives.

- Continue family work around communication patterns. There are a lot of feelings of anger and sadness connected to Jim's natural mom's death that interfere between Jim and his stepmom.

- Continue to emphasize Jim's ability and desire to do well and excel rather than Jim's past record of delinquency; emphasize his parents' desire to be the best parents.

- Make an effort to enlist the band elders to help provide a social support system for Jim and his family.

The worker in this example has made a start in breaking down the barriers between the parents and the child, the family and herself (and her white social service system), and the family and a source of support in the Native community. Recognizing that a long history of communal support is central to the Native culture can be a crucial step in strengthening the family. One finding of the child welfare study cited earlier (Shulman, 1991) was that regions of the provincial child welfare agency that established effective working relationships with the Native community had fewer Native children going into alternative forms of care, or if they did go into care, fewer leaving the Native community. (These working relationships involved friendship centers, homemaker and court workers, band chiefs and elders, and social workers.) Continued work with the family would need to integrate some discussion of the socioeconomic issues of oppression that had contributed to the struggles within the family so that the problem could be reframed from a personal pathology perspective to a social perspective. (For an additional example of working with a Native family whose daughter has been referred to a psychiatric hospital after a suicide attempt, see the Chapter 6 examples on the book's web page).

The Ending and Transition Phase

The general principles and interventions associated with the ending and transition phase described in Chapter 5 can be applied in the family situation. In the illustration that follows, we see that a social worker can do family work even when working with one family member. While many of the examples presented in this book so far have presented working with the female single parent, fathers also face similar problems and issues. These are explored in more detail in a later chapter, where an example of my work with a single parent group that includes men is presented.

In the following example we see a worker dealing with an ending and transition as a change in job status causes her to transfer the case. The agency is Big Brother and the social worker has been helping the client obtain services for her child as well as cope with her own difficult issues. Because the clients using this service have usually experienced large losses in their lives, the worker must pay particularly close attention to the demands of the ending and transition phase of practice. This is another example of how workers can integrate process and content.

WORKER: I have some news that I need to tell you.

CLIENT (MOTHER): Don't tell me you're leaving the agency.

WORKER: No, I'm not, but I will become supervisor of our new office, which will cause me to have to transfer the families I've been working with in this area.

CLIENT: I'm so happy for you, but it will be difficult for us not to have you as our social worker any more.

WORKER: I have mixed feelings also, because I'm excited about the new position, but it will be hard for me to give up certain people, like you.

After hugging, I said I'd be in touch to arrange a meeting with her and the kids to begin talking about the change. Later that week, we set up an appointment. The mother came in talking about what a difficult time her son was having due to rejection by his father and now her son's Big Brother was also rejecting him. I asked if he was also feeling rejected by me. The mother said that he was angry about finding out about the change by getting a letter, as he no longer felt special. I apologized for that and explained that I had meant to tell him myself, but didn't get a chance before the letter was sent. I added that he is special and that I was planning to tell him and apologize.

After discussing more issues related to her son's depression and making suggestions for follow-up treatment with the next worker, I asked how the mother was feeling about meeting another worker. She replied that she was ready. I commented on how nonchalant and accepting she seemed about the change, and mentioned that I was feeling sad. The mother acknowledged that, like her other son, she tends to deny difficult situations and then "fall apart" later on. I said that I hoped I wasn't pressuring her, but that I thought it was important for her to recognize how she was acting. She started to cry, and said she was glad to have known me. She spoke positively about our relationship and how much she has grown through her involvement with the agency. I told her that I would miss her cooperativeness, kindness, and appreciation, and that the next worker would be lucky. Mention was made of how it had been difficult to keep the professional and personal issues separate and how our relationship would change now. We then embraced again and made introductions to the next worker. The mother did call once after the day of my meeting with her child, but has not called since.

While the work clearly focused on the match between the child and the volunteer Big Brother, the worker also provided an important support service to the parent. At minimum, having a professional "friend" with whom to discuss the child's progress can take a significant load off a single-parent client.

Chapter Summary

The core skills outlined in Chapters 2 through 5 can be applied to working with families. Understanding this work in terms of the interactional model's phases of work is helpful. Family work differs from family therapy, in that the former focuses on helping the family work as a family and the latter focuses on a specific problem. Many of the concepts and strategies developed in family therapy theory can help in family work, especially in terms of family dynamics and strategies for intervention. The two-client concept is crucial in family work.

In this chapter, the beginning phase of family work was illustrated by a worker dealing with an angry parent; the middle phase by a worker developing an ongoing working relationship; and the ending/transition phase by a worker moving on in a Big Brother agency. Special circumstances, such as helping a single-parent family cope with their unique stresses, and assisting a Native family in dealing with their culture and their community, present particular issues for family work.

Related Online Content and Activities

Visit *The Skills of Helping* Book Companion Website at www.socialwork.wadsworth .com/Shulman06/ for learning tools such as glossary terms, InfoTrac College Edition keywords, links to related websites, and chapter practice quizzes.

The website for this chapter also features additional notes from the author and additional process recordings:

- Parent-Teen Conflict in a Native Family (White Worker): Mediating Family Conflict

- Working With a Single-Parent Family: The Child as the Ticket-of-Admission for Service

Problem-Centered Family Practice

I n this chapter we continue our discussion of work with families, focusing on practice in which the agency mandate or the client's particular problem is in the foreground, giving direction to the family work. Thus, the counseling focuses on a specific problem or issue, such as the physical or mental illness of a family member or a child's problems in school. The work with the family explores the impact of the particular problem on the family and the ways the family can be mobilized to cope with it more effectively.

Agency Mandate, Client Problem, and Family Counseling

As indicated earlier, this chapter continues to explore social work with families. In the cases described here, both the mandate of the setting and the specific client problems related to that mandate give focus and direction to the family practice. In effect, this chapter will revisit the contracting idea introduced in Chapter 3. There we saw that the worker's practice with a client must center on the common ground between the service of the agency or host setting (such as a school) and the felt needs of the client. This apparently simple but actually complex and powerful idea provides a boundary and structure that frees the client and the worker to be more effective. The worker needs to be asking him- or herself, at all times, "How does this conversation with family members relate to our service and the family's particular problem?"

The work must be guided by the specific agency function and not subverted by the worker or the clients and turned into family therapy. Fear of this outcome often causes clients to be defensive and resistant in early sessions. A family that is meeting with a school social worker about their child's educational problems will not necessarily appreciate the conversation turning to the parents' marital problems. Identifying marital stress as a factor affecting the child's schoolwork would be appropriate, as would a discussion of how to handle its impact on the child. It would also be appropriate for the social worker to offer to make a referral for the couple's marital problem.

The client's fears of invasive practice are not completely unfounded. Social workers who are unclear about the boundaries of their practice sometimes use the initial reason for the contact as an entry for family therapy. In one extreme example, a family support worker in a child welfare agency described working with a couple on their sexual dysfunctions. Although the worker was originally referred to the family to help them with parenting problems that had led to suspected child abuse, the sessions with the couple had revealed sexual problems that the worker had undertaken to treat through counseling. When I asked about the connection between this work and the agency mandate, the worker admitted that there was no connection. She went on to say that she had taken a course in counseling people with sexual problems, and this seemed like a good chance for her to practice. This worker's subversion of the working contract was inappropriate for many reasons, not the least of which was that while she was busy doing sexual counseling, she was ignoring the parenting-focused work that was in her domain.

In rural areas, with few services available, workers must often be all things to all people. In some cases, workers may have to provide a range of services as the "only game in town." Even in these situations, when a worker must offer help that may be beyond the normal service of the agency, social workers bear the responsibility of trying to close the gap between client needs and available services through professional impact on the community. By that I mean that while providing additional services that are unavailable to the client in that community, the social worker must also work with colleagues, the political system, the community leadership, and so forth to establish new agencies and/or new services. (The strategies and skills for this aspect of social work are discussed in more detail in Part V.) In trying to provide all services to all clients, workers often become less effective in providing the services that are clearly their responsibility. Each of the illustrations that follow will highlight this crucial idea.

Hiding the Family's Secrets: Dealing With Taboo Areas

Family members often have a family secret that they feel is so terrible, no one will talk about it. A **family secret** is an explicit or unspoken agreement in which all family members agree not to deal directly with a sensitive and taboo concern. Family violence, alcoholism, and sexual abuse are examples of family secrets often hidden behind a family facade. At times the oppressor in the relationship uses emotional or physical threats to maintain the secret through coercion. Other common secret areas are associated with physical and mental illness. Examples include family members who try to hide the onset of a potentially life-threatening illness, such as AIDS, cancer, or Alzheimer's disease. In some cases, the family knows about the illness but treat it as a taboo subject. Each family member may fear that the others cannot emotionally handle an open discussion. While genuinely wanting to protect the other family members, the guardian of the secret is also protecting her- or himself.

Family secrets that are kept out of sight and not discussed can impair a family's ability to function in a healthy manner. The inability to discuss the subject area, the norm of behavior that has declared such discussion to be forbidden, blocks the family members' ability to deal with the issue and discover their inherent strengths.

In one example, a young mother suffered from a degenerative illness that had already caused her to go blind. She had experienced strokes and memory loss, and the prognosis was an early death. The father was no longer in the picture, and the family living in the home consisted of the mother (Ruth), her 8-year-old son (Billy), and the maternal grandmother (Millie). A norm of behavior had evolved in which all of the family members covertly agreed not to speak of the illness or its symptoms and, in particular, not to speak of the mother's future. The child was seen as too young to be able to understand. The grandmother worried that discussing the illness would make the young mother more depressed and perhaps trigger a stroke. The young mother worried about the burden the illness placed on the grandmother and how that burden might affect her health. Both the mother and grandmother were deeply concerned about what would happen to Billy if the other died first.

Although the tensions and stress in the family were carefully covered up, there was no way for the feelings to remain under the surface. Billy signaled the underlying problems by acting out the anxieties he felt about what was happening to his mother and his family. As his behavior worsened, his mother and grandmother could not handle them, so they sought help from a child care resource to arrange a temporary placement in a foster or group home. The mission of this agency was to provide assistance to families in dealing with their children's behavior problems or offer resources for substitute child care. It was not, for example, a hospital social service department, for which the issue of the illness itself might be central.

The first response of the agency, along with the family worker involved, was to respect the grandmother's injunction against getting into the health issues. The grandmother involved the worker in a conspiracy of silence on the core issues. Given the child-focused service of the agency, the worker's agreement was understandable. Her early efforts focused on helping the mother and grandmother try to deal with Billy's behavior and on helping Billy control his activities. However, because this missed the real meaning of the deviant behavior and played into the family's use of Billy as the identified patient, little progress took place, and both the mother and grandmother expressed feelings of dissatisfaction with the results.

The family worker realized that the core issue was the family secret and made several efforts to open it up. She pointed out to the mother and the grandmother that Billy's behavior might well stem from his anxiety in sensing something wrong in the family. However, at the first sign of resistance from the grandmother, the worker backed off. The worker then had to examine her own feelings about death and dying that contributed to her willingness to go along with the illusion of work. As long as the family members sensed the worker's discomfort and resulting ambivalence, they would resist as well. By backing off, the worker indirectly signaled to the family her lack of readiness to help them with the issue. Once the worker had dealt with her own feelings, she could begin to see the resistance as a sign that the work was on target. When the meaning of "Resistance is part of the work" became clear to the worker, she made a demand for work on the family members by persisting in raising the underlying issue.

Recognizing she would need to confront the family about their conspiracy to keep the family secret, she took her courage in hand and challenged the obstacle. She confronted the mother and grandmother and tried to support them in opening up a discussion first between the two of them and then between them and Billy. She explored the resistance by asking, "What makes it hard for you to talk about this with each other?" The taboo subject was at least out in the open, yet the grandmother refused to continue this line of discussion and closed off further discussions by saying, "When the time comes, we shall deal with it." The mother, on the other hand, responded by dealing more openly with Billy on the issue of her death. This discussion seemed to help the situation and resulted in a decrease in the child's acting-out behavior. However, the mother remained reluctant to discuss death with the grandmother.

Although the worker could not help the family face the future at this time, she helped lay groundwork by creating conditions in which the unspeakable could be spoken. Given the service of the setting, the work succeeded in that the child was freed of the responsibility of signaling the family distress. The mother's and grandmother's denial was strong but understandable. In the last analysis, picking the time and place for facing a harsh reality remained up to them.

The Child Welfare Setting

A child welfare agency offers a good example of a setting in which functional clarity plays a crucial role in practice. Examples of contracting with the natural parents in a family and, in particular, dealing with the issue of the authority of the worker and the agency were discussed in Part II. In this section, family practice variations associated with work in a child welfare setting are explored through examples involving practice with two foster-parent families, with an 11-year-old child in residential care, and with a teenage mother. In each of these examples, the work involves helping the client deal with her or his family-of-origin issues at a point when she or he is not living with the family. The examples illustrate that clients take their families with them wherever they may go and that their families of origin can have ongoing and continued influence on their current experiences.

Work With Foster Parents

Child welfare family work often involves collaborative work with the foster (or group home) parents or child care workers in residential settings. Both the worker and the alternative parent often misunderstand the role of the social worker in relation to this parent (Shulman, 1980). On one end of a continuum, the foster parent may be viewed as a client. On the other end, workers may ignore important signals from the foster parents concerning their need for support. In reality, foster parents and other alternative caregivers are collaborators in the process of buffering the traumatic experience of children who find themselves in short- or long-term care. The positive impact of alternative caregivers is described in resiliency research (see Chapter 1), and the potential contribution to the foster child's plasticity is described in the life-span theory and research. These findings suggest that attention to the foster parents as contributors to the child's developmental reserve capacity can contribute significantly to the child's growth. The social worker can play an important role in mediating between the foster parents and the child, the agency, the natural family, the foster parents' own family, and other systems in the community, such as health care providers and the school.

Engaging and Working
With the Hard-to-Reach Client

Working With Other Professionals Here is a discussion of work with foster parents and the importance of maintaining the two-client idea. This example also raises the role of the social worker in dealing with other professionals and systems.

In my own work with foster parents and from my research studies, I have identified several areas in which problems may emerge. First, the foster parents may feel unappreciated and undervalued when the agency and the social worker make decisions without consulting them—the very people who may know the child best and will have to deal with the results of the decisions. Some foster parents report feeling particularly bitter when the agency or the workers tell them they are the most important members of the team and then proceed to ignore them. Second, difficult foster children can raise problems in the natural family between a foster mother and father, or in relation to other children in the family. Foster parents have described feeling torn between the needs of their own children and the demands placed on them by needy foster children. Finally, of all the issues raised in my workshops, two of the most difficult have to do with two kinds of overidentification with the foster child. The first results in unrealistic expectations for a return home, and the second results in anger and rejection of the biological parents. The next examples illustrate these two problems.

In the first example, the social worker tries to help a foster parent of a 9-year-old child deal with having been removed from his family. The social worker's role is to try to provide a source of support for the foster parent as she attempts to help the child. By recognizing the foster parent's caring for the child and her difficulty in dealing with the child's pain, the social worker strengthens her in her difficult role.

Mrs. Edwards, foster mother of 7 weeks to 9-year-old Tony, phoned me at 9:00 A.M. She told me in an angry, excited voice, "I had to call you and tell you that you need to hear the things that Tony told me this morning before he went to school. You people have things all wrong. I am convinced that the agency and that private school have done this boy and his family a grave injustice." I immediately thought to myself, "What has this kid cooked up now?" I said that this sounded serious and asked her to tell me more. She said that Tony insisted that his father had never beaten him and that his mother had never locked him out—he had just refused to go in the house and had gone away. Furthermore, Tony told her that he had decided to leave his last foster home 2 weeks early because he didn't want them to adopt him.

I asked Mrs. Edwards why she thought Tony was telling her these things. She replied, "Because he wants me to help him get home—he trusts me and he's hurting so bad that I told him that I'd get you to listen to him." I promised Mrs. Edwards that I would listen to Tony, but not on the phone as she suggested, because he played games on the phone and got her and himself upset in the process. I arranged to be there at 2:00 to talk to her before Tony got home from school.

When I saw Mrs. Edwards, we went over Tony's stories again. It appeared to me that Tony was using the information shared with him by another worker a month previously (when he decided to go home and not wait to be adopted) in an attempt to force me, through Mrs. Edwards, to get him home now. I reminded Mrs. Edwards of the tiny boy she had told me about, whom she had once fostered. He had been hospitalized after a beating from his mother, but had welcomed his mother when she had visited him in hospital. Mrs. Edwards responded that it was the same with Tony—blood is thicker than water, but she felt it would help Tony for me to listen to his story—he needed to be believed. I had told her that I felt that Tony needed most to know that she and I were on his side and would help him to get home, but that going along with his tall tales was not helping him wait or helping him learn to get along with people. Mrs. Edwards replied, "But he's only a little boy, he feels all alone and wants to get back to his mother." I said, "You really hurt when Tony is hurting, don't you?" She agreed that she was a "softie" and that Tony really got to her with his constant appeals for help to get home.

The worker in this excerpt avoided the mistake of identifying solely with the needs of the child. The two-client idea is illustrated when the worker understands Tony's needs and those of the foster parent at the same time. In addition to providing emotional support, the social worker offers resources including herself to help the foster parent get the child through the stress of the court process. An agency will often tell foster parents that they are the most important members of the foster care team, while simultaneously excluding them from any significant planning or decision making. This foster parent can instead be brought into a collaborative process by discussing a plan with the social worker. The worker should also convey the importance of involving the child in the discussion.

We discussed how the agency might see Tony through the waiting period until court on November 30. A child care worker to take responsibility for Tony after school is not acceptable to her—Tony needed to come home to her and discuss the school day and do his homework. Talking to a psychiatrist not connected with the agency or with the court appealed to Mrs. Edwards, although she felt Tony should not be told that he was seeing a psychiatrist. She agreed when I pointed out that this would not be fair to Tony or the psychiatrist and could not work because of Tony's alertness. We decided to ask Tony what he thought about this idea.

I suggested to Mrs. Edwards that Tony took advantage of her fondness for him and her wish for him to be happy. She replied that she knew he did, but he made her feel like she was the only one he could rely on. I told her that he could rely on me too, and that I could understand why he had doubts, since I had been absent during the most upsetting month of his stay in care—in other words, I had deserted him when he needed me. I told her I would try, with her cooperation, to spend more time with Tony and to reassure him that he would go home. I did not mention that she had balked at many of my attempts to see Tony during the early weeks of his placement in her home. Mrs. Edwards said that this should help a lot.

I told her why I thought that Tony was attempting to discredit the evidence used in court, pointing out that this was a plucky attempt on his part to take the responsibility for having been left in Canada by his parents, but reminding her that this information was in writing from Tony's mother, and that, although I was committed to returning Tony home, it could only be done through the court. Mrs. Edwards said she understood this.

Tony arrived home from school, gave me a fleeting greeting, collected his Halloween candies, and ignored Mrs. Edwards's request that he tell me what he had told her that morning. He finally went outside, and Mrs. Edwards turned to me in consternation and commented that she couldn't understand this behavior. I told her that it was OK if he wasn't ready to share this with me, as he probably hadn't decided whether he could trust me or not. After two more excursions in and out of the room and a brief period at his homework, Tony offered me a candy and sat down with us. Once more Mrs. Edwards urged him to tell me what was on his mind. Tony looked me straight in the eye and said, somewhat defiantly, "I told her I left Susan's two weeks early because I didn't want to be adopted by them." I told Tony that this wasn't the way I remembered it happening, and reminded him of visits and discussions about his leaving Susan's home, including his statements to me at the time. Tony wiggled a bit, conceded that was the way it had happened, shot Mrs. Edwards an amused glance, and looked at the floor. Mrs. Edwards's mouth was open. Then Tony looked up and told me firmly, "But my father never beat me!"

I told him that I wasn't going to get into a discussion of what had gone on in his family, because he had made his choice to return home and my job was to help him do this. I put it to him, "The fact is your mother left you in Canada, didn't she, Tony?" He nodded, looking at the floor once more. I went on to say, "The law in Canada is that, when children are left by their parents, it has to go to court and the judge has to decide if you will go home or go for adoption. I'm asking the judge to send you home because your mother wants you and you don't want to be adopted." I asked Tony if that was what he wanted. He said yes, with fervor. I told him OK, we all agree that's what we're working for. Now what can we do about the time between now and November 30? Tony observed brightly, "It's my birthday on November 7 and I'm having a party at McDonald's." I said that would be great, but what I meant was that things had to be a lot more peaceful in the Edwards home if Tony was to go home in good health and well behaved. Tony glanced at Mrs. Edwards, who chimed in, "I've been telling Donna that you're a hard boy to live with sometimes."

I told Tony that I felt that a lot of his behavior toward Mrs. Edwards and toward the girls (her children) was way out of line, so much so that I wondered if he really wanted to stay there until he left for home. Tony had been looking at me, but when I referred to the misbehavior toward the girls, his eyes glistened and he smiled a smug secret smile that caused Mrs. Edwards to widen her eyes in dismay. I told Tony that it was up to him to improve his behavior, since I knew that he was capable of this, and that I wanted to be able to tell his mother that he was happy, healthy, and well behaved when he left for home. When I asked Tony if he thought he could make this effort, he looked at Mrs. Edwards with an appealing smile and told me, "Yes, I'll try." We discussed whether or not it would be helpful to him to talk about his situation with someone outside the department and the court and, despite Mrs. Edwards's encouragement to do so, Tony declared that he didn't want to talk to anybody else. He then asked for permission to go outside and play.

Mrs. Edwards and I had a brief discussion of our talk with Tony, and she acknowledged that she had been taken in by him and that she now realized it had been deliberate. I, in turn, tried to get across to her the need to provide a structured, calm atmosphere in order to keep Tony on an even keel until he returned home. Although Mrs. Edwards verbalized intellectual understanding of this need, I was not assured that she could put it into effect, because of her own emotional needs.

The worker has begun to address the meaning of Tony's behavior but needs to focus further on the connection between Tony's acting out and his hope that he can return home. Teenagers have sat on the front porch of a new foster home, suitcase in hand, refusing to enter and demanding that they be returned to their natural parents. Foster children of all ages often act out in their alternative care setting, thinking that if they are rejected there they will most certainly be returned home. When their acting-out behavior affects the foster parent's natural children, it can lead to a call to remove the child. Rather than them returning home, the acting-out often leads to being placed in a new foster home. Foster parents need help in understanding the meaning of the behavior, and the children need assistance, from the social worker and the foster parent, in dealing with the pain of rejection.

In the next example, erratic visiting by the biological parent has upset a young teenager in care and angered the foster parents. The social worker needs to help the parents deal with their own feelings so that they can help the child with his. The anger toward the biological parent is in part a cover for their pain at sensing the child's hurt. One role of the foster care social worker is to help the foster family tune in to the meaning of the "deviant" behavior of the biological family. In this sense the foster parent also has two clients—the child and his parents. Before any work can be done, the worker must demonstrate a capacity to tune in to the foster parents. The worker's report follows:

I drove up to Ann and Tom's home. Kevin was standing outside with a friend. He ran up to my car and said, "I'm not going." I said I didn't understand. "Going where? What do you mean?" He replied, "I'm not going away this weekend. No one can take me." I said, "I'm taking you."

He said, "No. No one can take me at their house. My grandmother is taking two of my sisters, and she's tired and can't handle any more. My aunt is going away and my other aunt just moved and doesn't have a telephone." I said, "I'm sorry." He shrugged, looked away, and said, "That's okay. I've got stuff to do around here this weekend."

I said, "I was looking forward to taking you up. I also wanted to meet your grandmother." He asked, "When can I go home?" I asked him, "To Edison?" (where his mother and stepfather live). He nodded his head yes. I asked him if he had talked about this with his mother and stepfather. He looked at the ground and shook his head no. I asked him how his conversations with his stepfather were going. He said, "Good." I asked him if they had discussed the fight or had they just blown it off like it didn't happen. He said they had blown it off. I told him to talk about it with his mother and stepfather and see what they said. Then, if everyone felt comfortable, I would talk about it with his child welfare worker and maybe we could arrange a visit.

He walked back over to where his friend was waiting for him and I went inside to talk to Ann and Tom. Ann immediately started talking about how she couldn't believe that his family had cancelled his visit. She said, "They just don't want him. How could you do that to a child?" I said, "He must be very disappointed." She made a noise and said, "Yeah, he is." Then she started talking about how a previous foster child was supposed to come visit her this weekend as well as Tom's son. She also made a comment about how it would be difficult to keep Kevin occupied to keep his mind off his disappointment.

I said, "Kevin's family canceling the visit must be hard for you too. You have other plans, and you thought that Kevin was going away for the weekend." She reluctantly agreed. She said, "I just wish they had given us more notice. He has been planning on going all week, and they just call up the night before and say, 'You can't come.'" I said, "You are right. Their not giving more notice is not fair to you or Kevin. I will call them next week and discuss visitation. You shouldn't be expected to always conform to their schedules; they need to compromise and work with you. Kevin's feelings need to be considered, too."

She appeared relieved that I would address this. Tom entered the room and also began discussing how "Kevin's family doesn't want him." He said, "That kid isn't going home, I can feel it in my gut." Ann expressed her anger and repeated, "How can you do that to a kid?" several times.

I listened to them, but added, "We can't assume that his family doesn't want him."

I asked Ann if she voices these concerns to Kevin. She said she does not. I told her that as a person she was free to vent her frustration with his mother with me, but as a professional, she must try not to let her anger at his mother get in the way of working with his mother. She said she understood.

Tom expressed his feeling that Kevin needed to face the reality of not being able to go home because his family did not want him. I told him that I did not know what was going to happen when it was time for Kevin to leave our program, but I would ask the child welfare worker what the alternative to his going home would be. I also stated that he and Ann could help Kevin by developing some of his independent living skills. I took out a skills assessment, and we went over it together. We targeted some of the areas where Kevin might need their supervision, such as nutrition, what to do if there is an emergency, etc.

While we were going over this, Kevin came inside to tell Tom something. Tom asked him, "Are your ears ringing?"

Kevin looked confused and said, "No."

Tom said, "Well, we are in here saying a lot of good things about you."

The worker was supportive and offered to intervene with the biological parents to address limit-setting and visiting issues. She could, however, have taken this conversation even further. After tuning in to the foster parents, the worker could have explored with them the meaning of this erratic behavior by the biological parents. Were they canceling the visit because they did not care or because they cared too much? What current stresses influenced their capacity to take care of him? In addition, because contact between foster parents and biological family members can become extremely negative in such circumstances, the worker should consider with the foster parents how they might deal with the interaction. Was there a way to recognize the biological family's difficulty while sharing their own issues around the missed visits and short notice? The foster parents want the biological family to be more understanding of the child's feelings, and one way to do this would be for the foster parents to express some understanding of what the other parents are going through. The interview continued with the worker addressing the feelings of the foster child. However, the intensity of those feelings resulted in the worker changing the subject to one less painful to the child (and to herself). This is an example of how a worker's use of an assessment tool can block the immediate work instead of deepening it.

Kevin smiled and ran out. I followed him outside a few minutes later to talk to him. We sat down, and I started by telling him a few of the things Ann, Tom, and I had discussed such as his family contacting him earlier in the week if he couldn't go there for the weekend. I then said to him, "You must be disappointed about not going home."

He said, "Yes." I reminded him that I was not opposed to his visiting Springfield (an aunt's home town) if it could be worked out between him and his mother and stepfather. He said, "My aunt didn't call like she said she would." We were silent for a minute. Then I told him that I had brought him some exercises to work on since he wasn't in school. He asked me, "What does this have to do with school?" I said, "Well, it's not reading, writing, or arithmetic, but these exercises will give you something productive to do." He said, "Well, if I get real bored, I'll take a look at them."

At this point, Ann yelled out the window at his friend who was still in the yard, the friend started walking away. Kevin asked him where he was going, and he responded that he'd be back in a minute. I said, "I know there are a lot of distractions and you probably want to get back to what you were doing, but I have one more thing I want you to look at." I pulled out a family assessment. I said, "This is something to help you figure out ways your family interacts with each other. I made two copies for you so you could do one on your foster family and one on your other family." He said, "I don't know about my other family. I haven't been there so long." I said, "Well, do the best you can. We might be able to figure out things that need to happen in both families to help you feel more safe and comfortable." He said, "Okay. Leave it here and I'll do that one this week."

Kevin started telling me about some of the yard work he and Tom were doing. Then I told him I had one other thing on my mind that I wanted to talk about with him before I left. I told him I had been thinking about our conversation from last week, and I wanted to talk with him about keeping himself safe. He listened to me then told me he wasn't normally in the situation like the one we talked about last week. I said, "Okay, but still think about what I said." He said, "Okay."

I went inside to tell Ann good-bye. I also told her that I had addressed "safety" with Kevin. I told her to do the best she could and have a good weekend. Then I left.

Work With Children in Residential Care

In the next illustration, a worker helps an 11-year-old boy in residential care explore the connection between his feelings of loss and rejection and his ability to cope in the setting. In this example we see the worker dealing with the client's family issues even though the parents are not directly involved. One can do family work without working with the whole family. The example also illustrates how work with children can often take place in nonstructured settings. This could be called "steering wheel" or "fast food" social work. In residential treatment settings, where so many other children are around and competing for attention, a child needs to use these opportunities to capture the worker for his or her own needs. The issues, as in the example that follows, are often raised indirectly.

On October 15, Danny and I visited his grandmother. She is a terrifically "grandmotherly" lady who obviously cares for Danny a great deal. She, in fact, has no use for her daughter for rejecting Danny. Danny's birthday was the next day, and the occasion for our visit was to pick up his present and for me to meet her. We spent about 2 hours there—a very pleasant afternoon—and Danny was relaxed on the drive home.

Our conversation turned to Halloween, which Danny said he was looking forward to because he didn't get to go out last year. I asked why. He said that last year he'd stolen 50 cents from a friend of his and his mother found out and put him to bed right after supper. I asked him if he'd repaid the money, and he said yes he did when he got some money later that week. I asked why he'd taken money from his friend, and he said, "Well, he had money and I didn't." When I glanced at him he hung his head. I said, "Oh." But before I could make a further comment, he said that one time he'd stolen $4.65 from his mother and bought a whole shoe box full of bubble-gum cards. He said his teacher at school had found out about how he'd gotten them and made him rip them up and throw them away. His mother hit him and sent him to bed. This was relayed rather bitterly by him.

I was unsure at this point just where our pleasant driving-along conversation was headed, but I decided to explore how he was feeling about how he was handled by his mother vs. how the teacher handled him. When I asked him how he felt about having to throw the cards away, he said "Awful," because he wanted to give the cards to friends. I asked him if he thought it was fair, and he said yes, that he shouldn't have been allowed to keep them. When I asked the same questions about what his mother had done, he said that he got hit a lot whenever he'd done anything wrong, and it hurt when he got hit, but it also made him mad. I asked him if he'd ever expressed this anger directly to his mother and he said no, because, if he did, she (or her boyfriend) would have probably hit him more. He went on to say that Dale (his mother's boyfriend) had noticed 25 cents missing one night on returning from work and had really gotten angry and, although it was past midnight, Dale went into Danny's room and pulled him into the kitchen by his hair and in the final pull Danny crashed into the table and knocked over a glass which broke. Danny said he then had to sweep up the mess and was hit by his mother with a yardstick and sent back to bed.

At this point in the interview, the worker was probably feeling the pain involved in the child's description of the abuse. An understandable resistance to exploring this pain, coupled with lack of clarity about his role, caused the worker to respond as a "teacher-preacher," using the description as an opportunity to teach a lesson. This missed the signal of the child's real work, illustrating the problem described earlier as functional diffusion. Fortunately, the worker caught his mistake as the child gave him another chance, making a "second offering" of the theme of concern.

Danny's voice in this recital was getting more and more strained, and he sounded angry. I didn't answer for a couple of minutes (for one thing I wasn't sure of how to respond) and Danny calmed a bit. Then I said, "Well, it sounds like Dale and your mom were really fed up and angry with your stealing from them and other people. I guess I wouldn't like it much if you stole a lot around me either." He said, "I wouldn't steal from you, and besides you don't hit me." I said, "No, I wouldn't hit you, even if I was really mad at you for stealing."

I obviously still wasn't getting his point, however, because he was very tense and tight in the seat. He then said, "What would you do if your kid was fighting at school and got hurt and had a bloody nose and you had to leave work to take him to the hospital?" This came out in a rush and he started to go on with his "hypothetical" example when I interrupted him and asked if that had happened to him, and he said, "Yes."

WORKER: What did your mother do, Danny?

DANNY: She got mad at me for fighting.

WORKER: Well, I wouldn't be very happy if you got into a fight at school.

DANNY: I don't blame you. Kids shouldn't fight.

WORKER: I guess I'd also be concerned about how your nose felt. It must have hurt a lot if you were going to the hospital.

DANNY: That's what I mean!

WORKER: (To myself) I think I finally got it.

DANNY: All she did was nag me about how she had to leave work to take me to the hospital and how it upset her to do it, and she never once asked me how I felt about having a sore nose!

WORKER: That must have felt really awful.

DANNY: Yeah!

WORKER: Like she didn't care about you, only the problems you caused her.

DANNY: Yeah, all she did was nag, nag, nag about having to leave work and how it was stupid to fight.

WORKER: I guess you already knew about the fighting; you had the sore and bloody nose to prove it.

DANNY: (Laughing) Yeah, and it was the only time she ever had to do anything like that, but she acted like I did it all the time and I didn't. I know you're not supposed to fight, but kids do anyway sometimes.

WORKER: It must have been hard for you to act like a kid around your mother.

DANNY: Yeah, especially with Dale sticking his nose in all the time.

The issue of his painful relationships with his family finally emerged, although it surfaced just as the worker drove into the center parking lot. This is often how the client asks, "Do you really want to hear about this? Do I really want to talk about this?" If the worker uses the arrival as an excuse for backing off, the message to the client will close down the discussion. By continuing the discussion, the worker is saying to the client, "I'm ready if you are."

At this point we were a block away from the center, but instead of turning right onto the side street, I turned left into the parking lot of a park. He asked why I'd done that and I answered that it seemed to me that we were having a pretty good talk and that I wanted it to finish a bit more naturally than by pulling into the parking lot and getting mobbed by the rest of the kids. He said, "OK" and settled back in his seat.

WORKER: What do you mean about Dale "sticking his nose" into things?

DANNY: My mom and Dale would have meetings to discuss things and then they would vote on it.

WORKER: What did you vote on?

DANNY: We voted on my bedtime. I wanted to stay up til 9:00, but my mom wanted me to go to bed at 8:30, so we voted on it and he voted for her.

WORKER: Wow that sounds like they were sort of ganging up on you and pretending to be fair.

He agreed and said that they did that a lot. I asked if he was glad to be away from his mother, and he said yeah—that she didn't know how to treat kids and that all she did was nag or get mad and then stay mad, and he alluded to an incident that we had talked about before. I said that he must have gotten pretty angry sometimes when he was at home. He said yes and was sobbing. He said that he wished that she was right here now so he could tell her how much he hated her. I said he could hate her all he wanted and I didn't blame him.

He said that sometimes he felt like going by where she lived and throwing rocks through all the windows. I said it must have been hard to be angry a lot of the time he lived at home and not be able to tell anyone. He said that he'd like to tell her now and talked about how he'd like her to be a target in a shooting gallery so he could shoot at her. He laughed then and said that was a joke. I said he was saying that he was really angry, joke or not. He had relaxed somewhat by this time and said yes he was angry.

Having listened to the child's pain, the worker next made a connection between his family experiences and life at the center. The child had another social worker who focused on the ongoing relationship to family members. This worker would later share this information with the other worker, but at this point, our worker was concerned with the relationship of the child to the center (staff, other residents, and so forth) and to other parts of the child's life, such as school. In the next comments, the worker attempted to connect the discussion of the family experience to life at the center.

I said that he got angry a lot at little things around the center and sometimes screamed and raged at the adults. He agreed, and said he thought it was good at the center because he could get mad and nobody held it against him, I said yes, it was OK at the center to get angry and let people know about it, but maybe sometimes he wasn't yelling at the person he was really angry with. He said yeah, that sometimes he was really feeling angry with his mom and the least little thing would set him off. I said that he must have his mother and home on his mind a lot, and he said that he thought about it "sometimes," especially bedtime, but during the day, too.

I said that I thought I understood some of how he felt and that I was feeling right then really sad and hurt for him, and is that what he felt like, especially before he got angry, did he feel sad and hurt by his mother? He said yes, that most of the time before he got angry he felt hurt and that would help get him mad. I said that maybe he could come and tell me when he was feeling sad or hurt because he was thinking about his mother and home. He perked up a bit at this and said sure; he'd try to do that, but why? I said that maybe if he did that then he wouldn't have to get angry with the wrong person. He said maybe, but what would I do? I said, "Well, if you come and tell me when you feel hurt and sad, maybe we can just sit and feel hurt and sad together." He looked at me for a couple of seconds and smiled and said, "OK." I gave him a small hug, and we started back for the center.

In this last excerpt, the worker focused on helping the child to develop more adaptive ways of obtaining social support when he is hurting. The flight-fight mechanisms for dealing with pain are counterproductive. The child needs to learn how to make close connections with others who can help to fill the gap in his life left by parental abuse and abandonment. The worker has made a nice connection between the feelings of the client and the purpose of their work together.

Work With Teen Parents and Their Families of Origin

Children having children is a growing problem in North America. The stress of having to meet one's own teenage developmental needs, while simultaneously trying to meet the needs of a child, often results in a call for help through behaviors that bring the child welfare agency into the picture. In the following example, a family support worker attempts to help a teenage mother cope with her own feelings of rejection by her family of origin so that she can receive the support she needs as a parent under stress. The following excerpt is taken from the 15th session of counseling with Mary, a 17-year-old who is the mother of a 2-year-old daughter.

> Mary says that she has had little contact with her original family since she became pregnant. She has not wanted to talk about her family with me and has focused on her relationships with her boyfriend and foster mother. I felt that she might be ready to talk about her family, and I was looking for signals from her.
>
> Mary said that her father was shopping in the same store as she was this week. I asked what had happened. She answered, "Nothing." I smiled and asked her what happened when nothing happened. She laughed and said he pretended that he didn't see her. I asked her how she felt when he did that. She said, "I didn't care. He makes me laugh because he is so messed up." I said that when she says nothing happened, she seems to mean that they didn't speak to each other. I said I wonder if it really feels like nothing happened when her father passes her as if she didn't exist. She said that she really doesn't care.
>
> I said that I have known Mary since September and have seen her go through some really difficult situations. She has had some big fights with people close to her; she has had her boyfriend sentenced to 12 to 15 years in jail. However, in all this time, only once have I seen her with tears in her eyes. She asked, "When was that?" I answered that it was after the sentencing when she said that her child would not have a father just like she didn't and that it was so important to her that her daughter have it better than she did. Mary thought a moment and said that I was right. She really has a lot of feelings, but she can't talk about it. I asked her why she thought it was so difficult to talk about it. She said because it is so painful. I agreed with her. I asked her what she thought happened to painful feelings that a person can't talk about. I asked her where the feelings go. She said that she keeps them buried inside. I asked her if they stay buried.
>
> She smiled and said she had a dream about her father after she saw him in the supermarket. In the dream, her father and mother were both in the store

and, when they saw her, her father gave her mother some money and said to buy Mary whatever she needs. Mary said she knows what the dream means, but she doesn't want to talk about it. I said that she may not be able to talk about it today, but that she has done some really important work today. She took a tremendous step in moving from her statement that she has no feelings to saying she has a lot of feelings, but it is a difficult and painful subject to talk about. I said that she is sharing some feelings with me, but she is also saying that she needs to go slowly because it is so hard for her. I said that I will try to help her progress at a pace that is OK for her. I said that we know that there is some important work for us to do even if it is just a little bit at a time. Those bottled-up feeling are fighting to get out.

Mary was silent for a little while, and then she changed the subject. This was the first time that Mary discussed her father beyond the statement that they don't get along. I felt comfortable with the way I had handled this situation. I challenged her to work, gave her support, recognized her difficulty, gave her praise for beginning, and gave her permission to proceed slowly with my support. Finally, I gave her the opportunity to choose to continue or to change the subject knowing that we have agreed that it is an important area for us to work on. In the two sessions we have had since this meeting, Mary has been able to talk in detail about her family relationships.

Emotional support is one way Mary can get the help she needs in order to provide good parenting to her toddler. In one of my research projects, concrete support was also crucial (Shulman, 1991). To meet her own developmental needs, this client will require adequate financial support, child care, alternative schooling possibilities, respite care (someone to give her a break from child care duties), and so on. If this mother chooses to keep her child, the "goodness-of-fit" between her developmental needs and these formal and informal resources may mean the crucial difference between success and failure (Germain & Gitterman, 1996).

Family Practice in a School Setting

In this section, we examine an example of family practice in a school setting. The 15-year-old high school freshman had been diagnosed as having an attention deficit disorder (ADD) that affected his ability to negotiate his educational experiences. The social worker in this setting attempted to mediate between the client and his family as well as other professionals in the system. Family members and teachers often fail to understand the impact of this disorder and attribute the problems to "lack of trying" or "laziness." The illustration, in the form of a record of service, examines the social worker's efforts over time as she became clearer about her specific role in this educational setting.

Activities can be used with children and teens as a medium to create a comfortable setting for conversation. However, this informal activity does not take the place of some early conversation about purpose and role. In this case, the worker had not effectively contracted with the client and was using the activity to fill the time. It is not unusual for workers to feel they need to "establish a relationship" through small talk or an activity before they can get to work. Nothing could be further from the truth. The working relationship comes through the work, which requires clear contracting. Although activities can be useful, they do not substitute for effective contracting. In spite of the lack of contracting, the client raised several themes of concern.

RECORD OF SERVICE

Client Description and Time Frame

The client is a 15-year-old freshman, male, Jewish student. The time frame was from October 19 to March 22.

Description of the Problem

Jack is a young man who experiences considerable difficulty in dealing with his family and school system due to the effects of Attention Deficit Disorder.

Summary of the Work

October 19 (Second Session)

I wanted to find out how Jack was adapting to his new school. We began by talking about the fact that Jack had been absent last week. Since he is a freshman, I wanted to find out if he knew what he had to do to get his absence excused and if he had gotten his makeup work from his teachers. When I asked Jack how his classes were going, he said that he had received a supplemental (warning notice) in civics. We talked about how he could get help on his homework from the remedial services teacher. I should have asked Jack more about the situation—how he was getting on with his teacher, how his parents reacted to him getting a supplemental. I could tell he was becoming uncomfortable, but rather than acknowledging that, I allowed him to change the subject. We talked about the World Series and the earthquake out in San Francisco.

October 26 (Third Session)

I asked Jack to choose the activity and take some responsibility for the session. I asked Jack to choose the game, he decided on checkers, and we began to play. After a few minutes, Jack asked me if I had taken drafting in high school. I said that I hadn't, was there a special reason he was wondering about it? Jack replied, "Because I'm having trouble in drafting—I can't finish any of the assignments." I asked him what about drafting was keeping him from finishing the assignments, and he said, "It's just too hard." I asked him what part of it was hardest for him, and he said, "The measuring. If you have one line out of place, you get a zero." I said that I had taken mechanical drawing in junior high and that it is difficult and frustrating because it is so precise. Jack agreed but said that it wasn't really a big deal, because drafting was only the first 6 weeks of his Exploratory Shop Class and it was almost over anyway. I said if it was frustrating him I thought it was important. I offered to act as the mediator, but I didn't make Jack part of the process. I suggested that I talk with his drafting teacher and remedial services teacher to see if we could work together to make it easier for him. Jack agreed that I could do that.

   This interview led to a lot of running around. However, I did not take time to tune in to the other members of the system. I had my own agenda. After having seen the difficulty Jack had with hand-eye/fine-motor coordination last week when we played the game with the blocks, I was not surprised to hear that he had trouble in drafting. I spoke with the drafting teacher, who showed me one of Jack's papers. All of the lines were crooked, and I could tell that Jack had erased many times to try to get the lines straight. The drafting teacher said he couldn't understand why Jack couldn't make the lines straight. I said that Jack obviously has some trouble with this and that we need to find out how to help him. I did not empathize with the teacher. In fact, I felt annoyed that he hadn't recognized the trouble Jack was having and told someone in the Special Needs Department.

I then went to talk with the school psychologist about all of the testing in Jack's file. I wanted to know why Jack was having trouble and what we could do to help him be more successful in drafting. The psychologist took one look at the test results and said that a child with Jack's deficits shouldn't even be in such a class, that all of the testing showed that he wouldn't be able to do it. I was somewhat flabbergasted by this statement and confused by the fact that Jack was put in this class in the first place if the testing showed he couldn't do it. I was intimidated by the psychologist's authority. I asked her if there were any more tests to be done or any methods we could use to help Jack learn to measure. She said that all of the testing had been done, and that Jack should be removed from the class. I knew that she was giving up on Jack, and I felt uncomfortable about this, but I didn't verbalize it.

I then spoke with Jack's mother (who would have to give permission for Jack to drop the class). She said she wanted him to stay in drafting, that he probably wasn't trying hard enough. She said that he usually didn't try hard enough and wasn't motivated. I did not explore this statement or reach for the mother's feelings. At this point, I was identifying so strongly with Jack's predicament and how nobody wanted to help him, that I was very angry with all of these authority figures. I said that I would see if Jack's remedial services teacher could help him learn how to measure. I was very surprised that Jack's mother would not acknowledge that there must be more of a problem than just not trying hard enough when a 15-year-old can't draw a straight line, but I did not try to find out what was going on.

I then went to see the Remedial Services teacher, who said that she had her hands full helping Jack with his other classes and didn't know anything about drafting anyway. I didn't offer the teacher any support. She suggested that I ask Jack's Special Needs math teacher to help him. So I went to see the math teacher, who said that he would help Jack learn how to measure. Jack remained in drafting class and did a little better during the remainder of the 6-week period until they switched to a new area of study.

Over the next several weeks, we settled into an illusion of work. Jack and I continued to play games in our sessions. Jack was very uncomfortable and restless if we did not play a game, but when we did, he would open up and talk about himself. It became apparent that his mother hassles him a lot, always trying to get him to try harder. Jack became more able to talk about his feelings.

Last Week in January

Jack's mother called me and said that she was concerned because Jack had not been bringing any homework with him from school, and she thought he should have some. She said that Jack told her that he did his homework in Remedial Services, but she didn't know how that could be so, since he was getting such awful grades. I offered to act as the mediator between the systems, but I didn't actively include all of the parties involved. I said that I would mention her concerns to Jack, and if Jack agreed to it, I could go around and find out if he had been doing his work. She said that would be helpful to her, that it was really hard for her to get time off from work and come in to school. I told her I would call her back in a couple of weeks.

February 1

I worked to maintain Jack's trust by including him. I told Jack that his mother had called me about him not having any homework. I told him that I had been careful not to reveal to his mother anything that we talked about in our meetings. Jack said that it was fine with him if I checked around with his teachers about his homework, because he was doing it anyway. We talked a little about how hard it is when your parents don't believe you.

I spent the next couple of weeks going around to all of Jack's teachers. I started out with the Remedial Services teacher and the Special Needs math teacher, both of whom said that Jack wasn't the best student, but he came to class and handed in his assignments. At this point I think I was still overidentifying with Jack. I was looking for evidence that would show he was doing his best, so I didn't explore very much with these teachers. When I talked with the mainstream teachers, they all said that Jack was doing OK work (in the C range), handing in his assignments, and behaving well. I found out that Jack did have some difficulty with hearing and remembering instructions given verbally by the teachers and that he would sometimes blurt out answers before the teacher finished asking the question. I knew from the research I was doing into attention deficit disorder that these were common symptoms, and I found myself a little annoyed that none of the teachers seemed to be helping Jack with this (for example, by writing things down on the board).

Before I had the chance to call Jack's mother back, she called me, saying that she had found two supplemental reports in Jack's pocket when she was doing the laundry. The reports were from the Remedial Services teacher and the Special Needs math teacher. I told her I was surprised that he had received reports from those classes because I had just spoken with those two teachers within the last couple of weeks and they had given me no indication they were planning to send home a notice. I volunteered to take the role of the mediator, this time making suggestions that all parties take an active role. I suggested that perhaps it would be a good idea if we set up a time for a meeting. The meeting would include the two teachers, Jack, his mother, and me. I explained that maybe if we sat down together, we could figure out some strategies to help Jack do better. Jack's mother agreed that a meeting was a good idea, but she said that she thought the problem was that Jack wasn't motivated enough. We agreed upon a time for the next week, and I told her I would call back to confirm after I had spoken with the teachers and Jack. The teachers were open to the idea of a meeting, and in our next session Jack and I talked about it.

March 8

Jack started out by saying that things were going better in school lately except that he didn't like Remedial Services. I asked him what he did not like about it. I made a demand for work, asking Jack to define his own needs. He said, "Well, she makes up all of these rules like we have to come in and sit down and go right to work. We can't talk to each other at all. In classes like shop we get to talk to each other while we work." I asked him if it was hard for him to sit there and work the whole time without talking. He said that it was hard and usually he ended up forgetting and talking anyway. I said that it's hard when people expect you to do something that's really hard for you, and he agreed.

We went on talking about the meeting. Jack asked if everyone was going to yell at him and be mad that he was not doing better. I told him that I couldn't promise that there wouldn't be any yelling, but that the point of the meeting was to find out what we need to do to help him learn better, and that sometimes when people care they yell. I tried to reframe the situation. We then went on to talk about how this can tie in to his mother nagging him about school, that maybe it wasn't just because she wanted to bug him but because she really cares about him. We talked a little bit more about what Jack could expect the meeting to be like, and I told him that his input would be very important, that he had just as much to say as anybody else and that I would support him.

I later called Jack's mother back to confirm the meeting, and talked with her a little more about the purpose of the meeting. I found that we really had the same objective in mind, even if we had a different way of looking at it. I spent a lot of time over the next week doing research on ADD and tuning in to Jack, his mother, and the teachers.

March 16

Jack's mother arrived early for the meeting, which gave us a chance to get a little bit acquainted. I wanted to establish a rapport with Jack's mom, to tune in to her position and try to get her to work with me. I said that I was really glad that she had come and that I could tell she was really concerned about Jack and I thought it was very positive that she was so invested in making sure that Jack did well in school. I told her that a lot of parents aren't that interested in how their kids are doing, and that having a parent who really cares makes a big difference for the kid. I also said I thought it must be really frustrating for her. I had seen Jack's file and it was filled with years and years of evaluations and testing, yet things were still difficult. Jack's mother agreed, and seemed to relax a little.

Jack and the teachers arrived and we sat down in the conference room. I wanted to defuse any of the defensiveness people were feeling and set the stage for some work to be done right at the beginning. I introduced Jack's mom to the teachers and said I wanted to thank everyone for taking the time to be here, that our objective was to figure out how to help Jack to do better in school. I said that I knew everyone was working really hard already on this and that we weren't here to criticize anyone or get down on Jack, and I thought that if we worked together we might come up with some new ideas. I said that Jack's input would also be important and I wanted him to share his ideas with us too. I said I thought we could start out by hearing from the teachers. I asked them to tell about how Jack was doing, and to talk about not only the things that needed improvement but also the things that Jack was doing well. Each teacher took a turn, and when they brought up behaviors that were related to the ADD, I made a point of stating that those behaviors were tied to the ADD and not lack of control on Jack's part.

Jack's mom spoke next, saying that she still thinks that the problem is that Jack needs to be more motivated and try harder. I made a demand for work, asking Jack to say what he really felt. I asked Jack what he thought about that. He said it was probably true. I said that I thought he was trying pretty hard already and that some of the things he was being asked to do were difficult for him. Jack looked relieved and agreed that he does try, and no matter how hard he tries, everyone always asked him to try harder.

We then went on to talk about ways to help Jack to remember to bring his books and pencil with him to class, and how his mom could help him at home. The teachers came up with some really good ideas, and as the meeting ended, everyone thought the strategy was worth a try. We agreed to reevaluate the situation in about a month, and the teachers left. Jack, his mother, and I continued to work a little longer, talking about how they relate to each other at home. Once again, I tried to reframe their views of each other, and I gave them some suggestions about working together. This seemed quite successful, with Jack and his mom laughing a little and expressing some affection to each other.

March 22

I asked Jack to evaluate the meeting, to continue participating actively. We began by talking about the meeting with Jack's mother and teachers last Friday. I asked Jack what he thought about the meeting. He said that it was OK. I said that I thought it had gone well, that we had made some progress, but I had wondered what it had been like for him to sit in the meeting. He said that it hadn't been as bad as he thought it would be. I said that it is hard to sit in a meeting when it is about you and that I thought he had done really well. Jack smiled. I asked him how things were going now with his mom. He said they were still arguing a little over school, but that the new ideas were helping.

Current Status of the Problem

Where It Stands Now

A couple of weeks later, Jack's mom called me again to talk about how things were going. This time, I found myself really empathizing with her on the phone. In talking with her, I found out that in all the time that Jack has been diagnosed with ADD, no one has ever given her any real information about it or suggestions on how to deal with a kid with Jack's special needs. All this time I assumed somebody had given her that information and advice. I offered to photocopy an article I had about guidelines for living with a child with ADD and a list of some good books on the subject. She sounded really interested, and I mailed the materials off to her.

It then occurred to me that if nobody had spoken about these things with Jack's mother in all this time, probably nobody had spoken with Jack, which turned out to be the case. Since then, Jack and I have done some work on what ADD is, what might cause it, and what the treatment is. Jack said that all this time he thought that the ADD symptoms he experienced meant that he was stupid. I've learned never to assume that the obvious work has already been done. Even though we have not yet had our meeting to reevaluate the situation, Jack already seems to be doing better and feeling better about himself.

Strategies for Intervention

- Work with Jack on strategies for coping with the ADD symptoms (i.e., ideas for helping him remember things and helping him to expand his attention span).

- Find information about a support group for parents of ADD children for Jack's mother. This would help her learn more about ADD and talk with other parents about strategies for coping with and helping Jack.

- Work with Jack on expressing his feelings with his mother in a more constructive way to help their communication. Also, help Jack speak up more to his teachers and ask them to repeat directions or write them down on the board.

- Continue to work on the idea that the ADD symptoms are not Jack's fault.

- Help Jack learn to work effectively with his parents and teachers.

- Work on termination/transfer issues, including any ideas for talking with Jack's classroom teachers for next year and preparing them for his special needs.

By staying focused on education-related issues, and by bringing into the picture as many members of the family and school system as possible, the worker mobilized all parties involved to help Jack overcome the deficit and succeed in school. The repeated statements by the mother that all Jack needed to do was to try harder may have been a signal to the worker of an important area for discussion with the mother—her feelings about his academic problems and her difficulty in accepting that he may have physical barriers to success. The worker might want to explore the meaning of education to the mother's family and the cultural significance of education as well.

Chapter Summary

Family social work includes work that centers on agency mandates to address particular problems. Contracting and boundaries for service play a crucial role in these cases. The common ground between the services arising from the agency mandate and the client's perception of need gives direction to the work. Taboo areas in the family present special challenges to workers trying to achieve specific goals. Family work can occur in many settings, such as child welfare agencies or schools.

Related Online Content and Activities

 Visit *The Skills of Helping* Book Companion Website at www.socialwork.wadsworth .com/Shulman06/ for learning tools such as glossary terms, InfoTrac College Edition keywords, links to related websites, and chapter practice quizzes.

The website for this chapter also features additional notes from the author and on additional process recording:

- The Single-Parent Family and the "Big Brother" Service: An Acting-Out Parent

Social Work With Groups

I n Part IV we explore the interactional model of practice in the
context of social work with groups. In Chapter 8 we discuss
the group as a mutual-aid system, and in Chapter 9 we review
the principles of group formation. In Chapter 10 the beginning
phase of group work practice is examined in detail. Then, Chapters 11 and 12 explore the middle phase of practice, with special
emphasis on the importance of working with two clients: the
individual and the group. In Chapter 13 we examine the ending
and transition phase of practice in relation to groups, and in
Chapter 14 we look at variant elements of contracting introduced
by different types of groups.

The Group
as a Mutual-Aid
System

CHAPTER OUTLINE

The Fear-of-Groups Syndrome

The Dynamics of Mutual Aid

Obstacles to Mutual Aid

The Function of the Group
   Leader

I n Part IV we explore the dynamics of mutual aid that can
   occur when a group of clients with common concerns is
   brought together for the purpose of helping one another. You
will find that many of the processes and skills discussed in Parts II
and III can be used in the group context. We also explore some of
the unique features of group method, as well as specific obstacles
to mutual aid. In this chapter we outline the mutual-aid processes
and examine the function of the social worker in the group. We
also look at the concerns often experienced by workers as they
prepare to lead their first group session.

In our previous discussions of the underlying assumptions of the general helping model, we focused on the client in interaction with the various surrounding systems: family, agency, school, and so on. Perceiving the similarities between individual and group work is easier when one realizes that the group is a special case of the general individual-social interaction. In a sense, the group represents a **microsociety**, a special case of the larger individual-social interaction in our society. The potential for the "symbiotic" relationship described in the first part of this book is also present in each small-group encounter. In a seminal article entitled "The Social Worker in the Group," Schwartz (1961) defined the helping group as follows:

> The group is an enterprise in mutual aid, an alliance of individuals who need each other, in varying degrees, to work on certain common problems. The important fact is that this is a helping system in which the clients need each other as well as the worker. This need to use each other, to create not one but many helping relationships, is a vital ingredient of the group process and constitutes a common need over and above the specific tasks for which the group was formed. (p. 18)

The idea of the group as a mutual-aid system in which the worker helps people to help each other is an attractive one. However, workers with experience as members and leaders of groups have raised many legitimate questions about the potential effectiveness of such work. Exactly how can a group of people sharing the same set of concerns help one another? Isn't it a bit like the blind leading the blind? How will clients be able to talk about their most intimate concerns before a group of strangers? What about the coercive power of the group? How can individuals stand up against the odds? What is the job of the group leader if the members are helping one another?

My response is that the potential for mutual aid exists in the group, but simply bringing people together does not guarantee that it will emerge. Many obstacles can block the group members' ability to reach out to one another and to offer help. Many of these are similar to the obstacles described in earlier chapters; however, the group context can magnify their effect. Because all members will bring to the group their own concepts based on past experiences with groups (school, camp, committees, and so forth), and because many of these experiences may have been poor ones, the group worker is needed to help the group members create the conditions in which mutual aid can take place. The tasks of the group worker in attempting to help group members develop the required skills are related to these obstacles. Creating a mutual-aid group is a difficult process, with members having to overcome many of their stereotypes about individuals, groups, and helping. They will need all the assistance they can get from the group worker. Further, because the worker has also been affected by past group experiences, one of the worker's early tasks requires facing her or his own feelings and examining stereotypes. Without this self-examination, the worker may be unable to convey to the members a belief in their potential for helping one another. Faith in the strength of the group contributes greatly to the members' success.

Before we list the processes of mutual aid, let us discuss the common concerns experienced by students and workers when they first make the transition from working with individuals and families to work with groups.

The Fear-of-Groups Syndrome

In every one of my workshops for group work training, a moment arises, usually early on the first morning, when I sense a general unease in the group. Sometimes the first clue of what I call the **fear-of-groups syndrome** emerges during the introductions, when participants indicate they have never led a group, expressing this fact in a tone of voice that suggests that, if they had it their way, they would never lead one. When I explore these clues, I often hear that the workers were sent to the workshop by an administrator or supervisor who decided that group work would be a good idea. More recently, the pressures of managed care have led agencies to try to expand their group services, often for the wrong reasons.

Whether the participants are in the workshop voluntarily or not, and whether they are experienced workers or new workers, the underlying feelings are often the same: They are scared stiff of leading a group. As one experienced social worker said of group clients, "There are so many of them and only one of me!"

A common concern is having to practice with a group of people who are judging your work. Group work practice is seen as more exposed than individual work. If an individual client does not return after a few interviews, the worker can always chalk it up to the client's "lack of motivation." If ten clients fail to return to a group session, however, the worker feels he or she has failed.

Another concern involves the potential for direct negative feedback from clients. Anger from a single client or couple is one thing, but an angry group is something else. Of even greater concern is the possibility of a boring group. Workers feel completely responsible for the success of a group and dread the possibility of long silences, rambling conversations, individuals who dominate the discussion, or the sight of ten pairs of eyes glazing over.

Beginning group workers often raise their fear of lack of control. One workshop participant put it this way:

> When I'm conducting an individual interview, I know where it is going and can keep track of what is happening. In a group session, the members seem to take control of the session away from me. It feels like I am on my motorcycle, pumping the starter to get going, and the group members are already roaring down the road.

It takes some experience for a group worker to realize that moments such as these, when the group members take over the group, mean precisely that the group is well on its way to success. One of the benefits of caseworkers facilitating groups is that they begin to realize they can also let go of control in their one-to-one interviews.

The complexity of group work also intimidates workers. Whereas before they needed to concentrate on the relationship between themselves and the client, they now have to also concentrate on the relationships among group members. As they gain group work experience they become more conscious of the entity called the group-as-a-whole, which I will discuss in detail in a later chapter. In their one-to-one interviews they have to concentrate on the individual only, but now they must also pay attention to the group and somehow develop the ability to observe both the one and the many at the same time.

Such concerns are understandable. On reflection, however, experienced practitioners soon realize these concerns are similar to those they experienced when they first began to practice. Skills in work with individuals, which they now take for granted, seemed out of reach in their first interviews. They are continually learning more about the dynamics of the relationships between themselves and clients, as well as the dynamics of family relationships or couples. With some confidence in the skills they have, they worry less about those they need to learn and tolerate areas of ambiguity better. In learning the skills for working with groups, workers often start with no confidence at all; as in individual practice, they will build confidence through experience.

Further, I try to reassure these workers that they already know more about group work than they realize. Much of what they have learned about helping can be applied in the group situation, as chapters that follow illustrate. The areas of uncertainty represent exciting opportunities for new learning that can take place during the rest of their professional lives.

For the new worker or student, I suggest starting with individual work to develop some beginning confidence in basic practice skills, and then broadening these skills in the group context. Of course, students can also begin their learning with group work practice; I have seen many students develop quickly while working in the group medium. Nonetheless, talking to one client at a time makes the worker's task of beginning practice easier and more comfortable. If this can be supplemented with an opportunity to work as a coleader or observer with a more experienced group worker, then the learner has the best of all learning possibilities.

With both the new and experienced worker, I try to point out that the root of their fear is a misconception about their complete responsibility for the group work process. When they realize that they only have responsibility for their part, and that group members will do some of the most important helping, workers can view group work in its proper perspective. Certainly they will grow more helpful throughout their careers as they develop group skills and gain knowledge and confidence. They can, however, still give a great deal to their first groups.

Recall that new workers tend to underestimate the amount of help they can give to their clients. Group workers face this same problem. Continued group experiences help correct this misconception. The marvelous feeling a worker gets when he or she sees the power of mutual aid in group work helps to make up for the worker's anxiety along the way.

Finally, fear-of-groups must not interfere with the clients' right to receive the modality of service that is most appropriate to their particular needs. Consider, for example, populations of oppressed and vulnerable clients, as well as oppressors, for whom mutual-aid groups may well be the service modality of choice, providing a crucial complement to individual counseling. These clients should not be restricted to what may turn out to be less effective agency service simply because their social worker did not receive training in group work practice or feels more comfortable facing one client at a time. As you explore the many examples of mutual aid in the chapters that follow, the obvious healing power of groups will make the case for overcoming fear-of-groups.

The Dynamics of Mutual Aid

This section presents an overview of the mutual-aid process through several illustrations of specific dynamics. These will set the stage for understanding the more detailed discussions and examples of mutual aid in the chapters that follow.

Sharing Data

One of the simplest and yet most important ways group members can help one another is by **sharing data.** Members of the group have had different life experiences, through which whey have accumulated knowledge, views, values, and so forth that can help others in the group. For example, in a married couples' group (described in detail in Chapter 10), one of the couples was in their late sixties. They had experienced many of the normal life crises as well as those imposed by societal pressures, such as the Great Depression. As other group members who were in their fifties, forties, thirties, and twenties described their experiences and problems, this couple often shared insights that came from being able to view these crises from the perspective of time. As the group leader, I often found myself learning from the experiences of this couple. We created in the group a sort of extended family in which one generation passed on its life experiences to the next. In turn, the older couple used the group not only for their immediate problems but also as a place for reviewing their 50 years together. (This may be an important part of their work at this stage in their life cycle.)

In another group, working mothers shared ideas that had proved helpful in organizing their daily routines. The power of the Internet allows many clients to have access to information about resources that would never have been available before. Members shared the names of community services that they had discovered, and each mother tapped the experiences and the ingenuity of the others. Whether the data consisted of specific tips on concrete questions (jobs, available housing, money management, and so on), values, or ideas about relationships, each member contributed to the common pool of knowledge. The worker also contributed data that rounded out a rich resource for the members.

A group of clients with AIDS who were in early recovery from substance abuse (referred to as an AIDS/Recovery group) regularly shared specific information about the recovery process and coping with AIDS and its treatment. For example, one client told another, "This is the start of your second year in recovery—the feelings year—so don't be surprised about all of the pain you are feeling because you don't have the drinking and drugging to cover it up." At another meeting, clients shared their experiences with the new triple-drug therapy and provided information for those who were not in the trial groups about how to get connected. In the example that follows, group members provided tips on how to increase one member's chances for acceptance into a special housing program for people with AIDS. My job as group coleader was to help connect the group to the member to facilitate this form of mutual aid.

I pointed out that, earlier, Theresa had mentioned her interest in getting into this independent living facility. I wondered if we might help her just by addressing that issue, as well. She told us she was concerned about putting an application in because she didn't think she had established enough credibility in her single-room occupancy housing. At this point, Jake and Tania started suggesting strategies and ideas about how to approach the living facility and what would maximize her ability to get in. They strongly encouraged her to make an application right now, since there were openings, and a few months down the road these openings might close, and there would be no place for her. They said they thought it would be wonderful if she could move into the building.

Tania pointed out that the building—if you looked at it—the building was supposed to be for people with AIDS, but, if you took a look at it, your guess would be that it was essentially for gay men. She said she was the only woman in the whole building—the only single woman in the whole building. She said to Theresa that if worse came to worst, you could always tell them it's discrimi-nation, and that'll get their attention. She said, "That's how I got in."

They continued to talk with Theresa about ways she could demonstrate her responsibility, things that she had done, her commitment to recovery, the fact that she wanted to leave the place she currently lived in. Even though it was supposed to be a safe building, everybody knew drug dealing was going on there all the time, and it was scary to be there. She took it all in, thanked them for their advice, and said she was going to apply.

The Dialectical Process

The **dialectical process** is a mutual-aid process in which group members confront each other's ideas in an effort to develop a synthesis for all group members. An important debate can take place as each member shares views on the question under discussion. Group members can air tentative ideas by using the group as a sounding board—a place for their views to be challenged and possibly changed. Challenging ideas in the group is not always easy; I discuss later how such a culture for work can be developed. When this kind of group culture is present, the argument between two or more members becomes dialectical. Group members can listen as one member presents the "thesis" and the other, the "antithesis." As each member listens, he or she can use the discussion to develop a personal "synthesis."

For example, in a couples' group I co-led, one couple in their fifties discussed a problem they were experiencing with their grown, married children. They described their negative perception of the way in which their children were handling their marital difficulty. As they spoke, I could see anger in the eyes of a younger couple in their twenties. They were experiencing difficulty with the wife's parents, whom they viewed as "meddling" in their lives. When I reached for the verbal expression of the nonverbal cues, the battle was on. The older couple had to defend their perceptions against the arguments of the younger couple, who could see the problem through the eyes of the older couple's children. In return, the younger couple had to look at their own strained relationships with the wife's parents through the eyes of the older couple. For each couple, the debate led to some modification of their views and new insights into how the respective children and parents might be feeling. It was obvi-ous from the discussion that other group members were making associations to their own experiences, using the dialogue taking place before them.

Confrontation is a part of mutual aid. Instead of being suppressed, differences must be expressed in an arena where they can be used for learning. Group members often present strongly held views on a subject precisely because they have doubts and desperately need a challenging perspective. The skills involved in helping group members to use these conflicts constructively are explored later. Further, the group can be a laboratory for developing skills such as asserting oneself, so that the indi-vidual members can become more effective in their relationships outside of the group. In our example, the conversation between the older and younger couples con-stituted a rehearsal for the important discussion that needed to take place with their respective children and parents. The group members were able to use the experience for this purpose after the leader pointed this out.

Discussing a Taboo Area

Each group member brings to the group the norms of behavior and the taboos that exist in our larger culture. *Norms* are the rules of behavior that are generally accepted by a dominant group in society. These norms can be recreated within a social work group or other system. The existence of the norms is evident when the group members behave as if the norms exist. For example, one norm of group behavior may be to avoid discussion of a generally taboo area such as money.

In the beginning phase of work, the group recreates in this microsociety the general community culture, consisting of norms, taboos, and rules that the group members have experienced outside the group. Thus, direct talk about such subjects as authority, dependency (on people or drugs), death and dying, and sex is experienced as taboo. One of the tasks of the group leader will be to help the group members develop new norms and feel free to challenge taboos so that the group can be more effective. This helps the group develop a culture for work. The concept of a **culture for work** will be discussed in more detail in Chapter 12. For now, the term refers to an explicit or implied set of values, taboos, rules of interaction, and other concepts that are shared by the group members and that positively affect the group's ability to work at its tasks. Each client will feel the urgency of discussing the subject somewhat differently from the others, and each will experience the power of the taboo differently. As the work proceeds and the level of comfort in the group increases (the skills for helping this to happen are discussed in later chapters), one member may take the first risk, directly or indirectly, that leads the group into a difficult area of discussion. **Discussing a taboo area** is the mutual-aid process in which one member enters a taboo area of discussion, thereby freeing other members to enter as well. By being first, the member allows the more fearful and reluctant members to watch as the taboo is violated. As they experience positive work, they can see it as permission to enter the formerly taboo area. Thus, all the group members benefit from the particular sense of urgency, the lower level of anxiety, or the greater willingness to risk of the member who leads the way.

In my AIDS/Recovery group, one member spoke about her own abusive past history and how she had escaped her family and turned to the streets and "to every kind of drug and drink you could imagine." She described working as a prostitute in order to raise money for drugs and how she was not proud of herself or what she did. She said, "While I was on the street I was with many men but I was really with no man." These revelations opened the door for other members to share their own sexual experiences, often degrading and exploitive, as they went on "coke dates" to raise money for their drugs. The ability to discuss their emotions in a supportive, non-judgmental environment appeared to have a cathartic effect, creating a culture in which other taboo issues were discussed, such as their own illnesses, their rejection by friends and family, painful losses of people close to them, and their own fears of debilitation and death associated with AIDS.

The "All-in-the-Same-Boat" Phenomenon

The **"all-in-the-same-boat" phenomenon** is a mutual-aid process in which group members gain support from discovering that other group members have similar problems, concerns, feelings, and experiences. After the group enters a formerly taboo area, the members listen to the feelings of the others and often discover emotions of their own that they were unaware of, feelings that may have been powerfully affecting their lives. They also discover the reassuring fact that they are not alone in their feelings, that group members are "all in the same boat." Knowing that others share one's concerns and feelings somehow makes these feelings less frightening and easier to deal with. When, as a group member, one discovers that one is not alone in feeling overwhelmed by a problem, or in being worried about one's sexual adequacy, or in wondering who one is and where one comes from (as a foster teenager might), or in experiencing rejection because of "the virus," one is often better able to mobilize oneself to deal with the problem productively.

Discovering that other members of the group share his or her feelings often helps release a client from the power of the feelings. Guilt over "evil" thoughts and feelings can be lessened and self-destructive cycles broken when one discovers they are normal and shared by others. For example, a parent of a child with a physical or mental disability who hears that other parents may also feel that their child's condition represents "God's punishment" may be better able to cope with guilt. This can be one of the most powerful forces for change resulting from the mutual-aid process. A worker in individual work may reassure the client that others share the same feelings. However, it cannot compare with the impact of hearing them articulated by others in group sessions.

In another example from the AIDS/Recovery group, one member talked of her fears of being rejected by her boyfriend because she had AIDS and he did not. Even though the boyfriend knew about her AIDS and seemed to accept it, she was afraid to ask for a stronger commitment from him, because she thought he would turn her down and she would lose him. Although she was an attractive young woman, she feared that no one else could ever love her because of "the virus." A male member of the group responded, saying, "That's the thing you fear most—the rejection. I just disconnect my telephone and stay in my room because I know if I get close to someone, I'm just going to be rejected again."

Developing a Universal Perspective

Developing a universal perspective is a mutual-aid process in the group in which members begin to perceive universal issues, particularly in relation to oppression, thus allowing them to view their own problems in a more social context and with less personal blame. Expanding one's perspective is a special case of the all-in-the-same-boat phenomenon just described. Many clients, particularly those belonging to oppressed and vulnerable populations, may internalize the negative definitions assigned to them by the larger society. Thus, battered women, survivors of sexual abuse, people of color, the mentally ill, or people with AIDS may see their difficulties as a product of their own shortcomings. Mental health professionals who focus on personal pathology while ignoring the socioeconomic factors that created and constantly reinforce the negative self-image can reinforce this self-blame.

As members of a mutual-aid group share their common experiences of oppression, clients find it easier to recognize that a source of their problems may be external to them. For example, early in the women's movement, "consciousness-raising" groups arose to help women become more aware of gender stereotyping and oppression issues that affected their lives. A more universal perspective on one's problems can lift the burden of taking all of the blame for one's troubles. The anger against the oppression—anger that often lurks just beneath the outward signs of depression, submission, and apathy—can be released and converted into positive energy for dealing with personal as well as social issues.

In an example described in some detail in Chapter 13, a group of young female survivors of sexual abuse supported one another in recognizing the social roots of the gender oppression and violence they experienced. In a pivotal meeting, the worker announced that a "Take Back the Night" march would occur in their town the following week and wondered if group members might want to participate. An important discussion between the women, which highlighted how these women had been taught to accept their "victim" status, led to their decision to attend the march as a group. This experience, resulting from their ability to universalize their perspective, may well have been one of the most therapeutic aspects of the group practice.

In an example from the AIDS/Recovery group, one woman talked about the sexual exploitation she experienced both from her "Johns" while prostituting and from her boyfriends over the years. A transgender female member of the group angrily declared that, in her experience, sex is all most men are interested in and they will use and exploit you and your feelings, if they can, in order to get it. To underscore her point, she declared, "And I know, because I have been both!" After the group members stopped their good-natured laughing at her comment, there followed a discussion among the men and women of the group about intimate relationships, how hard it is to find people who really care, and how painful it is to lose someone who does.

Mutual Support

Mutual support occurs when group members provide emotional support to one another. When the group culture supports the open expression of feelings, members can empathize with one another. The group leader sets the tone through expression of personal feelings and understanding of others. Because group members share some concerns, however, they often understand one another's feelings in a deeper way than the worker. This expression of empathy facilitates healing for both the group member who receives it and the one who offers it. Specifically, as group members understand the feelings of the others, without judging them harshly, they begin to accept their own feelings in new ways. For a member struggling with a specific concern, the acceptance and caring of the group can be a source of support during a difficult time.

The idea of the acceptance and caring of the group introduces a new concept. It implies that the entity created when people are brought together—the group-as-a-whole—involves more than just the simple sum of the parts (members). For example, support from the mutual-aid group often differs from support received from a single empathic person. This is more than just a quantitative difference of more people equaling more empathy. At crucial moments in a group, one can sense a general tone or atmosphere, displayed through words, expressions, or physical posture, that conveys the caring of the group for the individual. This seems to have a special meaning and importance to the individual member. (See Chapter 12 for more on this and other properties of the group-as-a-whole.)

In the following example, also from the AIDS/Recovery group, the client who is reluctant to confront her boyfriend for fear of losing him asks the transgender member how she looks:

Once again, Theresa asked Tania how she looked. She said, "You're a woman. I know, as a woman, you will be honest with me and just tell me what you think. Do you think I look OK?" Tania seemed confused and said, "Well, sure, you look wonderful." I said, "I wonder if Theresa is really asking, 'Am I pretty enough? Am I attractive enough? If my boyfriend leaves me, can I find someone else who could love me even though I have AIDS?'" She said, "That's it," and came close to tears. She said, "I'm so afraid, if I lose him, I won't find anyone else." She said, "I know I could have guys, and I know I could have sex, and I like the sex. I sure missed it during the time I was in prison, but can another guy love me?"

The group members tried to reassure her that she was a wonderful person, and Tania said, "It's not what you look like on the outside, it's what you're like on the inside." And she said, "And you honey—you've really got it where it counts."

Mutual Demand

Earlier in this book, we saw how the helping relationship consisted of elements of both support and demand, synthesized in unique, personal ways. The same is true in the group context. In **mutual demand**, group members offer each other help by making demands and setting expectations on personal behavior. One illustration is the way group members confront one another. For example, in my couples' group two male members challenged a third who was maintaining that the source of the problem was his wife, that she was the identified patient, and he was coming to group merely to help her out. Both of the confronting group members had taken the same position at our first session and had slowly modified their views. They had lowered their defenses and accepted the idea that the problem was a "couples" problem. Coming from group members, this demand on the third member had a different quality from any that the group leader might have made.

As the group culture develops, it can include expectations that members will risk their real thoughts and ideas, listen to one another and set their own concerns aside at times to help one another, and so on. Such expectations help develop a productive culture for work. For example, the group may expect members to work on their concerns. At moments when clients feel overwhelmed and hopeless, this expectation may help them take a next step. The group cares enough about them not to let them give up. I have witnessed group members take some difficult action, such as confronting a boss or dealing more effectively with a close relative. When the action was discussed the following week, they indicated that one of the factors that had pushed them to make the move and take a risk was the thought of returning to the group and admitting that they had not acted. Mutual demand, integrated with mutual support, can be a powerful force for change.

In my AIDS/Recovery group, members often used their insights and understanding about the recovery process, gained through participation in 12-step groups such as Alcoholics Anonymous (AA) and Narcotics Anonymous (NA), to confront one another when their behaviors threatened their recovery. In one example, a group member who had just spent 2 weeks in a detoxification program after relapsing into cocaine use described how hard it was for him not to "hang around" the pool hall where all his friends were. He described how he wavered each day, wondering if he could connect up with them and not relapse again. Using an analogy obviously known by the group, one of the other members said, "You know, John, if you hang around a barbershop long enough" and then he paused. The rest of the group, in a chorus, replied, "You're going to get a haircut!" Everyone laughed, and John replied, "I know, I know, you're right, I would definitely be risking my recovery."

Individual Problem-Solving

A mutual-aid group can be a place where an individual asks for assistance with a particular problem. The group members help one member to solve a particular problem, receiving help themselves while offering it to another. For example, in one group a young mother discussed the strained relationship between her mother and herself. Her mother lived nearby and was constantly calling and asking to come over.

The group member had been extremely depressed and was going through periods where she neglected her work at home (dishes piling up in the sink and so on). Each time her mother came over, she felt, because of her mother's actions, that she was being reprimanded for being a poor housekeeper and a poor mother to her young children. The resulting tension produced many arguments, including some between the husband and wife. The client felt her mother still treated her like a child even though she was 27.

When the client presented the issue, at first indirectly and later with much feeling and tears, the group members reached out to offer support and understanding. They could use their own experiences to share similar feelings. The older members of the group provided their own perspective on the actions of the client's mother. They could identify with her feelings, and they pointed out how uncertain she might feel about how to help her daughter. When the group discussed conversations and incidents described by the client, they offered new interpretations of the interactions. It became clear that the client's perceptions were often distorted by her own feelings of inadequacy and her harsh judgments of herself. The worker also provided a new perspective by describing the problem as a normative crisis in life as the young couple sought new ways to relate to her parents, and the parents, in turn, struggled to find ways of being close while still letting go. There were other issues involved as well, related to some of the reasons for the client's depression, such as her feelings of being trapped at home and trapped as a woman. These emerged in later sessions.

Note that as the group members offered help to the individual with the problem, they were also helping themselves. Each member could make associations to a similar concern. All of them could see how easily the communications between mother and daughter were going astray. As they tried to help the client clarify her own feelings, understand her mother's reactions in new ways, and see how the mutual stereotypes interfered with the ability to communicate real feelings, the other members could relate these ideas to their own close relationships. This is one of the important ways in which giving help in a mutual-aid group is a form of self-help. It is always easier to see the problem in someone else's relationships than in your own. The general learning of the group members can be enhanced through the specific problem-solving work done with each member. The group leader can help by pointing out the underlying common themes.

Rehearsal

Another way in which a mutual-aid group can help is through **rehearsal**, in which the group provides a forum wherein members can try out ideas or skills. In a sense, the group becomes a safe place to risk new ways of communicating and to practice actions the client feels may be hard to do. To continue with the previous example, as the session neared the end, the group leader pointed out that the client seemed hesitant about taking up the issue with her mother. The following excerpt from the process recording starts with the client's response.

ROSE: I'm not sure I can talk with my mother about this. What would I say?
WORKER: That's a good question. How about trying it out right here? I'll pretend to be your mother calling to ask to see you. You can practice how you would respond, and the group can give some ideas about how it sounds. Does that sound all right?
ROSE: (She stops crying now and is sitting straight up in her chair with a slight smile on her face.) OK. You call me and tell me you want to have lunch with me and that I should keep the kids home from school so you can see them.

WORKER: (Role-playing) Hello, Rose, this is Mom.

ROSE: Hi, Mom. How are you and Dad feeling?

WORKER: Not so good. You know, Dad gets upset easily, and he has been feeling lousy. (The client had indicated that her mother often used her father's health to try to make her feel guilty.)

ROSE: That's it! That's what she would say to make me feel guilty. (The group members are laughing at this point.)

The discussion picked up, with the group members agreeing about how easy it is for others to make us feel guilty. The worker asked how Rose would feel at that point in the conversation. It became clear that the rest of the discussion would consist of her indirect responses to what she perceives as her mother's "laying on a guilt trip." After some discussion of what the mother might have been really feeling and having trouble in saying (such as how much she and her father really care about Rose and how much she needs to see her), the group brainstormed ways to break the usual cycle of indirect communications. The key moment in the role play came when the mother asked Rose to keep her children home for the mother's lunch visit. Rose had complained that the mother never wanted to see her alone—it was always with the children. She was always asking to have them at home when she visited. She thought her mother didn't trust her with the kids and was always checking up on her.

WORKER: (Speaking as the mother) I wonder, Rose, if part of the reason I always ask to have the kids there is that I'm uncomfortable when we get together. I'm not sure what I would say to you for a whole two hours. I want the kids around to help fill the conversation.

ROSE: You know, I'm not sure what I would say to my mother either. I really don't know what to talk to her about.

FRAN: (Another group member) Can you try to tell your mother that you get upset when she asks to keep the kids home because you want to have some time alone with her? Maybe your mother could understand that. (Silence)

WORKER: Rose, do you really want to spend some time with your mother?

ROSE: I'm not so sure I do.

WORKER: Then that's the first step. When you're sure, I think the words will come more easily. If you tell your mother how you really feel, it could be the start of some honest talk between you. Perhaps she could share some of her real feelings in response, instead of always doing it indirectly and in ways which are open to misinterpretation. Maybe if you could do this, then your mother would see this as a sign of your maturity.

Rose tried to articulate her feelings more clearly but was obviously still having difficulty. She reported the following week that she had talked with her mother about how it made her feel when the mother tried to do things for her (such as wash the dishes when she came over), and the mother had responded by describing how she never really knew what to do when she came over—should she help out or not? Rose felt it cleared the air, even though other issues and feelings were not discussed. The interesting thing about the role-playing device as a form of rehearsal is that is often reveals the underlying ambivalence and resistance that the client feels but has not expressed in the discussion. The rehearsal not only offers the client a chance to practice, it also reveals to the group, the worker, and the client some of the feelings that need to be dealt with if the client is to succeed in his or her efforts.

In the AIDS/Recovery group, the client who had raised boyfriend problems used the group at one point to consider how to approach him with her concerns. One member helped by role-playing how Theresa could handle the conversation:

We returned to Theresa, and I said, "Is the question really, Theresa, that you're afraid that he might not stay with you—that, if you actually confront him on this issue of the other women, he might leave you?" She agreed that it was her concern. At this point, I wondered if it might help Theresa to figure out what she might say to her boyfriend. Theresa said that would be helpful because she didn't know when and how to say it. Then she laughed and said, "Maybe I should say it in bed." Tania said, "Oh no. Don't say it before sex and don't say it after sex." And I added, "And don't say it during sex." Everyone laughed at this point, and Tania, a stand-up comedian, did an imitation of having a conversation with Theresa's boyfriend, while pumping up and down as if she were in bed having sex with him.

Tania said, "You have to find a quiet time, not a time when you're in the middle of a fight, and you have to just put out your feelings." I asked Tania if she could show Theresa how she could do that. She started to speak as if she were talking to Theresa's boyfriend. I role-played the boyfriend and said, "Oh, but Theresa you're just insecure, aren't you?" Tania did a very good job of not letting me put her off and, instead, putting the issue right where it was— whether I was prepared to make a commitment or if I was too insecure.

Theresa said, "I know I have to talk to him, but, you know, he's told me that he's not sure he wants to be tied down, that he likes to have his freedom." Jake nodded his head and said, "Yeah, that's the problem, they want their freedom and they don't want to make a commitment, and you're afraid, if you push him, he'll leave you because you got the virus." Theresa said she realized she had to sit down and talk to him because it couldn't keep up the same way. She would just get too angry and do something crazy and screw up her recovery. She said when she had a fight with him on Thanksgiving he did call his sponsor and came back much more gently. She felt she had gotten through to him, but she had to find another way to get through to him and talk to him. Otherwise, this thing was just going to continue and it was going to tear her up inside.

The "Strength-in-Numbers" Phenomenon

Sometimes it is easier to do things as a group than as an individual. The **"strength-in-numbers" phenomenon** is a mutual-aid process in which group members are strengthened to take on difficult tasks through the support of other group members. In one example, described earlier, a group of female survivors of sexual abuse attended a "Take Back the Night" march. In another example, described in Chapter 16, individual tenants in a housing project found it difficult to stand up to the housing authority on issues of poor maintenance service. When organized into a tenants' group, the "strength-in-numbers" phenomenon worked to decrease their feelings of isolation and individual risk, which encouraged the group members to make demands for their rights. An individual's fears and ambivalence can be overcome by participation in a group effort as his or her own courage is strengthened by the courage of others.

I have shared several examples to illustrate how the dynamics of the mutual-aid process can work. These examples should not suggest that working in groups is a preferred method. The choice of individual or group work is influenced by many factors, particularly the comfort of the clients in dealing with their concerns on a one-to-one basis as opposed to within a group setting. A client often finds both kinds of work helpful at the same time. Each would have a slightly different focus, and each could be expected to provide important stimulation for the other. For many clients, the group can offer unique forms of help in dealing with their life problems. I have attempted to identify some of these mutual-aid processes, but it is important to realize that groups will not provide this kind of help just because they have been brought together. In the next section, we briefly examine some of the obstacles that can make mutual aid a difficult process. These obstacles and others will be explored in detail in later chapters.

Obstacles to Mutual Aid

In the early phases of a group's development, one potential obstacle to mutual aid is the apparent divergent interest each group member brings to the engagement. Even in a group with a narrow, clearly defined purpose, group members might not identify their common ground. Various group members may feel their concerns and feelings are unique and unrelated to those of other members. The symbiotic attractions among members may be partial, subtle, and difficult to perceive.

In many ways, the small group is a microcosm of the larger society. The apparent diffusion of interest in the group between self and other group members is a reflection of the same inability to see the connections in our larger society. Thus, as each member becomes oriented to the group engagement, that member will be asking, "How am I the same or different from the other members?"

Given these concerns, one of the early tasks of the group leader will be to help group members begin to identify their common ground. As the group develops a mature way of relating, individual members can begin to understand that they can learn and grow by giving help as well as receiving it. As each member develops the skills required to offer help and to take help, these same skills will be found to be related to their individual concerns outside of the group. For example, group members who learn how to identify their feelings and to share them in the group may be able to apply these skills in other intimate relationships. Nevertheless, at the beginning stage and periodically during the life of the group, the inability of members to perceive their connections to the others will present an important obstacle.

A second set of obstacles emerges from the fact that even a small group can be a complex system that must deal with many developmental tasks if it is to work productively. As soon as more than one client is involved, a new organism is created: the group-as-a-whole. As we have seen, this group is more than the simple sum of its parts (that is, the individual members). For example, this new organism needs to develop rules and procedures that will allow it to function effectively. Some will be openly discussed, while others may operate beneath the surface by mutual consent. Roles such as scapegoat, deviant member, and internal leader may be subtly distributed to group members. Some of these role assignments allow the group-as-a-whole to avoid dealing directly with a problem. For example, the group gatekeeper may intervene to distract the group each time the discussion approaches a painful subject. Many of the unstated rules for relating will be counterproductive to the purpose of the group. Such factors are properties of this complex organism called the group and must be dealt with by the leader if the group is to function effectively.

A final major source of potential problems for the group is the difficulty of open communication. I have already discussed some of the barriers that make it difficult for clients to express their real feelings and concerns. These are related to a social culture that has implicitly and explicitly developed certain norms of behavior and identified taboo areas in which honest communication is hard to achieve. Each group member brings a part of this culture into the group, and thus the group culture, in early phases of work, resembles the culture of the social surroundings. This often makes it difficult for group members to talk with and listen to one another in areas of central concern. With the group leader's help, members will need to develop a new culture in which norms are modified and taboos lose their power, so that members may freely communicate with one another.

I have just outlined three major obstacles to mutual aid: the difficulty individual members have in identifying with other group members, the complex tasks involved in creating a mutual-aid system, and the difficulties in communicating honestly. Such obstacles define in part the job of the group leader. They do not argue against the use of groups as mutual-aid systems; rather, they represent an agenda for the group worker. If groups were not faced with these problems, and if people could easily join together to offer aid and support, then there would be no need for a group worker. The small group is a special case of the larger individual-social engagement described in Chapter 1; as such, it essentially carries the same potential for diffusion of the symbiotic relationship. Once again, the functional role of mediation will be used as a starting point for describing the tasks of the helping person—this time, however, in the context of group work.

The Function of the Group Leader

In the earlier discussion of Schwartz's mediation practice theory, the function of the helping person was illustrated using three circles (see Figure 1.2). The client was on the left, the systems to be negotiated on the right, and the worker in the middle. Because the group is a specific case of this larger engagement, the same diagram can be drawn with the individual on the left and the group on the right.

The general function of mediating the individual-social engagement is now translated into mediating the individual-group interaction. This leads Schwartz to present one of his most central and useful ideas about group work: that the group worker always has two clients—the individual and the group. The function of the worker is to mediate the engagement between these two clients. As the group process unfolds, the worker is constantly concerned with both. For example, when an individual raises a specific concern, the worker will help the member share that concern with the group. Chapter 4 detailed how difficult it often can be for clients to describe their concerns. All the worker skills described earlier—such as reading indirect communications and helping clients move from the general to the specific—can be employed to help individuals express their concerns to the group. As the leader helps the one talk to the many, she or he will also monitor the interaction to see if the members appear to be listening and relating to the individual. If they seem to be turned off, the worker will explore their feelings and reactions. Perhaps the individual's problem is painful to the group members, raising related feelings of their own and making it hard for them to listen. In any case, the group worker, with a clear sense of function, will pay attention to both clients at exactly the same time.

Like the first client (the individual), the second client (the group) needs help from the worker in dealing with the obstacles described earlier. For example, if the group culture is making it difficult for members to discuss their real feelings about a specific issue, then the worker can call this to the attention of the group. Bringing the obstacle out in the open is a first step in helping the group members become more conscious of their own processes. With the assistance of the worker, members can discuss how the blockage of open communication in a sensitive area frustrates their work. With understanding comes growth as the group becomes more sophisticated about its ways of working. A new agreement, including new norms that are more productive, can be openly reached. In many ways the group worker serves as a guide for the group members faced with the complex task of developing an effective mutual-aid system. The important point is that this is the members' group: The work to strengthen it is theirs, and the group worker is there to help them to do it.

In a general way, these two areas of work characterize the group leader's responsibilities: helping the individual and the group relate effectively to one another, and helping the group become more sophisticated about the group's way of working, so that it releases the potential for mutual aid. Of course, this process is more complicated than this simple explanation implies. In the remaining chapters of Part IV, we shall explore the underlying assumptions about how mutual-aid groups work and the tasks and skills required of the group worker.

Chapter Summary

Common fears of new group leaders, referred to as the fear-of-groups syndrome, are understandable and may be overcome. Clients have many ways of helping one another in mutual-aid groups. These include sharing data, the dialectical process, discussing taboo areas, the "all-in-the-same-boat" phenomenon, developing a universal perspective, mutual support, mutual demand, individual problem-solving, rehearsal, and the "strength-in-numbers" phenomenon. Three major areas of obstacles to the mutual-aid process in groups are the difficulty in identifying common ground, the tasks required to develop a positive culture for work, and the general difficulty of open communication. The role of the group leader is an extension of the mediating function into the group context. The group leader mediates between two clients: the individual and the group-as-a-whole.

Related Online Content and Activities

Visit *The Skills of Helping* Book Companion Website at www.socialwork.wadsworth .com/Shulman06/ for learning tools such as glossary terms, InfoTrac College Edition keywords, links to related websites, and chapter practice quizzes.

The website for this chapter also features additional notes from the author.

Group
Formation

In this chapter, we explore in detail the steps required to
establish a group and to increase its chances for success. Work
with the staff system is dealt with first, because much that
follows depends upon these efforts. Next, issues related to group
formation (timing, composition, and so on) are explored. The
impact of ethnicity and culture in the group formation stage is
discussed, as well as problems of recruitment. Finally, we return to
the tuning-in skill, this time applying it to a first session in the
group context.

Preparing for Group Work

Because several crucial issues must be dealt with before the first meeting takes place, the preparatory phase can be one of the most complicated in work with groups. The literature on group work pays surprisingly little attention to the problems of this phase, beyond discussion of group type (as in educational, therapeutic, support), structure (as in frequency and number of sessions), group composition, and so on. For example, one problem that is often ignored concerns staff dynamics. It is not unusual for a worker to decide that a group would be helpful for clients and then to approach colleagues for appropriate referrals. A staff meeting might bring general agreement to support the group; however, the worker waits 2 months without getting a single referral. In analyzing examples of this kind, I have consistently found that the worker had left out the important step of involving the colleagues in a meaningful way. I could often determine the moment in the staff meeting when the groundwork was laid for the frustration that followed.

Similarly, a worker may launch a group and prepare for a first meeting with ten members who have promised to attend. The evening of the meeting arrives, and after waiting 35 long and painful minutes for latecomers, the worker must face the reality that only two members have come. Once again, the source of the disappointment can often be traced to steps that were left out in the preparatory work with clients as the worker or other workers began the referral process. In analysis of interviews and telephone conversations, one can often identify the moment the worker sensed the ambivalence of the prospective group member but did not reach for it.

In the sections that follow, these and other group formation issues will be discussed, with an emphasis on describing and illustrating strategies for launching effective mutual-aid groups.

Work With the Staff System

An important first principle is that a group in an agency or institution must be related to the service. If a worker attempts to establish a group because of a desire to develop new skills or because he or she has decided (without involving the rest of the staff) that there is a need for such a group, the work may be doomed to failure. A common example is the student who is placed in an agency for practicum experience and is taking a course in group work practice. A requirement for the class is to have a group, so the student endeavors to set one up in the field. Quite often the group never has its first meeting, because the student's need for it is not a sound reason for developing a group. The idea for a group must begin with the identification of an area of clients' unmet needs that the group method might meet. The group must reflect the consensus of the department or team involved so that it is not seen as being personally "owned" by the group worker.

The difficulty or ease involved in establishing a group may depend on the group experience of the agency. In those settings where groups are a common form of service and where all staff members take their turn at leadership, many of the problems of formation can be minimized. In agencies that usually do not offer groups as a service, such problems may be intensified. For example, a worker who attempts to introduce group work into a setting that has never had groups must recognize that such a move might threaten staff. As we saw in the previous chapter, many workers are frightened by the idea of facing more than one client at a time. If they do not have a fund of good experiences to draw on or if they unsuccessfully attempted to establish a group when they were students, they may be hesitant about working with groups. The worker attempting to initiate a group service must recognize that colleagues may wonder whether they will be asked to carry a group next, especially if the first succeeds. This fear is often expressed indirectly with comments such as "Groups would be great in this agency, but do we really have the time?" The development of group service can have an important impact on the staff system, and the worker should make use of the tuning-in skill in preparing to negotiate the establishment of the group.

Staff resistance also occurs when the administration of an agency or organization, because of the pressures of managed care or other cutbacks in resources, has decided to move into group work as a measure of **cost containment**. In reality, group practice may actually increase costs, because it rarely serves as a substitute in those situations where individual work is required. In many cases, issues that emerge in the group for one client may generate the need for more intensive individual work, rather than less work, for other group members. Group work should be the practice modality of choice only if it is the best modality for the particular population and problem. When cost cutting is the only rationale offered, staff resistance due to fears about competency is often masked by staff anger at the "top-down" imposition of group practice. Whether the reasons for developing group work practice are sound or spurious, the use of group work has expanded explosively. Further, a documented decrease in group work content in social work education programs has accompanied this expansion. Any system considering moving into group practice must also consider the need for staff training and consultation to ensure the quality of the practice.

In the rest of this section, excerpts from an effort by a hospital social worker to establish a ward group illustrate the dynamics and the skills involved in preparatory work with staff.

Achieving Consensus on the Service

The idea of a group may emerge in an agency in many ways: client feedback, a worker discovering a common concern among individual clients, or a staff team discovering an important gap in the service. Wherever the idea starts, all staff involved must have the opportunity to comment honestly on the potential service. A common mistake is for workers to decide on the need for a group and then to set about "selling" colleagues on the idea. Rather than presenting their own views on the need for it and inviting feedback and discussion, workers may try to influence their colleagues, creating the illusion that they are involving others in the process. In the following illustration, a young social worker, relatively new to the hospital, approaches a long-time head nurse about forming a group on the ward. The nurse has a reputation for being tough and uncooperative on projects such as this, so the worker has steeled herself for the task of convincing the nurse of the need for the group. The illustration demonstrates the problems generated when one tries to "sell" an idea.

> I said to Miss Ford that I had been doing some thinking which I would like to share with her. I told her that I had been on the ward quite a bit and felt quite at home on it. I said to her that I, as everyone else on the ward, am here to try to service the patients to the best of my ability. I then asked her what she thought of a group having any value on the ward. She said that it has been

suggested before, so that it was nothing new. She said that the room full of ladies could do with something of that sort but that that's the only ladies' room there is. I asked if she thought that only ladies could benefit from a group experience and she said no, but that she was thinking in terms of room number 1403. She asked what the group would be about and for. I said that I'm open to suggestions but that perhaps the basic purpose could be for the patients to discuss their hospitalization, frustrations, etc. It would be open to all patients.

Although the worker said she wanted to explore the nurse's views, she really did not mean it. The nurse quickly sensed her purpose when she did not explore the suggestion that the patients in room 1403 might benefit from a group. The worker was still reacting, on an emotional level, to the nurse's first comment that the idea had been suggested before and that it was nothing new. Had the worker not been so set on convincing the nurse, she could have asked for an elaboration of the nurse's first comment. What had that earlier effort been like? Had there been any problems? The worker is new on the ward, and the nurse might have shared some past experiences that could have provided helpful feedback. Because the worker has already pegged the nurse as resistant, however, she did not reach past this first comment. The same lack of genuine interest in the nurse's views is demonstrated when the worker challenges her suggestion that the women in room 1403 might need the help. As the worker will find out later, this room contains patients with terminal cancer. It represents a room full of problems for which the nursing staff has genuine concern but few ideas for helping. It could represent an important area of missing service, but the worker does not know this because she has cut off the nursing supervisor's participation in the process.

After the nurse received the signals confirming her own stereotype of workers as outsiders who do not really appreciate the problems of the ward, she responded rather perfunctorily, asking crisp questions about the worker's proposed group:

Miss Ford asked how the patients would know or how I would tell them. I told her that in order to make it a voluntary thing, perhaps written invitations to each patient would be a good idea. She asked when and where it would be held. I told her that I hoped she could help make that decision, especially the time, because I realize they are busy. As far as the room goes, I suggested, perhaps an empty bedroom or the sunroom. She said that by October 16th all rooms should be filled up. I suggested we could decide on that at a later date. I asked if she could, however, talk to the doctors and staff about this, get some ideas, and we could discuss it again next week at rounds. She said that would be fine.

At the end of the worker's process recording, she included the following comment:

Miss Ford did not seem too enthusiastic and was quite resistant (mentioning no rooms, how would patients know, etc.). However, I feel she can see some value in a ward group. Next week I plan to give her some examples of why I can see a need for the group.

If the worker had done that, she likely would have met the same resistance. If she had continued to accept the nurse's superficial agreement, she would have proceeded to set up her group and probably been surprised on the day of her first meeting. Either the room would have been unavailable or the worker would have discovered that half the patients she had selected for the group session had been "inadvertently" scheduled for blood tests, X-rays, or other medical procedures that took them off the ward. The nursing staff would have apologized, and the problem would have repeated itself the following week. The worker would eventually have given up, adding one more story to the collection of examples of how "resistant" Miss Ford was to any new ideas.

The missing skill in this interview was described in Part II as "looking for trouble when everything seems to be going the worker's way." In this case, the worker sensed the underlying negative reaction in the interview but did not reach for it. For example, she could have said, "Miss Ford, you don't seem too enthusiastic about this group. Can you tell me why not?" This direct response to the indirect cue would have opened up Miss Ford's real feelings and reactions and might have turned a one-way selling job into an honest exploration of mutual thoughts about a new service. In many ways, the nurse's fair amount of directness about her feelings should have been an aid to the worker. At least her feelings were almost out in the open. By contrast, there are many instances, as when a worker is describing a group to other workers at a team meeting, when the worker might find an artificial agreement expressed through apparently unqualified support. Once again, the skilled worker would not leave the session without first reaching for the underlying reservations. For example, the worker might say, "It's great to see such quick support for my idea, but you know, it's going to cause some problems and inconveniences for the rest of you. Don't you think we should also talk about those?"

The worker often senses the underlying resistance but fears reaching for it. The belief is that if one leaves the negatives unexpressed, they might go away. They never do. These reservations, negative reactions, fears, and the like all come back to haunt the worker in the form of conscious or unconscious sabotage of the worker's plans. To establish a group successfully, the worker must insist that it be a service of the staff, not just the worker. It is not the worker's personal group that happens to be taking place in this setting. Without real support from the rest of the staff, the worker will be alone when problems emerge. I have seen excellent work done with school principals, for example, when after the principal has given perfunctory agreement to allow a group to meet in the school, the worker has asked, "Would you be very upset if we couldn't offer this group to your kids?" After a moment's pause, the principal has responded, "The only reason I OK these groups is that the people at the board like to see them in the schools. Actually, staff and I often find they are more trouble than they are worth." Only at this point does the real discussion begin, and the worker can start serious contracting with the agency or setting. If this stage is skipped over in the worker's eagerness to gain a toehold, then the lack of real investment will hurt when the going gets rough in the group.

Fortunately, as in work with clients, workers can usually go back after making a mistake and try again. After some consultation and discussion of the first process recording of the interview with the nurse, the worker returned to Miss Ford; instead of trying to convince her, she owned up to her mistake and tried to start over again. You will notice the change in the nurse's attitude as the discussion becomes real:

> I told Miss Ford that I felt I may have been too pushy about the ward group. I said that I had asked for her participation and interest, yet I hadn't given her a chance to express herself, and I wasn't really listening to her. I then apologized and suggested that we might go back to the beginning. I said I was interested in knowing her true feelings regarding the group. She said she thought the group would be very good for most patients, but she was worried about the manpower of nurses. She said it was difficult enough to get all the nurses to attend her

ward conference without having them attend a patients' group. I asked if she was thinking in terms of all the nurses going to the group at once. She said she didn't know and wondered what I thought. I said that the decision of nurses was up to her. I suggested that it might be just as effective to have one nurse drop in on the group or have the nurses rotate.

This may have been the issue on the head nurse's mind when she commented on the group having been tried before. The worker needs to pay attention to the problems that the group creates for the ongoing system. The worker must be able to empathize genuinely with the day-to-day difficulties of other staff members. Often, the recognition of these problems can lead to alternative solutions or to the willingness of the staff to extend themselves. As in all human relationships, the worker must truly understand how the other staff member feels. The discussion in the interview turned to the issue of purpose and contract:

I suggested that one important gap existed between patients and doctors or patients and nurses. I explained further that I believed that if a patient could release some of his anxieties or fears about his medical problems or share his hostilities in the group, he might be an easier patient to cope with. Rather than expressing his feelings in an undesirable way, he might be happier on the ward and easier to deal with. Miss Ford agreed with this and then asked about the resident on the ward. How could we keep him involved? We discussed this for a while.

Although the worker's contract statement is still unclear—reflecting her own lack of clarity—the general sense of the group dealing with issues related to hospital and illness and with communication between patient and staff is clearly suggested. This is important, because workers who do not connect the purpose of a proposed group to the general service of the agency are often seen as simply requesting space. When administrators and staff members perceive the connection between their service and the purpose of the group, they will be more likely to invest themselves in the group's development. A worker offering to lead a group for children who have been identified by teachers as having trouble at school will be more easily accepted by the staff than one asking to lead groups for general discussion (for example, "I would like to work with children who need a socialization experience").

As the discussion with Miss Ford continued, her more active involvement showed:

Miss Ford asked how the patients would know about the group, who would go, etc. I suggested that the nurses see all the patients, and they could tell who could benefit from a group experience, and who was ready to go. She asked how patients would find out about the group. I suggested we stick notices to their bedside tables. She said it would not be a good idea because the tables must be washed. She suggested we put them in the bathrooms where the beauty salon advertises. I said it was a good idea, and we went to the bathroom to select the best spot. I then brought up the subject of confidentiality.

The worker has used her tuning-in preparation to anticipate another sensitive area for discussion—the issue of confidentiality. Although the nurse has not raised this issue, she is likely wondering what would happen if patients complained about the nursing staff. This issue is often difficult for workers. It often lies under the surface when a worker proposes a group in a hospital, school, or residential setting, or when the worker is sharing clients with another worker but the first worker will continue to see the client on an individual basis. The group worker often suggests to the staff the need to maintain confidentiality, not reporting group discussion, so that the group members will feel free to talk. When group members talk negatively about staff, they often hope the worker will help improve a bad situation. They are also concerned about how the information will be used (the possibility of retribution from the teacher, nurse, and so forth). They are not, however, raising the concerns just for the sake of venting feelings.

Acting as a communication bridge between clients and the agency system—the mediating approach—is very much a part of the work. When the two-way flow of communication is not acknowledged, trouble results. For example, if the worker begins work with staff by stating they will not be included in discussion of group content, their fears and anxieties may lead to direct or indirect efforts at sabotage. In one such case, a worker in a home for unmarried mothers had completely ignored the housemother's concerns, particularly her fear of complaints, and had indicated that all discussions would be confidential. When the worker arrived, the housemother rang a bell and shouted, to the worker's consternation, "Group therapy time." In other examples, the worker's colleagues have described the group to their individual clients in a way that served to heighten the clients' fears of involvement: "We are going to offer this group for single mothers, but you don't have to go if you don't want to."

Clearly, the work of setting up a mutual-aid group involves careful contracting with staff, especially regarding confidentiality. That is, because the worker's sense of function involves communicating between client and system, including the agency, this must be part of the contract. Nurses, child care workers, teachers, and other counselors must be viewed as colleagues, with each having a part in the operation. Discussions should focus on how the group worker and the other staff members will handle feedback. The meaning of the feedback and the way in which clients might use either the individual worker or the group worker as a channel must be recognized. The agreement can include ways to achieve the optimum outcome, in which each will attempt to assist the clients' efforts to provide direct feedback to the other. I have found that this discussion often takes much of the threat out of the possibility of negative feedback and turns it into an important technical issue for both workers.

When I explore why workers are reluctant to follow this course of action—that is, to treat staff as colleagues and work out agreements for mutual sharing of relevant information—they raise several objections. First, they usually express concern about the client's acceptance of such a contract. Next, they express their own fears about confronting a colleague with "bad news." How do you tell a staff member with whom you have coffee each day that his client doesn't feel he understands her? Setting up a contract regarding what sort of information is to be shared—and in particular, obtaining agreements from colleagues to be open with each either even in regard to negative feedback—serves to protect the group worker from such scenarios. Finally, workers often reveal that they have developed stereotypes of their colleagues as "lousy" workers (poor teachers, insensitive doctors, and so on), so what good would sharing be? I can understand their reticence to take on this function, yet if the group worker accepts that the nurse on the ward, the teacher, a fellow social worker, or whoever is actually closed to change, such acceptance means that an important part of the service to clients will no longer be available. The worker will inevitably be in a serious quandary when the "strength-in-numbers" phenomenon leads the group members to share their real feelings. A situation will have been set up that makes it impossible for the worker to do anything about the problem except empathize, ignore it, or defend the system. This often leads to apathy and disengagement on the part of the group members.

The question of confidentiality has broadened during this discussion to encompass a much larger issue: the function of the helping person within his or her own helping system. This will be explored in detail in Part V. Clearly, this concern is often a central issue for staff members when group formation is discussed. It is best discussed out in the open, and contracting should take place with both staff and group members for freedom of communication of group content in a responsible manner. Returning to the interview, we find that this is precisely what our worker on the hospital ward does.

> I then brought up the subject of confidentiality. I asked how Miss Ford felt it should be handled. For example, if one patient or more complained about a certain nurse or herself, would she like to know or not? Rather than directly answering, she told me about a patient on the ward who would complain of different shifts of staff and play one against the other. I asked her if the gist of her story was that it was better to know the complaints so that they can be investigated and dealt with. She said yes. I told her I felt the same way and that I would like to know when patients made complaints about me.
>
> We then talked about where the group could be held. I again suggested the sun porch. This time, Miss Ford said that it would be all right because patients used it anyway. We then discussed further clearances in the hospital and set up a meeting with the nursing staff to clarify the group's purpose and to select members.

The result of this effort was active involvement on the part of Miss Ford in the establishment of the group. The frontline nursing staff quickly picked up the message of positive support for the group and offered their assistance to the social worker. The group was established and became integrated into the program on the ward, with nursing staff becoming involved as coleaders.

Identifying Group Type and Structure

Staff colleagues can also be helpful in considering the question of the group type and structure. For example, will it be a group of fixed membership meeting over a period of time, or will it be an **open-ended group** in which different members arrive and leave each week? Special problems and dynamics associated with open-ended groups will be discussed in Chapter 14; however, for some purposes and settings they provide a better alternative than a fixed-membership group. One ward group in a hospital consisted of women who arrived for a 2-day preparatory stay, a 1-day exploratory operation to determine the possibility of cancer, and a 2-day recovery period. Participation of both pre- and postoperative patients lent itself to the mutual-aid process, as those who had just gone through the experience were helpful to those preparing for it, and those who were newly admitted began the process of preparing to leave the hospital by helping those who were leaving.

In contrast, a group for teenage survivors of sexual abuse would need some time to establish the levels of trust required to explore painful and formerly secret experiences. An open-ended group with a continually changing membership would not be appropriate for such a population. Some members might join after the initial sessions, but at some point, such a group would need to be closed.

Groups are sometimes formed from ongoing natural groups, such as a group home. This living group operates 7 days a week, 24 hours each day. For 2 hours twice each week, house meetings are held at special times within the ongoing group life to focus on issues of group living, such as problems among residents and between residents and staff. These meetings represent structured incidents in the life of the ongoing group designed to improve their ability to live and work together.

Another issue is related to the content of the group meeting. People can provide mutual aid not just through talking but also through other "mediums of exchange" between people (Shulman, 1971). For example, senior citizens in a residential center might use activities that they have developed to structure their time, to provide enjoyment or education, to acquire new skills, or just to enjoy the company of others. In the formation stage, workers must consider whether interaction through activity represents an important part of the purpose of the group and fits within the general function of the setting.

A ward group in a psychiatric hospital involved in planning recreational activities for patients provides an example in which activities relate both to patients' needs and to the service of the setting. On the other hand, social activities offered during the school day to a group of children who are not doing well in their classes may be viewed by the school staff as a "reward" for acting badly, even if the worker argues that the students are helped indirectly. However, when such activities are used as a substitute for discussions about class problems or because the worker is concerned that the children will not come to a "talking group," they may frustrate the essential work rather than assist it. A decision on group type (talk, activity, or both) needs to relate directly both to the service of the agency and to the needs of the group members.

One widely used framework for describing group types was developed by the group work faculty at Boston University (Bernstein, 1965, 1970). The researchers identified four general types:

1. *Support and stabilization groups* are best suited for people experiencing a life crisis such as divorce, bereavement, or economic instability. As the name implies, group support is used to help members stabilize and begin to cope with the stress.

2. *Growth and education groups,* more familiar in traditional group service agencies, are applicable to people experiencing major life developmental challenges or transitions (such as teenagers) or people with delayed development of skills because of isolating, regressive, or stagnating influences (such as long-term chronic care mental patients). The focus of the group is on learning specific competencies and social skills related to the developmental tasks.

3. *Task and action groups* include committees, grassroots community organization groups, hospital ward governments, and so on. Their focus is on tasks to be accomplished, rather than support or individual development of the group members.

4. *Recapitulation and restitution groups* are more closely related to the classical psychoanalytically oriented insight groups for adults or play therapy groups for children. Their focus is on recapitulation of life events and restitution of member strengths and positive self-esteem.

While the various types of groups are helpful in conceptualizing the central purposes of the group, Bernstein points out that no group is ever a pure form of the model. In fact, most groups can be seen to contain elements of two or more of these "classical models."

Group Versus Individual Work With Clients

Another issue that can create problems for the group worker is the compatibility of group and individual work. Some group workers believe that group members should not be seen individually because that will lessen the intensity of the group experience. Individual counselors, as well, worry that clients will use their group session to discuss central issues. This can lead to a struggle over "who owns the client," a misunderstanding of the interdependence of individual and group work and an unacceptable attitude to client participation in decisions about service.

Clients may use both individual and group help for different issues, as they see fit. For example, as the group works on the concern of a particular member, the discussion may raise a similar concern for the client, who may want a chance to discuss a special case of the general problem and may not have enough time in the group to do this. Individual sessions can provide this opportunity. Rather than robbing the individual work of its vitality, group discussion often enriches the content of the individual sessions. As clients listen to issues and understand how others are experiencing problems, they may be put in touch with feelings of their own that were not previously evident. For example, finding out that others have fears related to taboo areas, such as sex, may greatly speed up clients' willingness to discuss their own concerns in individual work.

Similarly, the work in the individual sessions can strengthen a client to raise a personal concern in the group. For some clients, sharing their most private feelings and concerns with a group may be too difficult at first. As they find they can share these with an individual counselor and not be harshly judged, they may be more willing to share them in the group. Thus, the group and individual work can be parallel and interdependent, with the client free to choose where and when to use these resources for work.

Note here again that such choices, at any particular moment, rest with the client. Only clients can discern where they feel most comfortable dealing with a particular issue. Workers may share their opinions, offer support, and even provide concrete help (role-playing in an individual session to show how the client might raise an issue in the group), but the client decides in the end.

With two and possibly more helping people working with the same client, good communication between the helpers becomes essential. They should establish structures that guarantee regular communication, so that each understands how the client is choosing to deal with issues and so that the workers can help each other in their related work. For example, in a couples' group that I led, the two coleaders were also seeing most of the couples on an individual counseling basis. In the tuning-in session we held prior to each group meeting, they summarized the specific concerns dealt with in the individual sessions. We used this preparatory work to anticipate potential group issues. I maintain a policy of not directly raising concerns in the group that were discussed in the individual work unless the couples wish them raised. Through the tuning-in process, I became more effective at picking up their indirect cues. Because the coleaders sat in on each of the sessions, they could incorporate content from the group experience into their individual work. If they were not able to sit in, I shared copies of my group process and summary reports so that they would be aware of the couples' progress. When sessions were videotaped, the tapes were also available for their use. Rather than competing for client ownership, we had three professionals, each providing a service through different modalities. As pointed out in the earlier discussion on confidentiality, without freedom to share information, this open communication would not have taken place.

Agency Support for Groups

In addition to support from colleagues, help from the agency administration may also be needed. For example, special expenses may be incurred in carrying out a group program. Mothers' groups held during the day may require babysitting services. Recruitment publicity, transportation, coffee, and other items may need to be paid for in some group programs. In addition, the worker developing a group may need a reduced individual caseload and group work consultation from an outside consultant if one is not available on staff. These issues should be discussed when the group is formed.

In some settings, where groups have not been an integral part of the service, the approach to group work programs may require the worker to take personal responsibility for their implementation. For example, workers are encouraged to develop groups if they can do so "on their own time." Many workers, eager to see the service begin or to develop new skills in work with clients, accept this responsibility but soon regret it. If a service is part of the agency function, it should not have to be carried as a personal "hobby" by the worker. Groups take time, and if workers do not foresee the full extent of their responsibilities, the additional demands on them and their feelings about them will often negatively affect their work with the group.

Even when agencies support the development of group services, they sometimes do so for the wrong reasons. Administrators may believe that seeing clients in groups can save time and so encourage a swing to group programs as a way of providing more service to clients without increasing staff. With cost-containment programs on the rise, there are situations in which seeing clients in groups does save time. For example, orientation meetings for prospective adoptive parents or new foster parents can be an effective way of starting communications. As pointed out earlier, however, more often than not the development of group services tends to increase the staff's workload, because new issues and concerns that require additional individual work may be discovered. Groups should be viewed as an important service in their own right rather than as a service substitute. A worker in a group will need time to follow up with individual members, to meet with other staff, to develop a system for recording the group work for agency accountability, and to pursue personal learning.

To start a group service on a sound agency footing is best, even though the formation process may be slower and more frustrating. Time taken by the group worker to interpret the group's purpose as well as to identify the special needs and potential problems related to instituting new group services will pay off in the long run. In those cases where doubts exist about the benefits of group practice, the worker can propose the group as an agency experimental service to be closely evaluated. Records can be kept on the costs and benefits. The agency staff and administration can use the first groups as a way of developing experience with a new form of service. The important point is that the service be "owned" by the agency, not be the personal project of a concerned worker. With the latter, it is not unusual to have a good first group only to discover that the service dies when the worker can no longer provide it personally.

Group Composition, Timing, and Structure

A conversation I had with a group of students and health professionals helps illustrate some of the myths and questions involved in planning a group. I led a group for five couples in marital difficulty; sessions were videotaped and simultaneously observed on a monitor in another room. (Transcript excerpts appear in Chapter 10.) After each session, I met with the observers and my coleaders to discuss the session. At the end of a first session, which was marked by excellent group member involvement, the students and professionals peppered me with questions on how the group had been formed. The first request was for my principles of group composition, which had led to such a lively, interactive group. One couple was in their twenties, another in their thirties, a third in their forties, a fourth in their fifties, and the oldest couple was in their late sixties or early seventies. I explained, much to the disappointment of the group, that these were the only five couples referred for the group.

Another student asked how I had decided on five couples. I pointed out that we were using a studio for videotaping, and with myself and my coleaders, there was only enough room for five couples. Another effort to tease out principles followed as they inquired how we decided on the number of sessions. I pointed out that there were many long-standing issues involved, and a short-term group did not seem to offer enough time. "How did you settle on exactly twenty-three sessions?" was the next question. Once again I disappointed the group by explaining that we could not start the group before October 15, because we needed time to do the advance work, and we simply counted the weeks until the end of the academic year. We then went on to discuss the differences between what I felt to be the myth of scientific group composition versus the reality of how decisions were made.

The students wanted prescriptions and rules, and I argued, perhaps more strongly than was needed, that the rules were not really that clear. In reality, we often "take what we can get." Our experiences, and some research findings, have provided us with some guidelines. For example, we know that extremes often lead to problems. Groups can clearly be too large to provide an opportunity for everyone to participate or too small to provide a consistent core of members. While groups can tolerate some degree of age range, as in my married couples' group, extremes for some populations, such as teenagers, can create serious problems. For example, a 12-year-old foster child faces life tasks that differ significantly from the concerns of a 17-year-old who is preparing to leave the care of the agency at 18. One person of color in an all-white group, what I call the "only one" problem, may experience a sense of isolation that the addition of another might well alleviate. A group of survivors of sexual abuse may have significant difficulty in achieving intimacy if the group is open-ended, with new members constantly joining the group and other members leaving it.

The literature provides a fund of observations on questions of group composition and structure, but unfortunately it also provides conflicting scientific evidence in support of rules. For example, there are conflicting studies on the optimum size for effective discussion groups, with support for different numbers argued persuasively.

A balance has to be struck between ignoring these issues completely and depending too much on rigid rules and structures.

The position argued here is that each setting must develop its own rules, based on its experiences as well as those of others. As such, a worker must address several questions, using the experiences of colleagues and of other settings to develop tentative answers. Each group represents an experiment that can contribute to the fund of experience the worker will draw on in starting new groups. The remainder of this section highlights some of these questions. Rather than providing definitive answers, the discussion will offer a way of exploring the issues.

Group Member Selection

The crucial factor in selection of members is some common ground between their individual needs and the purpose of the group. Whether this purpose has been defined broadly or narrowly, each member must be able to find some connection between a personal sense of urgency and the work involved. Even if this common ground is not apparent to the prospective members at the start, the worker should have some sense of its existence. In the example of the couples' group, each couple was having severe marital problems. Another point in common was that all five couples had some commitment at the start to strengthen their marriages. Couples who had already decided to separate and who needed help in doing so without causing additional pain to each other or their families would not have belonged in this group.

In an AIDS/Recovery group I co-led, the five members included one white, gay man; a transgender woman; a heterosexual woman; and two African American men. Although their life experiences differed significantly, all the members had AIDS and all were in relatively early recovery from polysubstance abuse. Group members differed in their status with respect to AIDS. Two members were on an experimental treatment that had lowered their AIDS viral loads (counts) to almost zero and had raised their T-cell (protective) counts to near normal. One client was waiting for her viral load and T-cell count to reach the point at which she could enter the clinical trials with the new drugs. Another client was eligible but refusing treatment. The health of the fifth had been damaged so badly by her use of hormones and illegal substances that she was too ill for the treatment. This client's viral load was climbing each week, her T-cell count was nonexistent, and she was experiencing a range of infections common to late-stage AIDS. In spite of these significant differences, each member could eventually relate to the others on the basis of their shared struggle with AIDS, with early substance abuse recovery, and with the interaction between the two.

As the group leader defines the purpose of the group and considers potential members, common sense can help to identify potential differences that might create difficulty in reaching group consensus on the focus of the work. As mentioned previously, for example, although 12-year-old and 17-year-old wards may share their foster status, their issues and concerns may differ greatly. Combining these two age groups in a group to discuss life problems and issues related to being "foster" could create unnecessary obstacles. On the other hand, this may not be a problem, depending on the group's purpose. For example, I have seen groups developed by a child welfare agency to promote better communication between teens and staff and to provide social and recreational activities; here, a wide age difference between teens appeared to have a less negative impact. The older teens provided leadership for the group and looked on themselves as "big brothers" and "big sisters" to the younger ones.

As this example suggests, workers should consider group purpose when thinking about age and group composition. In the couples' group described earlier, the differences in the ages of the five couples also provided unexpected dividends. Each couple was experiencing the crises somewhat associated with their particular phase of life and phase of their marriage; however, common themes cut across all phases. In many ways, the older couples were able to share their experiences and perspectives with the younger ones, and the group often took on the appearance of an extended family. After one session in which some of the problems associated with the older couples' life phases were clearly delineated, the husband in the youngest couple said good-humoredly, "I'm beginning to wonder if this is what I have to look forward to going through!" The wife of the oldest couple, who had been married 49 years, responded, "But you will have the advantage of having had this group to help you face these problems."

Whether to include male or female members or both will similarly have to be determined according to the group's purpose. However, I find some of the other factors often discussed when deciding on group membership, such as judgments about a member's "personality," somewhat questionable. For example, I have seen a group meticulously assembled with the supposedly proper number of relatively passive schoolchildren balanced by a manageable number of active ones. The theory was to guarantee interaction, with the active members stimulating the passive ones. In addition, some limit on active members was thought to help the leader with potential problems of control. Unfortunately, nobody informed the group members about their expected roles. The leader was observed in the first session desperately trying to deal with the acting-out behaviors of the "passive" members while the "active" members looked on in shock and amusement. Clients simply do not act the same in every situation. A client who acts passively in an individual interview or classroom may act differently in a different context. Clients will not remain in the "diagnosed" box long enough to be clearly identified. Their reactions will somewhat depend on the actions of those around them, particularly the group leader.

Workers also need to consider race, ethnicity, and language issues when composing a group. Davis (1979, 1981, 1984, 1999; Davis & Proctor, 1989) has addressed the impact of race on group composition and practice, basing his observations on anecdotal as well as empirical evidence. In reviewing the literature on the impact of racial composition, Davis identifies several observed processes that emerge when a racial ratio changes and minority membership increases. These processes include cleavage, tipping points, and white flight. In **cleavage**, the group splits into distinct racial subgroups. The **tipping point** is the number that creates majority members' anxiety, resulting in aggression toward members of the "out" group. He suggests that white people are so often in the majority that when they are placed in a group in which they are in a smaller-than-usual majority—for example, with more than 10 percent to 20 percent people of color—they may experience a mental state of being in the "psychological minority," at times leading to a **white flight** reaction (Proctor & Davis, 1994). Conversely, members of the minority group faced with this ratio may experience being in the "psychological majority" even though their absolute numbers represent less than 50 percent.

As with many such observations, these concepts of psychological minority and majority may not significantly affect the decisions related to the composition of a group. Rather, they serve to attune the group leader to potential dynamics resulting from a composition that may affect the group's functioning. Awareness of the process by the group leader, as well as a willingness to address these issues when and if they emerge, may help the group cope more effectively.

In summarizing the literature on race and group, Davis and Proctor (1989) suggest the following:

> There is some evidence that whites and minorities may prefer different racial compositions: neither whites nor minorities appear to like being greatly outnumbered. The language spoken in the group may also be important. For example, if some members speak Spanish, while others do not, the non-bilingual speakers may become isolated. (p. 115)

Davis and Proctor also summarize the findings on group leadership:

> Leaders who differ in race from their group members may receive less cooperation. Biracial co-leadership may enhance communication in racially heterogeneous groups. However, biracial co-leaders must remain alert to the possibility of one leader being perceived as the leader and the other as his helper. (p. 116)

Finally, in addressing the paucity of empirical research, they suggest the following:

> There is no evidence which suggests that group treatment is more or less suitable for any particular ethnic group. Furthermore, there is little evidence that either racially homogenous or racially heterogeneous groups are superior in their outcomes. Very few studies have attempted to assess the effects of the group leader's race on group member outcomes. Furthermore, reports from studies involving the race of the leader are mixed. However, these studies are consistent in that they have found that prior group leader experience in working with minorities appears to have beneficial effects for the group. (p. 117)

Group Timing

When setting up a group, workers need to consider many time-related factors. How often will the group meet? How long will the meetings last? For how long will the group meet? Each of the answers must draw on common sense, the experience of the agency, and the literature, and all must be related to group purpose.

In the married couples' group, we chose to meet once each week, for 2 hours each session, for 23 weeks. Meetings had to be held in the evening so that the working partners could attend. The group was designed to provide long-term support to the couples as they dealt with their marital problems. The alternate option of intensive weekends was not considered. For couples in crisis, it seemed that the intensive, short-term experience might open up more problems while leaving the couples unable to deal with them. On the other hand, weekend workshops for marital enrichment groups, in which the relationships are strong to begin with, may provide successful educational and skill-development experiences. The decision to meet weekly was based on the recognition that longer breaks between meetings might diffuse the intensity of the experience, making each session seem like a new beginning. Two hours seemed to be enough time to allow for the development of central themes and issues in the beginning phase of each meeting, while leaving enough time to deal effectively with specific individual and group concerns. More than 2 hours might wear out group members and workers alike.

In every case, discussing and clarifying the plan with group members is important. Group members have a sense of the group's time frame and will be affected by the particular phase of the meeting or the phase in the life of the group. As pointed out earlier, the "doorknob" phenomenon can accelerate the presentation of important issues; however, the members need to know when the time to reach for the door is close at hand. Group members sometimes work more effectively if they have less time to carry out their tasks. Reid and Shyne (1969), for example, discuss the impact of time on both the worker and the client in their work on short-term treatment. There is a limit to how much can be dealt with; workers must balance the group's needs against the time limit, allowing the right number of sessions to deal with the anticipated themes of concern. This limit will come from experience as an agency evaluates each group, using the group members as part of the evaluation process. Before a group is established, workers can gain much help from group members by exploring their reactions to time proposals. Feedback on the day of the week or the specific time for starting may help a group worker avoid unnecessary conflicts.

An expression borrowed from architecture, "Form follows function," is useful in thinking about time in the group formation stage. The form of the group in relation to time needs to be connected to group purpose. Agency conceptions about time can change as experiences with new group services are evaluated. In one example, I served as a consultant to an agency providing extensive group services to people with AIDS as well as their friends, lovers, and family members. Under the original plan developed by the agency, a group would start with clients diagnosed as HIV-positive and continue as members progressed through the stages of the illness. The group would continue as a sort of community as members became progressively more ill and most finally died. This structure seemed to make sense if the purpose of the group was to provide an alternative source of support for its members, many of whom felt cut off from other systems in their lives (such as family, work, and friends). In reality, the groups did not work this way. Most of the groups began to dissolve as some members died or became seriously ill.

The experience caused a rethinking of group purpose. Rather than thinking of each group as a substitute community, the agency conceptualized the groups as time limited, with a focus on helping the members deal with transitions to the various stages of the illness. That is, one group would be for recently diagnosed HIV-positive clients, while another group would serve clients facing the onset of serious medical problems. This was not always easy to do, as the course of the illness was neither smooth nor predictable. However, instead of the agency attempting to provide the substitute community—a task that would eventually overwhelm the agency, given the number of potential clients involved in the pandemic of AIDS—the focus changed to one of helping group members mobilize existing support in their own friendship, family, and community systems. Analysis of process in the groups indicated that group leaders had been too quick to accept their members' contention that such support was closed to them and that only the group could provide it. Work in the groups became more demanding, and members were asked to look closely at their own efforts to connect with their social support systems. The move to time-limited groups greatly changed the nature of the work for the better. Once the "function" of the group had been clearly defined, the questions of "form" were easier to resolve.

In my more recent experience co-leading a group for people with AIDS in early recovery from substance abuse, new issues of timing presented themselves. For example, with several of our group members on the triple-therapy drug regime, and with their resulting improvement in health, we were viewing the group as one of the ongoing support systems designed to help members cope with living with AIDS rather than dying from AIDS. Also, the substance abuse recovery issues required more long-term support than if the members were dealing with AIDS alone. This group began in October, focusing on helping members get through the extremely stressful holiday season of Thanksgiving, Christmas, and New Year's Eve. The group reconvened in the new year and agreed to continue until a summer break period, with the understanding that the members would assess the need to reconvene in the fall. Individual group members received ongoing support from my coleader, who served as their substance abuse counselor.

Group Structure, Setting, and Rules

The formation stage raises many questions related to group structure and setting. For example, where should the group meet? Ease of access by public and private transportation might be a factor. Holding a session on sensitive and potentially embarrassing work (such as child abuse) in a public setting where members might fear being identified could be a mistake. The room itself should offer group members privacy and face-to-face seating (in a circle, around a table). Comfortable chairs and surroundings often add to the group members' comfort. On the other hand, work with children may require facilities that are relatively "activity proof," so that members and the group worker can relax without constant worries about order and decorum.

Group rules also need clarification prior to the first group meeting. For example, limits on physical activity may be set with children's groups. Some adult groups require boundaries regarding the use of physical force. In a group session for prison parolees, for example, one member pulled out a knife and begin to clean his fingernails in a manner meant to be threatening to another member. In this case, the worker must recontract with the members on the issue of bringing knives to the session. Many other "rules" need attention as well. Attendance requirements should be clear. Members' expectations regarding the agency and the group, as well as the worker's expectations regarding the members, should be discussed, especially concerning confidentiality. In my couples' group, we discuss three rules in the first session: (1) each member is expected to come each week as long as he or she is not ill, (2) a couple wanting to quit the group will come back for one additional week to discuss it, and (3) group members will agree to confidentiality. In my AIDS/Recovery group, meetings were held in a "clean and sober" residence. Members were not to bring substances to the group or be under the influence of substances when they attended.

There are many differences of opinion on the question of group rules. For example, some argue that group members should not have contact with each other outside the meetings. The field of group work is far from agreement on these questions. My general bias is that group members own their own lives and that my group is simply an incident in their week (I hope, an important incident). I would therefore have difficulty insisting on a rule preventing them from having contacts outside the group. In fact, in many groups the bonds of mutual aid that have developed through telephone calls and informal contacts outside the group have provided powerful support for individual members. Workers in some groups, who fear that group members may get involved in "acting out" outside of the group (having sexual contact, for example), appear to me to take more responsibility for their lives of the members than they should. Even so, in some groups, such as the AIDS/Recovery group, such outside activity could definitely threaten the members' recovery at a particularly vulnerable time in their lives. These issues need to be discussed as part of the structure of the group.

In addition, group members should be free to bring their outside interactions with each other into the group if they wish; such interactions can serve as an important entry into the content of the group work. In general, the rules stated in the beginning of the group should be firmly rooted to the reality of the situation rather than the arbitrary authority or personal preferences of the group leader. Group members should see them as emerging from the necessities of the work.

Issues related to group composition, timing, setting, rules, and structure have been raised here to show you some of the questions requiring consideration prior to the start of any group. I have shared my opinions on these questions merely to illustrate how one practitioner develops his own views from his experiences and those of others. As with all the ideas shared in this book, you will have to test them against your own sense of reality and ongoing group experiences.

Work With Prospective Members

After agency administration and staff support have been mobilized, potential obstacles to cooperation identified and discussed, and formation questions considered by the worker, then one more step remains: recruitment of group members. In contrast to individual and family work, a group of clients rarely arrive at the agency and request services. It may happen with some naturally formed groups, as when a group of teens in a school or a group of tenants in a housing project approach the social worker for help. These are the exceptions, however, rather than the rule. Most group work practice requires an **outreach process**, through which the social work service is brought to the potential clients. Recruitment of group members is therefore a crucial element in the formation stage.

This process can also be complex, because clients feel the general ambivalence about taking help (described in Parts II and III) as well as unique concerns related to the group context. Of course, workers who deal with groups in settings less focused on personal problems, such as community centers or community organization agencies, do not have to deal with the same reluctance to join a group activity. Nevertheless, when people consider joining any group, they face some degree of ambivalence. This discussion will focus on examples of mutual-aid groups designed to deal with problems of living—marital difficulties, parenting skills, alcohol or drug addiction, school difficulties, and the like—in the belief that some of the principles can be applied to other types of groups as well.

Clients may become prospective group members by identifying with advertisements for the group. They might respond to posters or newspaper stories, a letter from the agency, or other publicity of a group service. If handled well, the steps involved in making potential group members aware of the group can help to turn the potential client toward the service. For example, posters or letters should be worded clearly, without jargon, so that the prospective member has a clear idea of the group's purpose. It may be helpful to identify some of the themes of concern that may be related to the client's sense of urgency.

The embarrassment of the workers in being direct about the problem, discussed in the chapter on contracting with individuals, or the workers' concern that direct statements about the problem may turn potential clients off can result in the use of euphemisms or vague and general descriptions of the group. The result of this lack of clarity and directness may actually reduce the interest of the potential member in attending. Workers can test the letters or posters with colleagues and clients to get their sense of the meaning and suggestions as to how to make the wording direct but nonthreatening.

Other clients are referred by colleagues or other helping professionals or are selected by workers from their caseloads. Whatever the circumstance, even when the client has initiated the contact, the gap between thinking about joining a group and arriving at the first meeting can be a big one. Many of the skills already identified can increase the chances of a successful start. Two other skill sets, which we shall now examine, center on work with colleagues after they have agreed to recruit group members and telephone or in-person contacts between the worker and prospective members.

Strategizing for Effective Referrals

A worker may have done an effective job with other staff members regarding the establishment of a group but still be disappointed by a relatively low number of referrals. An important question often overlooked is how the colleague will conduct a referral interview. It is a mistake to assume that even a motivated colleague will be able to make an effective referral without some joint work and strategizing as to how it might be done. For example, the colleague may have a general sense of the group contract but be unable to articulate it clearly. One who has not worked with groups may not be sensitive to some of the underlying feelings and ambivalence that the client may share indirectly, thereby missing a chance to help overcome obstacles to group formation.

In a tuning-in session, either one-on-one or with a staff group, workers can pool their efforts to sensitize themselves to the concerns clients may have about joining the group and the indirect ways these may emerge. Staff can then share strategies for reaching for the underlying concerns. In addition, a brief role-play of the referral interview may reveal to the group worker that some colleagues cannot yet articulate the group purpose, and work can then proceed on that skill. Such a process may also bring to the surface any ambivalent feelings or unanswered questions that need to be dealt with prior to the actual referral interviews.

To see this process in action, consider a referral workshop that I conducted for social service professionals in connection with the establishment of a new and (at that time) experimental group service for men who had physically abused their partners. Recognizing the importance of professional referrals to launch the program and knowing that the referral process might be extremely difficult in this situation, we provided an opportunity for tuning in and joint strategizing. To keep the discussion focused on skills, I asked for examples of difficult referrals of a similar nature.

One worker described a referral he had recently attempted with the common-law husband of a client. The client was a prostitute who had been beaten by the husband who was also her pimp, but she had refused to report the incident or leave him. As the worker's interaction with the husband was analyzed, it became clear that the worker had never mentioned the physical abuse to the husband, attempting instead to lead him indirectly to agree to seek help. When this was mentioned during the analysis of the example, the worker revealed that he had feared angering the husband and risking that the husband might then take the anger out on the wife. An important discussion followed in which other workers spoke of their fears of possible retribution not only on the partners but also themselves. Their dilemma was discussed and strategies were developed for broaching the subject directly without exacerbating the partner's defensiveness. Without this preparatory work, workers would have been blocked in their attempts to offer this group.

The problem of stating group purpose came up for our group in another way as well. In a role-play, one of the workers described the group in a way that would lead the prospective member to believe his worst fears—that the group was designed solely to chastise him for his behavior and to educate him to appreciate his impact on his woman. When I pointed out that the worker seemed angry at the prospective group member, my comment released a flood of feelings, echoed by many in the room, of anger at the men. All of the professionals had agreed earlier that these groups could not be effective unless the men could both be held accountable for their violent actions toward women and also see the group as designed to help them as clients in their own right. This intellectual agreement evaporated in the role-play to reveal an essentially punitive and thereby ineffective offer of service. Enabling workers to discuss and be in touch with these natural yet often denied feelings might ensure a presentation of the group that will turn prospective members toward the service rather than reinforce their resistance. In this case, the workers recognized that, for many of these men, even the most effective offer of service might not elicit a response. Some of them would not come to the first meeting unless their partner left them or they received a court order. Although this group example may be extreme, I believe that in most cases the worker forming a group would be well advised to take some time with colleagues to discuss the technical aspects of making the referral.

Worker Skills in the Initial Interviews

Before the first meeting, group workers often contact individual members, in person or by phone, to discuss their participation in the group. These interviews can be seen as part of the exploratory process in which the worker describes what the group has to offer and checks with the client to determine what may be needed. The skills of clarifying purpose, clarifying role, and reaching for feedback are useful in this interview (see Part II). Describing the structure of the group (how it will work) as well as timing helps to provide the information needed for the prospective member to make a decision about using the service.

In addition to tuning in to the client's feelings about beginning a new relationship, the worker must also tune in to the specific concerns related to beginning in a group. For example, the public image of helping groups, ranging from group psychotherapy to encounter groups, might affect potential clients' attitudes. In addition, clients may bring other stereotypes of groups based on their past experiences (such as class groups at school, camp experiences) that will affect their feelings about attending.

Questions about how people with the same problems can help each other will also be on their minds. Much of this hesitancy and fear may lie just beneath the surface. The worker must listen and reach directly for any indirect cues. In the following example, a worker has been describing a foster parents' group to an agency foster parent, and the parent seems receptive. The cues of resistance emerge when the worker gets specific about the dates.

WORKER: We are going to have our first meeting in two weeks, on a Wednesday night. Can I expect you there?

FOSTER PARENT: (Long pause) Well, it sounds good. I'll try to make it if things aren't too hectic that week at work.

If the worker quits right there and accepts the illusion of agreement, she may be guaranteeing that the parent will not show up. Even though workers can sense the ambivalence in the client's voice, they often refrain from reaching for the negative attitude. When I ask why workers refrain, they tell me that they are afraid that if they bring the doubts out in the open, they will reinforce them. They believe the less said, the better. In reality, the client's doubts and questions are valid, and the worker is missing an opportunity to help the client explore them.

Without this exploration, the client may simply not show up at the first meeting, despite having promised to attend. When the worker later calls, then, the client will feel guilty and offer profuse explanations for his absence (as in "I really meant to come, only it got so hectic that day it just slipped my mind").

Returning to the interview with the foster parent, note the turn in the work when the worker reaches for the cue.

WORKER: You sound a bit hesitant. Are you concerned about attending the group? It wouldn't be unusual; most people have a lot of questions about groups.

FOSTER PARENT: Well, you know I never do too well in groups. I find I have a lot of trouble talking in front of strangers.

WORKER: Are you worried that you would have to speak up and be put on the spot?

FOSTER PARENT: I don't mind talking about fostering; it's just that I get tongue-tied in a group.

WORKER: I can appreciate your concern. A lot of people feel that way. I can tell you right now that except for sharing your name no one will put you on the spot to speak. Some people always talk a lot at the early meetings while others prefer to listen. You can listen until you feel comfortable about speaking. If you want, I can help you begin to talk in the group, but only when you're ready. I do this all the time with people who feel this way.

FOSTER PARENT: You mean it's not just me who feels this way?

WORKER: Not at all. It's quite common and natural. By the way, are there any other concerns you might have about the group?

FOSTER PARENT: Not really. That was the biggest one. Actually, it doesn't sound like a bad idea at all.

Once again we see the importance of exploring the indirect cue so that the worker has a clearer idea about the source of the ambivalence. Many workers hesitate to explore the cue, because they see it as a polite rejection of the group (and the worker). When asked why they see it this way, they often reply that they are unsure about their own competency and the quality of the group. They respond to the client's ambivalence with their own similar feelings. In the case just cited, the fear of speaking in the group needed to be discussed. Knowing that the worker understands and that it is all right to feel this way can help the client overcome the obstacle. Other obstacles might stem from memories of bad group experiences, horror stories recounted by friends or relatives about harsh and confronting group encounters, or embarrassment about sharing personal details with strangers. Workers need to clarify what will actually happen in the group, as compared with what the potential member may fear. The worker also needs to empathize genuinely with the fears, and still attempt to help the client take the first difficult step. With this kind of help from the worker, many prospective group members overcome their fears and doubts and give the group a try. A source of great support for the client lies in knowing that the worker understands his or her feelings.

Another type of resistance occurs when a group is offered to the caretaker, support person, or relative of a client. In one example, a worker was recruiting a group for relatives of elderly Alzheimer patients who were caring for these patients at home. In the face of the initial, hinted reluctance, the worker said, "You sound hesitant about coming to the group, Mrs. Smith. Can you tell me why?" The client responded, with some feeling, "Just one more thing on the list for me to do to take care of my mother. I don't have time for myself!" The worker replied, "Mrs. Smith, I think I can appreciate how demanding caring for your mother must be. But I don't think I made the purpose of this group clear when I described it. This group is not for your mother. This group is for you. Other group members will also be feeling overwhelmed by the demands made upon them by their relatives with Alzheimer's, and part of what we can discuss is how you can get the support you need." By reaching for the lurking negatives and the ambivalence, the worker creates an opportunity to clarify group purpose to a potential member.

A common trap that workers fall into when they hear the indirect or direct cues of reluctance is to try to "sell" the group even harder. Consider the following example of a worker in a convalescent home who is recruiting an elderly resident. In this case, the worker's honest caring and enthusiasm may well help the potential member consider the group, but her work would be stronger if she explored and acknowledged the obvious resistant responses. Also, the worker's focus on discussion of the "good old days" brings a response that surprises the worker but may actually suggest a different group purpose: to talk about both the good and the bad old days.

Purpose of the Interview

To explain the group and to invite 92-year-old female resident to attend. The prospective member is white, with a diagnosis of progressive dementia and agitated depression. She has been living in the nursing home for 3 years.

The Interview

Mrs. Franks was sitting up in a chair listening to music upon my arrival. I knocked on her door, entered, and introduced myself. She asked me to have a seat, which I did. I asked her how she was doing. She responded rather cheerfully that she was OK, but a little tired. I asked her if she generally napped in the afternoons (a common practice in the nursing homes). She replied, "Well, on Sundays I don't really have anything to do." "Oh," I replied, "so Sunday is your day of rest." We both laughed, and she agreed. "What do you do during the rest of the week?" I asked her. "I have my duties," was her reply. "Do you ever get down to any of the activities?" "Oh sure," she said.

"One of the reasons that I stopped by was to invite you to an activity that I am organizing. Beginning next week, we are going to be having a group called 'Jog Your Memory.' There will be five or six women in the group and we'll spend some time talking about the good old days. Do you think that you might be interested in something like that?"

"Well, I didn't have any good old days."

"Nothing good happened in your life?"

"Oh, sure," she said, smiling. "There were many good times. Some days were good, some days were bad."

"Each week there will be a different topic and we'll see what kinds of memories it brings back."

"Well, it sounds nice, but I don't think that it's for me."

"Well, it's going to be a small group of ladies, and we'll meet for about a half hour each Tuesday, just down the hallway in the nursing office."

"Oh, it sounds nice. We need something like that."

"Do you think that you'd like to come? I would pick you up and bring you back, so you wouldn't have to worry about that."

"Oh, wonderful; I might be older than some of the others though."

"Don't worry about that, Mrs. Franks. All of the ladies are in their eighties and nineties, and one woman is even over 100."

"My goodness." We laughed.

"Mrs. Franks, I am glad that you are interested in the Jog Your Memory group. I think you will enjoy it."

"Oh yes, it sounds like a wonderful opportunity. Thank you so much for thinking of me." I smile at Mrs. Franks and touch her hand. "You're welcome. Today is Friday. I will come back Tuesday morning to remind you about the 'Jog Your Memory' group. I will also let the nurse know, so she'll be sure that you are up."

Once again, the worker's caring comes through and may well lead to Mrs. Franks attending the group. The odds are good, because this is a residential setting.

Now that the worker has completed the group formation tasks and the clients are ready to attend, the worker needs to pay attention to the beginnings and the dynamics of first sessions. These topics are explored in the next chapter.

Chapter Summary

Three major areas of work are involved in the formation stage of group work practice. The first focuses on the skills required to work with one's setting and colleagues in order to engage them as active partners in the development of the group service. Several strategies help workers cope with underlying obstacles that can sabotage group work efforts. The second area involves issues of group composition, timing, and structure. Exploring issues in advance can maximize the possibility of success in forming the group. The final area of work centers on the skills required to recruit members who may be ambivalent about attending a group session. In particular, the skill of looking for trouble when everything is going the worker's way can help avoid the illusion of agreement, in which the client promises to attend but does not show up.

Related Online Content and Activities

Visit *The Skills of Helping* Book Companion Website at www.socialwork.wadsworth .com/Shulman06/ for learning tools such as glossary terms, InfoTrac College Edition keywords, links to related websites, and chapter practice quizzes.

The website for this chapter also features additional notes from the author.

The Beginning Phase in the Group

In this chapter we examine the dynamics of the first group session. The contracting issues explored in Parts II and III with individuals and families will be revisited, but this time we also explore the variant elements of practice introduced by working with a group. A detailed example of a first session with a married couples' group will illustrate the concepts. Next, we discuss five variations on first group sessions, relative to the age and relative articulateness of the members, the authority of the worker, the specific concerns of the clients, and the impact of the setting and time. We then examine the issue of recontracting when the initial contract was not clear, looking at examples of social workers modifying their working agreements with their own groups as well as with ongoing groups. Finally, the chapter ends with a discussion of coleadership.

Many of the issues related to beginning work that we described in Chapter 3 apply equally to first sessions with groups, with an important difference: The individual client must also deal with a new system—the group. The first two central questions for the client in the individual context were "What are we doing here together?" and "What kind of person will this worker be?" In the group context, a third question is added: "What kind of people will these other group members be?" Many of the uncertainties and fears associated with new beginnings will be increased by the public nature of a first group session. For example, the client's fear of being manipulated by someone in authority may increase at the thought that peers will witness any display of inadequacy, along with the resultant humiliation. For this reason and others, workers must pay special attention to first sessions in order to set a proper stage for the work that will follow.

This chapter provides an overview of the general structure of a first group meeting, reviewing some of the underlying assumptions outlined in Chapter 3 and considering some of the unique dynamics associated with group work. The tasks of both the worker and the group members are outlined, and specific skills are identified. With this overview as a backdrop, the dynamics of a first group session are illustrated through a detailed analysis of a first session of a married couples' group. Then, several variations on first group sessions are presented. We look at work with children and adolescents to see the impact of age and articulateness, then we examine involuntary groups to see how the authority of the worker affects group work. The specific concerns of the clients, as well as the impact of the setting and time, also present special challenges to workers and clients alike.

Next, we explore the issue of recontracting. This is the process in which the worker reopens the issues of contracting by providing a clearer statement of purpose or exploring the group members' resistance or lack of connection to the service. The skills in working with the coleaders and the group in initiating a recontracting process are illustrated using a detailed example from a student's experiences. The chapter ends with a discussion of the potential problems involved in coleadership and strategies for dealing with them.

The Dynamics of First Group Sessions

As in all new encounters with people in authority, clients begin first group meetings tentatively. Their normal concerns about their own adequacy may be heightened because the encounter is taking place in public view. Most clients bring to first meetings an extensive fund of group experiences, many of which are associated with painful memories. For example, we have all either witnessed or experienced the excruciatingly difficult moments in a classroom when an individual student has been singled out to answer a question or solve a math problem on the board. We have felt the embarrassment of a classmate exposed to sarcasm from an insensitive teacher. Whereas new encounters in a one-to-one counseling situation generate fears of the unknown, new group encounters tend to reawaken old fears based on past experiences.

As in individual work, early clarification of purpose is central in the group context. The clients' first question will be "What are we here for?" Once the boundary of the group experience has been clearly described, members will find selecting appropriate responses easier. When the expectations of the group worker and the setting or agency within which the group takes place are clear, the group members feel much safer than when the purpose remains ambiguous.

As the group starts, the members will watch the worker with keen interest. Having experienced the impact of powerful people in authority, they know it is important to "size up" this new authority figure as soon as possible. This leads to the clients' second central question: "What kind of person will the worker be?" Until the group members can understand clearly how this worker operates and will affect them, they will need to test the worker directly or indirectly. Defenses will remain in position until members are certain of their individual safety.

All these dynamics are similar to the ones described in Chapter 3. Again, the main difference in the group setting involves the presence of other clients. As the group session proceeds, each group member will also be appraising the others. Many questions will arise: "Who are these other people? Do they have the same problems that I do? Will I be embarrassed by finding myself less competent than they? Do they seem sympathetic and supportive, or are there people in this group who may attack and confront me?" While the client's primary concern in the first session is the group leader, questions about the other members follow closely behind. Not only do members wonder what they can get out of the experience to meet their own needs, they also wonder why it is necessary to get help in a group: "How can other people help me if they have the same problems I have?"

Groups also present a unique dynamic regarding leadership. The social work group leader is now the **external leader**, deriving his or her authority from external sources such as the sponsoring agency. This is in contrast to the **internal leader**, who is a member of the group. The internal leader assumes a leadership role in a situational or ongoing basis. That is, he or she leads in terms of one issue but not others or else leads in an overall way. Internal leaders cannot ultimately impose themselves on a group that is unwilling to accept them in this role.

With some of these issues in mind, the worker should design the structure of first meetings to meet the following objectives:

- To introduce group members to each other.

- To make a brief, simple opening statement that clarifies the agency's or institution's stake in providing the group service as well as the potential issues and concerns that group members feel urgently about.

- To obtain feedback from the group members on their sense of the fit (the contract) between their ideas of their needs and the agency's view of the service it provides.

- To clarify the group worker's task and method of attempting to help the group do its work.

- To deal directly with any specific obstacles that may obstruct this particular group's efforts to function effectively: stereotypes group members may hold concerning group work or people in authority, or group members' anger if attendance is involuntary.

- To begin to encourage intermember interaction rather than discussion only between the group leader and the group members.

- To begin to develop a supportive group culture in which members can feel safe.

- To help group members develop a tentative agenda for future work.

- To clarify the mutual expectations of the agency and the group members. For example, what can group members expect from the worker? In addition, what expectations does the worker have for the members (regarding regular attendance, meetings starting on time, and so forth)? Such rules and regulations concerning structure are part of the working contract.
- To gain some consensus on the part of group members as to the specific next steps; for example, are there central themes or issues with which they wish to begin the following week's discussion?
- To encourage honest feedback and evaluation of the effectiveness of the group.

At first glance, this list of objectives for a first meeting may appear overwhelming. Actually, many of them can be dealt with quickly, and most are interdependent—that is, work on one objective simultaneously affects the others. Obviously, however, these objectives cannot be achieved in the first session unless a clear structure for work is provided. The approach to creating such a structure, which is illustrated in detail in the remainder of the chapter, is offered as a general statement recognizing that the order of elements and the emphasis may vary depending on the worker, the group members, and the setting. Once again we see that a perceived dichotomy between structure and freedom is a false one. Freedom only comes with structure, and the structure must be of the type that encourages freedom.

The Couples' Group: An Illustration

This section illustrates a first meeting using excerpts from a videotaped recording of the first session of a married couples' group that I led. The group was conducted under the auspices of a community mental health setting. Five couples were referred from a variety of sources. All had experienced problems in their marital relationships, and in each of the five couples, one partner was the identified patient. The youngest were John and Louise, in their twenties, with two young children. Rick and Fran were in their thirties and had been married for 7 years with no children. Len and Sally were in their late forties, had been married for 20 years, and had borne children in their late teens and early twenties. Frank and Jane, in their fifties, were recently married after prior marriages and divorces. Jane's teenage sons were living with them at this point. Finally, Lou and Rose were in their sixties with several married children who had children of their own. Louise and Rose had recently been inpatients at a psychiatric hospital. Sally had been seen at the hospital and was considering entering as an inpatient. Frank, Jane, Rick, and Fran had been referred to the group for marital counseling. Each of the couples had been interviewed individually by one of my two coworkers in the group; however, they were meeting me, the senior group worker, for the first time that evening. My two coworkers, one male and one female, were also present.

The Initial Work

The group meeting room was carpeted and had comfortable chairs set in a circle. The session was recorded on video cameras placed in an adjoining studio. Cameras and cameramen worked on the other side of one-way glass partitions. The couples had met the coworkers in another part of the clinic and had been escorted to the meeting room so that they all arrived at once. The purpose of the videotaping had been explained to the couples, and they had signed consent forms prior to the first session. The group workers had tuned in to the impact of the videotaping and had developed a strategy to reach for their reactions at the beginning of the session.

As the couples arrived, I met them at the door, introducing myself to each partner and encouraging them to take a seat. Len, Sally's husband, had to miss the first session, as he was out of town on business. Frank and Jane, who had expressed the most ambivalence and uncertainty about attending the group during the week, were not present at the beginning of the session. After everyone was comfortably settled, I began by suggesting that we go around the room so that the members could share their names, how long they had been married, and whether they had any children. I said this would be a way for us to get to know each other.

LOUISE: I am Louise Lewis. We have been married six years, and we have two children.
WORKER: Go ahead, John (speaking to Louise's husband sitting next to her), please share it with the group members. (Leader points to the rest of the group.)
JOHN: My name is John. (Pause)
WORKER: (Smiling) With the same kids!
JOHN: (Laughing along with the rest of the group) Yes, I hope so.

The group members continued around the circle, giving their names and the data on their families. The advantage of introductions is that they help group members break the ice and begin to speak from the start. In addition, the worker conveys to them the sense that knowing each other will be important. Often during these introductions someone will make a humorous comment followed by nervous laughter; however, even these first contributions can help the members settle down. Because the contract has not been discussed, workers should request only a minimum of relevant information at this point. Later, clarification of group purpose will provide the necessary structure for the members to share why they have come. An alternative approach would be to make a brief statement of purpose before asking for introductions. This could be particularly important if group members had no idea of the purpose of the group.

Following the introductions, I brought up the videotaping issue:

WORKER: I realize you discussed the taping with my coworkers, but I thought I would like to repeat the reasons for taping these sessions and also to give you another opportunity to share your reactions. As you know, this is a training institution and we are involved in teaching other health professionals a number of skills, including how to work with groups. We find it helpful to use videotapes of groups such as these so that new group leaders can have examples to assist them in their learning. In addition, the coleaders and I will use these tapes each week as a way of trying to figure out how to be more effective in helping this group work well.

I went on to explain that if segments of the tape were kept, they would have an opportunity to view them and could decide if they wanted them erased. I asked if there was any response, and after a few moments of silence and some verbal agreement that there was no problem, I proceeded. I believed the tapes were still on their minds and would come up again; however, they were not quite ready at this point to accept my invitation.

With this acknowledgement of the taping issue, I moved to begin the contracting process. The first skills involved were similar to those described in Chapter 3: clarifying purpose, clarifying role, and reaching for client feedback. I had prepared an opening statement in which I attempted to explain the stake the clinic had in providing the group, to identify their potential interest in the work of the group, and to state our roles as workers. My coleaders and I had reworded this statement several times until we felt it was jargon-free, short, and direct.

WORKER: I thought I would begin by explaining how we view the purpose of this group and the role that we would be playing, and to get some feedback from you on what you see the sessions to be all about. All of the couples in the group—and there may be one more here later this evening—are experiencing some difficulties in their marriages. This is a time of crisis and not an easy time. The way we see it, however, is that it is also an opportunity for change, for growth, and a chance to make a new marriage right within the one you presently have. Now we know that isn't easy; learning to live together can be tough. That is why we have organized this group. Essentially, the way we see it, it will be a chance for you to help each other—a sort of a mutual-aid group. As you listen to each other, as you share some of the problems, some of the feelings, and some of the concerns, and as you try to help each other, we think you will learn a great deal that may be helpful in your own marriages. So that's pretty much the purpose of the group. Now, for our role as group leaders, we have a couple of jobs. The first is that we are going to try to help you talk to and listen to each other, since it's not always easy to do that, particularly with people you don't know. Secondly, we will be sharing our own ideas along the way about close relationships, some of which may be helpful to you. Does that make sense? Do any of you have any questions about that? Does that sound like what you thought you were coming to? (Most heads were nodding and there were murmurs of "yes.") I thought to get us started it would be worthwhile to take some time to do some problem swapping. What I would like you to do is to share with each other, for a little while, some of the problems and difficulties you have found between you as couples. I would like you also to share some of the things you would like to see different. How would you like the relationship to be? We can take some time to find out the kinds of issues that you're concerned about and then move from there. Would someone like to start?

The purpose of the problem swapping is twofold. First, it provides the feedback necessary to begin to develop the client's side of the working contract. These issues and concerns will be the starting point for the work of the group. In the initial stage, group members may share near problems, which do not bear directly on some of the more difficult issues. This is their way of testing, of trying to determine how safe it is to use the group. The group worker has to respect and understand their defenses as an appropriate way to begin a new experience. The second function of the problem-swapping exercise is to encourage intermember interaction. For most of their lives clients have participated in groups where the discussion has essentially been between the group member and the leader, the person in authority. This is a long-standing habit. They will need to learn new ways of relating in a group, and the problem-swapping exercise is a good way to start.

As each individual member shares a problem or a concern, the group worker pays attention to his two clients. The first client is the individual who is speaking at the moment. The second client is the group. The worker monitors their reactions as revealed by their eyes, their posture, and so on. The mediation function of the group worker can be seen in action during this exercise as he encourages individual members to speak to the group and share the concerns they are bringing to the forefront and at the same time helps group members respond to the individual. As group members hear others describing problems, they become better able to identify those issues for themselves. In addition, when they hear their own concerns echoed by other members, they feel relief at finding out that they are "all in the same boat." The onus that each member may feel over having somehow failed as a human being and as a partner in a marital relationship can begin to lift as they discover that others share their feelings and concerns.

Silence is not unusual at this point in the first group session. This silence can represent a different communication for each member. Some may be thinking of what they are willing to share with the group at that time. Others may be shy and afraid to be the first one to speak. Still others may be expressing their wariness of being put on the spot if they raise a concern, because they do not know how other members or the leader will react. These are the moments that inexperienced group leaders dread. The silence, they feel, confirms a recurring nightmare they have had about their first group session. They worry that, after they have made their opening statement and invited feedback, nobody will speak. At this moment the group leader will often think, "Why didn't I bring a film?" This anxiety may cause the group leader to take over the group and to offer subjects for discussion or, in some cases, to give a presentation on the topic. This, of course, leads to a self-fulfilling prophecy, where the message conveyed to the members by the worker is that although their participation is being asked for, there is no willingness to wait for it.

An alternative, after a brief delay, is to explore the silence by acknowledging beginning anything is difficult, as is discussing such subjects with people one does not know. Often, this supportive comment frees a member to risk speaking. If not, the group leader can ask if members would discuss what makes it hard to talk in a first group session. As the members discuss why talking is hard, they inevitably start the problem swapping as well.

In the case of this couples' group, Lou, the member in his sixties, had a strong sense of urgency about beginning to work and was ready to jump right in. He sat directly to my left. As he spoke, he directed his conversation to the other members. He began by describing the problem as his wife's depression. His voice was flat, and his wife sat stone-faced next to him. She stayed this way almost until the end of the session, not saying a word, although she appeared to be hearing everything said by others. She would speak at the end of the session in a powerful and moving way. As Lou spoke, the rest of the group listened intently, obviously relieved that he had started.

Lou: To begin with, as you heard, we have been married for 45 years. Our relationship has been on a rocky road due in a great degree to tragedies that have happened to our family. While that was a real contributing factor, social conditions, economic conditions, and family relationships were also contributing factors. I'm making this very brief because most of this will come out later on. I think the outline on this will be enough for us to get our teeth into. As a result of the things I have mentioned, Rose, particularly, went into some real depressions. All the threads of her family seemed to go. As a result, it became difficult for her to operate. The problems were so strong she decided she had to go to a psychiatrist. She went and I went with her for two and one half years. The psychiatrist opened up some doors for her but not enough to really make her free to operate.

The unfortunate thing about her depression is that it developed into hostility toward me and the children. Now as soon as the depression lifted, as far as she was concerned, things straightened out. As soon as her depression lifted, we had no problems. (This is said emphatically, facing the group worker.) We had differences of opinion, but we had no problems.

WORKER: It sounds like it has been tough for her and also tough for you.

LOU: Oh, yes! The unfortunate thing as far as we were concerned is that we did not have a psychiatrist who understood what the relationship was. He took our problems as a family problem. His suggestion after a while was that if we weren't getting along together, we should separate. I felt I really didn't like that because I knew that wasn't the problem. The problem was getting Rose out of her depression.

Lou had begun presenting the problem the way one partner often does in a couples' group. The problem was essentially the other partner who, in some way, needed to be "fixed." This is the way one partner often experiences things, and the group worker must attempt to understand and express that understanding of the members' feelings as they are presented. When I show this tape to students, one often confronts me for "allowing" Lou to talk about his wife as the identified patient. Many students in the class identify with his wife and become angry with Lou for not taking responsibility for his part in the problem. I point out that in the first few minutes of this session this couple is acting out the very problem they have come to get help with. Lou is in effect saying, "Do you want to see how I deny the problem and blame it all on Rose? Just watch me!" Rose is saying, "Yes, and watch how I sit here passively, letting Lou talk about me." I point out to the student that it does not make sense for me to get angry at these clients for acting out the very problem the group was established to deal with. Also, before I confronted Lou, I had to build up a fund of support. In this case I attempted to do that by my comment about this experience being tough on his wife and on himself. He talked about his wife, but I came back to him. Later in the session, this same client dropped some of his defenses.

Some observers also wonder about my letting Lou continue to talk instead of immediately involving other members. It seemed obvious to me that the second client, the group, was listening to what Lou had to say and did not mind his going on at some length. Group members begin first sessions with various patterns of behavior. Those who are used to being withdrawn in new situations will begin that way. Those who are used to speaking and jumping in quickly, such as Lou, will begin that way. Each member is entitled to his own defenses in the beginning, and the group leader needs to respect them. When a group member speaks for a while, keeping to the subject, usually only the leader feels nervous. The other members are often relieved that someone else is talking. In this case, the tuning-in work from the individual session had alerted us to Lou's strong feelings toward helping professionals, who he felt had not been helpful. I had decided to reach directly for the authority theme if I felt there were indirect cues related to us, the group workers. I did so at this point in the following way:

WORKER: Are you worried that I and the other group leaders might take the same position with you and Rose?

LOU: Well, I don't know (voice slightly rising with annoyance). I'm not worried; I'm past that stage (accompanied with a harsh laugh). I'm just relating what happened, because I know where I'm at (said emphatically). To be very frank, my opinion of psychiatrists is very low, and I can cite for two hours experiences of what I have been through, my friends have been through, to show you exactly what I mean. This was a good case in point, his making a suggestion that we should separate because of the problem.

WORKER: After 45 years I can imagine that must have hit you as a terrible blow.

LOU: Well, sure it did.

WORKER: Lou, do you think we could move around the circle a bit and also hear from the others as to what they see some of the problems to be?

In retrospect, I think Lou responded somewhat angrily partly because of the way I made my statement, "Are you worried that I and the other group leaders might take the same position with you and Rose?" I wanted to open up Lou's concerns about what kind of workers we would be; however, my effort was not direct or clear enough. Instead of asking for further elaboration from Lou, or asking if others in the group had similar experiences or relations, I suggested we allow others to exchange problems by "moving around the circle." Encouraging such an exchange of problems was important; however, further exploration of the authority theme was also important. Fortunately I had an opportunity to "catch my mistake" later in the session when I returned to the initial concerns raised by Lou. He responded to my suggestion that we "hear from the others" by turning to his wife:

LOU: Sure, you're on. Go ahead, dear. (He turns to his wife.)

ROSE: I think I'll pass right now (said in a slow, even way, with no evidence of affect).

WORKER: That's fine. How about some others? You don't have to go in order, and you know, you can also respond to what Lou just said if you like, as well as adding some of your own issues. We won't solve all of the problems tonight; I hope you realize that. (Some laughter by the group members.) But what we would like to try and do is get a feel for how they seem to you right now. That can help us get a sense of what we need to talk about, and I think Lou has helped us get started. (At this point, John takes off his coat and seems to settle back in his chair.)

LOUISE: (John's wife, who is now speaking directly to Lou) I can understand what Lou means because depression has been our problem as well. I have gotten into such a state of depression that I can't function as a mother or a wife. I feel I have lost my identity. (This is all said with a very flat affect.) And I don't think that separation is the answer either. And I have had some pretty bad psychiatrists as well, so I can really feel for you when you say that, Lou. I can understand that. But the problem is to be able to sort out and find out what feelings I really have and recognize them for what they are and try to get myself out of the hole that I fell into, and that's the tough part.

WORKER: How does it affect your relationship with John?

LOUISE: It's very strenuous. There is a lot of strain and tension when I'm sick and down and I put the responsibility for taking care of the household on John's shoulders. There is a breaking point for him somewhere there; I want to catch it before we get there. (Pause, worker is nodding and other members are listening intently.) That's about it. (Brief silence.)

JOHN: Our biggest problem, or Louise's biggest problem, is due to her migraine headaches. She's had them ever since she was five years old. This is where the whole problem stemmed from, those migraine headaches, and this new depression which she seems to have gotten in the last few months.

WORKER: Anything special happen within the last few months?

JOHN: No, it has been actually a very quiet time this summer.

LOUISE: I think it is things that have been festering for a long time.

WORKER: For example?

LOUISE: I don't know. I can't put my finger on what they are.

WORKER: (Speaking to John) This depression came as a surprise to you, did it?

JOHN: Yes, it did.

WORKER: How do you see the problem, John? What would you like to see different in the relationship?

John went on to describe how they do not do much together as a couple anymore and that he would like to see Louise get back on her feet so they can have some fun the way they used to. Discussion continued around the circle, with Fran and Rick looking at each other as if to ask who would go first. I verbalized this, and Fran begged off, saying that she did not feel comfortable starting right away and that she would get in a bit later. Her husband, Rick, responded to my question by saying he was wondering why he was there, because he knows that he has—or rather, they have—a problem, but what the problem is, is hard to define. Fran coached him at this point by whispering in his ear the word *communication*. They seemed to agree that that was the problem, but when I asked for elaboration, Rick said, "That's not my problem, that's Fran's problem." Rick then took a further step for the group by entering a taboo area.

RICK: I guess if you get right down to basics, it would have to be sexual intimacy. I have been going along for a little over seven years, and now I find that I'm all alone. Fran's gone on a trip, and we're really in the very rocky stages of breaking up. (There is shaky emotion in his voice as he is speaking.) For the last six months, we have sort of been trying to recover, but it's still pretty shaky.

WORKER: It must feel pretty dicey for you right now.

RICK: Right. (With resignation in his voice.)

WORKER: What would you like to be different? What would you like to see changed in your marriage?

RICK: (After a deep sigh to get his breath) There are times when everything is just fine, it seems to be going along smoothly, but just to say what I would like would be tough to put my finger on.

WORKER: How would you like the relationship to be with Fran?

RICK: I think I would like it to be peaceful at all times. We have been getting into a lot of fights and just recently we have been getting into a lot of physical fights. A peaceful relationship, that's what I would really go for.

WORKER: How about you, Fran, do you have any ideas now?

FRAN: No, can we come back to me?

WORKER: Sure.

The discussion continued with Sally talking about her marriage. This was difficult because her husband, Len, was not present. She described it from her perspective. Her description was filled with interpretations that had obviously been gleaned from years of involvement in various forms of analysis. The group listened intently to her stories. She also responded to Louise's comments about migraine headaches, mentioning that she had had them as well, and then she and Louise exchanged some mutual understanding. After Sally finished her description, there was a long silence as the group seemed unsure about where to go.

WORKER: (Turning to Lou) I didn't mean to stop you before, Lou, if you want to get in again.

LOU: No, that's OK (laughing). I could go on for hours.

WORKER: Oh, they won't mind, you know (pointing to the group), they would be glad. (Most of the group members laugh at this.)

LOU: I want to give others the opportunity to speak because, after all, I have been married over 45 years, so I have an accumulation of incidents.

During the problem-swapping exercise, I had attempted to express my empathic responses to the concerns as they were raised, taking care not to express judgments on the members' feelings and actions. Even this brief period had built up a fund of trust large enough to let me reach for some discussion on this difficult theme. For the group to develop as a healthy organism, it would need to begin to sort out the authority theme—its relationship to me as the leader and the person in authority. Because this is a taboo subject, I would have to work hard to open the topic for discussion. When I invited Lou to speak again, I decided to return to the theme of helpers who had not helped. Note that I returned to this issue directly by pointing out to the group members that I thought such a discussion might be important, so that they could be involved with full knowledge of the process. The group discussion that followed was led by Lou, an internal leader on this issue; it contributed to a striking change in the group atmosphere and to its successful beginning.

WORKER: I have noticed a theme that has cut across a number of your presentations that I think is important for us to talk about. A number of you have commented on helping people who have not been very successful—psychiatrists you have had in the past, doctors, and so on. (Group members all nod, saying yes.) Can you stay on that for a minute in terms of the things in your experiences that you found difficult? The reason I think it is important is because it would be a way of your letting me and my coleaders know what you would not find helpful from us.

This is the second time I reached for comments about the group members' concern about us. This time, because a relationship was beginning and because I reached in a way that was less threatening, they were ready to share. Lou volunteered to begin the discussion. He took us back to 1940, when he had his own business. He described some of the pressures on him concerning economic conditions and a rash he developed on his leg then. His doctor referred him to a psychiatrist who was brand new at the hospital. In fact, it was the psychiatrist's first job. Lou's enthusiasm and feelings while describing this experience captured the attention of the group. They smiled and nodded agreement with his comments.

As he was about to describe his encounter, the door to the group room opened and the fifth couple, Frank and Jane, arrived late. Group members often arrive late for a first session, but group workers many times feel doubtful about what to do then. In this case, I had the new couple introduce themselves, and I asked the other couples to give their names as well. I then briefly summarized the contract, explaining that we had been hearing about some problems to help get a feel for the concerns that had brought the couples to this session. I then pointed out that the theme of helping people who had not been very helpful had come up. I said that we were focusing on this right now and that just before they had entered we had been with Lou in 1940. With that, I turned back to Lou to continue, and the group picked up where it had left off. Workers should recognize the entrance of the new group members and help them connect to the group, but taking a great deal of time to start again would be a mistake. As will become clear later in this group session, the lateness of these group members was their way of handling a new and frightening experience.

Lou continued the story of his first encounter with the young psychiatrist, indicating that the psychiatrist had tried to lead him indirectly to recognizing that he had a marital problem. As Lou put it, "I was talking about the economic conditions and the problems of the time, and he kept coming back to the wife and the kids, and the wife and the kids, and the wife and the kids until I said to him, 'Are you trying to tell me my problem is with my wife and my kids?'" Lou went on to say that when the psychiatrist indicated it was, he stood up, called him a charlatan, and quickly got out of the office as the enraged psychiatrist came out from behind the desk shaking his fist at him.

LOU: OK. I knew that my wife and my family were part of the problem, but I also knew that they were not at the core of the problem. They were a contributing factor because of the social and economic conditions. I went to this guy to get rid of this rash on my leg and not to have him tell me that my wife and my kids were giving me the problem. It took a while for the rash to go away, but eventually it did. That was item number one. I am going to skip a lot of the intervening incidents that had to do with families, and I will go to the one which we just experienced recently. We went to a psychiatrist in the community for two and one half years (and then with emphasis) *two and one half years!* I knew I had to go with her to give her some support plus I wanted to find out what made her tick. I couldn't understand her depression. I had been down in the dumps and felt blue, but I had never felt depressed as she seemed to feel. He asked her a lot of questions, asked me a lot of questions, tried to have us do some play acting and had us try and discuss the problems. "You're not communicating" was his term. I didn't know what he was talking about when he said we didn't communicate, so we tried to communicate. But nothing really came of it because we saw we weren't communicating.

As Lou related his experiences, he was describing several techniques that professionals had apparently used to try to help him and his wife deal with their problems. The central theme appeared to be that of a helping person who had decided what the problem was and tried to educate them as to its nature. Lou resented this approach and resisted it in most of the sessions. Yet part of him deep inside knew that there was a problem that he attempted to deal with in his own way. He described an incident when he had tape-recorded a conversation with his wife, listening to it later. His description of the aftermath of this recording contained the first overt expression of the sadness and pain the couple had experienced but were not ready to share. In this case, I believe Lou needed to share the anger and the frustration at the helping people who had not understood him before he was willing to share his hurt and pain.

LOU: We talked for about 15 minutes, and I realized when we played the tape back, that I was screaming at Rose. Now I never realized that I was screaming at her. But I heard my voice. (Lou clears his throat at this point and begins to choke up, obviously feeling emotions and trying to fight back his tears.) This is a little rough for me, can I have some water?

WORKER: (Getting a glass of water from the decanter) Sure you can, Lou, take your time.

LOU: It's kind of tough to get over the fact that I was screaming at her. Then I realized that when I was screaming at her, I was treating her like a kid. I took this tape to the psychiatrist, and he couldn't hear the screaming. He got nothing out of it.

WORKER: He didn't seem to understand how it felt to you to hear yourself screaming?

LOU: That's right. He didn't even hear me screaming. The other thing he tried to get us to do which I found really devastating is he tried to get us to reverse roles; she should be me and I should be her. OK, we tried it. But while we were doing it, I was thinking to myself: "Now, if that isn't stupid, I don't know what is." (Turning to me at this point) But you're a psychiatrist—you know what the score is. How can you reverse roles when I'm not feeling like she's feeling and she doesn't feel like I do? How can I communicate? Well, it was things like that that had been going on for two and one half years, and when we had finished, I was nowhere nearer being helped to be able to live with Rose than I was when we started. Now that's two and one half years! It isn't that we didn't try; both of us used to discuss this. Rose went back to the doctor, but I said I wouldn't go because I found I was just getting more frustrated.

At this point, there was some discussion on the part of group members about the use of the tape recorder. Rick thought it was a good idea and wondered if Lou had tried it again. Lou said he had not. The conversation returned to his feelings of frustration and his sense of not having been helped.

LOU: I felt stupid. The psychiatrist kept telling me something, and no matter how hard I tried, I simply couldn't understand.

WORKER: You also seem to be saying, not only couldn't you understand him, but he didn't seem to understand you.

LOU: Well, yes. Peculiarly enough, that thought had not occurred to me. I felt, well you are a professional (facing the worker at this point), so what you're doing, you're doing on purpose. You know what you're supposed to be doing. And whether you understand me or not is immaterial. That's not what the game is. It's my responsibility to understand what you, if you are the psychiatrist, are saying. (There was anger in his voice.)

WORKER: If you're asking us (referring to the other coworkers) in this group, that's not the way I see it. I think that if we can be of any help to you or the other group members, the help will be in our listening and in our trying to understand exactly how you see it. The gimmicks and the things that seem to get tried on you is not my idea of how we can help. You'll have to wait to see if I mean that.

LOU: Yeah, we'll see.

WORKER: I think you folks have a powerful lot of help to give each other. And essentially, what I will try and do is to help you do that. And I'll share my own ideas along the way. But I have no answers or simple solutions.

LOU: Then, well, OK. (General silence in the group as the members appear to be taking in the meaning of the words.)

COWORKER: I'd like to know, Lou, as we go along, how you see things. So, if you're feeling stupid or whatever, you'll let us know.

WORKER: It might be because we've said something dumb (some subdued laughter in the group).

Although I had described the group as a mutual-aid group in the opening statement, only at this point did the members really began to have a sense of how the group might work. Also, they actually "heard" the clarification of the group worker's role contained in this exchange. As an internal group leader, Lou could articulate the fears and concerns that members felt about the potential power invested in the group worker's role. If the group leader is feeling insecure, as most beginners do, then she or he might see Lou as a "deviant member" challenging the leader's authority. In reality, he provided an opportunity for an initial clarification of who we were as group leaders and what we did. Skills of accepting and understanding his feelings and his frustrations, and of helping to connect his past experiences to the present moment, were crucial in this session. The feeling in the group was that we had moved past the first step in building our relationship. The authority theme would come up again; however, one could sense that an important start had been made. Following this exchange, the group members could move into work on their contract with more energy, involvement, and intermember interaction.

The Work Continues

The 2-hour session allowed the group to move past problem swapping and clarification of purpose and worker role into beginning efforts to define the primary work. Interestingly, Frank and Jane, the couple who had arrived late, provided an opportunity to do this. Frank began to share, with some elaborative assistance from the group worker, a problem that they were experiencing in relation to his wife's teenage sons who were living with them. It was an interesting example of a group member raising a problem tentatively, moving quickly back and forth between the implications of the difficulty for the couple and for his relationship to the children. He spoke of the sexual difficulty they had, attributing most of it to a medical problem he was having treated and also to the lack of privacy in their home. The bedroom door was never locked, and the children would wander in without notice. As Frank was sharing this concern, he phrased it in terms of his problem with his stepsons, but one could hear throughout the discussion hints of the implications for his relationship to his wife. Each time the worker would acknowledge, even gently, the implication for the relationship, Frank would back off slightly, and both he and Jane would quickly reassure the group, emphasizing the positive nature of their communications.

As we have seen, group members often use the early sessions to offer near problems in a way that presents them as issues and at the same time defends them from discussion. This move reflects the members' ambivalence about dealing with real concerns (see Part II), as well as their testing of the group to see if it is safe to share. The group members worry about sharing in front of not only the worker and the other members, but also their partners. Each of the couples has developed a "culture" in their marriage that has included certain norms, behaviors, taboo areas, rules for interaction, and so on. The group will in many ways be a place for them to learn how to change that culture, or at least those parts of it that are not conducive to their marriage. With so many factors to consider, group members often come close to a concern while watching to see how the partner, the other members, and the workers will react. Timing is important in a first session, and it would therefore be a mistake for a group worker to attack defenses at a point when the group member greatly needs them.

As Frank began to describe his efforts to deal with the children and privacy, I suggested that they might use this as an example of one of the ways in which the group members might help each other:

WORKER: (Speaking to the group) Perhaps we can use this as an example of how we can be helpful. Frank can describe the conversation he had with his son, and the rest of the group members might respond by suggesting how they would have reacted if they had been the son. We could do some thinking with Frank about how he might handle this kind of an issue.

The group members agreed, and Frank went into some details of a conversation in which he sarcastically implied to the son that they needed some privacy. After several group members supported his right to privacy, the coworker pointed out that it would be difficult to take his comments seriously because he always seemed to be joking as he described things and never seemed as if he could really get angry. This triggered a response from his wife, Jane.

JANE: Aha! That's it exactly. Frank has trouble getting angry. Ever since he has been a kid, he has been afraid to be direct and angry with people. I keep telling him, why don't you let yourself get angry and blow off steam? He says that he feels that it is just not the thing to do. You just don't do it. I do it all the time. I didn't use to, but now I do, and I get angry at least a couple of times a day.

FRANK: You know the kids are scared of you because you get angry so much.

WORKER: (Noticing that Sally appears to want to say something) Go ahead, Sally, get in.

SALLY: (Laughing as she speaks to Frank) You have got to meet my Len! (The whole group, including Frank, erupts in a great roar of laughter.) You sound like two of the same kind, and you're hard to live with.

WORKER: Frank, what made it hard for you to speak seriously to your son right then?

FRANK: I don't know. Well, you know the image of a stepfather like in the fairy-tale books, he is like a monster. I've got a nice thing starting to build with these boys, and I don't want to ruin it.

WORKER: You are afraid they would get angry if you were direct and honest.

JANE: (Laughing, but with a touch of anger) It's all up in your head.

WORKER: You know, Jane, I think Frank really is worried about that.

FRANK: I do worry about that. I really do.

In response to the worker's next question, "What are you afraid might happen?" Frank went on to describe the cold relationship the children had with Jane's former husband. Then he shared his fears of being unable to prevent the continuation of the same coldness and the problems that he envisioned in that relationship.

FRANK: It was because I didn't want to hurt that relationship that I more or less symbolized what I really meant.

WORKER: You kind of hinted at what you felt rather than saying it directly.

FRANK: Well, it's like you are in a washroom and you see a fellow peeing on the floor. You would probably say, "Hey, you missed, fella." (Group members roar with laughter at his story.)

Frank went on to describe, much to his wife's surprise, a very direct conversation in which he explained the problem to the son. Frank's point was that since that time, the son had been much more understanding about not interrupting. At this point in the group session, Lou, who had been listening intently, moved in and took responsibility for the group process. In a striking illustration of internal leadership at an early stage in the group development, Lou moved directly from the general discussion of anger and indirect communication to the implications for each couple. The worker had noticed during the discussion that on several occasions Lou had attempted to whisper to his wife, Rose, to ask her a question, but she had refused to respond, and remaining impassive and expressionless. Lou now used the group and this theme to deal with his concern—a concern common to all members. I believe that he was able to make this direct intervention and assume some leadership responsibility in the group because the way had been cleared through our earlier discussion of the role of the worker. This was an example of Lou accepting the worker's invitation for the members to begin to own their group.

WORKER: (Noting Lou's indirect communication of his desire to get into the discussion) Were you going to say something, Lou?

LOU: Something has come up here which I would like each couple in turn to answer if they can. (Turning to John, he asks his name, which John gives him.) I would like each couple to add to this in turn if they can. John, do you get really mad at Louise? I mean really mad, peed off? Do you yell at her, do you tell her off?

JOHN: Not really.

LOU: Why not?

JOHN: That's my style, that's the way I have been all my life.

LOU: Louise, how about you?

LOUISE: I'll probably hold back until as long as possible and then usually end up to where I'm in tears, or slam cupboards or dishes, or give John a cold shoulder rather than coming right out and saying that I'm angry. (As Louise is speaking, Lou is nodding and saying yes.)

LOU: Why? By the way, I am referring to Rose and myself right now when I'm asking this question and I want to hear from everyone.

JOHN: It happens sometimes, but it is really rare that we actually yell at each other. (Louise shakes her head, agreeing.)

LOU: Are you afraid to get angry, either one of you?

JOHN: I don't think I'm afraid. I don't have a problem yelling at other people. It's kind of strange. I don't know why.

LOU: How about you, Frank and Jane?

Jane and Frank both discussed her getting angry regularly, blowing her top all the time. She indicated that it worried her. Frank said he had trouble getting angry directly at Jane and gave an example of her not sharing her load of chores (they are both working), and he shared that he had been getting angry at that, because it was setting a bad example for the kids, but that he had not told her. He paused when he said that, and then said, "I guess I hadn't said that to you until tonight." As the conversation went on, the other workers and I were monitoring the members, making sure they were involved and paying attention. Occasionally one of us would comment on some of the feelings associated with the comments.

LOU: (Directly to Jane) You have no aversions about getting mad, I mean spontaneously mad?

JANE: What other way is there to get mad?

LOU: You don't build anything up and then have it boil over?

JANE: Not anymore, not now.

After a pause, I turned to Lou and said, "Stay with it." Lou responded, "Fine, because something is happening here that happens to us," (pointing to his silent wife, Rose) "and I would like to hear from everyone in the group on this." At that point he asked Fran, who had declined to speak thus far, if she got mad.

FRAN: I hold it for a little while, and then I start and I pick, and I can't stop at the issue. Often I can't even determine what the issue is at the time. Since I can't figure out what it is, I go through the whole gamut to make sure I get to the right one. And—maybe I should let Rick speak for himself—my opinion is that he's quiet. He listens to all of this without a comment back. That really drives me out of my mind. I can't stand the silence. If only he would yell! Even if I'm wrong, then I know I'm wrong. But like I said, I go over the whole ballpark because I know I may hit the right one, since the right one is in there somewhere. There's not much of a reaction, because Rick is the quiet type. He doesn't like to argue or fight. And the quieter he seems to get, the angrier I get. I have to push even harder. It's just recently, the last couple of months, that we've started to fight physically. We've been married for seven years, and this is just coming out now. Well, I didn't think that Rick had a breaking point and that he could get that mad. And I wasn't even aware that I could get that mad, but I can. I'm the pusher, I'm the one—the things that I could say could definitely curl your hair.

RICK: She basically said it all for me.

FRAN: And that's usual, too.

LOU: (Smiling in a supportive way) Your hair looks pretty straight to me, Rick.

RICK: (Sighing) It has been a long day. Yes, I am the quiet type, and I have a very long fuse, but once it gets to the end, look out. I've done some stupid things in my time, and they usually end up costing me. I guess I just reach my breaking point and take the frustration out somewhere. If it happens that Fran is taking hers out on me, I try and cool it as long as I can, but then I can only take so much of that, and we end up going at each other. That's about it.

LOU: Let me ask you a question, Rick. When Fran is at you like she does, is it that you don't want to or are you afraid of hurting her feelings so that she'll come back at you again and this thing will snowball, or is it that you have a reluctance and you feel you'll let her get it off her chest and then things will calm down again? Which of these is it?

RICK: I guess I'm just hoping that she'll get it off her chest and things will calm down again. But it doesn't work that way.

WORKER: (Turning to Lou) If I can just ask Rick this before you go on, Lou—what's going on inside of your guts when Fran is pushing that way? What do you feel?

RICK: (Takes a big sigh before he speaks) Well, I guess I'm trying to just block everything out of my mind. That's the reason I become quiet, even go to the point of reading the newspaper and just completely try to wipe it out.

WORKER: Because it hurts?

RICK: Right.

Lou continued, turning to Sally, who also described how she saw herself in Fran because her husband, Len, is like Rick, the quiet type. She described several similar examples, ending by saying, "I don't think I have ever found his boiling point. Heaven help me if I ever do."

WORKER: That must be as hard as having found it.

SALLY: Yes, I guess it is. The problem is that you hoard the hurts and when you get a chance, zap, you give them right back. The sad part is that I really don't think Len has a mean bone in his body.

There was a long silence after this as the group waited in anticipation. The next speaker was Rose, Lou's wife, who had not said a word nor changed her expression during the entire session. She had been watching and listening intently. Because of her silence, her comments at this point had a stunning impact on the group members as well as the group worker:

Rose: Well, I think there is a common thread running through with everyone and part of it is anger, and there may be some recriminations amongst the couples here. Some people have learned to live with it, but obviously, those of us here have not. And no matter how long you're married, it's still something you don't know how to handle. I found that I got very angry here.

Worker: You mean here tonight?

Rose: Yes, but I wasn't going to interrupt my husband to tell him that I didn't want him to say that or I didn't like what he was saying. So, I'm back to zero, not just one. I can pack my bags and go back to the hospital. (At this comment, her husband, Lou, flinches almost as if in pain and looked toward the worker.) And I don't feel comfortable talking about it.

Worker: It's hard even now, isn't it?

Rose: Yes, but I made up my mind I was at the point where I would pack my bags or talk. (Rose was referring to returning to the inpatient ward of the Center.)

Worker: I'm glad you talked.

Lou: (His face brightening) Well, I have been thinking that that was about the only way I could get Rose to talk and to burst open.

Rose: Sure, well, I knew that's what was going on.

Lou: She wasn't going to say anything to me. I asked her during the group if she was mad, and she said she was. I asked if she would say something, and she said no.

Rose: Right, I said no.

Lou: Plus the fact that what goes on is that all our lives both of us have always been afraid of hurting each other.

Rose: So, we kept quiet. Or else one spoke and said too much. I always felt that Lou had spoken lots more than I did. Now, I had an opportunity to do a lot of speaking at the hospital for five weeks, and certainly I found it helped me quite a bit. I told myself and the people there that I was going to try and remember to use everything they taught me. And there's really no way. Because different things come up and, say, they're not in the book that I went by.

Worker: I guess you have to write your own book, then.

Rose: That's right. I'm not very quick on my feet, and I don't think my mind operates very quickly either. But how to deal with anger seems to be everyone's particular problem. (There is a pause in the group as Rose's words sink in.)

Worker: It's close to the end of our session, and I wonder if what we haven't done is identify a common theme and issue that we might want to look at in more depth next week. Perhaps you could be prepared to share some of the incidents and difficulties, because I think if you can bring some of those arguments from the outside into here, where it is a little safer, and where there are people around to help, maybe it's possible to learn to do what Rose did just now without hurting. Perhaps it is possible to say what you are really thinking and what you're feeling without having to store up the hurts. My own feeling is that any real, intimate relationship has to have both some loving and some fighting. That comes with the territory. But it's a hard thing to do. We simply haven't learned how to do it. So maybe this could be a safe area to test it out. Does that make any sense to the rest of you? (Group members nod.) Maybe we could pick up on this next week as something that we're interested in. How do you find a way of saying what you're really thinking and feeling toward each other without wiping each other out?

JANE: Is there a way to do that?

WORKER: I think so, but why don't we test that out here in the group? If there isn't, though, then I think we're in trouble, because I don't think you could really care for each other if you can't also get angry at each other. Does that make some sense to the whole group? (Once again, there is some nodding in agreement.) What we could do is different couples could bring some examples. Maybe you'll have a hard time during the week that's tough to handle. Well, we could go over that with you here in the group and see if we can find a way of helping you identify what you were really feeling and also be able to say it directly and clearly in a way that keeps communication open. I think this is the way it would work. Even if one couple raises a specific example, the rest of us could learn in helping them with that example. So, you would get something out of each week's session even if you weren't talking about your own marriages.

With a clear contract and some work in the beginning of the session that helped create the safe conditions within the group, members felt free to begin to risk themselves. The group moved directly to one of the core issues in marital relationships. What is striking is the way the members themselves directed the emergence of this theme. Each group is different, reflecting the strengths and experiences as well as the weaknesses of its members. Lou brought a sense of urgency and a willingness to risk himself to the group that helped them not only tackle the issue of authority directly and constructively but also helped them to move past their early defenses into the common concerns they had about their relationships with each other. Although the particular way in which this group worked during its first session is unique, the level of its work or the speed with which it began is not unusual. It reflected the sense of urgency of the group members, the clarity of group purpose, and the workers' role. The members were willing to attack the issue of authority directly, and the workers consistently tried to articulate the feelings expressed by the group members, even being slightly ahead of them. Given these core conditions, the impetus of the group members carried them toward productive work.

Ending and Transition

Now that the session was nearly over and the group had agreed on a theme for additional work, the ending and transition part of this session continued with an opportunity for evaluative comments. The workers wished in the first session to encourage members to talk about the way the group was working.

WORKER: We have five minutes left. This was our first session. I would like you to take a few minutes to share with each other and with us what your reactions are. What are your feelings and your thoughts? How has this session hit you? What will you say to each other on your way home in the car about this evening's session? It's important that you say it now.

ROSE: Well, I have the feeling that the first thing out the door, Lou is going to ask me what it is he said that made me angry. I can't define it right now. I'd have to pull it out of my head.

LOUISE: That's tough. That's really tough trying to figure out what it is that makes you angry. I feel that way, too. When I was an inpatient and someone showed me that I was angry at a resident and why I was angry, well that was fine; I was able to do a little bit of yelling and get it off my chest. But it's not always easy to put my finger on what it is I'm feeling.

WORKER: Maybe that's what we can do here—help you figure out what those feelings are. (Turning to Lou) What's your reaction? I'm really interested in your reaction because I have a feeling that you came in here thinking about all of the people in the past who haven't been helpful. Where do we stand so far?

LOU: So far I feel that we're beginning to break a little new ground. Actually, the most important thing that happened to me tonight was Rose getting mad.

WORKER: Is it easier to handle it when you know where she stands?

LOU: No, not really. I don't know where she stands. I knew she was mad; I asked her to tell me what she's mad about, but she said no. The reason I am feeling good about this is that she has just gone through five weeks as an inpatient, and I can assure you (voice cracking) I've just gone through the same five weeks.

WORKER: I think these things change step by small step and perhaps tonight made a beginning. Perhaps if you aren't too harsh with yourself and demand too much, you have a chance of doing it. I am glad it hit you that way. How about the others, what will be your reactions tonight?

FRANK: Whew!

JANE: (Laughing) I think we were so apprehensive about what would happen here tonight it wasn't funny.

WORKER: What were you afraid of?

JANE: Well, I guess it was the fear of the unknown, and yet when we got here, we immediately started to sense that here are people who are concerned, who care, and this came right to the fore.

LOU: Larry, I'd like to make a comment here. Our youngest son is 36 and one of the things he complained about to us was that "you never taught me how to argue with my wife." I wondered where in the world did he get the idea that it was necessary to argue with each other. As time went on, I realized that we used to argue and keep things on the inside. My son today is having problems, and he even called me last night on the very same subject. The important thing he said was, "You haven't taught us how to argue." Oh, yes not only that but, "You haven't taught us how to argue and to win the argument." (The group roared with laughter.)

Other members of the group were given a chance to comment. Frank pointed out that he and Jane were late partly because they were ambivalent about coming. He had been telling my coworker all week that he was not sure whether he really belonged here. As he described his conversations, he laughed along with the other members of the group. They all acknowledged that coming to the first session had been frightening. Frank went on to say that what impressed him was the people in the group; they all seemed to be a really "super bunch," and that helped a lot. Lou commented that it was reassuring to find out that he was not alone and that others had the same feelings.

After some additional positive comments, I pointed out that it would also be important to share their negative reactions or questions; these were tough to share but were also important. Sally indicated her concern about whether or not the group would really help, if anything would really change. She was also worried about her husband, Len, having missed the first meeting. We talked about this, and I asked the group to strategize how we might bring Len into the second meeting quickly, because he would be feeling a bit like an outsider. This helped indicate to the group members that they all had a responsibility to make the group work well. After they made some suggestions for myself, Sally, and the group, I told Sally that there were no promises, no sure answers or easy solutions. Marriage is hard work, as she knew, but perhaps through the group we might be able to offer some support and help with their difficult tasks. She nodded in agreement.

Fran and Rick responded that they had felt a bit shy and found it difficult to talk in the group. John and Louise jumped in and reassured them, saying that they thought they had participated quite a bit. I pointed out that they had risked some very difficult subjects in the discussion with the group and gave them credit for that. Rick said that after a week or two he would probably find getting in easier; I told him to take his time and that he would get in as he felt comfortable.

As the evaluation seemed to be coming to an end, I pointed out that there were three rules we would follow in the group. I explained that members were expected to come each week and that it was OK to come even if your partner could not make it because of illness or some other reason. I said that they should treat what they shared with each other as confidential so that they could all feel that the other couples in the group would not be talking about them to outsiders. I also asked that if they wanted to drop out of the group at any time before the 23 sessions we had planned were over, they would agree to come back and discuss it with the group before quitting. All agreed that these seemed to be reasonable rules.

I then complimented them on what I thought was an excellent start. I told them that I could understand how nervous they must have felt at the beginning, because I felt a little of that nervousness, too, but that I thought they had launched some important work, and that boded well for our future. The session ended at this point, but people did not leave immediately; instead, they milled around talking to other members and the workers. Then, slowly, the group members left the room.

This has been a detailed description of the first session of one kind of group. You may already be thinking about some of the differences in the groups you have led. For example, these were generally articulate group members. They had volunteered to come to the group session and were not there under duress. The group leaders carried no additional functional responsibilities in relation to the members (such as a child welfare protective function). Of course, groups differ according to the setting, the members, the purpose, and so forth. Some of these are illustrated in the next section with brief excerpts from first sessions of groups from different contexts. Nonetheless, the basic dynamics and skills involved in effective beginnings with groups cut across these differences. You will find in the examples that when these dynamics are respected, they more often than not lead to an effective start. When ignored, however, they haunt both the group leader and the group members. First sessions are important because they lay a foundation for the difficult tasks to follow. If handled well, they can provide a fund of positive feeling as well as a clear framework, both of which will influence the remaining sessions.

One final note concerns a comment made by more than one social work student after watching the videotape of this session. Students are struck by Lou taking the initiative in asking the couples about anger in their relationships. The video images reveal my facial expression, which clearly indicates my delight at his moving into a leadership role. At one point I asked Lou if it was all right for me to interrupt him and ask a member a question. The surprised students ask, "Why did you let Lou take over your group?" My response is that it was not my group. The group belonged to the members, and the fact that they accepted my invitation to take over in the first session was a very positive sign and indicated the strength of the group members. This exchange often triggers an important discussion of the fear of an inexperienced group leader of losing control of the group. It takes some experience and growing confidence for the group leader to realize that leading groups effectively depends on the process of letting go.

Variations on First Group Sessions

In the previous section we explored common dynamics and skills related to first group meetings. These were illustrated using a first session of a group for married couples. However, not all groups are composed of articulate adults or of clients attending voluntarily. In this section we consider the most important variant elements that may affect the worker's strategy. These can be broken down into the following five categories: the age and relative articulateness of the members, the authority of the worker, the specific concerns of the clients, the setting of the encounter, and the impact of time. Each of these variations will be illustrated with one example of a first session. You can also refer to additional process recordings for Chapter 10, which are listed at the end of the chapter and available on the text's companion website.

Working With Children and Adolescents

The problem of lack of clarity of purpose or embarrassment about making a direct statement of purpose, discussed in Part II, is even more common with group work than individual work. The presence of more than one client may increase the reluctance of the worker to be direct. In the examples that follow, you will note a correlation between directness and honesty in the contracting and an effective start to the group.

Foster Adolescents in a Child Welfare Setting In this first extract, note the worker's reliance on safe and generalized topics in her opening statement to a group of foster adolescents in a child welfare agency:

> I opened the discussion by telling all the members that what was said in these groups would remain confidential. Neither workers nor foster parents would ever know what was being discussed. In addition, I pointed out that the same sort of commitment would be required on their part. I then mentioned the kinds of things we could discuss; for example, the trouble they have making their allowances stretch and whether or not the clothing allowance was sufficient. There followed a great period of silence, at which point I suggested that if they could think of nothing else, perhaps they would like to talk about the lack of conversation (which seemed to be a little too far advanced for the group to handle).

Nothing in the worker's statement recognized that they were all foster children. The examples she used could have been drawn from any discussion group for teenagers, and yet they all knew that they were foster children and that this group was sponsored by a child welfare agency. The worker omitted any comment about her role in the proceedings. The silence probably reflected their confusion about the group's purpose and their reluctance to begin. The worker's comment about the silence could reflect her own anxiety about their lack of immediate enthusiasm. In the rest of this session, the discussion was marked by wide shifts in subject matter, with youngsters talking about related topics (such as trouble with foster parents) and totally unrelated ones (such as TV shows).

Setting Limits: An Adolescent Acting-Out Boys' Group Ambiguity in contracting is common in work with children's groups. A good example is the "activity group" in a school setting, for children who are having difficulty with schoolwork or peers. A common problem with such groups results from having borrowed a traditional view of group work from the original group settings, which were leisure-time agencies, settlement houses, community centers, and the like. In this view, while members attended programs for what seemed like recreational purposes, the group leader actually had a hidden agenda related to agency purposes. In the school setting, the group worker might contract with the school administration to lead "clubs" that were designed for "teaching the youngsters how to get along better with each other and how to manage their own activities." A worker would argue that this would help the children get along better in school. The worker would view the group as a medium to "change the group members' patterns of behavior." The assumption is that a transfer of training will occur, and the learning from the group experience will make the children better students. A further assumption is that the worker can influence the group members indirectly by using the group activity as a medium for the "real purpose." The validity of both assumptions is questionable.

I have written elsewhere about the ways in which group members can use activities (singing, games, crafts, and so on) as important tools in their work (Shulman, 1971). There are many routes whereby group members can provide mutual aid for one another; certainly, it would be a mistake to view words as the only significant medium of exchange between people. The argument here challenges the view that program activity is the worker's tool for "changing" group members. For instance, the worker may withhold the real purpose of the group, leaving the members unclear as to the reason for the activity. When the youngsters look around during the first session, however, they know who the other children are and that they are the "losers," the "bad kids," or the "dummies" in the school. Because the contracting is not straightforward and honest, they become more anxious, often acting out their anxiety in disruptive behavior. The worker may assume that this behavior is intended to "test" authority or is an example of why the members have been referred in the first place. Early sessions may involve a great deal of limit setting by the worker, resulting in a battle of wills between the leader and the group. An alternative pattern is that the youngsters may involve themselves quickly in the group activities, which they might say are "a lot more fun than school." The worker would then find it harder to deal with school problems directly. Because the worker promised the teachers and the principal that the group would "change" the children's school behavior, the worker may be in trouble with the school staff when this does not happen and may then have to defend the rationale for the group against attacks by staff who view the group activities as "rewards for the kids' bad behavior."

In the example that follows, the worker makes an effort to clarify the real purpose with a group of 12- and 13-year-old sixth-graders described by the school staff as disruptive and noncooperative. The members respond to the worker's offer in two ways: First, they verbally describe their unhappiness with school as the worker encourages them to elaborate in this problem-swapping part of the contracting; second, they act out their anxiety through behavior that simultaneously shows the worker (the process) why they have been referred (the content). It is a new group worker's nightmare come true as she struggles to deal with the members' verbal and physical attacks on one another. In this excerpt, we see the worker integrating two roles. First, she sets limits on behavior in order to protect the individual members and the existence of the group itself. Second, she reaches for the meaning of the group members' behavior and points out the process-content integration.

> All five children know each other and are in classes together. Four are white, one Hispanic, and all come from troubled families. Juan has been physically abused by his estranged father. Greg has an older brother who is very violent and has terrorized this particular junior high school. James lives with his aunt, not his living parents. Jason (absent from the first meeting) has been sexually abused by his father. Collin's parents have separated. Three of these kids have had core evaluations and have been slotted for special education classes that have not started yet because of hiring difficulties within the school.

WORKER: I think that some of you could be nervous about being here. I want to try to reassure you and remind you that you are not in trouble, you have not done anything wrong, and this group is not detention or punishment. (James interjects.)

JAMES: We think it's great to get out of study period. (The others concur.)

WORKER: I hope this group becomes more than a way to get out of study period. The guidance director, Mr. Sher, and your teachers, Mr. Zacks and Ms. Trimble, are concerned because they want you to get more out of school and they feel you all can do much better. They thought I might be able to help you talk about some of the things that might be bothering you about school. You guys will be responsible for bringing up problems and solving them. My job will be to make sure we stay on the subject. Together, maybe we can think of ways to make things better for all of you at school, so let's get started. What is it like to be in sixth grade and in a brand new school for six weeks? (Greg raised his hand after I said the word *like.*) Greg, thank you for waiting until I finished, but it is not necessary for any of you to raise your hands in order to speak. I will ask that one person speak at a time and people should really listen to each other.

GREG: School sucks! (As Greg finishes, the others chime in.)

COLLIN: Yeah! School sucks! (Both Greg and Collin are trying to see whether I will react to the vulgarity. I do not react.)

JUAN: It's so boring.

JAMES: It's not as boring as elementary school.

JUAN: That is true; at least you are not stuck in the same room all day.

WORKER: In what ways is school boring?

> All the members begin talking at the same time, attempting to provide me with vignettes as to their own or present company's antics, making sure to hurl insults at each other; i.e., Greg stood on his chair and began to boisterously accuse Juan of never doing his homework. Juan snapped back that Greg was retarded and could not sit still. I told Greg to sit down in his chair and Juan not to name call. Collin asked permission to go to the bathroom (but didn't really need to go and did not ask again during the meeting). Then James spoke to me, stating that sometimes he finds schoolwork boring because he does not understand it. As I was focused on James and about to respond to him, Greg pulled the chair out from under Collin in such a way that Collin landed on his coccyx and was in severe pain.

WORKER: (Shouting) That's it! I want everybody to sit down and be quiet for a minute! (I gave Collin a brief neurological exam. I used to be an Emergency Medical Technician. Collin was OK. As his pain lessened, I helped him into his chair, and I sat back down.) I am sorry I yelled at you guys, but I felt things were getting out of hand. I got angry because I felt you guys were hurting each other with words, and, Greg, I know you did not want to hurt Collin, but you've all got to stick to our original agreement—no physical abuse. I think you guys were trying to hurt one another to avoid talking about what is hurting you inside about school. I wonder if this isn't what happens in class when things get uncomfortable.

The worker had to shout in order to get the group members' attention. In retrospect, given the reasons for referral for this group, acting out could be expected. Having a coleader might have helped the group leader feel more comfortable. The limit-setting intervention is familiar to the group members; they have experienced it in most of their classes. What may be different is the way in which she apologized for getting angry and then explained the limit as coming from concern about the members and her desire to provide a safe place in the group. The limit emerged from the reality of the group experience and was not expressed, as they may have often heard it, as an arbitrary imposition of authority (such as "In my class I will not tolerate this kind of behavior!"). Also, the worker did not fall into the trap of using this incident as an opportunity to preach or teach about "proper" behavior, as she had so unsuccessfully tried earlier ("Greg, thank you for waiting until I'd finished . . ."). If these children could work in this manner, they would not be in the group. Instead, she honestly expressed her own feelings, reinforced the element of the working agreement against physical abuse, and started to identify for the boys their maladaptive pattern of reacting. It will take some time until they learn to manage their feelings without using flight or fight to avoid their pain. Some may not be able to do it and may have to leave the group. However, with her first reactions, she let them know that this group (and she) will be different.

Impact of Authority: Involuntary Groups

The authority of the worker is always an issue in the first session. In some settings it can take on increased importance when the agency, and therefore the worker, carries functional responsibilities that may profoundly affect the client. Examples of workers with these additional functions include parole officers, child welfare workers in abuse situations, welfare workers dealing with income assistance, and adoptive workers who make judgments about who can or cannot receive a child. Fears of sanctions heighten normal concerns about the authority of the worker, and these fears can create a powerful obstacle that may block effective work. As with other obstacles, if the worker can reveal and explore them with the group members, then the power of the obstacle often declines.

A **mandatory client** group is one in which the members are required for some external reason to attend. For example, it may be a condition for getting their driving license returned, staying out of jail, keeping their children, or having their spouse return home. The common element is that group membership is involuntary; the members have not requested the service. They usually start the group presenting either passive resistance (through silence, apathy, creating an illusion of work, and so forth) or active resistance (through anger, confrontation, open denial of the problem). For the novice group worker, working with an involuntary group can increase the normal anxiety associated with new groups in the first session. The problems of engaging a reluctant client are similar to those raised in Parts II and III; however, in the group modality, the difference is characterized by the following statement of a young worker: "There are so many of them and only one of me!" Most new workers are so pleased at any conversation at all that they are perfectly willing to accept an illusion of work—a conversation in which the group members are "conning" the worker, each other, and even themselves.

The problem is that with the kinds of issues usually associated with involuntary groups, such as addiction, family violence, and sexual abuse, the denial itself is a problem. The requirement by the external authority that the group members must attend "or else" is a crucial part of the helping process and the only way to reach many of these clients. As long as the boss, spouse, agency, or court allows the client to continue to get away with behavior that is oppressive and dangerous to themselves and others, they will not seek help. Demanding that they face the problem is the beginning of the helping process. The tendency on the part of the client to minimize the problem lies at the core of the issue: They might say, for instance, "I only drink on weekends," "I only hit her with my open hand," "How can I raise my kids properly if I don't punish them to teach them right from wrong?" "The Bible says that to spare the rod is to spoil the child." One cannot begin to work effectively with such clients until their denial is dealt with. In one study, acceptance of a problem strongly and positively influenced client motivation, which in turn had a positive impact on the client's ability to use help (Shulman, 1991). Ability to use help influenced the working relationship with the social worker, as well as other outcome measures.

Stages of Change Model Some of the more recent conceptualizations about the nature of change and the change process can be helpful when one is working with involuntary clients, in that they try to reframe denial in a manner more amenable to intervention. The model developed by Prochaska and DiClemente (1982) describes the stages of change for people who are involved in addictive behavior. Their model is incorporated into a practice theory called *motivational interviewing*, in which the helping professional adapts her or his intervention to match the client's readiness for change (W. R. Miller & Rollnick, 1991). This model views clients as being at different stages of readiness for change and suggests that resistance is often the result of a counselor using the wrong strategy with respect to the client's stage of change. As DiClemente and colleagues suggest,

> A therapist can be understood as a midwife to the process of change, which has its own unique course in each case. The role for the therapist is to assist the individual, couple, or family in negotiating this process as efficiently and effectively as possible. In fact, the therapist can be a help or a hindrance to the process. . . . Skillful therapists will best facilitate change if they understand the process of change and learn how to activate or instigate the unfolding of the process. (DiClemente, Prochaska, Fairhurst, & Velicer, 1991, p. 191)

This stages-of-change model (DiClemente et al., 1991) suggests that clients can be in one of five stages:

1. ***Pre-contemplation: Resistance and the "Four R's."*** Individuals in pre-contemplation about a problem behavior such as smoking are not even thinking about changing that behavior. In fact, they may not see the behavior as a problem, or at least they do not believe it is as problematic as external observers see it. . . . There are many reasons to be in pre-contemplation. These can best be summarized as the "four R's": reluctance, rebellion, resignation, and rationalization. (p. 192)

2. *Contemplation: A Risk-Reward Analysis.* Contemplation is often a very paradoxical stage of change. The fact that the client is willing to consider the problem and the possibility of change offers hope for the change. However, the fact that ambivalence can make contemplation a chronic condition can be extremely frustrating. Contemplation is the stage when clients are quite open to information and decisional balance considerations. (pp. 194–195)

3. *Determination: Commitment to Action.* Deciding to take appropriate steps to stop a problem behavior or to initiate a positive behavior is the hallmark of the determination stage. Most individuals in this stage will make a serious attempt at change in the near future, and many have made an attempt to modify their behavior in the recent past. (p. 197)

4. *Action: Implementing the Plan.* What do people in action need from a therapist? They have made a plan and have begun to implement it by the time they come to the session. Often, making a therapy appointment has coincided with other change activity. Clients in the action stage often use therapy to make a public commitment to action; to get some external confirmation of the plan; to seek support; to gain greater self-efficacy; and finally to create artificial, external monitors of their activity. (pp. 198–199)

5. *Maintenance, Relapse, and Recycling.* The action stage normally takes three to six months to complete. This time frame is supported in our research on addictive behaviors, but may vary with the type of problem. Since change requires a new pattern of behavior over time, it takes a while to establish the new pattern. However, the real test of change for most problem behaviors, especially the addictive behaviors, is long-term sustained change over several years. This last stage of successful change is called "maintenance." . . . Relapse, however, is always possible in both the action and maintenance stages. (pp. 199–200)

By recognizing the difficulty associated with the change cycle, and by acknowledging relapse as part of the cycle, this approach allows the client to identify what she or he has learned from the relapse and to "recycle" into the stages to begin the action phase again, ideally this time in a stronger position to effect a longer or permanent "maintenance" of the change. Note that members of any group can each be in their own stage of change—from precontemplation to recycling. In the case of involuntary groups, many of the members may be in the precontemplative stage, not yet acknowledging the existence of a problem or the need to change. One way to view the requirement to participate in an involuntary group is that it may serve as the stimulus to help move a client from the precontemplative stage into the contemplative stage or further. While clients may not accept the idea that they have a substance abuse problem, for example, they can see that the use of the substance has led them to a conflict with the legal system, their boss, child welfare, their spouse or partner, and so on. One of the advantages of group practice is that a client in one stage of change may be motivated, by listening to a client in a later stage, to consider moving toward the action stage.

Most new group leaders are preoccupied with the potential negative impact of group members on each other and often miss the real strengths of mutual-aid groups with these populations. Once the worker deals openly with the authority issues in the first session, the group members may be the ones who most effectively identify each other's stage of change or confront denial. Further, by recognizing the involuntary nature of the group and encouraging a discussion of its impact on the potential for group effectiveness, the worker may be able to minimize this obstacle. In reality, while members may be forced to attend, they cannot be forced to participate in a significant way or to make real changes. The group leader's open recognition of this fact in a first session one may help to lower the barriers.

Male Batterers For example, in a first session with men who batter, Trimble (2005) included in his opening statement the following comment:

> I am sure it is possible to follow all of these rules and not change, not open up to facing yourself or the other men here. You can probably get through this group and really not change. That's up to you. The judge may order you to be here or your wife may be saying she won't come back unless you get help. And as I have just said, we require your anger diary and regular attendance in order for you to stay here, but no one can reach into your mind and heart and order a change. That's where you have complete control. (p. 360)

This honest recognition by the worker that change is in the control of the client helps to set the stage for the work to be done. The task of the group leader is try to find the faint lines of connection between the real, felt needs of the involuntary client and the potential services offered by the group. To do this, she or he must be ready to confront the illusion of work.

Driving While Intoxicated (DWI) This example comes from a mandatory substance abuse group for men who have committed a crime. It illustrates the worker's changing recognition of the meaning of denial, his recognition of his contribution to the resistance of the client, and his growing skill in involving the group members. In this case, the worker confronted the members early in the group, in an angry manner, failing to also provide the support the members need to face the problem.

According to the stages-of-change model, this form of confrontation of clients in the pre-contemplative stage, all exhibiting symptoms of the "four R's" described earlier (reluctance, rebellion, rationalization, and resignation), may stiffen their resistance. W. R. Miller and Rollnick describe it as the "confrontation-denial trap" (1991, p. 66). Essentially, as the group leader insists on the presence of a problem and the need for change, the client will argue the opposite—that there is no problem—until the interaction becomes an escalating battle. Another trap in early sessions is the "expert" trap, in which the group leader appears to have all the answers and tries to "fix" the client. A third and common one is the "labeling" trap, where the worker attempts to pressure the client to accept the socially unacceptable label of "alcoholic." Finally, the authors describe the "premature-focus" trap, where the counselor attempts to home in on the substance abuse problem when the client needs first to deal with broader issues (pp. 66–69).

The confrontation-denial trap in particular is illustrated in a third session of a mandatory group for drug users and alcoholics convicted of a crime. This is also an example of how contracting can take place over time and may not be completed in a first session.

August 28 (Third Session)

It was at this particular session where I was becoming very frustrated. I failed to interpret their resistance and came on too strong. In this group there was a lot of resistance and denial. John stated, "I went out over the weekend and got drunk." I tried to confront this and I felt like I was hitting a stone wall. He did not see this as a problem, and some of the other group members supported this type of behavior. I confronted those that continued to use but kept on stating that they did not have a problem, and they had a right to use.

I felt myself getting mad at the group, and they clearly sensed this. John asked, "Why are you picking on me?" Gary stated, "You don't have a right to tell us what to do." Gary was telling me that I cannot control their lives. Outside of the group they can do what they want. This made them more resistant, and one individual seemed to get a little angry with me. Steve, who is a marijuana addict and admits to that problem, has stopped using but continues to drink. I confront him on this, and he stated, "I don't have a drinking problem, so why is it a problem if I drink?" The tone throughout the session was my confronting and their denying. I really felt that I missed tuning in with their feelings about loss of control. For the next year or so the court will be in control of their lives. At the end of the group, I felt exhausted. I really never came to realize it until after I presented my case to the staff and our clinical supervisor.

Armed with the advice of supervisor and colleagues, the worker decided to stop pushing the clients during the next session and to relinquish control of the group. This led to a more comfortable meeting for the group leader and more active involvement in discussion by group members. However, the discussion was an illusion of work. A more helpful response during the first or second session would have been for the worker to explore with the members what makes it hard for them to face the problem. In addition, a focus by the worker on the negative consequences of the behavior may miss the important positives associated with the behavior that the client would have to give up. In referring to clients in the contemplative stage, W. R. Miller and Rollnick (1991) suggest using early sessions to explore "both sides of the coin," for example, by asking, "Tell me about your use of cocaine. What do you like about it? And what is the other side? What are your worries about using it?" (p. 72). This approach involves support integrated with confrontation and an effort to avoid the confrontation-denial trap.

September 18 (Fifth Session)

In group tonight, I had two new members beginning. I decided to have all the members speak about their drug and alcohol use, both past and present. Having the two new members was a benefit. This was one of the best groups in a while. The two new members were both sober. One stated, "I am an addict and I need to stay drug-free." This was helpful for other members to hear, because for them it seems to become more real. As I went around, some of the other members were now able to say that they may have a problem. A couple of the older members have also been sober for the last couple of weeks. In this group, people seemed to be more open. I still am confronting them on their denial, but not in a direct way. One tactic I have used is to ask all the members to stop using for a month, just to see how it feels for them. The ones still using refused but were willing to compromise. They agreed to cut their use in half. I told them that I felt that was OK. To me this seemed like a good intervention.

September 25 (Sixth Session)

The focus in this group session was on the difficulties of getting off of drugs. The members spoke about how some drugs are very difficult to get off of, particularly cocaine. There are two members, Bob and John, who continue to use. An interesting thing happened: A couple of the group members confronted them. This felt good, because for a change I did not have to do the confronting. It is now where I am beginning to feel that some of the denial is beginning to break down. The walls are slowly beginning to crack. I have to admit that part of the reason is because of the new members, who have brought in a positive attitude. There has been less silence in the group over the last couple of sessions.

Current Status of the Problem

I feel that this group is now beginning to head in a more positive direction. My role now in this group is to try and keep it heading in that direction. I feel that one thing I have learned is that it is unproductive to confront in a negative way. It only gets me and the other group members frustrated. Another ongoing problem is trying to keep this group feeling safe for the members. Since it is an open-ended group, there are new members coming in every ten weeks or so. At times this is helpful, but other times it seems like the group digresses. In the last few weeks, having a couple of new members begin was very productive for the group.

One thing I hope to do is to keep this group continuing to look at their own drinking or drug use in a more honest way. I need to let them decide when they are ready to get sober and not try to force it on them. I need to realize that the most I might be able to do is to educate them and at least give them respect and understanding about their addictions. It will be important for me to understand that at this time and space they are not ready to stop, and the reality is they may need to get into more trouble before they are willing to come to the realization that they are addicts and have to take more responsibility for their actions.

If this worker could go back and redo the first session using his current understanding his opening might have been quite different. For example, in another first session for men convicted of driving while intoxicated, when the worker sees men pointedly folding and putting away the schedule of topics for discussion, she directly confronts their reluctance to be present. When one of the men (an internal leader) says he does not want anyone calling him an alcoholic, instead of falling into the trap of the power struggle described in the earlier example, the worker writes, "Don't Want" on a flip chart and below it writes, "To be called an alcoholic." She then asks, "What else don't you want?" A second member says he does not want to be made to feel guilty. She writes that down as well. As the list grows, it becomes clear that by exploring the resistance rather than fighting it, the worker and the group members have actually developed a list of topics for the group. "Am I an alcoholic?" "What are the triggers that lead to my drinking?" "What are the things I have done with myself, my family, my job that I now feel guilty about?" When she summarizes the list at the end of the session and suggests these are the exact issues they can explore, she has demonstrated her understanding of the pre-contemplative stage and the way in which initial resistance (the process) may be understood as the beginning of work on the content.

All new workers face the struggle to synthesize support and demand, particularly with populations in denial (or the pre-contemplative stage). This skill comes with experience. The first step requires that the worker look closely at his or her own feelings and begin to manage them effectively. This frees the worker to deal with resistance by using the affective energy that comes from caring for the client. In the example of work with men who batter, described earlier, Trimble (2005) illustrates this synthesis by responding in the following way to a new group member's refusal to disclose the specifics of the violence committed toward his wife:

> I know it's hard to face it, to realize you hurt someone you love. Many men feel guilty and don't want to talk. But you can't change a problem that you try and forget. The basic goal here is to help you stop being violent. To do that, we start by asking you to tell exactly what you did when you were violent with your wife. (pp. 364–365)

The examples in this section and the additional process recordings on the text's companion website illustrate how the worker's authority is a crucial issue in first sessions of a group. It will remain an issue throughout the life of the group (see Chapter 11). However, the impact of authority is heightened in the early sessions before the development of a working relationship, which can cause authority to be a major obstacle to group development. Openly recognizing and clarifying the issue of authority diminishes its power to obstruct.

Working With Specific Client Problems

Some groups require attention to a particular problem. The specific concern facing the members of the group needs to be stated clearly and without embarrassment in the worker's opening statement. Providing examples can serve as "handles" for the group members. In the following example and those on the text's companion web page, we see how important this directness and specificity is to successful contracting.

Parents of Children With Cerebral Palsy In the next example, a worker begins a group for parents of children with cerebral palsy.

> Everybody had already introduced themselves, so I began by saying I wanted to give them an idea of what the group was about and then find out what they thought. I said that bringing up a teenager can be difficult, but when the teenager has cerebral palsy, a whole new set of difficulties and problems arises. In this group we are bringing parents together who are in a similar situation to discuss these problems. Hopefully, this will enable you to go back to your children with some new ideas of ways of coping with them. I also said that when I was talking to parents on the phone, they had mentioned several areas that were important to them right now. For example, what about starting high school? At this point Mrs. Boehm jumped in and said, "You know, that's exactly what I've been thinking about." She went on to describe her ambivalence about whether or not to send Stevie to a regular high school (he's 12). She talked about her desire for him to be with normal children, but she didn't really know if he'd be able to do it—it was a hard decision. She talked about this for quite a while. Finally, I said that the whole idea of the future for her son seemed to be an important thing to her now. She said, yes, it just began to be important in the last 6 months or so when she realized that he was getting older.

Women With MS: Crying in the First Session This group consisted of women, in their twenties to forties, all white and middle-class, who had recently been diagnosed as having the progressively disabling disease of multiple sclerosis (MS). This is the first session in which the women focused on the shock of the recent diagnosis and side effects. The group leader began with a request for introductions and a sharing of information about the illness. As is often the case, the sharing moved deeply into the work before the leader could make an opening statement. In retrospect, a brief statement about purpose and role prior to the introductions would have been helpful. As one member moved quickly and emotionally into the work, the group leader responded with support.

This was the first group meeting. As members arrived, those who had previously been in a group exchanged greetings with the leader. The newer people sat down quietly. Members were asked to introduce themselves and to share information on their illness. Specifically, members were asked to inform others when they were diagnosed, of the current status of their condition, and what they hoped to get out of being in the group. We went round in a circle. It was Cathy's turn. She appeared somewhat startled that it was her turn.

Cathy was asked to introduce herself. The group's attention focused on her as she tearfully began talking about herself. She related how she had been diagnosed with MS a few months ago and that she had been confused since then. "It must have been a very upsetting time for you; could you tell us more about it?" She related further how she had begun developing symptoms and after seeing doctors was diagnosed by a doctor who told her in a definitive way that she had MS. "It sounds like you heard about your illness in a very abrupt way and without any preparation or understanding of the implications it could have on your life."

Cathy went on to talk about her frustration with the illness. She described how her family and friends did not seem to understand what she was going through. "It would seem that the illness has not only been difficult for you, but also for others who are close to you." Cathy responded by saying that people did not know what to say to her nor did she know how much to tell them. "That is an understandable reaction when you first discover that you have MS." Cathy said that she felt very alone. There was silence. She went on to talk about how she could not remember things and would say incorrect words for what she meant to say. "That must be very frightening. You have brought up one of the side effects of this illness. In this group you will find that others may have had similar experiences, and it may be helpful to find out how they have coped."

Jane pulled from her purse a sticker notepad and declared that she used these everywhere to help her remember. Others agreed that these pads are very useful. I said, "You have made an important step in coming here tonight and sharing your feelings with the group."

At times throughout this exchange, Cathy was crying. When a group member cries during a session, the others may feel uncomfortable and embarrassed. Some models of practice argue that the group leader should control such expressions of emotion in a first session, so that they will not frighten other members. Unfortunately, this approach sends the wrong message to the members. They perceive the workers as being uncomfortable with the emotions, which reinforces the norms leading to an illusion of work. Rather than controlling the expression of emotion by ignoring it, changing the subject, moving to other members, and so on, the worker needs to reassure the member and the group that the expression of strong feelings is natural and appropriate. In understanding and accepting these feelings, the worker demonstrates a way of working that will help the group members create a new culture in which all the emotions of sadness, anger, joy, and so forth can be freely expressed.

When a group has begun with a particularly strong first session, in terms of emotional expression and quickly getting to core issues, the worker needs to use some time at the end of the session to discuss the members' reactions. At times, members will feel embarrassed after having expressed strong feelings or ideas that they think are theirs alone. Some attention to this issue often results in other group members reassuring the exposed members that they are not alone. For example, in the MS group, the worker could have said near the end of the session,

> I would like to take a few minutes to talk about your reactions to this first session. You all shared some strong feelings this evening about what you are going through—particularly you, Cathy. In my experience, sometimes people feel uncomfortable when they share so much or have cried at a first meeting. They wonder what the other group members are thinking and feeling. Could we talk about it for a moment?

Inevitably, some members will come to the support of the individual who cried and reassure him or her that they shared in the emotions. Some members may raise their concerns about how they are going to feel if so much emotion is shared at the meetings. This provides the worker and the group an early opportunity to discuss the impact of emotions on their lives and on the group itself. Whatever the outcome of the discussion, it is usually better to have it at the session than to have the individual (Cathy) or the other client (the group) worrying about these issues on their own.

Impact of the Setting

The setting for the group meeting will affect the group itself. One cannot simply invite the members into a meeting room, close the door, and pretend the system surrounding the group is not there. For example, in residential settings such as group homes, hospitals, or prisons, the members bring their common environmental experiences into each session. A suicide attempt on a psychiatric hospital ward will affect the content and process of the ward meeting that follows. Convicts in a group session will have to overcome the culture in the prison that makes being honest and vulnerable extremely risky. In their first sessions, members of a foster parent group may want to complain about agency policies and social workers, rather than focus on parenting. In many ways, the setting of service will affect the nature of the group contract.

Chapter 15 explores in detail the dynamics and skills involved in helping group members with the task of negotiating their environment. In this section we focus on contracting and beginning issues in groups where relating to the environment is central to the work.

In the following illustration, a social worker in a hospital contracts with a patient ward group to discuss their illness and hospitalization. He views the hospital as a complex system that patients must negotiate, and he sees the group as a vehicle for helping them do that.

> I introduced myself to the patients and asked them to go around and introduce themselves, which they did. I asked whether they had been told anything about this group. They hadn't. I told them we get together to discuss what it means to be a patient in the hospital, how it feels being in a strange place away from family and friends. I said that often patients found it difficult getting used to a hospital experience, and sometimes it helped to talk with other patients. Often they have the same feelings of anxiety, fear, and uncertainty; we get together as a group so that we can freely talk about hospital experiences and feelings around

being a patient. I mentioned that they will probably notice that I take notes from time to time, the reason being so that I can look back on the session to see where I could have been more helpful to them.

Mrs. Jones began talking about the doctors and how they change, just after you get used to one doctor. I said that it must be a frustrating and anxious time when the doctors change. She agreed. Mrs. Beatty said that this is her first hospital experience and it was upsetting. Mrs. Carter said that she's used to hospitals and she felt she adapted well. Mrs. Victor said that the system didn't bother her. I asked Mrs. Beatty why she felt so upset about the hospital. She said it was strange and she felt all alone. If it hadn't been for Mrs. Carter "adopting" her, she would never have stayed after the first hour. I remarked that it must have been terribly frightening, this being her first time here and her not knowing the ropes. She agreed.

Mrs. Carter said that the hospital system didn't bother her, but she's scared they won't find out what's wrong with her. She was very sick at home, and she hopes they'll be able to do something. I said that it's a natural feeling to worry about one's illness, particularly when the diagnosis is not known. At this point, an orderly came to take Mrs. Jones to X-ray.

Mrs. Carter said that when you're not told what's happening, you feel bad. I asked in what way she felt bad. She answered that all of a sudden you're told to go through a difficult test or examination, about which you know nothing, and you feel horrible. I remarked that you need time to adjust to the idea of a test and prepare yourself for it. She agreed. I asked whether the others had similar experiences. Mrs. Beatty said one day a doctor came in for a heart examination. She was very upset because nobody had told her anything about it and she was thinking she must have had a heart condition; otherwise, why would she have to have this examination? The nurse explained that this is routine and that every patient who is on the ward gets cardiac and respiration examinations while they're here, and it certainly does not mean that there is anything wrong with her. I asked Mrs. Beatty how she felt now, knowing that it's a routine examination. She said, much easier; she would have felt less upset had she known this before.

In addition to helping the patients adjust to the difficult situation and clarify their concerns, the worker can use this group as a vehicle for change within the hospital. Serious illness often makes patients feel out of control over their lives. When a system appears to treat them as objects, their feelings of helplessness and impotency increase. These feelings can affect their use of the medical services (as in following the treatment plan), their satisfaction with services, and their ability to hear, understand, and remember what is said in conversations with medical personnel (Shulman & Buchan, 1982). Involving staff in the group sessions can help bridge the gap between the providers and consumers of service. In Part V, I explore how a worker can use patient feedback to affect the way in which the system relates to the client. This is the mediating function applied to the second client, the system. As will become evident, before workers can empower their clients, they must feel empowered themselves.

Impact of Time

Time can significantly affect the worker's activities in the first session. For example, some groups meet for a single session and must incorporate the beginning, work, and ending/transition phases in that time frame. In this section, we discuss the variations in a first session of a *short-term group*—one that is designed to meet for only a single or a few sessions.

In the first session of my married couples' group, described earlier, I could use the entire session for contracting and setting the stage for work, because we had many sessions to follow. Knowing this affected the work of the group workers and members alike. For example, I did not feel the need to confront defenses; instead, I could concentrate on providing a clear framework and as much support as possible. The group members could take their time, as well, starting with near problems designed to test the waters until they felt safe.

This contrasts with a group I led for single parents, which illustrates the differences in a first session when time is limited. The entire group experience needed to be contained in three 3-hour sessions, held over one evening and a day. Community professionals in a small, rural town felt the need for a mutual-aid group for single parents, so I was invited to fly into town to spend one evening and one day. Local helping professionals also attended the group, with two purposes in mind. First, they could provide ongoing services to the group members after the sessions were over. I felt it was important that resources be readily available to pick up with clients on issues that might be raised through the group meetings. Second, they could observe my group leadership so that they might be better equipped to start mutual-aid groups of their own. The group was advertised as open to the public, and many community professionals suggested it to their clients. I met the 15 group members who attended the night of the first session. In this section, I focus on the implications for the first session only.

Before the group meeting, I had tuned in to the possible themes of concern and had prepared an opening statement that I hoped would focus us quickly on their most central concerns. I also tuned in to two difficulties. As an "expert" from out of town, who would not be around long, I imagined that getting started with such a new group, in a small town where people tended to know about each other, would be challenging. Also, I saw the difficulty in opening up issues in a short-term context. I decided I needed to move quickly from the problem-swapping stage into work on specific issues, because we did not have the luxury of a long contracting phase. In addition, I felt we needed to demonstrate quickly how helpful the group could be, if members were to risk sharing. Finally, I tuned in to my own hesitations about risking in a first session and prepared to raise the issue directly with the group whenever I sensed defensiveness or the illusion of work. The following is an excerpt from my recording of the session dictated immediately following the meeting.

> I explained the purpose of the group as providing an opportunity for single parents to discuss with each other some of the special problems they faced because they were alone. I explained that my role was not as an expert with answers for them, but rather, I would try to help them to talk and to listen to each other, and to provide help to each other from their own experiences. In addition, I would throw in any ideas I had that might be helpful. I then offered a few examples of possible concerns around dealing with friends and relatives after the split in the relationship, problems in relating to the ex-spouse, the financial strains, and problems that often accompanied being a single parent and the difficulties presented by the children. There was much head nodding as I spoke. I finished by describing briefly the phases that parents and children commonly go through after a separation (denial, anger, mourning, and finally, coming to terms with it). I then invited the participants to share their own

experiences and suggested that these could form an agenda for our work that evening and the next day.

There was a brief silence, and then Irene asked how long it took to go through the phases. I asked her why she was asking, and she said it was 3 years since her separation and she doesn't think she has passed through all of them yet. The group members laughed in acknowledgment of the meaning of the comment. I said I thought there must have been a great deal of pain and sadness, at the time of the split and since then, for it to still hurt after 3 years. I asked Irene if she could speak some more and she continued, in a more serious tone, by describing her ongoing depression. She described days in which she feels she is finally getting over things and picking herself up, followed by days when she feels she is right back to square one. Others in the group agreed and shared their own experiences as I encouraged them to respond to Irene's comments. I told them it might help just to know that they were "in the same boat" with their feelings.

I then asked if the group members could be more specific about what made it difficult. This resulted in a number of areas raised by members, which I kept track of in my written notes. They included most of the problems I had raised in my opening statement. There was much emotionally laden discussion of the first area, problems with friends and family, with a great deal of anger expressed toward others who "didn't understand" and related to them in ways that hurt.

Dick, a young man in his mid-twenties, spoke with great agitation about his wife, who had left him with their 6-month-old baby only 6 weeks before. The group seemed to focus on Dick, who expressed a very strong sense of urgency and was clearly still in a state of shock and crisis. I had earlier noted that Dick was the first to arrive that evening and, during the premeeting chatter, he had told the person next to him all of the crises he had gone through just to get there that night. I pointed out to the group that it seemed that Dick was feeling this concern about friends and relatives rather strongly, and in fact he had had a great deal of difficulty even getting here tonight. I asked if they would like to focus on problems with friends and relatives first, using Dick's example to get us started. They all agreed it would be helpful, including Dick.

My effort to move us more quickly into the work began with my contracting statement and continued when I responded to Irene's joking comment about "not getting through the phases yet" by reaching for the underlying hurt and bitterness. If we were to move quickly in the group, I felt I had to send an early message that I was ready to deal with the difficult feelings as soon as they were. The group responded by immediately moving into the painful feelings as well as the anger. Feeling the need to get into substantive work early in this first session, I moved to obtain group consensus on an initial theme of concern and to bring Dick's urgency to the members' attention. Thus, we moved into the work phase less than an hour after my opening statement. In the continuation of the first session description that follows, Dick's resistance to taking personal responsibility for his problems emerges. I responded with a demand for work, pointing out that we had little time in which to work.

After Dick described the details of his separation and his current living situation with the 6-month-old child, he went on to describe the problems. He emphasized the difficulty of living in a small town, and in his particular case, being in a personal service occupation that put him in daily contact with many town residents. He said, "Sure, I feel lousy, depressed, and alone. But some days, I feel I'm getting over things a bit, feeling a little bit up, and everywhere I go people constantly stop me to tell me how terrible things are. If I didn't feel lousy before I went out, I sure do by the time I get home."

Dick added a further complication, in that the baby had a serious case of colic and was crying all the time. He told the group that everyone was always criticizing how he handled the baby, and even his mother was telling him he wasn't competent and should move back home with her. He continued by saying he was so depressed by this that he had taken to not talking to anyone anymore, avoiding his friends, staying home alone at night, and going out of his mind. Others in the group shared similar versions of this experience. I said to Dick, "And that's the dilemma, isn't it? Just at the time you really need help the most, you feel you have to cut yourself off from it to maintain your sense of personal integrity and sanity. You would like some help, because the going is rough, but you're not sure you want to have to depend on all of these people, and you're not sure you like the costs involved." Dick nodded, and the other group members agreed.

After providing recognition and support for these feelings, I tried to move the group into examining how they handled their conversations with friends and relatives, as a way of dealing with these feelings. I encountered a good deal of resistance to this idea, with Dick balking each time I tried to get him to look at how he might have handled a conversation differently. He evaded this by jumping quickly to other comments or examples, or by expressions that seemed to say, "If you only knew my mother/friends, you would realize it is hopeless." When Rose, a member of the group in her early fifties, confronted him from the perspective of his mother—she had children close to him in age—he rejected her comments.

I pointed out what was happening. I said, "It seems to me that when I or a group member suggests that you (Dick) look at your part in the proceedings, you won't take in what we are saying." I said I only had a day and a half with the group, so I really couldn't pussyfoot around with them. I wondered if it was tough for Dick, and all of them, to take responsibility for their part in their problems. Dick smiled and admitted that it was hard. He already felt lousy enough. Others joined in on how easy it was to blame everyone else and how hard it was to accept any blame themselves. I agreed that it was tough, but I didn't think I would be of any help to them if I just sat here for a day and a half agreeing about how tough things were for them. The group members laughed, and a number said they didn't want that.

At this point, Doris, one of the three workers participating in the group, surprised us all by saying that she had intended to listen and not talk during the session, but that listening to Dick's problem made her want to share hers. She said she had come to the group as an observer; however, she was pregnant and unmarried and therefore was about to become a single parent. She thought she was having the same problem in communicating with her mother as Dick was having with his. It was a classic example of a conflict between a mother who is hurt and embarrassed and a daughter who feels rejected at a critical moment in her life. At my suggestion, Rose offered to role-play the mother as Doris tried to find a new way to talk to her mother. The group was supportive, but at the same time, following my example, they also became quite confronting with each other, in a healthy way.

Dick listened and participated in the work on Doris's problem and, as is often the case, was able to learn something about his own situation as he watched someone else struggling with the same concerns. When I asked him later if he had taken something from it, he said it had helped him a lot to see how he was holding back his real feelings from friends and his own mother. I pointed out to all of the group members what a shock their situation was to their friends and close relatives and how, at first contact, they could not respond in a way which met their needs. I said, "This does not mean they don't love you. It just means that they have feelings and aren't always able to express them. Your mixed messages also make it difficult."

Cerrise, another worker/observer in the group, joined the discussion at this point and described how she had felt when close friends had split up her marriage. She realized now that it had taken her a couple of months to get over being so angry at them for ending the marriage, because she loved them both. She hadn't been able to reach out to them to support them, but she was lucky, because they had not given up on her and she had been able to work it out. Dick said that hearing that helped a lot. That was what was probably going on with some of his friends.

Carrie, who was both an unmarried parent and a worker in the community, described her own experiences with her mother when she split up. She shared how she had involved her mother in the process, had let her know her feelings, and that she wanted her mother's love and support but felt she had to handle the problems herself. Dick listened closely and said that this was probably what he had not been able to do. We did some role-play on how Dick could handle the conversation with his mother—how he could articulate his real feelings. The group was supportive and helpful.

When I asked the group how they felt about this discussion thus far, Doris said it was helpful because I kept stressing the positive aspect, the reaching out and caring between people. Most of them were so upset they could only see the negatives. The discussion turned to how much they needed others to talk to about what they were going through. As the session neared the end, in typical "doorknob" fashion Dick revealed that a close male friend of his, in a similar situation with a young child, had told him he was considering committing suicide. He went on to tell us, with tears in his eyes, that the friend had just killed himself. I said, "It must have hit you very hard when that happened, and you must have wondered if you could have done something more to help." Dick agreed that was so, and the group members offered him support.

After some time, I asked Dick if he was worried about his own situation, since he had many of the same feelings as his friend. He said he was worried, but that he thought he would be strong enough to keep going, to have a goal in life, to make it for his child. I told him he had shown a lot of strength just coming to the group and working so hard on his problem. Carrie said that he was not alone, and that he could call her if he needed someone to talk to—as a friend or as a worker. Rose pointed out that there was a single-parent social group at the church, and Dick said he had not realized that. Others in the group also offered support. I asked Dick how he felt now, and he said, "I feel a lot better. I realize, now, that I'm not so alone." Irene, who had opened the discussion by saying she had not yet gone through all of the phases, summarized the evening's work when she said, "I guess we are all struggling to find ways of saying to friends and close relatives, 'Please love me now, I need you.'" The discussion ended, and we agreed to pick up again in the morning.

This example has illustrated how a group can move quickly into the middle phase of practice if the worker makes a demand for work. We shall return to this group example in Chapter 11 to explore the middle and ending phase work that followed this opening session.

Recontracting

After watching the videotape of the couples' group described earlier, many students feel intimidated. As they often put it, "My first session didn't go that way!" I reassure them that neither did my early efforts. Even if the new group worker has done excellent preparatory work, is clear about the working contract, and has role-played an opening statement with a supervisor, unexpected events and problems can occur. Retrospective analysis often reveals that the worker left something out or the actual opening statement did not resemble the carefully constructed and rehearsed version. New group workers are understandably nervous when leading their first groups and should not be too hard on themselves. They also need to realize that they usually have an opportunity to recontract with a group if they do not get it right the first time. **Recontracting** is the process in which the worker reopens the issues of contracting by providing a clearer statement of purpose or exploring the group members' resistance or lack of connection to the service. Even if they are able to begin exactly as planned, group members may not understand or even hear the opening statement. Contracting in an ongoing group always takes place over several sessions.

Another common problem may be encountered when workers join an already functioning group: They may have to recontract in terms of their role as leader and the purpose of the group. Joining an ongoing group as a coleader and discovering that the contracting was never done or has been done badly can also be disconcerting. One student put it this way: "This sounds great in class, but I don't think the psychiatrist running our group has ever read your book!" In some circumstances, the ongoing group leaders have adopted a group practice model that operates under assumptions that differ from the interactional, mutual aid model put forward here. I reassure students that there are many frameworks for helping and that this circumstance would provide them with an opportunity to see another model in action. Also, elements of the interactional model can often be integrated easily into other frameworks.

In some groups, there simply is no model at all. Groups can be disorganized and unfocused, with members and the group leaders unclear about the purpose. Group sessions can resemble individual counseling in a group, with each member being helped by the group leader in turn. In this case, it becomes the social worker's job to try to influence the process with coleaders and members to recontract for a more effective group.

In the example that follows, we look at recontracting in the context of one's own group. Then we explore further the concerns arising from contracting with an ongoing group.

Recontracting With One's Own Group

In the detailed example that follows, a worker with an open-ended group in a shelter for battered women begins a first session with a mixed message about the contract. In her opening statement she briefly mentions several powerful themes related to the abuse and oppression that have brought these women to the shelter. In her structuring of the first session, however, she moves immediately to her agenda of providing information on independent-living skills. Rather than structuring time for problem swapping, which would have allowed the women some control over the agenda, the worker makes the decision for them. If one applies the oppression psychology outlined in Chapter 1, encouraging these women to take control of their own group could be seen as an important step toward independent living.

Several group members signal that they are at a different place in their needs related to this group. While independent-living skills, job opportunities, and so on all matter to these women, at this moment their sense of urgency may be more connected to their abuse and their living situations. The worker continues to control the first session, providing a sermon about the importance of community support. Later, her understanding and skills evolve over the next few sessions as she recontracts with the women.

Session 1

As I was setting the room up for the group session, one resident of the shelter arrived. She helped me arrange chairs and, as other residents arrived, she introduced me to them. I had planned to go around the room so that each woman could tell me her name, her length of stay at the house, and the number of children in her family, but I decided against it since we had already been introduced. Now I feel that I still should have asked them for a little more information about themselves. I did tell the women a few things about myself and then I stated the purpose of the group. I said, "The purpose of this group is to provide you with some helpful information that you can use once you leave the house. The group will also provide you with an opportunity to talk about feelings, experiences, and concerns that you might have about the different topics we'll be discussing. Tonight's topic is independent living skills." I went on to say, "Some of you are here because of abuse either by a boyfriend or a husband. You may find tonight that you have some feelings in common with each other. Some of you may be here for reasons other than abuse, and you may have your own set of circumstances that you'll want to share. My role is to help you to talk and to listen to each other. So I hope that we can all learn tonight not only from the material I have brought but also from the comments that we share with one another."

I began by giving the women information about two job-training programs. One woman, Linda, talked about a job-training program that she had attended and how she had landed a job afterward. Two other women talked about the skills they had, one in accounting, the other in word processing and stenography. Four out of the seven women were interested. The other three women showed no interest at all. I didn't ask them why they seemed uninterested. I feel that I should have confronted them.

From there we moved on to the subject of community support. I stated that many people think asking for help is a sign of weakness. People, in many cases, think it's important to handle problems on their own. I said I disagreed with this type of thinking. I said people who think this way are oftentimes worse off because individuals aren't always equipped to handle situations that come up on their own. I said that people who look to their community for support could be better off in many ways. I then asked the women if they had any ideas or suggestions on where to find community support when they leave the house. No one had any suggestions off the bat, so I mentioned places such as churches, local community action programs, etc.

Although the worker wrote, "We moved on to the subject," she should have written, "I moved on"—clearly, the members did not move with her. In the next excerpt, an internal leader emerges to move the women to a discussion of the "here and now" of their experiences in the house and the pain of the abuse they carry with them.

One woman said she was very glad to be at the house. She said she came into the shelter wondering what the other women would be like and found out that many of the women were just like her. She said, "It feels good to be with people who have the same problem." She said that when she lived with her husband, he would be on her mind all day long. She would worry about what he would be like when he came home. Before she came to the house, she would stay with her parents when her husband became abusive. Eventually, her parents would talk her into going back with her husband. She said, "Here at the house, you get support. You're told he has a problem, not you." She said she was very glad to hear that. I said, "So it sounds as if you're relieved to be here." She said, "Yes."

Another woman said she used to wonder what her husband would find wrong when he came home. She also said he wouldn't allow her to talk with friends. I said, "You probably feel good that you don't have that pressure over you now." She agreed. In addition, she said she planned to attend Al-Anon meetings for support once she left the house.

In the next excerpt, one of the members sends a signal to the worker that the session is not meeting her needs. The worker's written comment about "reaction formation" indicates that she noted the negative feedback and reacted with internal anger and an external smile. The worker's early anxiety about doing a good job makes it hard for her to hear negative feedback. The group members' anxiety about their dependency on the shelter may make sharing such feedback difficult. The discussion finally turns to money and issues of economic oppression that are closely tied to a major source of anxiety experienced by these women—economic survival. The worker does not understand the meaning of the flight behavior and thinks that she will need to do a better job at setting out the rules—a step that would cut off the expression of feeling rather than dealing with it.

One woman who had left the group for 15 minutes came back and said, "What did I miss out on?" Angela, one of the uninterested women, said, "Oh, you only missed out on some boring information." I should have asked her why she found the information so boring. Instead, I just smiled at her (reaction formation?). Then Janice, a night staff person, joined the group. Everything was fine until she started talking with the woman next to her. They continued to talk between themselves for about 5 minutes. I didn't know how to handle this situation.

When we started to talk about the area of financial management and I mentioned budgeting, one woman said, "What do I want to know about budgeting? I don't have any money to budget." Then she said that actually she did want to know about budgeting. She felt that someone should have sat down with her at the welfare office and shown her how to get the most for her money. Angela said she was always worried about having enough money to make ends meet, and she didn't see what good a budget would do. Angela has four children, one of whom is handicapped. The group began to talk about how she could get help for the handicapped child with cerebral palsy. The women suggested that she or her social worker call a cerebral palsy foundation. I turned to Angela and said, "You must get very discouraged at times." She agreed.

As the discussion continued about financial management, the discussion became somewhat chaotic. People were talking at once, cutting each other off. The women were skipping from topic to topic. I finally asked them to please talk one at a time. For the most part three women were doing all the talking. I could see that the other women were not paying attention. Next week I'd like to lay down some ground rules for discussion and emphasize the fact that everyone has important comments to make and we should take the time to listen to one another.

With hindsight, the worker might have been able to address the second client, the group, by acknowledging that the discussion was not hitting home for all of them. She could have identified the flight behavior as an understandable expression of the anxiety associated with the economic oppression and humiliation of being on welfare. These women had to demonstrate remarkable courage to overcome the economic restraints that our society places on them when they consider fleeing an abusive home. Inadequate financial supports function as a societal "shackle" helping to keep women chained to oppressive family situations. The worker might have responded to the group with the same empathy she had demonstrated moments before when she said to Angela, "You must get discouraged at times."

Next, the worker is surprised when a shelter staff person intervenes with the offer of going to church the next Sunday. This staff member may have responded to the group members' anxious flight with what she felt might help.

Suddenly, Janice, the staff person, asked if anyone wanted to go to church the following Sunday. This question was somewhat disruptive because we were talking about managing money at this point. She may have been responding to our discussion earlier about finding community support. It's difficult to say. The discussion became focused again when Linda asked for information about apartment hunting. One woman said that transportation was a big problem. Everyone chimed in on this. One woman said they should write a letter to the governor asking him to supply a car for the shelter. The women got excited at this point. I agreed that it sounded like a good idea, and I asked who would be in charge of writing the letter. Pam volunteered. Janice, the staff person, said they could talk about the letter the next day at the house meeting.

I told them that we had discussed a number of important issues. I said I hoped they would be thinking about questions and ideas for next week's session on single parenting, and said I would see them next Wednesday night.

For the second session, the worker again planned an agenda without the involvement of the women. Even the best plans can go awry, however, and the worker had problems with a film projector. The worker's hidden agenda was selling to the mothers the importance of providing emotional support to their children, but the women needed support for themselves to strengthen them for their children. The "deviant" member of the group the previous week, Angela, who had said that the group was boring, sent another signal the second week through her nonverbal behavior of sitting outside of the group. The worker was still too insecure to reach for it. The response of the other women, to bring Angela into the group, may have represented their understanding of her role and importance. This time, the worker reached for Angela's individual needs by providing some concrete help. Although this was an effort at relationship building and an expression of individual caring, it did not deal with Angela's message on behalf of the group-as-a-whole.

Session 2

I started the group by asking the women if they had any questions about the material I had handed out the previous week. No questions. I told them, as I had the previous week, that tonight's topic would focus on parenting. I said that I had planned to show a 15-minute film called *Special Times,* but the projector I had rented didn't work correctly. Since I had watched the film twice, I said I would go over the main points of the film and we could have a discussion focusing on these points. I said, "Before we get started, let's go around the room so that each of you can tell me how many children you have, their names and ages." After the women told me about their families, I asked Angela to move in closer because she was outside the circle of the group. She said she was fine where she was. Two of the women got up, went over and picked up the love seat that Angela was sitting on, and moved her closer to the rest of the group. Everyone, including Angela, had a good laugh.

At this point, I mentioned to Angela (the woman who, last week, had said the group was boring) that I had called the Cerebral Palsy Foundation. "They gave me a few referrals that might be helpful to you." I said that I could make another call for more information or I could give her the number to call. I said, "You can think about it and let me know at the end of group whether you want to call or if you'd like me to call." Angela talked for 5 minutes about the problems she was having finding services for her handicapped son. Everyone in the group listened.

When Angela finished, the focus on parenting began. I told them the movie's main point is that a parent should set aside a special time—1 or 2 hours every week—to spend with her child. The parent and child should plan ahead for this time. Additionally, the parent should ask the child what he or she wants to do. The child should decide. Angela said, "My son would say, 'Ma, take me to Zayre's and buy me something.'" Everyone laughed. I said that there had been a scene in the movie where a mother initially felt uncomfortable with this special time. The son said he wanted to browse through the sports department at the store. They spent an hour looking at sports equipment (not necessarily buying anything). The time they spent together was enjoyable for both of them.

Linda said, "One day I brought my child to the store. I put her on the swing set in the children's department. She had a great time. While she was on the swing, I went to the sewing department and bought some material." I said, "Well, you know, there is a scene in the film where a mother and daughter are at a park. The mother is reading a book while the child is playing on the slide. The narrator says, 'Let's do this scene over.' When the scene is shown again, the mother and child are sliding on the slide together. The narrator says, 'The important thing to remember is that you do things together during this special time. Change your role from parent to that of a close friend.'"

Linda said she didn't remember her mother ever getting on a slide with her; however, she said she got the point. She said, "You don't care if the kid's face is dirty and you're not on their back saying don't do this and don't do that." I said, "You can see how important this special time is especially since most of you, as single parents, are the ones mainly responsible for disciplining your children. It's good for both you and your child to get a break from this role." Cindy said, "Yes, I'm always disciplining the children. Then when they go with their father, they're like angels." At first, she couldn't understand it. Then Kathy, the counselor, said, "Did you ever stop and think that maybe they're afraid he won't come back to see them if they don't act very good?" Cindy said she had never thought of that. She said now she sits her children down and says, "You have to listen to me. I'm your mother. I know what's best for you." These talks are helping her relationship with her children.

I told Cindy that I had read a little about single parenting. One writer had mentioned that sometimes the child will act very good with the parent who is not living in the household in hopes that the parents will get back together. The children think that somehow they can be responsible for the parents getting back together. She said, "You know, one time when Julie was only two, Matt and I happened to be with her one day together. We were walking and she was between Matt and me. We were both holding Julie's hands. Julie started swinging our hands back and forth. Then, she took our hands and brought them together." Cindy said, "I couldn't believe that at that age she knew that things weren't right between us and she wanted us back together."

I said that what Cindy had just mentioned brought us to another major point of the film. The narrator says that children should be encouraged to talk openly about their feelings. Cindy picked up on this point and said she agreed one hundred percent. She said when the children ask her questions she tries her best to answer them. "They ask me if I still love Daddy. I tell them that I do love Daddy, but in a different way. I tell them that it's not good for Daddy and me to live together." She said that her children listen to her. Linda said that she agreed with Cindy. She said that she's trying to explain to her daughter the changes that have taken place since they've come to the house. "My daughter doesn't know where she is or what's going on. She's clinging to me like a leech all of a sudden. I don't understand it." I asked Linda when she came to the house. She said 1 week ago. I said, "When parents split up, oftentimes the child is afraid that the parent the child is living with will also leave. Your daughter may be very afraid that you're going to leave her."

The next major point that the film made is that special time can take away the worries that parent and child have. I said, "I think all of you worry more than the average person because of abusive situations that you've been in. That's why special time is very important for you and your child. You can both put your worries aside." Cindy said, "The other day I took my two daughters to the beach. They were looking at snails, examining them closely." Pam broke in and said, "If that was my son, Jason, he wouldn't have looked at the snails, he would have eaten them." Everyone laughed. Cindy continued, "My daughters didn't fight, they didn't make a lot of noise. It was wonderful." I asked her how she felt. She replied, "I felt very relaxed." Pam jumped in to say, "One of the first days here at the house, I was playing with a couple of the kids. We started wrestling; we were laughing and playing for about an hour. We had so much fun. I felt great for the rest of the day. When I put Jason to bed at night when I'm relaxed, he falls asleep right away. I rock him and he falls asleep. If I'm aggravated or tense, I'll put him to bed and he won't fall asleep. He knows that something is wrong."

Linda said she feels that she is yelling at her child 24 hours a day. "My daughter does things that she never did before we came here." She said the other day her daughter was walking by Pam's son, Jason, and she slapped him on the face. Linda said she felt terrible about this. Pam said, "Don't worry about it. How do you think I feel? My son (who is big for his age) goes around trying to hug everyone. He's so big he knocks the kids over and they begin to cry. I feel the same way you do." I said, "Just the fact that you're expressing how you feel about your children's behavior makes it easier for you to understand one another." The women began to talk about how they discipline their children.

After a few minutes, I said, "Can we come back to Linda for a few minutes? I think she's very concerned about the changes she sees in her child since she came to the house." Linda said, "I wish I knew I was doing the right thing coming here with my daughter. I wish there was some research that said, 'It's better to leave your husband when the child is such and such an age'—then I could feel better. I don't want to be yelling at my child all day long." Vicki said, "But, Linda, every situation is very different from the next. It's not easy to say that for everyone who leaves her husband, the children should be a certain age. It takes time for a child to adjust to a new situation and a new environment." Angela said, "Look, as long as the kids aren't killing each other, I leave them alone. If one kid takes another kid's toy, at first they cry. But two minutes later they're playing with another toy." I was getting ready to ask Linda if she thought she should be home with her husband. But I didn't have to say anything. She said, "Well, I guess my only other choice is to go back home and have my child see my husband beat me up." I said, "Yes, that's right."

I wrapped up the discussion about the film by naming different activities that they might want to consider for special time. Then, I asked them how they thought the discussion went. Everyone thought it was a great discussion. They said they never have an opportunity during the week to get together to talk. At this point, Cindy started to talk about one of the children and the funny things he says and does. We sat and laughed for about 10 minutes. I felt very pleased that everyone seemed so relaxed—much more relaxed than last week. As everyone got up to leave, Cindy said, "This was a good discussion, even though you were only able to get a few words in." Linda said, "Yes, you might not think so, but you're really helping us." I thanked her and said I was glad that I could be of help to them.

The closing comment by Cindy, about the worker only being able to "get a few words in," reflects her sense of the worker's viewing her role as teaching. In many ways, these women used the film as a starting point and took the discussion to their own issues related to their stress and its impact on their children. As the worker felt more comfortable and started to refrain from giving advice, the members took over and the power of mutual aid became apparent.

In the third session, marked by changes in the group composition, the worker still began with an agenda; however, this time, she acknowledged that it was up to the group members to decide what they wished to discuss. The resulting conversation moved the group well into the middle phase.

The worker's fourth session presented a completely new group of six women. This gave the worker an opportunity to start again. The worker's continued growth is evident when we compare this session with the first, held only 3 weeks before.

Session 4

This week's group session included six new women. Because of the new group composition, I told the women some information about myself and then asked them to tell me their names, how many children they have, and how long they've been at the shelter. Then, I stated the purpose of the group session. I said, "This group will give you an opportunity to talk and to listen to one another. This is what's called a mutual-aid group. All of you here are experiencing some difficulty in your lives because of abusive relationships. This is not an easy time for you. In fact, it's a time of crisis. Because you've experienced similar difficulties, this group session will give you a chance to help each other. As you listen to each other, share some of your problems and feelings, I think you'll learn a great deal from each other.

"In order to get the group discussion started, I'd like you to do some problem swapping—share with each other some problems and difficulties you've experienced in your abusive relationships. If you want to, you can share some of the things you'd like to see differently in your lives now. By problem swapping, we'll find out what your major concerns are, and then the discussion can focus on these issues. There's no sense in having a discussion if it's not about issues that you're concerned with." I said, "Who would like to start?" Joyce said, "My problem right now is that I don't have any money, and the last time I tried to apply for welfare, they told me I wasn't eligible." The women talked about this for a few minutes and tried to offer Joyce suggestions about receiving welfare. Next, Linda said that her life was very disorganized. At this point, she doesn't know where she's going.

This example illustrates how the working contract with a group can evolve over time and how the group process can educate a worker to deepen his or her understanding of group dynamics, group skills, and the themes of importance to the clients. Now we turn to the dynamics of recontracting when a worker joins an ongoing group.

Joining an Ongoing Group

As we just saw, when workers start a new group, contracting issues are complex. They grow even more complex when a worker joins an ongoing group that may have been operating for some time without a clear working agreement or with an agreement that has not led to effective mutual aid. In this situation, the new group leader has to deal not only with the members of the group but also with the ongoing leaders, who have an investment in the current status. Students often raise this as a perplexing problem when they report sitting in on group discussions as coleaders and observing clearly the problems associated with poor contracting, coleader conflict over the contract, or simply a lack of understanding of the mutual-aid process. Tension develops as the students learn about alternative models and helpful examples while feeling that, as "mere students," they cannot or should not intervene and effect change. In a situation such as the one in the following example, their stress increases when the team leader is also of another discipline—in this case, a psychologist—which introduces issues of status and power.

This example simply represents a special case of the general problem in which the service offered in the setting does not meet the needs of the clients. As such, the definition of the social work function presented in this book—mediating the individual-social engagement—places this problem on the student's agenda for **systems work:** the set of activities in which social workers attempt to influence the systems and systems people important to their clients. Systems work was introduced in Parts II and III. It was discussed again in the chapter on group formation, where we saw how important it was to include all staff in establishing a new group. The issue will be addressed in detail in Part V of this book.

In the example that follows, two students attempted to be involved in the group formation process, with little success. Staff in the setting—a psychiatric hospital—had developed ideas about the limitations of the patient population. Under continued pressure by the students, a group was started, but its purpose and structure reflected the culture of the system. Although this is not an example of joining a group in progress, the principles are close enough for our purposes in this section. The record of service describes the effort over time as one of the social work students analyzes her own early efforts to influence her colleagues and develops interesting strategies for change that minimize defensive and territorial responses.

RECORD OF SERVICE

Client Description and Time Frame

This is an open-ended, support and stabilization group for chronic mentally ill patients on an inpatient unit of a large psychiatric hospital. The age range of the members is 33 to 64 years. The group is predominantly male (currently eight males, three females), all white, with various ethnicities. The period of time covered in the record is from January 18 to April 26.

Description of the Problem

The major problem this group faced from the beginning was a lack of agreement on the group's purpose, goals, and structure by the treatment team putting the group together. This resulted from uncertainty and disagreement as to what would be the most appropriate group format on the part of some members of the treatment team. The problem was reflective of and exacerbated by a hospital culture that was very hierarchical and did not easily tolerate discussion or disagreement among team members of various professions. Also, since specific alternative recommendations for group purpose, structure, and so on were coming from social work students, I believe the resistance to change was also a function of the challenge to the team culture. We were making our own recommendations, rather than just following the team leader's guidance. This restrictive hierarchical culture is an issue that is faced by both clients and staff in this setting, so resolution of the problem at the group level meant confronting the culture on the treatment team level as well.

How the Problem Came to the Attention of the Worker(s)

This problem was noticeable in my first semester at the placement, when development of a group kept being delayed—sometimes because there was "no one available" to co-lead the group, sometimes because we "just didn't get to that item" on the agenda of our weekly team meetings, and sometimes for no stated reason at all. Another student and I were both trying to begin groups, and it became increasingly clear that there was a resistance to beginning this process that was not being admitted or dealt with. In addition, once the groups did get a start date, there was continued reluctance to plan for them, to discuss what type of groups they would be, to discuss group composition, or to engage other staff from the dorm in the process of setting them up. The psychologist, Dr. Brown, expressed frequent concerns about our trying to do too much, or not being realistic in our expectations for the group, and cautioned frequently that "people with schizophrenia are different and the books don't tell you all of it."

Summary of the Work

I attempted to get clarification on the proposed purpose whenever a new group was recommended. Throughout the first semester, whenever possibilities for groups were mentioned, I expressed enthusiasm for getting started and asked about purpose, structure, and composition. It often seemed that a major purpose for the development of many group ideas was the fact that another student and I both needed to have a group experience at our placement, and our supervisor was trying to ensure that this happened. Specific concerns about group purpose and structure, therefore, often seemed to be secondary in our conversations to the possibility of getting a group at all. For example:

> SUPERVISOR: We may have a group for you. I was talking with Edward (the team leader, Dr. Brown) about a family group that you and Evelyn (a social worker on the team) could run.
>
> WORKER: Great! What kind of family group would it be?
>
> SUPERVISOR: Well, we're not too sure about the specifics yet, but it would be to help people deal with their families. Maybe we'd have a little party and have them serve refreshments to their families at the end.
>
> WORKER: So, would it be family members and patients?
>
> SUPERVISOR: Well, it's hard to get families in. It might just be for the patients to talk about problems with the families. But we don't know if it's going to happen yet. We have to check Evelyn's schedule to see if she'll be available to do it with you.

As noted above, purpose and structure were my concern, but my supervisor's interest was more in just getting a group started, and my questions about purpose and structure seemed to feel like pressure to her, or perhaps just irrelevant to the major concern, which was getting a group.

Once the group was decided on, I repeatedly brought up issues of group purpose and structure in group supervision meetings and in meetings with my coleader, initially just by asking for clarification, but later also by making recommendations. I asked about purpose and structure when the group was first decided on, and was told not to worry about it, that we'd be lucky just to get the members to stay in the room. I was also told that my coleader (the team leader) would be there and I should just follow his lead. When I pressed further for information, my supervisor tried to make it irrelevant:

> WORKER: Well, I can do that (follow his lead), but I think it's important to know what we're trying to accomplish so I can be more effective in helping to guide the group.
>
> SUPERVISOR: You probably won't get much of a chance anyway, in the beginning. They (the group members) are going to look to Dr. Brown mostly in the beginning.

When I continued to press at another time for group purpose, just before we were to begin our first group, Dr. Brown finally asked what I would suggest:

> WORKER: Well, we could say something like, "This is a place where people can learn how to support each other and how to get along better."
>
> DR. BROWN: Hmm. I think that might be too frightening for them to hear. Schizophrenics have a hard time with relating to others, and they may just get

scared if we try to tell them they have to talk to each other. I don't think we really need to tell them anything. We can just make it very general.

WORKER: Like what?

DR. BROWN: Well, we could say there's just so much to talk about and we don't get enough chance to talk that much, so this is a chance for us to be with them.

I did as he recommended at that point but continued to bring up the topic in future group supervision meetings.

By this point in the process the student was expressing, in class, increased feelings of frustration and anger. She decided to use this record of service to focus on her work with the system, recognizing that influencing her coleaders' and supervisors' perceptions about the group would require at least as much thought and skill as her work in the group did. This represented an important shift in her thinking from complaining about the existence of the problem to recognizing her functional responsibility to try to influence the system. At first, she still had difficulty tuning in to the concerns and feelings of her coleaders. The important change in her work, however, was her focus on taking some responsibility for her part in the interaction, which she can control.

I did eventually get some general answers about my coleader's (and by extension the hospital's) purpose, but I failed to tune in adequately to the team leader's place in the agency and its implications for what he could feel free to do. In the example above, Dr. Brown gave evidence of an important concern: the psychological feelings of safety of the clients. In the following excerpt, Dr. Brown notes other concerns:

DR. BROWN: I think you'll find that they don't react the way you're expecting them to. If we push them too far, I'm not sure what they'll do.

WORKER: Right. I wouldn't want to push them too far. But I think they may be able to handle some attention on relationships, and then we can see what happens and back off if someone is getting too upset.

By trying to convince him to do it my way, I failed to really give attention to his concerns or to explore what he thought might happen so that we might come up with some way to avoid it that really worked and that felt right to both of us. Since I wasn't really respecting his concern or trusting that it was a valid one, I was dismissing its importance and missing an opportunity to really tune in, to reach for the negatives, and to show empathy for the needs of the organization as well as of the clients. If I had this part to do over again, I would have asked for more information about his concerns, acknowledged them, and then tried to work with him to solve the anticipated problems. In fact, I did get to do it over again in a later session and did better at tuning in at that time:

WORKER: I thought it was great how they were able to challenge each other and really interact with each other.

DR. BROWN: Yeah, but I was concerned. Fred seemed to be getting upset at what was going on.

WORKER: Does he have any history of having problems when he gets anxious like that?

DR. BROWN: Yeah, actually he was at XXX (a forensic psychiatric unit) a number of years ago for attacking somebody with a knife.

WORKER: Well, no wonder you're so concerned! I didn't know about that.

DR. BROWN: Yeah, it was a few years ago, but you never know with some of these people.

WORKER: We have never really talked about what we would do if someone became violent in the group. I've had some training in nonviolent self-defense, but what is the procedure on this unit?

We were then able to talk about procedures and about other concerns about what could happen in the group. Again, I think I could have paid a little more attention to Dr. Brown's concerns by asking, "Do you think something like that might happen during group?" rather than by talking about procedures right away, but it did seem at least to acknowledge the importance of his concerns in a way I hadn't done before.

The tuning-in and empathic responses to colleagues must be genuine. Perhaps because of training that has often led professionals to respond with a pseudoempathy (speaking the words without feeling the feelings), an acute sensitivity to being "social worked," in the worst sense of the term, will result in a negative response. In this example, as the student examined and managed her own feelings better, her capacity for genuine empathy increased. In the next excerpts, the student describes a strategy she has developed for influencing the team leader. Instead of confronting him with his "deficiencies," she invites him to join her in her own analysis of her work. She does this through the sharing of her process recordings, which include her written self-analysis of her practice.

After the first session, I began to share my thoughts on what I would like to be doing in the group with my coleader via process recordings. I began writing weekly a description of what happened in group, the main themes I saw, my overall impression, and my plans for follow-up, and I gave a copy of this to my coleader each week. I hoped that if I shared my thoughts with him in a written format, he might be better able to take in my ideas without having to respond to them right away. I also felt that I could show in more depth in these recordings the scope of what I envisioned for the group, and that by giving me a chance to show him the things I would have liked to say, even when I wasn't yet able to say them, he might come to trust my judgment more. An example of what I shared with him follows, from the ninth group session:

Description: Helen started talking about her family and how her children and grandchildren kept her young. She also spoke about her job at the library and specific things she did there. I said it sounded like she really loved her job, and she agreed. She spoke more about this, addressing most of this to me, and I felt uncomfortable that the rest of the group was not being included, so I responded to her several times but then didn't pursue it further, hoping that others would be able to jump in then.

Reaction/Analysis: Not a great strategy, I see now! Perhaps I could have said how I felt and brought it to the group more, or said I thought it was interesting what Helen was talking about and wondered how other members were feeling as they heard Helen talk about her job, or asked her if she wanted anything from the group.

The second example, which is from an earlier session, shows my thoughts about my working relationship with my coleader, as well as some ideas on group structure. I hoped that by sharing some of my own transference issues with him, I might reduce any threat he might be feeling from me and engage him more easily in working through our differences to work together more effectively.

Description: Dr. Brown described why Fred was not on the unit today. There was no response to this, so I went on, saying, "We went over some ground rules last week, and I'd like to just review them quickly again today. The first is no smoking, which has already been mentioned. The second is that it's OK to leave if you have to go to the bathroom, but then we expect you to come back. Um, what else? Oh yes, we talked about confidentiality, that what we talk about here stays here, and that we won't talk about people who aren't here."

Reaction/Analysis: We had agreed to review the rules at the beginning of each of the first few group sessions at least, but we hadn't decided who would do which of these tasks. I felt Dr. Brown was giving me some space, so I went ahead and started. I noticed part way through that I wanted to share the task with my coleader, but we hadn't discussed it, so I wasn't sure if he'd jump in or not. I was glad when he did. I was also concerned about the confidentiality rule because, although we had discussed it in supervision group last week, I hadn't discussed it specifically with Dr. Brown. I guess the question arises as to whether or not I believe he can take care of himself in a situation like that. Clearly there's some transference here of me seeing him as a dad who would quietly disapprove but never talk about it directly. I guess we should talk about whether we can feel free to disagree or at least clarify things in front of the group (I hope so), and I need to trust Dr. Brown to discuss any differences that may come up openly with me, whether in group or later, and I need to trust myself that I can stand it if he disagrees with me sometimes.

This strategy seemed to work well. When I saw Dr. Brown after he had read my notes on the session, he said he had enjoyed reading it and looked forward to getting more. We then spoke more about the group and our plans for the next session. Although we rarely talked about the specific content of the process recordings, it seemed that giving Dr. Brown the recordings did help him get to know me better and trust me more, and gradually we did come to work together much better. I believe these recordings had a major impact on our relationship developing as well as it did.

I pointed out evidence of successful client interaction whenever I could to my coleader to support the notion of mutual aid. After one session in which a lot of participation happened, I mentioned in the "overall impression" section of my weekly recording my positive views of the ability the group shows to do mutual aid:

"This was a very exciting session! Lots of participation, including real, relevant concerns about what the group will be like. There was also a lot of evidence of people supporting each other (Ben trying to support Martha, Robert supporting Gene), and willingness of members to discuss and challenge (Ben, Martha, Jack, and Hilary on poverty; Martha and Jack on why people don't come; Robert on difficulty following conversation). Overall, it's much more participatory and interactive than I had imagined it would be. I see a lot of potential for this group!"

In our meetings as well, I consistently pointed out the positive evidence I saw of the effectiveness of the group, and Dr. Brown would usually acknowledge the evidence and acknowledge that he hadn't paid so much attention to that. I started to listen better to my coleader and became better able to hear his concerns and really take them in. We then became better able to work together to come up with strategies for working in group that achieved both our goals.

I continued to press for a more mutual-aid focus and more empowerment of group members to help each other and take control of the group. As my coleader and I continued to talk about purpose and structure, he gradually became more willing for me to try to promote interaction and a mutual-aid focus, and often agreed to suggestions

I made for ways to let group members decide how to run the group (regarding how to handle members who leave, for example). In fact, in the 10th session, Dr. Brown joined me in helping people talk to each other and in beginning to encourage members to take some control over their group (This time, when a new member showed up at group, instead of Dr. Brown telling the group he could stay, as he had done in previous sessions, he asked the group if it was OK if the visiting patient stayed!).

As my coleader and I started to agree more on the goals, purpose, and structure of the group, I brought up to the group the changes in how we were using the group, often using the introduction of new members as an opportunity to restate, review, and clarify any changes in those aspects of the group. For example, in session 14, after asking a new member to introduce himself, and having others introduce themselves to him, I continued as follows:

> WORKER: Michael, I know you've been to the Tuesday community meeting. I'd like to tell you a little about this group because it's different from the Tuesday meeting. In this group, we talk about all different kinds of things, but it's a smaller group, and people talk to each other more and try to help each other here. Sometimes someone will talk about a problem and others will try to help them figure out how they can make things better, or sometimes people will just talk about how they feel about something and they might find out that other people feel the same way.
>
> MICHAEL: Oh, like a support group?
>
> WORKER: Yes, have you been in groups like this before?

Finally, when problems came up for individuals in the group, I encouraged a mutual-aid focus. A pivotal session was one in which Gene, a patient whom I see individually, stated that he was going to leave the hospital in 3 days to get his own room. Although I was concerned about the inadvisability of this move, my coleader and I focused on the meaning to the group.

> WORKER: That's an important thing to be announcing here. I wonder how other people feel about your leaving.
>
> GENE: Well, I just wanted to tell you and Dr. Brown.
>
> WORKER: Well, we can talk more about it later. But, since you're here now, I wonder if you wanted to say good-bye to people in this group.

Other members then began to give Gene feedback, some supporting his move and initiative, some expressing concerns for him. And, instead of his being isolated by making this dramatic statement, as he had been in the past for similar statements, the group members were able to engage with him this time and help him think about his decision in a more realistic and fuller way.

Current Status of the Problem

Where It Stands Now

Tremendous progress has been made in getting the team leader to accept some different possibilities for goals and formats for use with these patients. Through much discussion, he has been able to accept the possibility of their interacting with each other in a safe and empowering way and, even more significantly, has begun to look at the system practices that work against the patients' being able to function independently in any areas. He has begun seeing possibilities that he didn't see before for them to have more independence in the group, and he is showing interest in continuing to encourage that kind of independence. The structure of the group has been pretty well set by now, although the goals and purpose still need to be more clearly stated to group members and to the entire treatment team. There is a lot of work yet to be done, but a lot has been accomplished toward creating more empowering and effective goals and structure.

Strategies for Intervention

- Use the remaining group supervision sessions to review with all involved group staff (myself, my coleader, the two coleaders of the other similar group on the ward, and my supervisor, who will be replacing me as coleader of this group) the progress of the group to date—what worked, what didn't, and so on—and discuss ideas for any changes that are needed now or in developing future groups.
- Write up a summary report of my impressions and analysis of the group to date, along with the recommendations below and any identified at the meeting above. Present this to my coleader and my supervisor.
- Continue to point out positive results of the mutual-aid focus in group supervision meetings, team meetings, and planning sessions with my coleader.
- Help group members use mutual aid to deal with my termination (and ask my coleader to do this as well).
- As I sum up my work with the group, point out how group members have been able to use mutual aid to help each other, and express hope that they will continue to do so.

This example has not only illustrated a recontracting process over time, it has demonstrated the importance of the two-client idea, with the agency or setting as the second client. The attitude toward group work practice in the setting reflected the general attitude toward work with psychiatric patients. The student social worker helped individual members of the group; however, her most important social work impact was on the system. Rather than just remaining distressed and angry about the deficiencies of the system, she began to see addressing these problems as central to her role as a social worker. The effects of her impact on the system would be felt long after she had left her placement. She had also learned that in order to empower clients, social workers (and other staff) must first deal with their own disempowerment.

Coleadership in Groups

The previous example brings us to the question of coleadership. Whenever the general subject of coleaders is raised by workers, I inquire if they have had experience working with another staff member in a group. Almost invariably they have, and the experience was usually a bad one. The list of problems includes disagreement on the basic approach to the group, subtle battles over control of group sessions, and disagreement during the group session over specific interventions—particularly those introduced by a coworker that seem to cut off a line of work one feels is productive. Underlying all of these problems is a lack of honest communication between coworkers both within and outside the group sessions. Workers often feel embarrassed to confront their coworkers outside the session and believe it would be unprofessional to disagree during the session. This stance is similar to the parental syndrome of "not arguing in front of the children." Coworkers usually face an unreasonable expectation that they must appear to agree at all times. This lack of honesty usually reflects the insecurity of both workers and often leads to defensiveness and the illusion of cooperative work.

Coleadership can be helpful in a group. Because a group is complex, assistance by another worker in implementing the helping function can be a welcome aid. In my couples' group, one coworker was female and brought perspectives to the work that were strikingly different from mine. For example, she reacted with a different mind-set to issues raised in the group related to women.

Several factors enabled us to work well together. First, we shared a similar approach to the helping process. While our theoretical frameworks differed and we used different conceptual models for understanding client behavior and dynamics, we shared similar attitudes toward clients and a commitment to mutual aid and the importance of reaching for client strength. Within this common framework, our different conceptual models served to enrich our work with the group.

Second, we set aside time to discuss the group. We met before the start of the first group session to strategize and also met before the start of each session to tune in, using the previous session as well as any additional knowledge gained from individual contacts with couples. We also set aside time after each session to discuss the group. In this case, the discussions took place with a group of students training at the school of social work who had viewed the group sessions on a video monitor. We made every effort to encourage honest communication about the sessions and our reactions to each other's input. This was not simple; because I was the senior group worker, coworkers found it difficult to challenge me. As our relationship grew and trust developed, direct communication increased. Finally, we agreed that we could disagree in the group. In many ways, the coworker and I would be a model of a male-female relationship in action. Supporting honesty and willingness to confront while maintaining professional "courtesy" toward each other in the group would make a mockery of our effort. Observing that coleaders could disagree, even argue, and still respect and care for each other can be a powerful object lesson for group members.

Group members can pick up subtle cues of tension between leaders, no matter how hard workers try to hide them. This came to light in the midyear evaluation of this couples' group. A third coworker in this group was a former student of mine, and although he had participated in the sessions up until that point, the presence of the other coworker and his feelings about working with a former teacher had inhibited him. We had discussed this in the sessions with the student observers, who had been quick to pick up his hesitancy. In the midyear evaluation session of the couples' group, I inquired how the group members felt we could improve our work during the second half of the year. Rose turned to my coworker and said, "I hope you don't take what I'm going to say personally. I think you have a lot to give to this group, and I would like to hear more from you. I don't think you should let Larry (the senior worker) frighten you just because he is more experienced." He responded, "You know, Rose, I've been worried about my participation, too. It is hard for me to get in as often as I want to, and I'm going to work on it."

As a final comment on coleadership, I would say that two beginning group leaders would find working together difficult, if not impossible. Their own anxieties are so great that they often become more of a problem for each other than a help. Working with a more experienced worker provides learners with an opportunity to test their wings without taking full responsibility for the outcome. When mutual trust and sharing develop between coworkers, the workers can be an important source of support for each other. The feelings of warmth and caring that develop among members and between the group worker and members must also exist between the coleaders as they tackle the complex task of working with groups. Of course, they need to keep the problems of coleadership, only partially elaborated in this brief discussion, in mind.

Now that we have explored the beginnings of group work, the following chapters will attempt to answer the question of what to do after the first session. They also examine the core dynamics of groups at work and explore the specific functions and skills of the group worker.

Chapter Summary

The core skills of contracting in first sessions, introduced in Parts II and III, apply to the group work context. These skills include clarifying purpose, clarifying the group leader's role, reaching for client feedback, and dealing with the authority theme.

The age and relative articulateness of the members, the authority of the worker, the specific concerns of the clients, and the impact of the setting and time each affect first sessions and in part determine the way workers handle contracting. Each worker brings a unique personal style to the beginning as well.

Recognition that contracting does not always go well the first time, or that it may take several sessions for the group to deal with all the issues, is central to the idea of recontracting—the process in which the worker raises contracting issues with an ongoing group. The worker must employ strategies and skills for working with coleaders and the system, regarding the system as the second client.

Related Online Content and Activities

 Visit *The Skills of Helping* Book Companion Website at www.socialwork.wadsworth .com/Shulman06/ for learning tools such as glossary terms, InfoTrac College Edition keywords, links to related websites, and chapter practice quizzes.

The website for this chapter also features additional notes from the author and additional process recordings:

- Acting-Out Adolescents in a Training Workshop: Recontracting and Clarifying Group Purpose
- Foster Parents: The Late-Arriving Members
- Older Foster Teens Transitioning to Independence: The Impact of Lack of Contracting
- Outpatient Psychiatric Group: Initial Resistance
- Parenting Group for Mandated Members Who Have Abused or Are at Risk for Abuse
- Pregnant Teens in a Shelter: The Power of Clear Contracting
- Teen Boys in a Residential Setting: Empowerment for Change
- Ten-Year-Old Girls in a School Setting
- Twelve-Year-Old Boys in Trouble in a School Setting: The Impact of Clear Contracting

The Work Phase in the Group

I n this chapter, we focus on the interaction between the
individual and the group and on the way in which the group
worker assists this interaction during the work phase. Using
time as an organizing principle, we first examine the contracting
phase of group sessions, emphasizing how the worker at the
beginning helps individuals present their concerns to the group
and simultaneously helps the group members respond. Next, we
look at the middle phase of a session, illustrating the dynamics of
mutual aid and the way in which group members can help each
other and themselves at the same time. Finally, our discussion of
the sessional ending/transition phase stresses the importance of
resolution and transition to next steps or next meetings.

Recorded material from a range of settings will illustrate each
of these phases and the requisite skills. Although this chapter
focuses on the individual-group interaction, note that both
clients—the individual and the group—require further examination. In the next chapter, we analyze the individual's role in a
group and also concentrate on the group-as-a-whole.

Beginning group workers, particularly those who have worked with individuals, often raise the following problem: In an attempt to deal with an individual's concern, they find themselves doing **casework in the group.** This is a common pattern in which the group leader provides individual counseling to a client within a group setting. This contrasts with an effort to mobilize mutual aid for the client by involving the other members. Suppose, for example, a member raises an issue at the start of a session and the worker responds with appropriate elaborative and empathic skills. The group member expands the concern, and the worker tries to help deal with the problem while the other group members listen. When this problem has been explored, the worker then begins with another client as the others patiently await their turn.

After the meeting, the worker worries about having done casework in front of an audience. In reaction to this feeling of uneasiness, the worker decides not to be trapped this way during the next session, but then makes a different kind of mistake. In an attempt to focus on only the "group" aspect of the work, the worker refuses to respond with elaborating skills when an individual opens the session with a direct or indirect offering of a concern. For example, one member of a parent group might say, "It's really hard to raise teenagers these days, what with all the changing values." The worker quickly responds by inquiring if other members of the group find this to be true. One by one they comment on the general difficulty of raising teenagers. The discussion soon becomes overly general and superficial, and meanwhile the first group member is anxiously waiting to air a specific concern about a fight with her daughter the evening before.

When trying to deal with individual concerns, workers may find themselves doing casework in the group, and when trying to pay attention to the group, workers may find themselves leading an overly generalized discussion. Both maladaptive patterns reflect the worker's difficulty in conceptualizing the group as a system for mutual aid and in understanding the often subtle connections between individual concerns and the general work of the group. Schwartz's notion of the two clients, discussed earlier, can help to resolve the apparent dilemma. He suggests that the worker simultaneously must pay attention to two clients, the individual and the group, and that the field of action is the interaction between the two. Thus, instead of choosing between the "one" or the "many," the worker's function involves mediating the engagement between these two clients. This is a special case of the general helping function for social work.

The worker's tasks in addressing these two clients are examined in this chapter against the backdrop of time—the contracting (beginning), work (middle), and ending/transition phases that characterize each group session.

Sessional Contracting in the Group

In Chapter 2 we examined some of the barriers to open communication in the helping situation. These included ambivalence toward taking help, because of the resultant feelings of dependency; societal taboos against discussion of certain topics, such as sex; the client's painful feelings associated with particular issues; and the context of the helping setting, such as the impact of the helping person's authority. These blocks often cause a client to use an indirect form of communication when sharing a problem or concern. For example, clients might hint at a concern (state a specific problem in a very general way), act it out (begin a session by being angry at the worker or other group members, using the anger to cover up the pain), employ metaphor or allegory as a means of presenting an issue (by telling a seemingly unrelated story, for instance), use art or other mediums (a child might draw a picture of an abusive parent), or send the message nonverbally (by perhaps sitting quietly with a pained expression or sitting apart from the group with an angry expression). The indirectness of these communications may cause the group members and the worker to miss important cues in the early part of the session. Alternatively, a member might raise a concern but hide the depth of feeling associated with it, thereby turning off the other group members. The worker's function is to assist the group in interpreting individual members' indirect communications.

Reaching for Individual Communication in the Group

Because of the problems involved in individual-group communication, the worker should in the early stages of each meeting concentrate on helping individual members present their concerns to the group. The beginning of each group session should be seen as a tentative, slow process of feeling out the group, endeavoring to determine which member or members are attempting to capture the group's attention for their own issues, and exploring how these issues may represent a theme of concern for the group. In a like manner, the group itself may be approaching a major theme of concern for that week, and the individual offerings may thus present specific examples of the central concern of the group.

Whether the concern originates with the member or expresses the feelings of many, the worker should focus on answering the question, "What are they (the group members) working on in this session?" For workers to rush in with their own agenda simply because the first productions of the group members are unclear would be a mistake. Likewise, workers should not believe that simply because the group had agreed to deal with a specific issue or an individual's concern at the end of the previous meeting, it will be the issue for the current session. Even if the discussion picks up exactly where the members had agreed it would, the worker should monitor the conversation in the early part of the session with an ear either for confirmation of the theme or hints that members are just going through the motions. In structured groups where an agenda for each session may be preplanned and a topic assigned for discussion, the group leader must still remain alert to the possibility that another or a related issue is emerging and must at least be recognized.

Two skills serve workers in this regard. **Monitoring the individual** involves observing individual group members, remaining alert to verbal and nonverbal clues signaled by each individual. This is an acquired skill and therefore requires practice. When this skill is integrated, a group leader can simultaneously monitor the group and each individual. **Monitoring the group** involves observing the second client—the group members—by watching for verbal and nonverbal clues as to their reactions while a member is speaking.

As they are monitoring the individual and the group, workers should remain aware that even though the conversation may not seem directed toward the group's purpose, it is always purposeful. For clarity of exposition, I shall focus here on examples in which the worker directs the early discussion toward a specific theme of concern. In a later chapter we shall explore examples where the purpose of the early conversation is to raise an issue concerning the working of the group or the leader. In both cases, workers should ask themselves early on, "How does this conversation connect to our work?" or "What is troubling this particular member?" By doing so, they stand a better chance of helping the individual relate a concern to the group.

An illustration from the couples' group described in Chapter 10 can demonstrate this process as well as the importance of sessional tuning in. The session was the 18th. At the previous one, Louise, who was then present without her husband, John, had revealed that he had a drinking problem. There was general agreement to pursue this concern with John present the next week. In my tuning-in session with coleaders prior to the start of the 18th session, I had learned that Fran and Rick had had a particularly difficult week and had threatened separation during their individual counseling session. Rick had questioned returning to the group. This couple previously had made substantial progress in the group and in a related sexual therapy group program. However, they had hit a critical point and were regressing. Over the course of the sessions, I had observed that Fran tended to express her own concerns and fears indirectly as she responded to other couples in the group, and Rick tended to physically retreat.

Having accomplished the preparatory work, the coleaders and I strategized to reach for Fran's indirect cues if they were evident, and we prepared to help the group discuss priorities for this session. The session began with some hints from the group about the ending process, a topic to which I had planned to respond directly. After I acknowledged the group's sadness, as well as my own, about ending, and the members briefly discussed their feelings, there was a silence that was broken by John:

JOHN: I know about your discussion about my drinking last week, since I met with Larry (the worker) and he filled me in. If you have any questions, let me have them.

At this point there was some relaxation of tension, and group members offered supportive comments for John for having raised this difficult concern. I noticed that Fran and Rick had turned their chairs so that they faced apart from each other. Rick was staring into space with a bland expression. Fran turned to face John.

FRAN: I want you to know, John, that I think it's great that you have come here prepared to talk about this problem. It takes a lot of courage on your part. It would have been a lot easier if you simply stayed away or refused to discuss it. That would have been the coward's way out.

WORKER: Fran, I wonder if that's what you think Rick is doing right now in relation to you. His chair is turned away from you and you seem to be upset with each other.

FRAN: (After a period of silence) I don't understand how you do this, how you read my mind this way. It must be a form of magic. (Pause) But you're right, we had a really bad fight this week, and we're not over it. Rick didn't want to come this week, and he won't talk to me about it. (Fran shows signs of becoming upset emotionally.)

WORKER: How do you see it, Rick?

After Rick's confirmation of the seriousness of the situation, both he and Fran stated that they were concerned because this was supposed to be the week for John and Louise. I raised the issue with the whole group and they decided to stay with Rick and Fran because of the degree of urgency in their situation. John and Louise felt they could wait another week. The session turned out to be an important turning point for Rick and Fran, as well as one that yielded important insights for the other couples into their own relationships.

There was no magic in picking up Fran's cues; tuning in and the identification of a pattern over time had helped, as had recognizing the often indirect nature of members' initial efforts to raise themes of concern. In another example from the same group, the problem of identifying the issue was compounded because the member, Lou, did not clearly understand the nature of the concern and presented it indirectly as a part of an angry attack on the group leaders. In the previous session, the group had viewed a videotaped segment of a meeting when one of the couples had blown up at each other. Although the couple had given their consent, Lou was upset that this painful exchange had been replayed in the group. He began with an angry attack on helping professionals, denouncing "the way they played games with people's lives." He was extremely upset at the way workers encouraged the expression of bitter feelings between couples, feeling that this tore them apart emotionally. He argued that this was not necessary. I reached for the specific meaning of his opening comments.

WORKER: Lou, I think you're talking about us and last week's session—when we watched the tape. (I had missed this session because of an accident but had reviewed the videotape. The session had been led by my coleaders.)

LOU: Of course I am! I've never been more upset. I tore my guts watching what you people put them through.

Lou went on to attack the helping professions in general as well as us in particular. The coleaders responded by attempting to explain what they had done. We were generally made to feel defensive and incompetent. Group members will often make the workers feel exactly the way the members themselves feel. When they are unaware of or unable to express their own pain and the hurt under their anger, they sometimes project it onto the leaders or other members. Bion (1961) describes this process as "projective identification," in which the client communicates his feelings by stimulating the same feelings in the worker. The difficulty for the worker is that there is always some element of truth in the attack, which is usually aimed at an area in which the worker feels less than confident. In this situation we stayed with the issue raised by Lou.

WORKER: Lou, you're angry with us and also feeling that we really hurt Len and Sally last week. Obviously we missed how hard it hit you to see their pain. Why don't you ask them how they felt?

LOU: Well, am I right? Wasn't that terrible for you to go through?

LEN: It wasn't easy, and it hurt, but I think it helped to get it out in the open. It also helped to have all of you care about us and feel the pain with us.

LOU: But there must be some way to do this without having to tear your guts out. (Lou seemed a bit taken aback by Len's comments, which were echoed by his wife.)

WORKER: When you attacked us, Lou, I have to admit it hit me hard. A part of me doesn't want to get at the anger and pain that you all feel, and yet anther part of me feels it's the way back to a stronger relationship. I have to admit you shook me.

ROSE: (Lou's wife) I think you have to understand this has been a hard week for us.

WORKER: How come?

ROSE: We just got word that Lesley, our granddaughter who lives in London, is splitting up with her husband.

Lou and Rose have spoken before in the group about their children and the pain it has caused them to see each of them experience difficulties in their own marriages.

Lou has been particularly angry with helping professionals who have helped neither him nor his family members. This was the first grandchild to experience marital problems, and it signified to Lou and Rose the continuation of the family's instability into another generation. Under much of the anger lay their pain as well as their defensiveness and doubt, to which Rose responded by clarifying Lou's signal.

WORKER: It must have hit you very hard, Lou, having the first grandchild experience marital problems.

LOU: (Seemingly deflated, the anger gone, slumped in his chair, speaking with a tone of resignation and bitterness) After 45 years, you learn you have to live with these things. It's just another notch that you have to add to all to the other hurts.

The discussion continued with Lou and Rose describing their feelings of helplessness as they watched their family disintegrating, as well as their desire to show the children that it did not have to be that way. The group members commiserated as they described how they also felt impotent in affecting the lives of their children and their grandchildren.

In the first illustration with Fran and in the second with Lou, the individual was reaching out to the group indirectly through her or his opening comments. With Fran the concern was presented in the guise of a response to a group member, while with Lou it appeared as an attack on the leaders. In both cases, the communication had two meanings. The first was the actual statement of fact, while the second was a disguised call for help. Unless workers are tuned in, are listening hard for potential offerings from group members, and are clear about their own function in the group, they can easily miss the early, indirect productions of group members. Of course, the member will often present a concern more directly, thus making it easier for the group to hear. And sometimes an issue may emerge at a later point in the meeting.

The following example involves a group for 10- and 11-year-old children who had lost a close family member. They were referred to the group because of behavior problems in school and elsewhere that signaled their inability to cope with death. The group members called themselves the "Lost and Found Group," because they had lost someone close but had found each other (Vastola, Nierenberg, & Graham, 1994). The authors describe how Mark, at the start of a group session following one in which members had begun to open up and discuss their losses, sends a mixed message using paper and pen. He repeatedly writes "Bob," the name of his grandfather who had recently died.

CARL: Mark, your grandfather died?

MARK: I don't want any damn body talking about my grandfather or I'll kick their butt.

LEADER: You sound pretty angry.

MARK: I'm not angry. I just don't want anybody talking about my grandfather.

LEADER: It's very difficult.

MARK: It's not difficult. I just don't want anybody saying that he died. (His anger is escalating.)

GLORIA: Nobody wants to talk about nobody dying.

DICK: Yes, we don't want to talk about that.

LEADER: How come?

GLORIA: That's why he (Mark) is running around. You can't force him if he doesn't want to.

LEADER: Are you saying that perhaps that's what makes you run around—so you won't have to talk about something upsetting?

MARK: Nope.

LEADER: Maybe you feel it's too hard to talk about.

MARK: No, it's not hard for me to talk about anything . . . but that reminds you, and you could be dreaming.

CARL: Yup, you dream for about a week when you talk about your mother, then it takes about five days to try to get over it, but it comes back again and it stops and it comes back again. . . . Nightmares, I hate. I hate talking about my mother. (p. 87)

Through his behavior, Mark demonstrated his difficulty in dealing with the loss. The group members moved to his defense, because this was their problem as well. The group leader's persistence sent a message to Mark (and the group) that she would not back off from this difficult issue. As she explored Mark's resistance by acknowledging the difficulty and asking what made it hard to talk about his loss, the members began to open up.

This worker was prepared to deal with the taboo subject of death and grieving—a very painful topic when children are involved. By responding to the behavior only and attempting to set limits and stop Mark from running around the room, the worker would actually have been signaling her own resistance to the discussion. The fight over the behavior would have allowed both Mark and the worker to avoid the pain. This is why social workers need to have access to support for themselves as they attempt to deal with these powerful issues (Shulman, 1991).

The final example of behavior as communication comes from the beginning of a session of an ongoing, open-ended group for friends, lovers, and relatives who were grieving the loss of someone from AIDS. A woman who had just lost her son was attending her first meeting. The meeting started with **check-in**, in which each member briefly shared what had happened to him or her during the preceding week. The new member began with an extremely rapid nonstop monologue about how busy she had been keeping herself since her son died. She described a daily, hectic round of activity, showing little emotion other than the hint of an underlying anxiety. She had clearly been in flight from her loss during the week and was indirectly communicating this flight by her opening conversation. It was as if she were saying, "Do you want to see how I am coping? Watch me!" The leader responded by cutting her off, after a while, pointing out that they needed to hear from all of the members as a part of the check-in. Later analysis by the leader revealed that he had sensed her anxiety and simply had not been able to deal with it. Had he been able to be honest about his feelings at the moment, he would have shared how he experienced her presentation—being uncertain about how to help, feeling her sense of overwhelming loss, and wondering about proceeding with the check-in. Any or all of these comments might have opened the door for further discussion and expression of emotion.

The group members joined in the collusion, in a flight process of their own. They were at a different stage in their grieving, and this new member's behavior may have reawakened feelings they would have preferred to have left behind. This example also reveals some of the problems associated with rituals such as check-in, which can take on a life of their own when adhered to dogmatically. Instead of providing an opportunity to deal with individual members' concerns, they can become a way to avoid deepening the work. In retrospect, the leader could have acknowledged the indirect communications of the member and raised, with the group, whether they wanted to respond right away or continue check-in. Either way, acknowledging the feelings underlying the individual's acting out of her pain would have laid the groundwork for dealing with her loss and the feelings evoked in the second client, the group.

This first section has focused on helping the individual reach out to the group. In many cases, particularly when the feelings expressed reflect those held by the group members, the worker's second client—the group—paradoxically appears to turn away from the individual. In the next section, we discuss the meaning of this dynamic.

Reaching for the Group Response to the Individual

It is easy to see how a worker can become identified with a particular client's feelings as a theme of concern is raised. If strong emotions are expressed, the worker may feel supportive and protective. Not surprisingly, if the other group members do not appear to respond to the individual, workers will often feel upset and angry. The worker is shocked and surprised to observe group members apparently not listening, to see their eyes glazing over as they appear to be lost in their own thoughts, or to witness a sudden change in subject or a direct rebuff to the client who has bared innermost feelings. At moments such as these, the worker's clarity of function and the notion of two clients can be the most critical. Instead of getting angry, the worker should view the group members' response as a signal, not that they are uninterested in what is being said, but that the theme may be powerfully affecting them.

The mediation function calls for the worker to search for the common ground between the individual and the group at the point where they seem most cut off from each other. This clear sense of function directs the worker simultaneously to empathize with the members' feelings underlying their apparent resistance and to express empathy with the individual client. The group leader must be with both clients at the same time.

The following example is from a day treatment outpatients' group for adult clients with a chronic mental illness. The group's focus was family issues. In this fifth session, a member raised her depression on the fifth anniversary of the brutal death of her child. The group members responded with silence, and the worker intervened to support the second client:

> At the beginning of our meeting, after group introductions and as people settled into their seats, Joan began speaking. She looked straight ahead of herself, eyes downcast most of the time, and occasionally made eye contact with me (one of the coleaders) or looked furtively around the group as she spoke.
>
> Joan said, "Well, I just want to tell everybody that the fifth anniversary of my daughter's death (the daughter was raped and murdered) is coming up this week and it's bothering me a lot. It always has bothered me. I try to deal with it OK, but I just don't always know how. I get to thinking about it, and the more I think, the more I'm afraid that I'm gonna lose it or do something against myself. I've tried to come to terms with it, but it's always hard when it comes around to when I lost her. So anyway, I've made arrangements to use the 24-hour bed (an emergency bed in the center) 'cause I'm too afraid when I get to feeling like this."
>
> There was complete and utter silence in the group. I remained silent for a few moments as well. As I looked around the group, the members too were looking straight ahead or acting uncomfortable and as if they didn't know what

to say. I said, "Wow, that's some pretty heavy issue that you're bringing up. It seems like it is hitting people pretty hard." The group was still silent, and I paused, although, just as Elizabeth was about to say something, my coleader said, "I'm wondering what people in the group are thinking or feeling about what Joan has just said, and if it's difficult to respond to it." There was a little more silence, and Joan went on, "Maybe I shouldn't have brought it up. Everybody here already knows that this is a problem for me. It's just that I felt so close to her. She was the one whose birth I remember. She was the one, instead of whisking her away and doing what they have to do right after they're born, they put her on me and I felt so much closer to her than the others. I remember it so much better. But maybe I just shouldn't bring it up here."

I waited a little and looked around the group once more and then said, "You're talking about a pretty big loss, here, and especially with it being your daughter, it's very appropriate to bring it to this group. Everyone has had some losses with people close to them; maybe some of them don't seem as earth-shattering as others, but we all know the experience of loss in our families, one way or another."

Then Elizabeth, who had been about to speak earlier, said, "Whew. That's just it. Thinking about your daughter and the 24-hour bed; that's pretty serious." Wendy spoke up, saying, "Yeah, that's scary. I mean I've been thinking about my accident (she had been in a car accident a few days before and has a long-standing fear that she may kill herself in a car) and thinking about losing my sons in the divorce like I did. It really troubles me." I said, "So, we're not only looking at family losses, but also at what we do to deal with them and look for ways to cope with them and feel safe."

With the worker's help, the group revealed that their silence did not reflect lack of feeling or concern for Joan. In fact, it was the opposite, as Joan's feelings about her loss triggered many of their own. Joan was reassured that the group was the place to bring these issues, and knowing she was not alone helped her.

As I have described the sessional contracting phase of a group meeting, many of the dynamics and skills discussed in Parts II and III of this book have reappeared. The worker's sessional tuning in, sessional contracting, elaborating, empathic, and demand-for-work skills are as important in helping the individual present concerns in the group session as they were in individual work. Such skills form the common core of practice skill. The worker's function is also the same, because the work centers on helping the client negotiate important systems in life. The differences in group work, compared with individual work, derive from the presence of one of these important systems—the group—and the need for the worker to pay attention to its responses. The core skills play a central role in implementing this aspect of the worker's function as well.

Reaching for the Work When Obstacles Threaten

In the analysis of work with individuals, we explored the connections between the process (way of working) and the content. For example, we identified the flow of affect between the worker and client—the authority theme—as a potential obstacle to work as well as a source of energy for change. Workers need to pay attention to these feelings—to acknowledge them before the work can proceed. This same issue was highlighted in our analysis of first group sessions, where I pointed out the importance of discussing the worker-group relationship. In the group context, workers must also deal with the interchange that takes place among the members—what Schwartz refers to as the **intimacy theme**. In the next sections, we look at authority and intimacy in the context of sessional contracting. For example, it may be important to discuss the process between members as a way of freeing individuals to trust the group enough to offer concerns in painful and sensitive areas. (We discuss both of these issues more fully in the next chapter.)

Teenager in a Residential Center, Raising a Difficult Subject In the example that follows, a youngster in a group for boys at a residential center wants to discuss a difficult issue but is hesitant about revealing himself to the group. By pausing and encouraging the group to discuss briefly the intimacy theme, the worker frees the member to continue.

> I began the meeting by asking if there was anything that anybody wanted to ask or say before we got started. Mike said, "Well, I have some things, but I am not sure that I want to talk about all of it." I said that Mike wanted to get at what was bothering him but he wasn't going to be able to do it right away. Perhaps he needed to test the group a bit to see if he could trust them? He said, "I don't know if I can always trust people." Terry came in here and said, "This is our group here, and we can say what we want to. What goes on in here does not go outside to others, isn't that right? If we have something that we want to talk about, something really personal, we won't let it out of our own group, right?" Terry got verbal approval from all the boys in the group. I also felt that Terry was demonstrating the basis of our contract. I said that I agreed with what Terry had said. To clarify the point further, I said that I saw our purpose as being able to talk about some of the feelings that we have around being here in the Boys' Center and that out of this might come family problems, work problems, and the problems of "what is going to become of me"—for example, am I really worth anything? Steve elaborated this aspect by referring to his willingness to share his feelings with the group.

The next move by the worker was important. After acknowledging the problem and restating the contract, the worker returned to Mike and his specific issue. This demonstrates the importance of not getting lost in a discussion of process. As will be illustrated later, there are times when a group needs to discuss obstacles and to explore them in depth; however, in most cases the recognition of the obstacle suffices. Workers can be "seduced" into expanding the discussion of the obstacle unnecessarily, thus subverting the contract of the group, even though the members themselves seem to want to talk about their work as a group rather than other concerns. In this case, however, this worker properly returned to the member, Mike.

> After this brief return to the contracting, I asked Mike if he thought he might feel like sharing some of the things he had said at the start of the meeting that were bothering him. He said that he thought that he could talk about part of it. John said that he thought that he knew what was bothering Mike. I let this hang. I wanted to see if Mike would respond to John or if the others would respond to either John or Mike to help us work on what Mike had come up with. Terry reiterated what he had said earlier: "What is said in the group is for the group." John said, "I think that it is about your family, isn't it, Mike? " Mike said, "Yes, that's part of it." I asked John what he meant by Mike's family. John said, "Well, Mike doesn't have any parents, and we are all the time talking about

troubles with our family, or we always have someplace to go if we make a weekend." Mike said, "Yeah, that's part of it. Like I make a weekend and I stay here."

Another way in which process and content are synthesized was described earlier in the discussion of resistance. For example, the client may appear to hold back from entering a difficult area of work, and the worker senses the client's reluctance to proceed. Such resistance is viewed as central to the work and a possible sign that the client is verging on an important area. In such cases, workers should suggest the need to explore the resistance. In much the same way, a group may resist by launching a tacit conspiracy to avoid painful areas. This is often the reason the members of a group hold back in the early stages of a group meeting. Once again, the worker's task involves bringing the obstacle out in the open in order to free the group members from its power.

Mothers of Children Diagnosed with Hyperactivity The following example concerns work with mothers of children who have been diagnosed as hyperactive. The early themes had centered on the parents' anger toward school officials, teachers, neighbors, and other children, all of whom did not understand. The parents also acknowledged their own anger at their children. The worker empathized by saying, "It is terribly frustrating for you. You want to be able to let your anger out, but you feel that if you do so, it will make things worse." After a few comments, the conversation became general again.

> I told the group members that they seemed to be talking in generalities again. Martha said it seemed they didn't want to talk about painful things. I agreed that this appeared to be hard. Every time they got on a painful subject they took off toward something safer. I wondered if the last session had been very painful for them. Martha said that it was a hard session, they had come very close, and she had a lot to think about over the weekend. Lilly said that she felt wound up over the last session, so much so that she had had trouble sleeping at night. I asked her to tell us what made it so upsetting for her. She said that she had felt so helpless when they had been talking about the school boards and the lack of help for children like her own. Doreen said it really wasn't so helpless. She had talked to a principal and had found out some new information.

Note that when the worker asked the group what made it so upsetting, the answer brought the group back to its work. This is a simple, effective, and usually underused technique for exploring and moving past resistance. When a client says, "I don't want to talk about that!" the worker often simply needs to reply, "What would make it hard to talk about that?" As clients talk about what makes talking about it hard, they usually find themselves talking about it. In the current example, later in the same session, the worker picked up on the acknowledgment of the members' anger toward their children and the difficulty of talking about that anger, with similar results. Workers find exploring resistance easier if they do not view it as a commentary on their lack of skill.

One final connection between process and task has to do with the power of specific examples in the work of the group. We saw earlier how moving from the general to the specific—an elaboration skill—could also powerfully affect the deepening of work with individuals. This skill is even more essential in work with groups. Because of its numbers, a group can sustain a general discussion about problems for quite a long time. The problem, mentioned earlier, of responding to a member's general comment by asking all the other group members if they too feel that way, and then forgetting to return to the original member, is one of the most common problems in the sessional contracting phase of group work.

Mothers of Sixth-Grade Underachieving Boys In the following example, the group is for mothers of sixth-grade boys who were underachieving in school. The purpose was to discuss how they could more effectively help their youngsters with their schoolwork. After the members had engaged in a general discussion of their feelings when faced with their children's resistance to homework, their own memories of failure at school, their identification with their children's feelings, and their recognition that they sometimes push their children because of their own need for success, the worker recognized the need for more specificity in the work. She began by focusing the members toward this end, then made a demand for work.

> I said that I thought it would be useful if they described what actually happens at home concerning the issue of homework—how they handle getting the kids started on and completing assignments—and then discuss the pros and cons of the various ways of handling this.
>
> I told them that they had come up with some good ideas during the past meetings and that if they could apply these to their own children, they might begin to resolve some of the difficulties they had been describing. I said that it seems to me that they already have found some alternate ways of dealing with their children related to schoolwork and homework, and it is just a matter of seeing where they can be applied in their own particular situations. I asked that each describe as fully as possible what goes on in their home concerning getting the children started on the homework and also to describe the means they may use to get them to complete it.

The members needed help at this point to get into the details of their experiences, for only in analysis of the specific details can the worker and the group provide the required help.

To summarize, in this section we have seen how individuals reach out, often indirectly, to raise their concerns with the group. We have also explored the group's ambivalent responses. In analyzing the worker's function in mediating this engagement and the importance of paying attention to the process in the group, we have concentrated on problem areas such as members' reluctance to trust the group, the resistance that sets in when the work gets difficult, and the problems arising from helping in general terms, rather than specifically. In the next section, we focus on the mutual-aid process in the middle stages of sessions, examining how individuals and the group are helped and outlining the tasks of the worker in this process.

The Work Phase in a Group Session

In Chapter 8 we discussed many mutual-aid processes, including sharing data, the dialectical process, exploring taboo areas, the "all-in-the-same-boat" phenomenon, mutual support, mutual demand, individual problem-solving, rehearsal, and the "strength-in-numbers" dynamic. In this section we look at some of these processes as revealed in recordings from work phase sessions of groups. The first set of excerpts illustrates how general themes of concern are presented and discussed over a period of time, emphasizing how individuals use the general discussion for help with their specific concerns. The second set of excerpts shows how individual problem-solving can influence the general concerns held by group members.

Note that work in a group is not neat and orderly—with general themes or specific problems presented at the start of the meeting, worked on in the middle segment, and then neatly resolved toward the end. In reality, themes and problems may emerge only partially in early sessions and then reemerge later in new forms as group members become more comfortable with each other and with the worker. For example, in the early sessions of an unmarried mothers' group, most of the conversation involved sharing the hurt and bitterness the young women felt over the reactions of the child's father, their own parents, friends, and others. Only as trust developed within the group and their feelings were accepted and understood could the members began to consider doing something about their relationships with significant others.

Change takes time, and group members need to explore their thoughts and feelings at a pace appropriate for them. Difficult issues may take weeks or months of "working through" before the group member is ready to face a problem in a new way. The worker needs to offer support during this process and at the same time stay a half step ahead of the client, thus presenting a consistent yet gentle demand for work. The sections that follow illustrate the process of helping group members work on themes over time and the process of facilitating problem-solving mutual aid. The latter also shows how workers confront members to take personal responsibility.

Helping the Group Work Over Time

Helping a group work over time involves a series of beginnings, middles, and endings. We therefore need to examine several sessions in order to gain a full understanding of the way help is given over time. The next example, of Puerto Rican pregnant teens living at home, illustrates this point.

The members of the group to be discussed are 14- to 16-year-old American girls of Puerto Rican descent. The transition through puberty and emerging sexuality is a central developmental theme facing adolescents at this age. While this may be a universal, life-cycle theme, it emerges in different ways within different ethnic groups. Devore and Schlesinger (1996) describe this stage for the Puerto Rican female child as follows:

> As the Puerto Rican female child learns the female role by imitating her mother, she receives much affirmation from the entire family. Gradually she takes on more female responsibility in caring for young siblings—the babies—but there is no talk of sex. She gains knowledge from friends with similar meager experience and from overheard conversations of adults. (pp. 69–70)

The lack of appropriate sexual information, or the inability to make use of this information, led to pregnancies for the group members in our example. The members found themselves facing adult responsibilities, but they still had the bodies, hearts, minds, and developmental needs of children. They found it easier to express their anger at their boyfriends, who emerged relatively unscathed from the experience, than to share their pain honestly. Within their ethnic group, Puerto Rican girls are often taught to adhere to the concept of "marianismo, referring to the importance of motherhood and of deferring to men in their culture" (Devore & Schlesinger, 1996, p. 229). The responsibility of caring for the family's babies is illustrated as one member must bring her 4-year-old brother to the meetings. Her anger at the impending changes in her life and the way in which they were already affecting her choices were acted out toward the child. Here we look at the first month of meetings.

RECORD OF SERVICE

Description of the Problem

This group of young, pregnant women of Puerto Rican descent have had no difficulty verbalizing their anger at their boyfriends, parents, and friends. They are expressive of their feelings of victimization. The challenge for this worker is helping them move beyond their anger and feel their pain and sadness. It is my hypothesis that only be after experiencing their grief as well as their anger will they be able to move out of the victim role, recognize their part in the negative aspects of their relationships, and find solutions for action to make the changes they desire in their lives.

How the Problem Came to the Attention of the Worker(s)

During the first few sessions of this group, an underlying current of angrily trashing men was established. In particular, they tended to focus this anger on their boyfriends. Beatriz emerged as the leader of this pattern, though the others eagerly joined in. In the second group session (10/9), Valerie brought her 4-year-old younger brother, whom she was looking after that day. During the course of the session, even though it was obvious that Valerie was very depressed and upset about something, she resisted looking at her own feelings and exhibited great anger at Dennis. At one point she exploded, striking him. After I asked her what she was feeling, she admitted she was having a bad day and looked like she wanted to cry. However, she almost immediately regained her composure and put up her tough defensiveness again. At this point Yardy defended Valerie's behavior toward Dennis, saying it was just discipline. Not much later in this same session, Valerie actually stood up and said the she was sorry, but she needed to leave immediately.

In session three (10/16), in response to finding out that her boyfriend had been cheating on her, Beatriz exhibited no pain but said instead that she couldn't wait until after her baby is born, so that she can "show him some."

Before proceeding, it is important to raise the issue of the striking of the 4-year-old child. Valerie acted out her issues by hitting her brother. The worker had been shocked and upset at the behavior but had withheld her response for fear of cutting off the beginning relationship. This was a mistake, because the worker needed to consider the protection of the child. In addition, Valerie may have been saying to the worker and the group, "This is going to be what it is like for me with my own baby." She may also have been raising issues about how she was raised as a child. If the worker could have responded honestly, using this as an opportunity to deal with the topic of confidentiality, it would have been helpful. It might also have opened up the issue of how these children having children were using flight and fight to run from their pain. Valerie would give the worker another opportunity at a later session.

Summary of the Work

October 2 (First Session)

I attempted to open up the conversation to explore a range of emotions. Early on in the first session, Beatriz expressed anger and the desire to break up with her boyfriend. I asked her what it would feel like to break up with him. She replied that it would be easy and that she didn't care about him. When I suggested that, as well as creating those types of feelings, mightn't it also be somewhat painful and difficult, she replied firmly that it wouldn't be at all, as she didn't really care about him. (They have been dating for 2 years.) This told me a lot about Beatriz. I saw right away how tough and hardened she was and how difficult it is for her to admit her vulnerabilities. This was an important signal early on that painful feelings would not be easily accessed in this group.

I pointed out the commonality and intensity of the feelings in the group. I said, "Are you angry, Beatriz? You sound like it." She replied with an enthusiastic "Yes!" Then I said, "In fact, it sounds like something you are all feeling is very angry—am I right?" Once again, there was a round of enthusiastic agreement. It seemed helpful to put into words the emotion that was present in the room. They all seemed to experience some relief in having it named and noticing that they were all feeling the same. At the time I did not realize how this one emotion would dominate the group, and how by openly noticing the anger now, it would help me later to be able to point out how other emotions were so blatantly missing from the group culture.

Valerie shared some very rejecting behavior by her mother since she had become pregnant. I asked how this made her feel. She said that it made her feel very alone and like she didn't have a mother. Valerie took the lead at that point as the person who was the most willing to share deeply about painful feelings. She created an opening for Yardy to share about some of the rejecting behavior of her mother.

October 9 (Second Session)

I ignored strong signals that Valerie was giving me and stuck to concrete questions. Valerie arrived with her younger brother and within the first few minutes threatened to hit him. Just before this, she said that she had broken up with her boyfriend that week. I ignored her behavior toward her brother and asked her another question about her situation with her boyfriend. My thinking was that if she could talk about her boyfriend, it would relieve some of the pressure and her attitude toward her brother would shift. However, I was wrong. She did not answer my question and instead yelled at her brother again. Then she sat with her eyes down. I asked Yardy a question. In fact, I think I was shocked and immobilized at her aggressive behavior and the possibility of abuse happening in the group itself. I was reluctant to make her upset or step in and set limits around her treatment of her brother.

I attempted to open up a space for Valerie to share her painful feelings. As Valerie grew tenser and tenser during the session, I noticed out loud how tense she seemed and told her in a gentle voice that I was wondering what was going on with her. She told us that she had a toothache that had been bothering her for 3 days. She also said that she was supposed to have started high school that day (under a special midyear promotion program) but that she hadn't been able to because she had to look after her younger brother. Seconds later she leapt from her chair and hit Dennis.

I didn't know what to do and was frozen in my chair. The group stopped dead while I was in shock and trying to figure out what to do. I was torn between acting parental and setting limits around abuse in the group and helping her reach for her feelings.

I shared my feelings and attempted to help Valerie reach for her pain. I said that I felt very tense when she hit Dennis and I was wondering what was going on for her just beneath the surface. Valerie was not able to talk about her pain. I think if I had a second chance, I would have acknowledged out loud all the different, difficult things that were going on for Valerie that gave her a reason to be upset, i.e., her toothache, missing her first day of high school, being pregnant, and the fight with her boyfriend. I would have attempted to articulate for her the underlying pain, saying something like, "All of these things have happened and I imagine you may be feeling very alone right now, like there is no one there to support you. And yet you are expected to look after somebody else. I imagine that might be very difficult." I also would have arranged for Dennis to either leave the room and have someone else look after him or have him come closer to me, giving him a coloring book or something to do near me, and I would have taken over looking after him for a while.

I attempted to define a group norm that would be different from the norm in their homes. Valerie said that when she felt like this she didn't like herself and she just preferred not to say anything at all. I then said that, as the group continued, I hoped that it would become more and more a place where people felt that they could say anything on their minds and express whatever mood they are in. I told her that I wouldn't judge her for being sad or angry or depressed or whatever mood she was in on any particular day. This kind of expressed permission may be something the group needs to hear often at the start, since I imagine it contradicts the situation at home. It may also address their reluctance to express themselves fully that may evolve from their mothers' unavailability to all their feelings (transference).

Although the worker was more direct about the abuse of the child, she did not take it the next step and clearly indicate that as a mandated reporter she would need to let the child welfare authorities know if she feels a child is at risk. I believe the young woman had been letting the worker know that she cannot control herself, because of her anger at having to take care of Dennis. This was also an important signal of the kind of problems they will all have when they have children of their own while still trying to grow up and be a teen. The process and content integration is clear.

October 16 (Third Session)

I intellectualized and jumped in, cutting off the group process. We were talking about hitting people and whether it was OK to do that. I suggested that perhaps it was never a good idea, and I asked them why they thought I said that. Yardy said that it didn't work—it wasn't effective. Beatriz said that she thought it made things worse. Yardy said it was better to talk things through. When Beatriz said that didn't always work, I jumped in and said that I hadn't said it would be easy, and that hitting always created bad feelings. Beatriz replied that men deserve it sometimes and then went on to complain about men, something she frequently does. I notice that I jumped in, wanting to be right, and I stopped allowing the group to explore the issue themselves. This whole session was very different from the last one. For one thing, Valerie wasn't there (she was at the dentist), and a new member had joined the group. This week I kept the group more intellectual, posing questions and asking the girls to think about things from different perspectives. I know there is part of me that is put off by Beatriz's constant raving against men. I know that I am looking for a way into her deeper self, and I haven't found that way yet. This is probably why it is bothering me so much.

October 23 (Fourth Session)

I try to call Valerie during the week to touch base with her. Interestingly enough, her phone number has been changed and is now unlisted. I have no idea whether or not she will come. Sure enough, she does not show. One of the other members also cannot come, because of an appointment at the hospital. There are only two members present, and it is an educational group, with one of the nurses coming in to talk about fetal development and birthing. It is a good group; the girls are excited to be learning these things—new to both of them. There is little chance, however, to open up deeper feelings. There is a lot of giggling and squeamish faces as they look at the pictures and try to imagine themselves pushing out a baby.

October 30 (Fifth Session)

During the week, Carmen gives birth to a baby girl. I make plans for us to go to the hospital to visit her. I have written a letter to Valerie, telling her we will be celebrating both her and Yardy's birthday at the next meeting and I hope she can make it. Sure enough, she comes early to the group and is in the waiting room! I am very glad to see her. It turns out that she had come to last week's session. She had gotten a ride with her boyfriend, and they had had a fight in the car, and they ended up driving back to her house. This taught me that the circumstances in these girls' lives are complex and play a larger role in their getting to group than I had thought.

I let Valerie know that she was missed. I told Valerie how disappointed the group was that she didn't come the week before. Beatriz agreed and said that the group wasn't as good without her. By doing this I emphasized that she was important and that her open display of strong emotions 2 weeks before had not created negative reactions in the group or from me as leader. By fully welcoming her back, I set a group norm that it is OK to display strong feelings and/or not be able, for whatever reason, to attend group for a few weeks and you will still be accepted for who you are and remain part of the group.

Although the trip to the hospital [to visit Carmen and her baby] did not allow for an in-depth talk in which we were able to have a conversation about painful feelings and the group's tendency to avoid them (a conversation I know we will need to have at some point), I felt it was essential to set a culture of being there for each other at those critical and special moments just before, during, and after giving birth. As each girl picked up Carmen's baby and held her, they expressed a lot of feelings about being pregnant themselves. They were able to see the eventual end result of their pregnancy and ask Carmen lots of questions about her experience. As we were leaving, Yardy asked Carmen, "Are you still going to be able to be part of the group?" and Carmen responded, "Of course, I'll bring my daughter!" I knew, in that moment, that they had become a group. I knew this because the girls named it and gave it a life.

Current Status of the Problem

Where It Stands Now

Although I do not feel that we have cracked the shell of defensiveness and entered a new arena of free expression of painful feelings, I believe that this will happen in the next stage of the group. It has taken these first five meetings for the group feeling to gel. There is now a bond established, created in part by the return of Valerie to the group after we had all given her up as possibly lost, as well as Carmen's commitment to be a member of the group after having given birth. Given the fact that it is a small miracle that these girls get themselves to each group meeting, given the complexity of the circumstances in their lives, I think we have done well. I know I underestimated all the factors that would make it difficult for them to get to group, especially before it became clear to them what was in it for them. I also think I underestimated the influence of culture in their ease with anger and the unfamiliarity with expressing their pain, particularly in front of others.

On the other hand, the stage we are at could be considered normal for a group that has only had five sessions. It takes this long to establish a group bond and a culture of safety in which deeper sharing can take place.

Strategies for Intervention

- For the next two to three meetings, we will not go out anywhere, but stay in and "talk." This is so we can get down to the next level of work.

- The next time someone in the group points to painful feelings but indirectly expresses them through other channels, I will confront the group with their pattern of avoiding painful emotions and ask them why they think they do this.

- I will support the "emotional leader" of the group (which thus far appears to be Valerie) in any risk taking she does in sharing painful or difficult emotions.

- I will tell them that I think it is helpful and important for them to share their pain with one another.

- I'll ask them to look and see how the norm of falling back on anger and blaming appears in their families and, in particular, with their mothers and have them look and see how that has been helpful and unhelpful.

- I will model unconditional acceptance of their feelings when they do share them in the group, creating a culture of acceptance.

Focusing the Group on Problem-Solving Mutual Aid

Mutual aid is also offered in relation to specific concerns raised by an individual member. As group members help an individual to look closely at a particular problem and find a new way of dealing with it, they are helping themselves to deal with similar issues in their own lives. Thus, mutual aid can also start with a specific issue and move to a general concern.

This process will now be illustrated using excerpts from a group offered in a family agency. The five women and two men in the group were separated, divorced, or widowed. All of them had experienced heavy depression and difficulties in their interpersonal relationships. The group contract was to discuss these concerns and to find some solutions. The session began with a young woman, Sheila, asking for help. The first response from group members was to offer consolation. The worker asked for elaboration while offering empathic support.

> Sheila suddenly broke in and in a choked voice said, "I am feeling so down tonight." Bob quickly responded, "You, too?" Sheila continued that she had called Don in Montreal; he had been busy and had not wanted to talk to her. I said, "You sound very hurt." Tears filled her eyes, and Sheila said, "Yes, I am. I blew up and acted like a baby and now I have to apologize when he comes down on Saturday." Roberta and Bob rushed in to support Sheila saying they would be hurt, too, if they called someone and he was too busy to listen. Libby nodded but said nothing. I asked Sheila why she had called and why she blew up. She softly and sadly replied that she had called Don because she was lonely. Evelyn questioned if she had told Don this. Sheila hadn't. Bob asked why. Sheila smiled and said, "That wasn't the only reason I telephoned. I sometimes call to check up and see if he is really working." Roberta said, "You can't dwell on the fact that he had an affair, and Joan is going to have his baby."

Sheila began to talk about Don and Joan and the baby. I suggested, after listening a few minutes, that it seemed to me that Sheila's relationship with Don right now was important, rather than again talking about what had happened in the past. I asked the others in the group, "What do you think?"

The worker refused to allow Sheila to discuss ground that had already been covered in the group. Instead, she made a demand for work by focusing Sheila on the here-and-now details of her discussion with Don. A major step in such work involves asking the group members to take some responsibility for their part in their problems. Our defenses often cause us to explain our problems by projecting the blame onto others in our lives or justifying the present difficulty by describing past reasons. In this case, the worker focused the client and the group on the immediate situation in the belief that this was the only way to help. The client's responses elaborated on the specifics of the concern.

Sheila did not wait for a response and replied directly to me, "I feel so tense. I don't know what to talk to Don about. I don't want it to be like it was before we separated." I said, "You sound scared to death." Sheila became very sad and nodded. Evelyn added, "I have felt the same way with Jacques. I was his shadow. When he left and moved in with a girlfriend, I thought I could not exist on my own. I have learned to do so. Sheila, you talk as if you had no life of your own." Libby continued, "Do you always do what Don wants?"

Sheila then revealed the reason she was angry on the telephone with Don. She had earlier thought of going on a trip to England on her own and had wanted Don to say no. He had not, and when financially she had been unable to make the trip, she called Don expecting him to be very happy that she was staying. He was busy and did not say much. Sheila then accused him of not caring and hung up crying.

As the details emerged, so did a fuller picture of the problem. The worker recognized a common problem in intimate relationships—one partner feels that the other should "divine" what she is feeling and wants to hear, but when this does not happen, the first partner feels hurt. This is a specific example of a general problem: that risking ourselves by sharing real thoughts, feelings, and needs directly with those who are important to us is hard to do. As a group member began to provide feedback to Sheila on her part in the proceedings, she cut him off, and the worker moved quickly to point this out:

Bob started to say that Sheila had put Don on the spot, when Sheila interrupted and continued talking. I stopped her and said to the group, "Did you notice what just happened?" Everyone except Sheila and Bob smiled but said nothing. I said to Sheila, "Bob was trying to say something to you when you cut him off." She cut in to say anxiously, "Did I? I'm sorry, Bob." Bob quietly said, "My God, I didn't even notice. It has happened to me so often I guess I just expected to be cut off." She picked this up and said Don and Bob were alike and that Don let her get away with talking too much and cutting him off. Roberta commented, "Don seems hard to get close to," and there followed a few more comments on how Don seemed unapproachable.

The worker then challenged Sheila's view of the event and asked her to take responsibility for creating part of the problem. Because the worker had already built a positive working relationship with the group, Sheila could accept the confrontation and examine her own actions. As the group worked on the details of this specific example, it is easy to see how they were also working on their own variations on the theme.

I then went back to Sheila's telephone call and asked Sheila why she had called Don at work when he was likely to be busy, rather than calling him at home. She stumbled around and didn't answer the question. I kept pressing her with the same question and then asked the group if they had any ideas on this. Bob said, "I don't know what you are getting at." I said, "Let me check this out with all of you. My feeling is that Sheila called Don when she knew he would be likely to be busy and set it up so that he would probably be annoyed with her. Once again, she got very hurt." Evelyn added, "You did that with Don around the trip. Had he told you not to go to England, you would have been angry. If he told you to go, you would have said he did not care. I did the same thing with Jacques, and I never knew what I wanted. I was the little girl who asked her father's permission for everything."

Sheila said, "I guess I set things up so that I am the sad little girl and everyone feels sorry for me, just like I am trying to do tonight. How do I stop?" Bob said, "How do we stop hating ourselves—that is what it comes down to." Sheila continued thoughtfully, "You know I took the job at the airline so that Don and I could travel, and he really doesn't like traveling. I also bought him a bicycle to go cycling, but then found out he hates it." I said, "It sounds like you assume things about Don but somehow never check them out with him—how come?" There was a short silence, and I continued, "Is it because when, as Bob said, we hate ourselves, we are too scared to say what we feel or want?"

Sheila talked about how horrible and stupid she feels she is, and the group members gave her much support. They also reminded her of the one area where she feels she has accomplished something—teaching piano. She brightened and talked of her love of music and how she enjoyed teaching.

Roberta then remarked on how much everyone needs to be told they do some things well. She recounted an incident at work where she had been praised and how pleased she was. The others in the group, except Libby, agreed. She said it depended on whether or not you believed it. Sheila agreed and stated it was hard for her to accept praise. Evelyn went back to Sheila's relationship with Don, saying Sheila had given indications that she knew the marriage was breaking up, although she had said Don's decision to separate was a complete surprise. Sheila said she partly knew but did not want to admit it to herself. She had been withholding sexually, although they had had good sexual relations prior to marriage. I asked if she often gets angry at Don, and Sheila replied angrily, "I get furious at him, but I end up being bitchy, which I don't like. I am also scared he will leave." As the end of the group session was approaching, the members began making some suggestions around dealing with Don on the weekend. She should be a little more independent, say what she is feeling and not always what she thinks she should say.

As the group members work on a specific problem, workers should share any of their own thoughts and ideas that could help place the problem in a new perspective. To do this, they must draw on their own life experience; the information they have gathered by working with people, either individually or in groups, who have had similar concerns; and the professional literature. For example, in this brief excerpt, group members were learning something about taking responsibility for one's own actions, the difficulties involved in interpersonal communications, and specific interactional skills that might promote more effective interpersonal relationships. These agenda items were set in the context of their own experiences as they explored their often mixed feelings about themselves and others. Workers often serve to provide data that have been unavailable to the client and that may provide help with the problem or issue of the moment. In working with a couples' group, for example, the leader could draw on communications theory, ideas about "fair fighting" in marriage, developmental life theory, game model theory, gestalt, and the like. As workers deepen their own life experiences, as they use group experiences to learn more about the complexities of life, and as they review the literature, they can enrich their contributions to the group members' struggle.

Sessional Endings and Transitions

In Chapter 4 we discussed sessional endings and transitions, pointing out that each session requires a resolution phase. We saw that summarizing, generalizing, identifying next steps, rehearsal, and exploring "doorknob" comments were helpful skills for the worker at this stage. Each of these skills from work with individuals applies to the group session as well.

In the illustration that follows, a worker helped mothers with children diagnosed as hyperactive move toward more realistic next steps in their work as a mutual-aid group. In making this demand for work, the worker endorsed the power of resilience, suggesting that no matter how hopeless the situation may seem, the group could begin by taking steps on their own behalf.

> There was a lot of exchanging of problem situations, with everyone coming out with her problems for the week. There seemed to be some urgency to share their problems, to get some understanding and moral support from the other members. Through their stories, themes emerged: an inconsistency in handling their children's behavior (lack of working together with husband), the tendency to be overprotective, and their hesitancy in trusting their children. The issue of "nobody understanding" was again brought up, and I recognized their need to have someone understand just what it was that they were going through. Betty said that her son was never invited to play at the neighbors' houses, because he was a known disturber. Others had the same experiences with neighbors who didn't want their hyperactive son and daughter around. I expressed the hurt they were feeling over this, to which they agreed.
>
> After further discussion about the impact of their children on others (teachers, neighbors, children), they moved to a discussion of how their children's behavior affected them. Rose said that she ends up constantly nagging; she hates herself for it, but she can't stop. Her son infuriates her so much. Others agreed that they were the biggest naggers in the world. I asked what brought the nagging on. The consensus was that the kids kept at them until they were constantly worn down and they gave in to them. Also if they wanted the children to do something, they had to nag, because the children wouldn't listen. I said that the children really knew them, how they reacted, and also exactly what to do in order to get their own way. They agreed but said that they couldn't change—they couldn't keep up with the badgering that these children could give out.
>
> The group members expressed two divergent ideas: On the one hand, they "couldn't change," and on the other, they could not "keep up with the badgering."

They quickly moved to a discussion of medications as a source of hope for change. The worker pointed out that their hope in this solution was mixed with their recognition that the drugs were addictive and that they could not provide an answer in the long run. This is an example of a process in groups that Bion (1961) calls *pairing*, in which the discussion of the group members appears to raise the hope that some event or person in the future will solve the problem.

For these group members, drugs provided this hope but also gave them an opportunity to avoid discussing what they could do to deal with the problem. In a way, it represented a "primitive" group response: attempting to deal with the pain of a problem by not facing it. As the session moved to a close, the worker sensed the heaviness and depression caused by the group's sense of hopelessness. She had empathized with these feelings but now needed to make a demand for work on the members, asking them to explore what they could do about the problem. When the members raised another hope for a solution in the form of an outside expert who would help, the worker pointed out their real feelings that no "outsider" could help and that they needed to find the help within themselves. In this way, the worker helped them resolve a difficult and painful discussion by conveying her belief in their strength and her sense of the concrete next steps open to them.

> There was further discussion around the children's poor social behavior and the mothers' own worry about how these children will succeed as adults. What will become of them? Will they fit in and find a place for themselves in society? I was feeling the heaviness of the group and pointed out what a tremendous burden it was for them. Our time was up, and I made an attempt to end the meeting, but they continued the discussion. I recognized both their urgency to solve the problem and their need to talk with each other and get support from each other. Marilyn said that it was good; she came away feeling so much more relieved at being able to talk about how she felt, and she certainly was gaining some new insight into herself.
>
> Discussion diverted to the problem with the children and how they were to deal with it. I asked what they wanted to do. Edna suggested they ask a behavior modification therapist to help them work out solutions. Others thought it was a good idea. I said that was a possibility, but I wondered if in wanting to get an "expert" involved, they were searching for someone to solve their problems for them. They agreed. I asked if they thought all these experts could do this. They said that it hadn't happened yet. I wondered if we could use the group for the purpose it was set up, to help each other problem-solve. I suggested that next week we concentrate on particular problems and work together to see what solutions we could come up with. They seemed delighted with this and decided that they should write down a problem that happened during the week and bring it in. Then we could look at a number of problems. Consensus was reached as to our next week's agenda, and the meeting ended.

This illustration of one form of sessional ending and transition work brings to a close our description of the work phase in a mutual-aid group. Having seen the general model of the individual-group interaction, we can now examine the elements in depth and explore some variations on the theme. In the next chapter, we examine the individual's role in the group, concentrating on how members are informally assigned to play functional roles such as scapegoat, deviant, and internal leader. We also explore the needs of the group-as-a-whole and the way in which the group leader can help the group work on its central tasks.

Chapter Summary

The sessional skills for helping individuals also apply to the group setting. In the beginning stages of a session, group workers need to work with the individual and the group as they reach out to each other. During the work phase, mutual aid deals with general themes of concern explored over time as well as specific problems of individuals. Such concerns require the worker to make demands for work and show the members how to take responsibility for their part in problems. Groups can move from the general to the specific and from the specific to the general. Finally, as meetings draw to an end, successful helping involves striving for resolution.

Related Online Content and Activities

 Visit *The Skills of Helping* Book Companion Website at www.socialwork.wadsworth .com/Shulman06/ for learning tools such as glossary terms, InfoTrac College Edition keywords, links to related websites, and chapter practice quizzes.

The website for this chapter also features additional notes from the author and additional process recordings:

- African American Public Welfare Clients: Dealing With Issues of Authority and Racism
- Alternative Public Day School: Parents of Children With Emotional and Behavioral Difficulties
- Parole Group for Ex-Convicts: Dealing With Issues of Authority and Internalized Negative Self-Image
- Preadoption Group: Authority and the Illusion of Work
- Preadoption Group: Clarifying Purpose and Acknowledging Concerns
- Preadoption Group: Dealing With Friends and Relatives
- Welfare Mothers' Group: Mediating Between the Client Group and the Agency

CHAPTER TWELVE

Working With the Individual and the Group

The interactionist model presents the notion of two clients: the individual and the group. In this chapter an artificial separation of these two clients is employed to deepen your understanding of each in interaction with the other. First we focus on the individual within the group, discussing how clients bring their personalities to bear in their group interactions. The concept of role is used to help describe how individual personality is translated into group interaction. Many common patterns of individual-group relationships are described and illustrated; for example, we look at scapegoats, deviant members, gatekeepers, and monopolizers. As these individuals are isolated for closer analysis, you will see that understanding individual clients without considering them in the context of their group interaction is often impossible.

In the latter half of this chapter we examine the concept of the group-as-a-whole. This is the entity created when more than one client is involved at a time. I introduce an organismic model and illustrate some of the worker's tasks when he or she must intervene to help in the growth of the second client, the group.

The Concept of Role in a Dynamic System

Two ideas central to the discussion of the individual in a group are role and dynamic system. Ackerman (1958) describes the ways in which the term **role** has been used and proposes his own definition:

> Sociology, social psychology, and anthropology approach the problems of role through the use of special concepts and techniques. They apply the term in two distinct ways, meaning either the "role" of the person in a specific, transient, social position or the characteristic "role" of the individual in society as determined by his social class status. Working in the psychodynamic frame of reference, I shall use the term to represent an adaptational unit of personality in action. "Social role" is here conceived as synonymous with the operations of the "social self" or social identity of the person in the context of a defined life situation. (p. 53)

Ackerman suggests that the individual has both a private "inner self" and a social "outer self" that emphasizes externally oriented aspects of his or her personality. I shall use this idea of social role in the following way. When clients begin a group, they present their outer self as their way of adapting to the pressures and demands of the group context. Their pattern of action represents their social role. Ackerman argues that incongruity between the reality of the inner self and the outer self that is presented in a group can cause tension there. In many ways, the task of the group worker involves helping individuals find the freedom to express their inner selves in the group. The central idea is that each member brings to the group an established pattern of translating a unique personality into social action.

When considering oppressed and vulnerable groups, we can integrate Ackerman's notions about role with the oppression psychology concepts described in Chapter 1. The outer self of survivors of oppression represents their adaptive behavior to the defined situation of oppression. We can understand the incongruity between this outer self, which they present in social situations, and their inner self as one of the defense mechanisms employed in an effort to cope. This resulting incongruity is a form of alienation from self-identity, as described by Fanon (Bulhan, 1985). The effort in the mutual-aid group is to help members use the group to integrate their inner and outer selves and to find more-adaptive mechanisms of coping with oppression, including personal and social action. The small group is a microcosm of the larger society. If we consider the impact of oppression, our understanding of the role played by a survivor of oppression within a group context deepens.

Keeping in mind the concept of individual roles, we can view the group as a dynamic system, (see Chapter 5) in which the movements of each part (member) are partially affected by the movements of the other parts (the other members). This view is rooted in the work of Kurt Lewin (1935, 1951), who is often considered the founder of group dynamics. Thus, members bring their outer self into this dynamic system, then adapt to this system through their social roles. All group members engage in this process of adaptation. The model presented thus far provides a general description of the individual-social interaction in group. For our purposes, however,

I shall concentrate on specific social roles emerging over time and requiring special attention by the group worker.

Patterned social roles are most easily illustrated using an example from a formal, organized group, such as a tenants' association. To function effectively, the association usually identifies specific tasks that group members must assume and then assigns these jobs by some form of division of labor. For example, the association may need a chairperson, a secretary, a treasurer, and a program coordinator. The essential idea is that group roles are functionally necessary and are required for productive work. In taking on any of these roles, specific members will bring their own sense of social role to bear. For example, depending on their experience, their background, their skills, and their sense of social role, various members would implement the role of chairperson differently. Because the group is a dynamic system, the group and its individual members will also somewhat affect the chairperson's implementation of this role. The actions of the chairperson are best described as the product of the interaction among the individual's sense of social role, the role of chairperson as defined by the group, and the particular dynamics of the group and its members.

The roles just described are formal. Every group also creates less formal roles to help in its work, even though these might never be openly acknowledged. For example, in a group led by a worker who leads the discussion as an external leader, one or more internal leaders may emerge as if they had been formally elected. The individuals who assume internal leadership in a group often bring a concept of social role that includes this function. By responding positively to them, group members encourage the internal leaders' assumption of this important role.

Other, less constructive functional roles can emerge in a group; these reflect maladaptation rather than healthy development. For example, scapegoats are often selected by the group because they have the personal characteristic that members most dislike or fear in themselves. Thus, a group of young teenage boys who are worried about sexual identity may select as the group scapegoat the teen who seems least "macho" or least sure of himself. The members, of course, do not hold an election for such roles. It is not as if the group members held an informal meeting in the coffee shop, prior to the group session, and asked for volunteers to be the group scapegoats, internal leaders, deviant members, and so on. If the group has a need for these roles, however, they will go through a subtle, informal process to select members to fill them. The dysfunctional aspect of employing a scapegoat is that it often leads the group to avoid facing their own concerns and feelings by projecting them onto the scapegoat.

Similarly, individuals do not raise their hands and volunteer to act as scapegoats, pointing out that they have successfully played the scapegoat role in their families and social groups for most of their lives. The scapegoat in the group usually subtly volunteers for this role, because it is consistent with that individual's concept of his or her social role. Adapting to groups by playing this social role is as dysfunctional for the individual scapegoat as it is for the group as a whole. Once again, the idea of the group as a dynamic system helps us to understand the process of scapegoating in a dynamic way. (The next section explores the role of scapegoat in greater detail.)

In the sections that follow, we look at informal roles developed in groups, such as scapegoats, deviant members, monopolizers, and gatekeepers. (See the book's website for discussion and examples of other roles in the group.) In each case, the discussion focuses on analyzing the dynamics as they reflect the individual's social role within the group. In addition, we examine the skills of the group worker as he or she implements the individualizing part of the work.

The Scapegoat

The discussion of individual roles in the group begins with the scapegoat because it is both one of the most common and one of the most distressing problems in work with groups. The **scapegoat** is a member attacked, verbally or physically, by other members. These members are usually projecting onto the scapegoat their own negative feelings about themselves. The scapegoat role is often interactive in nature, with the scapegoat fulfilling a functional role in the group. Whether it is overt scapegoating in groups of children and adolescents or the more subtle type in adult groups, the impact on the group and the worker can be profound. As we explore this particular role in detail, I shall introduce several important concepts regarding social role in the group and the function of the group worker. These central ideas will reemerge as we examine other roles. This discussion can then serve as a general model for analyzing individual roles in the group.

First, we must consider the history of the term *scapegoat*. Douglas (1995) attributes the origin of the term to the 15th-century biblical scholar and translator Tyndale. Tyndale's translation of sections of Leviticus referred to an ancient ritual among the Hebrews practiced on the Day of Atonement. Two live goats were brought to the altar of the tabernacle. One was killed as a sacrifice. The second goat, after the high priest transferred his own sins and the sins of the people onto it, was taken to the wilderness and allowed to escape. Douglas suggests, "If Tyndale had read into the Hebrew idea that the goat was 'suffered to escape,' then his coining of the word 'scapegoat' becomes much clearer" (p. 8). Douglas describes the scapegoat ritual as

> essentially a process of purification, which means in essence that its practitioners felt that they were contaminated by the transgressions of their daily lives and that the ritual of scapegoating was one that would disperse that contamination and reinstate them as clean in their own eyes and, more importantly, in the eyes of their god. (p. 14)

Whole populations, such as African Americans, Jews, and homosexuals, have experienced extreme forms of scapegoating as part of the systematic oppression described in Chapter 1. These have included the projecting of negative stereotypes as an underlying justification for slavery as well as more current forms of economic and social oppression; anti-Semitism and the Holocaust in which millions of Jews (as well as many homosexuals, gypsies, and others) were systematically killed; and gay-bashing activities in which gays and lesbians are physically attacked on the street or serve as the butt of homophobic jokes.

Bell and Vogel (1960) have described the dynamics of this phenomenon in the family group, emphasizing the functional role played by the scapegoat in maintaining equilibrium in the family by drawing all of the problems onto him- or herself. Many scapegoats in groups have been socialized into this social role by their family experiences and are ready to assume it in each new group they enter.

Scapegoating is also discussed by Garland and Kolodny (1965), who provide an interesting analysis of the forms of scapegoating prevalent in practice:

> No single phenomenon occasions more distress to the outside observer than the act of scapegoating. Frequently violent in its undertones, if not in actual form, it violates every ethical tenet to which our society officially subscribes. As part of that society, the group worker confronted with scapegoating in the midst of interaction often finds himself caught up in a welter of primitive feelings,

punitive and pitying, and assailed by morbid reflections on the unfairness of fate which leaves one weak and others strong. (p. 124)

Another article addresses the common mistake in practice of the worker moving into the interaction between the scapegoat and group in a way that preempts the opportunity for either the group or the individual to deal with the problem (Shulman, 1967). Most often, when the worker protects the scapegoat, the hostility merely takes more covert forms. Appeals to fairness or requests to give the member a chance do not seem to help, and the worker is usually left feeling frustrated, the scapegoat hurt, and the group members guilty.

A Scapegoating Example

As we think about scapegoating in the social work group, the concepts of social role and the group as a dynamic system provide us with clues to the meaning of this interaction. We cannot understand the behavior of the scapegoat simply as a manifestation of his or her "personality." Rather, it is a result of the interaction between the scapegoat's sense of social role and the group's functional needs. The relationship between the individual role and the group need becomes clear if the group loses its scapegoat—if, for example, the member leaves the residence or drops out of the group. As though operating on an unconscious command, the group immediately searches for a new candidate to take the scapegoat's place. One member is usually waiting to do so.

The example that follows illustrates the scapegoating process, some of the pitfalls the worker faces, and effective strategies for intervention. In this example, we see a new worker's interventions with a group of teenage girls for 2 months in a school setting. The worker was white and the girls were African American and Hispanic. The worker started by developing insights into the scapegoating process and tuning in to her own feelings. Her protective responses toward the scapegoat were subtle; she tried to deal with the problem indirectly because of her concern over the possibility of hurting the member who was scapegoated. Although she never directly confronted the process, she did deal with the concerns of the second client, the group, which led the group to have less need for a scapegoat.

RECORD OF SERVICE

Client Description and Time Frame

A seventh-grade girls' peer support group of 12- and 13-year-old adolescents (3 African American and 2 Hispanic girls) from a racially mixed, low-income part of the city. The time frame is from 12/5 through 2/6.

Description of the Problem

This group is projecting its dependency needs onto one individual, causing the group to remain in the beginning stage of development. This individual, Rachel, acts out these dependency needs for the group. Rachel does her own thing, not involving herself in any group activities, keeping to herself. Thus, the group temporarily remains in the power and control stage, as described by Garland, Jones, and Kolodny (1965)—a stage in which authority, permission, autonomy, and confidentiality are crucial issues for these adolescent girls. The group's investment in the role of the scapegoat both hinders and helps the development of the group as it pushes toward its next stage, intimacy.

How the Problem Came to the Attention of the Worker(s)

On January 23, I observed that Rachel sat away from the other members of the group and refused to join in the group activity (which was painting) and was unwilling to speak. This behavior brought a negative reaction from the group, and the other girls hypothesized about why she was acting as a loner. The group soon ignored this behavior when Lisa brought up a "hypothetical" situation in which she was involved. Lisa stated that she was tired of a girl whom she used to be friends with and now does not like anymore. Lisa asked the group for advice about what to do and how to tell this girl. At this point, I saw that the girl she was discussing was Rachel. When questioned by the other girls as to who this girl was, Lisa would not say. At this moment I was very unsure of my position as a worker and what I should do about the situation. My first instinct was to see this as an issue that needed to be dealt with by Rachel and Lisa only, but, in thinking about it further, I decided it was indeed a group problem, especially considering our group goal of improving peer relations. It became clear to me that this need for the role of a scapegoat was an issue for the entire group.

Summary of the Work

December 5 (First Session)

We were discussing the purpose of the group, and I asked them what they thought some of the rules should be. Most of the members jumped in and offered suggestions, many of them expressing concern about confidentiality and "secrets." Rachel and Kim sat on either side of me, neither of them saying anything, but they nodded when Lisa and Amy asked them what they thought of a rule or idea they suggested. I attempted to engage Rachel and Kim in conversation, and I gave the group permission to make their own rules. I asked them both what they thought we should do as a group if someone broke our rule of confidentiality. They both replied by looking confused and shrugging their shoulders. Rachel said, "I don't know—what do you mean?" Lisa immediately jumped in, asked Rachel if she was "deaf or what?" and gave her idea of a "punishment," causing Rachel to sink in her chair and look down at the floor.

I could sense what was going on, but did not know how to respond to it. Looking back, I can see these were all issues related to the theme of authority. I did not want to discourage anyone from saying what they wanted, and did not want to push anyone into talking if they did not want to. I was simply thrilled that anyone was saying anything, and that they were enthused about the group.

December 12 (Second Session)

Kim had a problem and I supported her bringing it to the group. Kim told the group that she had a problem and that she wanted to ask everyone what she should do about it. She had been involved in a fight earlier that week and now she had to go to court. She said that she was afraid that she would be sent to a school where "they are real strict and don't let you do nothing you want to do." She asked me what she could do about this and asked if I could help her by talking to the principal for her. I told her I was glad that she brought this to the group. I asked the group what they thought about the situation. Lisa stated that, if the situation happened to her, she wouldn't worry about it because she knew her mother would not get mad at her and would not care. I completely missed the boat on this statement! Kim was discussing the entire incident with Mary, and the group became interested in the details of the fight. I became interested in who did what to whom and who was responsible for what, trying to determine if Kim was indeed going to be punished severely by the court system.

Kim told the group that the reason she got into the fight was because someone in the school had spread the rumor that she was pregnant. She said that she had to let everyone know that she was not, and so she had no choice but to get into this fight with the person who started the rumor. The group agreed that she did have to fight this girl because, after all, she had no business saying such things and she ruined Kim's reputation. (I missed an important issue the group was raising and asked the group to work on the more obvious issue.) I asked the group about other things they could do to avoid fighting in such a situation, and did not focus in on the pregnancy issue which, in retrospect, I think was the real problem. Almost everyone in the group was actively involved in a discussion of who can and cannot be trusted in their class, and who the people are in the school that spread rumors. I missed the significance of Rachel not participating in the discussion. I realized toward the end of the group that Rachel did not participate actively in the conversation and, in fact, had sat next to me again. I also was able to recognize the fact that I was quite uncomfortable in addressing the issue.

At a later session, the worker realized that she had missed the central theme of concern for Kim. Although Kim raised her problem in terms of the fight and the discipline, this was actually a first offering of her deeper concern—the fact that she was pregnant. The issue did not resurface until the fifth session.

December 19 (Third Session)

I avoided an issue that I was having a difficult time dealing with. The fact that Christmas is often a sad time for many poor people was an issue that I was unable to confront in this session. It was the last day of school before Christmas vacation, and only four of the members were there. We had a Christmas party and spent most of the time talking about what they would be doing with their time off. When I asked them what they would be doing, Lisa said nothing, and that it would be boring. I allowed countertransference to take over and I felt very guilty that I was excited about my own vacation and Christmas. I tuned out as a result of this guilt. Mary seemed very quiet; I assumed that it was because Kim was not in school that day (they are best friends). Cindy said that she was going to stay home, watch TV, and sleep.

Rachel asked if we could "have group" even though they did not have school. (She was sitting next to me again and I was aware of her need to be close to me and have me recognize her presence.) I used this as an opportunity to tell them that I would be on vacation and that we would not meet until the second Monday that they would be back in January. I then stated that, if I was going to be around, I would love to get together with them, and that maybe we could do something on a Saturday to make up for lost time. Lisa stated that under no circumstances would she want to get out of bed during her vacation or on a Saturday. I did not verbalize the feelings of the group. Rachel asked me where I was going and why I couldn't come back early. Mary immediately jumped in and told her that I obviously had another life and had important things to do. Lisa said that I was lucky to be leaving "this dirty and boring city." Although my first instinct was to side with Rachel and protect her, I reminded the girls that this was their group to do what they wanted with and it was up to them if they wanted to meet on a Saturday. In retrospect, I realize that I missed the issue they were raising: the fact that Christmastime is not fun for them and that they recognize differences between me, a middle-class, white worker, and themselves.

January 23 (Fourth Session)

Before group started, Rachel came in and told me that Lisa had been acting unfriendly toward her and that this upset her a great deal, because they were supposed to be best friends. We discussed some ways that she could confront Lisa on this and the friendship in general. Rachel told me that she wanted to meet two periods a week instead of one. I encouraged her to bring this up in group.

When everyone arrived for the group, the girls all asked why Rachel got to get out of class early to come and talk to me. They appeared annoyed that Rachel may have received "special attention" but soon forgot this discussion when Lisa brought up a problem. I supported Lisa for coming to the group for advice, but missed an underlying issue. Lisa told me that she had a problem this week and asked if we could please talk about her this week. She went on to say that this was a hypothetical situation and that it did not involve anyone they knew. Lisa said that she has a friend who is always doing everything she does, is always wearing the same clothes she wears, says the same things she says, and even likes the same boys she likes. I sensed that Lisa was talking about Rachel, and I felt a strong urge to protect the individual being scapegoated.

The group members jumped in on this subject and stated how they all hate this behavior. Rachel sat in the corner of the room, watching the group and looking out of the window. I suggested that maybe this friend really likes Lisa a great deal and she wants to be like her. Kim jumped in and agreed with me and told Lisa that she should be complimented. I made a demand for work. I asked the group what they would do in this situation. I made the assumption that I was the only one who knew the entire picture and acted accordingly. Everyone was very involved in the pictures they were drawing and did not seem to feel like discussing the subject.

In retrospect, I see that the group knew exactly what was going on and that it was my own feelings of discomfort that allowed me to avoid the issue. I avoided the main issued being raised in an attempt to protect the scapegoat. Lisa insisted on getting my opinion on the subject, even though I threw it out to the group for answers. I picked up on a conversation that Kim and Mary were having, and began talking with Cindy about a teacher they disliked. Lisa put her problem back on the table for discussion. I was feeling very annoyed at her insistence and I told her that we had answered her question and that she could come and discuss it with me later if she wanted to. As the members left that day, Lisa pulled me aside and told be that this person was Rachel and that she did not want Rachel to know. I was able to support her as an individual group member and told her that I would be free to speak with her later that morning and gave her a pass to get out of class.

The pattern of scapegoating is not directly addressed. Rachel, the group members, and the worker all know it is going on. The worker's reluctance is rooted in her not wanting to hurt Rachel, yet the persistent pattern of scapegoating is more painful than any direct discussion might be. Workers are also often afraid to open up an issue such as this because they are not sure what will happen and where it will go. The worker's indirect efforts to deal with the problem match the group members' own use of indirect communications, thus frustrating the growth of the group. As the group culture becomes more positive, the group members are able to deal with some of their issues and lessen their need for a scapegoat.

January 30 (Fifth Session)

I supported Kim for bringing a problem to the group. Kim brought up a problem she was currently dealing with and asked the group for advice. She said that she has a friend who thought she was pregnant. Her friend's cousin told her to drink "this awful stuff" to get rid of the baby. She said her friend did not want the baby, but that her friend's boyfriend wanted it very badly. Now her friend does not know what to tell her boyfriend. I reached for the group's feelings. The group immediately confronted Kim and wanted to know if she was speaking about herself. Kim said it was a friend. I said that this must be very difficult and was a scary situation to be in. I verbalized the group's nonverbal behaviors. I acknowledged that there seemed to be a great deal of tension around the subject of pregnancy and that it was a difficult topic of discussion. Cindy said that her mother would kill her if she ever came home pregnant and that she felt sorry for this girl. I pointed out to the group that the problem was not only an individual issue, but also an issue for the group. The members appeared uneasy discussing the topic of pregnancy and even willing to change the subject and talk about something else.

The group tried to avoid the issue by concentrating on who in the school they thought could be pregnant. I made a demand for work. I stated to the group that a member had raised an important question and that it was an issue that demanded their attention. I asked the group what they would tell their boyfriends in a similar situation. Lisa stated that she would simply dump him and not tell him, since he must be crazy to think a 12-year-old should have a baby. Rachel stated that she did not have a boyfriend, and Mary said that she would tell him and hope he did not leave her. At this point, Kim broke in and told the group that it was her whom she was talking about. I said that everyone might be feeling a great deal of emotion and that it must have taken a great deal of courage and trust to come to the group with this issue. The members focused in on the situation, giving Kim advice, and reflecting the situation onto themselves, talking about what they would do in such a situation.

In this session the group did not appear to need the scapegoat; the conversation was intense, and everyone worked together on the issue at hand. I began to feel that the group was progressing, and I felt much more in tune with my own feelings about things that happened in the group. I was able to catch myself more quickly and did not feel such a strong urge to protect everyone.

February 6 (Sixth Session)
A girl, Sandy, was very interested in joining our group and, because she was a good friend of the other members, I considered it and brought it up in group. I encouraged the group to state their feelings. The group had very divided reactions. Kim said, "There is no way I'm going to stay in this group if Sandy comes here . . . it's either her or me!" I reminded the group that they are in control. I told them that this is their group and that they are the ones who make the rules, and that the decision about Sandy is up to them. Rachel said that she liked Sandy, but that she knew that Sandy already came to the Collaborative for individual counseling. "She already gets to come down all of the time, so why should she get to come when we are here?" I made a demand for work and asked for clarification. Rachel stated that it is not fair that some people get to come to talk one-on-one whenever they want, but that they themselves can come only one time a week for only one period. Mary said that she likes Sandy also, but that she has too many problems and would not fit in with our group.

I missed the racial issue that came up in Lisa's next statement because I was so wrapped in the issue at hand. Lisa (who is African American like Mary) said to her, "You dumb nigger, what you think this group is for, anyway?" I used the current issue to talk about how they may be feeling about the group. I told the girls that it is OK if they want to keep the group the way it is now, and that they all seemed to be happy with the way it has been going. I then suggested that many of them need a place to come and talk about their feelings and that they've found this to be a good place to do that. Rachel (sitting next to me) said that she was glad that they could keep me "all to themselves." Lisa said, "I don't think that's fair; we don't need to be here as much as Sandy does . . . I don't see why this is so important to you, Rachel."

I verbalized the feelings that appeared to be present. I said I think that you are all saying that you don't want Sandy in the group, because you all need this group for yourselves and that, because you like it so much, you would rather not let someone new in. We have a great group here and you are happy with who we have in the group now. It's not easy to show that you need something and like something. Sometimes when you are a teenager you need to be really independent and don't want to rely on anyone. That's OK to do; it means that you are growing up! But it's also OK to need to talk about these feelings and to need your friends. Lisa said that she could not wait to grow up so that she could move out of the house and be on her own. I focused on what she was saying. Mary said yeah, she didn't always like it at home either, so growing up and moving out as soon as possible was a good idea. I made a demand for work. I asked them what it was like for them at home and how it felt to want to leave.

As soon as a reason for scapegoating was identified, the group steered away from Rachel and did not seem to need to scapegoat her. Instead, they began discussing their home situations and saying to me indirectly that they did, indeed, need someone to talk to about growing up. They were able to begin to show me their individual dependency needs and not feel like they had to scapegoat Rachel for outwardly showing hers.

Current Status of the Problem

Where It Stands Now

The group has entered the intimacy stage and, although power and control remain essential issues in the group, they are not issues that dominate our entire group sessions. We are able to do "real work" and discuss issues that they want to talk about. Scapegoating still occurs at times, but I am able to recognize it and address it at some level. I have found that, when I call attention to the scapegoating, it is no longer an issue (at least at that time). Rachel has been integrated into the group more often and has not been in the role of the scapegoat in our last few sessions. The group is able to discuss issues that are of concern to them, such as boys, friendship, and the violence that they frequently see in their neighborhoods.

Other issues are still very difficult for them to talk about, such as racism, what it's like to be black or Hispanic in the city, and the fact that I am a middle-class, white worker in a group for minority girls. The theme of authority remains an issue for the group, as they have a difficult time understanding that they have control of this group. I need to work on letting them know this more often. It is when the members fully understand and accept the purpose of the group that they will no longer need the role of the scapegoat and will be able to move completely into the stage of intimacy.

Strategies for Intervention

- I will be aware of the group's occasional need for a scapegoat and will investigate the reasons behind such a need.
- I will verbalize and bring out in the open issues that are hidden and are under the surface.

- I will continue to make demands for work and challenge the group to explore their feelings on issues that are difficult for them to discuss.

- I will let the members know that the group and I are there for them and that it is OK to express dependency needs.

- I will try to make myself and the group available on an occasional Saturday and vacation day so that the members recognize that the group is also important to me.

- I will continue to address the power and control issues that the group has and will let them know that the group belongs to them.

- I will empower both the individual members and the group to feel comfortable with both their emerging feelings of independence and their dependency needs.

- I will challenge the group about their need for the role of a scapegoat and bring to the surface my feelings about what is happening.

- I will encourage Rachel's need to be dependent on me and the group, yet at the same time I will look for meaning in her need to take on this role.

- I will make quicker verbalizations of what I am observing, pointing my impressions out to the group.

- I will continue to make the group aware of the fact that I'll be leaving in May and will challenge them to discuss their feelings about this.

Note that this student-worker identifies race as an issue for the girls in their lives and an issue between the girls and herself. She even includes it in her assessment of where the problem stands; however, she identifies it as an issue that the members are having difficulty discussing. However, her list of strategies for intervention does not include any in this area. This is an agenda item for her professional growth. Her struggle in dealing with this crucial issue is not uncommon, and she will need support and supervision to recognize that her group members' difficulty in exploring the potentially explosive area of race reflects her own reluctance. When they are clear that she is ready, they will respond. This would be important to free her to attend to the meaning of the clues that emerge, including the African American member's use of the self-derogatory phrase "dumb nigger" to refer to the scapegoat.

By understanding the dynamics of scapegoating, the worker can more easily avoid the trap of siding with either the individual or the group. This natural response misses the essential message: that the group and the scapegoat are using the process as a means of raising a theme of concern. The process can best be understood as an attempt, albeit maladaptive, to offer a theme of concern. Because scapegoating may be the only way the group members know to deal with their thoughts and feelings, the worker should not get too upset with either the group or the scapegoat. The worker's task involves helping the group and the scapegoat to recognize their patterns and helping them find a new way of dealing with concerns common to both. By viewing both the individual and the group as clients in need, the worker can become better at understanding and empathizing with the feelings the two share.

Dealing With the Scapegoating Pattern

Work with the scapegoating pattern involves several steps. First, the worker observes the pattern over time. Second, the worker must understand his or her own feelings in the situation to avoid siding with or against the scapegoat. By using the tuning-in skill, the worker can attempt to search out the potential connections between the scapegoat and the group. If the worker is not clear about these, he or she can ask the group to reflect on the question. The next step involves pointing out the pattern to the group and the scapegoat. Thus, the worker asks the group to look at its way of working and to begin the struggle to find a more positive adaptive process.

When workers challenge this scapegoating process, they must not criticize either the group or the scapegoat for having developed this way of dealing with their underlying feelings. In fact, the capacity for empathy and understanding of how hard it is to face these feelings is the very thing that allows the worker to make this demand for work. This demand includes two tasks: asking the group to consider why they are scapegoating and asking the scapegoat to reflect on reasons for volunteering for the role. Discussion of this process is designed to free the members to explore further their underlying feelings. It would be a mistake to support ongoing discussions of the individual's life pattern of being a scapegoat or the group's analysis of its process. When the discussion is honest, invested with feeling, and touching all the members, then the group will no longer need a scapegoat. The discussion may help them moderate their harsh judgments of themselves that lead to the need for a scapegoat. In turn, the scapegoat may discover his or her feelings are not unique.

The Deviant Member

One of the most difficult clients for workers to deal with is the *deviant member*. In this discussion, the term is used broadly to describe a member whose behavior deviates from the general norm of the group. This deviation can range from extremely inappropriate and disconnected behavior (as in a participant who refuses to stop talking at the first meeting or a member who manifests psychotic behavior) to one whose actions deviate only mildly or sporadically (as in a member who stares out the window while the rest of the group is deeply involved in a discussion). In my practice, I have made two major assumptions about such behavior. First, deviant behavior is always a form of communication. The worker's problem lies in figuring out what the member is saying. This difficulty is compounded by the fact that workers often experience the deviance as directed toward themselves, thus activating powerful emotions in the workers. For example, workers may see acting-out behavior in a children's group as testing their authority. Second, deviant behavior in a group may be expressing a communication that has meaning for the group as a whole. That is, just as the group may use a scapegoat as a means of dealing with difficult feelings, a deviant member may be serving an important social role for other group members. This assumption is related to the view of the group as a dynamic system. In this section we explore these two assumptions.

Again, we can consider deviant behavior on a continuum ranging from extreme to slight. On the extreme end would be a client or group member who evinces bizarre behavior that is totally inappropriate for the group. This can happen on occasions when meetings are open to the community or screening of prospective members has not taken place. When this happens in a first session, the impact on the worker and the group is profound. As the member speaks, one can sense the group shrinking in embarrassment and at times in fear. The leader needs to take responsibility for gently but firmly asking the member to withhold comment or, in extreme cases, to leave the session. Group members are not prepared, in an early session, to deal with extreme deviance and therefore depend on the group worker to clarify the boundaries and to enforce the limits if needed.

Extreme Versus Mild Deviance

In one such example, a woman attending a foster parent recruitment session responded to the worker's opening contract statement and requests for group feedback by beginning a long, and essentially unrelated, tale of personal tragedy. When the worker tried repeatedly to clarify the contract or to discover how the woman's concerns might relate to the discussion, she met with no success. The woman refused to allow others to speak and went on in detail about her personal problems and her fears that people were after her—even that the room was bugged. The discomfort in the eyes of the group members was clear. The worker, herself uncomfortable, finally moved to control the situation.

WORKER: Mrs. Pane, it is obvious that you're having a tough time right now, but I simply can't let you continue to use this group meeting to discuss it. I'll have to ask you to leave, but I would be glad to talk with you further about your concerns at another time.

MRS. PANE: You f—ing workers are all alike. You don't give a s—t about us, you're no different from the rest. You took my kids away, and I want them back.

WORKER: I'm sorry, Mrs. Pane, I can't talk with you now about that. You will have to leave, and I can discuss this with you tomorrow.

Mrs. Pane finally left, and the worker turned to the group to acknowledge how upset she was feeling about what had just happened. The group members expressed their own feelings. After emotions had settled, the worker picked up the group members' reactions to Mrs. Pane as a parent of children in the care of the agency. This led to a discussion of parents, their feelings about placements, and contacts between natural parents and foster parents. The worker followed up the next day with Mrs. Pane and did get to see her. There was a long, sometimes rambling and disjointed conversation during which the worker consistently tried to reach Mrs. Pane and acknowledge her feelings. Mrs. Pane turned to the worker as she left and said, "I'm sorry for what I said last night. You know it's just that I'm so angry—I miss my kids so much." Mrs. Pane's behavior at the meeting was an extreme example of the use of deviant behavior to express deeply held feelings. The worker could not allow the session to be captured by Mrs. Pane and, using all of her courage, she protected the group's contract.

Most workers do not experience such extremes of deviant behavior. This example has been included because workers often fear that such an experience will happen to them and because it demonstrates how even bizarre behavior contains a message for the worker. On the other end of the continuum is an example drawn from another group for foster parents who already had children in their homes. The worker was well into the presentation of introductory material on the agency and fostering policies, when a member arrived. She was dressed elaborately, wore a big hat, and sauntered up to the front of the room. All eyes in the group followed her as she made a grand entrance. The worker was shaken by her entry but continued to speak. As the woman sat there, the worker noticed what appeared to be a scowl on her face and occasional grimaces in response to the worker's comments. The worker later described how she tended to "speak to this member" as the evening drew on. After the session, unable to contain herself because of the implied negative behavior, the worker inquired why the member seemed so antagonistic. The member, who had not said a word during the evening, was surprised by the worker's question. She explained that she was not angry at all, and that in fact, she was having a really hard time with her new foster child, because it was her first time fostering, and she was looking forward to getting help from these sessions.

Reaching for the Underlying Message of Deviant Behavior

It is striking how often group leaders are surprised to find relatively normal reactions and feelings underlying initial deviant behavior that they have taken as personal attacks. For example, a group member whose first comment is to challenge the need for the group itself or who responds defensively about his own need for help may seem deviant at first but not later, after the source of the behavior comes to light. All that is needed, at times, is to confront the group members directly and to ask about the meaning of the behavior. Two skills are involved: the ability to tolerate deviant behavior and the ability to reach for the underlying message. Consider the following example from a group for children having trouble in school. The meetings were held at the school in the afternoon, and John started acting up as he entered the meeting room. He picked a fight with Jim, knocked over the desk, and appeared ready to tackle the group worker next.

WORKER: John, what the hell is up? You have been roaring mad since you walked in here. (John remains silent, glaring with his fists clenched.) Did you just come from a fight with someone? Or was it Mr. Smith [the teacher]? Did you have an argument with him?

JOHN: (Still angry, but slightly more relaxed) He's always picking on me, the bastard.

WORKER: OK, now slow down and tell me what happened. Maybe we can help you on this one. That's what the group is all about.

The worker was able to reach for the meaning behind this behavior, instead of getting caught up in a "battle of wills" with John, because he understood his own function, was clear about the purpose of the group, and understood that children often raise their problems indirectly by acting out. The group member does not always immediately respond to the worker's efforts to reach past the behavior; however, he often understands the worker's meaning and will sometimes pick up the invitation later. Clarity of function is important, because if the worker is concentrating solely on his limit-setting function (as in stopping the fight), he may miss the other part of the work. The skill often involves setting the limit and reaching for the meaning of the behavior at exactly the same time.

Deviant Behavior as a Functional Role

As mentioned earlier, deviant behavior may in some way reflect the feelings of the group-as-a-whole. This notion stems from the idea of the group as a dynamic system, in that the movement of one member is somewhat affected by the movements of the others. The deviant member can be viewed as simply a member who, for various reasons, feels a particular concern or emotion more strongly than the others in the group do. This greater sense of urgency causes the deviant member to express the more widely held feeling, often in an indirect manner.

Schwartz (1961) refers to the function of the deviant member in the client group as follows:

> Such clients often play an important role in the group—expressing ideas that others may feel but be afraid to express, catalyzing issues more quickly, bringing out the negatives that need to be examined, etc. This helped us to see that such members should not immediately be thought of as "enemies" of the group, diverting it from its purposes, but as clients with needs of their own, and that these needs are often dramatic and exaggerated versions of those of the other group members. (p. 11)

It is critical, therefore, that the group leader not dismiss a deviant group member too quickly as simply acting out a personal problem. This would constitute the mistake of attempting to understand the movements of one member of a dynamic system (the group) apart from the movements of other members of the system. While this member may bring this particular social role to bear in all groups, one cannot understand him or her simply as a separate entity. The first hypothesis should always be that the member may be speaking for the group-as-a-whole. In the first session of the couples' group described in detail earlier, the member (Lou) who attacked "professionals" was carrying out the important task of dealing with the authority theme, an issue for the whole group.

The following examples demonstrate two specific ways in which deviant behavior operates functionally: in opening up a discussion of group function and in deepening the work already in progress.

Opening a Discussion of the Group's Functioning In the following excerpt, a member attacks the purpose of the group in a counseling session at a psychiatric hospital:

MR. WRIGHT: (Who has been quiet for most of the first two sessions, although he seemed to have a critical look on his face) I think this is really all a bunch of crap! How in the hell is it going to do us any good sitting around and talking like this?

MRS. SAMUELS: Well, you know, you really haven't had much to say. Maybe if you spoke up, it would be more worthwhile.

For most inexperienced workers, the force of the attack would be taken personally because the worker felt fully responsible for the success of the group. It would not be unusual for the worker to view Mr. Wright as negative, hostile, and resistant and to set out to challenge him or encourage the group members to "take him on." For example, "Mr. Wright doesn't seem to think the group is too helpful. Do the others feel that way, or do they feel the way Mrs. Samuels does?" If Mr. Wright's behavior is viewed in the context of the dynamic interaction, and if the worker sees him as a potential ally, he might instead help him to elaborate.

WORKER: I think it's important that we hear Mr. Wright out on this. If there are problems with the group, maybe we can work them out if we can talk about them. What's bothering you about the group?

MR. WRIGHT: Well, for one thing, I don't think we are leveling with each other. We're not really saying what's on our minds. Everybody is too busy trying to impress each other to be honest.

WORKER: You know, that often happens in the first few sessions of a new group. People are unsure of what to expect. How about it, have any of the others of you felt that way?

Mr. Peters: I didn't last week, but this week I thought the discussion was a bit superficial.

By treating the deviant member as an ally rather than as an enemy, the worker gave permission for the group to begin a frank discussion of how they were working. Others in the group felt the freedom to express their dissatisfaction, and as a result, the members began to take responsibility for making their group more effective. This kind of discussion is essential for all groups, but it is often considered impolite to be direct in such areas. Members feel they do not want to "hurt the worker's feelings." As the group proceeded, the worker found that Mr. Wright, rather than not wanting to work, had several pressing issues he wished to deal with. His sense of urgency had forced him to speak out. Often in a group, the member who seems most negative and angry is the one who wants to work the hardest. It is easy to understand, however, how the worker's feelings might make it hard to see Mr. Wright in a more positive way.

Deepening a Discussion Expressions of deviant positions in a group are often a lever for the group leader to deepen a discussion. For example, in one group on parenting skills, a major argument occurred when Mr. Thomas expressed the view that "all of this talk about worrying about the kids' feelings is nice for social workers but doesn't make sense for parents. Sometimes, the back of the hand is what they need." The other members pounced on Mr. Thomas, and a verbal battle royal ensued. Once again, for new workers who are not clear about their function, the expression of an idea that ran counter to their view of good parenting would arouse a strong reaction. The new worker would be particularly angered by the jibe about social workers and might set out to "educate" Mr. Thomas. Instead, this worker saw Mr. Thomas as expressing a feeling that in part was true for all the parents but was not considered "proper" in this group. The worker reached to support Mr. Thomas:

Worker: You are all attacking Mr. Thomas's position quite strongly; however, I have a hunch there must be many times when all of you feel the same way. Am I right? (Silence.)
Mr. Fisk: There are times when the only feelings I'm interested in are the ones he has on his behind when I let him have one.

With the worker's help, Mr. Thomas gave permission for the parents to begin to discuss the reality of parenting, which includes anger, loss of temper, and frustration. The worker continued by asking Mr. Thomas why he felt he had to express this position so strongly.

Worker: You know, Mr. Thomas, you come on so strong with this position, and yet you don't strike me as someone who doesn't care about how his kids feel. How come?
Mr. Thomas: (Quietly, looking down as he spoke) Feelings can hurt too much.
Worker: What do you mean?
Mr. Thomas: It wasn't easy to talk with my kids when their mother died.
Worker: (After a silence) You really know what that is like, don't you? (Mr. Thomas just nodded.)
Mr. Simcoe: I've never had to handle something that tough, but I know what you mean about it being hard to listen when your kids are pouring out the hurt.

In summary, the deviant member who challenges the authority of the leader provides negative feedback on the work of the group, raises a point of view contrary to the group's norm, or fights strongly and with emotion for a position may be playing an important functional role in the dynamic system of the group. The deviant member can be an ally for the worker if the worker can deal with personal feelings and then listen to the deviant member as a messenger from the group. In this last example, we can see how a deviant member can turn into an active participant over time.

The Internal Leader: Ally or Enemy?

Group workers who are unsure of their function often experience internal leaders as a threat to their own authority, even viewing them as deviant members. Actually, if the mutual-aid process is central to the work, workers know that the work is going well when an internal leader emerges. The mistake of viewing the internal leader as a deviant member is most evident in work with teenagers and children, when the internal leader challenges the authority of the worker.

The following excerpt is from a first meeting of a group I led during my first year of social work professional training. I share this example for several reasons. First, students need to realize that all workers start out with similar feelings, making most of the same mistakes. Many students who read examples of my more recent work with married couples, single parents, or people with AIDS do not know about the many mistakes I made, and still make, during my professional development. Second, this particular group—acting-out adolescents—can be one of the most painful and stressful groups to lead. I still vividly remember dreading the early sessions, which seemed like a perpetual battle of wills—a battle both the group and I were destined to lose. Third, it provides a good illustration of how the worker may at first see an internal leader as "the enemy" rather than as an ally. Finally, it is an example of a community center group in which activities are a central part of the work. These kinds of groups often make up the bulk of early group practice of social workers.

The group consisted of acting-out adolescents (13 and 14 years old) who were members of a community center club. I had been warned that they were a difficult group and that they had given other workers a tough time in the past. Although the group was set up so that the club members planned their own activities, the agency had structured the first night by planning a mass sports program in the gym. The first issue on the group members' minds was "What sort of worker will this be?" but my supervision had mistakenly led me to think that I must "demonstrate my authority in the first session and assert myself as leader," which in effect began the battle of wills.

> Only five boys had shown up by 7:45, so we spent the first 10 minutes talking about the club last year. At this point, Al showed up and completely changed the tone of our meeting. It seemed as if the first five boys had been waiting for the catalyst that had finally arrived. Al was bubbling over about the school football game he had played in that afternoon. It was their first win in 3 years. When I asked how it had gone, he described it abruptly. He then wanted to know what we were doing that night. When I explained the prearranged evening program he became very negative about it. "Rope jumping" (one of the competitive events) "is for girls," he replied. I told him boxers use rope jumping for training, and he replied, "I'm not a boxer, and I'm not a girl." Although the other boys had not been overly enthusiastic about the evening program when I had described it earlier, their tone changed sharply as they agreed with Al.

Lack of clarity of function and initial nervousness led me to defend the program and to see Al as competition. Contracting was unclear, and an important discussion about the role of the worker in relation to the group members was missed because of my own fears and misconceptions. As the meeting proceeded, I got myself deeper into trouble:

> I tried to discuss at least next week's program with the guys. Girls from another club started pressing their faces against the window of the door, and before I could stop him, Al was racing to the attack. The contagion was immediate, and what had been a quiet group of boys were now following their leader. I jumped up and asked them to ignore the girls. Instead, they chose to ignore me. I went over to the door, closed it, and politely guided them back to the desk. This time, when they sat down, Al's feet were on the table (one of the wooden-finish types). Five more pairs immediately joined Al's (the testing was in full swing). I asked them to remove their feet, because they could damage the table. Joe and Ken responded, but the others didn't. I tried to maintain a light and firm stand. They slowly responded, stating that last year's leader let them keep their feet up that way. Another said there were a lot of things their leader let them do last year that I probably would not. I said that I would only allow them to do these things that were acceptable to the agency. One of the boys asked me what an agency was. I explained I meant the center (first week of field work and I was already overprofessional). It was time to hit the gym for the games (much to my relief).

It is clear that my sense of function, that of "taming the group," led me to miss important issues. Discussing the last leader's role would have been helpful. In addition, relationships with girls was an emerging and uncomfortable theme for this group, given their age. Al was the only club member to dance with girls later in the evening during the social part of the program. He asked about having a party with a girls' group, and I put off his request by saying, "We would need to plan this ahead of time." Al provided leadership in several areas, expressing the feelings and concerns of the group, but because I missed the importance of his role, a battle over "who owned the group" resulted.

Because I missed the signals, the indirect testing continued. Al led the members in throwing paper around the club room and leaning out of the windows, spitting on other center members as they left. I kept trying to set limits while not allowing myself to get angry (not thought to be professional). Finally, my instincts got the better of me.

> I said I would like to say a few words before we finished. I was attempting to reestablish the limits I had set earlier, but my own feelings got the best of me. I explained that this evening was really difficult for me and that probably it was so for them too. I said that if we couldn't relax enough to discuss further programs, there probably wouldn't be any. At this point, I said something that surprised me as I said it. I said their behavior better improve, or they could find themselves a new leader. They replied by saying that compared with the group members who hadn't shown up this evening, they were well behaved. My reaction to this group was mild panic.

It is easy to understand my panic in this situation. My idea of being professional was to be able to "handle" the group without losing my temper. Actually, in these moments at the end of the meeting when I revealed my real feelings, I was starting to develop a working relationship with the group members. After a few more sessions of off-and-on-again testing, I moved to discuss the issue of the authority theme and to help the group members develop their own internal leadership and structure.

> I told the boys that because I had been with them for 5 weeks, they might be interested in hearing what I thought about the group. They perked up at this.

Bert said, "You love us," and everyone laughed. I said that during this time I had been able to talk to each one of them individually and seemed to get along well. However, when we got together as a group, we couldn't seem to talk at all, right from the beginning. In spite of what they said, I thought that each one of them was concerned about stealing, acting wise all the time, and being disrespectful. Al said (very seriously this time) that it was different when they were in the group. I asked why that was so. Bert asked all the guys if they had stolen anything, and they all agreed that they had. After some discussion I told them I thought they were really afraid to say what they thought in the group. Bert said he wasn't afraid. I asked about the others. Al mockingly put up his fists and said, "I'm not afraid of anyone in the group." I laughed with the rest and said I thought it was easy to be brave with your fists but that it took a lot more courage to say something you thought the other guys would not like. I said it was their club, and although it was important to me, it was really more important to them. Joel made a wisecrack, but he was silenced by Ken, who said, "That's just the kind of thing he [the worker] was talking about."

As the discussion continued, the boys explained that they often didn't like my suggestions for activities, and I encouraged them to say so in the future, because it was their club. A surprising amount of feeling emerged about the kidding around in the group, much of it directed at one boy who acted out a great deal but was not present that night. They talked about how they could plan their own programs. The group members suggested that I could bring in ideas from other clubs and that they would then decide what they wanted. At this point, Al suggested they have a president. After some discussion about the respective positions, a president (Al), vice-president (Bert), and treasurer (Ken) were elected. A social committee was also formed to speak with the girls' club to discuss a party.

At this point in the meeting, I realized we were actively talking about something with no kidding around and no testing of me. I felt at ease for the first time. I commented to them about this. Al said, "We won't be able to do this all the time." I said I realized this and that there still would be a lot of kidding around. It would be OK as long as they could pull themselves together at times to get their work done. Al said that would be his job, and that I could help by telling them when they got out of hand. I agreed.

At the end of the process recording, I commented that "all of the boys gave me a warm good-bye" as I left the building. From this point on, much of the work shifted to helping the group members develop their own structure. For example, I met with Al before sessions, at his request, to help him plan the agenda and to discuss his problems in chairing the sessions.

These group sessions were a painful initial lesson on the need to clarify my function and recognize the group's internal leadership. I had experienced Al as the groups' deviant member, when in reality, he was their internal leader. I had told them it was their group but, following a different paradigm of practice, I believed it was really my group for implementing my "social work purposes." I encouraged them to plan activities when I already had the "appropriate" activities in mind. I experienced Al as my enemy, when in reality he was my main ally. Chapter 15 includes further illustrations of my work with this group, in which I describe what the group taught me about helping clients to negotiate the system—in this case the community center.

The Gatekeeper

The previous section pointed out that the deviant member is often the one who feels the strongest sense of urgency about a particular issue. In a sense, the deviant behavior is an effort to move the group toward real work. The internal leader often serves this function in a healthier, more direct way. A group can be ambivalent about work in the same way an individual can be, and members can take on the function of expressing that ambivalence for the group. This is sometimes seen in the form of a **gatekeeper** role, in which a member guards the "gates" through which the group must pass for the work to deepen. When the group discussion gets close to a difficult subject, the gatekeeper intervenes to divert the discussion.

In one group, for example, every time the discussion appeared to approach the issue of the worker's authority, one female member would light up a foul-smelling cigar or in some other way attract the group's ire. The group would rise to the bait, and the more difficult authority theme would be dropped. The worker pointed out the pattern, describing what he saw: "You know, it seems to me that every time you folks get close to taking me on, Pat lights up a cigar or says something that gets you onto her back. Am I right about this?" The group rejected the interpretation and turned on the leader with anger, thus beginning to deal with the authority theme. Later in the session, Pat commented that the worker's observation might be accurate, because she had always been fearful of seeing her parents fight and probably had done the same thing in childhood. It was not appropriate in this group to discuss the reasons for the pattern, either Pat's or the group's reasons, nor did the group members need to agree with the observation. The mere statement of the pattern offered the group an opportunity to face the worker directly, and Pat no longer needed to carry out this role.

People often use humor to protect the gates in difficult and painful areas. A group member, usually one who has learned to play this role in most areas of her or his life, will act out, crack a joke, make a face, and so forth in an effort to get the group members and the leader laughing and distracted. Note that humor can also be used to help advance the work of the group and does not always represent a means of gatekeeping. It helps, at times, to be able to laugh when facing painful work. Staff groups, for example, often use macabre humor to deal with their tensions. However, when this the only means of releasing tension, and the underlying feelings resulting from the stresses and traumas are not dealt with, such humor can cause worker burnout rather than preventing it. With the client group, the worker needs to observe the pattern over time and to note the results of the use of humor. If the humor consistently results in an illusion of work, then the gatekeeper function is a likely explanation.

In the following example of gatekeeping through humor, a worker in a residential setting picks up directly on the sexual innuendo involved in an apparently casual conversation in the lounge. The boys are young teens.

FRANK: (Watching a television show) Wow! Look at the build on that broad. Boy, I wish I could meet her after the show.

LOU: You wouldn't know what to do with her if you had her, you big jerk. Besides, your pecker isn't big enough. (At this comment there is general kidding around and teasing of a sexual nature.)

WORKER: You know, you guys kid around a lot about this sex business, but I bet you have a lot of questions on your mind about it—a lot of serious questions.

FRANK: What kind of questions?

WORKER: Well, I'm not sure about your questions, but I bet you are interested in what would make you attractive to women, sexually, and how you actually handle sexual relations as well as other relations with women. It's probably a tough area to talk about seriously.

LOU: My old man never talked to me about sex.

TERRY: (Who has a pattern of clowning in the group) Did you hear the story about the kid who asked his father where he came from? The father gave him a 15-minute sex talk, and then the kid said, "That's funny, and Jimmy comes from Chicago." (Some of the boys laughed and others groaned.) I got another good one . . .

WORKER: Hold it, Terry! There you go again. Every time we get to some serious discussions in tough areas, you start with the jokes. And the rest of you guys go right along with it. What's wrong? Is it tough to talk about sex without kidding around?

The boys returned to the conversation with several serious questions specifically related to sex, as well as others related to the whole question of intimacy with women. Terry sat quietly during the discussion and did not participate. The worker later talked alone with Terry about his discomfort in such discussions. The worker asked if it was related to some of his difficult sexual experiences. Terry's mother had been a prostitute, and he had been a male prostitute for a time when he was 12. He could not talk about this in front of the other boys, and the worker had respected this. In most cases the gatekeeper carries out this functional role because he feels the resistance aspect of the group's ambivalence a bit more strongly than the rest of the members do. In a sense he is the spokesman for this feeling, in the same way the internal leader or the deviant may speak for the opposite pole.

The Defensive Member

Defensiveness represents its own social role, although other social roles may involve it. The defensive member refuses to admit there is a problem, to accept responsibility for his or her part in a problem, or to take suggestions or help from the group after a problem has been raised. Group members often respond to a defensive member by attacking the defense and then eventually giving up and ignoring her or him.

Lewin (1951) described a model for change that can be applied to defensive members on several levels—individual, group, family, organizational. Stated simply, the individual personality in relation to its environment has developed a **quasi-stationary social equilibrium** in which some form of balance has been worked out. For the defensive member, denial has worked as a way of dealing with painful problems. The three steps for change involve "unfreezing" this equilibrium, moving into a phase of disequilibrium, and freezing at a new quasi-stationary equilibrium. The important point is that defenses have value to the individual, and to expect the unfreezing process to be easy misses the essence of the dynamics. The more serious the issue—the more deeply the individual feels a challenge to the sense of the core self—the more rigid the defense. Like resistance, a group member's defensiveness is a signal that the work is real. To begin the unfreezing process, the worker or group must challenge the individual. However, the individual will need all the support, understanding, and help possible to translate unfreezing into movement and then into a new level of quasi-equilibrium.

Workers often underestimate the difficulty of what they and group members are asking people to do when calling them to move past defensiveness and denial. The difficulty of this process needs to be respected. Only a delicate integration of support and demand can create the conditions in which the group member may feel free enough to let down the barriers.

A Defensive Father in a Parents' Group

In the example that follows, a father has described a conflict with his 18-year-old son that has resulted in the son's leaving home and the family's being in turmoil. As the situation plays out in some detail, other parents point out how the father has been stubborn and failed to listen to what his son is saying. They try to pin him down to alternative ways of relating, but to each he responds in a typical "yes, but . . ." pattern, not able to take in what they are saying. Finally, after a few minutes of this, the group grows silent. The worker intervenes by pointing out the obstacle.

WORKER: It seems to me that what has been going on here is that Ted has raised a problem, you have all been trying to offer some answers, but Ted has been saying, "Yes, but . . ." to each of your suggestions. You look like you are about to give up on him. Are you?

ALICE: We don't seem to be getting anywhere. No matter what anyone says, he has an answer.

WORKER: Ted, I think you must feel a bit backed into a corner by the group. You do seem to have a hard time taking in their ideas. How come?

TED: I don't think they can appreciate my problem. It's not the same as theirs. They all seem to be blaming me for the fight, and that's because they don't understand what it really is like.

WORKER: Maybe it would help if you could tell them how this struggle with your son makes you feel.

TED: I gave this kid so much, raised him since he was a baby, and now he treats his mother and me like we don't matter at all. I did the best I could—doesn't he understand that?

WORKER: I think it's tough when you feel you love your child the way you do and you still see him as your kid, but he seems to want to pull away. You still feel responsible for him but you also feel a bit impotent, can't seem to control him anymore. Can any of you appreciate what Ted is feeling right now?

The group members moved to support Ted in his feelings, with others recounting similar experiences and feelings. The focus had shifted for a moment to the common feelings between group members rather than the obstacle that seemed to frustrate them. The worker sensed that Ted needed to feel understood and not be judged harshly by the other parents, precisely because he tended to judge himself more harshly than any of them. Having established this support, the worker reached for the feelings underlying the resistance.

WORKER: Ted, if I were you, I think I would spend a lot of time wondering what went wrong in the relationship. I would be wondering how this could have happened when I had tried so hard—and if I could have done things differently. Is that true for you?

FRAN: (Ted's wife) He stays up nights these days, can't get to sleep because he is so upset.

TED: Sure, it's tough. You try your best, but you always wonder if you should have been around more, worked a little less, had some more time . . . you know?

WORKER: I guess that's what makes it hard for you to believe that anyone else can understand, and you feel so lousy about it yourself. Can the rest of you appreciate that it would be tough to listen if you were in Ted's shoes?

RAY: I think we are in Ted's shoes. When I see him getting stubborn in this group, I see myself and my own defensiveness.

The group discussion focused on how hard it was to take advice in the group, especially when they felt uncertain themselves. As the conversation shifted, the worker could sense Ted physically relaxing and listening. After a while, Ted asked the group to take another crack at his problem. He said, "This is really tough, but I don't want to lose the kid completely."

Often, defensive members need more time than a single session to feel safe enough to "move." Workers will often find that the member has thought deeply, after the meeting, about the way he reacted, so that readiness to change and unfreezing appear in a later session. This is the client's part in the procedure; once again, the worker can only take responsibility for establishing the best possible conditions for change—the rest is up to the client and depends on many factors. One of my studies found that clients' acceptance of a problem contributed to their motivation to change as well as their ability to use help (Shulman, 1991). For some clients, the stress of the issue was so great, or the issue so loaded, that they could not accept any help at that point. Although such situations are frustrating and often sad, they exist. Accepting this is one of the most important things a new worker can do. He or she must avoid taking responsibility for the client's part in the proceedings. Nonetheless, workers often feel guilty because of lack of clarity on this point and feelings of failure, and this guilt leads workers to feel angry at a defensive client for not cooperating. Note in our example that the anger from the other group members appeared to be a result of their seeing some of their own feelings and attitudes exaggerated in the defensiveness of the member. In fact, the more they pushed him, the more they heightened his defensiveness. The issue of the functional role of the defensive member is explored more fully in the next example.

Denial in a Living-With-Cancer Group

The following illustration explores the denial exhibited by cancer patients and family members in a group designed to help them cope with this life-threatening disease. We focus on the role of one defensive member, Al, who helps the group avoid the taboo subject of death. In addition, the members' different responses to the disease of cancer illustrate the impact of gender and ethnicity. The two men in the group, for example, respond by using increased work activity as part of a strong pattern of denial of their emotions about their wives' cancer. At one point, Al says, "You have to understand what it's like to be an engineer. Engineers are used to working with problems that can be resolved, and her cancer is a problem that I can't resolve."

Further, as a Hispanic mother and daughter describe their reactions and those of their husband and father with cancer, we can see a contrast with the white members of the group that reflects the influence of culture, as described by Schaefer and Pozzaglia (1986):

Unlike their uninhibited expression of grief and sadness, Hispanics try to control their anger. This, however, is not necessarily the case with white, middle-class families who are more comfortable in openly expressing their anger at the disease and their frustration with the hospital system. The Hispanic family's strong belief in God and His will is used to explain why the child is ill and minimizes their anger. (pp. 298–299)

The Hispanic father contemplates suicide rather than becoming a burden on his family; his reactions of shame to his diagnosis of cancer can be partly explained by *machismo*: "As macho, he is the head of the family, responsible for their protection and well-being, defender of their honor. His word is his contract" (Devore & Schlesinger, 1991, p. 81).

RECORD OF SERVICE

Client Description and Time Frame

A weekly support and education group for cancer patients and family members. It is a 6-week, time-limited, closed group. The setting is a large teaching hospital, and the group is offered free of charge through the social services department.

Age Range of Members: 30–78 years old. Ten group members are Caucasian American. Two members, a mother and daughter, are Latin American. There are ten women and two men in the group. There are five patients and seven family members.

Dates Covered in the Record: February 1 to March 8.

Description of the Problem

The problem is the group's avoidance of painful issues that would lead to a discussion of the taboo subject of death. The taboo needs to be breached so that the group may begin to redefine its norms to include direct discussion of the reality of cancer. Though there is reality-based discussion of living with cancer, there is resistance to discussing the reality of dying from cancer. An additional problem is our collusion as coleaders in the process of avoidance.

How the Problem Came to the Attention of the Worker(s)

As an observer of a previous 6-week cancer group, I was witness to and aware of the incredible courage and depth of hope displayed by two patients in the group. They and their struggle were an inspiration. As the group ended, I wondered if they had gotten what they needed from the group. I had a sense that they had never faced up to the harsh reality and finality of cancer as they had maybe hoped they would in the group. I felt they may have been cheated of an opportunity to confront the reality of the disease. Though raising the more painful issues seemed taboo, I suspect it is part of the reason the group members chose to attend the group. As a coleader of this new group, though aware of the issue of false hope, I found myself again caught up in the gifts of inspiration shared among members. In an attempt to refocus the group on more painful issues, I felt a resistance to their discussion and retreated from making interventions, thus colluding with group members in their hopefulness and avoiding discussion of the virtues (?) of cancer.

Summary of the Work

February 1

I overlooked the group's response to a member as an introduction of a major group issue: the desire to resolve the unreasonable. I kept my observation to myself. Rosina and her mother, Maria, talked quite a bit about their father and husband, who had lost interest in everything since his diagnosis of cancer. They talked about what he had been like before cancer and how he had changed. People were trying to be very helpful and supportive in giving advice to them. I wondered if the members responded this way because if you give advice and people accept it then you have helped and possibly resolved a problem—the very thing you cannot do with cancer.

I failed to reach for the feelings underlying the statement of hope. Faith, a daughter of a nonlocal patient, said her mother described cancer as the great liberator and she said that this part of the disease was contagious. Both she and her mother were becoming more assertive as well as expressive. She talked about friends who are there for her parents and how wonderful they are. I wondered (to myself) what about cancer was liberating.

I allowed the group to gloss over the pain and return to the hope. I succumbed to my own fear of discussion of death. Frances (a patient attending the group with her daughter, and the widow of a cancer victim) began to talk about her husband after Rosina said her father would rather have died of a heart attack than lived feeling like a burden to her and her mother. Frances said her husband felt the same way. He had lung cancer (here, she pointed to Sara, who has lung cancer) and was given a year to live. He died in 7 months. She said she was working when he was first diagnosed, but one day she came home and found him trying to commit suicide. She said, "We held each other and cried and I said 'We're going to fight this thing on my shirttails' . . . and we did . . . one day at a time." Sara, always an inspiration, said, "You need to fight, you need to find something to make every day count," and she began to talk to Rosina and Maria about ways they could help their father and husband make every day count. I wondered (to myself) if the return to advice giving was the group's response to the pain of Frances' disclosure about her own husband's painful and conflicted death.

February 15

I failed to recognize the underlying disappointment that there may be no satisfactory resolution and to note the pain masked by a hopeful discussion of drugs and experts. As in the two previous groups, Doris talked about her allergic reaction to the chemotherapy drugs. She focused on how much she had been "digging" for information, calling the manufacturer and even the inventor. She was discouraged to find out she was the only patient to have such a severe reaction to the drug, but she seemed to feel better by taking some action. Group members seemed to admire her initiative.

I missed the connection of an individual's themes to the purpose of the group. Al, Doris' husband, talked about what a hard week it had been for him. He had overslept that morning after working night and day for 3 weeks on a contract that was meant to be in the mail that day.

I missed the group's attempt to resolve the problem with more advice about drugs and experts. I was caught up in the hope of resolution. Faith asked Doris if the dosage of the drug might be diluted. Christine shared that her mother was participating in a drug study and gave Doris the name of the physician conducting it.

I thought about reaching for feelings, but I held back. Doris talked about having no pain and discomfort except for the rash on her legs. I wondered what it was like for her to have no pain and discomfort and still be sick with colon cancer.

I would have liked to support a group member's progress, but I remained silent. Faith read a poem from her mother. She began to cry as she read it. She reiterated her mother's description of cancer as a blessed, terrible happening. Faith said she had been crying daily for 10 weeks. She said in all that time she thinks it never quite sunk in that her mother has cancer and she said the word that she previously could not say. She said she was angry about it.

I attempted to generalize to the rest of the group. I said I wondered if anger was something they had all experienced. There were many nods. Maria asked Faith who she was angry at and why she was angry. Faith talked about how her mother had not taken care of herself, though she did not directly say she was angry at her mother. She said she did not know whether or not to blame God. Al said, "You can't blame the person with the disease and you can't blame God. It's nobody's fault, it just happens." Christine asked Maria if she was angry. Maria said, "No, never." She had never been angry at God or her husband. She talked about how wonderful their life had been and said she thought God needed to give them some pain and that whatever happened they would accept. Rosina said, "You haven't always felt this way. In the beginning you were really depressed and feeling badly when he was sick." Maria said, "That's true." Rosina said she even got sympathy pains. Maria said they don't talk that much about his cancer. They just hold hands and that's enough; they don't have to talk about cancer.

Al said he understood where she was coming from, but that you cannot sacrifice and change your life because of your husband's illness. He said, "I haven't. I go to work and do what I need to do and, of course, I've given up some things." "Not many," Doris said. "No, not many," he said, "You just have to go on with your life, otherwise you'll just get depressed. You just can't let yourself get depressed." I attempted to bring the reality of the disease into the room and connect his intellectual discussion with the emotions he was trying to avoid. I said, "I understand what you're saying about needing to have a life of your own, but what do you do with the feelings? You may not want to get depressed, but the disease is depressing." Al responded somewhat angrily, saying, "I only allow myself 15 minutes of depression a year. Any more than 15 minutes is too long."

I backed off in response to his response and remained silent. Al said he gets depressed around Christmas but always brings himself out of it. Grace (coleader) said his feelings around Doris's disease were coming out somehow and that it sounded like he was avoiding them by being away so much. He denied this and talked about how crucial it is that he put in the evening and weekend hours at work. Christine said, "With all due respect, I don't know about your relationship, and I think I'm talking to you so much because I'm thinking of my parent (her mother has colon cancer like Doris), but I think Doris is asking you to spend more time with her and be there more."

All group members got involved in this discussion, speaking for Doris to Al who, when people said they did not want to attack him, responded by saying this was nothing, he was used to handling this kind of argument at work all the time. He defended his need to be at work. Sara said, "But Doris needs you there too." I missed an opportunity to ask if Al may have been speaking for the whole group and allowed the discussion to return to a struggle between the group and Al.

February 22

I attempted to connect present group activity and previous content with the issue of avoidance. Al talked for a while about the pressures on him at work. He talked about having spent 35 years building his career. Sharon (Frances' daughter) said, "I'm sitting here listening to you, Al, and I'm not sure what went on last week (she and her mother had been absent because of poor weather), but I can say that I see a lot of myself in how you're dealing with this." She talked about when her father had gotten sick. She was in Washington and her parents were in Pennsylvania. She talked about the sense of relief every time she got on the plane to go back to D.C. She did not want to and couldn't face her father's illness. She said when her mother called and said, "You'd better come," she even waited then to go to Pennsylvania. She said, "I know about career pressures. I work for an agency that regulates the type of company you work for and I know about those pressures. When my mother got sick, it was the same time that a promotion came up that I'd been working toward for years and I passed it up because I needed to be with my mother."

I failed to point out that Al's need to see himself as different was a common reaction to defend against a painful reality. Al said, "But there's a difference. You're at the beginning of your career—I'm in the last 10 years of it when my entire pension and retirement are determined." Sharon said, "None of us know if we're even going to be here tomorrow."

At that point, Sylvia and Sid came in with their daughter, Laura (not a member of the group). Grace briefed them on what was going on, and everyone quickly introduced themselves. Sid asked what they had missed last week, because they had also been absent. Al laughed as he said, "They all ganged up on me." He had already been through this with the other people who'd been absent the previous week. Sid said he was sorry he'd missed it. Al said, "So you could join in?" Sid said, "Who knows, maybe I would have joined in with you against everyone else." (These two were the only men in the group.) Frances asked Sylvia (the patient) how she was doing. She said her treatment had been going well, though she had been sleeping a lot. Laura said that she always sleeps a lot and said she even falls asleep at movies.

Then Doris and Al got into a discussion with them about how he loves movies and she hates to go to them. I said I wondered, as I thought Sharon had been saying to Al, if there was a tendency to avoid thinking, feeling, and talking about cancer— even in the group right now. I wondered if people found that they tended to or felt like avoiding it all. Frances said, "You avoid it and then don't know that you're doing it." Al said, "I'm not avoiding it, it's just my way of coping. You just can't think about it all the time."

I failed to clear a space for Al to be able to connect his feelings about his past losses with his current situation, by my tuning in to Doris's fear of that connection. Al said, "This isn't the first time I've been through it." "But it's not the same," Doris said. "But I was 10 when my father died of cancer," said Al. "You were just a child, it's not the same." "My mother died of leukemia," said Al. "But you weren't in the house, your brother and sister took care of her." Al said, "That's true." I neglected to share my thoughts about how he managed to distance himself from his mother's illness as he seems to be trying to do with Doris. Frances said, "It's different when you're living with the person than if you're away." I said it's different and it's the same. Al said, "No, it's definitely different when you're living with the person."

I mistook Sylvia's successful attempt to steer the conversation away from the topic of how difficult it is to live with a cancer patient as an inappropriate interjection into the conversation. Sylvia asked if anyone had seen the show *20/20* that week. Group members said they had not. Sylvia said it had been about chemotherapy drugs.

I responded to my own desire to avoid pain instead of tuning in to the probable pain of many of the group members. I allowed an eloquent expression of a painful experience to be perceived only as moving and inspiring. Frances asked Maria how her husband was doing. Maria and Rosina looked at each other and Rosina said it had been a discouraging week for them. Her father was no longer responding to the chemotherapy. Maria talked some but mostly cried as Rosina talked about a new lump her father had found behind his ear. Frances said that was the last thing he needed, to find that lump. She said her husband had gotten a great big tumor on his neck and couldn't stand it so she had to shave him. She spoke eloquently about her husband, her experience with him and his death.

I overlooked Frances's own need to confront her own cancer, which she only talked about in terms of beating. The group was engrossed. Al asked, "How do you do it?" Frances looked at him and said, "Sometimes you just hold each other and cry." She said again, "I told him to grab on to my shirttails and we'll make it though this thing." After a while her husband had said, "I'm not going to make it." She told the story of how he had died, in the hospital, not at home. I wondered how everyone felt. I imagined that everyone was moved by Frances's story but that they also related it to themselves or their own loved one. We missed the boat.

March 1

Grace mentioned that this was the fifth group and that we had one more left before the end. Doris said, "That's a bummer," and that was all that was said by her or anyone about the group ending. I failed to tune in and connect Al's feelings to Doris's illness. Al talked about what a tough couple of weeks it had been. He said it had been emotionally draining, and he attributed it mostly to work.

I attempted to confront the group's denial around its ending, but I was unable to connect their difficulty in confronting the group's end with how it related to cancer and the pain of having to say untimely good-byes. In the middle of the group, I said that Doris had said it was "a bummer" that the group was ending next week and I wondered how others were feeling about it. After an attempt to confront the denial, I copped out and colluded with it, allowing their discussion of how they could keep the group going. Sid asked if it could be extended. Doris said that it was a bummer and that she always felt better after the group. Then everyone talked about ideas for how it could continue rather than talking about what it was like that it was ending. I wished I had said, "But this group as it exists now is ending next week."

Grace said how the tone of the group seemed different tonight and wondered if it had anything to do with the two unexplained empty chairs. I missed the opportunity to comment on the very depressing reality and finality of cancer that group members were now unavoidably facing in the form of two glaringly empty chairs and to ask how it related to themselves. Rosina and her mother, Maria, were unexplainably absent after having spoken of their father and husband's turn for the worse the previous week. Frances, often the "cheerleader" and major source of group inspiration, said they were occupying her mind. The conversation for the next 10 minutes revolved around the group's concern for the missing members and their loved one.

March 6

I listened intently to information I wished had been shared earlier in the 6 weeks. I felt sad that I had not helped facilitate its earlier entrance into the group. At the end, Christine talked about what had gotten her to come to the group. She said she didn't know if people could tell what kind of person she was, but that she went on a cross-country bike trip alone and hiked and camped and was very independent. She's also organized and likes to keep things in order and be healthy. She said a few weeks after hearing her mother's diagnosis she had a terrible headache one night and realized she hadn't eaten in 3 days. She said she made some cream of wheat but couldn't eat it. She looked around her apartment. There were clothes in every room and dirty dishes in the sink. She said she didn't know who was living in her apartment. She saw the flyer the next day and said, "I've got to get into that group."

I regretted that I had not trusted and acted on my instincts, which told me that this group was not dealing directly enough with the issue of death. Christine said the group had been keeping her in touch with the disease, but that she wasn't really facing that her mother could die from this. She said she talked to her boyfriend and he got so upset and said to her, "I can't believe you're in this group and you're not dealing with death." She said it as if she were the only one in the group who was not. I looked at Grace and thought that Christine said what I had been thinking throughout the 6 weeks of group. We had 5 minutes left of our final group. Sadly, this group did not confront death.

Current Status of the Problem

Where It Stands Now

This group ended, though they have made a commitment to informally continue their meetings. Possibly they will begin to confront their own avoidance, particularly if members begin to become sick. I am looking forward to the start of another 6-week group March 22. I hope to be more cognizant of the ways in which avoidance surfaces and be more assertive in noting and helping the group confront their avoidance without letting the discussion drop. I am also more acutely aware of how attractive it is to collude with the hope of group members as a defense against not only their fear death and dying but mine as well. I want to support their struggle to heal from the disease without cheating them of an opportunity to talk openly about the painful reality of cancer. Having taken a closer look at the issues of avoidance, I feel better prepared to facilitate that process.

Strategies for Intervention

- Be more active about listening for and speaking to the group's underlying messages as they relate to cancer.
- Point out a pattern of flight and be persistent in raising the issue.
- Believe that death is something that group members are thinking about, then raise the issue, breach the taboo, and bring it into the group for discussion.
- Communicate with my coleader about my need to confront the issue of avoidance.
- Notice my own discomfort with discussing taboo areas and share it with the group in an effort to help group members free up the energy that is bound up in their discomfort.
- Do not fall into the trap of believing that group members are doing my job for me by asking questions of each other.

The worker in this illustration has used the experience to deepen her understanding about her clients and herself. Typical of new workers, she overly criticizes her work, focusing on what she did not do while not crediting herself enough for what she accomplished. A little guilt is helpful for professional growth; however, workers should not undervalue their work along the way.

In exploring the worker's hesitancy about dealing with the subject of death, you may have noticed a piece missing—the support system for staff that is essential in such emotionally draining practice. Case-related stressors on staff can directly affect practice (Shulman, 1991). Davidson (1985) examined the impact of the special stresses affecting social workers who work with cancer patients and their families. He hypothesized that workers experience their work as stressful and lack adequate support to help them cope with the emotional impact of working with clients affected by a chronic and life-threatening illness. Pilsecker (1979) found that social workers, like other hospital staff, used strategies to deal with their painful emotions, including reduction of their direct involvement with patients. By recognizing, accepting, and trying to meet their own needs, social workers can better support their clients.

The Quiet Member

The **quiet member** is one who remains noticeably silent over a an extended period of time. In small groups the worker and the other group members notice after only a few sessions that someone has said very little or nothing at all. A quiet member can create problems for the group, because they do not know what thinking and feeling goes on behind the facade. Group members will tend to believe that the quiet member is sitting in judgment of them, does not share their problems, or feels that others in the group talk too much. Workers, too, often grow uncomfortable, feeling that a member who is not speaking may not be involved.

The silence of a member in a group is similar to the silence in an interview. It is a form of communication that, as we have seen, can be difficult to understand. For some group members, it simply means they are uncomfortable speaking in the group. This is one of the most common explanations. Others feel left out or uninvolved in the group because they feel their problems are different. Some sit in judgment of the group's activity (as was the case in one of the deviant member illustrations). In my experience, sitting in judgment is the least stated reason for silence but interestingly is the interpretation most often put on silence by the active group members and the worker, probably reflecting their own feelings. The two examples presented shortly will examine the quiet member who is afraid to speak, then the quiet member who is left out. First, let us see how the worker can help the group when they react to a quiet member.

Worker Strategies

Believing that all members need to speak equally is a mistake. Social roles developed by individuals include patterns that involve active participation through speech as well as active participation through listening. A member may get a great deal out of a discussion without directly participating. On the other hand, small groups carry a sense of mutual obligation: Members who risk themselves feel that others should do the same. In fact, the silent member often feels uncomfortable about "taking" and not "giving." In addition, many silent members have been so used to being quiet in groups for so long that they have not developed skills required for intervention. Some quiet members say that they are always too slow with their thoughts. The group moves too fast for them, and by the time they can get in, the idea has been stated and the group has moved on. Others say that after they have been quiet in a group for several sessions, they are afraid the group members will "fall out of their chairs if I open my mouth." So although all members should be able to move into a group at their own pace and although equal participation is not a goal, the quiet member often needs some assistance in participating in the group.

Workers sometimes try to deal with this problem either directly through confrontation or indirectly. Each tactic can backfire. For example, if a member has been quiet because of discomfort in speaking, a worker who suddenly turns and says, "I notice you haven't spoken yet in the group and wondered what was on your mind?" may find the member even further immobilized by embarrassment. This direct confrontation may be exactly what quiet members feared would happen.

Indirect means can be just as devastating. The worker has noticed a member not verbally participating in a discussion and turns and says, "What are your ideas about this question, Fran?" A member who is afraid of speaking often finds that any ideas she did have completely disappear in this moment of panic. The other indirect technique, of going around the room to get all opinions when it really is only the quiet person's opinion the worker seeks, may be experienced as manipulative and artificial by members.

The task, then, is to be direct and nonthreatening at the same time. My own strategy is based on the belief that people have a right to their defenses and their characteristic patterns of social interaction. As the worker, my job is to mediate the engagement between each member and the group, so I feel a responsibility to check with a quiet member and see how that engagement is going. If there is an obstacle between the member and the group, I can offer to help.

The Member Who Is Afraid to Speak

As we have seen, members sometimes are merely afraid to speak. They have likely always held back in groups. The following conversation took place after the second meeting of a group. Richard had been particularly silent in both meetings, although his eyes seemed to indicate he was involved.

WORKER: Do you have a second to chat before you go?

RICHARD: Sure, what's up?

WORKER: I noticed you haven't spoken in the group these two sessions, and I thought I would check to see how it was going with you. I know some people take longer than others to get involved, and that's OK. I just wanted to be sure there were no problems.

RICHARD: Well, you caught me.

WORKER: What do you mean?

RICHARD: I managed to get through all of my years in school without ever saying anything in class, and now it looks as if I've been caught.

WORKER: Is it hard for you to speak in a group?

RICHARD: I always feel unsure of what I'm going to say, and by the time I've figured it out, the group has gone past me. Sometimes, it's just hard to get in with everyone speaking at once.

WORKER: Look, I can tell from your eyes that you are actively involved in the discussion. However, after a while, you will probably feel uncomfortable not speaking, and then it will get harder and harder to talk.

RICHARD: That's the way it usually is for me.

WORKER: Not just you, you know. Lots of people feel that way. If you would like, I can help by watching for you and if I sense you want to get into the conversation by the look on your face, or your body, or if you give me the signal, I can reach for you and help you in. Would you like me to do that?

RICHARD: That sounds OK. If I give you a signal, you'll call on me?
WORKER: Exactly! I find that has helped people in the past.

At the next session, Richard avoided the worker's eyes for the first 15 minutes; he was probably afraid of giving a false signal. The discussion was heated and the worker kept glancing at Richard. After a while, the worker noticed Richard leaning forward a bit, with his eyebrows arched, looking at the worker. The worker simply said, "Come on in, Richard." The group paused, and Richard began to speak.

The Member Who Feels Left Out

Another type of quiet member is one who feels that his particular concerns and issues may not be of interest to the group or that his problems differ from those of the others. Such members do not share problems with the group members, and after a while they feel left out and the group members wonder what is happening.

In the following example, Mrs. Trenke, who had shared some difficult experiences with the group, stated that she felt let down when the group did not respond to her feelings. Mrs. Davidson, who had been quiet in the group, supported Mrs. Trenke's comment.

> The worker said, "Maybe we could hear how Mrs. Trenke felt let down by the group?" Mrs. Trenke continued, "I felt that I was not a part of the group and that I was not going to get anything out of it." Mrs. Davidson cut in, "Yeah! We didn't listen to other people's troubles because we had enough of our own!" The worker turned to Mrs. Davidson and said, "Have you felt let down and left out of the group?" "No," said Mrs. Davidson, "I don't feel I have the same situation—they have husbands." (Mrs. Bennet reached out and touched Mrs. Davidson on the arm.) The worker asked Mrs. Davidson how she felt about not having a man. Mrs. Davidson replied, "Sad, depressed—I wonder if he could be as proud of the kids as I am?" She went on to say that maybe things would be different if her husband were still alive—maybe they could have made a go of it. The worker said he felt that Mrs. Davidson had been cut out of the group for some weeks. Mrs. Davidson agreed.
>
> Mrs. Bennet said that was probably due to the fact that she had not been able to share with the group the concerns she had. All agreed. The worker cut in after a silence and said, "I felt the group would like to know what it is like, what it feels like to be alone. What do you need help with?" Mrs. Bennet cut in, "There you go on that feeling theory again." The worker asked if it worried Mrs. Bennet when we talked about feelings. "No," she said, "but is it important?" The worker said that it seemed important because everyone in this group was having trouble talking about and sharing feelings while at the same time they were interested in what others were feeling. "Do you see what we have done here? When we began to find out about Mrs. Davidson's feelings, someone suggested that we avoid it and we all agreed. Let's go back to Mrs. Davidson's feelings!"
>
> Mrs. Davidson said, "I feel like an s-h-i-t (spelled out) at home with the kids." The worker cut in and said it was OK with him if she said *shit*—why did she feel that way? "It rips me right across here (indicating midsection) when they are fighting—I've had nothing but fighting all my life—first in my own home—then with my husband—now with my kids." "How do you see the

fighting—what does it mean to you?" asked the worker. "I feel on my own, all alone." Mrs. Trenke cut in, "I know that feeling—I had it with my husband—we used to argue. . . . What can I do? Why is it always me?" The worker asked if Mrs. Davidson could share a specific problem with the group, and she did. It involved setting limits, then wavering on them and letting the kids have their own way.

The Monopolizer

The previous section on the quiet member brings up the opposite side of the issue: People who talk a great deal and are sometimes referred to as **monopolizers.** My observation is that people who talk a lot are often more of a problem for the worker than are quiet members. In first sessions in particular, group members are pleased to see someone pick up the discussion. A problem arises, however, when the person talking does not also listen to others, cuts them off, and creates a negative reaction in the group. The worker who sees this happening can raise the issue directly. Usually the discussion between the member and the group helps to ease the problem. If the group worker inquires why the member acts this way in the group, the individual will often reveal that talking is a way of covering up feelings, avoiding a problem, or expressing concern about actions in the group. The overly verbal member's words are often a way of handling the same feelings that the quiet member handles, but in a quite different manner.

The following brief excerpt illustrates how immobilized both the group leader and the other group members can feel when faced with a monopolizer. This member, Dawn, acted out her anxiety by responding to a doctor's presentation with an unstoppable stream of talk.

Agency Type: A hospital and rehabilitation center for children and adolescents.

Group Purpose: To educate the group members about their children's medical and therapeutic conditions, as well as to inform them of safety precautions for children who have had a traumatic brain injury.

Gender of Members: 3 men and 11 women (including worker).

Age Range: Mid-twenties to early forties.

As soon as Dr. Thomas began to explain that children who have experienced traumatic brain injuries tend to be impulsive, Dawn started to describe what had happened with her child to demonstrate that she agreed with the doctor. She went on and on for almost 10 minutes, and nobody intervened. Then, she started to talk about her other child, Lisa, and what had happened at home during the past weekend. I turned to Dawn and said, "Dawn, I know you have many things to say, but why don't we go back to Eileen's behavior?" Dawn replied, "I know. I know. But let me finish. This is related to Eileen, too." People in the room rolled their eyes, but I did not object. She spoke another 3 minutes or so and finished her story by saying, "So I told my children that school is always number one." I jumped in and said, "Good. Why don't we ask Melissa (the hospital tutor) about school?" People, including Dawn, laughed. When Melissa finished reporting about Eileen's school issue, I encouraged Dawn to ask Melissa questions. Then, I announced to the treatment team that we were running out of time so I would like to ask everyone to be short and precise. They nodded.

In retrospect, this first meeting focused almost entirely on the concerns of one member. Although the other group members signaled their displeasure by rolling their eyes, the group leader, perhaps feeling unclear about how to intervene, let Dawn continue unchecked. The leader would have been helpful to Dawn and the other members if she had intervened more directly and firmly. In a session such as this one, the monopolizer often feels embarrassed afterward for having dominated the conversation, and the other members wonder about the value of the group. In a first session, the group leader must take responsibility for providing structure. In doing so, the leader needs to be both direct and empathic, saying something like this:

> Hold on a second, Dawn. I know your child's injury and this discussion provokes a lot of feelings in you, and you probably feel you want as much help as you can get for your own child. But we need to allow room for everyone to ask their questions and make their comments, so I'll play traffic cop if it's OK with the rest of you.

If Dawn continued to test, such as by saying, as she did in the session, "Let me just finish," the worker would need to say something like "Nice try, but we need to give someone else a chance." Continued persistence would require some discussion of the significance of being so full of one's own feelings that very little room remains for anyone else's. There is also a good chance that Dawn has also just acted out the problem she has with friends and other family members—of overwhelming them with her issues and not being able to respond to theirs. Once again we see the integration of process and content.

If the worker handles such interventions directly, openly, without anger, and where possible with nonhumiliating humor, he or she will be reassuring the group that the worker will not let them subvert the purpose of the group or act out their anxiety. The problem is that such interventions go against societal norms, which encourage passively allowing the monopolizer to go on at length, intervening indirectly with little success, or intervening from anger as the group leader feels frustration at one member's dominating the group. In most cases the monopolizer wants the worker to set limits, because structure helps to bind anxiety and helps the member feel more in control over what must be a devastating situation. In this case, the other members reacted negatively to the monopolizer.

The Group as an Organism

As promised, we have explored the various roles individuals play in a group setting— the interplay of one member in a dynamic system. In the second half of this chapter, we take a more detailed look at the group as an entity much like an organism, with its own properties and dynamics, and then we explore a strategy for the worker's intervention in relation to it. Next, we trace the tasks of the group as it attempts to deal with the relationships of members to the worker (the authority theme), relationships among members (the intimacy theme), the group's culture for work, and the group's internal structure (communication patterns, roles, and so forth). A fifth task requires the group to relate to the environment—the setting that houses the group (the school, agency, institution). We address this task in Chapter 15, when we examine the role of the worker in helping the client (the group in this case) relate to other systems.

It is not easy to describe this second client called the group-as-a-whole. In part, the difficulty comes from the fact that we cannot actually see the properties that describe a group. When we watch a group in action, we see a collection of individuals. Compare this to a solid object, such as a chair. When we are asked to describe its properties, visual references such as materials (plastic, wood, chrome), parts (back, seat, legs), shape, size, and so on immediately come to mind. With a group, describing the properties is more difficult. For example, **cohesion** in a group can be defined as a bond among members—a sense of identification with one another and with the group-as-a-whole. An observer cannot see "cohesion," but if we observe a group for a time, we can see all of the members acting as if the group were cohesive. Other properties of groups include shared norms of proper behavior and taboo subjects. We cannot see a norm or a taboo, but we can see a pattern of behavior from which we can infer that a norm or taboo exists. Our discussion will focus on the unique properties that help to define the group.

Practitioners who wish to better understand group dynamics can draw on a large body of group theory and research. As we discuss these dynamics, we shall use theoretical models and research results to develop an integrated model of group practice. I have selected two classic theoretical models and one relatively new framework for discussion in relation to the group tasks: developmental (Bennis & Shepard, 1956), structural (Bion, 1961), and self-in-relation (Fedele, 1994; Schiller, 1993). Each of these theories offers ideas relevant to all of the group tasks.

Before we discuss developmental tasks, we need to explore the very idea of a group. When attempting to describe something as complex as a group, using a model is helpful. A **model** is a concrete, symbolic representation of an abstract phenomenon. To develop a model for describing a group, we must find an appropriate metaphor. Two common metaphors are the machine and the organism. In the mechanistic model, the observer describes processes such as "input," "through put," and "output" to describe the group. Many theorists interested in human social systems have adopted the **organismic model** as the most appropriate. The choice of an organism rather than a machine as a model reflects the organism's capacity for *growth* and *emergent behavior*. These terms describe a process in which a system transcends itself and creates something new that is more than just the simple sum of its parts.

To apply this idea to the group, we need to identify what is created when a group of people and a worker are brought together that goes beyond the sum of each member's contribution. What properties exist that are unique descriptions of the group, rather than descriptions of the individual members? An example of such a property is the creation of a sense of common purpose shared by all the members of the group. This common purpose is a catalyst for the development of a tie that binds the members together. **Group culture** is a second example. As the group process begins, activities in the group are governed by a group culture made up of several factors including accepted **norms of behavior.** In a first session, the group culture generally reflects the culture of the larger society from which the members have been drawn. As sessions continue, this culture can change, allowing new norms to emerge and govern the activities of the members. Thus, common interests and group culture are two examples of properties of the group that transcend the simple sum of its parts, the individual members.

A third example is the group's relationship with its environment. As the group is influenced by its environment—for example, the agency, school, or hospital—or the worker as a representative of the agency, it must develop adaptive behaviors to maintain itself. This pattern of adaptive behavior is yet another example of a property of the group.

To summarize, we cannot actually see a group as an entity. That is why a model, such as the organism, is helpful. What we can see, however, are the activities of a group of people who appear to be influenced by this entity called the group. For example, when group purpose is clear, we can explain the members' actions as contributions in pursuit of that purpose. Again, group pressures, group expectations, and the members' sense of belonging all influence the members' behavior. The fact that a member's behavior changes as a result of believing in the existence of the group makes the group real. In the balance of this chapter, we shall refer to the group as an entity, employing the organism as a metaphor, and focus on the group's developmental tasks.

Developmental Tasks for the Group

Two major group tasks have already been discussed without having been specifically described as such. These illustrate how a group can have tasks that differ from the specific tasks of each member. In the chapter on group beginnings we addressed what could be called the group's formation tasks. The group needed to develop a working contract reflecting the individual members' needs as well as the service stake of the sponsoring agency. In addition, a group consensus needed to be developed. This consensus reflected the common concerns shared by members as well as agreement as to where the work might start. Reaching consensus on the work is a task unique to work with multiple clients (group, family, couples, and so on), because individual clients simply begin where they wish, with no need to reach a consensus with other clients. The group's formation tasks also include initial clarification of mutual obligations and expectations. The effectiveness of the group depends on how well it accomplishes these formation tasks. The skills of the worker in helping the group to work on these formation tasks are described as contracting skills.

A second critical group task involves meeting individual members' needs. For the group to survive, it must have individual members. Members feel a sense of belonging and develop a stake in the work of the group when they can perceive that their own related needs are being met. If these needs cease to be met, then members will simply drop out of the group, either by not attending or by not participating. In the chapter on the work phase of the group, we saw how easily the group can miss the offered concerns of a member or turn away from these concerns when they hit the group members too hard. In still other examples, individual members did not immediately see the relation between the work of the group and their own sense of urgency. In the first part of this chapter, we saw how members can play functional roles in the group, some of which cut them off from being able to use the group to meet their own needs. In each of these cases, workers attempted to help the members use the group more effectively, helped the group reach out and offer mutual aid more effectively, or both simultaneously. All these efforts were directed toward helping the group with its task of meeting individual members' needs.

Thus, in order to grow and survive, a group must address the tasks of formation and meeting individual members' needs. Other sets of tasks linked to the developmental work of the group are those in which the group works on its relationship to the worker (the authority theme) and relationships among members (the intimacy theme). Schwartz (1971) describes these two critical tasks as follows:

> In the culture of the group two main themes come to characterize the members' ways of working together: one, quite familiar to the caseworker, is the theme of authority in which the members are occupied with their relationship to the helping person and the ways in which this relationship is instrumental to their purpose; the other, more strange and threatening to the caseworker, is the theme of intimacy, in which the members are concerned with their internal relationships and the problems of mutual aid. It is the interplay of these factors—external authority and mutual interdependence—that provides much of the driving force of the group experience. (p. 9)

The group's ability to deal with concerns related to authority and intimacy is closely connected to the development of a *working culture:* common interests and group norms of behavior. Finally, the group needs to develop a structure for work that will enable it to carry out its tasks effectively. For example, responsibilities may have to be shared through a division of labor, and roles may need to be assigned formally or informally.

These four major task areas—the relationship to the worker, the relationship between members, the development of a working culture, and the development of a structure for work—will be introduced in the balance this chapter. Obviously, these tasks overlap a great deal, in that work on one area often includes work on the others. Although somewhat artificial, the division is helpful. Recall that discussion of these tasks will draw on elements of group theory from three major models, focusing on constructs that seem relevant. For example, Bennis and Shepard (1956) address the themes of intimacy and authority in their model of group development, and several of their key concepts are useful in explaining group process. Their observations, however, are based on their work with laboratory training groups (T-groups), in which graduate students studied group dynamics using their own experiences as a group. As a result, some ideas in their theory may be group-specific and therefore not apply to groups of the type discussed in this book. Our analysis will illustrate how a practitioner can use what he or she likes from a good theory without adopting it whole.

Dealing With the Relationship to the Worker

In the early phase of the group development, the group needs to sort out its relationship to the worker. Much of the group's beginning energy will be devoted to this theme. An early question concerns issues of control. Like work with individuals, group work includes the dynamics of transference and countertransference. Members bring their stereotypes or fantasies about group leaders to the first meeting, and these generate a fear of a powerful authority person "doing something" to them. Thus, in my description of the first session of the couples' group in Chapter 10, the member named Lou raised the authority issue by sharing his negative experiences with workers in the helping field. Open discussion of the implications of this issue for the workers present helped the group members relax and become more actively involved in the session. However, such an open discussion does not resolve the question, in that feelings and questions concerning the relationship to the worker always remain. What the group and the worker do achieve is the ability to address this issue openly as it emerges. The comfort of the group may increase, but the theme remains. In the second session of the couples' group, the members were watching to see if I would carry out the role I had described in the first session. Once again, Lou signaled the members' concern about this issue:

> One couple was presenting a problem that they were having that involved the husband's grown children from another marriage. I noticed each spouse was telling the group things about the other, rather than speaking directly to each other. I interrupted Frank and suggested he speak directly to his wife. After a noticeable hesitation, he began to speak to her, but he soon returned to speaking to me. I interrupted him again. Once again, he seemed slightly thrown by my action.
>
> As this was going on, I noticed that Lou was looking distressed, staring at the floor, and covering his mouth with his hand. After watching this for a time, I reached for the message. "Lou, you look like you have something to say." He responded, "No, that's all right. I can wait 'til later." I said, "I have the feeling it's important, and I think it has something to do with me." I had been feeling uncomfortable but unaware why. Lou said. "Well, if you want to hear it now, OK. Every time you interrupt Frank that way, I think he loses his train of thought. And this business of telling him to speak to Jane is just like the stuff I described last week." I was surprised by what he said, and I remained quiet while I took it in.
>
> Frank said, "You know, he's right. You do throw my line of thought every time you interrupt that way." I said, "I guess I ended up doing exactly the kind of thing I said last week I would try not to do. I have not explained to you, Frank, why I think it might help to talk directly with your wife rather than to me. I guess you must feel my comments, because you don't really understand why I'm suggesting this, as sort of pushing you around." Frank said "Well, a bit." Lou said, "That's exactly what I mean." I responded, "I won't be perfect, Lou. I will also make mistakes. That's why it's so important that you call me on it, the way you just did. Only why wait until I ask?" Lou said, "It's not easy to call you; you're the leader." I said, "I think I can appreciate that, only you can see how it would speed things up if you did."

This second week's discussion was even more important than the first, because the members had a chance to see me confronted with a mistake and not only acknowledging it but also encouraging Lou to be even more direct. The point made was that they did have rights and that they should not let my authority get in the way. At this point you may be thinking that reaching for or encouraging such negative feedback would be difficult for a beginning group leader. Ironically, the worker needs this kind of honesty from group members most when she or he is least confident and prepared to hear it. Beginning group workers should expect to miss these signals in sessions, but as their confidence grows, they should start to reach for the negatives later in the same session or in the session that follows.

The authority theme appeared many other times in similar discussions, for example, about the agenda for our work. When I appeared to return to an area of work without checking on the group's interest, members would participate in an obvious illusion of work. When I challenged the illusion, we could discuss why it was harder for them simply to let me know when they thought I was leading them away from their concerns. Issues of control also emerged in connection with responsibility for the effectiveness of the work. In this example, one couple had spent an unusually long time discussing an issue without getting to the point. I could see the reactions in the group and inquired as to what was going on.

> Fran responded by saying it was getting boring and she was waiting for me to do something. Because this was a middle-phase session, I found myself angry that everyone was waiting for me. I said, "How come you are waiting for me to do something? This is your group, you know, and I think you could take this responsibility, too."

The resulting discussion revealed that members felt it was risky to take each other on, and so they left it to me. We were able to sort out for a time that members, too, needed to take responsibility for the group's effectiveness.

These excerpts help to illustrate the two sides to the members' feelings: On the one hand, they were afraid of the worker and the worker's authority; on the other, they wanted the worker to take responsibility for the group. Bennis and Shepard (1956) attribute these two sets of feelings to two types of personalities in the group: the **dependent member** and the **counterdependent member.** They believe that the dependency invokes great uncertainty for members and that the first major phase of group development, the **dependence phase**, involves work on this question. They describe three subphases within this first phase. In the first subphase, **dependence-flight**, the group is led by the dependent leaders, who seek to involve the worker more actively in control of the group. In the second subphase, **counterdependence-flight**, the counterdependent leaders move in to attempt to take over the group. The group often shows much anger toward the worker in this phase. Two subgroups develop—one arguing for structure, the other arguing against it.

In the third subphase, **resolution-catharsis**, members who are **unconflicted**—independent and relatively untroubled by authority issues—assume group leadership. According to Bennis and Shepard (1956), this "overthrow" of the worker leads to each member taking responsibility for the group: The worker is no longer seen as "magical," and the power struggles are replaced by work on shared goals. The groups studied by the authors were marked by group leaders who were extremely passive in the beginning, which, in my view, increased anxiety about the authority theme. While many of the specifics of the model are restricted to the particular groups observed, we can apply to all groups the general outline of this struggle over dependency.

Issues of control are just one aspect of the general theme of relationship to the worker. A second area concerns the worker's place as an outsider to the group. This comes up particularly in groups where the worker has not had life experiences central to the group members' themes of concern. For instance, in a group for parents of children who have been diagnosed as hyperactive, the question arises of whether the worker who has no children can understand them and their problems. This is a variation on the similar question raised in the discussion of the beginning phase in work with individuals. The following excerpt illustrates this aspect of the authority theme struggle in the group context:

> Discussion got back again to causes of hyperactivity. Ann, who had thought it was hereditary, explained that her husband thought that he had been hyperactive as a

child, except that nobody gave him the title. Marilyn said that her husband had also said that he had been like her son and had felt that her son would grow out of it. The group picked up on this idea and seemed to like the possibility. I was asked by Betty what I thought. I said I didn't know the answer, but that from what I did know, not enough research has been done. The group began throwing questions at me, related to general conditions, medications, and I couldn't answer them. I admitted that I knew very little about hyperactivity. I was certainly nowhere near being the experts that they were.

Someone asked if I had children. I said that I didn't. Beatrice wondered what work I had done with hyperactive children and extended this to children with other problems. I answered as honestly as I could. She wondered whether I was overwhelmed by their feelings. I replied that she and others present were really concerned about how I felt toward them, and whether I really understood what it felt like to be the mother of a hyperactive child. She agreed. I added that last week when I had said I was feeling overwhelmed I was really getting into what it felt like to have such a child. It was pointed out to me that I was the only one in the group who didn't have a hyperactive child, that I was really the outsider. Beatrice offered to lend me her son for a weekend, so that I could really see what it was like. Everyone laughed. (I think they were delighted at this.) I said that they were telling me that it was important that I understand what it's like, and I wondered whether I was coming across as not understanding. They didn't think so. I said that the more they talked, the better the feeling I got about what they were going through. Toward the end of this there was a lot of subgroup talking going on, and I waited (thankful for the break).

The third area of the authority theme has to do with the group's reaction to the worker as a person who makes demands. For the group to be effective, the worker must do more than contract clearly and be empathic. The group will often come up against obstacles, many of which are related to the group members' ambivalence about discussion of painful areas. As the worker makes demands, group members will inevitably generate negative feelings. If the worker is doing a good job, group members will sometimes get angry at the worker for refusing to let them off the hook. Of course, clients also have positive feelings associated with the fact that the worker is empathetic and cares enough about the group to make these demands. The angry feelings, however, need to be expressed; otherwise they can go under the surface and emerge in unconscious expressions such as general apathy. As we have seen, the worker must feel comfortable in the role to be willing to deal with this negative feedback. In the same group of parents of hyperactive children, the worker picked up the signals of this reaction and reached directly for it:

Millie began talking about her son's learning disability. After a little while I cut in and asked the group what was happening here, to the conversation and to the members. (My feeling was that they were way off the track again.) Marilyn said that they had gotten off the subject again; they were supposed to be discussing how they felt and their attitudes. I added that indeed this was what was happening; it seemed that they were unable to keep on talking about themselves. Millie and Marilyn thought that it was probably because it was hard to accept the fact that they get angry. I started to say something in response to this, and I noticed that Claudette kind of sighed and made a face. I pointed this out to her and suggested that perhaps she didn't want to discuss some of the things I thought they should. She nodded.

I told the group that perhaps this was a good time to talk about how they felt about my forcing them to look at themselves, to keep on the subject, and to talk about what they didn't want to talk about. I said that they must have some feelings about me; perhaps every time I open up my mouth and point this out to them and try to refocus them, they say to themselves, "Why the hell doesn't she get off our backs and let us talk about something easy?"

Beatrice said that she had the feeling that was true, every time I brought them back to talking about how they felt, she could feel people moving back in their chairs, as if they were looking for a place to hide, and then they would hide by talking about school, teachers, and so on. She said that her own behavior has changed considerably with these sessions, and although it has been hard, she's been able to see herself a little more clearly. But not everyone in the group has moved at the same pace; some people are really changing their attitudes because they are willing to risk and look at themselves, but others still hide behind the facade. I said that I agreed. Often I felt how terribly hard it was for them to face things, and I kept pushing them at it. Sometimes I pushed them hard, like two sessions ago. And then other times I felt it was too hard, and like last week, I hardly said anything and really let them talk about anything and everything. I don't think that is being helpful to them if I let them do that, even though I can feel their hurt so much, and my own gut reaction is "I should let you alone; it hurts too much to look at yourselves." People nodded in agreement.

A fourth issue here is the need for the group to come to grips with the reality of the worker's limitations. Members hope that the worker, or some other expert, will be able to solve their problems. This is, in part, a result of the emerging dependency of the group. When the group members realize the worker has no solutions, then their own work really begins. However, this realization is painful for the members and often for the workers as well. At the end of one particularly painful and depressing discussion in the same parents' group, when the members recognized that the drugs and the professionals were not going to "make the problem go away," a member appealed to the worker to cheer them up:

We were way over our time, and I started to sum up some of the feelings that came out today. I said that they had really been saying all along how helpless they felt that they couldn't do anything to help the children, and how hopeless they were feeling that there wasn't a solution for them. Marilyn said to me that that's how they felt, depressed and helpless. She said that I always came up with something at the end to make them feel better. I had better come up with something really good today, because they needed it. I said that I was feeling the same way, thinking to myself, "What can I say that's going to take the depression and hurt away?" I told her that I didn't have a magic formula, that I wished that I could suggest something. I knew how much she and all of them wished that I could help them with a solution. Rose said that they were feeling depressed, but they shouldn't blame themselves. I said that perhaps part of the depression was related to the fact that they themselves hadn't been able to help their children more, and they felt terrible about it. She seemed to be so terribly depressed, more than ever before. I know because that's exactly how I felt.

There was not too much discussion on the way out, as I didn't to know what to say to them (usually we joke around a bit). Marilyn said to me I let her down, I didn't come up with my little blurb to pep them up. I said that she was feeling very depressed and she looked to me to say something to make things easier. I said that she wanted a solution, and I didn't have one. She said to me that perhaps I had, and I was holding back. I said to her that she was very disappointed in me that I hadn't been able to make things easier. I wished that I did have the magic solution that they all wanted so desperately, but I didn't have one. After this, the members left.

A final aspect of the authority theme requires the group to deal with their reactions to the worker as a caring and giving person. The group members watch as the worker relates to them and to the others in the group. They can see the pain in the worker's face if he or she feels the hurt deeply; after a while, they can sense the genuineness of the empathy. This side of the worker provokes powerful responses in the group, and a mutual flow of positive affect results. An interesting discussion in my couples' group illustrates the importance of this aspect of the authority theme, as well as the group's awareness of this issue. In the session before the Christmas break (the eighth), one member arrived late and distraught. She sat down in the empty chair to my right, and for the first time in the group she shared a frightening problem she was facing. Until then, the member had appeared to be "without problems," because her husband was, in her mind, the identified patient. I comforted her while she told her story, and I tried to help her verbally and nonverbally—touching the back of her hand, communicating my empathic responses to her feelings. The group also reached out with support. In the second part of the session, after the immediate issue had been somewhat resolved and the member was in better shape, we carried out a midpoint evaluation of the group. In discussing the way we worked as a group, one of the members raised the authority theme.

Fran said, "I knew that this was Jane's night to get help the minute she walked in the door." (Jane was the member who had been crying.) When I inquired how she knew, she said, "Because she sat in the crying chair." She went on to point out that all of the people who had cried in sessions, 4 of the 10 group members, had all sat down in that chair at the beginning of the session. In fact, some had sat apart from their spouses for the first time in the group. Other members nodded in recognition of the accuracy of Fran's observation. I inquired if they had any thoughts about why that was so. Rose said, "Because that's the chair next to you, and we sit there to get some support when the going gets rough." I responded, "Could you talk a bit about what it is about me that causes you to sit there or feel I can support you? This is important as part of our evaluation, but also, it can tell us something about what it is you might want from each other."

The request for specifics was designed to encourage discussion of the members' feelings about the worker reaching out to them with caring. In addition, as is often the case, the process in the group can serve to assist group members in understanding their own relationships more clearly. The record continues:

Louise said, "It's because we can feel free to say anything to you, and you won't judge us. We can tell you our feelings." Rose continued, "And we know you really feel our hurt. It's not phony—you really care." Lou said, "It's safe next to you. We can share our innermost feelings and know that you won't let us get hurt." As I listened to the members, I felt myself deeply moved by the affect in their voices, and I shared that with them. "You know, it means a great deal to me to have you feel that way—that you can sense my feelings for you. I have grown to care about you quite a bit. It's surprising to me, sometimes, just how hard things in this group hit me—just how important you really have become."

The authority theme is a two-way street, and the worker will have as much feeling toward the members as they have toward the worker. The countertransference dynamics, described in Chapter 4, need to be made a part of the discussion. The honest feelings of the worker, freely expressed, are often the key to aiding the group as it comes to grips with its relationship to the worker.

In summary, some aspects of the authority theme to be dealt with during the life of the group include the worker's control, responsibility, and status as an outsider and the group's reactions to the worker's demands, limitations, and caring. Although the phases in which a group deals with issues are never neat and orderly, a pattern emerges: As the issues of authority are dealt with, the group becomes more ready to turn to its second major developmental task, the relationships among members (the intimacy theme).

Dealing With the Relationship Among Members

Once again, Bennis and Shepard's (1956) theory can provide helpful insights. In addition to concerns about dependency, a second major area of internal uncertainty for group members relates to *interdependence*. This has to do with questions of intimacy—that is, the group members' concerns about how close they wish to get to one another. In Bennis and Shepard's model, the group moves from the first phase, concerned with dependence and marked by a preoccupation with authority relations, to the **interdependence phase**, characterized by issues of peer group relationships. The two sets of member personalities that emerge in relation to this issue are the *overpersonal* and *counterpersonal* group members. These parallel the dependent and the counterdependent personalities of the first phase. Once again, three subphases are identified: the **enchantment-flight** subphase, in which good feelings abound and efforts are directed toward healing wounds; the **disenchantment-flight** subphase, in which the counterpersonals take over from the overpersonals in reaction to the growing intimacy; and finally, the **consensual validation** subphase, in which the unconflicted members once again provide the leadership needed for the group to move to a new level of work characterized by honest communication among members.

While the specifics of the Bennis and Shepard model relate most directly to the dynamics of T-groups (training groups), ambivalence toward honest communications among members can be observed in most groups. After dealing with the authority theme, the group often moves through a phase marked by positive feelings among members, as the enchantment-flight subphase suggests. As the work deepens and members move beyond simply supporting each other and begin to confront each other, more negative feelings and reactions arise. As members begin to rub up against each other in their work, these feelings are quite natural and should be an expected part of the process. However, group members have learned from their experiences in other situations (family, groups, classes) that talking directly about negative reactions to the behavior of others is not polite. This conditioning is part of the worker's experience as well. Often, then, the worker and the group get angry at members but nonetheless withhold their reactions.

Without direct feedback from the group, individual members find it difficult to understand their impact on the group, to learn from that understanding, and to develop new ways of coping. The worker's task is to draw these interpersonal obstacles to the attention of the members and to help the group develop the ability to discuss them. Workers often fear "opening up" discussion of the angry feelings they sense in the group, because they are concerned that things will "get out of hand," they will be overwhelmed, individuals will be hurt, and the life of the group will be threatened. Actually, the greatest threat to the life of the group is overpoliteness and the resulting illusion of work. Expression of anger can free the caring and other positive feelings that are also part of the group's intimacy.

Of course, the worker needs to take care that the contract of the group does not get subverted. Sometimes the discussion becomes centered on intermember relationships, thereby losing sight of the original reason the group was formed. This is one of my major criticisms of the type of groups (T-groups) studied by Bennis and Shepard. They have no other external group purpose other than to analyze the interactions among members. They are usually described as educational groups wherein members can learn about group dynamics and their own interpersonal behaviors. A second possibility to which the worker must be alert is that the member involved may attempt to use the group to deal with a personal pattern of behaving in groups, another attempt at subversion of group purpose.

College Student Counseling Group and the Intimacy Theme In the following illustration from a counseling group for college students experiencing difficulty in adjusting to their first year on campus, one member developed a pattern of relating in which she consistently cut off other members, did not really listen to them, and attempted to raise her own questions and concerns directly with the worker. The worker sensed she was relating only to him. The other group members showed elevating nonverbal signals of anger at her behavior that she did not perceive. The record starts after a particularly striking example of this behavior.

> I noticed the group members had physically turned away as Louise was talking. Their faces spoke loudly of their negative reaction. I decided to raise the issue: "There is something happening right now that seems to happen a lot in this group. Louise is asking a lot of questions, cutting some people off as she does, and I sense that the rest of you aren't too happy about that. Am I right?" There was silence for a moment, and Louise, for the first time, was looking directly at the other group members. I said, "I know this isn't easy to talk about, but I feel if we can't be honest with each other about how we are working together, we don't stand a chance of being an effective group. And I think Louise would want to know if this was true. Am I right about that, Louise?" She answered, "I didn't realize I was doing this. Is it true?" Francine responded, "Frankly, Louise, I have been sitting here getting angrier and angrier at you by the minute. You really don't seem to listen to anyone else in the group."

The worker opened the door by pointing out the pattern in the group and breaking the taboo against direct acknowledgment of an interpersonal problem. This freed members to explore this sensitive area.

> After Francine's words there was a moment of silence, and then Louise began to cry, saying, "You know, I seem to be doing this in all areas of my life. All of my friends are angry at me, my boyfriend won't speak to me, and now I've done it again. What's wrong with me?" The group seemed stunned by her expression of feeling.

Because this was the first real discussion of an interpersonal issue in the group, the worker needed to clarify the boundary of the discussion, using the contract as his guide. The group felt guilty, and Louise felt overwhelmed. The worker acknowledged both of these feelings:

"I guess you all must feel quite concerned over how strongly this is hitting Louise?" Members nodded their heads, but no one spoke. I continued, "Louise, I'm afraid this has hit you really hard. I should make it clear that we won't be able to talk about the other areas in your life that you are finding tough right now—that wouldn't be appropriate in this group. I'd be glad to talk to you after the group, however, and maybe, if you want, we could explore other avenues of help. For right now, could you stick to what is happening in this group? How come you seem to be so eager to ask all the questions, and why do you seem so cut off from the group?" Louise was thoughtful for a moment and then said to the group, "I guess it's just that I'm feeling really concerned about what's going on here at school and I'm trying to get some help as quickly as possible. I want to make sure I get as much from Sid [the worker] as I can." I paused and looked to the group. Francine responded, "You know, that's probably why I got so mad at you, because I'm the same way, and I'm sitting here feeling the same feelings—I want to get as much help as I can as well." Louise: "Well, at least you were straight with me, and I appreciate that. It's much worse when you can sense something is wrong, but people won't level with you."

After the exchange between Louise and Francine, the group seemed to relax. Louise's readiness to accept negative feedback without defensiveness had an impact on the group. In other circumstances, members may feel more vulnerable and would need all the help the worker could give in terms of support. When Louise was able to express the underlying feelings she experienced, other group members were able to identify with her, and this freed their affect and concern. Louise could sense their concern for her, making it easier for her to feel more a part of the group rather than relating only to the worker. The worker proceeded to underline the importance of honest communication among members and then guarded against preoccupation with process, by reaching for the implicit work hinted at in the exchange.

"I think it was really tough just now, for Louise and the rest of you. However, if the group is going to be helpful, I think we are going to have to learn how to be honest with each other. As Louise pointed out, it can be tougher not to hear sometimes. I think it is also important that we not lose the threads of our work as we go along. I noticed that both Louise and Francine mentioned their urgency about getting help with their problems right now. Could we pick up by being a bit more specific about what those problems are?"

Francine accepted the invitation by expressing a concern she was having about a specific course. From that point on, Louise was more attentive to the group and appeared a good deal more relaxed. The few times she interrupted, she good-naturedly caught herself and apologized. The worker spoke to her after the session and arranged an appointment for personal counseling. Members from that point on also appeared more involved and energetic in the discussion.

A group needs to develop a climate of trust that will allow members to lower their defenses. A powerful barrier to trust can be raised and maintained by what members leave unsaid. Group members can sense both positive and negative reactions by other members. The effect of these reactions increases when they remain beneath the surface. On the other hand, open expression of these feelings can free members, who feel more confident when they know where they stand with the group.

Workers usually experience intermember issues as particularly difficult. As they develop group experience, they become proficient at reaching for issues related to the authority theme; however, they take longer to risk dealing with the intimacy theme. So powerful are the taboos and so strong is their fear of hurting, and being hurt in reaction, that they will try many indirect routes before finally risking honesty. The reluctance may be partly rooted in workers' feelings that they are responsible for "handling" anything that comes from reaching for intermember negatives. As this excerpt has illustrated, a group that has developed even a small fund of positive feelings is better equipped for handling its own problems. They need the worker's intervention to act as a catalyst, giving them permission and supporting them as they enter the formerly taboo area.

Intimacy and the Relational Model Another theoretical model (mentioned in Chapter 1) that helps us to understand the intimacy theme is the relational model. It has emerged from the work done at the Stone Center in Wellesley, Massachusetts, which is dedicated to studying the unique issues in the development of women and methods for working effectively with them. The center has built on the early work of Jean Baker Miller, whose publication entitled *Toward a New Psychology of Women* (Miller 1987; Miller & Stiver, 1991) laid the groundwork for the relational model.

Much of the evolving work in this area can be found in publications and a series of working papers from the Stone Center. Recall that this framework is often classified under the general rubric of self-in-relation theory. In one example of a group work elaboration of this model, Fedele (1994) draws on three central constructs repeatedly found in relational theory: *paradox* (an apparent contradiction that contains a truth); *connection* ("a joining in relationship between people who experience each other's presence in a full way and who accommodate both the correspondence and contrasts between them"); and *resonance* ("a resounding; an echoing; the capacity to respond that, in its most sophisticated form, is empathy") (p. 7).

Referring to therapy, Fedele (1994) identifies several paradoxes: "Vulnerability leads to growth; pain can be experienced in safety; talking about disconnection leads to connection; and conflict between people can be best tolerated in their connection" (p. 8). She also identifies the paradox between "transferential" and "real" relationships in therapy as well as the "importance of establishing a mutual, empathic relationship within the context of the unequal therapist-client relationship" (p. 8) as additional primary paradoxes in therapy. She says,

> These dilemmas are dramatically apparent in group psychotherapy. The therapists and group members collaborate to create an emotional relational space which allows the members to recapture more and more of their experience in their own awareness and in the group. The feelings of the past can be tolerated in this new relational space. It allows us to reframe the experience of pain within the context of safety. The difficulty of creating an environment that allows vulnerability in a group format involves the complexity of creating safety for all participants. (p. 8)

In applying this theory to group therapy, she identifies the "basic paradox" of a simultaneous yearning for connection accompanied by efforts to maintain disconnection as a form of protection from being hurt—a need generated from earlier painful experiences. The paradox of "similarity and diversity" describes a tension between connection around universal feelings and fears of isolation because of difference. She points out that "the mutuality of empathy allows all participants to feel understood and accepted. The leader, creating a safe relational context, fosters connectedness within that safety by working to enlarge the empathy for difference" (1994, p. 9). Another related paradox is the fact that the very process of sharing disconnection can lead to new connection. For example, "When members phone the leader to report anger or dissatisfaction with the group, the leader can encourage them to share this experience in the group. Often, if one feels the disconnection, it is very likely that one or more of the other members experience similar feelings and resonate with the feelings of dissatisfaction" (p. 10). Thus, when members share the sense of disconnection, these feelings can lead to connection. Finally, the paradox of "conflict in connection" describes the importance of managing conflict and keeping anger within the context of safety and acceptance of divergent realities. As she points out, "One way to view anger is to see it as a reaction to the experience of disconnection in the face of intense yearning for connection" (p. 11).

In describing the second major construct of relational theory, the idea of "connection," Fedele (1994) says,

> The primary task of the leader and the group members is to facilitate a feeling of connection. In a relational model of group work, the leader is careful to understand each interaction, each dynamic in the group as a means for maintaining connection or as a strategy to remain out of connection. As in interpersonal therapy groups, the leader encourages the members to be aware of their availability in the here-and-now relationship of the group by understanding and empathizing with their experiences of the past. But it is the yearning for connection, rather than an innate need for separation or individuation, that fuels their development both in the here-and-now and in the past. (p. 11)

Finally, the third major concept, "resonance," asserts that the "power of experiencing pain within a healing connection stems from the ability of an individual to resonate with another" (Fedele, 1994, p. 14) She suggests that resonance manifests itself in group work in two ways:

> The first is the ability of one member to simply resonate with another's experience in the group and experience some vicarious relief because of that resonance. The member need not discuss the issue in the group, but the experience moves her that much closer to knowing and sharing her own truth without necessarily responding or articulating it. Another way resonance manifests itself in a group involves the ability of members to resonate with each other's issues and thereby recall or reconnect with their own issues. This is an important element of group process in all groups but is dramatically obvious in groups with women who have trauma histories. Often, when one woman talks about painful material, other women dissociate. It is a very powerful aspect of group work that, if acknowledged, can help women move into connection. It can also cause problems if women become overwhelmed or flooded. The leader needs to modulate this resonance by helping each member develop skills to manage and contain intense feelings. (p. 14)

Many of the constructs of this theory, particularly its group work implications, fit well with the interactional framework presented in this book. For example, a former colleague of mine, Linda Schiller (1993), was able to use the self-in-relation framework to rethink a classic theory of group development known as the Boston model (Garland et al., 1965), adapting it to a feminist perspective.

In the example that follows, from a support group for women with cancer, we can use the relational model to explain the patterns of interaction over time. We can see examples of paradoxes, connections, and resonance in each session of the work.

RECORD OF SERVICE

Client Description and Time Frame

Members: Four 45- to 58-year-old white women from different ethnic and socioeconomic backgrounds. All have been diagnosed with breast cancer and either are in the midst of treatment or have just finished. The group was created in response to inquiries made by each of the members to the outpatient oncology clinic in the hospital. All members are voluntary.

Dates Covered in Record: 11/14 to 12/5.

Group Task: Individual need satisfaction.

Description of the Problem

The task of this group is for members to reach out to one another in order to find support around painful issues in dealing with their cancer diagnoses. One member in particular seems to be expressing the pain and anger for the group. The problem that I began to recognize was that this member was carrying a great deal of emotion about her cancer diagnosis. She demonstrated her emotion through anger and distrust projected onto group members and the medical staff in general. I suspect that all members shared similar feelings to some extent but were unable to recognize them as related to their illness. My coleader and I found ourselves faced with two problems: (1) we needed to find appropriate ways to address the emotions expressed by the angry member, or what appeared to be the deviant member, in order to get at the underlying message, and (2) we needed to help the group as a whole find the freedom to express and address their painful feelings rather than allowing this individual member to bear the responsibility.

How the Problem Came to the Attention of the Worker(s)

Through conversation and telling of individual stories, it seemed apparent from the beginning of the group that this particular woman was distrustful of people in general. I had originally suspected that she was someone who generally had not found people trustworthy throughout her life. After the second session, I began to wonder if this quality was not somehow related to her recent cancer diagnosis as well. She called my coleader and expressed a desire to quit the group because her "ways of dealing with her illness were diametrically opposed to the other members' ways." At this time she also mentioned the name of one member specifically. Although she continued coming, it was apparent that she was carrying anger with her, especially toward the member she had named. She would roll her eyes or mutter something under her breath whenever this woman spoke. The other members did not acknowledge this, nor did the woman to whom the behavior was addressed.

Summary of the Work

Session 1

For the first session, although I was very anxious about its newness, I was truly excited about the nature of this group, as the women attending had taken the initiative to request its formation. I felt that it was going to be an exciting and rich experience for all of us. My coleader and I began the group by introducing ourselves and then having each of the four members introduce themselves. I then went over confidentiality issues as well as the rules and the purpose of the group: This was a support group for women with breast cancer. It was created because of their requests in the oncology clinic, and I hoped that it would become a safe place for each of them to share their experiences and feelings around their illness as well as a place in which they could learn from one another. My coleader then stated that she, too, hoped to make this a safe place for the women to share their stories, and then she invited each one to talk about her experiences.

Each member told her story, offering an account of what she had been through. I noticed that none of the women expressed their stories with much emotion, only offering descriptive accounts of their experiences. However, one woman, Joan, did stand out in her account. She expressed distrust in the medical system and said that so far she had not found any of the doctors or nurses helpful. "I do my own research and reading. I can't count on them to give me the answers. They're in and out in a flash." Another woman, Judy, added that she had had a similar experience in the past and ended up switching doctors. Joan snapped at Judy, making an excuse for not being able to switch doctors, and said, "I just deal with it." I made a mental note of this exchange and gave some thought to Joan's account of her experiences as well as her stating that change was not possible. I, at this time, thought that she seemed to be a person who did not trust others, probably because of her own life experiences. I did not make a connection between her feelings about the medical staff and her cancer at this time, nor did I think much about why her reaction to Judy was so strong. In retrospect, I would guess that Joan was offering the group some insight into how she was feeling in the group and about her cancer.

Once each woman had shared with the group, my coleader asked if any of them had been in groups in the past. Only one woman had been in a prior group, and she talked about how each member in that group had died. The room was silent. Instead of letting the silence stay and then addressing its meaning, I asked the woman what it felt like to be starting another group. She commented that it was a little scary and added, "But we have to keep going on. We have no other choice." I then asked the other members what it felt like to hear her talk about the other group. They all commented about how it must have been an awful experience for her. My coleader pushed, "Does it make you start to think about your own mortality?" A couple of members said that they had not really given it much thought, and Joan said that it did make her think about it but that was all. Instead of pursuing this, both my coleader and I let the conversation drift back to the members' telling Barbara how it must have been hard to be part of that group. Again, Joan had given us an opportunity to recognize her as really wanting to do the work in the group. First, she brought up the anger and then acknowledged thinking about death. Both are very real issues for all the members in this group. We failed to pick up on her desire to work.

Because of time constraints, we ended the meeting. My coleader offered a summary of what she felt she had heard as being common among the women's experiences as they had portrayed them to the group, and she used this as a way to reiterate the goal of finding support from each other within the group. Death and anger were not mentioned. We both thanked them for coming to the group.

Session 2

This session began with all members arriving on time. We asked each member to give a brief check-in so that everyone could get an idea of how the others are doing. Joan was the last one to check in, and she brought up the fact that her daughter was going through chemotherapy at the time and that she herself was presently taking care of a depressed friend. This opened up a discussion for all the women to find something in common. It turned out that each of them was caring for elderly parents; thus, all these women were acting as caretakers while dealing with their illnesses. I asked, "What's it like to not only have to worry about your own health and ability to live from day to day, but have to worry about taking care of someone else as well?" Barbara said, "You gotta do what you gotta do." Everyone agreed. Judy then began to change the subject and talk about how when she's not caring for her mother she is working on a proposal that addresses research around tobacco- and cancer-related issues. She wanted to know if any of the other women would be interested in helping her out. Barbara and Gayle inquired about it, while Joan sat quietly, appearing to be somewhat annoyed. Neither my coleader nor I said anything. I did not realize at the time that this was Judy's way of avoiding the work of addressing painful feelings, the group's way of going along with it, and Joan's silent plea to do the work.

The women continued to talk about their own efforts in keeping busy, and then Joan chimed in, "I haven't been able to go back to work because of the amount of chemotherapy I receive. I have enough trouble trying to take care of everyone else and myself." Judy responded by stating that she knew how she felt because she wished she had more time to work on her proposal. She then went into how long a proposal takes to draft. Joan rolled her eyes. The other members seemed to fall into Judy's trap again. My coleader said, "I've noticed that the group sort of shifts a focus off issues that seem to bring up some painful emotions for each of you. Have you noticed that, Sandra? Has anyone else noticed that?" Gayle asked what she meant. She explained, without using names, that whenever the group got close to having to share how experiences or "realities" were affecting them, they seemed to shift to talking about less emotional topics. She then said, "I wonder why this happens." Here we began to point out the pattern that the group was establishing in addressing painful issues. What we failed to do was to recognize and to use Joan's experience in the group as a way to name the painful feelings that the members were avoiding discussing. Gayle stated that she hadn't noticed this. Judy and Barbara stated that they had not noticed either. Each of them was sort of smiling an embarrassed smile. Joan would not look at the group members; she just let out a very heavy sigh that caused everyone to look at her. No one said anything. Once again, we had missed an opportunity and had failed to answer what seemed like Joan's plea for work. We let the group sit for a little while and think.

Barbara commented on how quiet it had gotten. This broke the silence, and the other members began to admit that they "might" have been avoiding painful issues. Joan still sat quietly. I remarked that she had been very quiet for a while and that our time was running out. I wondered if she wanted to share anything with the group. She said no. My coleader said that she imagined her silence meant something. She said, very angrily, that it was sometimes easier to "just not talk." The group then began to inquire and stated that the reason they were together was to help one another and that if they could help her they wanted to. Joan just shook her head and said that she was fine. We, again, avoided bringing up the anger that was present. Maybe we (my coleader and I) did not want to deal with it?

The group then began to talk about some side effects of their chemotherapy. Judy was the only one in the group without hair. She expressed feeling fine about not having it: "It will grow back." Others talked about hair thinning and other side effects that they had read about. Joan joined in the conversation minimally. We still ignored the possible significance of her deviation from the group norm.

The group ended, and that afternoon my coleader got a call from Joan saying that she felt her way of dealing with things was very different from the group's, especially Judy's, and that she felt as though she wanted to quit coming. After talking it through with my coleader, Joan decided to return to the group for at least one more time. When my coleader and I discussed this, I did not see that Joan's phone call was probably a plea, again, for us to help her work with the group on addressing the pain she was feeling. We simply chalked it up to her not getting along with one of the members and feeling as though she was just not getting the kind of support that she needed from the group. My coleader expressed to her that the group was as much hers as anyone else's and that she hoped she would bring her concerns up to the group during the next session. In retrospect, what I think we were missing was that Joan was representing the ambivalence of the group to face painful issues. In addition, we failed to really note what Judy represented to her, and possibly other members. Judy is the only one who has completed chemotherapy and/or radiation, she is the intellectualizer (or initiator of flight), her baldness is a reminder of what might happen to others in the group, and she is getting back into her work and other parts of her life that she has put on hold, unlike the other members who are still faced with much uncertainty.

Session 3

The group opened again by checking in with each member. Joan appeared somewhat more cheerful than I had expected. Barbara brought up feeling worn out about caring for her mother and herself. This opened up a discussion around how they each were giving support to other people. Directing the question to any member, I asked, "Who gives you support?" Judy began to talk about how her friends used to provide her with transportation and/or come over with meals when she was sick from treatment. Each of the other women shared their "support" stories as well. I finally stated that the kind of support that they had all just talked about was support around concrete needs: food, rides, and so on. I then asked who gave them emotional support. The room got silent. Judy began to intellectualize. Joan rolled her eyes and shook her head. I pointed out that they were "doing it again," referring to their established pattern of avoiding painful issues.

Everyone but Joan smiled embarrassedly. I said to them that everyone was smiling but Joan, and I wondered what they were really feeling. They were silent. I said that I imagined it was hard for each of them to be here and to talk about their illness, especially while they are still in treatment. Here I failed to acknowledge or name the ambivalence and did not make its connection to Joan's desire to quit the group. Judy offered a reminder that she was finished with her treatment. My coleader took this opportunity to ask the group what it was like for them to still be in treatment and to have a member present who was through with it. Joan remained quiet. Gayle got tearful and began to pour out that she was "scared shitless" of what might happen to her hair, of how sick she might become and of how there's no real guarantee the chemo would work. I stated that I had just seen more emotion pour out of her than I had seen before. I named what I saw: "You seem like you're feeling sad and scared and angry all at once." She had tears rolling down her cheeks. I looked at Joan, who was tearful. My coleader asked the group, "What do you do with all of these feelings every day?" Joan made a sound of irritation. My coleader asked her what that sound meant. Joan just shook her head. My coleader stated that Gayle's outpouring of emotion was understandable and that she thought it must be hard for her to carry those feelings around. I then took the opportunity to narrow the focus to the anger, because it seemed to be an emotion shared at that moment by more than one member (both Gayle and Joan). At this time, I ended up taking advantage of an opportune moment to address Joan's anger without making her feel alone with it. When I mentioned that it must be hard to deal with the anger and asked how they managed it, Joan started right in about how angry she was at the hospital and about her depressed friend. The discussion continued until Gayle said that she just wished that she could get back to where she was before she got sick. Through this discussion the group was able to talk about their anger, an emotion that all of them admitted to feeling. They acknowledged that it "might" be about their "unlucky" confrontation with cancer, but no one would give a definitive "yes" on that.

As the group ended that day, there was a sense of peace in the room. At this time I was not sure what we had accomplished. But on reviewing my notes from this session it appeared that much work was done in breaking through the obstacles that the literature speaks to. By reaching for the underlying feelings and the meanings of the nonverbal messages, we were able to open up some painful areas that the group obviously felt ambivalent about sharing. We were also able to take the individual's issue (the anger) and bring it out as a common feeling among all the group members, rather than leaving it in one person's possession. One thing that was not addressed, though, was Joan's anger directed at Judy. I think the leaders were too afraid to touch this.

Session 4

The group started as usual with check-ins. The members shared some events that had taken place that week regarding new drugs that two of them were put on. A discussion opened up around side effects again, and this led Joan into discussing her anger about her visit with her doctor that week, as he had been "in and out in a matter of minutes." The group started to ask her questions about why she could not switch doctors if she was so unhappy. I noticed that Joan's response was somewhat different from how she had responded the first time the group had confronted her regarding switching doctors. She was less hostile, and her anger did not seem to be directed at the members. She was able to discuss with them the possibility of switching but came to the conclusion that she would rather still do her own research than switch doctors midtreatment. At this point, Barbara said to Joan, "You seem so angry at the doctors. I wish that your experience with them wasn't so dreadful. It makes it much easier if you feel like you are in good hands." The group began to discuss this thought, and Joan sat back and listened. She did not appear angry, just deep in thought. My coleader asked her what was going through her mind. Joan said, "I just feel like my life is in their hands. They have all the power, the cancer has the power, the drugs have the power, I have none."

For the first time, the group started to really talk about feeling helpless to their cancer diagnoses. After we had recognized and called attention to Joan's nonverbal messages, the group was able to benefit once again from Joan's ability to bring a common issue to the forefront. In addition, the members were beginning to feel comfortable in bringing up the issues themselves. This was evident when Barbara commented to Joan about her anger. No one other than the leaders had pointed this out before.

Current Status of the Problem

Where It Stands Now

At the time that these excerpts were compiled, it was apparent that the group had begun to address painful issues with one another. The leaders' push to address one member's obvious feelings of pain allowed these issues to emerge. The group also began to point out one another's nonverbal reactions, thus opening up deeper levels of discussion and understanding. Although the issues were constantly put in our (the leaders') faces, it took Joan several tries to finally reach us. The group continues to need prodding and reminders that they are "doing it again." Joan continues to display anger, but the group has begun to talk to her directly about this. However, the fact that her anger is often directed at Judy has never been brought up. My coleader and I have begun to discuss our hypotheses about Joan's anger being directed toward Judy. So far, however, neither of us has brought this observation to the forefront, nor has any of the group members. What is clear, still, is that Joan seems to carry the group's internal struggles. What I hope is that the group will somehow find a way to share that responsibility, and Joan will no longer be responsible for vocalizing their needs. Not only will the group benefit from this, but this will help to decrease the alienation that I suspect Joan has felt as her "deviant" way of dealing with issues has set her apart from the group.

Specific Next Steps

- I will continue to zero in on nonverbal messages and bring them to the attention of the group.
- I will continue to encourage group members to discuss painful issues and to point out the obstacles that are created to avoid this work.
- I will continue to collaborate about and review sessions regularly with my coleader so that we can gain greater insight from each other regarding group process.
- I will continue to search for connections between an individual's behaviors and those of the group in order to help the members become more aware of internal struggles.
- I hope to create an educational session for members to have their questions answered by a physician in order to address feelings of disempowerment and helplessness.
- I will continue to work on my group skills and to actively engage in seeking materials to increase my awareness about specific group tasks and problems.

The descriptions of the difficulties group members face in dealing with two major developmental tasks, the relationship with the worker and the relationship among members, refer to a yet more general task, the development of a culture for work. In the following section, we explore the question of group culture in more detail.

Developing a Culture for Work

The term *group culture* has been used thus far in its anthropological/sociological sense, with a particular emphasis on group norms, taboos, and roles. Earlier in this chapter we addressed the concept of role in some detail, so we focus here on norms and taboos. Hare (1962) has defined group norms as

> rules of behavior, proper ways of acting, which have been accepted as legitimate by members of a group. Norms specify the kinds of behavior that are expected of group members. These rules or standards of behavior to which members are expected to conform are for the most part derived from the goals which a group has set for itself. Given a set of goals, norms define the kind of behavior which is necessary for or consistent with the realization of those goals. (p. 24)

Taboos are commonly associated with primitive tribes who developed sacred prohibitions making certain people or acts untouchable or unmentionable. As we have seen, the term *taboo* in modern cultures refers to social prohibitions related to conventions or traditions. Norms and taboos are closely related; for example, one group norm may be the tradition of making a particular subject taboo. As groups are formed, each member brings to the microsociety of the group a strongly developed set of norms of behavior and shared identification of taboo areas. The early culture of the group therefore reflects the members' outside culture. As Hare points out, the norms of a group should be consistent with those necessary for realization of its goals. The problem, however, is that the norms of our society and the taboos commonly observed often create obstacles to productive work in the group. A major group task then involves developing a new set of norms and thereby freeing group members to deal with formerly taboo subjects.

We have already been dealing with the problem of helping group members develop their culture for work. For example, authority and dependency are generally taboo subjects in our culture; we do not talk freely about our feelings regarding either. Group experiences in classrooms over many years have taught us not to challenge authority and yet alerted us to the dangers involved if we admit feelings of dependency on a person in authority in front of a peer group. The discussions of the authority and intimacy themes in the first part of this chapter described the worker's efforts to help the group discuss these taboo areas and to develop a new set of more productive norms. The effort is directed neither at changing societal norms nor exorcising taboos. There are sound reasons for norms of behavior, and many taboos have appropriate places in our lives. The work focuses instead on building a new culture within the group, but only insofar as it is needed for effective group functioning. Transfers of this experience beyond the group may or may not be relevant or appropriate.

For example, members in a couples' group had to deal with taboos against open discussion of sex, an area critical to the work of the group. The frankness of the group discussion freed the couples to develop more open communications with each other outside the sessions. This change in the culture of their marriages was important for them to develop and was therefore an appropriate transfer of learning. On the other hand, if the couples used their newfound freedom to discuss issues of sexual functioning at neighborhood cocktail parties, they might quickly discover the power of peer-group pressure (or perhaps be invited to more parties).

To illustrate the worker's function of helping the group work on its important tasks, we shall examine five efforts of workers to develop a group culture. Then we examine the impact of ethnicity on group culture. This section uses the group theory outlined by Bion (1961) to illustrate again the way in which practitioners can draw on the literature to build their own models of group functioning.

Parents of Hyperactive Children: Accepting Difficult Feelings The first illustration is of a worker's efforts to help a group of parents of hyperactive children share their painful and angry feelings about their children's problems. This is the same group cited earlier to illustrate the need for group members to deal with feelings that result from demands for work.

RECORD OF SERVICE

Client Description and Time Frame

This is a group for parents of children with a hyperactivity diagnosis. It is a gender-mixed group. All of the members are white. The setting is an outpatient clinic at a general hospital. The time frame is five weekly sessions.

Description of the Problem

Members found it very difficult to talk about their own feelings about their hyperactive children. Instead, they continually focused on what other people—such as teachers, neighbors, husbands, and relatives—felt about the children. Despite their reluctance to focus on their feelings, they occasionally gave me clues that this was their underlying concern, and as this was also part of the contract, I felt we had to explore their feelings and work on them.

How the Problem Came to the Attention of the Worker(s)

During the first few meetings, the members continued to talk about how important this group was for them, as it gave them a chance to get together to discuss their problems related to their hyperactive children and get support from each other. The feeling was that no one, not even their husbands or wives, understood what they were going through and how they felt. Any time they would begin talking about their own feelings, they resorted back to discussing medications, school, etc.—in other words, a safe topic. Yet the need to talk about how they felt was always raised by members in different ways. This pattern began in session two, when one member raised the question of hyperactivity due to emotional deprivation at an early age—the group superficially touched on it but dropped the subject, resorting back to something safe. As their pattern of flight became more obvious to me, I could help them understand what they were doing, and thus help them deal with their feelings.

Bion (1961) can help explain such difficulties with emotions, a characteristic common to groups. His work was based on observations of psychotherapy groups, led by himself, in which he played the relatively passive role of interpreting the members' behaviors. Once again, as with the earlier theory, some elements of his model are group-specific, while other aspects lend themselves nicely to generalizing. A central idea in Bion's work is the **work group.** This consists of the mental activity related to a group's task. When the work group is operating, one can see group members translating their thoughts and feelings into actions that are adaptive to reality. As Bion describes it, the work group represents a "sophisticated" level of group operation. Most groups begin with a more "primitive" culture in which they resist dealing with painful emotions. Group development is therefore the struggle between the group's primitive instincts to avoid the pain of growth and its need to become more sophisticated and deal with feelings. The primitive culture of the group's early stages mirrors the primitive culture in our larger society, where the direct and open expression of feelings is avoided.

In the example of the parents' group, the worker described how the problem came to her attention, pointing out how the more painful subjects were dropped as the group took flight into a discussion of more superficial issues. This conforms to one of Bion's key ideas—the existence of basic assumption groups. He believes that the work group can be obstructed, diverted, and sometimes assisted by group members experiencing powerful emotional drives. His term **basic assumption group** refers to the idea that group members appear to be acting as if their behavior were motivated by a shared basic assumption about the purpose of the group—an assumption other than the expressed group goal.

One of the three basic assumption groups he identifies is the **flight-fight group**. In a primitive group, when the work group gets close to painful feelings, the members will unite in an instantaneous, unconscious process to form the flight-fight group, acting from the basic assumption that the group goal is to avoid the pain associated with the work group processes through flight (that is, an immediate change of subject away from the painful area) or fight (that is, an argument developing in the group that moves from the emotional level to an intellectual one). This process in the group context parallels the ambivalence noted in work with individuals when resistance is expressed through an abrupt change of subjects. Bion's strategy for dealing with this problem is to call the group's attention to the behavior in an effort to educate the group so that it can function on a more sophisticated level.

As we return to the worker's record of service on this problem, we see that her early efforts were directed at systematically encouraging the expression of feelings and acknowledging these with her own feelings in an effort to build a working relationship. As the pattern developed, the worker drew on this working relationship to point out the pattern of avoidance and to make a demand for work.

Summary of the Work

Session 3

I listened to what the members were saying, and I encouraged them to talk about their feelings toward their hyperactive children. Marilyn told us that since she had begun coming to the sessions, she noticed that she had changed her attitude in relation to her hyperactive son, and now he was responding more positively toward her. She had always thought of him in terms of being a normal child, and it had frustrated her that he was unable to react as normal children do. In fact, she had set up expectations for him that he couldn't meet. I encouraged her to continue talking about her feelings toward him. She said that she supposed she really couldn't accept the fact that he was hyperactive, and then after coming to the meeting she began to accept this. I asked how she felt now. She felt better, but the hurt was there.

By the fifth session, the group had come close to discussing some of the more difficult underlying feelings; however, each time they had come up, they had used the flight mechanism to avoid the pain. Some of the feelings experienced by these parents ran so counter to what they expected themselves to feel that they had great difficulty in admitting the feelings to others and at times even to themselves. The worker had developed a fund of trust during the first sessions through her efforts to understand the meaning of the experience for the members. In the following excerpt, she draws on that fund and makes a demand for work by pointing out the members' pattern of flight. Even as she does this, she tries to express her empathy with the difficulty the group experiences in meeting this demand.

Session 5

The group sometimes picked up on their feelings, and I tried to put a demand for work on them; that is, to stick with the subject and to really talk about their feelings. I pointed out their underlying anger and did not allow them to take flight. Betty started talking about George and the school again, and the others became very supportive, offering concrete help. She expressed anger at the school but also talked about George and how he didn't fit in—he couldn't read and cope with the courses, and he didn't care. I detected that some of her anger was directed toward him, and I asked how she felt toward him at this point. She said that she pitied him. I wondered if she wasn't also feeling somewhat angry at him for causing her so many problems and irritating her so much. I said that there were times when George made her very angry. Mildred agreed that she has reacted negatively, too.

The worker's synthesis of empathy and demand helped the group modify its culture and create a new norm in which they would not be judged harshly for their feelings, even those they felt were unreasonable. As they expressed feelings of anger toward their children, the group moved to a new level of trust and openness. With the worker's help, they described moments when they felt like "killing" their child, and, under her gentle prodding, they explored how they experienced having an "imperfect child" as a reflection on themselves as bad parents. This attitude, in turn, affected the children's sense of acceptance by their parents, which sometimes led to further acting out. Understanding and accepting these feelings was a first step toward breaking this vicious cycle. The worker's comments at the end of the session acknowledged the important change in the discussion:

I recognized how hard it was to talk about their feelings, and how much pain they felt. I credited them for their work and tried to create feeling among them that I understood. Denise had been talking about her own feelings about her son, and she seemingly had her feelings well under control. She had said that she was very sensitive and had trouble talking about it. I said that perhaps she was saying that she, too, had feelings that the others had mentioned, but she found them very hard to discuss. The others said that it was hard to talk about their concerns, to admit that these children weren't the same as the others, that you wanted to be proud of them but couldn't. I agreed that it was hard—they were living the situation 24 hours a day, and they had feelings about these children. . . .

The members discussed how much they were criticized by their relatives and were very upset. I said that people just did not know what it was like to be a mother of a child like this, and also they did not feel the pain and frustration that the parents felt. I waited, and there was silence. I noticed that our time was long ago up, and I said that they had done some very hard work. It was not easy to talk as they had today, to share the feelings of depression and hostility toward their children and to admit that they had wanted to kill them at times. I wondered how they felt now. Marilyn said that she couldn't understand everything I tried to get them to do, but I made her think and try new things, and also I made her look at things differently. I said that it wasn't easy for them to do this, I knew that, and I often felt their pain.

We have already seen in an earlier excerpt how the worker needed to help this group articulate its anger in response to her demands for work. Bion might describe those exchanges as examples of the flight pattern of reaction in the flight-fight group. Another basic assumption group, as described by Bion, is the **dependent group**, in which the group appears to be meeting in order to be sustained by the leader. This is another form of avoidance of the work group and was illustrated in the earlier excerpt by the group wanting the leader to "cheer them up." The third and final assumption group in Bion's theory is called the **pairing group.** Here the group, often through a conversation between two members, avoids the pain of the work by discussing some future great event. The event can be the discovery of a new drug or procedure that will cure the person who is ill. Another example would be the arrival of some person or organization that will solve the problem. The discussion in this group of "new drugs" or "outside experts" who would provide a solution to their problems is an example of the pairing group in action. Now let us see the rest of the record of service.

Current Status of the Problem

Where It Stands Now

The group is beginning to work on their feelings, although not all members are equally willing to take a good look at themselves. They are starting to share with each other the pain, guilt, and anger they have toward their hyperactive children. Also, they're sharing feelings of helplessness—of wanting to be the perfect parent but knowing that they're not—and their desire to find ways to deal with their children better.

Strategies for Intervention

- Keep the focus, and continue making the demand for work. Continue making this a work group and not a fight-flight group.
- Use the deviant member's behavior to point out their own underlying feelings.
- Continue to recognize their feelings and credit them for their work. In crediting, make them aware of their progress, as a means of encouragement.
- Credit the internal leaders for taking over leadership and focusing the group on the work.
- Help the group work on solutions to their feelings and problems. The group needs this if they are to lose their feelings of helplessness—they want to learn how they can function better as parents and help their hyperactive children.
- Help the group move into the ending and transition stage.

Married Couples: Legitimizing the Expression of Anger In a second example of helping a group change its norms to develop a culture more conducive to work, a worker in a different married couples' group notices the group members' reluctance to get involved when couples share very personal and angry feelings. She brings this to their attention.

By the sixth session (following Christmas vacation, during which the group had adjourned for 2 weeks), most of the group's work seemed to involve each couple presenting problems that had been decided on by both partners and within limits felt by both to be fairly comfortable. If there was intracouple disagreement and challenge, such conflict seemed to be on safe topics—e.g., related to problems of the others in the group or, if pertaining to their own marriage, then almost always at the level of the more reluctant spouse. Don, at the fifth session, challenged Liz directly. Liz responded to his charge that she was "always covering up the truth" by a return challenge, asking him why he had married her—daring him to share with the group the real reason, her pregnancy.

When he tried to evade her by deliberately misinterpreting her question, she stuck with it and said she had always suspected that he had felt an obligation to marry and had never really loved her. The group seemed reluctant at first to step into this interchange—they seemed to be giving the couple a chance to "unsay" what had been said. I pointed out the difference between their reaction to this problem and others they had picked up on unhesitatingly, and I asked if they agreed that there was a difference. A few members did, and I asked why they thought they hadn't wanted to get involved. Most felt it was "extremely intimate," and that made the difference. I agreed that it was and that I felt it really took guts to bring up something intimate. I said that problems were not often brought up, because they were so personal and that we were so used to keeping anything personal as private as possible. The group talked about family and friends and "how far" one could go in these relationships and how this group was different from "out there." Something clicked for Reisa, because without even checking it out with Jack, she told the group that she and Jack had been forced to marry because she had been pregnant, too. They talked about her family's reaction and how this had affected their marriage and their feelings about their first child.

Married Couples: Dealing With Sexual Taboos I described earlier how the skill of helping individual clients to discuss subjects in taboo areas was important to the work. The social nature of taboos magnifies their impact in the group setting. Many of the taboos have their early roots in the first primary groups, such as the family, and thus can represent a powerful obstacle to group work. Sometimes the worker simply needs to call the group's attention to the obstacle, but in the case of some of the stronger taboos, such as sex, the group may need more help.

In the couples' group described in Chapter 10, sexual concerns between members were hinted at toward the end of an early session. I pointed this out to the group and suggested that we pick up on this at our next session. The group agreed enthusiastically. I did not expect it to be that easy; because of the strength of the taboo in this area, simply calling the group's attention to the subject probably would be insufficient. At the start of the next session, the members immediately began to discuss an unrelated area. I called their attention to the existence of the taboo. I asked the group members to explore the obstacle that made it hard for them to discuss sexual subjects. As they discussed what made it hard to talk about sexuality, they were talking about sexuality:

I said, "At the end of last week we agreed to get into the whole sexual area, and yet we seem to be avoiding it this week. I have a hunch that this is a hard area to discuss in the group. Am I right?" There was a look of relief on their faces, and Lou responded, "Yes, I noticed that as well. You know, this is not easy to talk about in public. We're not used to it." I wanted the group to explore what it was about this area that made it hard. "Maybe it would help if we spent some time on what it is about this area, in particular, that makes it tough to discuss. That might make everyone feel a bit more comfortable."

Fran responded, "When I was a kid, I got a clear message that this wasn't to be spoken about with my parents. The only thing said to me was that I should watch out because boys had only one thing on their mind—the problem was, I wasn't sure what that thing was." Group members were nodding and smiling at this. Lou said, "How many of you had your parents talk to you about sex?" The group exchanged stories of how sex was first raised with them. In all cases it had been done indirectly, if at all, and with some embarrassment. Those with older children described their own determination to do things differently, but somehow, their actual efforts to talk to their children were still marked by discomfort. At one point, Frank described his concerns as a teenager: "You know, from the talk I heard from the other guys, I thought everyone in the neighborhood was getting sex except me. It made me feel something was really wrong with me—and I made sure not to let on that I was really concerned about this." The conversation continued with the group noting that they had been raised in different generations, and that while some things were different in terms of attitudes toward sex, other things, particularly the taboos, were the same. I could sense a general relaxing as the discussion proceeded, and members discovered that there were many similarities in their experiences. I said, "It's easy to see how these experiences would make it difficult for you to talk freely in this group; however, if we can't get at this critical area, we will be blocked in our work."

By encouraging discussion of the taboo and the reasons for its power, I was helping the members enter this area. It was important that I did not blame or criticize them for their difficulty in getting started, but at the same time I needed to make a demand to move past the taboo.

"I can imagine that this difficulty in talking about sex must carry over in your marriages as well. I believe that if you can discuss some of the problems you are having here in the group, we might be able to help you talk more freely to each other—and that might be the beginning of a change." Rick responded, "We can never talk to each other about this without ending up in a fight." I asked Rick if he could expand on this. "We have this problem of me wanting more sex than Fran—sometimes we can go for months without sex, and I'm not sure I can take this anymore." Fran responded, "A relationship is more than just sex, you know, and I just can't turn it on or off because you happen to feel like having sex."

The rest of the evening was spent on Fran and Rick's relationship. The group was supportive to both as the couple's early conversation centered on who was to blame: Fran for her "frigidity" or Rick for his "premature ejaculation." During the next few sessions, the group kept discussing the sexual area as members explored the intricate patterns of action and reaction they had developed that led them to blame each other rather than take responsibility for their own feelings about sex. Once the taboo had been breached, and group members found that they were not punished, it lost some of its power and the discussion became more personal. Note that the process and the task are intermixed. As the group members discuss their difficulty in speaking about sex (the process), they are actually beginning to work on their concerns about sex (the task).

The final two brief excerpts in this section focus on helping young people deal with violence in their families. In these excerpts, the workers attempt to help group members share with each other the pain and posttraumatic stress that has become a part of everyday life for many of our most vulnerable children. In the first example, the worker helps the group discuss violence in their homes directed toward their mothers. In her analysis the worker shows how the violence also affects her feelings and actions. In the second example, the worker and the group try to help an older teen in a juvenile delinquency detention center deal with the result of his having accidentally shot and killed his best friend. As with the first example, we clearly see how hard it is for the workers to stay with the pain expressed by the group member. In the second example, one worker reaches for the member's underlying feelings while the other moves away from them, focusing instead on questions of responsibility. Both examples underline the importance of support for helping professionals so that they can manage their own feelings while helping clients manage theirs.

Inner-City Elementary School: The Impact of Violence in the Family

Purpose: Discussion group (with special attention to violent school behavior).

Gender/Age of Members: Female; age range: 9 to 10 years.

Cultural, Racial, or Ethnic Identification of Members: Two are African American and the third is African American and Hispanic.

Session 2

I asked if anyone had something they wanted to talk about today. Both Shaquandra's and Asia's hands shot up. I told them to decide who goes first. They pointed at each other and said, "You go first." Maria said nothing. It went back and forth for a few minutes with, "You," "No, you," "No, you," when finally Shaquandra said, "Oh, I will." She launched into a long, detailed account of how her stepfather tried to kill her mother. He was hiding in the room and she tried to get a gun but she could not get it because he pushed her down. She was talking very rapidly and staring blankly. She made no direct eye contact with anyone.

Finally, she paused, taking a deep breath. I said, "Wow, that's a lot of information all at once—sounds scary." She said, "Yeah." I asked her how that felt to her. She said, "It feels bad. I'm scared of him, but he's going to jail." Asia quickly chimed in, "Yeah, it feels bad." Then she launched into a similar story about an uncle who tried to kill her mother, but Asia hit him. "He's going to jail too, but I'm scared if he gets out he'll try to kill my mother again." I asked how it felt to hit him. She said it felt good. I said, "Wow, you girls have a lot to deal with. It must be hard for you. Did you know that sometimes when kids have a lot going on at home, they sometimes have unhappy times at school?"

Analysis

The major thing I would want to do if I had a chance would be to encourage a fuller development of statements the girls made. Because of my inexperience, and its having been only the second group meeting, I was feeling my way and did not explore as much as I would now. At the time, there was nothing coming from the group that could explain my last intervention statement. I think it meant I was scared, so I threw in a safe (for me) training manual statement! The Student Support Program at the school prepared a manual with suggested wording of statements for working with the kids. "Did you know that when kids are unhappy at home, they often have problems at school?" is a vintage example, which I used verbatim. In retrospect, I would still want to tie the school behavior together with the home problems at some point, but I would not feel so compelled to run away from the violence issues. I have a much better comfort level with tougher issues now.

Residential Center for Young Men in the Criminal Justice System

Purpose: To provide education and support to male juvenile delinquents with histories of anger and violence control problems.

Gender/Age of Members: Male; age range: 14–18.

Cultural, Racial, or Ethnic Identification of Members: Caucasian, African American, Native American, Hispanic, Cape Verdian.

Session 33

Jon (coleader) reminded Bill of family group when his mother was so angry with his apathy and resistance to treatment that she threatened to "leave her kids and get on with her life." There was silence in the room as Bill stared at the floor. In a soft voice, I said, "Bill, I was wondering about last week in family group—what was it like to hear your mom talk about stepping over the spot where Jim died?" Bill looked up at me as a group member asked, "Where did you shoot him? It was in your house?" Bill's gaze returned to the floor and he replied, "Yeah, it was in my living room. . . . My mom had new carpeting put in and stuff, but it's that spot, we know where it is."

I asked, "Had you considered what she continues to go through on a daily basis, or was that the first time you had heard she is stepping over it to close the drapes every night?" He raised his voice and responded, "I don't know, it made me mad to hear that she wants to sell the house or burn it or something! That made me mad." I replied, "She has a lot of memories there that she faces each day." There was silence. Then Bill said, "I used to sit on that spot on the floor and think about Jim." I said, "You have memories too, Bill?" He shared the moment of Jim's death on his living room floor. "I held on to him so tight . . . they pulled me off . . . the paramedics, they had to hold me so they could take him away . . . I just want him back." Bill began to sob uncontrollably. Jon encouraged Bill to feel the pain because that would be the only way it would go away. The group supported Bill with "Let it go, Bill," and "It's OK, guy, we're here for you." Jon then said, "You killed your best friend, Bill. You were out of control. You killed him and you cannot afford to forget that." The group remained silent.

The Impact of Ethnicity on Group Culture As the previous examples show, the worker faces many issues in establishing group culture. One such issue that deserves special attention is ethnicity.

One of my most important learning experiences occurred when I served as a consultant for the Hong Kong government department of social services. I provided short-term training workshops for social service professionals on how to organize and lead mutual-aid groups for clients. Although I had tried to get ready by reading about ethnic-sensitive practice and tuning in, nothing quite prepared me for the emotional impact and challenge to my adaptive skills I would face. I quickly understood that the process in the training groups would parallel what these social workers would face as they attempted to lead their client groups. Also, I realized that my task would be difficult: I would probably learn at least as much as I taught. The staff of the Hong Kong Social Service Department helped me in my efforts.

My first important insight was that fundamentals of human and group behavior are universal across cultures, but we can trace the roots of these norms, taboos, rules of behavior, and so on to quite different sources; thus, the intensity of their impact and the way they emerge vary among cultures. For example, I had prepared for the fact that the authority theme would be central in this group, as it is in all groups, in the beginning phase of work. With the Hong Kong groups, however, I was the "Professor," to be accorded status and deference in a manner that persisted for the life of the group. One group member pointed out to me that Chinese tradition bestows great prestige and authority on the group leader. This echoes the father in the Chinese family. As a person of knowledge, the group leader is entitled to respect and obedience from the group members who come to learn from him or her. Respect involves more than just ordinary politeness; it also involves agreement with the leader's view or at least abstention from open expression of disagreement. To disagree with a leader is to challenge his or her social role and hence harm his or her prestige. The leader would be seen as losing face. These values toward authority and others that stress harmony and order in all personal relationships can be traced to the three major streams of thought in Chinese history: Taoism, Buddhism, and Confucianism.

A second major insight was that principles of good practice also applied across cultures, but respecting and working with ethnic and cultural differences required me to make adaptations. For example, rather than opening each training group session with problem swapping and discussion, I prepared a brief and expected presentation. However, I did not abandon my requests for active discussion and involvement; I just delayed the demand, because I needed to respond to their expectations of me. I also respected their early resistance to disagreeing with me; however, I pointed out my awareness of their reluctance and my hope that, during our work together, we might find a way for them to provide feedback. Here is an excerpt from my notes from one of the early groups:

> I am very pleased that I will have an opportunity to share my ideas about leading mutual-aid groups with you. However, I have a problem with which I will need your assistance. These ideas were developed in my work with groups in a Western culture. I believe many will be useful for your groups as well, some will need to be adapted to respect your Chinese culture, and others may not fit at all. I understand and appreciate that your respect for me as a professor and your thoughtfulness will make you hesitant to disagree or suggest different ideas. It is my hope, however, that as we get to know each other, you will see that I very much value your ideas and will find your opinions helpful. I am prepared to teach what I know about group leadership, but I am also hoping to be a student as well.

There was no response to this offer, but I believe it was heard and understood. After the session, one group member, who had been educated at Berkeley University, where the cultural expectations governing the interchange between faculty and students differed somewhat from tradition, approached me privately to reassure me that it would take some time before I could expect a response and that I should not be discouraged.

I continued to try to find ways to encourage the group members to participate and provide feedback within their own cultural tradition. For example, when our groups had reached the point where they felt safe enough to share some of their difficult experiences leading groups, and we had reached a point in the analysis of an example where the skill of reaching for feelings or making a demand for work was appropriate, I would comment as follows:

> If I were faced with this problem in a group I was leading back home, I would probably say the following at this point: (I would then share my specific intervention). Can you help me to see how we could modify this so that we can accomplish the same end but do it in a way that would be comfortable for your culture and your groups?

This often generated an excellent discussion in which the workshop members artfully found their own ways of making the same intervention. Because my request was presented in a cooperative, rather than confrontational, manner, workshop members appeared to feel free to respond without fearing that they would be offending their group leader. An important additional benefit here was that I was modeling the same respect for culture in the workshop group that they would need to demonstrate in their own client groups.

One final tradition was observed with each of the groups I led: I was taken out to a celebratory luncheon banquet following the last session. This is one ethnic cultural practice I made no effort to modify; in fact, I would like to import it into my Western classes. This personal example has been provided to introduce the idea of respect for ethnic and racial variations in understanding and supporting the development of an effective group culture.

Developing a Structure for Work

As a group develops, it needs to work on the task of building a **structure for work:** the formal and informal rules, roles, communication patterns, rituals, and procedures developed by the group members to facilitate the work of the group. Regarding rules, some are established by the agency or host setting and are not in the control of the group members. At times, the group leader may try to help a group change a rule when conflict persists (see Part V). In other cases, the rules emerge from the members themselves.

In the following example, one member of an outpatient group for recovering addicts raises the issue of bringing her baby to the group sessions. Underlying the issue of structure are several other concerns for this client as well as questions for the workers about the need for additional agency support for the group.

The setting is an outpatient alcohol and drug clinic in a hospital. This is a group for young recovering addicts. The purpose of the group is for the members to learn from and support each other as they cope with a sober lifestyle. Two men and two women are at the first meeting, and up to four more members could be added. The members range in age from 19 to 27 years. The two women are black; one of the men is black and the other is white. The coleaders are white, and one is a counselor at the clinic.

> We had just finished going over the group rules and the group members were quiet. Beth (my coleader) asked the group if they wanted to add any more rules. There was a brief silence, and then Amanda said (to Beth), "You know what I would like to have for a rule." Beth nodded and said that maybe Amanda could explain what she meant to the group. Amanda turned back to the group and said that she had a 3-month-old baby. The social service department had the baby now, but she hoped to get the baby back soon. She was not

sure that she could find someone she trusted to watch the baby while she came to group. This was her first child, and she had been separated from her for so long that she didn't want to leave her. She said that while she was in group she would worry about the baby and that she had asked Beth in the pregroup interview if it might be OK for her to bring the baby along, but that we (Beth and I) had told her that she couldn't bring the baby. Amanda looked at Beth.

Beth said that traditionally the clinic hasn't had very many female clients and that this issue hadn't come up before at the clinic, so she hadn't given Amanda an answer right away but had talked to me and to the other staff members; she said that she and I had thought that it could be disruptive and distracting to have a baby in the group. Amanda, still speaking to Beth, said that probably the baby would just sleep most of the time. Beth said that the problem was that the baby wouldn't be 3 months for very long. Beth said that maybe Jen (another member) had some thoughts about the issue. Amanda turned to Jen. Jen smiled and said that she could remember when her daughter and her son were babies and that she had never wanted to leave them. She said that it's hard to leave your baby, but if there's a baby in the room, it's hard to ignore it even if it is asleep, because babies are so cute you always want to pick them up or play with them or touch them, so having a baby in the group could be disruptive.

Amanda appeared to take this comment in thoughtfully, and then she turned to Leo and Herb and said, "What do you think?" There was a brief silence and then Leo said that he didn't personally have children, but that he had a real soft spot for children and old people. He said from what he could tell it was going to be hard for Amanda to leave her baby, and he could see why. He said it seemed like Amanda was between a rock and a hard place, because if she brought the baby, it might distract her and the rest of the group, and if she didn't bring the baby, it might also distract her because she would be thinking about her baby and worrying about her. He said that it was important for Amanda to take time to focus on her own recovery, and bringing the baby to the group could get in the way of that as well as being distracting.

Amanda seemed satisfied with this and turned to Herb, who said that he basically agreed with Leo. Herb said that he liked kids a lot, but that he thought that a baby probably would be distracting and that it would be good for Amanda to take the group time to focus on herself. Amanda said that she could understand where everyone was coming from, but she still felt like she didn't want to leave her baby, but she'd do the best she could to get a babysitter. Leo suggested that maybe Amanda shouldn't get too worked up just yet, because it would be a few more weeks before she got the baby back and maybe a solution would turn up between now and then. He finished off by saying, "Easy does it," prompting Herb and Jen to follow quickly with two more AA slogans and everyone, including Amanda, wound up laughing. Then there was a brief silence.

I agreed with Leo and said that it was good this issue had come up because it might be the first time it had come up in the clinic, but it almost certainly wouldn't be the last time. I said that I thought it showed a gap in the clinic's services and it was something Beth and I could explore a little more and see if we could find a solution for. The members nodded, and Beth mentioned that there was a babysitting service in the hospital during the day, but that there clearly was a gap in the availability of services at night. Amanda said that she had not known about the daytime service and it made her mad to know it wasn't offered at night. She said she thought that probably a lot more women would come to the clinic if there was someone here to watch their kids. The other group members agreed. Beth said that maybe something could be worked out such as cooperative babysitting, and she asked me if I would bring that up at the staff meeting on Monday morning, because she isn't there on Mondays. I said I would be sure to, and I'd let them know what happened.

The discussion of the rule often raises many issues for the client, for example in this case Amanda's concern about caring for her baby and not losing it to the child welfare agency again. The worker remains responsible for enforcing the agency policy on the issue of Amanda bringing her baby to the group. In this case, the worker involves other group members in addressing the rule and its impact on Amanda and the group. Most important, the worker's sense of the mediating role between client and system leads her to begin immediately to identify potential systems work on the issue of providing child care resources so that members can attend the group without being concerned about neglecting their children. In exploring the other issue that may be being raised indirectly by the member—that is, her concerns about the demands on her life that emerge from her parenting responsibility—the worker provides an example of how process and content can be integrated. By bringing the baby to the group, the client may be indirectly saying, "Look how hard it is for me to take care of my own life and the baby at the same time." The worker might also want to explore this as a theme of concern for Amanda and for other members as well.

Chapter Summary

In this chapter, we have examined common examples of individual roles in the group, exploring the worker's helping role in relation to them. The concept of social role helps to explain patterned reactions by scapegoats, deviants, and gatekeepers, as well as defensive, quiet, and monopolizing members. In each case, the worker can best serve the group by understanding the individual member in terms of the dynamics of the group.

The worker's second client, the group-as-a-whole, is much like an organism: The sum of its parts is greater than the whole, and it goes through a developmental process. Early tasks include problems of formation and the satisfaction of individual members' needs. Problems of dealing with the worker as a symbol of authority (the authority theme) must be faced, as well as the difficulties involved in peer-group relationships (the intimacy theme). The worker also must attend the culture of the group so that it can develop norms consistent with the achievement of the group's goals. Taboos that block the group's progress must be challenged and overcome if the discussion is to be meaningful. A formal or informal structure must also be developed. This structure includes formal or informal rules, roles, communication patterns, rituals, and procedures developed by the group members. Effective work in the group develops a sense of cohesion, which in turn strengthens future work.

Related Online Content and Activities

 Visit *The Skills of Helping* Book Companion Website at www.socialwork.wadsworth.com/Shulman06/ for learning tools such as glossary terms, InfoTrac College Edition keywords, links to related websites, and chapter practice quizzes.

The website for this chapter also features additional notes from the author and additional process recordings:

- Boys in a Residential Center
- Boys in a Residential Treatment Center: Identifying With the Scapegoat
- Canadian Pregnant Teens in a Maternity Home: Development of Themes Over Time
- Developing a Group Structure Over Time: Teen Psychiatric Group
- Geriatric Reminiscence Group
- Homosexual Veterans with AIDS—Dealing With the Effects of Oppression
- Male Batterers: Moving From a General Problem to a Specific Concern
- Men's Counseling Group
- Men's Group: A Member Reaches Out to the Quiet Member
- Pregnant Teens in a Shelter: Mediating the Scapegoat—Group Interaction
- Teen Boys in a Residential Treatment Center: Raising a Difficult Family Issue and Dealing With the Group as the Second Client
- Teen Residential Group: Acting-Out Behavior as a Means of Communication
- Veterans With HIV/AIDS: Powerful Feelings and Powerful Fears
- Veterans' Outpatient Clinic: Management of Chronic Pain and Posttraumatic Stress

Endings and Transitions With Groups

The dynamics and skills involved in the ending and transition phase for individuals were discussed in detail in Chapter 5. All of these processes apply equally to work with groups. After offering a brief review, this chapter illustrates the variations that come with group work. The chapter concludes with a full description of an ending group session that demonstrates the unique aspects of endings in groups.

Ending and Transition Phase Summary

The ending stages of work with individuals, described in detail in Chapter 5, are also apparent in group sessions. First, there is the **denial of the ending**, in which group members appear to ignore the imminent end of the group. This is followed by **anger over the ending**, which emerges in direct and indirect forms and is often directed at the worker. The **mourning period** is usually characterized by apathy and a general tone of sadness in the group. Next, we have **trying the ending on for size**, in which the group members operate independently of the worker or spend a great deal of time talking about new groups or new workers. The *farewell-party syndrome* is seen when group members appear to protect the group by avoiding its negative aspects. It is not at all unusual for group members to suggest an actual farewell party in an attempt to avoid the pain of the ending.

Like the ending phases, worker strategies for dealing with endings in group work are similar to those described in work with individual clients. The worker should bring the ending to the group members' attention early, thereby allowing the ending process to be established. The stages should be pointed out as the group experiences them, with the worker reaching for the indirect cues and articulating the processes taking place: denial, anger, mourning, and so on. Because the group ending has meaning for the worker as well, he or she should bring personal feelings and recollections to the group. Discussion of the ending feelings should be encouraged, with the worker participating fully in the exchange of both positive and negative reactions. The worker should also help the group be specific as they evaluate their work together. For example, when a member says, "It was a great group!" the worker should ask, "What was it about the group that made it great?" Finally, the worker should reach past the farewell-party syndrome to encourage members to share negative feedback.

Because members have different reactions to endings, the group worker should encourage the expression and acceptance of differing views. The worker must also pay attention to the transitional aspect of the ending phase. For example, if members are continuing with other workers, how can they begin the relationship in a positive manner? If members have finished their work, what have they learned, and how can they use their learning in their new experiences? If they have found the group helpful, how can they find similar sources of support in their life situations? In this way, the worker can ensure that the ending discussion deals with substantive matters as well as the process of ending. In some situations, help can also take the form of a physical transition (such as a visit to a new school or institution). Finally, the worker should search for the subtle connections between the process of the ending and the substantive work of the contract. For example, endings for a group of unmarried mothers may coincide with separation from their children; foster teenagers who have provided mutual aid to each other may have learned something about giving and taking help from their peer group. These and other connections can help to enrich the ending discussion. The next section illustrates these dynamics and skills drawn from the group context.

Group Illustrations

The ending phase of work offers a powerful opportunity to deepen the work by integrating process and content. The losses involved in ending a group often provoke issues of intimacy and loss in other areas of the client's life. By constantly searching for the connections, however faint, between the dynamics of the ending process and the substantive work of the particular group, the worker can help the members use the ending as an important learning experience.

In the example that follows, a worker opens up the discussion of her leaving with a group of people who have multiple sclerosis (the group will be continuing). The announcement of the impending ending initiates a powerful conversation about intimacy and loss related to the illness. Note that the worker brings the group members back to their own endings in the here-and-now of the group experience.

Patients With Multiple Sclerosis

WORKER: As you know, I only meet with you one more time after today. You all will continue to meet until June. What are your thoughts about the group ending in a couple of months?

BOB: I am not looking forward to the summer because of the hot weather . . . it makes my MS flare up.

ALBERT: I know . . . I always feel tired and run down when it gets too hot. And then the group breaks up and I don't have anyone to really talk to about my MS. I used to look forward to the summer, but now I almost dread it.

BOB: I'm going to miss everyone too. I don't have anyone to talk to either. My wife is great, but she doesn't really understand what I am feeling.

WORKER: Do you guys keep in touch even when the group is not meeting during the summer months?

ALBERT: Not really . . .

FRED: I often talk to Rob from the other group pretty regularly.

BOB: Albert, you live not too far from me. We should get together once in a while this summer. Or at least talk on the phone.

ALBERT: I like that idea . . . I do want to stay in touch.

JAMES: (Who had been quiet up to this point) I used to dance and run track . . . and now I can't anymore. People look at me like I'm weird.

BOB: I always liked to dance too.

WORKER: James, you said people look at you weird. What do you mean by that? How does that make you feel?

JAMES: I get mad because I am not weird. I am just in a wheelchair. They don't know what I used to be able to do. All they see is what I look like on the outside.

WORKER: You're right. Strangers do not know who you are or what you are like, as we do. They don't know you as a person, and it isn't fair that they should judge you by your appearance or being in a wheelchair.

FRED: That's the trouble—no one can see the MS. They can't see the pain we feel in our legs, or the burning we have in our joints.

ALBERT: (He is one of the members whose MS is not as extreme. He still walks.) People don't even know anything is wrong with me because I am not in a wheelchair. But I still experience the MS symptoms. When they flare up, I get tired and sometimes walk off-balance, like I am drunk or something.

WORKER: It must be hard for you, Albert, because people cannot see your illness, and may not understand when you try to explain your physical symptoms.

ALBERT: Yeah, that happens a lot. When people find out I have MS, they don't believe me, because I am not in a wheelchair and they automatically associate MS with being in a wheelchair.

FRED: I went through that a lot when I was first diagnosed. I fought going into this wheelchair for as long as I could. I was lucky to be able to work until I was 60. But a short time after I retired, I had to get the chair.

JAMES: Yeah . . . when I first got those symptoms, the MPs on base used to stop me to ask if I was drunk because I staggered so much. That's when I first realized something was wrong. And then it just kept getting worse until I wound up in this wheelchair.

WORKER: You guys have lost important things associated with your identity because of this disease. Many of you had to quit working before you wanted . . . some of you lost important relationships.

JAMES: That's what I miss . . . having a girlfriend. (He pauses.)

WORKER: (After it looks like he won't continue on his own) Tell us more, James.

JAMES: I just miss the company. I don't care about the sex. I just wish I had the companionship. Someone to talk to, who will do things with me. I love my son and my parents, but I wish I had someone more my age to be with. (James is a young guy, in his early thirties and, in addition to being confined to a wheelchair, he has speech difficulties and shaking in his arms and neck. In retrospect, I wish I had explored more about how the change in his appearance and increasing disability affects his romantic possibilities. He has an 8-year-old son, but I don't know what his relationship with the mother was or if she left him when he became disabled. I'm sure this is something all the men have had to face—changes in their manhood, and how society views a disabled man.)

FRED: I know, James. Companionship is important.

BOB: There are a lot of symptoms of MS that people don't see and we don't talk about. Like our bladder and bowel problems. It's very degrading and embarrassing not to be able to control them all the time. (The others all voiced their agreement.)

WORKER: I know you were interested a few weeks ago in having Dr. C. (urologist) come to speak to you about these problems. Did she ever come?

ALBERT: Not yet.

WORKER: I will talk to the RN again and try to schedule her as a speaker in the future. (I bowed out of a sensitive and embarrassing subject here as well. I probably should have explored their feelings more around this subject, too.)

WORKER: I want to talk some more about our ending. I know I've been mentioning it the last couple of times we've met. It's really hard when people come and go from your life.

ALBERT: Yeah, it is. It seems like we just started with you and now you are leaving already.

WORKER: I want you to know that it is hard for me too. I am in a field where I will have to say good-bye many times to people whom I have grown to care about. But I believe that when I leave here, I will take a part of you all and internalize it, especially your courage. I have learned a lot from all of you about what it is like to live with MS, and how hard it is to deal with all the symptoms. But mostly I have seen how courageous and positive you are in light of all you have been through, and that encourages me. I believe I will be able to help other people in your position because of what you have taught me about dealing with a chronic disease like multiple sclerosis, and I thank you for this group and this experience.

Bob: I know you are going to do well. You are a kind person, and genuine and caring. I think I speak for everyone when I say we've enjoyed having you here. (The others nodded and voiced their agreement.)

Worker: Thank you. That's nice to hear. I've really enjoyed being a part of this group and getting to know all of you. (The time was up and we finished by saying good-bye and talking about meeting again in 2 weeks.)

As the ending approaches, there is always unfinished business between the group and the worker that needs to be explored. In the next example, we see the variation on the theme with children's groups.

Children's Group in an Elementary School

Sometimes the expression of anger can emerge indirectly as acting out. This is particularly true of endings in children's groups, as the members seem to revert to the behaviors exhibited in the beginning sessions. In the following illustration, a student worker returned after a 2-week absence from her group of grade-school children who had been meeting with her weekly because of trouble in school. The group had only 2 weeks left before its last meeting. The worker reached for the cues of the anger expressed in the children's behavior.

> The children were sitting in the middle of the room in a circle waiting for me. This was different from usual. There was a big table at the back of the room, and we usually sat around it. The boys started cheering and clapping when I came in. I said hello and told them that I was glad to see them too. I had missed them, and it was good to be back. They asked me a lot of questions about where I had been, what I had done, and so on, and I had to give them a rather detailed description of my vacation. After a while of this joking around, I said that it had been a long time since I had seen them last, and I asked what was new.
>
> They started talking about Chang, the Chinese boy in the class whom they hated, and how they had beaten him up. While I was trying to get the story straight about what had happened, a couple of the kids started becoming rowdy and rude, cutting each other off more than usual and cutting me off, too. I was surprised because, although they had the habit of interrupting each other and me as well, they had never been so belligerent. George continued telling me about the fight he had had with Chang, and how he had given him a bloody nose and sent him to the hospital for stitches. (I later found out the stitches part of the story was exaggerated.) Warren, Bobby, and a couple of others joined in and they all proudly described in detail the way they had beaten Chang up. I wanted to remark on this and finally had to tell them to hold it, I wanted to say something. They quieted down a bit, and I finally was able to say what I had wanted—that I couldn't get over how excited and proud they were about what they did to Chang, and I asked them why they did it.
>
> They totally ignored my question and continued in depth about the fight. I waited for a while and tried again to say something, but they were so noisy, I couldn't finish my sentence. There was a lot of horsing around, and they continued extolling the merits of beating Chang up. I tried to speak but kept getting cut off. I let them continue for a couple of minutes and kept quiet. Finally I was

able to ask them what was happening. I said that I got the feeling they were mad at me because they wouldn't let me speak. Jimmy nodded yes. Costa said, "We've wasted time, we've spent enough time talking about Chang, we only have a half hour left and then next week and that's all." I said that I thought maybe they were angry at me because I went away for 2 weeks, and maybe the group didn't go so well while I was away. They nodded yes. I said maybe also they were angry because the group was ending next week. John said he didn't want the group to end.

The worker astutely picked up the ending stage being acted out both in the children's behavior in the school and the process in the group. She chose to focus on the underlying meaning for the group and reached for the anger toward her. In retrospect, because the children were also describing an incident of a racist physical attack, the worker needed to at least acknowledge her distress over the idea that a child was "hated," potentially because he was Asian. While she might have needed to wait until later to go into this in more detail, she should not have let the discussion continue without her comment. Children need adult models, with whom they identify, to make clear a value system that their own homes or communities might not express. The skill involves the worker "lending a vision" by sharing her own views without falling into the trap of preaching or teaching and missing the underlying anger over the ending.

George asked why it had to end, was I leaving the school? I said no, I'd be in the school until the end of May, but did they remember that in the first session we had all agreed that we'd have 6 to 10 sessions and then it would end? They agreed. Costa said, "We'll miss you. I know we fool around a lot, but we'll really get down to talk about something properly." I said that I guessed that they were sad the group was ending, and they thought that it was ending because I was punishing them for being noisy and rowdy. They nodded. I said that this wasn't so; it was ending because I had other things that I had to do in the school. But, I said, the group was not supposed to end—it was supposed to continue with their teacher leading it, as we had all agreed. There was a lot of complaining about their teacher and what had happened when I wasn't there, how she had made them do health instead of having a discussion.

I said that they were saying that the group wasn't the same when I wasn't there, and I got them to elaborate on how the two sessions had been during my absence. The boys felt that it was terrible. Jimmy complained that next week would be their last session, so they had better make the most of it. I said that in part they were angry with me because I was saying that I could no longer come in after next week, and maybe they were feeling let down and deserted. They quietly nodded. I said that I could understand how they felt; I was also sad that I would no longer be able to come in on Tuesday mornings, because I really enjoyed working with them, but I would still be in the school for a while and they could come to see me alone if they wanted to, and I would come in from time to time to see them. One of the boys asked if I would come to their next party, and I said that I would love to. I added that besides talking about me and them, I knew that they were angry at Mrs. Morris, and I wondered if we could talk about that and see if we could work something out.

Mrs. Morris was a classroom teacher who had offered to continue the group. The worker focused on the transition question, realizing that she might be able to help the group members continue their work after she was gone. A discussion of the group sessions while she was away revealed that the children had been upset at her absence. They had not given Mrs. Morris a chance. They had acted out, causing her to abandon the group meeting and turn to a general health discussion. The worker strategized with the boys about how they could handle things differently with Mrs. Morris. She also offered to meet with Mrs. Morris to assist in the transition.

In addition to unfinished business with the worker, groups face unfinished business among members during the last sessions. These issues, particularly the negative feelings, often emerge only toward the end of the group. Workers tend to pass over these issues in order to end the group on a high note. However, the worker who trusts in the group will encourage exploration of the negative feelings as well as the positive ones, as illustrated in the next example.

Male Batterers' Group

In the next illustration, the worker encouraged group members to share negative reactions to the helping efforts. The worker asked the group, "How can I be more helpful to groups in the future?" The group was composed of men who had been violent with their wives or the women they had lived with. The members responded to the worker's first question by referring to a coworker, who was not present. Note how the worker brought the discussion back to himself.

WORKER: What I want to ask you is what do you think I could have done better? What did I do that I shouldn't have done? I would like some feedback about me in relationship to the group and what's been going on here.

CHARLES: I always felt like he [the coworker] was giving me the "third degree," but at the same time it brought out answers that probably wouldn't have come out any other time. I didn't feel like he was pushing, but at the same time he asked penetrating questions. And you had a choice, you could either lie about them or you could just fade out and go around them—or tell the truth; most of the time instead of hiding it I would answer his questions and I think I got a lot more said that way than talking on my own.

WORKER: Do you think I could have asked more questions?

CHARLES: Yeah, you could have, but . . . I don't like criticizing.

ALAN: I don't see where you could have asked that many more questions. I think you've done well at bringing things out. It always takes somebody to start it . . . and I think you've tried to get it going.

CHARLES: Yeah.

ALAN: I think it has slipped quite a few times, but I don't think that is necessarily your responsibility; I think that's the group's responsibility.

CHARLES: Yeah. For some reason we did seem to digress quite often, I felt. But I think it's my responsibility just as much as it is yours. Alan thought maybe we could have talked about some things more.

WORKER: How do you mean "slipped?" Do you mean we got off the topic?

CHARLES: Yeah,

BEN: We used to bullshit a lot!

ALAN: But I feel that's really good because you have to be comfortable with the people you're talking with, therefore you have to bullshit sometimes. You have to get off the subject in order to get back on to it because we always manage to get back onto the topics. I think it's good to get off the subject—it's a rest . . .

BEN: I'm just questioning how much we do, that's all.

ALAN: Yeah, well, we did quite a bit . . . but I think we got things done.

CHARLES: But we always noticed it, eh? If it got carried too far, one of the group would say something about it, but I think it helped in a way because it made things more relaxed. We weren't always discussing somebody's hang-up or anything.

WORKER: I won't say that I don't mind being criticized because I do—(laughter) OK! But at the same time, I recognize that . . . Larry [Shulman], the consultant in this outfit, says, "We make mistakes, we learn from those and then we make more sophisticated mistakes"—that kind of thing. I need that kind of input, not only for me as an individual, but for other guys who are going to be leading these groups.

CHARLES: Well, I think you're OK then—you haven't reached the sophisticated stage yet.

WORKER: You mean I'm just making the gross mistakes?! (Laughter.)

CHARLES: No, you're just making the everyday, ordinary ones.

WORKER: Like what?

CHARLES: I don't know, I haven't noticed you making any mistakes.

WORKER: What would you like to see me doing differently?

BEN: Going back to what I said earlier this evening about becoming more aware of how pervasive (maybe) this anger is, how it manifests itself in different ways, and one way is just kind of a sense of being uptight. And it seems to me that the only way I'm gonna change is that I first have to become somehow aware. I mean, I don't know how you ask questions to help another person become aware, but I think that's the kind of question that is helpful and maybe you could have asked more of those. Now, specifically, I can't say because I don't have a firm grasp on that. Do you (turning to John) have any idea of what I am talking about?

JOHN: Yes. Maybe we are putting too much responsibility on the worker? I don't think so. If I could do everything myself, I wouldn't be here in a group.

WORKER: I agree with that.

BEN: And I'm not sophisticated enough, I guess, to have penetrating questions . . . or to draw out . . . to help me become aware, I guess that takes . . . first of all that you have the knowledge or something and being able to see more than I can—or at least have an idea, so that you can ask the questions that will help me rather than telling me, but help me become aware of what, you know, uh . . . Because I'm just seeing now that I don't think I'm very aware of all the waves in my life—and I don't know why, but I think it's important that I gain that knowledge for myself. I'm not sure how to go about it. Because I don't think that my being is just going to change in the sense of my violence toward women—not just toward women; I think it has to change in other areas, it will carry over. (Pause.)

WORKER: (Speaking to Alan) I was really moved when you talked about your feeling of being set up and you were obviously very upset talking about it. Maybe I could have reached a bit more, I don't know, helped you get in touch with . . .

ALAN: Yeah, I think that you might have and I probably showed it too, because I was uptight that night, I was getting into it—I think maybe you should have pushed me a little more. It was a very touchy subject for me, because it's a helpless . . . I never really had a totally helpless feeling in my entire life; I've always been able to do something about it, but this is one thing that I can do nothing about; every time I try it gets worse, and the frustration that comes from that really gets me. I get hit by this almost every day . . . the feeling that I can do nothing.

By making a demand for work, the worker demonstrated that he really wanted the feedback, and the members responded. Of course, the worker had to have enough confidence in himself to invite the negative responses and to stay with them when the members tested him to see if he really meant it. In addition to making the ending discussion honest and receiving important professional feedback, the worker demonstrated a view of manhood that said it was all right to make mistakes and to accept criticism. This was critical for this group because of their tendency to avoid owning up to their own mistakes and taking responsibility for their abusive behavior.

Adult Survivors of Childhood Sexual Abuse

As the previous examples illustrated, the ending and transition phase of a group takes place over time. The stages are noticeable over the last three or four sessions for an ongoing group, beginning with the worker's reminder that the group is coming to an end. The next example provides excerpts from the last six sessions of a group for adult survivors of childhood sexual abuse.

The members of this group all experienced oppression on many levels. They were all sexually exploited as children, most often by people whom they knew and should have been able to trust. As women, they continued to experience oppression in relation to their gender. Some of the members were Hispanic and faced racism, which when combined with sexism strongly affected their lives. Finally, some were lesbians or bisexual, which also placed them in a group that commonly experiences prejudice and oppression. Thus, all of the group members carried a great deal of pain and internalization of their oppression.

As the group members moved into their ending and transition phase, and they reviewed and evaluated their work together, note their courage, their love for each other, and their social worker's conviction about their inherent strength not only to survive oppression but to overcome it and fight it. In many ways, the work of the group followed the three developmental stages described in Chapter 1, in which oppressed people attempt to free themselves from the oppressor within and the oppressor without.

RECORD OF SERVICE

Client Description and Time Frame

This 24-week group for adult survivors of child sexual victimization is a combination of support and stabilization and growth and education models. It is offered by a community rape crisis center and is led by two coworkers. The time frame of the meetings is August 28 to October 16.

The seven members range in age from 22 to 28. All members are women from working-class or middle-class backgrounds. Two members are Hispanic, and the rest are white or from various other ethnic groups. Two women are lesbians, one is bisexual, and four are heterosexual.

Description of the Problem

As the group begins its ending stage, members are reluctant to face the pain and loss of the impending termination and the potential effect of this transition on their lives. As survivors of sexual abuse, many of the women feel acute fear and discomfort when confronted with strong feelings. They have described families of origin in which the development and ending of relationships has been poorly modeled and they have learned to keep silent about their feelings and fears. The tasks of the workers will be to help build a group culture in which the taboo subjects of endings and losses can be explored, freeing the members to grapple with the tasks of termination. We must help the group establish a norm that supports intimacy and risk but also profoundly respects each member's need for safety and self-protection.

How the Problem Came to the Attention of the Worker(s)

As my coworker Jane and I prepared for termination, we tuned in to the potential problems of this stage, using both general knowledge of survivors' issues and our knowledge of the work and struggles of this particular group as a guide. Since the first sessions, safety had been vital to meaningful and productive work in the group. Members had worked hard to recognize when they felt unsafe or at risk and had learned to take steps to protect themselves. Because bonding and connection had been central to the group's creation of a safe and trusting culture, we hypothesized that the group might begin to feel unsafe as members began to separate. We believed that the group might need to create a different "safe culture" that could tolerate the coming ending. On August 28, we learned about the group's norms for saying good-bye and about subjects and feelings, related to endings, that were forbidden. Members responded with silence when asked direct questions about what the group's end meant to them and informed us that they usually run away from and ignore endings.

Summary of the Work

August 28

I tried to reach for the pain behind a group member's description of self-hurting behavior. Linda was describing how she felt compelled to binge on salted and high-cholesterol foods lately and how it was very dangerous for her high blood pressure. I observed that in the past she had done this when she was having really strong feelings and asked how she was feeling these days when she seemed compelled to binge. She began to cry and said, "There's just so much pain, so much loss." She described her fear of losing her whole family if she confronted her mother (the perpetrator of her sexual abuse), the death of a cousin who had been missing and whose body had been found, the anniversary of a rape in which she had nearly been killed at age 18, her loss of me as her individual therapist, and the impending loss of the group, the first people who had ever believed in and supported her. In the face of this she said that she was really isolating herself and wanting to eat.

I felt guilty for "abandoning her" at this difficult time and felt an impulse to fix things for her. I decided this was a signal that I should involve the group rather than respond as her individual therapist. I tried to enlist the support of the group to combat her isolation. I said, "Linda, it sounds like you're feeling overwhelmed by all this pain, and at the very time you could use some support, you're all alone. Is there any way the group can help you right now?" She responded that she isolates most when she's most in pain but that the group could help by reaching out to her, that she needs to be with people when she feels this way. Some group members responded with expressions of support and offers to talk on the phone or be with her. People shared how hard it was to see her pain but how important it was that she share it.

I used Linda's expression of loss to raise the issue of termination again for the group. I said that Linda had shared feeling really sad about the group and I wondered how others in the group were feeling about the end approaching. There was silence. I waited, thinking they might need time to respond. Jane, the coleader, asked group members how they usually say good-bye. Group members responded: "I just take off, usually." "Hey, I don't say good-bye, I say see you later." "I never say good-bye, I just disappear." "I try to pretend nothing's changed." Jane said that she felt it was important for members to understand how they usually cope with good-byes so that they can make choices this time about how they want to handle this ending. Issues of trust, intimacy, and loss had been important in the group's work, and we could do vital work in these areas during our final weeks. Time was up, and I said that we would be spending more time next week talking about the approaching end of the group and how people wanted to work on it.

September 11

I reframed a member's inability to reach a stated group goal and attempted to unite ending process with content. A major goal for Martha had been to spend time in the group telling the story of her abuse, but each time she had planned to do it she had felt unable to go through with it. She had felt flooded with fear and pain. The group had processed why it was so difficult and suggested different ways she could prepare and cope with this "disclosure," but to no avail. This time, what came up was that she felt unable to risk and be vulnerable in the group when it was so close to ending and she could be rejected and abandoned by the group members. She said that it no longer felt safe in the group. I said that perhaps what she was telling us was that this goal was not right for her right now, that keeping herself safe was most important and that she was making choices about how she needed to protect herself. Because child-victims often learn to feel that they are not worth protecting and can never feel truly safe, safety and self-protection had been important in the group's work.

I offered the group a new norm for endings. I said that we needed to strike a careful balance as we approached the ending, trying to work as hard as we could and risk as much as we could but also respecting each person's needs for safety. I said that if she wanted to do her disclosure we would help her, but that no one would force her to do it. Martha and the group discussed this for a while, and then Jane talked about Martha's goal and goals in general and how it was important for us to review them and take stock of the work we needed to address in the next 4 weeks.

I attempted to demand work from the group, evaluating progress and exploring feelings, but blew it by asking for too much information at once. I asked if we could spend some time right now hearing from everyone about what they had accomplished so far, what they still needed to work on, and how they were feeling about the group ending. I immediately sensed my error but didn't know how to correct it. The group was silent. Jane then said that she understood how hard it was for the group but that it was important for us to take stock of where we were. We could still accomplish a lot but we needed to know . . . Jodi burst in and said," I just feel like telling you to shut up. You both keep talking and talking about this and I'm feeling really angry. I wish you would let us move on to what we want to talk about and stop wasting time."

I attempted to address her anger directly and put it in context. I said that she was clearly feeling really angry, and that it felt to her like we were pressuring the group. I waited and then said that people often feel very angry when they face losing something that has been really important to them. I wondered if some of her anger was related to the ending itself. Rita said, "But we're not losing the group. We'll still see each other." Others agreed. I confronted the group's denial. "That's true," I said, "You can choose to continue your friendships as individuals and as a group, but this Monday night group is special, the way we work together here. It's like it has its own identity. That's what's going to end." Michelle said that she wouldn't know what to do with herself on Mondays anymore. Others joined in, saying how they would miss the group. Both workers reflected these feelings and shared their own feelings about the group ending.

I attempted to correct my earlier mistake and reach for more feelings. I said that I had asked for rather a lot at once during my earlier question about goals. This was really hard to talk about and might require some reflection. Perhaps group members could review their progress and future needs during the week and we could set aside time to discuss them next week. We would also need to talk in more depth about the final session. For now, I wondered if we could just spend some time talking about how it felt right now to be dealing with this. We discussed this for the last few minutes of the session.

September 18

I renewed the previous week's demand for work. I reminded the group that we had planned to spend some time this week taking stock of what the group has meant to people and where we needed to put our energy during these final four sessions. People had put quite a bit of thought into this, and the group spent some time evaluating and prioritizing. Martha had clarified the issue of disclosure for herself. She had discovered that, in trying to force herself to discuss the abuse before the group "audience" while feeling unsafe, she had been recreating the dynamics of her abuse as a child in which her father had taken her to bars where she had been sexually abused by various strangers while others observed. With the support and understanding of the group, she was able to carry out a disclosure related to this specific abuse, checking with the group whenever she began to feel unsafe. We credited her growing ability to protect herself while achieving her goals. Both Jane and I offered positive feedback about Martha's growth and her ability to both keep herself safe and move forward with her goals.

Later, Jane raised the issue of the final session, explaining to the group that it is generally structured around feedback, both negative and positive. She asked the group to consider a structure that has worked well for other groups, in which each group member in turn gives feedback to each of the other members and the workers. Past groups have chosen to write a special message to each individual so that the feedback would be kept and remembered. Some members were eager to do this, while others expressed considerable anxiety about evaluating themselves and others. I reached for feelings while giving the group responsibility for its own structure. I said that some people seemed eager to do this while others seemed really uncomfortable with it. Ultimately the decision of how to handle the last session lay with the group, but I wondered if we could explore how people felt about it right now. What made it seem scary, and what seemed positive about it? This was explored for a while.

Then group members asked me to review information about the local "Take Back the Night" march with them. We had told them about the march against sexual violence against women a few weeks before and, after some exploration of their fears about participating in a public demonstration, they decided to march as a group. I supported the group's readiness to act independently and support one another in new experiences. I shared with them how good I felt that they wanted to march together, and I gave them the information they needed.

September 25

We supported the group's growing independence and shared our feelings with them: As the group processed how the march had felt for them, Jane and I shared how powerful it had felt for us to see them there, marching, chanting, and singing. We also shared that it was hard for us to see them and know that the group was ending. The group was special for us, and it would be hard to let it go.

I fell for the illusion of work and let the group get off the track. Rita had been talking for some time about her problems and conflicts with her parents. At first both workers and group were active in discussing her problem, but I gradually began to feel that we weren't going anywhere and my attempts to involve the group proved fruitless. They seemed to have "checked out." I now think that some of the anger Rita was expressing was indirectly aimed at the leaders and/or the group, but I missed this at the time because she had ample reason to be angry with her parents.

I tried to regain focus by demanding work of another member. I had noticed for some time that Linda seemed very agitated and seemed to be struggling to contain herself. Rita had come to a long pause, and I asked, "What's going on with you, Linda?" Linda seemed startled: "Who me? Why? What's the problem?" I answered, "Well, Rita's been talking for a while now about her family, and I know your family has been a source of a lot of your pain. You seem really upset right now and I wonder what's happening." Linda began to talk of having a great deal of pain all the time. She said that her losses had totally overwhelmed her lately and she just didn't know how she was going to make it. I immediately felt the group come back to life. I checked with Rita that we could move to Linda's issue. It would have been better to clarify what had occurred with Rita first, but I wasn't sure how to handle it.

Linda and various group members talked for some time about how hopeless she felt. I reached for her ability to cope with her pain. "I'm just hearing that you have so much pain and sadness right now, Linda, and I wonder, what are you doing with all this hurt?" She said that she was crying a lot, just letting herself feel the sadness, and that she was also writing in her journal and writing poems. She mentioned that she had just written a poem today about her pain and where it was taking her. Several people asked her if she would read it, and she did. It was called "Children of the Rainbow," and it described how beams of light are shattered and broken as they pass through a drop of water and how they emerge to form the vibrant colors of the rainbow. The poem said that she and all survivors in recovery are like beams of light; if they can make it through their pain, they will become vibrant, beautiful, and whole. Several of us had tears in our eyes (me included) and there was a powerful silence when she had finished.

I remained silent to let the group control this moment. People thanked her for sharing such a personal, painful, and hopeful part of herself. I had been Linda's individual worker for some time and I was finding it very hard to leave her and leave the agency. I acknowledged her feelings, shared my own, and credited her ability to cope. I shared that I found the poem very moving, that I could feel that she had incredible pain, but that her art and ability to create were powerful vehicles for carrying her forward and transforming her pain. The group ended soon after.

October 2

We credited a member's growing independence. Martha told the group that she had confronted her father with the abuse since the last group. We were all amazed, because this had been a goal that Martha had not hoped to attain for several months, if not years, in the future. Her abuse had been very sadistic, and her father had continued to hold incredible power over her when he was able to have contact with her. She had been with Linda before he called and described "just feeling very powerful and safe. I was able to see Linda and my roommate right there, and I could hold the whole group right in my mind and feel you supporting me and helping me to be safe. I've never felt anything like that before. And he was weak! He was the one who seemed powerless." Martha had burned a picture of her father after the call as a way of exorcizing his control over her, and she had brought the ashes to group. Later the group gathered and flushed the ashes down the toilet. Both leaders credited Martha's incredible and rapid growth and related it to the ending and how she had taken control of how she wanted to accomplish her goals and approach the end of group. The group gave Martha feedback and discussed how it felt to be part of her sense of safety.

I missed two important opportunities to discuss anger in relation to the group's ending. Linda discussed feeling intense anger lately and feeling like she was about to explode and be violent. The group and both workers addressed her anger extensively, relating it to her abuse and her current pain and exploring coping strategies. Although I mentioned her several losses as being related to her anger, I neglected to focus on the group's ending as a major source of her pain and thus missed a potentially important piece of work.

Next, Donna raised the issue of her psychiatrist and how he had told her to get on with her life and stop indulging herself with her depression and dwelling on her abuse. The group responded with explosive anger. I allowed my own anger and the real differences between my approach and the approach of the psychiatrist to blind me to the part of the group's anger that might have been directed at me had I invited it. We did good work in helping Donna evaluate her therapy, but we missed another chance to explore the group's anger about the ending and our role as workers. I think that this group felt so special to me, and I was finding termination from individuals, the group, and the agency so hard, that I kept myself unaware of their anger.

October 16—Final Session

We assisted the group in sharing feedback and establishing closure, but we neglected to reach for negative evaluation. Each member and each worker had prepared written feedback for the other members and workers, and members took turns reading their messages to each other. (Workers passed out written individual feedback and gave verbal feedback to the group as a whole.) The material was very personal and moving and related the work of the group to strong feelings about ending. Workers assisted members in preparing to read and helped the group to respond. Some members cried and expressed deep feelings of pain and loss. Workers also responded directly to their own feedback.

A few of the women chose to hand out the personal feedback and speak to the group generally while members read the personal material. Although I believe that the material was genuine, it focused on positives only, and both workers missed the opportunity to reach for negative feedback, falling for the farewell-party syndrome. Although this important task was not accomplished, the workers did accomplish their goal of creating a safe culture in which members could risk being intimate and trusting as the group ended. I reinforced the culture that permits people to risk even as they are separating. Martha had read each note and closed with "Love, Martha." At one point, Rita said, "This is really hard, but I have to ask. You said "Love" to everybody, but you didn't say it to me. I'm sure you just forgot, but I have to say, it hurts. Don't you love me too?" She began to cry with these last words. Martha had clearly just forgotten and turned to Rita, saying, "I'm so glad you told me. I was just finding this all so hard that I didn't even realize . . . I do love you. I'm sorry it hurt that I forgot you. Here, let me write it on yours."

I asked Rita how it had felt to risk this question, and I said that I remembered that she had entered the group 6 months ago saying she never let herself be vulnerable with others. Rita responded that this was a safer place than she had ever been in before. She had shared her story, her shame, and had been vulnerable with people here. She knew she could trust us. "It's true," added Martha, "I've never been anywhere that was safe the way this is, even more than individual therapy." Michelle added, "This place is like the safe home we never had. You guys were almost like parents for us. You were honest with us and we learned to be honest with each other. And it never mattered, we could feel good, feel bad, disagree with each other and be mad, but it was OK. We could learn to be ourselves. You were there for us the way our parents should have been." Soon after, we ended the group. There was a long "group hug" at the suggestion of the members, and we ate some cake a member had ordered. The message on the cake said, "Survivors—Striving and Thriving!"

The metaphor of the poem in which survivors in recovery are viewed as "beams of light; if they can make it through their pain, they will become vibrant, beautiful, and whole" is extremely powerful and moving. It captures beautifully the struggle of these young, oppressed, and vulnerable women to free themselves from the self-image of being "damaged goods" that had been imposed upon them by those who should have been nurturing them. Their courage in joining a "Take Back the Night" march, when they felt so personally uncomfortable in doing so, was an affirmation of their willingness to fight and overthrow their oppressors. It was a social parallel of their individual revolutions against oppression described in one member's efforts to confront her offending parent. The unique power of mutual-aid groups is amply demonstrated in the content of their work together and in the "Survivors—Striving and Thriving" lettering on the cake at their final session.

In the next section, a detailed analysis of a single session in the ending phase of a group of teenagers in a residential setting completes this chapter. Many of the teens in that group have experienced emotional, physical, and sexual abuse in their families of origin. The example illustrates all of the ending phases described thus far.

A Termination Session: The Worker Leaving the Group

The following description of a group meeting with teenage girls in a residential treatment center illustrates some of the unique dynamics that emerge when the group continues and the worker leaves. The session took place 1 week after the worker told the group members that she was leaving the agency for another job. This worker in this example demonstrated both an advanced level of skill in group work and skill in dealing with endings. Of particular interest is the impact of the worker's sharing of her own powerful feelings. The entire meeting is presented, together with a detailed analysis of the skills employed. The process in the meeting is classic, as one can see elements of all the ending dynamics in one session.

Three of the girls came in with each other and seemed in a very happy mood. They said that they'd had a good week in school. I said, you know that sounded real nice and that this was one of the enjoyments of finally being a senior, and I teased about that. I asked about where Gladys and Beth were, and they said that they had to speak with a teacher about some arrangements and that they'd be there in a little while. The three of them continued talking about school and the rehearsals and the senior trip and stuff like that. Then Beth came in, and she was singing "Everything Is Beautiful," a rock-and-roll song. She took her seat and was laughing with everyone.

The good feelings expressed by the group members represented a denial of the ending. Because there was only one meeting left after this one, the worker strategized to reach past the denial for the opposite feelings she knew would be there. The members responded to her demand for work.

After a while I said, "Hey, it's great to see everybody in such a good mood, and I hate to be a party pooper, but I feel that I have to say that this is our next-to-last meeting, and a lot of things between you and I will be drawing to an end." Margie said, "You have a hell of a nerve." I said, "You mean about my leaving?" She said, "Yeah, that and a whole lot of things." I said, "OK, let's hear them. I'm sure that my leaving and the ending of the group has caused a lot of reactions in all of you." Nobody picked up on that, and Margie said, "Are we going to have a group next year?" A couple of girls said, "Yeah, we want to have another group next year," and Beth said, "Let's have a party in honor of your leaving."

The group's anger was expressed in Margie's comment "You have a hell of a nerve." The worker acknowledged this anger and encouraged the members to continue. The anger they felt and the pain underneath it were too much for them at this point, so they backed off. They began, instead, to discuss the continuation of the group and a farewell party. The worker allowed them to move away from the anger but held them to discuss the importance of the group.

There was a lot of mixed-up talk, and I tried to pick up about continuing the group. I said, "You're saying that the group has meant something to you and that you want to continue even without me." Beth said, "Naw, the group wasn't all that good," and Margie said, "Sometimes it was and sometimes not. Sometimes the meetings were very good, and sometimes they were a waste of time." I said, "Can you tell me more about that?" Margie said, "Well, sometimes it just seemed like we weren't in the right mood and we couldn't get down to work." Jill said, "Yeah, we were just fooling around all over the place," and Donna said, "Like the mood we were in Sunday night," and they all began to talk about a riot that had happened in the cottage, and they started fooling around. I said, "Hey, can we get back to the thing about the group, and what you thought about it, and what it meant to you? I think it is important for us to take a look at it now that you're nearing the end."

The members attempted to evade the discussion once again, and the worker showed great skill in not letting them put her off. She made another demand for work and insisted that the group discuss their specific reactions to their time together. As the members described the mutual aid they had experienced, the worker attempted to explore this aspect of their learning; however, they were not ready for this discussion and still needed to express their angry feelings.

Donna said, "Well, the best meeting we had was just with three of us—me, Jill, and Gladys. That's when we really talked about ourselves." Margie said, "You mean without me and Beth, is that what you mean?" Jill said quickly, "No, I don't mean that. We did have a good meeting with everybody, but I guess that was really the best," and I said, "Well, what made it the best?" Donna said, "Because we talked about our families, and we got to understand how we were feeling," and Margie said, "Yeah, I agree. The best meetings were when we talked about our families, and the worst meetings were when we talked about the cottage and the cottage parents." I said, "How come?" Gladys said, "Because we couldn't do anything about the cottage parents or even about the cottage, and at least when we talk about ourselves and about our families we can understand more, we can know why we are like we are," and Beth said, "Yeah, we can help each other." I said, "You have helped each other a lot. Is that something important that you've gotten from these meetings?" Nobody picked up on that.

Beth began talking about a party that they had been to, and all of a sudden in the midst of a whole big discussion Beth turned to me and said, "You're leaving, you God-damned fink." And everybody stopped, and everybody looked at me. I said, "I'm leaving, and I guess that makes me a fink." And everybody began, saying, "Why are you leaving? Why do you have to leave us? Why can't you stay?" Then a whole torrent of emotion came pouring out. Finally Jill said, "Why are you leaving?" I said, "I tried to explain the reasons on Friday, but if you'd like me to I'll explain them again now. But I don't know if it's the reason that really matters. It's more how you feel knowing that I'm leaving, for whatever the reason." They said, "No, no, we want to hear the reasons, we don't understand." I said, "OK, let me try to explain. I'm leaving because I've been here for a number of years and I feel that it's time for me to move on, to move into another situation. Working here has meant an awful lot to me, and you all have meant an awful lot to me. Yet I feel that a combination of things, the long traveling, working a lot of nights, have become very hard for me and I feel like I want to work nearer to where I live, and that I want to have a new kind of experience and not work in a residential treatment school. That's pretty much the reason. If there's anything you don't understand, ask me and I'll try to explain more."

As the anger emerged, the worker struggled with her own feelings in order not to block its expression. Her acceptance of their feelings demonstrated in her response, "I'm leaving, and I guess that makes me a fink," freed them to explore the feelings of dependency and hurt that were below the surface feelings of anger. Although she had explained her reasons for leaving the week before, the group members had been too shocked to heed and understand. She agreed to explain them again while acknowledging that their feelings were what really mattered, rather than her reasons. As the group began to express their emotions toward the worker, she asked them to identify the specific things about her they had found helpful. These would be the qualities they must look for in other workers. She also stayed with their hurt feelings, and she reached for their fear about establishing a relationship with a new worker, for their sense of rejection, and for their anger. Most important, the worker also shared her own pain at leaving them. The open expression of her feelings provided the impetus for the members to respond with theirs.

Beth started to cry and said, "You can't leave. We need you." I said, "You mean you won't be able to make it without me?" Margie said, "You're the best social worker I ever had. I won't be able to talk to anybody else." I said, "We have been real close, me and every one of you, and I guess the thought of starting over with somebody else scares the hell out of you. What do you think there was about me that made it easier for you to talk to me?" Beth said, "It's because you cared about us. It's 'cause we knew that even when you were mad at us, you were really sticking up for us, and you were really with us." Donna said in a soft voice, "Yeah, but if you cared so much, you wouldn't be leaving." And I said, "That's a thing, isn't it? How could I leave you if I really care for you?" Gladys said, "We know you care for us. We know you're leaving because you really feel that you have to." And then she just kind of shrugged, and I said, "But the words don't help very much, huh? They don't take away the bad feeling." Beth said, "That's right, what good does it do me to know that you care if you're not here?" And Jill said, "Yeah, you've been my social worker for a whole year. I don't want anybody else." There was a lot more talk about the idea that they didn't want anybody new.

I said, "You're angry as hell at me. You have a right to be, and even though your anger hurts me and a big piece of me wants to say, 'Don't be angry at me,' I can understand that you are, and I know the kind of pain that must be underneath, and I feel some of that pain also. It's hard as hell for me to leave you." Beth said, "If it was hard for you to leave us, then you wouldn't leave us." Margie said, "No, Beth, that's just not the truth. It was hard for me to leave home . . ."

At this point in the session, the pain of the discussion caused the group to adopt its pattern of using a scapegoat when things got rough. Gladys, the group scapegoat, began to cry, expressing many of the emotions felt by the other members. Their anger at her was an expression of their anger at the same feelings within themselves. The worker demonstrated her group work skill, at a time when she herself was feeling somewhat overwhelmed by emotion, by paying attention to her two clients—Gladys and the group. In the next excerpt, we see an illustration of the worker's functional role, as outlined in the discussion on scapegoating in Chapter 12.

Gladys put her head down and began to cry, and one of the kids hollered, "Oh, cut it out. This hurts us as much as it hurts you." I said, "Maybe it hurts each of you in a different way, and this is how Gladys is reacting." She picked up her head and said, "Oh, leave me alone. None of you care about me," and Margie said, "Yes, we do, you don't want help. You just want to feel sorry for yourself." I said, "You're all getting so angry at Gladys, and it seems that all she's doing is acting out how you feel. Is it that you hurt so much that you don't have room for anybody else's hurt?" Jill said, "She cries all the time. Who gives a damn about her?" Donna said, "I care about her, but I don't know what to do." Beth said to her (by this time Gladys had moved away from the table where we meet and was sitting alone on a chair, crying), "Gladys, why don't you come over here?" and Gladys just shrugged, and one of the other kids said, "Aw, leave her alone," and there was kind of an uncomfortable quiet in the room, and I said, "I don't think that you feel right leaving her alone," and Beth said, "Hell, what can we do?" and I said, "What do you feel like doing? Do you feel like reaching out to her?" Beth got up and walked over to Gladys and put her arms around her and said, "You're scared because everybody's leaving, right?" Gladys nodded her head. Beth said, "We're all in that situation, too. She's leaving us, too. Miss S.'s leaving us, too. Not only you." Beth said, "But maybe it is different for

Gladys." Gladys said, "You have a mother and father. Every one of you has at least a mother or a father. Who do I have?" Beth said, "You have foster parents." Gladys said, "Big deal. They don't want me." There was a hush in the room at the pain of those words, and I said, "Wow, you really know how that feels."

The worker's trust in her group was rewarded as they reached out to Gladys to offer aid. As they spoke to Gladys, they were really speaking to each other and to the part of them that was facing the same set of problems. The faith of the worker was important at this point, because with her help they were able to experience the power of mutual aid in the peer group. As they move into their young adult years, they will have to seek out support and help from their peers; this was possibly the most important learning for them.

Beth said, "I think I know how it feels. I think I know how bad it feels. And if you want to cry, that's OK, but you gotta live. You gotta pick yourself up. You gotta face it." Gladys shook her head. "No," she said, "I can't." I said, "It seems that she can't pick herself up." Donna said, "Even when you're alone, you have to trust yourself." Margie said, "That's pretty hard to do." Beth said, "But you're not alone, Gladys, you have us. We'll help you, and somebody else can help us." Donna said, "And maybe we'll also have to help ourselves." Gladys said, "I know what you mean. I know that in the end I do have to help myself." I said to her, "But are you scared that you won't be able to do that?" She nodded her head yes, and once again she began to cry. Beth said, "We'll help you, too. Just like we did here this morning." And I had tears in my eyes, too, and I said, "Wow, you kids are fantastic." And they all kind of laughed, and somebody said, "Maybe we'll become social workers, too," and that kind of broke the tension of the moment, and we never really got back to the thing of them helping each other.

The feelings associated with endings stir deep and powerful emotions in all of us. When I use this example and the earlier ones in my workshops, workers have been visibly moved by the power of the feelings expressed; they have perhaps moved you as well. Workers also react to the degree of skill demonstrated by this worker and the workers in the example involving the survivors' group. They reflect on endings they have handled poorly by missing the cues or not facing their own feelings with enough honesty. This record represents an advanced level of skill. This same worker handled endings quite differently in her training days; she would have cut and run at several key places in this meeting. There were many group endings along the way in which she made mistakes, learned from them, and ended her next group with more skill. However painful, this process represents the only way to develop professional skill. It is a process that continues throughout a professional's working life.

Chapter Summary

The ending and transition phase of practice and strategies for intervention, as described in detail in Chapter 5, apply to group work as well as individual work. Workers help groups move through several ending stages: denial of the ending, anger over the ending, mourning, and trying the ending on for size. Helpful skills include pointing out endings early, reaching for feelings, and dealing with the farewell-party syndrome. Special dynamics arise when the worker leaves and the group continues.

Related Online Content and Activities

 Visit *The Skills of Helping* Book Companion Website at www.socialwork.wadsworth .com/Shulman06/ for learning tools such as glossary terms, InfoTrac College Edition keywords, links to related websites, and chapter practice quizzes.

The website for this chapter also features additional notes from the author and additional process recordings:

- Ending With a Hearing-Impaired Teenagers' Group
- Pregnant Teens in a Group Home: Integrating Ending Process and Content
- Welfare Mothers: Conflict in the Last Session

CHAPTER FOURTEEN

Variations in Group Practice

Part IV has focused on the common aspects of group work, but many key variations exist. The three such variations that appear most often are open-ended groups, single-session groups, and activity groups. This chapter discusses each in turn.

The Open-Ended Group

As we saw in Chapter 9, an *open-ended group* is one in which the membership is continuously changing. New members arrive and old members leave throughout the life of the group. This is in contrast to a **closed group** (or fixed-membership group), where the same people meet for a defined period of time. Members may drop out and new members may be added in the early sessions, but in general, the membership of a closed group remains constant.

The decision to run a group as open-ended or closed depends on several factors, including the nature of the contract, the characteristics of the clients served, and the structure of the setting. For example, in a couples' group dealing with marital problems, the difficulty of discussing personal issues such as sexual incompatibility would increase if membership in the group were constantly changing. The same would be true in a group for survivors of sexual abuse, where disclosure of traumatic experiences is difficult in a group context. A stable membership is essential for such groups to develop the necessary mutual trust and culture for work. On the other hand, an open-ended group is more appropriate for teenagers in a group home, where residents are entering and leaving at different times. The problems associated with shifting membership in this type of group are outweighed by the advantages of having all the residents present. Thus, the decision to operate open-ended or closed groups must be made with the unique characteristics of members, purpose, and setting in mind.

An open-ended group provides certain advantages. For example, a group that has developed a sound culture for work can bring in a new member quickly. As the new members listen to the discussion, their own willingness to risk may be accelerated by the level of openness of the others. In addition, those who have been in the group for a while can assist new members with issues they themselves have already dealt with. A technical problem associated with open-ended groups is that each session may be a new beginning for some members, an ending for other members, or both. In short-term groups, where members do not remain for a long time, the worker can take responsibility for bringing in new members and acknowledging the departure of the old ones. In groups with longer-lasting membership, the group members themselves can discuss this process and develop a system for dealing with the changing group composition. Either way, the skills involved require that the worker be able to state purpose clearly and briefly to a new member so that the ongoing work of the group can proceed in spite of the changes.

Hospital Group on a Gynecological Ward

The following example involves an open-ended group on a gynecological ward of a general hospital. The women on this ward had all been admitted to the hospital for operations because of suspected cancer of the uterus. The usual routine was that they stayed for 2 days prior to the operation, 1 day for the operation, and then, depending on the results, they could be released from the hospital in as little as 2 days. Thus, some group members were in the preoperative state, while others had completed the procedure. The worker restated the group's purpose at the start of each meeting.

WORKER: This group meets each day at the same time to give you a chance to talk with each other and with me about your feelings and concerns about being a patient in the hospital. We realize your illness and hospitalization have caused a great deal of stress, and we feel your having a chance to discuss your reactions may help. In past groups we have discussed the food, hospital procedures, how patients get along with staff, and of course, your concerns about your illness.

The particular theme for each group changed each day with the composition of the membership. When appropriate, the worker arranged for attendance of the dietitian, nursing staff, or doctors to facilitate communication between patients and the hospital system. In the following illustration, we see how one member, who had just been told she had cancer, used the group to deal with her initial shock even though it was her first day of group attendance:

After some preliminary chatter, I turned to Mrs. Bourne (an elderly, delicate-looking lady), who had been silent. She didn't respond. I pointed out that she still seemed shocked. The group members asked about her family. She said she had a son and daughter. Her son had just gone to South Africa. They said she had to tell her daughter. She should be told, and talking about it with family would make her feel better. She said her daughter would cry. I said it is a hard thing to face. Mrs. Powers suggested having her chaplain talk to her at this time. It was helpful. She had found it supportive. Mrs. Bourne remarked that there was no use having the priest talk to her: She is disenchanted with her religion. Mrs. Powers then went into a brief monologue on cancer being just another disease like alcoholism and how it used to be something to be ashamed of and now it's treated openly as a disease. She expressed her present despondency because her cancer had reached a point where they might not be able to operate. Someone asked how her husband felt. He felt terrible. They asked about the children, but she had none. She said at the end she was depressed and wanting to get this all over with. It was no pleasure for her husband, and she's not getting any younger. Then she immediately changed her mood and said you need a sense of humor, to which all the ladies agreed. Our time was up.

At this point it was too difficult for Mrs. Bourne to take in the words because of the shock of the diagnosis. However, she had been able to begin the process of talking with others about her first reactions. The worker picked up with her after the session for individual work in this area, and other group members offered their support through their informal contacts on the ward. The report of this group session was also used later for work with the medical staff on the problem of how staff communicates a diagnosis to patients.

Just as each group meeting may be a beginning for a member, other members are leaving. Workers can deal with the ending process by calling attention to the departure of each member at the start of her or his last session or sessions, depending on the length of attendance. Workers can allow some time at the end of the last session for each to say farewell and for the group to say good-bye as well. The following excerpt illustrates a worker structuring this process at the start of the session:

WORKER: This will be Mrs. Lewis's and Mrs. Peter's last day with us. We have enjoyed having both of you in this group. If it's all right with the rest of you, perhaps we could leave the last five minutes of the session to say good-bye and to give both ladies a chance to share their thoughts and feelings about the group.

Open-ended groups, particularly short-term groups, are characterized by the need for more worker guidance. Because the group has little continuity, the worker needs to actively provide the structural supports. This does not mean, however, that the group members are excluded from taking some responsibility for dealing with structural issues. One common example is when a new member joins a relatively stable open-ended group. Often, the new member initially feels like an outsider. In turn, the ongoing group members may resent a new member and be concerned about the possible impact on the group dynamics. Ongoing members may not be direct about their feelings, because they sense it is not OK to feel that way. Their heads may say, "Because I am receiving help, shouldn't it be available to others?" At the same time, their hearts may say, "I like the group just the way it is, and I'm afraid a new member will screw it up!" Unless this issue is openly explored, their real feelings may be acted out in the way they relate to the new member. The worker may have some ambivalence as well, accepting the agency policy of keeping the group open, yet feeling concerned that a "good group" might change with the addition of an unknown new member. The result may well be an illusion of work, in which the worker announces a new member is coming the next week and the group quickly moves on to a different topic. Or, if the group raises objections, the worker may side with the new member and completely miss the concerns of the second client, the group.

The alternative is for the worker to tune in to his or her own feelings, as well as the feelings of the group members, and to use the skill (described in Chapter 4) as looking for trouble when everything is going the worker's way. This is illustrated in the next example.

Bringing a New Member Into an AIDS Group

The following example from a group for people with AIDS illustrates how the worker asks the group members to take real responsibility for bringing in a new member.

WORKER: I wanted you to know that we have a new member joining the group next week. As you know, agency policy is that we stay open to new members if we have room. I'm not asking for a vote here, but since we have been maintaining a regular membership recently, I wondered how you all felt about adding some-one new.

JOHN: It's not a problem. After all, we were all new at one point or another.

WORKER: I appreciate that thought, John, but in my experience, even though it isn't completely rational, ongoing members sometimes resent and even fear adding someone new to a group that's working well. I wonder if anyone feels that way.

TED: Does it mean we are going to go back to square one—I mean, starting all over? I've gotten to trust these guys, and I'm not so sure a new member is a great idea.

WORKER: That's exactly what I meant, Ted. How about the rest of you? You have worked hard to build a good group here, and it wouldn't surprise me if the new member might make a problem for you.

RICK: I'm not sure I want to see someone going through what we all went through when we first had that diagnosis. I mean, I'm past all of that now, and I want to work on other issues.

WORKER: I think it's also a little scary to have someone come in who may reawaken all of the fear and anxiety. I hear three issues: Is the new member going to set us back to going over old issues? Are we going to lose our sense of trust in the group? And, How are we going to feel facing all of our initial feelings again?

Let's discuss these and see if we can come up with a way to bring this new member in and cope with it effectively. I am willing to work with him in advance to help in the entry to the group, but I think you are all going to need to help as well. The faster we integrate him, the better chance we will not lose what we have.

At the worker's suggestion, the group members used the rest of the time to tune in to some of their own feelings when they first joined the group and what it was that either helped them to connect or put them off. As the members put themselves in the shoes of the new member, they developed strategies that both the worker and they could adopt in greeting the new member. These included acknowledging that he was coming into an ongoing group and that it might take some time for him to feel connected; making some room for him in the first session to handle the initial shock issues, while still making sure that they picked up on their own ongoing issues; letting him know he could get involved as he felt comfortable; and offering to provide a "buddy" from the group whom he could contact by phone if he wished.

After some further discussion, the worker raised another potential underlying issue associated with the entry of the new member. This was the fact that the space had opened up because of the sudden and unexpected death of one of the ongoing members. Even though it had been discussed when it happened, he explored with the group how their ongoing feeling of loss might affect their ability to attach to each other and to the new member.

The worker did not need to have this conversation for every new member who joined. Rather, the worker monitored the changing composition of the group and periodically raised the issue when circumstances required it. This concept is clearer if we conceive of the group as an organism, which is more than the sum of its parts (see Chapter 12). If we think of the group as an entity independent of its members, existing with a continuously changing membership, then the need to address its tasks in relation to new members is clear.

The Single-Session Group

Some work is done on a short-term, or even a single-session, basis. Examples include informational meetings (such as foster parent recruitment) or educational sessions (such as a session at a school designed to help parents assist their children with homework problems). These groups will often be larger than the small, face-to-face groups I have been describing thus far. Workers leading such groups often feel that the time limitations and size of the group will eliminate the possibility of group interaction or involvement, so they substitute direct presentation of the information to be shared, followed by a question period. Sessions structured in this way can be quite effective, but one drawback of straight didactic presentation is that people do not always hear, understand, or remember the material presented. Questions raised at follow-up sessions too often suggest that, although the worker has shared the data, the group members have not taken it in. The challenge for the worker is to structure a session in a way that allows participants to interact with the information given and make it more meaningful. Size of group and restricted time do not automatically rule out active participant involvement, and many of the principles discussed thus far can be adapted to such situations.

The worker should begin by thinking about each group if it were a "small group" and by attempting to adapt the basic model to the group's limitations. For example, the idea of phases of work is still helpful, but the beginning, work, and ending/transition phases all must be encompassed in one session. Contracting in the opening phase of a session is critical, as the following example from a foster parent recruitment meeting demonstrates.

Information Group: Foster Parent Recruitment

I explained that the agency was holding these meetings to encourage families to consider providing a foster home for our children in care. The purpose of this first session was for us to share some information about fostering with the group, to try to answer their questions, and to discuss the concerns they may have on their minds that might help them to determine if further exploration were feasible. I pointed out the group was large (over 40), and I realized that might make it hard for them to talk, but I hoped we could treat this evening as a conversation rather than a lecture. I would be interested as much in hearing from them as in sharing my own information. I then asked if this is what they had understood to be the purpose of the meeting. There was a general nodding of heads, so I continued. I said I thought it might be helpful if I could begin by asking them what some of their questions were about fostering—some of the things that were on their minds. I would keep a list of these and try to make sure we covered them in our discussion. There was silence for a moment, and then a hand was raised.

In this example, the worker chose to obtain feedback from the group before beginning her presentation. This can be termed the **listen first—talk later** approach to leading an informational group session. One advantage to this approach is that it helps the worker identify and address members' needs. If people have an urgent concern about the subject, listening to any other conversation can be hard for them until that concern has been dealt with or at least acknowledged. Once they know they are "on the agenda," their energy is freed to invest in absorbing other data. The amount of time taken to raise questions or, in other groups, swap problems, is determined by the overall time available. For example, in a 2-hour meeting one would not want to spend more than 15 minutes contracting and problem swapping, while in a 3-hour session, more time might be used to explore issues and develop a group consensus on the agenda. Timing is always important in group sessions, but it naturally takes on a special urgency in a single-session group. The worker needs to keep track of time and point out continually to the group the relationship between time and their work. For example, the worker might say, "You are raising so many good issues that I think we could probably meet for a week. However, we only have 2 hours. I wonder if it is possible for us to focus on one or two central concerns and dig into them." Or the worker could explain, "I would like some time at the end to discuss this evening's program, to evaluate the session, and to see what you feel you have gotten out of it. Can we be sure to leave the last 15 minutes to do this?"

Workers often suggest many reasons for not involving clients in single-session or large groups more actively in the work. First, they are concerned that they have so much to "cover" they do not have time for group process. However, as most of us have noticed in our own educational experience, a teacher who is busy "covering" the agenda does not necessarily teach anything. We are often better off narrowing the field of work and limiting our goals. Effective work with a manageable agenda is preferable to going through the motions of trying to cover a wide area. The first skill in handling such meetings, then, is to narrow down the potential area of work to suit the time available.

A second area of concern is that the group may raise questions that the workers are not prepared to answer. This is a particular concern for new workers, who are nervous enough as it is. They may have little experience in the field and have prepared extensively to deal with the specific areas they have predetermined as important. Their notes are written out in detail, and the last thing they want is someone asking a question for which they are unprepared. This is understandable, because it takes confidence to allow the group to shape the direction of the work. When workers realize they are being judged by group members not on whether or not they have all the answers but rather on how well they involve the group in the process, they are often more willing to risk opening up the session in novel and unexpected directions. When they do so, they find they learn as much from such sessions as the group members do. Each session helps the worker to tune in and prepare for the next one, so that the ability to deal with the real concerns of the group grows with experience.

A third area of concern, particularly with large groups, is that a single member may take over the group for individual or personal issues unrelated to the contract. Our discussion of deviant members illustrated how the worker may need to be assertive in such a situation and guard the contract vigorously (see Chapter 12). This ability also comes with experience. Once again, the worker has to be willing to risk the hazards of such an approach if the benefits of more member involvement are to be gained.

Informal Event Group: Remembering the Holocaust

A short-term, informal, spontaneous group can be brought together to deal with an event or immediate circumstances. For example, social workers have reached out to relatives and friends in the waiting room of an emergency ward to form an informal group to help them cope with their immediate stress. School social workers have organized groups for students following a classmate's suicide. Groups have been held in residential settings or schools following a catastrophe (hurricane, earthquake, flood, September 11th) or the assassination of a political or movement leader. In each case, the work is short-term and focuses on the impact of the event and ways in which group members can more effectively cope with it.

In the following example, a worker works with a group of elderly members of a Jewish community center day program. As part of a program designed to focus on the World War II Holocaust, when millions of Jews, as well as others, were killed, the center staff had mounted a photo exhibit during Yom Hashoah—the day set aside for remembrance. An informal group had spontaneously begun a discussion in the hallway, and the student social worker was present. She noticed Sara, who often played the role of group scapegoat, expressing angry feelings.

SARA: Why are we talking about this nonsense? Photo whatnots. Didn't used to be what we did for Yom Hashoah. We didn't used to have a bunch of foolishness pictures—it was taken more serious.

VICTOR: (Referring to Sara) She doesn't know how to talk. There were community gatherings to remind us about what happened. Yom Hashoah isn't taken seriously now.

WORKER: Somehow I get the feeling that we're not just talking about this particular day being taken seriously.

SARA: No, we're talking about death gonna happen again if we don't do something about it.

ROBERT: (To Sara, laughing mockingly) Well, what could you possibly do about it anyway?

WORKER: I wonder what's going on that people are talking to Sara this way.

VICTOR: Because she is so strange!

WORKER: I wonder why people are talking this way to Sara right now. To be honest, people seem angry.

ROBERT: (To worker) Yeah, sure we're angry. You want us to dance? I would never dance with Sara!

WORKER: I wonder if people are actually angry about the Holocaust not being taken seriously. (Silence.)

WORKER: Or maybe angry that nothing stopped it from happening in the first place.

SARA: (To worker) *Gei kaken* (Yiddish for "Go shit"). You're a nice girl, but . . . (To Robert, loudly) Did you live in the War?

ROBERT: (Stands up, loudly, to Sara) "I'll tell you something! I saw my father shot, my mother was gassed, and my sister (makes gesture of hanging by a rope). You never had such a life! (Puts hands in pockets, jingles change, and begins to sob quietly, turns back to group. Silence follows.)

SARA: (To Robert) That's a terrible thing. I wish I could say something to make you feel better.

Remembering an event as powerful and awful as the Holocaust is bound to generate many reactions to the associated pain. The flight-fight reaction in the group was maladaptive in that it turned survivors of oppression into antagonists, just when they needed each other the most. The worker's brief intervention illustrates the beginning of helping them to rediscover their connections.

In summary, clients in a single-session group, even a large one, can be involved actively in a group process with beneficial results. I have asked groups with as many as 900 people to attempt a discussion, with some degree of success. There are many situations where direct didactic presentation at the beginning of a session can be extremely helpful. However, the worker must keep the presentation of material to a reasonable time (more than 40 minutes may be too much) and should monitor the group's reactions as the presentation progresses. The ability of group members to work effectively and with feeling in a single-session group, when the proper conditions are set by the worker, has never ceased to amaze me.

Activity Groups

Activity group is a term usually applied to groups involved in a range of activities other than just conversation. *Program* is another term used to describe the activities implemented in such groups, such as the expressive arts (painting, dancing), games, folk singing, social parties, cooking—in fact, almost any recreational or social activity used by people in groups. In one of my earlier articles, I examined the ways in which people relate to each other, suggesting that to dichotomize talking and doing is a mistake (Shulman, 1971). Relationships between people were best described by a mixed transactional model. Let me explain.

In the complex process of human interaction, people express feelings, ideas, support, interest, and concern—an entire range of human reactions—through a variety of mediums. A **mixed transactional model** presents the idea that all of these mediums—words, facial and bodily expressions, touch, shared experiences of various kinds, and other forms of communication (often used simultaneously)—should be included when one considers the means by which transactions are negotiated and consummated. Workers should not fragment human interactions by forcing them into categories such as "talking" and "doing" but should focus instead on the common denominators among *transactions,* defined here as exchanges in which people give to and take from each other. Group workers are concerned with helping people who are pursuing common purposes to carry out mutually productive transactions.

In my analysis of the ways in which group members might use shared activity for mutual aid, I rejected grandiose claims that suggested specific activities might lead to creating "spontaneous or creative individuals" or "strengthened egos." Instead I suggested the need to describe the specific and immediate functions that the activity in question may play in the mutual-aid process. Here are five of these identified functions:

1. *Human contact*—activities that focus on meeting a basic human need for social interaction (such as golden age clubs for isolated senior citizens)

2. *Data gathering*—activities designed to help members obtain more information central to their tasks (such as teenagers, preparing for employment, arranging a series of trips to business or industrial complexes)

3. *Rehearsal*—a means of developing skills for specific life tasks (such as a teenage party in an institution creating an opportunity for members to practice the social skills necessary for the courtship phase of life)

4. *Deviational allowance*—activities creating a flow of affect among members that builds up a positive relationship, allowing members to deviate from the accepted norms and raise concerns and issues that might otherwise be taboo (such as young teenage boys who have gotten to know each other and the leader through many shared activities being more willing to accept a worker's invitation to discuss their real fears about sex)

5. *Entry*—specific activities planned by a group as a way to enter an area of difficult discussion (such as the playacting of young children as they create roles and situations that reveal their concerns of the moment, or artwork expressing issues for people in recovery from addiction)

Besides these functions, we can see activity groups in terms of two general categories of groups in which activities are used as a medium of exchange. In the first, the activities themselves constitute the purpose of the group. Examples include a teenage club in a community center or a patients' committee in a psychiatric hospital charged with planning recreational activities or an evening lounge program. The group exists for the purpose of implementing the activity. A second category includes groups established for curative purposes, in which an activity is employed as a medium of exchange with specific healing goals in mind. A dance therapy group in a psychiatric center is an example of this type of group. These two categories will be covered separately, because each raises special issues.

The first type of group—for example, a teenage club—can often be found in the agencies that gave birth to group work practice in the social work field: community centers, YMCAs, and national youth organizations. This type of group is used in other institutions as well, as a vehicle for involving clients in planning their own leisure activities. The most typical problem with this type of group is that the worker or the agency ascribes therapeutic purposes to the group that constitute a hidden agenda. The group members may think they are attending a YMCA teenage club, but the workers view the group as a medium through which they can change the members. This view reflects an early and still dominant view of program activity as a "tool of the worker," which grew out of the social work profession's early efforts to distinguish the group social worker from the recreational worker. The professional worker, so the thinking goes, would bring to bear special skills in selecting programs that would result in the desired behavioral changes. Take, for instance, the problem of the child who was scapegoated in a group. In this early model, the worker might ascertain what area of skill this child had and then select or influence the group to choose an activity at which the scapegoated child would shine.

My own training was rooted in this view of practice. In one setting, my agenda involved attempting to influence group members (teenagers) toward their religious association. The agency was sponsored by the Jewish community, which was concerned that second-generation teenagers might be "drifting away." Program was the tool through which I was to influence the members by involving them in agency-wide activities—for example, in connection with religious holidays and celebrations. When such activities were conducted with the direct involvement and planning of the members, they offered powerful opportunities for deepening a sense of cultural connection and community. Unfortunately, at times I was so busy attempting to covertly "influence" the membership that I ended up missing the indirect cues group members offered about their real concerns related to their identity as a minority group in a Christianity-dominated culture. There were important moments when the concerns of the community and the felt needs of the group members were identical; the common ground was missed because of the misguided view that I was to use program as my tool to accomplish the agency's ends.

The program is an effective tool—but it is the members' tool, not the worker's. A group of teenagers in a community center or a residential setting sharing a "club" in which they plan their own social and recreational activities is an important service in itself. It does not have to be embellished with "professional" purposes. The worker's function in such a group is not to secretly influence members but rather to help them to develop their own club. The worker's suggestions for activities related to the group members' needs can be shared freely, as a worker with any group would share relevant data, but it is the group members who must sort out those activities and decide which ones they wish to pursue. If the agency has other agendas it feels are important for groups, then these must be openly presented in the contracting phase, and the group worker must attempt to find whatever common ground may exist. However, just as the worker will guard the group's contract from subversion by members, he or she must also guard it from subversion by the agency. Members will learn a great deal about relationships, problem solving, and other areas as they work to create and run their groups; however, the worker must see the club as an end in itself, not a tool to be used for hidden professional purposes.

The second category of activity group is the type in which specific purposes other than the activity are the major focus and the activity is used to help achieve these ends. This is illustrated in the following two examples. In the first, the workers help a group of 8- and 9-year-old children deal with the trauma of separation and divorce through activities using drawing and puppets as mediums of expression. In the second example, a group of Vietnamese women use sharing tea and homemade

Vietnamese food as their medium for sharing the traumatic experiences associated with their transitions to a new country and culture.

Children Dealing With Their Parents' Separation and Divorce

RECORD OF SERVICE

Client Description and Time Frame

Type of Group: This is an ongoing group to give children the opportunity to discuss their fears, to face change, and to find solutions to the painful crisis of family disruption.

Members: 8- and 9-year-olds; white; lower- and middle-income; two girls and one boy.

Dates: 10/31 to 11/28.

Group Task: Developing a structure for work and maintaining it.

Description of the Problem

The task this young group faces is understanding that the sharing of feelings, thoughts, and attitudes with one another about the theme that unites them (having lived through the separation and/or divorce of their parents) can be a powerful mechanism through which each member can identify and relate to others, recognizing that their experience is not unique and that divorce is a change with both positive and negative aspects to it, thereby decreasing each member's sense of isolation, loneliness, guilt, and grief. Two major challenges are faced by members within this group. The first is the likelihood that they are unaccustomed to or discouraged from sharing their feelings, particularly with regard to separation/divorce, in their respective families. The second is learning to speak to teachers and to parents (people in authority) to have their needs met and questions answered rather than looking to their peers.

Given the ages of the children, their looking to adults to provide some guidance and support is natural and healthy. However, the challenge for me, as the worker, is to create an environment in which increased communication and the sharing of affect among the children can be encouraged, as opposed to allowing only the continuation of the more familiar process of the children's dependence and reliance on authority figures to meet their needs. My role is to continually find ways to foster and strengthen the members' ability to speak with, and find support and solace from, one another. My hopes are that (1) the members can begin to feel freer to acknowledge their feelings with regard to the endings of their families as they once knew them, as well as to the reconstruction of their newer families, and (2) the members, through this group experience, can practice new ways of sharing, cooperating, and finding within and among themselves a greater capacity to cope with the struggles that life presents.

How the Problem Came to the Attention of the Worker(s)

I noticed in the first group session, and again in the second, that the members seemed most comfortable speaking in response to a question or statement that my coleader or I would raise. I was aware that the group takes place immediately after the children leave school, an environment in which it is expected that they speak only when they raise their hand and/or are acknowledged by their teachers. Given their ages and the newness of being in this particular kind of group experience, I suspected that the children might not know what was expected of them. As a result, in both the first and second sessions, I asked the members to share with one another to encourage not only communication, but also collaborative problem solving. They were able to do this when it was suggested, but unless the suggestion was explicit, I noticed that the members looked to the leaders for instructions on how to proceed. I knew that it would be essential to continually set a tone where discussion among the members could occur to best create a sense for the members that they were in this group for a shared purpose—a purpose, I realize, of which they may have been unaware, but which would need to be clarified through the leaders' function of helping the members put their thoughts and feelings into words, pictures, or play and helping the members reach out in new ways by making connections among their shared experiences.

Summary of the Work

First Session

I was anxious about starting a group whose members were so young. My coleader, Joanne, had a lot of experience working with children and did not share my anxiety, and this offered me some relief. She had some written activities for children from a former group she had run, and she and I together modified the activities to meet the needs of this group, knowing that it was important to allow for input from the members as well. Two of the members showed up early. For the first session we had expected three members and had been told one member would arrive late. We had a snack prepared and tried to make the two members comfortable, explaining that we would wait for the third member to arrive before actually starting group. I felt a need to reach out to these two members. I introduced myself, asked their names and ages and where they went to school, and encouraged them to help themselves to the snack. Henry (age 9) and Stacy (age 8) were initially shy but with this invitation helped themselves to juice and crackers. Stacy began talking about her family. Time passed; the third member never arrived. Joanne and I decided to formally start the "group," recognizing that, with only two members, we might need to alter some of our planned activities to decrease the intensity for these two children. I asked if they knew why they were here. I wanted to get a feel for what they had been told about the group and note any reactions. Both were able to share that it was because their parents were "going through a separation."

I was confused, because my understanding was that in both these families the separations had occurred long ago and that in Stacy's family, the divorce had been finalized. I tried to assess what I suspected was denial by eliciting information from them concerning these separations. I wasn't sure if it was denial operating or a misunderstanding of the term *separation*. Not wanting to assume that it was denial or to confront it so early in the group's life, I asked each child who he or she lived with. Then I asked when this change in the living situation happened. Both Henry and Stacy were able to respond to these questions and clearly understood their parents were, in fact, separated. Maybe they were thinking that it was the divorce that was in progress, but Henry's father had literally walked out 4 years earlier, and Stacy's parents had been divorced for several months, following a separation 2 years earlier. I chose not to ask at this time what it had been like to make these changes in their living arrangements. It may have been a missed opportunity to discuss how their parents' separations directly affect them, but because it was the first session and because at least one member was missing (we were working on getting more members), I did not seek further elaboration.

We began our first activity, which involved having the members draw or write their responses to benign questions: something they like, something they don't like, an animal each would like to be and one they wish they had, and then share their work as an effort to increase their comfort level with sharing. Henry drew a picture of not liking when kids fight, which he said was happening at school. I wondered, given this was a group dealing with separation and divorce issues, if he also had not liked when his parents fought—how that felt, the position it put him in. Stacy said she does not have to worry about this because "everyone in my class likes me."

I tried to encourage mutual aid. I wanted to set a precedent in this first group that there would be an expectation that members would speak with one another and that by doing so members might find new ways of problem solving. I asked Stacy if she could give Henry some advice about how to avoid getting into situations where fighting might occur. Her response to Henry was to fight back if you had to. She said that is what her father had taught her to do. A wish that both Henry and Stacy had was illustrated by a great amount of money (green rectangles). I missed the significance of this wish until a review of the literature helped me to understand how money, in the children's minds, could fill the void that each of them feels.

The next activity involved each member drawing a picture of his or her family. Henry had great difficulty here. He drew a door, then a window, then asked to go to the bathroom. Stacy drew her entire family: all five members were smiling, Mom and Dad were next to each other, and a big heart encircled all of them. Henry's inability to draw his family members and Stacy's wishful illustration seemed to reflect some avoidance and some denial, respectively. (Henry did complete his drawing on his return and drew a smiling child with his mother's arm around him.)

Because of their ages and the fact that this was the first group session, as with issues mentioned earlier, I chose not to explore the significance of how this activity was played out. I knew these would be ongoing and necessary themes to explore, as the artwork demonstrated, and that my coleader and I would need to help these children name their feelings if the group was to be effective. I was able to identify many messages in the session, but unsure as to when to probe and when to just let the members be. I knew, too, I would need to pay attention to my own resistance or hesitation to explore these emotional, painful issues.

The group leader's recognition of her own resistance to explore painful issues is an important step in helping her to reach for the members' underlying feelings of hurt, anger, and tremendous loss. At times such as these, workers need supervision or consultation to help them explore their own resistance. These children are astute observers of adults around them and have already received the message that the feelings are taboo and not to be discussed. When they perceive that these adults are ready to hear them, the chances of their responding greatly increase.

Second Session

Henry, Stacy, and Tara (age 9) participated in group today. Because Tara had missed our first group, I asked Henry and Stacy if they could share with her what took place in the first session. Rather than my telling Tara what had occurred the previous week, I hoped that this would be a nonthreatening attempt to encourage intermember communication; my intent was to set the tone right away in that the two initial members would recognize that this new member was an equal participant in the group and to encourage her sense of inclusion. Henry and Stacy could feel important by sharing with her, while Tara could feel that the other members, and the leaders, were reaching out to admit her. Both Henry and Stacy were able to tell Tara the activities we had done, and Henry even recalled the details of each of the drawing activities. Joanne and I asked the members if they could recall why each of them was here. Tara was able to say, as Henry and Stacy had the week before, that she knew it was because her parents had separated.

We gave Tara an opportunity to draw her responses to the previous week's activities while Henry and Stacy embellished their pictures. Repeating the previous week's activities felt awkward to me, but my coleader, and I to an extent, felt it was important for each member to participate in this early task. After Tara was done, the members shared their drawings with one another. I frequently asked members if they could tell the others what something represented to him or her in the drawing. I understood that this was like a first group, because Tara had not been able to come the week before, and that it might take a while for members to become comfortable sharing with one another without prompting from a leader. Still, I continued to make a demand that they speak to one another. I felt that my coleader was excellent at drawing each child out, but the result seemed to be that the child would respond to her. I seemed to be more focused on drawing each child out in an attempt to increase dialogue with his or her peers. I am aware that this is a function of the training I have received and my belief that peers engaging one another can provide a more powerful mechanism for support and growth than that provided by the interaction between members and leader.

For this session, the plan was to focus on the word *divorce.* The children were asked to brainstorm words that come to mind when they hear this word and determine whether the words have positive ("good") or negative ("bad") meanings to them. The members eagerly responded to this activity. Each took turns writing a word or phrase on the blackboard, and after they finished, we discussed what they had written. Their list was quite comprehensive: the "good" list included "no more fighting" and "parents still love us," and the "bad" list included "separation," "lots of crying," "children feel sad," and "some people think it's their fault." Because "children" was a big word and Stacy had trouble writing it, Henry suggested that she simply write, "We feel sad." I heard this as his ability to identify with her statement and bring its context closer to home.

When Henry wrote, "Some people think it's their fault," I asked him, "Which people?" I wanted to reach into his words and bring what he was saying closer to the group. He responded by mentioning "the children," which led us into a discussion as to whether each of the members had ever felt it was their fault that their parents had separated/divorced. None of them believed that it was; each sounded as if she or he was repeating messages heard from their parents about not feeling responsible. Whether they really believed it was not their fault was not clear to me at this time.

Following this discussion, the members drew pictures illustrating aspects of what had just been discussed. Henry's picture was incredible; the top of the page said, "Separation" and under this heading, he drew a crying child, alone, in the middle of the page with Mom walking off the right-hand side of the page and Dad walking off the left side. All you could see was one leg and one hand of each parent. It was a powerfully vivid and moving depiction of Henry's understanding of "separation."

The last part of the session involved reading a series of statements and the members deciding if these statements were true or false. Somehow, animal puppets had gotten passed around, to the leaders as well, and we all agreed to respond through the puppets. I did not know if it was due to difficult subject matter or the lateness of the hour, or perhaps a combination of both, but the group all seemed to be responding at once. I asked that one puppet speak at a time. While recognizing that this exercise was the most sensitive one in which the group had participated so far, I wanted to review the rule that we had discussed last week and at the beginning of this group that one person talks at a time. I hoped that stating this through "one puppet," as opposed to "one person," would honor the acceptability of "working" through the puppets and keep the members engaged, while pointing out the need to be respectful.

I saw that the use of puppets seemed to be very freeing for each of the members; they were immersed in their puppets but were able to remain attentive to the activity. Even though each member had done well up to this point, the use of puppets seemed to elicit much more spontaneity and free associating. Each child had much to say about each statement and was clearly speaking from his or her realm of experience. Again I noticed, however, that discussion seemed to travel between each member and my coleader or the members and me. I once more tried to encourage discussion among the members. Each time someone responded to a statement, I would say, "Stacy and Henry, Tara thinks this statement is true because . . . what do each of you think?" My effort at this time only resulted in their responding to me.

I wished that this last exercise could have been given more time. The statements had evoked a lot of feeling and a lot of sharing, but the session was over. In comparison with the previous week's session, I did feel discussion of feelings associated with separation and divorce had taken place and that through their words, pictures, and puppets, much had been shared. It was only the second group, and the first group for the three members together. I am actually struck, as I write this, at the courage and vulnerability the members displayed. I hoped that next week's session would provide another opportunity for the members to share their feelings and recognize their capacity for mutual aid.

In the next excerpt, the leader notes the difference in interactional style between her and her coleader. She strengthens their work together by raising the issue in a nonthreatening manner. Crucial to this conversation is her recognition that they both are contributing to the group's development and that they can learn from each other.

Third Session

Prior to session, I spoke with my coleader and mentioned that, while writing this record of service, I became aware of the different functions she and I seemed to play in the group. She found my observation interesting. I told her if this was a group for adults I would think downplaying member-leader interaction would be important and that encouraging mutual aid would be critical. In a group for children, however, I wondered if both functions were in fact necessary to model healthy adult interaction for the children on the one hand and help the children learn to enhance their interpersonal skills with peers on the other hand. We did not get to finish this discussion, but I did notice that she made different kinds of interventions in this group session than she had previously done. Simultaneously, I felt freer to explore each member's comments in more depth than I may have in previous weeks, while still continuing to make demands for mutual aid.

All three members were present for this third session. After everyone had had a snack, I asked members if they could recall what we had done the previous week. I wanted to see what the members would find significant to mention and if they would specifically mention our activity around divorce. I was impressed, as I had been the week before, with the members' ability to cite details from what we had all done together in our previous session. I then asked members if they had thoughts or feelings they had wanted to bring up since the last meeting. I wanted to demonstrate that although we only meet weekly, our work together continues between meetings, and to give them permission to share anything that might have arisen for each of them. No one felt a need to respond to this question. My next question was to ask them if family members had asked any of them what was happening in their group. I again wanted to see if there had been carryover from the group meetings into their homes. Surprisingly for me, each child said no one had discussed group with them. Henry, however, did offer that his mother had stopped smoking since our last meeting. He sounded proud of her, and this led into a discussion of when our partners make us proud of them versus when they make us sad or angry at them. Although the members had started off quietly, 10 minutes into the group each child seemed ready to share.

In this session, the focus was to acknowledge that divorce means change and that change is something that occurs all the time. Joanne asked the group what changes when parents separate or divorce. I overheard Stacy and Henry both say the word *disappear.* I commented that they had both used this word and asked each of them to share what they meant by this word. I was trying to create a bridge by showing the members there was similarity in their response. Stacy said that things disappear, like the couch or the television—one parent gets the couch, one the television. I looked to Henry for his response, and he immediately offered that a parent can disappear. Because I had learned through Joanne that Henry's father had left 4 years earlier, I knew there was a lot of feeling behind what Henry had shared. The two other members in the group had both parents very much in their lives, as well as brothers and sisters and new partners for their parents; Henry had only his mother. I do not believe the other members were aware of the significance of Henry's remark and therefore were not sensitive to what he had shared. I struggled with how to proceed. I chose to mention how divorce can be different in different people's homes. I discussed that for some people divorce may mean new people in their lives if mom or dad gets a new boyfriend or girlfriend and that this can be positive or negative; I also said that it can mean being single for a parent, which can be lonely for the parent and maybe for the child; and I added that it can mean leaving a place one has lived; leaving school, friends, grandparents, other family members; or perhaps moving to a place where one is closer to relatives or family friends. This created discussion among the children as they began to relate stories about their parents' partners, their grandparents, and their friends who were also experiencing parental separation/divorce.

Our activity for this session involved giving each member a sheet of paper with three faces on it, one face reflecting happiness, one reflecting sadness, and one reflecting fear. Each child was to write underneath each face the best, worst, and scariest thing about divorce, respectively. The children immediately responded to this task; all were clearly concentrating on what they were writing. When they were finished writing, they shared what they had written. All of them agreed that "no more fighting" was the best thing about divorce, a theme they had perhaps recalled from the previous week. A variety of answers were written, and both Joanne and I encouraged each of the members to think about whether what the others had written applied to them. My purpose here was to demonstrate once again any similarities in their experiences. Not surprisingly, the children could identify with several of the examples. They all agreed with Tara's comment that another "best" thing about divorce is that "your parents still love you" and with Henry's comment that a "worst" thing about divorce is that "some kids think it's their fault." While many of these themes had been discussed the previous week, I saw that the members were incorporating some of what was being shared in our group. In addition, this week it seemed there was more feeling behind the words. I wondered if Joanne and I were functioning well as leaders and creating a safe environment in which the children's feelings could emerge, as the group seemed to be feeling more comfortable with one another, and in turn, more comfortable sharing.

Fourth Session

With the Thanksgiving holiday occurring this week, I thought it would be appropriate to focus our fourth session on how the members were feeling about the upcoming holiday and what it represented to them in terms of how and with whom they had spent it in the past, what has changed for each of them, and what they anticipated for this holiday. I spoke with my coleader about this idea, and she agreed that it would be useful and that we could modify any activity to include this event. As has been described, each week so far had revisited discussion about expressing feelings of sadness, anger, and happiness in response to divorce. While in some ways it seemed redundant, my coleader and I recognized that the purpose of this group was to get the members to feel increasingly comfortable acknowledging and voicing their feelings. The Thanksgiving holiday seemed a perfect vehicle to elicit current struggles each member might be experiencing.

When this session started, I noticed that all three members immediately began chatting, eating their snack, and asking about today's plans in a more animated display than I had seen in previous weeks. I used this opportunity to get right down to work, and I asked what was happening this week that made this week special. Each child mentioned that it was Thanksgiving. I asked if they could tell the group how each one would be spending the time. All three members began speaking at once. I asked the group if we could review the group contract. Tara and Henry raised their hands. I explained that hand raising was not necessary, but that it seemed that they had the right idea. Tara said that only one person should speak at a time. I commented that it seemed all three of them had something interesting to say and that I did not want to miss anyone's contribution. Stacy asked if she could go first, because she was the youngest. The children described how they would be spending the holiday and then drew pictures of how they envisioned feeling on that day.

All three members reported that the previous Thanksgiving had been their favorite Thanksgiving; Joanne and I looked at each other skeptically, because we knew that for Stacy in particular, her parents' marriage had already been in serious trouble. I reached for more feelings in order to confront the denial and avoidance I was sensing. I asked the group what had made the previous Thanksgiving so special. Each child commented that they were with family and had good food. Stacy talked in great detail about her grandmother's soup. I recalled Stacy's difficulty in focusing on her personal situation in our first group session. When I tried to verbalize the pain that members of the group may have been feeling, I missed an opportunity to point out to the group that talking about painful emotions seemed to be difficult for them. I mentioned that holidays can be very special because for many people they are spent with loved ones, but that they can also be difficult when families change or when someone wants to be in two places at once. The members continued to draw. Tara commented that she has an aunt who draws well, but not as well as Henry.

Despite the members' inability to tolerate what I was attempting to raise, this was the first time I had heard an unsolicited comment from one group member to another. While this may have demonstrated a member's aligning with another member rather than dealing with the issue at hand (flight), other examples of this interaction occurred in the session that supported my initial sense that the members seemed more connected and willing to speak to one another. Nevertheless, Joanne and I looked at each other and agreed we needed to move on to another activity; the members had become absorbed in their artwork and needed a push.

Joanne and I took turns creating vignettes, and the members had to decide whether someone described in the vignette would feel happy, sad, angry, or disappointed. We spontaneously created scenarios that seemed relevant to what the children might be facing this week. I went first and offered: "Mary's father is supposed to pick her up at 10 A.M. on Thanksgiving. He calls her at 11 A.M. to say he can't make it because he's decided to go to his girlfriend's house. Mary feels . . ." The scenarios became more complicated as Joanne and I introduced stepparent and stepsibling issues and other conflicting themes that might involve the members. Each child responded quite positively to this activity. They were spirited and engaged, and each contributed sound reasons for feeling as the character might have felt. Often the members personalized the scenarios by saying how he or she would feel. After Joanne and I had each done two scenarios, Tara asked if she could make one up. Stacy followed. She described a situation where a mother's boyfriend was angry at a child and threw the child down the stairs. She wanted to know how the mother should feel.

Henry and Tara responded together that the mother would be sad the child was hurt. I felt an urgent need to make a stronger statement, as well as model for the members the acceptability of their own strong feelings. I added, in a very firm voice, that if I was the mother, I would be furious that my boyfriend had hurt my child and that no matter how my child behaved, no child deserved to be hurt and that my boyfriend's behavior was absolutely unacceptable. Recalling the activity we had played in a previous session, Stacy acted like the judge and said I had given the best response for that scenario. It was a scenario Joanne and I would need to be alerted to.

The scenario raised by Stacy raised a warning flag for the workers that they need to address in an individual session. The social workers leading this group are mandated reporters, and even an indirect communication of possible abuse must be explored, and if confirmed, shared with the appropriate child welfare agency. Even if the individual conversation does not provide confirmation, the workers should alert the child protection office so that a more thorough investigation can take place.

The children's vignettes were complicated and revealing. Each member seemed to be an internal leader—creating a vignette and listening to each person's discussion as to why someone might feel as he or she did. This activity seemed to reduce the amount of denial and avoidance I had sensed earlier; by removing the focus from the three members, which in a group of three may have simply been too intense, the members could be more spontaneous in exposing their feelings. Time had run out, and the members did not want to leave. I told the group that everyone had made wonderful, creative, and sensitive contributions and that we would talk more next week. I wanted to praise and reinforce their willingness to take risks and to take ownership of their group by conceiving their own stories. I also hoped to imply that next week would provide another opportunity to do more of the same.

Fifth Session

My coleader and I decided to focus this week's session on anger. Prior to group, she and I had agreed that we would use vignettes again because they seemed to be an effective way of getting each of the members to reveal their own feelings, sometimes in the guise of sharing through what the characters might feel and sometimes through making identifications with the characters as to how they, the members, would feel.

The group opened as it did last week; the members were snacking and chatting with each other and seeming comfortable as they discussed how they had spent their Thanksgiving holiday. The members asked what we were going to do today, and Joanne responded that we would be talking about anger. I felt a need to review why we were all together and to remind the group that there was a shared purpose to our meeting. I asked the group what we had been discussing in our previous weeks together and what it was that brought us all together. Tara immediately responded, "Divorce." I nodded and then asked if anyone could be more specific. Stacy said we talked about "happy, sad, and mad." I asked the group if this is different from what they do in school and, if it is, in what way. Everyone said it was different and that in school people do not discuss their feelings. I asked the group why they thought this was so. A silence followed. I thought that the members might be feeling uncomfortable and that their silence reflected their own discomfort and sense of isolation regarding their ability to discuss their family situations freely at school, and perhaps even in the group. I missed an opportunity to acknowledge their discomfort and instead tried to educate them and normalize their experience about the common occurrence of divorce. I asked the members if they knew other children at school whose parents were separated and divorced. My coleader pointed out that almost half of all marriages end in divorce. Not surprisingly, the intellectualized response by my coleader, and perhaps by me, generated little response, and my coleader and I moved on to our planned activity.

The workers here took the children to the edge of an important discussion. The question about what makes it hard to talk about these subjects was on target; however, the children's silence in response moved the workers away from an important discussion. This was the moment when reaching into the silence, perhaps by offering some specific possible reasons why it is hard, could help the children deepen the conversation. The group leader showed important insight in her learning process as she recognized her own intellectualizing response. Perhaps the silence and intellectualizing arose because talking about anger—the focus of the session—was particularly difficult for both the workers and the children.

We asked the children what makes them angry about divorce. They came up with several responses. I tried to draw them out to have them reveal the depth that they had in previous sessions, and I pointed out connections to other responses when similarities were evident to me. Joanne and I then took turns creating vignettes that we knew would resonate for the members in our group. What followed was a lengthy discussion about absent parents, new partners in their parents' lives, and contending with the children of these partners. This presented an opportunity for helping the children to engage in some problem solving. Tara and Henry both described wanting to kill a new baby who was born to "Walter's mother and her boyfriend," characters in a scenario. I thought it was important to acknowledge the expression of their feelings and again tried to elicit from them why might they want to kill this baby, whom else might they be angry at, what would happen if they really did kill the baby, and what their loved ones might feel about them. Following this opportunity for them to play out this scenario, I asked if it was really OK to kill a baby. The members all said no. I then asked if anyone could think of other solutions to this dilemma, because killing a baby is really not OK. I hoped that this would instill confidence in the members' own capacity to problem-solve. Henry and Stacy smiled. Tara, who had a newborn in her home, did not. Henry, an only child, said maybe "Walter" could play with the baby; I asked Henry what that would do. He replied, "Walter might like it." I acknowledged that Walter might enjoy having a younger sibling after all, even though his feelings might remain mixed. This seemed to give Tara permission to discuss that it is hard having only younger siblings and that she wished she were not the oldest in her family.

In an effort to increase members' sensitivity to the experiences of others and to demonstrate tolerance, I tried to articulate the idea that members in the group have had different experiences in their families from which they draw their feelings and attitudes. I commented to the group that it sometimes sounded like Henry found it lonely to be an only child and that Tara, having two sisters and now a newborn, would often prefer more privacy. Both children nodded.

One of the vignettes created a scenario of a friend wanting to talk to someone about his parents' divorce. I wanted to show the group that each of them had a lot to offer, not only in the presence of the group, but outside the group as well. I asked the group whom this friend could speak with. Henry said that he would tell this person to speak to a counselor or teacher. I said that this was a very good suggestion. I then highlighted for the group that each of them could be very supportive to a friend because they have gone through a similar situation and that it might help the friend to feel less alone. We again began discussing why talking about these feelings is difficult. I noticed that all three children had moved into the corner and were focused on a doll house, standing with their backs turned toward Joanne and me. This time I was not going to miss the opportunity to acknowledge their discomfort. I said to the group, "I have asked all of you a question. Is it hard for you to talk about this stuff right now?" I was stunned by the honesty of their reactions. Henry immediately nodded, and Stacy and Tara said, "Yes." I chose to reach further to have them identify their discomfort. "How come?" I asked. There was no answer, and this session was over. I again wanted to praise their willingness and bravery to take risks and share their feelings. I commented, "That's OK. You've all been doing a great job today talking about issues that are hard for everyone. It's not easy, and you've all been very brave."

Current Status of the Problem

Where the Problem Stands Now

Each week the group members have appeared increasingly comfortable with one another, as evidenced by their spontaneous interactions when they enter group. They seem to recognize that they share similarities as children of divorced parents. Even though the children admit that it is hard for them to discuss painful events they have experienced, they have each shown a greater willingness to tolerate sensitive issues. It is my hope that the structure and maintenance Joanne and I strive to continually sustain has resulted in a group culture that is different from what they may experience elsewhere and that it has made the members feel safer to express themselves when they choose.

The members still look to Joanne or me to guide the session, but this may be a function of their developmental stage and being more accustomed to looking to adults than to themselves for guidance. Movement toward mutual aid is apparent, however, as I have noticed that greater interaction does take place among the members, with less prompting from me, as we progress into each session. The members are increasingly showing that they can share and cooperate with one another. Perhaps because this group is so small, or because we have not yet faced these problems, power and control struggles have been negligible; the only manifestation of this kind of struggle that I have been aware of has been when the children, together, decide they no longer want to discuss the issue at hand and begin to play with or focus on something else. I am trying to not only recognize this but, as I did in this last session, point out to the members areas that are troublesome for them. I suspect that, many times, they can identify certain feelings and are conscious of holding back, but remain confused as to how to express themselves. If their attention is directed to these areas, the members may slowly become less constricted and freer to externalize through an appropriate means of communication the confusion and the turbulence they feel inside.

Specific Next Steps

- I will continue to discuss with my coleader the importance and value of encouraging mutual aid, as opposed to only encouraging member-leader interaction.

- I will continue to be sensitive to the age and developmental stage of the group members so as not to create any unreasonable expectations for myself or for them.

- I will continue to recontract—to remind the members that they are here because they are all children who have experienced their parents' separation and divorce.

- I will continue to create an environment that feels safe for each member so that each can feel increasingly safe to disclose aspects of his or her inner self and know that he or she will be heard.

- I will be sensitive to each member's outside reality in terms of the defenses, learned behaviors, and coping mechanisms each may have developed, while encouraging them all to adopt a different way of relating while within the group.

- I must make demands for work (reach for feelings of sadness, loss, anger, frustration, confusion) and continue to help the members explore painful themes that are difficult for them to examine and verbalize.

- So as not to sabotage the critical work of this group, I must stay in tune with my own need to intellectualize or avoid painful feelings.

- I will try to listen for and understand the underlying messages members may be communicating.

- When silences occur, or lapses in process (reluctance to draw, to participate in an activity, and so on), I will mentally make note of the seeming resistance to understand what the members are experiencing, while gently helping them to identify, or identifying for them, what this might be.

- I will continue to demonstrate support to any of the members who demonstrate initiative and take risks by sharing their feelings and thoughts with the other members.

- Similarly, I will continue to credit the group's efforts at working together.
- I will continue to reveal and create connections for the members as I see and understand them.
- I must take a more active role in acknowledging my own feelings with the group, to demonstrate my own humanity and to help model for them the sharing of feelings.
- As I sense the members' feelings emerge, I must help the members put their feelings into words rather than internalize them or put them into actions.
- As I prepare the group for its eventual termination, I must continually work to reflect the value of connection and to instill in each member an enhanced sense of being able to trust, interact with, and depend on others for support and validation, as well as a firmer, more confident sense of self on which to rely.

Vietnamese Immigrant Women

The group in this example was set up to help Vietnamese immigrant women deal with their transitions to a new country, language, and culture. Each meeting began with tea and Vietnamese food already prepared by the members. This activity provided a medium for maintaining old customs as well as for discussing difficult issues. Conversation was in English, as much as possible, to provide an opportunity to practice this second language. Written English exercises were also integrated into the group's activities. The contract included using the time to discuss their weekly experiences related to the transition. In this session, held close to the Christmas holiday, the worker explored their feelings of loss. This is also an example of practice without a translator, with the worker depending on an internal leader for help.

Session 5

We began the group as we always do, with food and tea. We then talked about the week's activities (one woman getting a letter from Vietnam, another's daughter having a cold, and another's having been to a Housing Authority meeting). My opening statement for the group went something like this: "Last week when I brought in the picture of a Christmas tree, you talked a little about your feelings about being away from home during the holiday season. I thought maybe today you might like to talk a little more about those feelings." I looked around the room to see if the women had understood what I had said. It's still very hard for me to "read" their expressions. I then said, "It must be difficult coming to a new country and having to learn so many new things." Hoan was nodding her head so I asked her what the hardest thing was for her. Hoan said she didn't realize snow was slippery, so during her first snowstorm in America she slipped and fell on a sidewalk and broke her wrist.

Thu asked something in Vietnamese, and the four women spoke together in Vietnamese for about 5 minutes. I feel certain that none of the women understand everything I've said. I think this is their way of processing all the pieces they do understand and putting them together to form a whole.

When they stop talking, I always ask if there's something I've missed. They always smile, and then Hoan gives me a brief synopsis of what they were discussing. (Hoan is the spokesperson for the group. She's the oldest, as well as the one who speaks English the best—I'm not sure which is the most important in making her the spokesperson.)

Hoan told me they had been discussing coming to this country. I asked her what she meant. (I am always unclear where the group is when we reconnect in English.) Hoan said it was very difficult to leave Vietnam. I said it must have been difficult to leave her family. She said it was that she had many brothers and sisters still in Vietnam. I asked her why she had left Vietnam, and she said it was because of her son (age 16) and her daughter (age 18), who is the Thu in the group. (Thu is developmentally delayed from a fall she had when she was 3 years old.) She didn't want her children to have to grow up under the Communist rule. She said she probably wouldn't live another 15 years, so she didn't care for herself, but she cared very much about her children.

Toi spoke up and said she had left Vietnam because of her children, too. She has five children; two are by her first husband, a Vietnamese man who was killed in the war. Her other three children are by her second husband, an American GI. Her Amerasian children bore the brunt of a lot of racial criticism by the Communists. Toi went to the Communist government and asked them if she could leave the country to go to America with her three Amerasian children. (Her other two children are still in Vietnam with relatives.) After a 2-year bureaucratic struggle, she moved to the United States, only to find her American husband had divorced her last November. Hoan said that it really hurt Toi to find out her husband had divorced her. I said that would hurt me too.

Hoan said it took her (Hoan) 7 months to leave Vietnam. First she fled to Cambodia, then to Thailand, then to the Philippines, then to California, and finally to Boston in November 1984. I said it seemed like a lot of things happened in November—Toi's divorce and Hoan arriving in the United States.

Again, there was discussion in Vietnamese. After a few minutes, Hoan told me they had been talking about Vietnam. I asked her what she meant by Vietnam (trying to reconnect with them again). She said they all wished things were different—that the Communists weren't in power.

Toi said she wanted to bring her other two children to America, but that she didn't think the Communists would let them leave. I asked her if she had made a formal application for immigration and she said yes, but that it had taken her 2 years to leave the country when the government had wanted her and her Amerasian children to leave. I asked Toi if there was a lot of discrimination in her country against Amerasian children, and she said yes. I asked her if she faced any discrimination here and she said sometimes. Hoan said Toi has had windows broken in her apartment. I asked Hoan if she had felt discrimination and she said no, she was an old woman and people left her alone.

The phone rang, and they lapsed into Vietnamese again. When we reconnected, Hoan said she knew we didn't have much time left, and could I go over the English paragraph she had written. The rest of the session was much less intense and formal. We did some grammar and some English pronunciation, and I left a short time later.

In later group sessions, the women used the activity group meeting to explore current issues of cultural clash, as they attempted to help their children integrate into a new country while holding on to some of their own culture; their own struggles with changing gender roles and rules in relation to their families and husbands; and the painful memories of their passages—in particular, the experiences of those who had endured the atrocities committed on the "boat people."

Chapter Summary

Variant elements in group practice include, among others, the unique processes and skills required in working with (1) an open-ended group, in which members join and leave the group continuously; (2) a single-session group, often large, which meets for informational proposes or in response to a particular event or trauma; and (3) activity groups, in which activities are used as "mediums of exchange" among members, for various purposes such as sharing information or working through problems. Workers can apply to such groups all the core dynamics and skills discussed throughout this book.

Related Online Content and Activities

 Visit *The Skills of Helping* Book Companion Website at www.socialwork.wadsworth .com/Shulman06/ for learning tools such as glossary terms, InfoTrac College Edition keywords, links to related websites, and chapter practice quizzes.

The website for this chapter also features additional notes from the author and additional process recordings:

- Housing Complex Group for Elderly Persons
- Teenage Girls' Dance Group in a Residential Setting: The Use of Singing and Dance as Therapy

Social Work
With the System

Part V consists of three chapters that focus on the social worker's role in relation to the professional, organizational, and community systems of both clients and workers. In Chapter 15 we explore the worker's efforts to help the client negotiate the system. The skills and dynamics described in the first four parts of the book reappear in the analysis of working with other professionals. This chapter also focuses on the social worker's responsibility to have professional impact on his or her own setting and the larger society. Chapter 16 describes the function of the social worker in various settings within the community. Finally, Chapter 17 shows how systems, in turn, affect social work practice; agency culture, ethics, and legislation all make profound impacts on workers, who must take care to evaluate their work in this context.

Professional Impact and Helping Clients Negotiate the System

I n Parts I to IV of this book, we explored the helping model in the context of work with individuals, families, and groups. Much of the emphasis was on preparing and helping clients to deal with important systems. In Part V, we consider another level of interaction—the relationship between clients and the social institutions with which they come into contact, such as schools, hospitals, housing agencies, political systems, residential care centers, community organizations, and social agencies. As we examine this interaction and the worker's function and skills required to facilitate it, we shall see that we can apply to this interaction much of the material already presented. The use of an approach based on systems theory makes this possible: Because different levels of systems have universal properties, insights into one level can serve as hypotheses for understanding another.

Chapter 1 introduced the systems or ecological approach as a general framework for understanding the client in his or her broader social context. Parts II, III, and IV focused on the worker's efforts to help the client negotiate the various important systems in her or his life (such as family, school, the mutual-aid group). We saw that the worker always had two clients—the client and the system—and that many of the principles developed in work with one can apply to work with the other. Practice examples included illustrations of social workers attempting to have professional impact on doctors, residential care workers, other social workers, and so on. In this chapter and the next, work with professional, organizational, and community systems comes to the foreground of the discussion for special focus. This level of systems work, an essential element of all practice, is what distinguishes social work as a unique profession.

Hearn (1962) was one of the first social work theorists to describe the potential value of general systems theory to the development of a unified social work practice theory. He said,

> If there are principles which apply to organismic systems in general, and if individuals, groups, organizations, and communities may be regarded as such systems, then these principles collectively might find their place in a unified theory of practice. This would provide a common framework for conceiving the individuals, groups, organizations, and communities as "clients," or as the means by which service is rendered to "clients." (p. 67)

Hearn suggests here that we use our understanding of one level of system to better understand another level. As an example of this idea, recall our discussion of the dynamics between a family and its deviant member; often, the behavior evidenced in this role was sending a message for the family as a whole. Recall also that the functional role of the deviant member in the small group worked in the same way. In this chapter and the next, we take the same concept of the role of the deviant member and apply it at the organizational and community levels. For example, in my consultations with large organizations, such as hospitals, I always find a service that is considered the deviant member of the system. This is the department that is constantly in turmoil, faces frequent staff changeovers, is in conflict with other departments, and so on. In child welfare, the protection unit often plays this role.

Following our analogy, we can interpret the behavior of an organizational department the way we would do so for the deviant member of a group. Thus, as hospitals come under increasing stress because of cost-containment efforts resulting from managed care, specific departments might act out the stress of the whole system. As with the small group and the family, the deviant member is usually the unit that is having the most difficulty coping with the general stress. In hospitals, it is often the emergency room, the intensive care ward, or the surgical service department that plays this role. These parts of the system normally have high-stress operations. In a larger entity, such as a state or a province, a statewide agency, such as the child welfare service, may send the signal of stress for all of the other human services systems. As another example, scapegoating is also common; some social service systems regard others as "less professional" and project their own problems onto the workers in those systems.

Once this systems approach is integrated into a social worker's theoretical framework, he or she can view all levels of systems dynamically and as potential targets for intervention. In addition, this point of view gives direction to conceptualizing the social worker's function and identifying the required skills. This chapter examines the individual-system interaction in much the same terms used thus far and describes the social worker's role in terms of mediation, which includes advocacy. Examples from several settings will show work with clients who sometimes individually and at other times in groups are endeavoring to negotiate systems and their representatives (such as teachers, principals, doctors, housing authority administrators). You will see that many of the skills already identified are as helpful in dealing with system representatives as they were with clients. Because change also often involves confrontation with the system and social pressure, we discuss these processes as well.

This chapter also demonstrates how a worker can use experiences with clients to guide efforts to affect agency policies, structures, procedures, and programs to better meet the needs of clients. This specific responsibility to influence the larger systems—the second client concept—is historical and gives the social work profession its unique and crucial role in our society. In short, social workers need to stop complaining about the system (school, hospital, agency, community) and to start doing something about it.

The Individual-System Interaction

In a modern, industrial, and largely urban society, the relationship between individuals and society has grown quite complex. A large number of institutions and agencies have been established to deal with the individual on behalf of society. For example, welfare agencies care for those who cannot support themselves (although efforts at "welfare reform" have brought that function into question), schools provide the education needed for individuals to become integrated into the community and to play a productive role, hospitals provide medical care for physical illness, and psychiatric centers treat people with emotional disorders. However, the very institutions set up to solve problems have become so complex themselves that they have generated new problems. Social, medical, and educational systems can be difficult to negotiate even for individuals who are well equipped to deal with them, let alone those with limited education and resources. The services established for people are often so complex that individuals find making use of them difficult.

In addition to complexity, other factors compound the individual-system interaction. For one, many services inherently approach clients ambivalently. Thus, although welfare has been established to meet the needs of the poor, it is often administered in a way that reflects a judgmental and punitive attitude. For example, welfare recipients are often made to feel that their checks are public "doles," gifts from a generous community rather than a right, and that acceptance of welfare is a sign that the individual is neither a productive nor an important member of society. Changes in the welfare legislation over the past few years have reinforced such views. Anecdotal reports indicate that welfare-to-work efforts may help some recipients—in a good economy, when appropriate day care, training, and other supports are in place. These reports also suggest that the undifferentiated application of the new rules to families and individuals who cannot make the transition may result in unacceptable hardships for the most vulnerable members of our population.

A third factor contributing to breakdowns in the individual-system relationship is the size of bureaucracy. For example, finding the right department in a large government agency can be a frustrating, even overwhelming, task. Entering a large high school as just one student in a class of 2,000 can easily lead to getting lost in the system. This may prevent the student from getting the special help needed for successful completion of a program.

A fourth complication is the difficulty of human communication. For instance, a student may, even in a small setting such as a specific class, feel that the teacher does not care, and the teacher, in turn, may feel the same way about the student. Both may well be mistaken. In another example, a student of color may experience a white teacher as racist and punitive. In some cases this perception may be accurate. In others, it may reflect the tremendous complications involved in relationships among members of different races and cultures. You can surely provide your own examples in which the size and complexity of a system, difficulties in communications, or the ambivalence of the system toward its clients cuts them off from services they require. Because the individual who needs to use the system is also complex, feels some ambivalence toward the service, and has difficulty in communications, breakdowns become almost inevitable.

Of course, we all know that simply establishing a service to meet a need does not guarantee that the need will be met. Recognizing this reality led Schwartz (1961) to propose the function of the social work profession to mediate the individual-social engagement. He suggests that this is the historical reason for the development of the social work profession: to stand as a buffer between clients and the systems they need to negotiate. Other professionals (psychologists, nurses, and so forth) may appropriately play this role; however, only the social work profession, according to Schwartz, embraces this role as a functional responsibility, that is, an essential part of the work.

Mediating the Individual-System Engagement

One of the major problems facing workers in implementing this role is their own feelings. They often tend to overidentify with the individual client against the system and its representatives. In our earlier discussion of work with the family and work with scapegoats in the group, we saw how workers, because of their own life experiences, often identify with one side in an engagement. Because we have all known complex bureaucracies, authoritarian and insensitive administrators, teachers who seemed not to care, and the like, such an initial reaction to a client's problem with a system is understandable. I have seen workers develop a fine sense of tolerance for deviant behavior on the part of clients, an ability to see past a facade and reach for clients' underlying strength, and an understanding of clients' ambivalence. Yet these same workers lack tolerance for deviant behavior, are fooled by facades, and cannot accept ambivalence when they see these same characteristics in a system or representatives of the system.

Sometimes anger is the only appropriate response, and confrontation the only answer. However, workers often react in this way before they have attempted to understand the dynamics involved, and so they may respond to teachers, doctors, welfare workers as if they were stereotypes. At the very point when a client needs the worker's help in negotiating a system, the worker may respond in a way that further cuts off the system from the client. The worker may then point to the system as impossible to reach, rather than examining personal feelings and critically analyzing his or her own part in the proceedings.

First Reactions to a System

A striking example of how workers can move beyond their initial reactions arose in a workshop I conducted for Native Canadian Indian women who work as social aides for their local bands. Their job was to help the members of the band in their dealings with many white-dominated agencies and institutions (schools, welfare, and the like). One worker presented an example of her efforts to help an Native teenager who was close to failing a course taught by a white teacher. This worker had often attacked the inadequacy of the school. The following record presents the conversation between the worker and the white teacher.

WORKER: I hear you're having problems with Albert's English.
TEACHER: It's not my problem, it's his.
WORKER: I do think you're leaning on him too hard.
TEACHER: Look, if he wants to get anywhere, he'll have to shape up. I really don't have the time to argue. If he wants to pass English, he'll have to try harder.
WORKER: Speaking about time, we do pay some of your wages, you know. I do think you could be a little more lenient.
TEACHER: I'll try to keep that in mind.
WORKER: You do that.

In discussing this brief interchange, the workshop participants, all Native Indian workers, felt that the worker had come on too hard with the teacher. Both appeared to be defensive: The teacher may have felt the worker wanted her to let Albert pass in spite of his poor performance, and the worker felt that the teacher did not really care about Albert. The group agreed that the relationship between the worker and the teacher was in poor shape and that, as a result of the interview, not much hope remained for an improved relationship between the teacher and Albert. The teacher had gained neither a better idea about Albert's feelings nor a sense of what was interfering with Albert's learning. In addition, the worker interpreted the teacher's expectations for Albert's performance as a rejection of Albert. However, many workshop members pointed out that some teachers made no demands on Indian students at all; they just passed them along—a real form of rejection and racism. The workshop group members strategized how the worker might go back to meet with the teacher and negotiate a contract for their relationship and try to begin again. Although the worker seemed to agree, I sensed her hesitation, particularly in respect to admitting to the teacher that she had come on too strong. I reached for her feelings:

WORKSHOP LEADER: You seem hesitant. I get the feeling you're not anxious to go back and try again. Am I right?
WORKER: (After a very long silence) It would hurt my pride to go back and talk to that teacher. (Another long silence.)
WORKSHOP LEADER: Could you explain why it would hurt?
WORKER: I don't think you understand. Thirty years ago, I was one of the first of five Indian children to go to that school when it was all white . . .

She went on to describe her experiences in a white-dominated school in which she and other Indian students were made to feel ashamed of their race and their heritage. They had been forbidden to speak their native language, were ridiculed by teachers and white students for their poor dress and manners, and were generally made to feel like outsiders. One example of the cultural shock was related to the use of silence. When asked questions in class, Indian students would take a long time to respond because they were thinking about the answer (as was the custom in conversations they heard in their families) or trying to translate into their native language and then back to English. Teachers who did not understand the importance of silence would often interpret the delay as indicating the student did not know the answer, and they would move on to another student. After a while, the Indian students did not even try to speak, and the teacher failed to ask.

In the workshop group, others shared their own experiences. Some participants gently pointed out it was not the same today and that some of the white teachers tried hard to understand their students. I tried to acknowledge the feelings of the worker.

WORKSHOP LEADER: I guess every time you walk into that school it must bring back a great deal of pain and feelings of humiliation. I can understand now why you would feel it would be a blow to your pride. I'm not sure if I can help right now. What is hitting me hard is that for you to work differently with this teacher, you have to deal with your feelings about the white world—all the hurt you have experienced—and that's a tall order.

Other workshop members moved in at this point and the discussion focused on how they needed to avoid the tendency to see the world of today's Indian teenagers as being exactly the same as the one they had dealt with. There were still many similarities, and evidence of ongoing prejudice and oppression clearly existed. The anger they felt toward present injustices was clearly stated. Nevertheless, if they were to help things be different for their children, they had to do something to try to change things themselves.

In this specific case, the workshop members felt it would not help Albert if the worker simply gave up on the school. For Albert to make it, someone had to open up communications between his teacher and him. The worker agreed that she could see this and said she would have to think about what she would do. I pointed out that this example opened up a larger question about the relationship between the children of the band and their parents and the staff of the school. Had they thought about the possibility of trying to do something on a band- and schoolwide basis? Were other Indian parents also feeling somewhat intimidated by the school? Perhaps the school staff felt cut off and intimidated by the band. Would this be an area to explore? Discussion continued on the implications of this specific case for the general problems of Indian children in the school. Moving from the specific example to more general problems is an important line of work that the next section will explore. For now, understand that the worker's feelings can have a powerful effect on perception of the system and its representatives. If the worker only sees that part of the system that shows resistance, then the worker may fall into the trap of missing the part of the system that is still reaching out.

Of course, workers do not need to have gone though this specific sort of experience in order to feel intimidated by a school setting. For example, one graduate student of mine described his first day of fieldwork. He was placed as a student social worker in the same school he had attended as a child. On his first morning he met his former fourth-grade teacher in the hall, and she said, "Terry, what are you doing here?" He replied, "I'm the new student social worker." He described her face as broadening into a maternal smile as she said, "Isn't that nice." He blushed and felt that the possibility of doing any effective work with this teacher was finished. A first step, therefore, in functioning more effectively in systems work is for the worker to become aware of her or his personal feelings about a system's representatives, particularly those in positions of authority. This is essential.

Work With the School System

The following example, about a youngster who was suspended from school, illustrates the mediation role in action. The worker demonstrated her ability to be with both the youngster and the system representatives in the engagement. This was the key to her success. The client was a 61-year-old woman who had contacted the worker at a community psychiatry department of the local hospital. The worker had been seeing her son in a group at the hospital, and the client, Mrs. Jones, had called to inform the worker that she was not able to get her son Bobby accepted into school, despite a court order requiring her to do so. The worker described the client as being somewhat inept at handling school matters and vague about why the school was failing to comply with the court order. The worker felt that Mrs. Jones was worried and depressed about the school problem. She visited the client at her home to help her talk about her problem.

Summary of the Work

WORKER: I know that with all of the criticism you have had regarding your children, it is very hard for you.

MRS. JONES: (Looking depressed) I am trying my best. I don't want the courts to send Bobby away, but the school won't let him return and he is getting into more trouble.

WORKER: It's like going around in circles—everyone's telling you what to do, and no one is showing you how.

MRS. JONES: Now they will say I'm neglecting Bobby. (In an exasperated manner) The court says put him in school; the school says he can't go. I don't know what to do!

She continued to talk about her inability to understand why the school has refused to allow Bobby to return. While we were talking, the other children were yelling and screaming. Mrs. Jones was very edgy. Several times she grabbed the little ones to make them be quiet. I said she seemed overwhelmed and I asked how I could help. She said I could do better if I talked to the school. She didn't understand "those people." Maybe I could. She explained how difficult it is for her to travel to school when taking care of all the other children. I said I would speak to the school and keep in close contact with her as to what was happening. She seemed relieved and thanked me.

I later talked to Bobby to see how he was feeling. He was out on the block when I spoke with him, and he seemed unhappy but perked up a little when he saw me. His immediate comment was, "You going to get me in school?" I gave him some information about the steps I had in mind and added that I knew he and his mother had been trying very hard. My comment led to further discussion.

BOBBY: I know why the school doesn't want me.

WORKER: I'd like to know why.

BOBBY: The teachers don't like me, and they don't want me in that school.

He was sulking and seemed quite torn inside. He looked at me, and his eyes were watery. I reached out and probed for what he was feeling.

WORKER: I know it's hard, but get it out of you; tell me what you are feeling.

BOBBY: (Who was crying) I want to go back into school. There's nothing to do on the block! The court is going to send me away, and my mother keeps hollering at me!

We talked at great length about his feelings, and he continued to express his fears about getting into school. If he gets into school, he is not sure he will do well. He is afraid the same experiences will repeat themselves. Mostly, I just listened, giving support where I could.

WORKER: I know it's hard, Bobby. I want to help you by trying to help your parents as well as the school to see that you want to do the right thing. But it's not easy. You'll have to help me do this.

BOBBY: I'll try.

WORKER: You're trying already. It must have been very hard for you to tell me what you were thinking.

Bobby was silent, but I felt he understood what I was saying. When I was leaving, he reminded me of the group's trip that evening, and I said I would be there.

The worker had begun the process by contracting with Mrs. Jones and Bobby about how she could help. She tried to get a sense of how they saw the difficulty and attempted to encourage their expression of feeling about the problem. After these conversations, you might expect that the worker might have gone to the school to do battle for Bobby. With a court order in the background, the worker might have tried to use the power of the court to force Bobby back into school. This effort might have worked, but the worker recognized it would have been a short-lived victory. If the problems between Bobby and the school system were not dealt with, they would just return to haunt him later, and he would soon be suspended again. In addition, while the worker might have been able to force the school to take Bobby back, she wanted more from them—she wanted them to work to help Bobby stay in. To enlist their aid, she needed to treat the staff at the school as allies, not enemies, in the struggle to aid Bobby.

Instead of creating a self-fulfilling prophecy by attacking the school representatives and provoking a defensive and negative response, the worker began the first contact with the school guidance counselor by contracting, employing the skill of clarifying purpose. Often, because of their hidden agendas, workers begin their systems work without a clear and direct statement of what they are about. Lack of clarity as to purpose can be just as threatening and unproductive with systems representatives as it is with clients. She also encouraged the guidance counselor to elaborate her perceptions of the problem. A worker who saw the counselor as the enemy might have begun a counterattack after the counselor's first responses. As the worker said,

I visited the school for the purpose of getting clarification on the reasons why Bobby was not allowed in school and to trace the source of his difficulty there. I met Ms. Gordon, the guidance counselor, and after briefly describing my involvement with the family, I told her what I was after.

WORKER: The court has requested that Bobby be returned to school. Mrs. Jones has informed me that the school has refused to readmit him.

MS. GORDON: I know that the court has ordered Bobby back to school. However, when he was suspended, it was done by the district superintendent. Therefore, only that office can admit him to school.

I then asked for some clarification as to the meaning of Bobby's suspension. I wanted to know if it was common for suspended pupils to have to wait so long for readmission. She said Bobby's situation was different because he had been so disruptive (emphasis on disruptive) in school. She was emphatic about his fight with the lunchroom teacher last year. Further discussion revealed that there was a possibility that Bobby had been provoked. This came out when I shared with her Bobby's feelings about the situation. I revealed some of Bobby's characteristics that I felt the school should know about. My purpose was twofold: (1) I knew Bobby's record at that school would follow him, and I wanted to clear it up; (2) because of the demands placed on teachers, a child's struggles with the school and himself can often go unnoticed.

In response to the worker's direct statement of purpose and her willingness to listen, the guidance counselor began to open up with the worker. The worker listened and attempted to empathize with the counselor and her difficulties. It is in this sense that the worker tries to "be with" the client and the system at the same time. It would be easier not to hear the problems facing the system, but just as with any relationship, there must be genuine understanding before making demands is possible.

MS. GORDON: I have noticed that Bobby is a sensitive boy, and under all his toughness there's a scared child.

Ms. Gordon seemed frustrated by her inability to reach for the positive aspects that Bobby has, and I suspected that she was feeling defeated and threatened by my probing into the particulars surrounding Bobby's suspension. I said to her, "There's probably a desire on your part to be more responsive. You probably feel uncomfortable about not reaching Bobby." Miss Gordon, in a sincere but hesitant manner, had this to say:

MS. GORDON: Many of the teachers are insensitive, and there is a lack of cooperation on the part of the principal. Also, there is a large population of disruptive children who are frequently sent to the office. The lack of sufficient personnel for these children inhibits us from doing our job.

She continued for some time, talking about her frustrations. I made several unsuccessful attempts to refocus the discussion on Bobby. I then decided it was best to allow her to ventilate her feelings. I listened while she told me how she tries to help the children and how in the past she has had some real struggles in terms of getting the teachers to relate to the disruptive students. In an exasperated manner, she said, "The pupils do need help, but it is hard for the teachers to give it to them—especially with so many!" I chose this opportunity to get back to Bobby's problem.

WORKER: Ms. Gordon, I can understand how frustrating it is for you and the teachers, but it is also frustrating for Bobby. He wants to belong to the school, and I know that the school wants to help him.

MS. GORDON: (Very concerned) I will not send any record of this to Bobby's new school. I wouldn't want to prejudice the teachers against him. I will write in the records that Bobby is a sensitive boy who is bright and capable but who needs some special help. I feel this will give him a better chance of adjusting.

Ms. Gordon then gave me some names of people to contact at the district office. She said she had enjoyed talking to me because it is rare that she gets a chance to talk about her frustration. I suggested that we could talk some more and this comment led to a long discussion about obtaining a social worker for the school.

Because of the worker's stance and skill, the guidance counselor became an important ally in the effort to get Bobby back into school. Workers often wonder about the use of empathic skills on other staff. They ask, "Isn't it like 'social working' a staff member, and won't they resent it?" I believe that when they say this, they are using the term *social working* in its worst sense and that what they are referring to is an insincere, ritualistic empathic response, which the other staff members quickly experience as an attempt to manipulate them. In this case, there are real difficulties in dealing with children like Bobby in a school system, and if the worker expects the counselor and the staff to listen to Bobby, to understand his difficulties, and to empathize with his feelings, she must do the same with them. Of course, the guidance counselor and other staff people at the school are not clients; the worker needs to keep in mind that they are professional colleagues, each with different functions in relation to the same client. However, mutual respect and understanding between colleagues and a willingness to understand the complexities of a situation matter greatly if the worker is to help Bobby and his mother, as well as have a positive effect on the interaction between Bobby and the school. In process recordings of work with systems representatives, workers often run into trouble in the sessions just after the point where the problems in the system start to be shared. Workers demand empathy for clients despite refusing to empathize with colleagues.

The worker in this example next approached the supervisory level for further information. When she found out there might have been some reactions to her involvement, she reached for possible negative reactions.

At the district office, my strategy was to find out just what or who was preventing Bobby's return to school. I spoke with Ms. Reardon, guidance coordinator. Upon introducing myself, I was told that she had heard of me. I was surprised and asked what she had heard. She said she had seen my name on several court reports as the family social worker for St. Luke's Hospital. Ms. Gordon had also called and told her I was coming. Ms. Reardon seemed nervous, and I decided to explore her feelings about my involvement:

WORKER: Here I am trying to get back in school a child who has been out for a long period of time. You must feel somewhat annoyed by my efforts.

MS. REARDON: At first I felt that way, but my conversation with Ms. Gordon changed my mind. I am impressed with anyone who is interested in listening to problems of the school as well as the child.

WORKER: You must have had some bad experiences with social workers?

MS. REARDON: (With some irritation) Too many social agencies attack the schools. They make a big stink, and when the child is returned to school, they drop out of the picture. I don't like the fact that Bobby has been out of school so long, but I am waiting for a report from Child Guidance before returning him to school.

I began to reach for her positive feelings.

WORKER: I know you want the best for Bobby as well as for any child. With so many demands on counselors, it is easy for a child to get lost.

MS. REARDON: This is true. There are so many students like Bobby who have been out of school long periods of time. The parents think we don't care; but the children need so much and the teachers are unable to give it. We need help!

I then attempted to focus on Bobby's situation and at the same time recognize the global problems of the school system. I said I knew how difficult the school situation is.

WORKER: We need social workers and psychiatrists right in the school, and most of all we need sympathetic teachers. But I am concerned with what we can do together for Bobby.

MS. REARDON: (Seeming rather embarrassed) Oh! Forgive me! It's just that I had said to Ms. Gordon that I would explore the possibility of getting social services in at least one of the schools in the district.

I invited her to a meeting that Ms. Gordon and I were going to have to work to secure services for the school. I then made some suggestions about what we could do for Bobby. I asked her to call Child Guidance to determine when the report would be ready. When she phoned, she discovered that Child Guidance was under the impression that the court was going to do a psychiatric evaluation. Ms. Reardon then phoned the court and spoke to the probation officer, who informed her that their psychiatric evaluation was to be done on the parents only, and Child Guidance was to do the one on Bobby. Ms. Reardon told me, frustrated, "No one really communicates with each other." She angrily phoned Dr. Bennet, head of Child Guidance, and obtained a commitment to do a psychiatric on Bobby.

After acknowledging the problems, the worker made a demand for work by concentrating on the immediate problem facing Bobby. The supervisor's conversation with the probation officer was one illustration of how the complexity of the system can often lead to clients "falling through the cracks." In the following excerpt, the worker sensed the coordinator's underlying ambivalence and reached directly for the feelings. She wanted to be sure that her conversation with the coordinator was "real," because any unexpressed doubts would return to haunt Bobby later. An important additional step was the worker's recognition that she would have to begin a working relationship with the staff in Bobby's new school; she thus suggested modifications in the coordinator's description of the worker's role, in order to prevent misunderstanding.

I told Ms. Reardon of my earlier conversations with Bobby and Mrs. Jones and expressed their desire to have him back in school right away. Ms. Reardon said she also wanted him in school immediately, but I sensed some reservations. I reached for her ambivalent feelings.

WORKER: Part of you seems to want him back, and part of you doesn't.

MS. REARDON: You're right. I'm concerned about what school to send him to. Most of the other schools in the district are loaded with problem kids. There is one school that is better than others, but they are somewhat rigid. I want Bobby to have the best possible chance, but that's the only school that has room for him.

I offered a plan of action and reached for some feedback:

WORKER: If you could introduce me to the principal of the new school, perhaps we could work together with the teachers in a supportive role to broaden the chances of Bobby making a satisfactory adjustment.

Ms. Reardon felt that this was a good plan. She thought the school would appreciate my help. However, she suggested that I work with the school social worker and the teachers because they might resent my working directly with the principal. I said that I didn't fully understand what she was trying to tell me. She explained that the principal and the teachers have a "pretty rocky relationship," and she didn't want to get in the way of my attempts to help. She wrote a letter to the principal explaining who I was and what role I would have in working closely with the school to help Bobby. She ended the letter by stating that I should be consulted before decisions were made regarding anything Bobby has become involved in. I suggested that the letter be reworded so as not to give the impression of taking away decision powers. I told her to simply ask that I be involved as a resource person to enable them to make more informed decisions.

I gave recognition to Ms. Reardon for her assistance in getting movement on the reinstatement of Bobby:

WORKER: I know it isn't an easy decision to return Bobby to school, but I will be around to help when you need me.

As I was leaving, Ms. Reardon said I should contact her about the meeting to get social services in Ms. Gordon's school.

This worker recognized that getting Bobby back into school was just the beginning of the work, certainly not the final solution to the problem. She managed to keep in contact with the school and to monitor Bobby's progress so that when trouble arose, she would be there to help. In this important part of her work, her earlier efforts to develop a positive working relationship with the school staff paid dividends, giving her a basis of trust from which to work. The following is the worker's assessment of where things stand.

Bobby is in school. He is feeling quite nervous because the school is new, and he is having difficulty adjusting to a structured setting again. So far, he has not made any friends, and his relationship with classmates is strained. Bobby's teacher is kind of rigid, but she has begun to use me when she feels he is heading for difficulty. She is somewhat overexcited and afraid of not "bringing Bobby around." Her preoccupation with having a good class is strong, and she lets it get in the way of reaching for and understanding Bobby's needs.

The social worker in the school is in a rather precarious position. She is the only social worker in the school and is walking a rather thin line by trying to please everyone and "not rock the boat." She is also frustrated because she has strong feelings about teachers' insensitivity. Mrs. Jones is worried that Bobby might not continue in school. Therefore, she is constantly threatening him. Her threats seem to discourage Bobby and put ideas into his head about "playing hooky."

The worker continued by identifying her next steps in this case.

- Meet on a regular basis with the teacher to talk with her in an attempt to help her see that her feelings about success are preventing her from reaching Bobby.

- Work with the social worker who is in a bind and torn between the demands of the teachers and those of the children. I would like to see her work more closely with Bobby.

- Point out to Mrs. Jones that her negative attitude toward Bobby's progress in school can only complicate things for him—as well as for herself.

- Continue to encourage Bobby to talk about his fears and anxiety about being in a new school. Also, support him when things are going rough and let him know I am available to him.

- Secure tutorial help for Bobby.

These first steps by the worker, predicated on the assumption that it was best to reach for the system's strength and to "talk softly" rather than begin with a confrontation, led to the client's reconnection to the school system in a new and more helpful way. In addition, the worker made a major contribution toward strengthening not only her own professional relationship with the school system, but also with the relationship between her hospital and the schools. She would likely reap important benefits from this careful systems work if she needed to deal with this school system again. In addition, the worker's recognition of her responsibility for working with other professionals around the larger issue of availability of resources for children like Bobby reflects the broader social work function in action. Examples in the next chapter illustrate the steps involved in moving from Bobby's "private troubles" to the "public issues" affecting all of the children like Bobby.

Finally, although the worker was acting appropriately in working for Bobby's mother to overcome the immediate roadblocks to Bobby's readmission to school, the worker should also try to strengthen the relationship between Mrs. Jones and the school system. Other problems will come up and the worker may not always be available. Specifically, she should explore Mrs. Jones's description of the school's staff as "those people." Mrs. Jones was an African American, and the worker was not. An underlying issue of racism may exist. Certainly, Mrs. Jones may think that an African American parent would not be respected by a largely white school system. She may have found it difficult to be direct about this issue with the worker, and the worker may have been uncomfortable about raising it.

Work With a Psychiatrist in a Hospital Setting

In an example from a hospital setting, we see the classic conflict called **Who owns the client?** This is a maladaptive struggle in which helping professionals appear to fight over "ownership" of functional responsibility for a client. As the worker comes to grips with her feelings of anger toward a psychiatrist and works to clarify her role in her own mind and with her colleagues, she begins to play a more effective role as a third force.

RECORD OF SERVICE

Client Description and Time Frame

Cynthie is a 23-year-old woman, diagnosed schizophrenic, with whom I worked intermittently over a course of 6 months.

Description of the Problem

Cynthie's medical records revealed no fewer than 11 psychiatric admissions since the age of 14, three of these being at this hospital. During the time I knew her, she was in fact discharged and readmitted to our ward twice with a serious suicide attempt in between. To say the least, the ward staff considered Cynthie to be a chronic patient. It seemed clear that they had pretty well given up on her. They felt discouraged, exasperated, and disillusioned with what they interpreted as her lack of motivation, her lack of compliance to treatment (specifically, medication) and her recurrent readmissions. In my view, Cynthie had also taken on much of their discouragement and pessimism, which compounded her already hopeless and depressed view of her life.

My task, in the narrowest sense, was to find a suitable placement for Cynthie upon discharge. However, as time progressed, I soon realized that placement was the least of Cynthie's problems. I became aware that if I was to be of any help to her at all, I would need to redefine the problem as follows: First, by virtue of her admission to hospital, Cynthie had been thrown into a complex maze of hospital life. Within 6 months, she had been subjected to no fewer than three psychiatrists, two psychiatrists-in-training, two psychologists, four primary nurses, an agency social worker, the ward social worker, three boarding home coordinators, two day care program coordinators, two occupational therapists, two student nurses, and myself. She had been spared being assigned to medical students, but only because her "case" was considered chronic and thus not very interesting from a psychiatric point of view. Here was a multilayered hierarchy of staff, difficult for even the well-equipped person to deal with, let alone a frightened, depressed, sometimes psychotic, and definitely overmedicated woman like Cynthie. Second, two further issues became crucial: Cynthie's medication (and her refusal to take it) and Cynthie's plea (revealed to me in an interview with her) that, and I quote, "I just want to be a normal human being."

Over and above the placement problem, my task became at least threefold: First, to help Cynthie negotiate this complex hospital system to her advantage: a system whose representatives were making demands of her (e.g., insistence on medication) that Cynthie saw as being incompatible with her goal of becoming "normal." Second, to help the system reach past the image of Cynthie as a chronic, unmotivated, and hopeless patient. Third, to persist in my efforts to reach out to both these "clients": to Cynthie, on the one hand, who much of the time was so withdrawn, depressed, and uncommunicative that it was very difficult for me to reach her; and to the staff, on the other hand, who were often resistant and rigid in their view of Cynthie as "sick" and definitely short of "normal." The following record of service highlights some of my attempts and many of my misses in my effort to stand as a buffer between Cynthie and the system.

Summary of the Work

My Early Attempts to Reach for Cynthie's Feelings

Our first few meetings revealed an image of Cynthie not unlike the one described in her chart: depressed, withdrawn, rigid in posture, and almost mute. She rarely spoke, and when she did, she answered my questions with one or two words at best. I entered her room, having tuned in to her possible concerns, or so I thought. I asked if I could talk with her. No response. I sat beside her, gave a brief introduction, and stated my purpose: "Cynthie, I'm the social work student. I'll be helping you find a place to stay when you leave the hospital." (My sense of role was not clear yet.) Silence. "Have you thought about where you might live?" Long silence, not even looking at me. (I'm missing the boat here, I thought. Probably the hospital's concern, not hers.) "I'm sorry, Cynthie, I guess a place to stay is the least of your worries right now." No response. I continued, "I know it's been scary for you, being in hospital." No response, but now looking at me, although rather vacantly.

I reached rather hesitantly, for the taboo issue: "I know about Jean-Paul too, Cynthie, and I'm so sorry." (Three weeks prior to my arrival on the ward, Cynthie had been abruptly informed by a social worker that her 4-year-old son, Jean-Paul, had been permanently taken into care. The loss of her son had compounded Cynthie's anxiety and depression and had precipitated 2 solid weeks of pacing up and down the ward's corridors, screaming and wailing, "I want my son back" and prostrating herself on the corridor floors, refusing to move, particularly when offered medication.) I felt torn: reluctant, on the one hand, to broach the subject of Jean-Paul, knowing that the ward staff discouraged Cynthie's outbursts and fearing that I would precipitate one; and feeling, on the other hand, that she had little opportunity to express her grief. There was no outburst. (I admit to having felt relieved about that.) Just a long silence and then, looking at me, she simply said, "Can I have my son back?" She looked so sad. I didn't know what to say. "No, Cynthie, you can't." It sounded so blunt. "I'm sorry," I said. Long pause. I shared my feeling and made an offer: "I feel sad too, Cynthie. Do you want to talk about Jean-Paul?" No response. Long pause. "Or maybe you'd like to be alone now?" Another long pause. Finally, she said, "I'm OK, I'll be OK." I reassured her that I wanted to talk to her about Jean-Paul, if that's what she wanted. Long pause. "Perhaps tomorrow then," I said.

Making Demands for Work

In my later meetings with Cynthie, she continued to show little response. Her affect was blunted; her face was masklike and vacant. Occasionally she would say, "I'm sad," sometimes "I'm OK." I continued making efforts to put her feelings into words, to reach inside of silences (of which there were many), largely to no avail. I felt I was getting nowhere. Finally, I said, "I feel frustrated, Cynthie. I don't know what you're thinking. I don't know what you're feeling. I'd like to help you, Cynthie, but if you never talk to me I don't know how I can." Long silence. What was to come showed me a side of Cynthie I hadn't seen—one I would later convey to her psychiatrist on her behalf. "I just want to be a normal human being," she said. Now I was silent. Actually, I was floored. She said it without emotion. It sounded so pathetic and tragic. And not much to ask for, really. The least she deserved. I felt like saying, you're in the wrong place for that, Cynthie. (My resentment toward her treatment was surfacing.) But I didn't want to cut her off from the help she might get here. I believed, perhaps naively, that this system could help her be normal. I sensed her feelings of being stuck and overwhelmed. Or maybe these were my own feelings. I partialized her concern: "It's just hard sometimes to know where to start," I said. I asked for clarification: "What would normal mean to you, Cynthie?" to which she replied rather solidly, "No more psychiatrists, no more mental hospitals, no more medication."

Identifying With Both Cynthie and Her Doctor

It was unlikely I could help her negotiate these goals within the context of this system. But perhaps in some small way, I wanted her to know that there was a next step. I know Cynthie had become less and less compliant to taking her meds—a growing concern for the staff. Having experienced a round of antidepressants myself at one time, I recalled my own feelings: feeling numb, deadened, unreal, not myself, slowed down, too numb to talk or care. In short, not normal. I wondered if Cynthie was feeling the same way. I shared this experience and reached for her feedback. Long pause. "The pills make me crazy," she said. "I'm scared. . . . They're trying to kill my brain. They're killing my brain." I acknowledged her fear and tried, with difficulty, to be with her and the system at the same time: "The side effects are scary, Cynthie—I had them too—like you can't control your own body. But the doctor gives you the pills to help you, not to kill you. Remember how you felt before?" I hoped to help Cynthie see that the pills had helped. She said, "Before, I thought

I was Jesus. I thought demons were crawling on my body. I covered my body in paint. I felt crazy." Cynthie was unable to talk to her doctor about her fear of the pills. We agreed that I would talk to her doctor and that I would help her talk to him.

Helping Cynthie's Doctor Understand Her Feelings

First, some background: My first encounters with Dr. Renton were something short of positive. I had found him patronizing and condescending and wondered if Cynthie experienced him in a similar way. He was the patriarch on the ward, with the nurses—all women—seemingly willing to jump at his every command. Everyone knew their place, and although there were resentments, these were never directly expressed (including my own).

From the moment I was introduced as the social work student, I sensed he had written me off as brainless. He rarely missed a chance to "put in a dig." Like the time in rounds, when we were discussing Tourette's (a central nervous system disorder). I'd studied Tourette's and knew of its treatment. To which Dr. Renton asked, "Oh, did you see that on *Quincy*, or something?" I rose to the bait, responding defensively, "No, actually, Dr. Renton, I read it in *Harrison's*" (a well-known and standard text-book in internal medicine). That shut him up. I had won the point, but not the war.

Dr. Renton insisted on seeing me as "the placement person." Therapy, as he called it, was psychiatry's domain. It frustrated him, he said, that "everyone around here wants to do therapy." He actually approached me one time while I was talking with Cynthie in her room and demanded to know what we were talking about. I was beginning to wonder—who was more paranoid, patient or doctor? Dr. Renton's argument was that the only one qualified to understand the patient's "complete clinical picture" was the psychiatrist. And one could not understand the so-called complete clinical picture, according to Dr. Renton, without medical training, of course. It started looking like a contest of "Who knows the patient best?"

It also really bothered me that Cynthie's case was always presented last or close to last in Dr. Renton's rounds. This indicated to me the low degree of Cynthie's interest or importance to him, or maybe his level of frustration. The focus rarely shifted from diagnostic issues and from endless discussions about which medication and in what dosage to use. Cynthie's feelings were always overlooked.

In retrospect, two things were clear: First, I had let my resentment toward Dr. Renton get in the way of any real work with him. I had written him off as a "jerk" and refused to reach for his feelings, convincing myself that he probably had very few. Second, I had missed every opportunity to clarify my role (mostly because I wasn't yet clear on what that role was). If I didn't want to be seen simply as a "placement person," it would be my responsibility to tell Dr. Renton exactly how I could help. Cynthie's medication problem gave me this chance, as the following account shows.

I approached Dr. Renton and asked if he had a few minutes to talk to me about Cynthie. "I'm still working on a placement for her," I said, reminding him. "You know, I guess I've never said it this way" (in an attempt to clarify my role) "but I also think an important part of my work with Cynthie is to help you help her, and that's why I need to talk to you." Crediting his work, I continued, "I know how hard you've been working to stabilize Cynthie on her medication," then empathizing with his situation, "and how frustrating it must be for you and for the nurses with Cynthie acting out all the time and refusing her pills." I had his full attention. "Well, that's true," he said, "It isn't easy." Sharing my own experience, I said, "I find it hard to reach her at the best of times too, but while I was talking to her today she said some

incredible things I thought you should know about . . . about not taking her pills."
"Oh, like what?" he asked. "Well, this probably won't surprise you, but she's really
scared. She's scared of taking her pills. And do you know why?" (He shook his head
to say no.) "She thinks we're trying to kill her brain." "Did she say that?" he asked.
"Yes, she did. I wouldn't take them either, if I thought that, would you?" "Obviously
not," he said.

I continued, "She also said—and this was really sad—that all she wants is to be a
normal human being. Do you think she'd feel more normal without side effects?
I was wondering if you thought she might be toxic." "Well, I think you have a point.
I'll check into it today," he said, "and we'll get this cleared up." I suggested a three-
way meeting with Dr. Renton, Cynthie, and myself. "I've had some luck getting her
to talk about her medication," I said, "but I think she needs some reassurance from
you." He agreed.

Ignoring the Lurking Negative and Paying for It Later
All the while, I continued to look for a suitable placement for Cynthie. I soon came
to realize that Cynthie's "private trouble" was indeed a "public issue": There was a
serious shortage of suitable homes for women like Cynthie, and those that did exist
had incredible waiting lists. Finally, en route to a home that was willing to take her,
Cynthie announced to me, "I want to live with Jurgen" (her ex-husband). Oh no,
I thought, I don't want to hear this, here we go again: Cynthie had bounced back
and forth from Jurgen to hospital to Jurgen to hospital. At one point, Jurgen even
had Cynthie prostituting herself. I felt she needed a supportive environment, some
stability in her life—something she'd never had. "Cynthie," I said, "I can't force
you to go to the boarding home, but I really think you should give it a try." What
I failed to do was reach for her feelings. She was probably scared stiff. Living in the
boarding home was my agenda, not hers. Besides, what gave me the right to
make that decision for her anyway? Five days later Cynthie was back in hospital,
having stabbed herself in the abdomen with a kitchen knife at the boarding home,
missing all her vital organs, thank God. I came away feeling that I had set her up
for failure.

Sabotaged by the System
The final blow came in early February. Cynthie, it had been decided, would be
transferred to another hospital. "She's too chronic for our ward," announced
Dr. Renton. "She needs long-term care, so I'm transferring her. And I've decided
that she's not to be told." The orders were written in the chart, just like that. I was
furious and shared my feelings with Dr. Renton: "I can understand the transfer,
Dr. Renton" (I guess I had rationalized that perhaps they could help her) "but not
preparing her for it! I think that's pretty crummy! She deserves at least that, don't
you think?" "Look, I know it seems crummy," he started. I interrupted, "It doesn't
seem crummy, it is crummy." He went on, "Look, in my opinion, she's a serious
suicide risk, and if she's told now, she'll probably elope and kill herself. I can't and
won't risk that." "I see your dilemma," I said, "but I can't agree with your decision.
I think you're shortchanging Cynthie." (Actually, I also felt shortchanged and ripped
off. Without choice, my ability to help her had been cut off.) Dr. Renton and
I agreed to disagree.

I was on the ward when they came to get Cynthie. She cried when they told her.
Within 10 minutes, she was gone. I did manage to stop her in the hall on her way
out. I felt like a traitor. I gave her a hug. "I'm sorry you're going, Cynthie," I said.
"It's OK," she said to me, exactly as she had many times before. And off she went.

Current Status of the Problem

Where the Problem Stands Now

Cynthie is out of the hospital and back with her parents, in another city. Fran, the student nurse who was also working with Cynthie, had taken it upon herself to phone Cynthie's parents. Up until then they had been unsupportive and had "written Cynthie off." Fran was "severely reprimanded" by her nursing supervisor for having acted in an unprofessional way and for putting her own needs ahead of Cynthie's. I thought what Fran had done was great, and surprisingly, so did Dr. Renton.

Strategies for Intervention

- To continue "working on" Dr. Renton. I think he has potential.

If the worker is going to be able to tap the "potential" she sees in Dr. Renton, she will have to tune in to the implications of patient suicides in a psychiatric setting. The strong reactions of the system to Cynthie's suicide attempt can be viewed as a signal of serious, unresolved issues in this area. Helping systems can be very unhelpful to their own staff members during times of stress. Crisis heightens the defensiveness of the system so that it places blame instead of providing support through some form of mutual aid. Chapter 16 explores ways in which a worker can move from a specific example, such as this case, to trying to deal with the underlying problem in the system.

Confrontation, Social Pressure, and Advocacy

If we think of agencies and institutions as social systems, by employing the organismic model used earlier to describe the group, some of the processes observed in small groups may also apply to larger systems. One such idea is Lewin's (1951) description of systems as maintaining a quasi-stationary social equilibrium in which customs and social habits create an inner resistance to change (see Chapter 12). This resistance to change is found in the individual, the family, the group, the community, agencies, and institutions. In the model presented thus far, the worker has endeavored to open up communications between clients and relevant systems (between the individual and the group, for example) in order to help overcome the obstacles to the inherent common ground. The worker has at all times been reaching for the desire for change within both the client and the system.

Because of their inherent resistance to change, systems and their representatives do not always respond with a willingness to deal with the obstacles. Even with a worker who understands the system's problems and who makes every effort to influence the system in a positive manner may make no progress. In such situations confrontation and social pressure are required. That is, some additional force is needed to overcome the system's resistance to change and to show the system it needs to respond in new ways to the client. This additional force upsets the quasi-stationary equilibrium and makes the system more open to change.

This argument resonates with crisis theory, which suggest that individuals and families are most open to change when a crisis makes maintaining a situation untenable. Under conditions where negotiation has failed or has been declined, the resistance of the system's ambivalence is so strong that it dominates the interaction. Something is needed to upset the dysfunctional equilibrium.

The following example illustrates how a worker did just this by acting as an advocate for an overwhelmed client who was facing a housing crisis after being ignored by an unyielding bureaucracy. As with the previous example, the worker was not hired as a client advocate per se, but considered advocacy part of his role as a worker. In this case, the worker was employed by a child welfare agency in a large Canadian city. His client was a French-speaking woman named Mrs. Belanger, age 35, who was a single parent with four children. She had requested placement of her children with the agency because of her severe depression after her husband left her. After several interviews, the worker saw one of Mrs. Belanger's precipitating crises: She had been forced to move twice within the past 6 months because of changes in ownership of the buildings she lived in. Adequate and affordable accommodations were not available. As an alternative to accepting the children for placement, the worker proposed the following plan: Mrs. Belanger would continue seeing a psychiatrist to help her with her depression; the worker would arrange for homemaker services to help her with the children; he would also work with her to try to solve the housing problem. The client agreed. The worker felt this was a good example of a situation in which, with personal support and help in dealing with the housing system, the client had the strength to maintain herself and her children. By not providing adequate housing for this family, society bore part of the responsibility for the problem. Thus, the worker began a 4-month odyssey that provided a lesson in the complexity of the housing system and evidence of the power of persistence.

As a first step, after consulting with Mrs. Belanger, the worker addressed a letter to the city housing authority. An excerpt from that letter follows:

September 26

This letter is on behalf of Mrs. Belanger and her application for a 3-bedroom unit.

Certainly this is a matter of urgency, as Mrs. Belanger and her children have been obliged to move twice in a very short time as her landlords have sold out. There is cause for serious concern, as Mrs. Belanger's health demands a stable environment. Due to the limits of her financial situation and her health, her choice of adequate shelter depends on your assistance.

Mrs. Belanger, as I know her, is a quiet, reserved woman with very good housekeeping standards and well-behaved children. It is my opinion that she would be a very good tenant.

To keep her family together and maintain the home, it is imperative that she relocate to a suitable unit in a French-speaking area of her choice as soon as possible.

Thank you for whatever assistance you can offer to the Belanger family.

As the worker developed his case for Mrs. Belanger, he enlisted the aid of allies. The first was the psychiatrist who was treating the client. The psychiatrist's letter to the placement manager read as follows:

September 26

The above-named client, who is on your waiting list for housing, has been under my direct care for 2 years. She has exhausted her own possibilities in seeking housing for herself and her four children. It is imperative and urgent that suitable accommodation be found this month, as otherwise her mental health may decline once again with repercussions for herself and the children.

A return letter indicated that the client did not meet the residency requirements for housing within the city limits. The area Mrs. Belanger lived in was technically in another municipality surrounded by the larger city. The placement manager suggested that the worker should contact the provincial government housing authority for help. The worker repeated the letters to the housing authority of the smaller municipality. Because of a shortage of housing in the French-speaking area—a shortage that the municipality had done little to rectify—the only help available to Mrs. Belanger was an apartment in an English-speaking area. Becuase Mrs. Belanger could not speak English, she would have been socially isolated in this area, which would have compounded her problems.

The worker made sure to consult with Mrs. Belanger at each step of the process to be sure she understood and agreed with the next steps. She felt identified with her present housing area and feared moving into an English-speaking housing project. They agreed to try to have the residency requirements waived in order to obtain housing in the city. A second letter was sent to the placement manager of the city housing authority with additional letters of support from the homemaker service. In addition, the worker arranged a meeting with the mayor of the smaller municipality, at which time he raised the problem of Mrs. Belanger and received assurances that the mayor would do his best to help.

Despite such promises, the months dragged on with no action. The worker arranged a meeting with the placement officer of the city housing authority and his client. His impression was that the officer was not as interested in the client's dilemma as he was in applying the regulations. As the worker encountered one frustration after another, he noted his own increasing depression. After only 2 months in the shoes of the client attempting to negotiate government bureaucracies, he felt it would not be long before he began to show clinical symptoms of depression. This increased his anger at the way his client and her children were lost in the complexity of agencies supposedly established to serve their needs. With the agreement of Mrs. Belanger and his supervisor, the worker wrote the following letter to the federal government representative (Member of Parliament):

November 21

I am writing on behalf of one of your constituents, Mrs. Belanger, who is having serious difficulty in finding adequate accommodations within her budgetary limitations.

The enclosed letters indicate a series of steps that we have taken on behalf of the Belanger family in support of her application for low-rent housing. I urgently requested that her doctor and visiting homemaker outline their involvement to support the request. Letters were delivered and immediate personal interviews were held with the mayor, Mrs. Johnson of the Provincial Ministry, and Mr. Rolf of the Housing Authority. Unfortunately, we have come to a dead end.

As you will note in the accompanying letter from Mrs. Helflin, Mrs. Belanger has exerted many frustrating efforts on her own behalf. She, too, has been unsuccessful. She has been forced to move twice within the past year, due, in both cases, simply to a change of landlords through sales. Another move will occur at the end of the month, as she has received a notice to vacate.

These necessary moves, due to no fault of Mrs. Belanger and her children, are very seriously affecting her health, as is documented in the attached letters written by various agencies on her behalf. Needless to say, the housing problem and a resulting depression of the mother can only have negative consequences for the children. Our concern is to prevent what will inevitably occur as Mrs. Belanger's health deteriorates further: placement of her children in foster homes.

I am asking that you intervene immediately on behalf of your constituent. I have no doubt that you will be far more effective than my efforts have been.

Over the telephone, the secretary of the Member of Parliament promised to look into the situation. The urgency of the problem increased as Mrs. Belanger received an eviction notice. She was to be out of her apartment by the end of the week. It was at this point in the process that the worker presented this case at a workshop I was leading for his agency's staff on systems work—the skills involved in helping clients negotiate agencies and institutions. He reviewed his efforts to date, reading excerpts from the letters and describing his interviews from memory. At the end of the presentation, he shared his utter frustration and anger at what was happening to his client and his feeling of powerlessness to do anything about it. I could tell from the reactions of his colleagues, and the looks on their faces, that they were feeling the same sense of impotency as they reflected on similar cases from their own caseloads. An excerpt from the workshop follows:

WORKSHOP LEADER: I can tell this case has come to mean a great deal for you. It probably symbolizes all of the cases where you feel deeply about the injustices your clients face and how little you seem to be able to do about it. It must hurt and make you feel bitter.

WORKER: What good is all the talk about systems work if Mrs. Belanger ends up with lousy housing and depressed, and then turns her kids over to us?

WORKSHOP LEADER: I don't think it is over yet. There is always some next step you can take. Does anyone have any ideas?

WORKSHOP PARTICIPANT: The only thing I would feel like doing is screaming about how mad I am about this.

WORKSHOP LEADER: Well, why don't you? If Mrs. Belanger is willing, isn't it time somebody brought her problem to the public's attention? How are they going to know about this kind of thing happening to people if you don't tell them?

WORKER: I'm a representative of the agency. How can I go to the papers?

WORKSHOP LEADER: Sounds like you need to do some work within the agency to gain support for taking a more public step. Have you spoken to the agency director about that possibility?

WORKER: No, I haven't. I assumed the agency wouldn't want this kind of publicity.

WORKSHOP LEADER: Why don't you ask your director? He's right here.

In the conversation that followed, the director indicated that he felt social pressure was needed at times, and that this seemed to be one of those times. He defined the parameters within which he felt his staff could operate. He wanted to be informed about cases as they progressed and to be assured that all steps had been taken before going to the press. After that, he would cooperate with staff if they felt that public awareness was the only step left. The director and the worker agreed to meet after the workshop to plan how to use the media in this case. What I found interesting was that the worker had assumed, without asking, that the agency administration would reject going public.

Workers often take this position, and in some cases they indeed run into stiff opposition. This means that they have some work to do within their own agency systems to obtain allies and to try to change a policy that categorically rejects the use of agency social pressure on behalf of the client. If unsuccessful, they may have to consider changing jobs or taking other steps to bring about changes in agency policy. It would be a mistake, however, to assume the rejection in advance without even trying. In such a case, the worker avoids getting involved in a confrontation but can still blame the agency for the problem. Workers have said that it takes a lot of courage to challenge their own agency system, and I agree. Social change is never easy. However, a sense of professional identification that extends beyond being an agency staff member requires that workers take some risks along the way.

After a discussion with the client in which she agreed with the strategy, the worker contacted the local reporter who covered the social services in that city. The following edited excerpt is from the newspaper story on the case of Mrs. Belanger, entitled "'Take My Children,' Mom Pleads."

November 29

If Mrs. B. doesn't get help within the month, she will be forced to turn her children over to the Children's Aid Society.

Ron Strong, a Children's Aid Worker, said the separated woman's plight is critical as she and her four children continue to survive on a $464-a-month mother's allowance she receives.

This has been her only source of income since her husband left in April.

The problem is housing. The family finds itself forced to move this weekend for the third time this year because the house in which they are living has been sold.

She has two boys and two girls between the ages of 8 and 12 and needs a three-bedroom accommodation that will not eat up half the monthly income, Mr. Strong said.

An added problem is that Mrs. B. only speaks French and must live in a French-speaking area. She has been living in ———, which, Mr. Strong said, is causing her another problem.

In living outside the community boundary, technically she is not eligible for a housing unit under the Housing Authority until she has been living in the city for a year.

"And the Provincial Housing Corp. has no units in other sections of the city—only further out—and even then they haven't offered her anything," Mr. Strong said.

"She has given up all hope," he said. She has already asked the Society eight times if they will take the children.

"The Society is trying to prevent taking them," Mr. Strong said. "I have been working almost full time to find some solution to the problem."

Is there a solution?

"City Housing can waive the eligibility in December, and they must do it—there is no other route to go," he said. "If it doesn't happen, the Society will have to take the children."

"She is a good mother and tenant," Mr. Strong said. "But another month and the situation will move to emergency proportions."

A few days after the appearance of this article, the worker and Mrs. Belanger met with the federal representative, the Member of Parliament, who was somewhat upset at the publicity. Nevertheless, he offered his support. A call was received soon after from the placement officer of the city housing authority informing the worker that the 1-year residency requirement was being waived. Soon after, Mrs. Belanger was offered a suitable apartment. Interestingly, the psychiatrist treating Mrs. Belanger reported that during the time she and the worker were involved in the fight for housing—a period of almost 4 months—her psychotic symptoms disappeared. Acting in her own self-interest and starting to affect others, rather than being passively acted on by the system, proved quite therapeutic. The experience appeared to be good for the worker as well, as some of his symptoms of depression, sometimes known as the "child welfare worker blues," were also relieved.

This example shows that mediating between a client and the social system sometimes requires the worker to act as an advocate for the client. In this example, the worker made sure that the client was involved in each step of the decision-making process. In dealing with the system (the agencies), he was acting as if he believed they could provide the services if social pressure were employed. In a sense, he used pressure to make a demand for work and reached for the strength of the system. Another key factor was that he acted openly and honestly along the way. My view is that, although tactics involving deceit may seem helpful in the short run, they always return to haunt the worker in significant ways. The worker involved allies wherever he could (the psychiatrist, homemakers, and so forth). He was persistent and did not give in after encountering the first obstacles. Nor was he fooled by the system's efforts to "cool him off" by passing the buck or making vague promises of action. He made sure to involve and inform his own agency system, so that his agency (the director, supervisors) would feel part of the process. Most important, he maintained a belief in the idea that there is always some next step that can be taken.

Because we do not have detailed process recordings of the conversation between the worker and the representatives of the systems he dealt with, we cannot analyze the use of skills that characterized the work. However, Heyman (1971) addressed the questions related to worker skills used in establishing a relationship with the systems representative at points of conflict. Using the example of a social worker identified with tenants about to implement a rent strike, he describes in detail the way a worker attempted to play a mediating role and provide assistance to the landlord, which in turn could prove helpful to his clients. The key to the worker's effectiveness was that he was always open to the side of the landlord's ambivalence that ran counter to the strong forces of resistance to accepting the worker's help. As long as workers do not view the system as completely closed, one-dimensional, and without ambivalence, they can employ all of the helpful skills identified thus far.

The earlier example concerning the housing system raised another area of concern for the agency. Mrs. Belanger was one example of a client experiencing problems with public housing. However, many poor people in town who were not clients of the agency also had these problems. This worker had invested a great deal of time in this case, something that clearly would not be possible for every case on a worker's caseload, let alone the larger population. What would happen to a Mrs. Belanger who did not have a worker-advocate? In this way, the individual example of the problem facing Mrs. Belanger raised for the agency and its professional staff the general problem of housing for the poor. Almost every individual case raises some issue of public policy. Although workers cannot tackle all such issues at one time, they have a responsibility to deal with some of them. In this agency, a social policy committee was established to provide leadership in identifying and developing staff programs for dealing with the social policy implications of the problems facing individual clients. In the next chapter, we explore this aspect of the professional's dual responsibility for both clients' private troubles and society's public issues.

Professional Impact on the System

In the rest of the chapter we discuss ways in which social workers can have professional impact on policies and services within their own and other agencies and institutions as well as on broader social policies that affect clients. We also examine how social workers can bring about positive change in the interprofessional relationships within a setting and between settings. Illustrations of social workers attempting to influence larger systems, professional teams, and so on will demonstrate the functional role of mediation that lies at the core of the interactional model.

The term **professional impact** is defined in this chapter as the activities of social workers designed to effect changes in the following two areas:

1. Policies and services in their own agency and other agencies and institutions, as well as broader social policies that affect clients
2. The work culture that influences interstaff relationships within their own agency and with other agencies and institutions

This breakdown is somewhat analogous to the division cited earlier between the content of the work and the process (way of working). Interest in the first area emerges directly from the worker's practice experience. As workers address the concerns of individual clients, they become aware of general problems affecting categories of clients. For example, in our recent illustration, the worker saw that Mrs. Belanger's particular difficulty was a specific example of the general problem of inadequate public housing. The worker's attempt to heighten his agency's interest in the problem of housing and his efforts to influence housing policies as part of his role as agency worker and as a member of a professional association are examples of professional impact on the agency, community institutions, and social policies. Similarly, a worker may point out, to the agency administration, an agency policy that negatively affects service to his clients; this is also an attempt to have professional impact within the system.

The second arena for professional impact is the work culture that exists within the agency staff system and between staff members of different agencies. When dealing with clients, workers constantly meet and interact with other professionals. Services to clients are directly affected by how well interdependent staff members work with one another.

The staff system in an agency develops a culture similar to that of a group. The barriers to the effective development of staff culture are also similar. In fact, my observations of staff systems have indicated that difficulties between staff members often occupy the greatest portion of staff time and energy. When one asks staff members what their prime source of frustration is (particularly in large and complex systems and especially if the staff is interdisciplinary), they usually answer, "Interstaff relations." Similar problems often exist between staff members of different agencies within the community that are supposed to be working in partnership to meet clients' needs. Some clients suffer because workers in two settings are no longer talking to each other. Efforts by staff members to improve interstaff relationships and to create a more productive culture for work constitute the second area for professional impact.

In addition to providing direct service to clients, then, helping professionals have a functional responsibility for attempting constructive impact on these two major areas—policies and services, and the work culture of the system. Of course, a worker cannot deal with every social policy, program, or staff interactional issue that emerges from the work; indeed, merely identifying all of the concerns would be a major task. Nevertheless, a worker can tackle a limited number of issues, one at a time. For instance, a group of colleagues can begin working on an issue even though it may take months or even years to resolve. Recall from Part II that the process of taking a problem and breaking it down into smaller parts (partializing) and then attacking the problem by taking a first step, followed by a second, and so on, is helpful for clients. This same process is also useful for tackling questions of professional impact.

Nonetheless, attempting professional impact is not easy. Let us review some of the factors that can make it hard. In addition to the magnitude of the problems, workers have to deal with many of their own feelings about change. Workers too often feel helpless, viewing themselves as incapable of exerting meaningful influence. Our socialization experiences have generally encouraged us to conform to social structures. Families, schools, peer groups, and work settings do not always encourage individual initiative. Although all systems have a profound stake in encouraging members to differentiate themselves and to make contributions by challenging the system and asserting their individuality, neither the system nor the members always recognize this need, let alone act on it. Encouraging members to be an integrated part of the system is an important imperative; however, the system often achieves this at the expense of individual initiative. Efforts to integrate individuals can develop system norms that encourage conformity.

Given such life experiences, many workers tend to view taking responsibility for professional impact as a major change in their relationship to systems in general and to people in authority in particular. Even if workers are willing to strive for social change, experiences in agencies often discourage any further efforts. When workers face resistance to their first attempts, they often fail to recognize the agency's potential for change and give up. The same worker who skillfully deals with resistance from a client, understanding that resistance is a central part of the change process, forgets this insight when dealing with the agency system. If workers remember that agencies are dynamic systems, open to change but also simultaneously resistant, then an initial rebuff does not necessarily mean closure to the worker's effort. Change may require persistence on the worker's part. Timing is also important. Like individuals and groups, agencies grow and change over time. An attempt to deal with a problem at one point may be blocked, but the agency might welcome the same effort at a later stage in the agency's development.

In many situations, workers are simply afraid to assert themselves. If the agency culture has discouraged previous efforts, or if workers feel they will be viewed as "troublemakers" and that their jobs may be on the line, then they will be reluctant to raise questions about services or policies. In some cases, such as extreme defensiveness of administrators or political pressures on the agency, these fears are well founded. Workers in such situations have to decide for themselves, in light of their personal situations and their feelings about the professional ethical issues involved in the problem, whether they are willing to take the risk. If an effort to bring about change is risky in a particular setting, then workers would be wise to gather allies before they try.

While I have advocated these views over the years in my teaching and writing, I have done so from a relatively safe position as a tenured faculty member in a university. Tenure is designed to create the freedom to take risks in teaching, research, and participation in university governance. Many years ago, while acting as chair of the Faculty Council in a university whose employment I have since left, all of my theories, practice principles, and skills related to professional impact were put to the test over an issue of academic freedom. After exhausting all avenues of negotiation, the Faculty Council faced the need to release a controversial report. When I received a letter from the university administration containing a thinly veiled threat to revoke my tenure and fire me if I proceeded, I felt the full impact of the risks involved in attempting to confront an unyielding system. The report was issued without execution of the threat. Although my position on the responsibility of the social worker to improve her or his system has not changed, this experience has helped me to understand better why acting is not possible in some situations.

In some situations, workers remain uninvolved because they held preconceived notions about the administration, not because any actual experience in the agency had led them to fear reprisal. Nonetheless, trying to make a professional impact often requires courage. Lack of time also greatly affects a worker's ability to challenge the system. Some agencies demand impossible caseloads; in such circumstances, becoming involved in agency or social change seems completely unrealistic. However, simply dealing with the working situation would be a first effort at systemic change. Often, outside organizations such as professional associations or unions are the best mediums for effecting such changes.

In summary, the complexity and magnitude of issues tend to discourage professional impact efforts. Workers' general feelings about asserting themselves, as well as specific experiences in agencies, may act as deterrents. Fear of losing their jobs or experiencing other retribution may also be an obstacle to involvement. Finally, unrealistically high caseloads may obstruct workers' attempts at professional impact.

From Individual Problems to Social Action

In developing his position on the function of the social work profession, Schwartz (1969) argues that the worker must be concerned with both the specific problems faced by the client and the social issues raised by those problems. Objecting to a professional trend of splitting these two concerns, so that some professionals deal only with the problems of the individual (clinicians) while others focus solely on problems of social change (activists), he argues that every professional has a responsibility for addressing both concerns. He cites C. Wright Mills (1959) as one who refused to accept this dichotomy between individual concerns and issues of policy:

> In our own time, C. Wright Mills has seen most clearly into the individual-social connections identified with social struggle. He pointed up the distinction between what he called the "personal troubles of milieu" and the "public issues of social structure," and noted that trouble is a private matter, while issue is a public one. Most important, he stressed that each must be stated in the terms of the other, and of the interaction between the two. (Schwartz, 1969, p. 37)

Schwartz points out that splitting these two worker responsibilities is impossible if "we understand that a private trouble is simply a specific example of a public issue, and that a public issue is made up of many private troubles" (Schwartz, 1969, p. 37). Recognizing that agencies and social institutions can be complex and ambivalent, he suggests the worker's function should be to act as a "third force" or a "hedge against the system's own complexity" (p. 37).

> Where . . . such a function originates within the agency itself, the image is that of a built-in monitor of the agency's effectiveness and a protection against its own rigidities. From such a position, the social worker moves to strengthen and reinforce both parties in the client-agency relationship. With the client—and with mutual aid systems of clients—the worker offers the agency service in ways designed to help them reach out to the system in stronger and more assertive ways, generalizing from their private experiences to agency policy wherever possible and avoiding the traps of conformity and inertia. In many instances, the activity thus produced is similar to that desired by the advocates—except that the movement is towards the service, and the workers are interested in the process rather than having lost faith in it. With the system—colleagues, superiors and other disciplines—the worker feeds in his direct experience with the struggles of his clients, searches out the staff stake in reaching and innovating, and brings administration wherever possible into direct contact with clients reaching for new ways of being served. (p. 38)

Earlier in this chapter, we saw several examples of workers helping clients reach out to the system "in stronger and more assertive ways." The following examples show the worker raising general issues with the system that result from his or her experience with clients.

Illustrations of Agency Change

The worker who is alive to the dynamic tension between clients' needs and the agency service will look for opportunities to generalize from direct practice experience to policy issues. Noticing a particular problem emerging regularly in the caseload may signal a need for modification in agency service. For example, one worker who dealt with groups of unmarried mothers noted the strain that the mothers' parents seemed to feel. When she shared her observations with other workers in her department, a highly successful group was developed for these clients. Several illustrations of this process follow.

Hospital Emergency Room Service For a hospital worker, repeated comments from patients in his ward group about the strain of their first contact in the emergency room (as in lack of attention for hours, which heightened their anxiety and that of their relatives, and difficulty in getting information) led her to explore the problems with the emergency room staff. The record of the start of this work follows.

> I asked for a meeting with the head nurse of Emergency. I met Ms. Thomas at the end of her shift, and I commented on how tired she looked. She told me it had been a particularly rough day complicated by two car accidents with four victims. I acknowledged that I could see it was really hectic and thanked her for taking some time to talk with me. I explained that I had been meeting with ward groups on 2 East and that a common theme had been patients complaining about their entry into the hospital through the emergency room. I told her I was raising this because I thought she would want to know about the problems and also I wanted to better understand the difficulty from the staff's point of view so I could handle this issue when it arose at meetings. Ms. Thomas seemed irritated at my statements, stiffened physically, and said

she and her staff didn't have time to sit and talk to patients the way social workers did.

I quickly reassured her that I was not coming down to criticize her or her staff. I told her that I had worried that she would misinterpret my intentions, and I thought that she had done just that. Would she give me a chance to explain? I said, "I realize it's no picnic down here, and part of the reason I stopped in was to see if there was any way social service could be of more help. Working under pressure the way you do is rough." Ms. Thomas seemed to relax a bit, and I asked how I might be able to help. She said she thought it would be helpful to have a social worker around more often. I told her that might be one way. I wondered if we could arrange a meeting with the other staff members where I could share the feedback and get their reactions. I had no set ideas yet but perhaps if we put our heads together, we could come up with some. She agreed, and we set a time to meet.

The worker's directness and statement of purpose helped to clarify the boundaries for the discussion. She responded directly to the indirect cues of defensiveness by sharing her own concerns. By acknowledging the real difficulties and offering to examine how she, in her function as social worker, might help, the worker quickly changed the situation from one staff member criticizing another to one in which two staff members, each with their own function, carry on the work of using patient feedback to examine their services. The meeting that followed was successful, with staff members telling the social worker about the difficulties they were facing. In addition, they identified changes they could make in response to the patient feedback. The worker, for her part, developed an open-ended group in a quiet corner of the waiting room for waiting patients and relatives. The group met for half an hour at midmorning to allow patients and relatives to ask questions and to deal with some of their anxieties about the emergency situation. Both staff and patients found the group to be helpful.

At a later date, the worker suggested that occasional meetings be held with patients, before they left the hospital, to discuss their experiences in the emergency room and to provide feedback for hospital staff. The bimonthly meetings proved to be effective. Both the social worker and the other staff members in Emergency approached other parts of the hospital to enlist their aid when required. For example, a trial program was established with young volunteers to run a children's group in the adjacent outpatient clinic waiting area to address the problem of bored children roaming the halls.

In both the case of the group for parents of unwed mothers and the example of the emergency room problems, a sense of dual responsibility for dealing with both the specific problems and the policy issues led the workers to take their first steps. In these examples, the workers made use of direct client feedback in their efforts to influence service. Sometimes the feedback is more indirect, so that the worker must examine the relationship between client problems and agency service closely to observe the connections. In such situations, again, the worker can apply some of the dynamics used to understand processes in the group and family. For example, earlier chapters pointed out how deviant group members may be signaling a problem in the group-as-a-whole. Problems in a system, such as irregular or deviant behavior by groups of clients, may also be providing an indirect form of feedback.

Rehabilitation Institution for Paraplegics One example of using principles from group work to understand more complex systems is drawn from a rehabilitation institution for paraplegic patients. The institution had a rule against patients going home on weekends, because of a government policy that paid for a patient only on days they slept at the hospital. Systematic work by the staff and administration, including organizing feedback by patients to government officials, led to a change in the policy, and weekend passes were authorized. Three months after implementation of the new policy, the administrator called in the worker to raise a problem. He pointed out that patients were returning to the hospital with serious bedsores and that if this continued, he would have to suspend the pass program. Before instituting such a change, however, he asked the worker to meet with the patients' council to discuss the issue. The administrator had been criticized before when he had instituted changes without patient consultation and was thus hoping to avoid another confrontation.

The following excerpt is from the worker's meeting with the patient council.

WORKER: Dr. Mansfield met with me and told me that many patients are returning with bedsores. He is deeply concerned about this and feels he may have to revoke the weekend-pass policy.

LOUIS: (With great anger) He can't do that. If he takes away that privilege, we will wheel down to his office, and he'll have a sit-in on his hands.

JOHN: Who does he think he is anyway? We fought hard for that right, and he can't take it away. (Others murmur in angry agreement.)

WORKER: I can understand why you are so angry. The pass is really important to you. It's important to see your families. But, tell me, I don't understand: Why is it so many people come back with bedsores? (Long silence.)

TERRY: (Speaking slowly and staring at the floor as he does) Here at the center the nurses turn us in our beds all the time. When we get home, our families do not.

WORKER: (Suddenly understanding) And you are too ashamed to ask them, isn't that it?

In the discussion that followed, the group members talked poignantly about their feelings concerning their newfound dependency. Many felt they had lost their "manhood" and were ashamed to need help suddenly for going to the bathroom and for turning in their beds. So, they simply did not ask for help. As they discussed their families' reactions, it emerged that their wives were often too embarrassed to ask what kind of help they needed. It soon became clear to the worker that the problem of bedsores was an indirect communication of the need for an important new area of service: addressing the problem of dependency, patients' and family members' feelings about it, and how to handle it. The worker's next step was to ask for a meeting of the various department heads so she could report back on her session with the council.

WORKER: A most interesting issue was raised when I talked to the patients about the bedsores, and I wanted to share it with you to get your reactions and ideas.

After the worker recounted the discussion, the staff fell silent as the department heads thought about the implications of this feedback for their areas. The worker suggested it might be helpful to explore this question of dependency as it was handled throughout the institution and to see if some special attention could be paid to the problem. Once again, the worker took the stance of involving her professional colleagues in mutual discussion of an issue relevant to their work. From this discussion emerged a plan for raising the issue in the various departments and developing new services to deal with the problem, such as groups for relatives of recently paralyzed patients that would specifically focus on their reactions to the accident and their questions about their ongoing relationships, particularly how to handle the feelings of dependency they were sure to encounter. Programs for patients were also developed, and staff training implications were discussed. Because the worker was open to the idea that her setting was a dynamic system and that change was possible, she could enlist the aid of her colleagues to set important changes in motion.

Sexuality in a Home for the Aged Another example in which a worker's mind-set dramatically affected how she described a problem is taken from a home for the aged. At a staff conference, a ward aide raised a problem concerning one patient who was regularly masturbating in public places. This was affecting both staff and other residents, and the social work student was asked to speak to her about the problem. The discussion at the staff meeting was brief, and the discomfort of staff who had noticed this behavior and had been at a loss as to what to do was evident. Not happy about having to see the woman, the student was not sure what she could do, but after some discussion with her supervisor, the student began to see that her discomfort, and the discomfort of the staff, was related to the fact that sexual issues were never raised at the home. In fact, the staff system operated as if all of its residents were past the point of sexual interest. This had a great deal to do with the staff's view of the aged and their embarrassment about considering the question at all. The result was lack of attention to the real sexual needs of residents. This was, in many ways, a form of institutional oppression. In entering the institution, the adult resident was cut off from opportunities to engage in any form of sexual activity.

The student began to check out her hunch that this was a signal of a larger issue. When she approached various staff members and raised her feelings, she was amazed to find that she had unlocked several major issues that the staff had not addressed. Staff members were uncomfortable about this area and had not known how to raise the question. For example, there were elderly senile men who continually tried to get female residents and staff into bed with them. Staff joked about these occurrences, although their real feelings reflected discomfort. After a preliminary survey, the student returned to the meeting with her findings. The result was a decision by staff to develop a survey to identify the problem as seen by staff and residents, to discuss ways to deal with the feelings of the staff, and to develop new approaches for handling the issue with residents. The staff attended a workshop, run by outside consultants, on geriatric sexuality. The student social worker's sense of the connection between "private trouble" and a "public issue" opened up important work in a formerly taboo area.

Social Action in the Community

Workers' contact with a client often puts them in a unique position in relation to community and social policies. Their firsthand experiences can provide insights into client needs, gaps in services, and the impact of existing policies that need to be brought to the attention of policy makers and the community. The complexities of our society often make it difficult for the wider community to know what is happening with the many "left-out" groups. In addition, society has some stake in not finding out the real nature of the problems. Once again, the functional role of mediating between the client and the system—this time, the community—can provide direction for the worker's efforts. These can consist of letters to a newspaper; briefs for government bodies prepared by the worker as an individual or as part of a professional organization, organized lobbying efforts in relation to specific legislation, and so forth.

One illustration of this process comes from my early practice in a small, suburban community on the outskirts of a large city. I was a youth worker in a Jewish community center serving a middle-class population. Over time I noticed two teenagers who were attending our lounge program but who were not members of the center's client population. After I made contact with these youngsters and a working relationship developed, the boys began to discuss their gang activities in town. It became obvious that they were coming to the center in an effort to move away from their peer group because of fear of getting seriously hurt or in trouble with the law. As a new youth worker in town, I had not been aware of the existence of this problem and had not seen any reference to it in the local press. Conversations with other teenagers in the program confirmed the extent of the problem.

At about the same time, I was invited to participate in a mayor's committee on youth that had recently been established to plan the town's priorities in the area of youth programs. More than one hundred workers and volunteers in local youth organizations attended the first meeting. As I listened to the presentations, it became clear that each organization was presenting a brief in support of its own activities. It was also clear that the gang youth population was not going to be part of the discussion. In fact, because of their difficult behavior, these youngsters were usually barred from participating in the organizations represented at the meeting. I attempted to raise the issue and was naively surprised by the reluctance of the group to admit the problem. My notes of the session describe the process:

> After being recognized by the chair, I said we were missing an important youth problem in town. I pointed out that no one had mentioned the gang problem, and yet it was one that must be troubling all of our organizations. There was a long silence. The chairman of the committee, a town councilman, said that he didn't think the town had a gang problem. He felt the gang trouble was usually caused by kids who came over from a neighboring town and that perhaps those were the youngsters I was referring to. He turned to the planning and research coordinator for the county government and asked if they were aware of any serious juvenile delinquency problem or gang problem in this town. He pulled a folder from his briefcase and outlined statistics that indicated very little difficulty in this area, with the exception of some limited informal gang activity in the neighboring town. The chairman of the committee then suggested that because I was new in town, it might explain why I believed the spillover problem from the neighboring town was really our concern.

I sat down, resolving to keep my mouth shut in the future. I can still remember the embarrassment I felt in response to the patronizing tone of the chairman. A week later, after some reflection, I realized that a community was not much different from a family and that admitting a problem was not easy. Many of the members of the group were unaware of the extent of the problem, and reassurance from the officials was all they needed to return to questions such as the adequacy of the number of baseball diamonds in town. Some were aware of the problem but chose to deny the extent of the difficulty.

I decided to develop, before the next committee meeting, a way of bringing the problem to their attention more effectively. I also decided that I needed both allies and some initial ideas about how to deal with the problem. When the two teenagers met with me that week, I explained what had happened at the meeting and asked how they felt about audiotaping a conversation with me about their gang activities, in which I would maintain confidentiality, leaving their names out; they agreed to help me. I also inquired if there were any other people in the community with whom they had good relations and who might be helpful in convincing the committee that the problem really existed. They mentioned a police sergeant who had been involved with the kids when there was trouble and who most of the youngsters felt was OK. I called the sergeant and met with him for lunch. My notes of that meeting follow.

> I detailed my involvement in this issue, including my abortive attempt to raise the problem. He told me that he had heard about it the next day and had a good laugh at the response. When I asked him why, he told me he had been raising this issue with city hall for 2 years and getting nowhere. I asked him what he thought needed to be done. He felt the town very badly needed a youth bureau that could concentrate on working directly with the gang kids. He tried to make contact, but this was not officially part of his job, and his being a police officer created real conflicts. I told him I thought this mayor's committee might be a great place to bring pressure to bear on city hall, which would have a hard time ignoring a recommendation from its own committee. I asked if he would support me at the next meeting when I played the tape and raised the issue again. He said he could not raise the issue himself, for fear of sanctions, but he would attend. If the committee asked him questions directly, then he could respond. We agreed that I would raise the problem and he would respond.

My next step was to record an hour-long conversation with the two teens. In the first part, I asked them to discuss the gang structure and activities in town. In the second, I asked them to talk about themselves, their hopes and aspirations, the problems they faced in trying to accomplish them, and what they thought might be helpful. I felt that it would be important for the committee members not only to be shocked out of their complacency but also to gain a sense of these teens as the community's children who needed their help. We reviewed the tape together, with the teens editing out parts they felt might reveal too much about themselves and strategizing with me about which parts I should play for the committee for the greatest effect. I then made an appointment to play the tape for the police sergeant to alert him to its content.

At the next session of the mayor's committee, I explained what I had done, and I requested time to play the tape excerpts. The committee members were intrigued and agreed. They listened with attention as the two boys, in response to my questioning, described in detail the gang structure in town, the names of each gang, whether they were white or black, the number of members of each gang, their relation to larger gangs in the county, and the internal structure of the gangs. They then reviewed several gruesome incidents in town of recent gang fights at movie theaters, in pizza parlors, and at the local high school. They gave detailed descriptions of their involvement in "stomping" kids with hobnailed boots. I asked them how they felt about all of this, and one responded, "Lousy, but what can I do? If I don't go along with the gang, I would be on my own, with no one to back me up." The boys then talked about their future plans:

WORKER: What kind of work would you like to do?
TOM: I'd like to be something like a bank clerk, or work in an office somewhere—
　　but you need high school for that, and I don't think I'm going to make it out.
WORKER: What do you think you will end up doing, then?
TOM: Probably, I'll end up like my brother—going to jail.

At the end of the tape there was another silence in the room, but this time the expressions on the committee members' faces indicated that they were stunned by the detailed description of the gang structure and moved by Tom's fatalism. One member asked if all the gang fights that had been described had actually taken place. The police sergeant was asked if he knew about these fights, and he confirmed that they had occurred. He was then asked if he knew about the gangs described, and in response he detailed his experiences with gangs over the past 2 years. The committee chair asked him what he thought they could do about the problem. The police sergeant described the possibility of a youth bureau such as had been created in other communities. The story of the gang groups received front-page publicity in the town paper the next morning, along with an editorial stressing the importance of dealing with this problem. Several recommendations emerged in the final report of the commission, including the establishment of a youth bureau and the development of special programs at the other youth organizations, as well as activity centers that would make the programs accessible to the gang population. The youth bureau was funded in the town's next budget, and the police sergeant accepted the job as the first director with a field staff of two.

In this instance I had many advantages: dealing with a small town that was relatively open to influence, finding an effective ally in the sergeant, working with a ready-made forum provided by the mayor's committee, having the support and encouragement of my agency administration and board, and finding two youngsters willing to risk themselves. In other situations, moving from identifying a problem to changing policy might not be as easy.

Professional Impact and Interstaff Relationships

The second area of professional impact concerns the work culture that influences staff relationships both within and between agencies. This is partially analogous to the "process" aspect of the helping relationship, but I am referring here to the way in which staff members relate to one another. Let me clarify several points. First, I am concerned with working relationships. Staff members need to deal with one another effectively while pursuing their own functions. Personal friendships may develop within a staff system, and they may enhance the working relationship, but it is not necessary to be friendly with a colleague in order to work well together. Poor interstaff working relationships usually have a strong negative effect on the provision of services to clients. For example, an interesting research project by Stanton and Schwartz (1954) indicated an association between staff tensions and evidence of psychiatric symptoms in patients in a psychiatric hospital. In addition, the emotional drain on staff members and the amount of time and energy expended on such issues can be extraordinary.

Second, the responsibility for strengthening staff working relationships and for dealing with obstacles that block effective collaboration rests with supervisory and administrative staff. If we think of the staff system as a group, then we can use the discussion in Part II to develop a model of the supervising and administrative functions. In workshops I have conducted for supervisors and administrative staff, I have helped participants analyze problems in the staff system by using many of the constructs and models described earlier. For example, staff systems often have a member who plays the same role as the deviant in the client group. In larger systems, as we have seen, a whole department or section may take on the scapegoat role, with the system avoiding its problems by projecting them onto its weakest part. Through analysis of process recordings, one can identify all the skills described thus far—contracting, elaborating, empathy, demand for work, and the rest—as useful for staff management functions. Helping staff members develop a positive working culture is thus analogous to dealing with the intimacy theme described earlier in this book. A discussion of the use of this model in supervision and staff management can be found in my supervision text, *Interactional Supervision* (1993a). Although further discussion of supervision issues lie beyond the scope of this book, understand that the functional responsibility for dealing with problems in the staff system rests with the supervisors and administrative staff. Nonetheless, in spite of this general position, each member of a staff system can contribute to effective staff interaction. This is part of his or her responsibility for positive professional impact.

The Agency as a Social System

In one of my earlier publications, I described the agency as a social system and argued for the importance of paying attention to interstaff relationships:

> The complex organism called "agency" consists of two major subsystems: staff members and clients. The client subsystem is further divided into smaller units, such as families, groups, wards, cottages. The staff subsystem is subdivided along functional lines. We have administrators, social workers, supervisors, clerical staff, and so on. In order to analyze a part of a complex system we must set it off with a boundary—an artificial divider which focuses our attention. In social work, it has been the client subsystem. We study family dynamics, ward behavior, group process, and so forth. While this is necessary, there is the danger that we can take this boundary too seriously. We examine our client interactions as if they were in a "closed" system in which interactions with other subsystems did not have significant impact. For example, we will try to understand the deviant behavior of some hospital patients as their problem rather than seeing this behavior as a signal of a problem in hospital care. Or we will describe our clients as "unmotivated" when they stop coming to our agencies rather than interpreting their dropping out as "voting with their feet" against poor service.
>
> If we view our agencies as open, dynamic systems in which each subgroup is somewhat affected by the movement of the other subgroups with which they come in contact, we cannot isolate our clients as discrete entities. Instead, we must see the total interaction between clients and staff as an essential part of the helping process. In turn, to the degree that staff interactions have a direct impact on the agency service, they must also be placed on our agenda. The way in which staff members' relations affect the "productivity" of the agency is thus directly connected to issues of client service. (Shulman, 1970, p. 22)

Staff relations can profoundly affect service. The cultural barriers that prevent open discussion of problems in the staff system are similar to those described in the chapters on group work. In any complex social system, conflicts of interest, hidden agendas, residues of bad feelings, misunderstood communications, and so forth are bound to arise; nonetheless, the system treats discussion of these concerns as taboo. The organizational theorist Argyris (1964) describes how the formal organization stresses "cognitive reality" (as opposed to expressions of real feelings), unilateral control in human relations, and the artificial separation of "process and task." He points out how this interferes with genuine interpersonal feedback; openness to new ideas, feelings, and values; owning one's own views and tolerating others; experimentation and risk taking—all factors that vitally affect the productivity of an organization. Organizations continue to function in spite of these problems, operating under what Argyris calls a **pseudoeffectiveness** that corresponds somewhat with the previously described illusion of work. The most important conversations about the real problems in the system then take place in the halls, over lunch, or within subgroups gathering over beers on Friday afternoons to complain about staff members they find impossible to work with. Obviously, client service must suffer under such conditions.

Recognition of the importance of the way in which staff members work with one another has grown. For example, Braeger and Holloway (1978) wrote an excellent book dealing with this area of practice. They focused on the problems involved in effecting "changes from below" and explored forces affecting stability and change, the initial assessment stage, and the change process itself.

In contrast, agency efforts to deal with such problems sometimes use approaches borrowed from the "sensitivity training" movement, such as weekend retreats, encounter groups, and ongoing T-groups (training groups). Outside organizational development experts are often enlisted to assist staff in developing more authentic communications. Under some circumstances, these efforts can pay important dividends, but often they create more problems than they solve. Staff members may be stimulated in the artificial atmosphere, created by the trainer, to share thoughts and feelings with which other staff members or administrators cannot cope. When the session has ended and the trainer has left, the ongoing repercussions of this honesty can deepen rifts and intensify bad feelings. In addition, staff members who may have felt "burned" by the experience are confirmed in their views that any attention to process is destructive, and their resistance to any form of open discussions of inter-staff relationships is heightened. Periodic opportunities for a general review of the working relationships in a setting can be helpful only if the setting is already operating at a sophisticated level of open communication on an ongoing basis.

Because most staff systems do not yet operate on that level, an alternative process is needed. Rather than attempting a full-scale analysis of the working relationships in a system—a threatening process at any time—focusing on specific problems directly related to service issues is often more helpful. By this I mean that the discussion should not deal with the question "How do we work together?" but rather "How do we work together on this particular case or in this area of agency concern?" This discussion needs to be built into the ongoing operation of an agency, as opposed to being reserved for special retreats or meetings. By keeping the discussion related to specific issues, one can avoid the trap of becoming personal, as in staff members dealing with each other's "personalities." Agency staff meetings are not "therapy" sessions, and staff members have a right to relate to each other in their own, unique ways. The only issues appropriate for discussion are those directly concerned with the business of the agency. It is precisely the fear that sessions will turn into personal encounter groups that generates resistance by staff members to a discussion of process.

Focusing on specific issues on an ongoing basis allows a staff to develop the skills needed to be honest with one another at their own pace. As staff find that risking their feelings produces effective results, they gradually lower their defenses, building on their first experiences to increase their capacity for authentic communication. As stated earlier, this process is greatly facilitated when administrative and supervisory staffs are skilled at helping staff members deal with one another. Of course, this is not always the case. In either situation, staff members can develop their own skills in relating to others individually and as a group in order to improve the agency culture for work. Although strong leadership speeds the process, change can begin anywhere in the system, as the examples that follow will show.

These examples present several common situations faced by social workers. In the first, a staff member tries to sort out her relationship with another staff member who shares work with her regarding a particular client. In the second, a unit in a large organization takes a first step at opening up communications in a system and is surprised to find that this leads to major changes. In the third example, staff members in one system face their responsibility for developing a better working relationship with staff in a related agency. This final example deals with the problem of discovering that a particular client is being served by a multitude of agencies and workers, none of which ever talk to each other. Some of you will find these problems familiar.

Interdisciplinary Collaboration in Work With a Client

A common area of tension between staff members occurs when different workers deal with the same client. The strains are often intensified if the workers come from different disciplines. As we have seen, one variation of this struggle appears in the form of a contest over "who owns the client." (Of course, it is the client who owns the client, in the last analysis.) In larger systems, one group of professionals often becomes quite concerned if they believe another group is impinging on their role. Status is often at stake. More recently, with cost-containment efforts in full force, loss of a professional responsibility can threaten the continued employment of a whole professional group.

In one example, when nurses began to lead ward groups in a hospital, other professionals felt their traditional territory threatened. This type of conflict has emerged with new force recently, as the impact of managed care has led various professional groups to attempt to carve out their "territories." In this specific case, efforts to discuss the questions of role in order to resolve the conflict failed because of the vagueness and generality used by the two professional groups when asked to describe what they did.

Often, one cannot attend an interdisciplinary meeting and hear a single sentence that is not full of jargon. When a professional group is clear about its function and the way in which that function is implemented in a particular setting and with particular clients, members feel much less defensive and do not need to resort to jargon. Interprofessional conflicts over territory often signal lack of functional clarity within each group. A first step toward resolving such conflicts is for each professional group to develop its own sense of role and then present it—not with reams of jargon, but by sharing specific examples of their work in action. In this way, different groups can become more aware of their similarities and differences concerning what they do with clients. Division of labor within a system can emerge from a joint discussion of what the clients' needs are and how each group can play the most effective role in meeting those needs.

Give-and-take can begin within the same staff, as members of different professional groups clarify how they will work together with specific clients. In the example that follows, a social worker dealing with Cindy, a 17-year-old girl attending a hospital clinic, is concerned about the lack of cooperation between the doctor on the case and herself. She feels he does not respect her contribution to the work, a complaint often voiced in interdisciplinary settings. Rather than simply complaining to colleagues, the worker confronts the doctor with the issue:

> I was alarmed that Cindy would cut off all contact with the clinic and thus a potential source of help. I was also concerned with how the doctor viewed the case, what his intentions were, and if he felt that my role and opinions in the case were relevant.
>
> I confronted him with these concerns and initially he reacted defensively, stating that he felt she needed an experienced psychiatrist and not a social worker. I replied that perhaps he was correct but that I felt at present she was having enough difficulty in accepting and receiving the aid of doctors, social workers, and school counselors, let alone a psychiatrist. (She had expressed some very strong and negative feelings about psychiatrists.) He calmed down, and I empathized with his difficulty in dealing with her during the interview. I then attempted to get some clarification of our roles in relation to a treatment program. We discussed at length where we might cross each other up and confuse her and decided that we would consult one another before tackling certain problem areas involved in the case.

The important result of this discussion was not that the two professionals no longer experienced conflicts in their work but that they began to develop a working relationship in which they could anticipate conflicts or raise them with each other more quickly. The worker's taking the first step of raising the question lifted the strong taboo against direct discussion in this sensitive area. If staff members begin joint work with the understanding that there is bound to be some conflict and confusion, then they will be more likely to establish a maintenance system for early self-correction.

Interdepartmental Communications in a Large System

A common problem in large systems is for subgroups of professionals, such as departments, to blame all the problems in the system on other departments. One group of staff members might even be identified as scapegoats or serving the "deviant member" function. Because of rules or politeness, as well as the fact that each department has some stake in maintaining the status quo, no formal discussion of the problems and the "problem" department follows. The talk in the informal system often consists of speculations on how things would be much better "if only the other department straightened out." When the problem department is expressing a widely held concern, then its members will continue to bring the problem to the system's attention through indirect means. However, when this department finally starts to affect other departments directly, the response is often to deal just with the content of the issue. This is a mistake: Even if the specific issue is resolved, it will be replaced with another issue if the underlying problems are not addressed.

To illustrate this process and the way in which staff can use a specific confrontation to deal with the larger question of staff relations, I shall draw on an experience I had, early in my academic career, as a full-time field instructor for a school of social work. In this case I was working with a unit of graduate students placed in a residential institution for adolescents diagnosed as mildly retarded. After 3 months in the setting, the students and I had observed many practices with which we disagreed, particularly the control procedures used by the cottage staff. The cottage life department was responsible for supervising residents and for maintaining the rules of the institution. The staff in this department was not professionally trained, and they had a serious communication gap with the professionals (social workers, psychologists, educators, counselors). Informally, the professionals often expressed distaste for some of the more restrictive policies, but they never raised objections in formal meetings. Our unit went along with this state of affairs, content to carve out our area of service while ignoring the general problems.

This quasi-equilibrium was upset when a cottage supervisor refused to allow group members to attend a session led by one of my students. Some of the residents were on restriction (a punishment for behavioral offenses), and the cottage staff viewed the club group as a reward. The supervisor informed my student that he could only see his members one at a time and that he was to use the session to "give them a good lecture on how to behave." Our first reaction at our unit meeting the next day was shock at being instructed how to do our job. After reflection, however, and by analyzing the staff system of which we were a part, we began to see that this incident was a symptom of a larger problem of lack of communication between departments.

We could have easily "won the battle" by gaining permission to see our group members on our terms, because the administration wanted to maintain federally funded student-training programs at the institution. However, we would have further alienated cottage staff and would probably have found our program subverted in indirect ways. We chose, instead, to attack the larger communication problem, using this incident as a specific example. We clearly saw that a split in the institution between the training and therapy services formed a major obstacle to work.

The combination of overlapping boundaries and underdeveloped communications resulted in areas of conflict with limited opportunities for resolution. In such a situation, staff frustration grew, and a process of withdrawal had begun. Instead of increasing lines of communications, staff members made those that were open less meaningful by avoiding discussion of conflict issues. Cottage life staff, who bore the brunt of implementing the control function in the institution, became the convenient target for criticism. It became more difficult to mobilize the potential within the staff to make those adjustments that would keep the system in a "steady state." The most serious consequence of these problems was that the feedback essential for system adjustment was blocked.

Our strategy for action involved three lines of approach. First, I requested permission to attend a weekly meeting of department heads on the training side of the institution. This was the first formal bridging of the therapy-training gap and provided a forum for the discussion of conflict issues. By disregarding the taboo against real talk, I could raise concerns directly, and the resultant discussions served to clear up mutual misconceptions. It became clear that staff in all departments were reacting to people in other areas as if they were stereotypes, which led to consistently missed communications. Face-to-face contact made dismissing each other out of hand more difficult for staff. As communications opened up, the interdependence of department heads began to emerge, and the group became an arena for mutual aid. Members found they could help each other with their problems, particularly those in relation to the administration.

In a second line of work, each student in the unit requested weekly meetings with respective cottage attendants to help bridge the communication gap. One result of these meetings was that students obtained a more balanced perspective on the problems faced by cottage attendants in dealing with residents. They found that their stereotypes of the attendants, developed by hearing only the residents' point of view and hardened by the general attitude toward cottage staff held in the institution, quickly faded as cottage attendants shared their "binds" in trying to do their jobs. Students also took turns coming in on a weekend to get a sense of the issues facing staff and residents at these less structured times. As the students began to listen and to understand, cottage staff dramatically changed their views about student social workers. As the students better understood the realities of the attendants' jobs, they were perceived as "having their feet on the ground." This outreach effort continued in other areas of the system. For example, to gain a greater appreciation of the problems in the vocational training areas, students took turns helping prepare meals or working in the center's laundry.

The third line of work had the most dramatic impact. In an effort to break down the isolation between departments, we tried to improve communications with the social service department itself. I outlined the problem in a meeting with the head of social service, as indicated in my notes:

> I explained to Mrs. Paul that I was concerned because the students felt they were an enclave in the institution and that they were even cut off from social service. I told her that we felt that we had contributed to this isolation by not attending meetings and by not raising these feelings earlier. I asked if a meeting could be held with the department staff to discuss this and to see what might be done to rectify the problem. Mrs. Paul told me she was glad I raised this, because she had always felt uncomfortable about the lack of connection but wasn't sure about what to do to correct it. She said she was always afraid to raise it. I asked her why, and she indicated that she didn't feel she could make demands on the unit as she would her staff, so she didn't want to seem to be pushing us for more involvement. I laughed and pointed out how we were both worried about the same thing but afraid to raise it. She agreed that other staff members might feel the same way, and we decided to make it an agenda item at the next social work meeting.

At the meeting, everyone could clear the air, as the staff members and the social work students raised their mutual concerns and discovered several misconceptions about each other's attitudes toward student involvement. They then discussed specific strategies for more meaningful student involvement in the work of the department. I generalized the question by pointing out that we felt an estrangement between social services and the rest of the institution, particularly cottage life. As an example, I related our recent experience of a cottage supervisor withholding permission from residents to attend a meeting and shared our beginning efforts to open up better communications. I asked if others felt the same way, and a flood of examples and feelings emerged.

It became clear that we were articulating common feelings held by the department members but never expressed. The balance of the meeting consisted of strategizing how we might reach out to the cottage life department to discuss the working relationship between social workers and cottage attendants. We extended an invitation to the head of cottage life and his supervisors to discuss this problem, and we all agreed on a date. As the time approached, word of the meeting spread quickly, and comments in the informal system revealed some clues as to why such a meeting had not taken place before. It was variously described as a "showdown," a "shooting match," and a "confrontation," and all staff members were tense when the meeting time arrived. To our surprise, the heads of all of the other departments also attended the meeting on their own initiative.

Three meetings were held, and those expecting fireworks were not disappointed. Many work issues were aired for the first time, often with great feeling. Interestingly, my attending the training department heads' weekly meetings paid dividends at this point. A beginning working relationship had been developed that led various department heads to offer support when a particular area was under attack, including the activities of my student unit. As we owned up to the ways in which we helped to make the work of others more difficult and as we attempted to be nondefensive, the defensiveness of the other staff members lessened. The focus of the discussion soon shifted from recrimination to identifying common problems, some needing to be dealt with by the departments and others requiring policy changes by the administration. As the list of concerns was drawn up, it became obvious that much work was needed even to begin to attack it. The group decided to form four task forces to deal with each general category of problems. Line and supervisory staff from each department sat on each task force so that all opinions could be represented in the discussions. The group formed a steering committee with a department head or supervisor from each area to monitor the process, and a deadline was set for reports.

At this point the group approached the administration for official support of this ad hoc effort. Some staff members had been concerned that the administrator might not value their efforts to institute change. They had developed a stereotyped view of the administrator as being someone who would object to anything that would disrupt the status quo, but when he was approached, his response was, "I'm always besieged by people telling me about all of the problems. It's a relief to have the staff coming to me with some solutions, for once." A memo to all staff clearly outlined his support for the project. What had begun as our student unit raising questions about our relationship to the social service department had become an institution-wide, formally sanctioned effort to attack long-standing problems. In addition, a new structure was developed that greatly enhanced interdepartmental communication at department head, supervisor, and line staff levels.

Thirty-eight recommendations for changes in policy and structure eventually emerged from the task forces. After line staff in each department approved the reports, the changes were instituted. A sample of the recommendations provides a sense of the range of the topics:

- Establishment of a representative resident council to meet monthly with the superintendent of the institution and department heads.
- Elimination of a "gold-card" system that rated residents on their behavior and controlled their access to the recreation program. This system had been generally described by staff as ineffective.
- A change in the dining room procedures to allow for coed dining.
- Allowing residents to have a degree of choice in selection of on-campus work assignments.
- The expansion of social services into evening and weekend time, when the greatest need was felt by staff and residents.
- The combining of the training and therapy services committee into one committee.

Of course, these changes did not solve all of the problems in the institution. The crucial result was that staff members discovered that they could talk to one another and that doing so might yield positive results. Structural changes (such as a resident council and combining training and therapy committees) would also increase the chances for better ongoing feedback. Most important, the experience released a flood of staff energy that apathy and a related feeling of hopelessness had suppressed. Staff learned that change could begin anywhere in the system and that they had to risk and invest themselves for those things they really wanted. The lesson was not lost on the social work students or their instructor.

Impact on Relations With Staff at Other Agencies

While providing services to clients, workers make contact with staff from other agencies working with the same clients. After repeated contact, patterns of staff relationships develop. When positive, these relationships strengthen the cooperation among professionals. When negative, because of either direct or indirect cues of hostility or lack of mutual trust, they act as barriers that can cut a client off from the required service. In one example presented at a workshop, emergency service workers described how they had been cut off from using the services of a hospital psychiatric department that was refusing to accept their clients with drug-related psychotic episodes when they brought them to the hospital. Because several workers had undergone similar experiences or had faced hostility from the hospital staff, the agency had written off the hospital as being noncooperative and no longer attempted to use it as a resource. A negative judgment about staff members of another agency thus can quickly become part of the agency culture. New staff members, who have had no experience with the other setting, are warned not even to try. In another illustration of this process, parole officers would not tell their parolees to use a particular government employment service because of past experiences that they felt had indicated a bias against their clients.

When the example of the uncooperative psychiatric service was examined in some detail and the actual conversations between workers and the hospital staff analyzed, it became clear that the workers had approached the hospital staff as if they expected to be rejected. Their aggressiveness in dealing with the nursing staff, for example, was answered with hostility and defensiveness. The nursing staff viewed workers in an equally stereotyped way, and both sides began each encounter ready for a fight. When I inquired if any efforts had been made, either individually or as an agency, to explore this poor working relationship, I was not surprised to find that the answer was no. The workers sensed the tension and hostility during the encounters, but they never directly reached for it to explore the reason for the difficulty. As a staff group, they had never thought to ask for a meeting with the hospital staff to discuss the obvious difficulties in communication. As often happens, the staff of each setting had decided, in advance, that the situation was hopeless.

Numerous examples of conflict between different staff groups suggest that the root of the problem lies in the stress each group experiences in its work. The stress may come from the nature of the client's problem. For example, dealing with teenagers who have had drug-related psychotic episodes is difficult at best, and the possibility of suicide makes this line of work particularly daunting. Lack of support for frontline workers in these high-stress jobs often leaves them unable to tune in to the feelings and concerns of workers in other settings. The conflict between staff groups often represents the flight-fight syndrome, described earlier in the text, when running from a problem or angry confrontation becomes a maladaptive means of coping with pain. During times of cutbacks in funds and services—so-called "restraint" programs—tensions among overworked, threatened, and unappreciated frontline staff members and their groups escalate. The unfortunate result is that the social services staff groups are cut off from one another just at the time when they need the most support. The cycle can be broken, however, if staff members begin to examine the process systematically rather than viewing the conflicts as personality based.

After the workshop analysis of the example dealing with teenagers and drug abuse, the agency workers held a meeting with the hospital staff. The skills of tuning in, contracting, and the other skills helped the social workers develop a strategy for opening up honest discussion without backing the hospital staff into a corner. Reports from workers after this session indicated that the hospital staff had been equally upset about the relationship with this agency. They had sensed the workers' hostility and particularly the workers' lack of understanding that the hospital was understaffed and somewhat overwhelmed by the cases brought in by the workers. The workers, in turn, shared their problems in dealing with such cases. Many of their problems were similar to those faced by the hospital staff—for example, providing help to a spaced-out youngster, receiving a report of child abuse in progress, and being expected to be involved in both cases at the same time.

The session resulted in a better delineation of the mutual responsibilities of the two settings and the development of a procedure for handling the immediate problems when either system was under strain. In addition, the groups agreed to cooperate in bringing the staffing problem to the attention of the respective agency administrations and supervisory government bodies. Although the problems were not solved immediately, the hospital and the agency workers were once again open to each other. In the earlier example of the parole officers and the employment agency, a joint meeting resulted in better understanding on both parts about the special problems involved in finding jobs for parolees and the establishment of a special group of workers to handle referrals and to provide a liaison with the parole service.

Clearly, workers can become so overwhelmed by the demands placed on them that they have little patience with problems in other systems. Communication breakdowns lead to the formation of stereotypes, which then become self-fulfilling prophecies. Client service suffers in the end. Workers argue that they do not have time for these efforts to improve working relationships between agencies, yet close analysis reveals that poor communication often results in greater expenditures of time than would be needed in order to face and resolve the problems.

Another example of professional impact concerns the common problem of "too many cooks." The following excerpt provides a good illustration. One worker reported an interview with a young mother of six children who was seen by the worker because of her potential for child abuse. After a good contracting interview, the worker tried to arrange a second session, but, much to her amazement, she discovered another problem faced by the mother:

WORKER: I'm glad you found this interview helpful. Can we get together on Friday?

CLIENT: I would love to, but I'm afraid I'm seeing Ted's probation officer Friday morning.

WORKER: OK, how about in the afternoon?

CLIENT: No, I have an appointment with the visiting nurse who is helping me out with my youngest.

WORKER: Would Monday be OK?

CLIENT: I don't know, the homemaker comes then, and the family support worker is here as well.

WORKER: (Beginning to feel a bit frustrated) Can you tell me your schedule for next week, and maybe I can find a time?

CLIENT: Well, Tuesday I'm supposed to see Leslie's psychiatrist at the mental health center, and Wednesday the family court worker wants to speak to me, and . . .

WORKER: My God, when do you have time for yourself?

CLIENT: You know, it's a real problem—but some of these people I have to see, and others are so nice, I don't want to hurt their feelings.

WORKER: Mrs. T., I wonder if all of these people know that you are seeing the others?

CLIENT: Probably not.

WORKER: Would it help if I tried to call a meeting of all the workers you are seeing, just so we can all find out what is going on with you, and perhaps work out some way to cut down on all of this?

CLIENT: Please! Anything would help.

This interview is not unusual. Families with many problems often find themselves involved with such a complicated and intricate system of services that they need a worker just to help them sort it out. This worker called a meeting with the mother in attendance. Everyone was shocked to discover 14 different services and workers involved with the family, some of whom were providing overlapping services. They decided the social worker would serve as key worker for the mother and help coordinate the other services as needed. The group also discussed how the services could use registries better to stay informed of each other's work with the same families.

A final example summarizes in a way the process we have been discussing. In my training workshops, when I discuss issues of professional impact, workers usually follow a pattern of response. First, they tend to externalize and place complete blame for the problem on the "others" in the system. When I challenge this, they usually become defensive and angry. Often they claim that I simply "don't understand the particular situation." Detailed examination of the specifics of the interactions often leads to a lowering of defenses, particularly if I can be genuinely empathic with the difficulties involved and the feelings generated in the workers. Recognition that they may have had some part to play in the proceedings often leads to expressions of guilt about past or present experiences that workers feel they could have handled differently. This is followed by a renewed enthusiasm about the possibilities for action.

Situations that seemed hopeless may remain hard to deal with, but some possible next steps are evident. Workers are reassured when they realize that they need only take responsibility for their next steps and that the systems have responsibility for their own. Workers generally want to believe that there is a next step and that they can have some impact. Even though they may fight this idea initially, they would be very disappointed if I agreed with their apparent fatalism. I do not think workers need to be motivated to attempt professional impact on their systems. Rather, they need support for their existing impetus toward action.

Chapter Summary

The social worker plays an important role in mediating the engagement between her or his client (individual, family, or group) and the systems that are important to them. Examples of mediation between clients and the school, hospital, and housing systems illustrate the two-client concept, in which the worker attempts to work effectively with both the client and representatives of the systems. At times, advocacy and confrontation are necessary strategies for "unfreezing" systems that prove to be unresponsive.

The worker needs to pay attention to opportunities for professional impact both to improve agency and community social policy and to promote better interstaff relationships. In so doing, workers must overcome initial feelings of apathy and hopelessness, avoid being overwhelmed by the enormity of problems, have faith in the potential of systems to change, and use interpersonal skills in improving relationships.

Related Online Content and Activities

 Visit *The Skills of Helping* Book Companion Website at www.socialwork.wadsworth .com/Shulman06/ for learning tools such as glossary terms, InfoTrac College Edition keywords, links to related websites, and chapter practice quizzes.

The website for this chapter also features additional notes from the author and additional process recordings:

- Adolescents: Acting-Out Behavior in a Community Center
- Helping Group Members Negotiate the Environment
- Senior Adults in a Jewish Community Center: A Changing Neighborhood and Feelings of Abandonment
- Sixth-Grade Girls and the Transition to a New School
- A Women's Assertiveness Training Group: Dealing With the Hospital as the Second Client

Social Work in the Community

I n this chapter we examine the role of the social worker as she
or he works with clients in the community. The concept of
community will be applied broadly, including neighborhood
communities as well as milieu communities (such as residential
institutions, psychiatric wards). Work with clients in the community is often termed **macropractice,** in contrast with work with
individuals, families, or support groups in a clinical setting, which
is called **micropractice.** Many social work activities fall under the
term *macropractice.* For example, a social worker may undertake
social policy research designed to influence legislation. The social
worker may never actually work directly with clients. This would be
an example of what is called **indirect macropractice:** activities of a
social worker on behalf of a community that do not involve direct
work with clients. In contrast, working to organize tenants in a
housing project to help them influence their housing conditions is
an example of **direct macropractice:** social work involving direct
work with clients in pursuit of community goals and objectives.
This chapter focuses on direct macropractice.

Community Practice in the Social Work Context

Mizrahi (2001) argues that there is a growing need for social workers with community practice skills. She points to the growth in community organizations that need well-educated practitioners who can focus on such issues as the impact on those who are "left out" during times of economic boom and are harshly affected during times of economic bust. Cox (2001) traces the development of community practice in social work as it has changed and reemerged over the past 10 decades.

> The *focus* and *emphasis* of community work has changed to and from primary emphasis on (a) community organizing (community/locality based), (b) issue-based social action efforts (local-state and/or national in scope), and (c) planning and coordination emphasis (service delivery systems–related efforts). Shifts in emphasis have been strongly related to political/social/economic circumstances of the period. (p. 39)

She points out that those different forms of community practice have existed at different times and have overlapped, particularly during times of transition. She continues:

> Frequently, targets of concern evolved from the social aspects of community issues to the economic aspects of these issues, as in the civil rights movement. . . . Community practice . . . has also been characterized by degree of relationship to social movements (including the union movements of the 1920s and 1930s, socialist activity of the 1940s and 1950s, the civil rights movements of the 1960s and 1970s, the self-help movement of the 1980s, and now the new social movements of the 1990s. (p. 39)

Although many models of community organizing practice exist, our discussion will emphasize empowerment-oriented and progressive practice models, in keeping with the direct practice approach of this book. Cox (2001) draws on Lee's stated goal of empowerment practice as "socio-economic justice, reduction of institutional power blocks and social pollutions, changed socioeconomic structures and institutions to make them empowering structures" (Lee, 1994, p. 24). Cox sees the intervention strategies of empowerment practice as including a wide range of knowledge and skills used in other social approaches, including group work and community practice. Consciousness-raising processes with respect to personal, interpersonal, organizational, and political aspects of issues and egalitarian worker-client relationships are also critical components of most empowerment-oriented practice approaches.

Thus, although the focus of the work tends to be on community, larger systems, or political processes, many of the principles of practice and intervention strategies are similar to the work with clients described in earlier chapters. However, as we have seen, goals, values, and strategies need to be attached to the clear sense of function and role that is unique to the social work professional. So, although other professions may work to organize communities, I propose that the mediating function described earlier—the worker's standing between the client or clients and the systems that matter to them—offers a role that is consistent with the professional roots and historical professional development of social work.

Thus, we shall return to the two-client idea, with the second client being the social institutions and political systems that impact the lives of clients. The social work community organizer works with clients in the community to empower them to engage effectively with larger systems that are often more powerful and at times threatening. As one strategy, workers may employ advocacy; however at all times they should help clients develop the skills, strength, and confidence to advocate on their own behalf. Consistent with their functional role, social work community organizers should work skillfully to identify barriers that could impede the ability of clients to impact these important systems. When faced with clients' internal barriers, such as the need to develop leadership skills or the need to address real fears and concerns that involvement may be risky and result in retribution, social workers must address these issues directly in order to help clients overcome them.

The worker also works with the system as the second client in need of effective intervention. As seen in the previous chapter, skillful implementation of this role often results in effectively helping the service system, organization, or political system become more responsive to the needs of the client or client community. By first attempting to engage the system representatives effectively and to develop a positive working relationship, the social worker increases the possibility of assisting both the community and the system in identifying and acting on areas of common ground. Not to be seen as naive, I recognize that, no matter how effectively the worker tries, reaching some systems may be impossible. Powerful socioeconomic and ideological forces too often work to maintain an unsatisfactory status quo. This is why people often need advocacy and confrontation in order to move past system denial and resistance to change.

Effective social work community organizing respects the following principles:

- It is important to develop internal leaders from among the clients and not to take over the leadership when problems occur.

- In the last analysis the client must control goals, objectives, and strategies even though the social worker may have other views.

- A key role of the social worker is to help the group members develop and own structures and a culture for effective work. Many of the concepts related to group development described in earlier chapters (such as the authority theme, the intimacy theme, and formal and informal roles) will be just as relevant in a community-focused group.

- The social worker must respect the existence of barriers, both current and emerging from prior experiences, that may make taking the next step difficult for the client group until they are ready. This respect involves recognizing and accepting the process of change, as well as an understanding of the stages cited earlier in the book. These include precontemplation, contemplation, preparation for action, action, and so forth (Prochaska & DiClemente, 1982).

- The social worker needs to know when to help clients to speak "softly" to systems in an effort to reach for the system's strength (that is, to negotiate) and when to speak "loudly" to move a system to respond (that is, to confront).

- Social workers must understand the importance of shifting from confrontation to collaboration once the system's attention and response has been obtained.

- The social worker needs to fully understand that all of the dynamics and skills described earlier as crucial for so-called clinical practice are equally important when the client is a community. The purpose and goals of the group may differ, but the process does not.

Community Organizing Philosophy and Models

Social work, drawing on practice wisdom, has from its inception as a profession attempted to define a role that includes working with communities. In an early effort to conceptualize community organization, Rothman (1979) pointed out that this practice tended to play a peripheral role in social work and similar fields. He also described a "considerable degree of variation, transition, and confusion" in the theory development at that time (p. 25). To conceptualize this practice more clearly, he described three orientations regarding purposive community change:

> Model A, locality development, presupposes that community change may be pursued optimally through broad participation of a wide spectrum of people at the local community level in goal determination and action. . . .
>
> Model B, the social planning approach, emphasizes a technical process of problem solving with regard to substantive social problems, such as delinquency, housing and mental health. . . . Community participation may vary from much to little, depending on how the problem presents itself and what organizational variables are present. The approach presupposes that change in a complex industrial environment requires expert planners who, through the exercise of technical abilities, including the ability to manipulate large bureaucratic organizations, can skillfully guide complex change processes. . . .
>
> Model C, the social action approach, presupposes a disadvantaged segment of the population that needs to be organized, perhaps in alliance with others, in order to make adequate demands on the larger community for increased resources or treatment more in accordance with social justice or democracy. It aims at making basic changes in major institutions or community practices. Social action as employed here seeks redistribution of power, resources, or decision-making in the community and/or changing basic policies of formal organizations. (pp. 26–27)

Grassroots Community Organizing

The area of community practice that this chapter focuses on could be described as a hybrid of Models A and C, which most closely fits the empowerment model described earlier. Another term commonly used to describe such a model is *grassroots organizing*. Staples (1984) provides a manual for organizers that presents an organizing model by starting with a basic philosophy and then describing strategies for implementing an organizing effort. After providing examples of government and corporate actions that directly and adversely affect people in disadvantaged communities, he suggests that these are typical problems faced by low- and moderate-income people across the United States. The problems stem from people not having control of the institutions that affect their lives; this lack of control, in turn, stems from the unequal distribution of power, money, and prestige in U.S. society. This is true at the local level as much as in the state and national arenas. Inequality is a fact of life.

> To solve problems, people need to get some control over the concrete circumstances of everyday life. Organizing seeks to do this. The person who acts alone has very little power. When people join together and organize, they increase their ability to get things done. The goal is to strengthen their collective capacities to bring about social change. (p. 1)

Grassroots organizing implies active and involved leadership by members of the community. Given that most members of many communities, even those who have already demonstrated leadership traits, have not been trained in organizing and leadership skills, then a program of leadership training often precedes effective community organizing. Zachary (2000) conducted an exploratory case study of a major training project called the Parents Leadership Project (PLP), conducted by the City University of New York. During the study period, over 400 parent leaders participated. They were mostly female (over 90 percent), African American or Latino (over 80 percent), and not college graduates (80 percent). The purpose was to assist parents in developing their knowledge of contemporary educational issues and their leadership skills so that they could be more effectively involved in influencing public schools.

Qualitative interviews with 40 participants during summer 1995 explored the aspects of the training that participants experienced as most helpful. Zachary's study participants identified the following elements as critical in developing their leadership skills and encouraging them to take significant risks:

> rituals of engagement; the sharing of power; a culture of participation characterized by safety, respect and high expectations; and skillful, yet humble, facilitation to create solidarity and equality within the group. (2000, p. 71)

This community organizing model of social work practice is emphasized in Specht and Courtney's (1993) critique of a trend in the social work profession to abandon its traditional mission of working with the poor and the disenfranchised. They call for a return of the social work profession to its historic and "unfulfilled" mission:

> to build a meaning, a purpose, and a sense of obligation for the community. It is only by creating a community that we establish a basis for commitment, obligation, and social support. We must build communities that are excited about child care systems, that find it exhilarating to care for the mentally ill and the frail aged, that make demands upon people to behave, to contribute, and to care for one another. (p. 27)

Examples of community-based social work interventions that address several problem areas have emerged. For example, Mulroy (1997) describes an effort to build neighborhood networks to prevent child abuse and neglect. Mulroy and Shay (1997) illustrate how neighborhood-based collaboration of nonprofit organizations can lead to innovative prevention programs for child maltreatment. Amodeo, Wilson, and Cox (1996) describe lessons learned in an effort to develop a community-based alcohol and drug abuse prevention effort in a multicultural urban setting.

Community Organizing Around a Specific Issue

Communities can also be brought together to deal with what may be experienced by some as a specific threat or raise a significant and controversial issue. One example would be the expansion of casino gambling within an economic development area. Simmons (2000) uses an example of a 1992 proposal for the development of a casino in Hartford, Connecticut. The author points out that casino development is a type of proposal that ignites a not-in-my-backyard (NIMBY) scenario. In addition to the usual issues of scale, public funding, property values, "fit," safety, and infrastructure, casino development, Simmons suggests, raises unique concerns:

> Casinos as venues for gambling raise an entirely new set of issues and elicit deep value conflicts. Gambling, itself, becomes a central controversy. Some forces

want to debate gambling on purely economic grounds; others debate the issue from a moral perspective; and there are still others who are concerned about its social impacts without asserting a moral judgment. The discourse becomes extremely strident as powerful financial interests who develop casinos clash with opponents who hold strong views about the harm of gambling. (p. 48)

Simmons describes the complex interplay of powerful political and financial forces and the strong desire by some to see casino gambling as a force for economic development for a generally depressed downtown Hartford area. This issue came to a head after the 1992 opening of the giant and extremely successful Foxwoods Casino by the Mashantucket Pequot Indians on tribal land. The State of Connecticut took in $120 million from the arrangement that provided the Pequots with exclusive rights to operate slot machines. With this kind of money at stake, we can easily understand how forces for expansion of casinos would be powerful and organized. Simmons describes in detail the battle fought in town meetings and informational sessions. The experience was both dramatic and exhausting. In the end, Hartford rejected the casino. This settled the problems that came from organizations and community groups taking opposing positions instead of uniting to battle for social justice issues, as they usually did. Simmons concludes:

If proponents want to bring a casino to town, an uproar surly follows. Yet community organizations have considerable leverage in the fate of these projects because they can reveal the inflated claims of casino proponents and articulate an alternative vision of local economic development. More than most other "big projects," casinos provoke genuine arguments of costs and benefits, who will gain and who will lose. Community organizing can be critical in protecting a community from a highly questionable form of development. (2000, p. 67)

This example is but one of many reflecting a growing interest in how problem-specific community organizing efforts can enhance traditional treatment approaches.

Rurally Based Community Organization Practice

The literature on community organization contains many examples from urban settings but few from rural areas. This distinction is important. As Soifer (1998) points out, "Socio-cultural, economic, and political differences between urban and rural areas are present. To be effective a rural social work practitioner must recognize and spend time learning about these differences" (p. 2).

Soifer provides an example of a rural-based community organizing effort in Vermont that combined several different community organizing models. The project arose in response to the many problems faced by low- to moderate-income and mobile home park residents. Foremost of these problems was that residents felt extremely intimidated by their landlords. In spite of significant protections built into state law, residents feared retaliation and loss of their homes in a state with a tight housing market for people like themselves.

The approach used to address the problem was the development of local tenants' associations that were linked statewide in an organization called Tenants United for Fairness (TUFF)–Vermont.

The primary goal of the organization was to empower tenants to bring about qualitative improvement in their living conditions on a local, regional, and state level. . . . The methods used to achieve this objective include grassroots organizing, developing indigenous tenant group leaders, educating tenants about their rights under Vermont law, and mobilizing tenants to advocate for fundamental changes in state law concerning tenant-landlord issues. (Soifer, 1998, p. 3)

By August 1993 a network of 23 tenant associations representing 750 Vermont renters was organized. A statewide meeting of representatives that fall included training and educational programs. Soifer describes significant successful impacts on a state and local level. The step-by-step process involved in this organizing project included the selection of appropriate locations, door-to-door organizing drives, organizing committee meetings, tenants' formation meetings, and developing organizational officers' meetings. Soifer believes that building an organizational basis for an action plan, as well as developing and implementing such a plan, depends on this process.

According to Soifer, the differences between urban and rural community organization include the small size of many of the local organizing housing complexes (in this case, 15 units); driving distances, combined with poor roads and winter conditions, making attendance at state meetings difficult; and the essential difficulty in using militant actions in small towns where people must deal with neighbors and friends and politicians they know on a first-name basis. Further, high rates of poverty may be less visible in a rural area than in an urban one.

One additional difference, not mentioned by Soifer, that I have often observed in workshop presentations is the "only game in town" problem. Smaller and more rural areas tend to have fewer services and resources to address economic, health, education, and other issues. Working on major community organization projects is difficult without associated agencies willing to help. Also, individual workers often have to provide all services, and this can lead to overwhelming caseloads and limited time for agency sanctioned community organizing activities. In spite of such significant obstacles, many social workers find ways through their jobs or personal lives to address the social issues impacting their clients.

The Use of the Internet in Community Practice

With the growth in the ownership of computers and access to high-speed connections, community organizers are finding new tools for implementing their goals. Where the term *community* might originally have been limited by geographic location, it now can refer to a cybercommunity in which common interest and concerns bring members together. While this can be a powerful tool for social organization and social change, many people with low incomes or limited education do not have the equipment, technology, and knowledge needed to use it. This can result in what is called the *digital divide,* a sharp distinction between those who can take advantage of "digital democracy" and those who cannot (Shelley et al., 2004). Thus, any effort to use this powerful tool for organization and social change among the poor and less educated, many of whom may have been left out of the computer revolution, needs to incorporate access to computers and computer training to empower community members to become actively involved. Recognition of this issue has led workers to establish learning projects, among others, that directly address this issue.

Nartz and Schoesch (2000) identify four models of Internet community practice: information dissemination, community building, mobilization, and community planning. They suggest that these models use six primary Internet tools:

- ***E-mail:*** Allows users to compose messages and transmit them in seconds to one or more recipients anywhere in the world.

- *Text:* Allows users to read printed matter on pages of a website, and to navigate the sites and the web via clickable links.

- *Search engines:* Help a user find information or resources by searching for keywords that the user specifies.

- *Listservs:* Allow users to receive and post messages about topics. Each message is sent to all subscribers to the list.

- *Newsgroups:* Allow users to go to one place on the Internet and view previous messages on topics and add new messages.

- *Chat:* Allows a group of users connected at the same time to send messages to each other in real time. (p. 45)

These tools are powerful aids in the development of community action. Once again, the potential digital divide problem needs to be kept in mind. If that can be resolved, then the ability for a few to mobilize, educate, and lead the many in community building and community and social policy change is evident. The Internet can give grassroots organizations the ability to confront and impact large organizations, government bodies, financial institutions, businesses, and so forth without being frustrated by the lack of matching financial resources and power. I believe we have just begun to understand and use this powerful method in the fight for community and social justice.

The Neighborhood as Community

The social science literature reflects growing professional interest in community concepts. One such area of interest centers on the concept of "neighboring" and its social, cognitive, and emotional components. Unger and Wandersman (1985) have reviewed the literature from several disciplines, including social psychology, environmental psychology, community psychology, and sociology. The authors define *neighboring* as involving "the social interaction, the symbolic interaction, and the attachment of individuals with the people living around them and the place in which they live" (p. 141). Their review identifies many important areas of social support:

- *Personal/Emotional Support.* The extent to which neighbors are willing to greet and visit with each other can serve as a source of social belonging and reduce feelings of social isolation often fostered within cities.

- *Instrumental Support.* Neighbors may serve as informal helpers for one another.

- *Informational Support.* Neighbors provide information to each other as they interact. This information may be helpful in locating needed resources.

- *Personal Social Networks.* Neighbors establish linkages with key individuals in their neighborhoods for individual benefit. They use these connections to find and further link themselves to resources in their neighborhood and wider community to solve problems.

- *Neighborhood Social Networks.* Neighborhood social networks are the linkages developed by a group of neighbors. (pp. 142–149)

Unger and Wandersman (1985) also describe *cognitive mapping* as "an activity neighbors routinely engage in. It has significant implications especially in transient and unstable neighborhoods for determining where neighbors feel safe to travel and where they choose to socially interact with others" (p. 150).

Finally, Unger and Wandersman address the affective bonds within a neighborhood:

> Being a neighbor involves an affective dimension. As neighbors live in interaction or isolation within their neighborhood, various feelings often develop which characterize their relationship to neighbors and the neighborhood. These feelings may affect residents' satisfaction with their neighborhood and may influence their motivation to become involved in ways to solve neighborhood problems. . . . Three affective bonds are suggested: (a) a sense of mutual aid, (b) a sense of community, and (c) an attachment to place. (1985, p. 154)

Clearly, work with the neighborhood as community will involve specific sorts of knowledge as well as skills. As in the earlier discussions of social work with individuals, families, and groups, the first question to be addressed is the role of the worker. In working with communities, the worker often faces a more complex role because she or he must work within a task-focused group that has a formal structure. For example, if the group has a member who serves as a chairperson or president, and that person leads the discussion, what does the social worker do? While we saw earlier that all groups informally develop internal leaders, in these task-focused community groups the internal leader may be elected, with well-defined responsibilities spelled out in the group's charter.

So, then, what is the role of the community social worker? As one answer, Staples (1984) addresses the distinction between leading and organizing:

> It is the organizer's job to get other people to take the lead. They have to be motivated and recruited, encouraged and convinced that they can really do it. Their knowledge and skills must be developed, their self-confidence bolstered, and their commitment to collective action deepened. Whoever acts as organizer shouldn't be a formal officer or the organization's public voice. S/he shouldn't make policy decisions or tell people what to do. (p. 8)

Structure and Maintenance: A Citizen's Antipoverty Action Group

In the excerpt that follows, we examine worker interventions with an antipoverty action group that was formed to encourage poor people to use strength in numbers to try to change some of the local welfare and school policies that affected their lives. More than 50 members signed up at an initial organizational meeting. Because 50 people cannot operate together without some form of organization, they clearly needed structure. One early task was to identify roles required for effective operation. The term *roles* is used here more narrowly than before, relying on Hare's (1962) definition: "The expectations shared by group members about the behavior associated with some position in a group, no matter what individual fills the position, are called roles" (p. 24).

A small steering committee met to draft an outline of the group's structure and to identify functional tasks that group members needed to carry out: leadership (a chairperson), responsibility for relations with other community groups (a co-chairperson), responsibility for the group's funds (a treasurer), and responsibility for maintaining the group's records and correspondence (a secretary). As the group developed, other roles became necessary and were created (such as committee chairpersons for special projects). By creating these roles, the group was engaging in **division of labor**—the development of group structure in which the tasks to be performed are distributed among members in a formal or informal manner. Dividing the labor among group members allowed each member to carry some part of the burden but not all of it. When division of labor and responsibility are not handled well—for example, when a chairperson attempts to do all the work—the overworked member can become overwhelmed while the other group members feel angry, left out, and apathetic. The greater the apathy, the more the chairperson feels the need to take responsibility.

In these circumstances, clarity about the worker's function is crucial. In addition to helping the members develop a structure for effective operations, the worker must monitor how well the structure is working and bring any problems to the members' attention. This group task, called **structure and maintenance**, refers to the work done by group members to develop, examine, and maintain in good working order their structure for work. In the example of the chairperson who does not share responsibility, the worker's function would be to mediate the engagement between the chairperson and the other group members.

The following excerpt illustrates this work in a steering committee session of the antipoverty action group described earlier.

> I had gotten signals from a number of members that they were upset with the way things were going and especially with Sid's leadership. He had taken responsibility for a number of follow-up items and had not handled them well. As a result, the group faced some serious problems on a planned sit-in action that weekend. The meeting began as usual, with Sid reading the agenda and asking for any additions. There were none. Discussion began on a number of minor items. It finally reached the question of the plans for the action, and I could feel the tension growing. Sara began, "Is it true, Sid, that we may not have the buses for Saturday?" Sid replied abruptly, "I'm working on that, so don't worry." There was silence. I said, "I think there is something going on here. What's up?"
>
> Sara continued, "Look, Sid, I don't want you to take this personally, but there are a number of things screwed up about this Saturday and I'm really worried." Sid responded defensively, "Well, what do you expect? You know I have a lot of responsibility to carry with not very much help." Terry broke in, "Every time we try to give you some help, you turn us down." Sid looked hurt. I intervened: "I think there has been a problem going on for some time, and you folks have not been able to level with each other about it. Sid, you feel you have to carry a lot of the burden around here and the group members don't really appreciate how hard it is for you. Am I right?" Sid nodded in agreement. I turned to the others. "I think the rest of you feel that you would like to pick up a piece, but you sense Sid seems to hang on—so you don't offer. Then you feel angry later when things don't work out." They nodded as well. I said, "Look, I know it's hard, but if we get this out, maybe we can work out a way of sharing the responsibilities that would be more helpful for the group."

The community social worker needs to be clear that his or her function involves helping group members work on their tasks. Workers with such groups are often just as uncomfortable about confrontation as the members. As a result, they may try to use indirect influence, or to take over some of the chairperson's functions, or even try to get the group to replace the chairperson. This reflects a lack of understanding about group developmental tasks. Groups often run into such problems in maintaining their structures for work. Indeed, if the group could work easily, without such obstacles, it would not need a social worker. The real problem for a group such as this one arises when the members cannot openly discuss these difficulties as they emerge. This is the work of the helping professional: not managing the details of the structure itself, but facilitating the way in which group members develop and maintain their structure. In our example, the worker helped the group in this way, in this case by knowing that feelings have a great deal to do with most communication problems and that skill in this area can prove helpful.

> Although they were uncomfortable, they agreed to take some time to discuss the problem. I asked the group members why they had not leveled with Sid before. Rudy said, "Sid, we all like you a lot. That's why we asked you to be chairman. I didn't want to hurt your feelings. Since you became chairman, you seemed to forget the rest of us—and frankly, I started to get pissed off." I said, "Did you get the feeling, Rudy, that you weren't needed?" Rudy said, "That's it! All of a sudden, Sid was gong to do the whole ball game himself." I asked Sid how come he felt he had to take all the responsibility. He said, "Look, this is my first time chairing anything. None of us has much experience at this stuff—I'm worried that we will fall on our faces. I've asked some people to do things, and they have screwed up, so I don't ask anymore, I just do it." I said, "Are you worried, Sid, that you're going to fall on your face?" He was silent and then said, "You bet." I waited.
>
> Rita said, "I'm probably one of the people you feel let you down, aren't I?" Sid nodded. She continued, "Well, I meant to follow up and hold that subcommittee meeting. I just kept putting it off." I asked, "Have you ever chaired a meeting before?" Rita said, "No." I continued, "I guess you were probably nervous about it." She agreed that she had been nervous. Rudy said to Sid, "Look, Sid, I can understand your feeling worried about the group. We all feel the same way. But you really don't have to carry it all on your back. That's not what we expect of you. We can help out, and if we flop, we all flop." Sid relaxed a bit and said, "It would make it easier if I didn't have to feel completely responsible." I pointed out that the whole group was probably feeling shaky about their jobs and how well they could do them—just like Sid and Rita pointed out. "I don't think that's so unusual—in fact, I think that the fact that you are talking about this is a great sign. At least you can do something about the problem and not let it tear your group apart." They agreed that it was a start and spent the next 20 minutes analyzing the jobs to be done and redistributing the responsibilities.

In addition to overcoming division-of-labor problems, groups must develop formal and informal communication patterns. In our current example, the group needed to decide who reported to whom, how often various subgroups would meet, who would get copies of the minutes, and how communications at meetings would be governed. Another task required the development of a decision-making process that would be efficient but still allow individual members to feel involved.

In addition to paying attention to the formal structure, the worker observed the informal system at work. For example, shortcuts in communication were found that facilitated the coordination of subgroups within the structure. This had to be monitored because the informal communication system could also serve to subvert the formal system, thus becoming an obstacle in itself. The worker also observed the informal assignment of status to various members of the group. Members who performed their functions well and demonstrated the most-admired skills in the group gained higher status, and their contributions to discussions tended to carry more weight because of this. Because differential status could cause friction in the group, the worker needed to monitor the members' reactions to it.

In a sense, the worker is assigned the special responsibility of paying attention to the way in which the group works on these important structural tasks, monitoring the process to pick up cues that signal difficulties and helping the group members pay attention to these problems. Community group workers often ignore these critical group tasks, however, concentrating instead on a strategy of action in relation to the outside systems (the welfare department, the school board, government officials, and so forth). After a while these workers may find that the internal struggles of the group have grown so much that they have begun to sap the group's strength. This decline results in a loss of group cohesion, the mutual attraction members feel for one another. Attempts to develop greater cohesion through social activities (such as parties) or, even more commonly, by attacking another system and trying to unite members against a common enemy are only useful in the short run. Striking similarities exist between work with community (task-focused) groups and the work carried out with groups concerned with growth and development, support and stabilization, or therapy. The developmental group tasks are similar, and the skills required by the worker to assist this second client, the group, are similar as well.

In the following example, we broaden the role of the community social worker to examine how it is implemented in helping the group deal with its formation tasks. The example addresses many of the contracting issues and skills first raised in earlier chapters. Of particular interest is the social worker's skill in dealing with the underlying fears and anxieties of the potential group members. This step is often overlooked, with the community organizer taking over the tasks of the members rather than exploring the barriers to organizing.

Contracting: A Tenants' Group in Public Housing

In the following example, a social worker contracts at a first meeting of public housing tenants he is attempting to organize. Public housing tenants are usually economically oppressed. They also often belong to minority groups or face gender discrimination as single mothers. When they accept public housing, they sometimes find themselves treated as second-class citizens, lacking even basic tenants' rights. Poor housing, inadequate maintenance, and nonresponsive bureaucracies add a new level of oppression and increase their sense of hopelessness.

As described in our discussion of oppression theory in Chapter 1, oppressed people may internalize this oppression as a negative self-image, and this can lead to their acting out the physical or emotional violence imposed on them. They often act out the violence on one another. Thus, they may become "autooppressors as they engage in self-destructive behaviors injurious to themselves, their loved ones and their neighbors" (Bulhan, 1985, p. 126). In turn, the oppressors use this self-destructive behavior as a justification for additional oppression.

Workers can break the cycle only by helping such clients to find their common ground and to assert themselves by confronting the oppression. In our example, the worker saw the tenant's group as a way of helping the tenants deal with both the results of the oppression (such as their neighborhood conflicts) and the oppression itself. Oppression theory offers a helpful prism for understanding the problems raised in the first meeting.

The social worker in this example had done his preliminary phase work through door-to-door contacts and interviews, thereby gaining a sense of the issues of concern to the tenants. The meeting had been publicized by circulars and posters. Natural leaders in the housing complex had been identified through the interviews, and the worker had requested their help in getting a turnout for this first session. Because the first session began without a structure in place, the worker made the opening statement to a room of 45 tenants.

After introducing myself, I explained that I was a community social worker employed by the local neighborhood house and that my job was to work with citizens' groups to help them organize themselves to improve their community—that included their housing, schools, recreational services for kids, etc. After spending some time in this housing project, it became clear to me that the tenants had a number of gripes that they felt the management was not doing anything about. The purpose of tonight's meeting was to discuss these gripes and to see if they felt it would help to organize a tenants' group to deal with the management more effectively. I would try to help them get started and would stick with the group to try to help it operate effectively. However, it would have to be their group, because I couldn't do anything for them by myself. I asked what they thought about that.

The discussion began with group members complaining about poor maintenance, a haughty administrator who ignored simple requests, and so on. There was a great deal of anger in the room, which the worker acknowledged while he kept track of the issues raised. He did little to intervene other than to help the group members speak in order and respond to one another when appropriate. After a while, the members were speaking more to each other than to the chair. The discussion also moved to complaints tenants had about one another (such as noise at night, loud radios, littering) and about gaps in service for kids (such as no safe place to play). The discussion was animated. When the list seemed complete, the worker returned to the question of his role.

"You have many issues here that I think can be dealt with if you organize yourselves as a group. There are issues with management, issues between each other, and new services you feel are needed. Now I told you at the beginning that I was getting you started, but that you would have to form your own group to deal with these concerns. I would like to recommend that you select a steering committee tonight that could meet to discuss next steps. For example, they could discuss whether you need an association: if yes, what kind should you have, etc. What about it?" There were murmurs of agreement. I then asked for volunteers and was greeted by silence.

In the remainder of the excerpt, we shall see how the worker reached into this silence for the underlying concern to which he had tuned in prior to the meeting. If it were easy to get together as a group to take on these problems, why had the tenants not done so on their own? The worker had tuned in to the residents' fear of reprisals if they became identified as "troublemakers" in the housing project and decided to reach for it at this point.

As the silence continued, I asked why they seemed hesitant to volunteer. With no response, I risked my hunch and said, "You know, I was thinking about this before the meeting, and I wondered if you might be concerned about reprisals if you get organized. You know you are dependent on this place for housing, and if you were afraid that management might be upset, I could understand that."

Mrs. Cain, who had been identified as one of the community leaders, spoke up at this point, "You know, Mr. Brown used to raise a ruckus and complain all the time. He got drunk a while back and they used that to get him." I asked if they were afraid that this might happen to them. Discussion began to explore what might happen, their mutual fears, etc. Mrs. Cain finally said, "I guess we do take a chance, but if I knew you other folks would stand behind me and not run for cover if it got hot around here, I would think about doing it."

At this point, others indicated they would help out on the committee. I said, "It seems like some of your neighbors are willing to take some responsibility for leading this off and getting the group organized, but they want to know that you will back them up." Another member, a tall, older man with gray hair, who hadn't spoken all evening, said, "It's about damn time we stood up to the bastards!" Laughter broke the tension of the moment, and one could sense an agreement had been reached. I wanted to complete the contracting about my role before I finished the evening. "I want to be clear that I will help you folks get yourselves organized and help you work together, but it will have to be your group. You will need your own chairperson; you will have to make your own decisions." Group members murmured agreement to this. "We can discuss this later, but perhaps I might be able to speak to management at a later point and help them see how the group could be in their interest as well." The meeting ended as I complimented them for making a great start and set up a brief meeting with the steering committee to get ourselves organized.

This example demonstrates, again, the importance of process in dealing with groups and the importance of using the skills described thus far. The principles of contracting, clarifying purpose, clarifying role, and reaching for feedback were central to the effective start of this group. In addition to the contracting skills, the worker's tuning in and effective elaborating and empathy skills helped the group examine and overcome a major obstacle to their formation. If the worker had ignored their fears, tried to overcome them with a lecture on "strength in numbers," or simply jumped in and agreed to take the responsibility for the next steps for them instead of with them, then the group development that is central to the worker's purpose would likely have been seriously delayed. Instead, his empathy and demand for work helped them find their own strength.

Work with a task-focused, community organization group also requires that the boundary between individual problems and the work of the group be clearly defined. For example, if a group member raised a specific problem related directly to the member's child (such as drug issues, getting into trouble after school, getting suspended for behavior problems in school), turning the group into a problem-solving support group for the parent would be a mistake. In a sense, the member would be using the group for his or her own purposes, thereby subverting the group's goal. Although the worker would need to acknowledge the specific problem, perhaps even offering to talk with the client after the meeting, the worker should during the meeting relate the individual problem to a larger issue appropriate for the group's task. For example, should the group be working on drug prevention activities for all children? Should the shortage of after-school recreational opportunities be on the agenda for discussion? Is there a need to open up a dialogue with the local school principal on the issue of suspensions and how parents and the parent group can collaborate with the school to help children in trouble? These sorts of issues could be included in a task-focused community organizing group without subverting the group's task. It is the role of the social worker to help "guard" the contract in this way when personal problems surface in a task-focused group.

In the next example, we broaden our definition of the worker's role even further by focusing on how she or he helps the members negotiate their environment. In this case, the group consisted of welfare mothers in a public housing setting somewhat similar to the one described in the previous example. This time we explore the "third-force" role as the social worker attempts to work between the group and the systems that they must negotiate. we shall see how the worker's mediating role can include confrontation and advocacy when the system representative is not responsive.

Negotiating the Environment: Welfare Mothers and the Housing Agency

In this example the state welfare agency established this group to explore the problems faced by welfare families and to provide help with these problems when necessary. (This example of practice preceded the welfare reform act and the welfare-to-work movement.) Seven women, aged 23 to 45, made up the group's membership. Discussion during the group's second session indicated that their problems with the Housing Authority and the housing project in which they all lived were central concerns:

MRS. BROWN: I don't have any complaint about the building or rent, but if we get more money from welfare for any reason, they [Housing Authority] raise our rent. But if our checks are reduced, they say they can't break our lease to reduce the rent.

MRS. MELTON: They also make us pay for things that people not on welfare do not have to pay for.

WORKER: Like what?

MRS. SMITH: During the summer a man from the gas company came and put a tube on my stove so that I could move the stove, and the Housing Authority sent me a bill for $26.00.

WORKER: Did you call the gas company for repairs on your stove?

MRS. SMITH: No, he just came.

WORKER: Did you discuss this with the office?

MRS. MELTON: That doesn't do any good.

MRS. SMITH: I told them I couldn't pay the bill because I didn't have the money. They said I broke the pipe, so I had to pay the bill or move. So I paid it. But I didn't break any pipe.

MRS. LESSER: Last summer the children were playing in the court and broke four windows in my apartment, and I had to pay for them. I called the office when they were broken and told them how they were broken, but I had to pay for them anyway.

MRS. SMITH: There is no such thing as wear-and-tear items that most landlords have to replace for tenants when you live in the project.

MRS. BROWN: That's what they tell us.

MRS. MELTON: If they come into your apartment and see the shades are worn, we have to pay for them.

WORKER: Do you know of any repairs or replacements that the Welfare Board will pay for?

MRS. SMITH: Yes, Miss D. told us to send in these bills and the welfare would pay for plumbing, shades, oven doors, and things like that.

WORKER: What does your lease say that the Housing Authority is responsible for replacing or repairing?

MRS. SMITH: It has all "don't" on the back and nothing else.

MRS. MELTON: They make us pay for everything, and I don't think this is fair.

WORKER: Do you have a tenants' group that takes complaints to the office?

MRS. SMITH: Yes, but they [Housing Authority] choose the officers, and they don't do anything about the complaints. They call us troublemakers and try to keep us out of meetings. (Group members all agree.)

WORKER: Would you like for me to invite Mr. Murray [housing project manager] to one of our meetings so that you can find out just what the Housing Authority is responsible for and what your responsibilities are?

MRS. MELTON: It won't do any good. He's great for listening and taking no action on complaints.

MRS. SMITH: Yes, let's ask him. But I don't think he'll come.

WORKER: Do you want him to come, or not? (Group members all indicate yes.)

As they discussed their relationship to the housing project, they found they shared many of the same complaints. Strength in numbers made them believe some change might be possible in spite of their past experiences. In her enthusiasm for moving the work forward, however, the worker missed the underlying fears and doubts hinted at in the conversation. If taking on the housing project was so easy, why had they not done so before? At the next session, the worker corrected her mistake and began by trying to determine if the housing issue was still the central concern.

Note that the worker did not determine which issues the group members should tackle. A common error in community organizing is for workers to choose, in advance, what issues citizens should focus on. They see their work as applying direct or indirect influence to convince the members to act on the hidden agenda. However, the driving force for the work must emerge from the client's sense of urgency. The encounter may be rough, but the clients need to feel a commitment to the issue to carry them through. At the next meeting in our example, the conversation reflected some of the fears and doubts that had occurred to the group during the week. The silences hinted at these feelings.

To give the group perspective on where the group stood, the worker redefined the purpose of the group and gave a brief summary of the concerns expressed in the last three meetings before the holidays. The worker then asked group members what topic they would like to focus on. They agreed that their problems with the Housing Authority needed immediate attention (14 welfare checks had been stolen from the mailboxes).

WORKER: I called Mr. Murray's office and his secretary said that she thought Mr. Murray would be willing to meet with the group. Maybe we should use this time to plan for the meeting with him. Make a list of questions you want to ask and what approach to use.

MRS. MCIVER: I would like to know if we can have more secure mailboxes or a different type of lock on them.

MRS. MELTON: Anybody could open these boxes—even a child with a stick or nail file.

MRS. KING: I'm there when the mailman comes, so no one gets my check.

MRS. MELTON: I can't sit by the box and wait for the man. I've got other things to do.

MRS. SMITH: Why should we have to wait? If the boxes were better, this would not be a problem.

MRS. McIver: I've complained about those boxes, but they [Housing Authority] say we talk too much about our business. He said the thieves know who gets the most money and when the checks come.

MRS. Smith: That's common knowledge that the checks come on the first.

MRS. King: I'd never tell anyone I was on welfare.

MRS. Smith: People assume that you are on welfare if you live in the project.

MRS. Stone: Why can't the police be there on check day? Someone broke into my box, and I had to pay $2.50 for it.

MRS. McIver: That's right. They [Housing Authority] say we are responsible for the boxes whether we break them or not.

MRS. Smith: That's not fair. Why should we have to pay for something we did not do?

MRS. McIver: Most people are afraid to call the police.

MRS. Melton: You're right. You never know what those people [drug addicts] will do to you or your children.

MRS. McIver: You remember when that brick was thrown through my window? It was because I called the office [Housing Authority] about those big boys hanging out in the halls.

MRS. Melton: They can sure make it bad for you.

MRS. McIver: The other tenants call you a troublemaker if you complain about noise or dirty halls or anything like that.

MRS. Smith: I complain to the office all the time, not that it does any good. I don't care what the other tenants think. I've got my family to look out for.

MISS Brown: That's right! And look what happened to you last summer. (Laughter from the group.)

WORKER: What happened, Mrs. Smith?

MRS. Smith: There were a lot of older boys outside my door making noise. I asked them to leave because my mother was sick, but they wouldn't do it, so I called the office. The police made them move, but they came back and turned on the fire hose and flooded my apartment. (Silence.)

MRS. Wright: They'll get you, all right. (The group agreed.)

The worker sensed the fear in the silences but did not reach for it. Workers in these situations are sometimes afraid to acknowledge underlying feelings of fear and ambivalence. One worker told me, "If I reach for it, I might get it, and then they would be so scared they would back out." This view underestimates the strength of people to face difficult and frightening tasks when they have a stake in the proceedings. Rather than frightening the group members off, the acknowledgment of the fears may provide the added strength needed to make the second decision about the confrontation. The first decision to act for their rights was made in the heat of the exchange of complaints. The second decision, the real one, must be made after the members have had a chance to react to their own bold steps. They must reflect on the risks involved and feel the fear that is associated with taking an action such as this. Workers who do not pay attention to helping clients with these feelings often find that when the crunch comes, clients are not ready to take the next step. Then the worker often takes over for the clients—for example, becoming the spokesperson in a confrontation—when, with more preparation, the clients might have handled the problem themselves. In this group, however, the housing manager's refusal to come to the meeting and a threat against one of the members by a local welfare rights group brought the issue to a head.

Plans had been made for Mr. Murray, manager of the Housing Authority, to attend this meeting. The worker told of her meeting with Mr. Murray and his refusal to come to the group's meeting. A general attitude of pessimism, disappointment, and "I told you so" was expressed by all members.

MRS. MELTON: I think we should go over his head, since he refused to come. (All agree.)

MRS. SMITH: Let's talk to Commissioner Long. He is black and just recently appointed to the Housing Authority Board. (All agree.)

At this point in the meeting, Mrs. King arrived late, appearing upset. In response to the concerns of the worker and the other group members, she revealed that, because of her participation in this group, she had been threatened by members of a welfare rights group to which she and others belonged. What follows is an example of the problem of advocates taking the position that the system—in this case the Welfare Department and the welfare worker leading the group—is always the enemy. Rather than exploring the genuine common ground between their own group's goals and those of the agency, they attempted to coerce members into quitting the group:

MRS. MELTON: I told you, Mrs. Payne, that he would not come. He does not care about us. None of them do. (At this point Mrs. King came in, looking upset. She apologized for being late and stated that she almost had not come at all.)

WORKER: I'd rather that you be late than not come at all.

MRS. SMITH: What's the matter? Is Ronny [her son] all right?

MRS. KING: He's all right; that's not it.

MRS. MELTON: Don't you feel all right?

MRS. KING: (Silent for a few minutes.)

WORKER: If you'd rather not discuss it, we'll go on to our discussion about the Housing Authority.

MRS. KING: No, I'll tell you.

She then explained in detail how some members of the welfare rights group had come to her apartment and accused her of starting trouble with the people in the project by being in this group and told her that she should get out. She denied the charges but stated that she was upset when they left and was worried that they might cause trouble for her because of her participation in the group. She stated that this morning she got mad with herself for letting them boss her around, so she got dressed and came to the meeting.

MRS. MELTON: How can they cause trouble for you? They don't have any power.

MRS. SMITH: How did they know you belonged to this group?

MRS. KING: I don't know. I didn't know any of the people. I've seen two of them who live in my building. I don't bother anyone. I stay to myself and mind my own business.

WORKER: Were any of you approached by this group? (All said no. Two of the five present belong to the welfare rights group.)

MRS. MELTON: Have they bothered you any more?

MRS. KING: I don't really know. I had two slips in my box to come to the office [Housing Authority]. The lady under me complained that I let water run down her walls from my apartment.

MRS. SMITH: I remember your telling me about that.

MRS. KING: I knocked over the pile of scrub water and it went through the holes between the radiator pipes. I said I was sorry, that it was an accident.

MRS. MELTON: They [Housing Authority] should close up the holes anyway.

MRS. KING: The other was that my son made too much noise.

WORKER: Have you received complaints before these?

MRS. KING: No.

GROUP: (Long silence.)

This time, the worker had strategized to reach into the silence and explore the group members' feelings and ask them to face the second decision.

WORKER: I believe that this has troubled all of you, and I can understand your concern. Let's take a few minutes and think about the group and your participation in it. How do you feel about it? Are you getting anything from the group? (Silence.)

MRS. KING: I've been thinking about it a lot. I'm not going to let people tell me what to do. I don't really know what I'm getting from being here. I like to come and I've been able to meet some new people. I think I understand your agency better.

MRS. MELTON: You see, Mrs. Payne, people are afraid of reprisals. I'm older so they don't bother me. I get a lot out of these meetings. Things are clearer to me. And you helped me with those bills from the Housing Authority. Besides, this gives me a chance to get out.

MRS. DAVIDSON: I've learned a lot. I think my attitude about the caseworkers has changed. I know now that they are not all bad, and it's my responsibility to see that they know what my family needs. Certain things that I did not know about came up, and other policies were explained to me. I don't feel sorry for myself anymore, because I see other people's problems are worse than mine.

MRS. MELTON: I like coming here; a lot of things that were on my mind about welfare are clear to me now. You have helped me a lot. Besides, if we can get somewhere with the Housing Authority about our complaints, that alone will be a great deal.

MRS. KING: I've learned a lot about welfare, too, that I did not know before. I enjoy the group and I'm going to keep coming. It's too bad more people don't come. It makes me mad to know that they will benefit from all our hard work.

GROUP: That's the truth.

WORKER: Then I take it that you want to go on? (All agree.)

WORKER: I'll follow through and will let you know before the meeting if we will have a guest.

After contact was made with the city commissioners, the project manager, Mr. Murray, changed his mind about meeting with the group. The group members found that if they understood the political system, they could use it by applying pressure in the right places. Decisions concerning public housing are political in nature, and as long as there are no public complaints, problems can be ignored. Using the political system as a tool for citizens is an important step for change. All too often, members of poor and repressed groups give up hope of trying to deal with the "system." An attitude of "you can't fight city hall" predominates, leading citizens to give up on the institutions, structures, and agencies established to meet their needs. The worker must convey the idea that there is always a next step.

After the worker clarified the purpose of the meeting with Mr. Murray, the group members began their confrontation.

MRS. SMITH: I'd like to know what the Housing Authority considers wear-and-tear items. I don't think I should have to pay for shades that were worn when I came into my apartment or if they have been hanging for five years.

MR. MURRAY: If the shades are worn when an apartment is vacant, we replace the shades. All apartments are in good order when you people move in.

GROUP: (All disagree.)

MR. MURRAY: When you move in, you sign a statement that everything is in good order. If you don't agree, don't sign it.

MRS. SMITH: I wrote on the list that the shades were worn. You replaced them, but you charged me for them. Ask Mrs. Payne, she gave me the money for them.

MR. MURRAY: You should not have been charged for those shades.

MRS. MCIVER: You see, that's what we are complaining about. We don't know what we should and should not pay for. Your men make us pay for everything. Even if we disagree, you take their word for it.

GROUP: That's right.

MR. MURRAY: You should come to me when you feel you are being charged unjustly.

GROUP: (Laughter.)

MRS. SMITH: You're never there, and no action is taken if we leave a message.

GROUP: (Agreement.)

As the meeting proceeded, the manager expressed his feelings about the tenants. It became clear that he had a stereotyped view of the tenants based on those who had damaged property and not maintained their apartments.

MR. MURRAY: The problem is that you people don't take care of your apartments. You let your kids wreck the place because you don't own it. You've got a responsibility, too, you know.

MRS. MCIVER: I resent that. Most of us keep our places clean. I know there are some people who don't care, but why should the rest of us have to suffer?

MR. MURRAY: We clean the grounds, make repairs, paint the halls every four years. It's the tenants' responsibility to care for the upkeep of their apartments.

MRS. BROWN: Gin bottles, beer cans, and urine, stay in the halls for days, and your men don't clean it away.

MR. MURRAY: Call me. I'll see that it gets done.

MRS. MCIVER: What about the mailboxes? Can't we have better boxes with pick-proof locks? Our checks are always stolen and boxes broken into and we have to pay for them.

MR. MURRAY: There's no such thing as a pick-proof lock. I know the trouble you are having with your checks, and I'm sorry, but if we assume cost, then you people will break in every time you lose your key.

MRS. MCIVER: I disagree. I don't think the tenants would deliberately break into boxes.

MR. MURRAY: They do, and they will do it more often if I change that rule.

The white manager of this housing project with a majority population of people of color was treating tenants in a racist and stereotyped manner. His offers to take care of things were largely efforts to disarm this group, probably because of his fear of their strength in numbers. When the members felt they could not get past the defensiveness of the manager, they again resorted to political pressure, which had worked the first time. The manager responded by inquiring why they had not brought their complaints to him, and the issue of retribution was out in the open. The worker intervened to try to help the manager see that the residents were motivated to improve their living situation.

MRS. SMITH: Who makes appointments to the Housing Authority?

MR. MURRAY: The city commissioners make the appointments.

MRS. SMITH: Can one of us go to the commissioners to let them know our problems?

MR. MURRAY: My board meets once a month. It's open to the public. The board is autonomous. It sets its own rules within the federal guidelines. We will listen to your complaints.

MRS. SMITH: We want them to take some action, too.

GROUP: (All agree.)

MRS. MELTON: We don't feel that the building representatives represent us. I did not know about the elections of officers.

MR. MURRAY: You were all told about the meetings, and I know it.

GROUP: (Disagreement.)

MRS. MCIVER: (Member of one of the committees) Maybe the representatives do not take the time to tell all the people in their buildings.

MRS. SMITH: That man in my building does not represent me. He's not qualified; besides, he does not care about us.

MR. MURRAY: You people have lots of complaints, but you never bring them to the office.

MRS. MCIVER: Most people don't complain because they are afraid of trouble from the office.

MR. MURRAY: We have not put anyone out because of making complaints. I don't see why you should be afraid. There's no reason for it.

WORKER: What the group is saying is that the office has ways to put pressure on these people. The fear is here and cannot be changed overnight. These people are not here to attack you personally but the people who make these unjust rules. These people are motivated—that's why they are here. They want to improve their living circumstances. It's up to you and your board to help them.

MR. MURRAY: If the tenants think the representatives do not meet their approval, then I'll see to it that new elections are held.

MRS. MCIVER: The people don't feel that you are willing to meet with them. They don't feel that you are interested.

MR. MURRAY: I'll do what I can and take your complaints to the board. If you like, you may form your own committee.

MRS. SMITH: We will be at your next meeting.

The meeting had to be called to an end because it had run 45 minutes over the scheduled time. The housing manager's reaction to the confrontation was predictable—inspections were suddenly ordered for all apartments. At the next meeting, the worker again attempted to explore the members' feelings about the reactions to their assertive behavior.

MRS. SMITH: Everybody's talking about it [group's meeting with Mr. Murray] in the office. The janitor who came to inspect my apartment got mad because I refused to sign the inspection form. I told him why and he asked who had I been talking to, Mrs. Payne [the worker]?

GROUP: (Laughter.)

MRS. BROWN: They think we are wrong. He [maintenance man] said that there were over $6,000.00 in repairs this year in the projects and that we were responsible for them.

MRS. KING: Andy [maintenance man] said it's about time someone spoke up. Some of my neighbors are blaming us for the inspection because they have not been inspecting apartments.

GROUP: (All agree.)

MRS. SMITH: I knew Mr. Murray would do something to get back at us.

GROUP: (All agree.)

WORKER: Well, how do you feel about the things that are happening to you?

MRS. SMITH: I don't mind. I knew he would do something to get back at us. But with the agency [Welfare] behind us, he knows he cannot get away with these things anymore.

MRS. BROWN: I heard they were inspecting the apartments so I was ready for them. My apartment was really clean and in order.

MRS. MELTON: They [Housing Authority] have not inspected our apartments in two years or more. Why now?

GROUP: (Agreement. They seemed to make light of the situation and to take it as a joke.)

WORKER: But you still have not told me how you feel about all this, the criticism and pressure from the Housing Authority and your friends and neighbors.

MRS. BROWN: I don't mind. Something had to be done, so we are doing it.

MRS. SMITH: I don't mind either being the scapegoat. I think we can still do a lot more. We will benefit if they [Housing Authority] approve some of our requests, as will those people who call us troublemakers. It's for them, too, not just us.

MRS. KING: The only thing I did not like was their going into my apartment when I was not home.

GROUP: (All agree.)

WORKER: Were you notified of the inspection?

GROUP: No.

MRS. SMITH: They [Housing Authority] can come into your apartment anytime they want to—it's in the lease. They can do it as long as it's a reasonable hour.

MRS. KING: I still don't want them walking into my place.

WORKER: Were nonwelfare tenants' apartments inspected also?

GROUP: Yes.

MRS. KING: They wouldn't like it if it was their place.

MRS. MELTON: They did not miss a thing. We even had to pay for tassels on the shades and missing screws.

WORKER: In other words, they went over your apartment with a fine-toothed comb.

GROUP: (Laughter, agreement.)

MRS. BROWN: They even took the screens out of the windows to be cleaned and fixed. I asked the man not to take mine because those windows are high and the children might fall out, and he said I should put parachutes on all of my kids. I could tell he was mad. (There was a great deal of conversation between members about what they did and did not sign for in regard to the inspection. Their general attitude was surprisingly light and gay.)

WORKER: Am I correct in assuming that you want to go on with the plans for the meeting tomorrow?

GROUP: (All agree, saying, Of course, Why not? and so on.)

MRS. SMITH: We all have asked the tenants in our buildings, but most people won't come because they are afraid of reprisals. They are always asking what we are doing and are interested.

WORKER: Are you afraid of the reprisals?

GROUP: (All chime in) No, of course not.

MRS. SMITH: No, I've always complained about things, not that it does any good. We think we are right. We are not asking for anything that is unreasonable.

MRS. BROWN: My friend said she would not come but would babysit so I could go. (Group all agreed that they were not afraid and would all be there Thursday night.)

The worker then suggested that they consider their strategy for the meeting. The members were concerned about speaking in public and asked the worker to read their requests. She refused, emphasizing the importance of tenants' speaking for themselves. The worker's belief in them was important. She offered to be there to help but said that it was their fight and she believed they could do it.

WORKER: What approach are you going to use?
MRS. MELTON: Can't we do like we did at our meeting?
GROUP: (All agree.)
MRS. BROWN: Maybe one person should read the list of requests. Can't you do it, Mrs. P.?
WORKER: No, one of you should read it. The board will want to hear from you as tenants. What I will do is make a list of your requests and have one for each of you and the board members. Then they can ask you questions. I'll be with you and give you all the support I can, but it's up to you to present your side of the picture.
MRS. KING: That's a good idea, and it will help a lot if they ask us questions.
MRS. MELTON: Sometimes I get all confused and can't say what I want to say.
WORKER: Let's all try to be calm and above all be polite.
GROUP: (Laughter. Personal joke on Mrs. Payne was told.)

Discussion continued about the painting of apartments—cheap quality of paint used, lack of color selection, penalties for not painting, and differential treatment of some tenants. The meeting adjourned with plans to meet Thursday night at 8:00 for the board meeting.

At the meeting with the board, the members acquitted themselves well, and the board immediately approved 9 of their 11 requests. Two of the requests were complicated and required further study, but the board indicated a positive response would be forthcoming. The members of the group and the worker were elated. By using the political system, the members found they could exercise their rights. The balance of power shifted and the pattern of inaction and conformity because of fear was broken; the positive reaction to the first steps taken by this group encouraged other tenants as well. Of course, many issues remained. The relationship with the project manager was still poor, but the worker strategized how to help him see that recognizing tenants' rights would serve his interests. The problem of intertenant friction also needed to be attended to, because peer pressure might well be the most important factor in getting tenants to take responsibility for better maintenance of the project. These next steps seemed more manageable to the group after their initial success.

In addition to the roles described thus far, the community social worker with a task group has many of the same functions described in the earlier chapters on working with clinical groups. Many of the dynamics described earlier, such as the emergence of the deviant member, arise in task groups such as the one described in the next example. This example also raises a fundamental issue common in community-based groups: "What if the worker has a strong opinion about an issue or the direction the group should take?"

The Deviant Member: Community-Based Citizens' Advisory Board

In previous chapters we saw how the deviant member in a group can be seen as a possible spokesperson, an ally for the worker rather than an enemy of the group. We saw that the worker should not identify with the group versus the individual but instead focus on helping the two clients. This clarity of role becomes particularly difficult when the deviant member expresses a point of view at variance with that of the worker.

One example of the functional role of the deviant member in a community group can be drawn from a community-based citizens' group charged with the responsibility of distributing a portion of community social welfare funds. Mr. Fisk developed a reputation in the group for being outspoken, angry, and intimidating, and usually taking a minority conservative point of view on an essentially liberal board. Given that the worker usually agreed with the more liberal view of the majority, she needed to overcome the strong temptation to work with the group against Mr. Fisk. In the first encounters, the worker lost sight of this role and attempted to rebut Mr. Fisk, thus siding with the majority.

The purpose of the board was to represent community opinion in the distribution of funds. On the agenda the evening of the meeting was the funding of a local women's center that was both politically active and provided community social service. As the group worker expected, Mr. Fisk began by attacking the funding on the grounds that the center was essentially political. Feeling a strong attachment to the work of the women's center, the worker attacked his position by offering additional information in favor of the center. The debate between group members and Mr. Fisk continued, and he ended up losing the vote.

In a retrospective analysis of the process, the worker granted that when Mr. Fisk spoke, some members were silently nodding in agreement. Other members were obviously disagreeing. The group was also clearly uncomfortable about taking on Mr. Fisk, because of the way he argued his point of view. As can easily happen, the worker was so intent on her agenda of getting the center funded that she ignored the communication problem in the group and jumped in to take sides. An alternative line of work might have been to help other members in the group express the feelings and thoughts behind the nonverbal signals, including those members who agreed with Mr. Fisk. The worker could bring into the open the difficulty in discussion caused by Mr. Fisk's strong presentation, but she would do this only to help the group members and Mr. Fisk in their communications.

With hindsight, it is easy to see that Mr. Fisk represented a larger body of opinion in the community, and if the board was to do its job effectively, then decisions had to take into account a broad range of opinions. There was a good chance that some of the most ardent supporters of the women's center had some mixed feelings about funding the political action component, which was outside of the center's current mandate. In turn, Mr. Fisk and his supporters probably had a sense of the importance of the social service aspect of the center's work. If not, then the discussion would be enriched by a full debate on these ideas, in which the worker helped the members from both sides say what they felt as well as listen to those who disagreed with them. The worker would be free to add her own views on the matter, but she should not abandon the crucial function of group worker. Often, in withholding personal views so as "not to influence the group," the worker ends up indirectly attempting to manipulate opinion to the desired outcome. The irony of this is that the same worker may feel and express a deep conviction in the importance of the community decision-making process. Once again, the deviant member, Mr. Fisk, could have been helpful in strengthening the debate on a contentious issue.

Relationship to the Environment: Adolescent Peer Leaders

In this next community group example, we examine a common type of program in which adolescents and teens in a housing project are organized to provide service to their community. The social worker focused on helping the teens to overcome their internalized sense of inadequacy, which had been reinforced by negative community stereotypes regarding their competency. The example demonstrates that each individual member of such a group brings her or his own strengths and problems to the process and not all members will be able to achieve the hoped-for positive results.

RECORD OF SERVICE

Client Description and Time Frame

Type of Group: Task group for adolescent peer leaders.

Age Range: 13–19 years old.

Gender and Ethnicity: Four male African Americans, one female African American, two female Hispanics, and one female Caucasian.

Dates Covered: 10/15 to 1/13.

Group Task: Relationship to the environment.

Description of the Problem

The peer leaders' lack of credibility in the community in which they worked and lived led to criticism from parents, the funding agency, the Housing Authority, and the Tenant Council. Few believed this group could organize positive events in this housing project, an attitude that undermined the peer leaders' potential and purpose.

How the Problem Came to the Attention of the Worker(s)

During my twice-weekly training sessions with the peer leaders, the group would talk about the rumors and comments that their mothers, neighbors, Tenant Council, or Housing Authority Task Force were alleging against them. I watched the group go from joking about the newest rumor to growing discouraged, doubting their own abilities to create positive events. In late November I announced to the group that the funding agency was going to drop this project because of the negative press that this housing project was beginning to receive in relation to teenagers.

Summary of the Work

Thirty teenagers from this small housing project interviewed for the peer leader position. Eight were hired: four male and four female. At the first formal meeting, during their first day on the job, the contract became the tool that disclosed the group's task: negotiating its relationship to the environment.

Keith (17 years old, African American) mentioned that Mary, the Tenant Council chair, probably would not let them use this community center every day. Amy

(15 years old, African American) elaborated on how the "green monster" yells and screams at them just for looking at her. I asked why they named her the "green monster." Bruce (15 years old, African American) answered by pointing to a green partitioned office in the corner of the center. Everyone laughed. I asked if there were any rules connected with our use of the building. They all grunted and chuckled, and Lucy (19 years old, white) enlightened me by asking if I had all day to sit and listen to her list them. I was reaching for their perceptions of their own environment as well as conveying my willingness to learn from them.

As the group began defining the problems they wanted to tackle and the events to work on, they became more aware of what a peer leader group is. The group struggled, however, with the idea of serving as positive youth role models.

Jake (15 years old, African American), Amy's twin brother, mentioned that there is nothing for a teenager to do in this city. "All we do is go to school, come home, and get into trouble." Gwen (14 years old, Hispanic) added that the weekends are boring and "someone needs to make some changes around here." I asked who they thought should make these changes. I wanted to assist them with connecting their purpose as peer leaders with the task of creating change. Bruce answered by insisting that the Housing Authority were the only ones who could create change, because they had all the money. Danny (14 years old, African American), Keith's younger brother, jumped in and said, "Yes, if they were the cops we'd all be in the state pen." They then went on to exchange stories about their bad encounters with the Housing Authority.

I asked if they thought they could make some changes. Once again, I was hoping to help them make the connection between themselves and their purpose. Karen (13 years old, Hispanic) nodded her head yes, vigorously. The Housing Authority was perceived to have all the power, and they continued to have a difficult time envisioning their own abilities to create positive changes. I too was feeling oppressed by this powerful organization, but I also realized my need to know the Housing Authority Task Force so decided to attend meetings on an irregular basis.

In the excerpts that follow, the reality of living in a neighborhood in which crime, drug dealing, and murder are all too common is brought home dramatically to the social worker. These teens face many environmental stressors, and the worker must have faith in their resilience to survive and thrive in the face of adversity.

In early November the group ran their first meeting with teenagers from the Project. Forty-five youth showed up for the meeting. The basic goals were to build an organization of youth, brainstorm ideas for future events, and establish themselves as leaders among their peers. On the following Monday I went prepared to process the success of their first organizing meeting; however, they came to work discouraged and quiet. I inquired about their gloomy faces. A few shrugged their shoulders, and then Danny looked over at Keith and said, "Just tell her."

Keith went on to tell me that he was arrested for assault on the weekend. I immediately responded by asking if Keith had been convicted. He informed me that he was given a court date in 2 months. I avoided details of the arrest intentionally because I did not want to set myself up as the moral teacher or the judge. Lucy, however, was upset with Keith and asked him how he ever thought the group was going to look good if they all went around beating up people. This conversation lasted for 45 minutes and ended with major changes on their work contract. They decided that they needed to be accountable as positive role models

"24/7" instead of just the 2 hours they worked each day. They also put in writing that, if any of them are arrested, caught in possession of illegal drugs, or caught carrying a gun, that they are immediately terminated. They all agreed that Keith should not be fired, because he had not known about the rule.

During the last week of November, one of their friends, Jed, was shot seven times and killed in front of the community center. Jed was a local hero because he had just signed on with a record label and already had a rap album produced. He was also selling cocaine, resulting in his death, a fact that the group refused to accept verbally. They romanticized Jed's death. It appeared to me that Keith, Danny, and Jake were struggling internally with the decision to choose positive behavior over negative. The world that surrounds them daily is so full of pain and negative options. Their ambivalence about their role as peer leaders showed itself often in the group, putting them at higher risk for negative actions.

After an hour of talking about Jed's death, I asked them to think about how his murder affected them as a group. I saw this tragedy as an opportunity to clarify the need for peer leaders in this community. Keith said, angrily, that the world would do anything to keep the black man down. Jake agreed, adding that Jed was going somewhere, and someone had to go and "take him out." Once again I asked them to focus on the group as it related to Jed. I was aware of their avoidance to address the facts of the murder such as the drug charges and the sad reality that the killers were also black youth. It did not seem appropriate to address this at this time, because their grief was so new. Therefore, I felt a deep need to look at the relationship between themselves as peer leaders and an environment where other youth are being killed.

After a brief silence, Gwen said that no one really gives a "fuck" about them. Danny jumped in and shared that his mother thought they were all a bunch of hoodlums and that she is surprised that any of them could even get out of bed in the morning. No one laughed. Bruce added that he thought the whole community was against them and that they all thought the members of this group were just like Jed. "We are just like Jed," blurted Jake. "I won't live past 18 years old." Silence fell over the group.

The silence was powerful. I was deeply affected by their comments. I was angry along with them. I was also sad as I felt their pain. "I'm tired of the killing," shouted Amy. "First my older brother is murdered, and then you (looking at Jake) were stabbed this summer, and now Jed, dead!" Amy turned to me and looked straight into my eyes and said, "Tina, no one gives a shit about us. What can we do to change anything?" "Amy, you can prove to yourself by proving to others that you care very deeply about life and you want to see it improve," I responded.

I could see a lot of hope in the anger that we were all feeling. I felt like we were closer to sharing a common vision than ever before. I could see some lights clicking on in the midst of the pain and a new energy for the work being rekindled. I also felt a sense of urgency about our work. The time was now, and we needed to take the opportunity.

Instead of a teen dance, or party at Christmas, they decided to plan an event that would serve the whole community with an emphasis on celebration and healing. They needed money, credibility, and success.

The Holiday Bazaar would offer international foods, raffles, free presents for all the children, Santa Claus, a craft corner, face painting, a graffiti wall, and speeches delivered by Amy and Keith. They sent out press releases to several newspapers and TV channels. They especially wanted Channel 7 news because they were the station that had covered the story on Jed. They liked the idea of the news team coming back to cover a positive story on youth. I overheard Amy telling the news reporter, "I believe youth need to be heard in America. We have a lot to say and a lot to give you adults, so listen closely."

During the event, the director of the Housing Authority stood behind the microphone, asked for attention, and proceeded to deliver a speech to the community about how crucial he felt these peer leaders were for this housing project, and how proud he was of them. He then announced to the group, in front of their parents, friends, siblings and neighbors, that the Housing Authority was giving the peer leaders $9,000 to continue their work. The group was stunned by this announcement. Lucy, Amy, Keith, and Bruce flew over to me confused and disoriented by the good news. They were firing questions at me, such as "Did he say he was giving us money?" "Did you know about this?" "What does he mean?" "Did you hear all the cool things he said about us?" I asked them how it felt to be such a success. I saw their shock at being delivered encouraging news from the Housing Authority, the very agency that they had felt so oppressed by during the past 3 months. I felt I needed to help them connect the director's announcement with their success. They were slow at internalizing good news, and I was hoping they could absorb the glory as they were experiencing it and not just in retrospect. Finally as the good news began to sink in, the peer leaders started hugging me and one another, exclaiming, "We did it!"

We all broke for the holidays for 2 weeks, then held our first meeting after our big event on January 6. Jake had taped the 7-minute excerpt from the local news the night of our event, so I arranged for us all to view it. We watched it two times and then discussed what our favorite part of the event was. "Being told we could continue working," said Lucy. Bruce commented, "Yeah, I was shocked when the director got up there and said those cool things about us. I was scared that he was going to kick us out of the community center." We all laughed. I then told them I had some more good news. Not only did the Housing Authority commit to donating money, but the drug prevention funding agency also donated some. In unison, they shouted, "How much?" I was so excited to tell them that the amount was $10,000. I really wanted them to absorb their success as a group, so I lingered in the details.

"That's $19,000" Bruce declared. "We were hoping to raise $200 from selling the food and sodas. Shit, we really showed them." "Who are 'them'?" I asked. I hoped we could reconcile some of the pain that months of criticism had brought them. I was also hoping that they would really start seeing themselves as creative and positive people. Naming the "enemies" and realizing that they too could change could reveal to them some very important truths about their own personal power. We discussed every detail that was observed concerning their success as a youth organizing group.

During the next training session on January 13, we focused on our next big event. I started the group with a bit of new information that was being discussed in the Task Force meetings. "Because of your success as a group, the Housing Authority, in conjunction with the funding agency, wants to create five more peer leader groups in this city. They see the success of teenagers working to improve their own environments. Isn't that great? The youth voice in this city will be strong." I was personally so excited about this new development. From my perspective, this was the best news yet because it would provide more jobs for youth as well as reach a large constituency.

The group was silent. I was surprised that they did not seem excited. Lucy then blurted, "What about us?" I was lost and said, "What do you mean? It's because of you that this is happening." I really missed the point here. Lucy continued, "What about us? They could be taking care of us and trying to improve our voice." "Yeah," Danny added, "they have completely forgotten about us." "We need a youth center," Bruce joined, "we can't keep meeting in this ugly building, on these metal chairs." "We can't even hang up a poster in here," Keith added. "They won't even let us have snacks in this center."

These comments went on for 15 minutes before I asked what was wrong. I felt there was something else going on that I wasn't aware of. They were back to being upset with the agencies and their surroundings. They continued talking about not wanted to be forgotten. I then asked if they would like to help train other peer leader groups. I was beginning to see how much they needed to be recognized on an ongoing basis and how fearful they felt of having their victory robbed. Perhaps if they were given some status among these other groups they might feel more in control.

They changed their tune completely after this comment. They started making plans on how to teach these other young rookies the ropes as youth organizers. They fantasized about their position as the top youth workers in the city and how the mayor would give them all outstanding citizen awards. I felt both sad and happy by their need to be accepted. I realized that the ongoing, daily reality of living as poor minorities in a housing project where they feared eviction was a very heavy burden that I so quickly forgot. Listening to them dream, however, was also beautiful. They had a very difficult time dreaming of a positive future.

Current Status of the Problem

Where the Problem Stands Now

The problem still exists. However, the opportunity for the group to see agencies that felt so powerful and so oppressive be affected by the peer leaders' dedication has made them realize that they do have some control over their environment. The ongoing struggle of daily life, however, feels like an endless battle for some of the youth. Danny was fired in late January because he was caught in possession of cocaine by his mother. The only reason she reported her son was to beat the eviction letter. If tenants confess their mistakes before the Council writes them a letter, they avoid eviction.

Jake is also struggling with his street-self. He was present when two of his friends were killed; he experienced the death of a brother, and another has recently been arrested; and he experienced violence personally when stabbed in the summer. Rumor is floating around that Jake bought a gun. We have no proof, and Jake denies the allegation.

Keith, on February 8, was convicted of an assault that he committed in October. He will be on probation for a year. Lucy, 2 weeks before the Bazaar, married a 38-year-old man at the state penitentiary. He's been a "friend of the family" since Lucy was a child, and he is now serving time for rape charges.

These hard realities have certainly impacted the group's newly attained credibility. One step forward, two steps back.

Specific Next Steps

I am now working 3 days a week with the peer leaders. We are currently planning a month of prevention in this city where the peer leaders will perform plays in the high schools, have a poster and essay contest, and host a banquet/entertainment night where city officials and those who provided the funds will be invited. The internal issues in the group, which are directly related to the environment in which they live, continue to undermine the group's work. However, much of my time is spent negotiating with parents and agencies to believe in these youth and encourage their efforts.

Dealing with the dysfunction and the group dynamics is an area that is demanding much more attention, requiring sensitivity and skill, but this is a whole new story.

What is so impressive about this example is the worker's never-failing faith in the capacity of the teens to overcome adversity. She understands the meaning of the deviant behavior that they have evidenced and still reaches for their strengths.

The Milieu as Community

In the final section of this chapter on community work, we focus on the milieu as community. For many clients, their community is a residential center or a hospital ward. Although treatment programs affect their lives, the day-to-day experiences of living and working with staff and other residents always have the most powerful effects. If a treatment group teaches about life empowerment while its members feel they are disempowered in the setting, the real message reinforces weakness rather than strength, pathology rather than resiliency.

In the example that follows, the social worker uses the medium of a ward newspaper to help psychiatric patients negotiate their community more effectively. The newspaper becomes a vehicle for communication with staff as well as a means for the members to discover their own strengths. It also becomes a medium through which the members can communicate their inner feelings about having to deal with the oppression associated with mental illness.

RECORD OF SERVICE

Client Description and Time Frame

Members: White male veterans who are patients in a VA psychiatric setting.

Dates: 9/30 to 12/2.

Group Task: Relationship to the environment.

Description of the Problem

The task this group faces is one of negotiating the larger system in which it is situated, in order to produce a patient newsletter. Some of the challenges faced by the group are resistance from the larger system (the hospital), resistance within the group (fear of making waves), members' fear of retribution from staff, feelings of disempowerment, and suspicion from inside and outside of the group. The major problem centers on the feelings of disempowerment embodied by the group members. This is illustrated by the reluctance to express themselves honestly in the newsletter. A second, related, problem is the hospital's low expectations of the patients and the ambivalence of the hospital toward change. The problem I face is to find a way of mediating between these two systems.

How the Problem Came to the Attention of the Worker(s)

Several incidents led to this assessment. In beginning the newsletter, I observed a great deal of enthusiasm initially, both from group members and staff, but this enthusiasm began to falter after the first few meetings. Many of the members failed to complete the assignments they had volunteered for, and support from the outside system was not forthcoming, as had been promised. Staff members discussed the need to censor the newsletter before it was distributed, which heightened and rein-forced group members' fear and reservations. I realized that some of these issues would need to be addressed if the group were to proceed any further.

Summary of the Work

The first session was exciting. It was filled with hope and expectations on the part of the worker as well as the members. It was a large group with 17 members in all. There was a sense of expectation in the air. I had been preparing for the group for several weeks, and the newness of it was intriguing to the members. Most of the vets had gotten to know me well enough to suspect that something different was happening, that this group would be different from other groups at the program.

In the beginning of the session, I explained to the group what I had in mind for the newsletter, in order to clarify its purpose. "As some of you already know, I had an idea to start a newsletter. The newsletter would be created by all of you. You would write the articles, decide what went into it, how often it would be published, and things like that. In other words, it would be your newsletter. I also thought of it as a way of helping the members of this program get connected with one another and keep one another informed as to what kinds of things happen around here. We could send copies to your friends and families to let them know what kinds of things you do here. I would also contribute my own ideas from time to time and be avail-able to help members with any problems they might have. There will also be some other students and volunteers who have offered to help in any way if you have trouble with writing. I'd like to hear from you now. Do you have any thoughts on this idea?"

Many members expressed interest and said it was a good idea, though I sensed some doubt on the part of the members. I had the vague sense they were just humoring me. Instead of confronting it directly I just went on, hoping in time they would become more invested. Had I confronted it then, it might have opened up the discussion and raised some of the concerns and doubts they were feeling.

We decided on a name for the newsletter, and people volunteered for jobs. There was much debate about what to call the newsletter. One member offered the *Elite Newspaper of the East* as a possible title. He seemed very angry. I added his title to the rest of the titles to be voted on, and I commented that I thought it was an inter-esting name. He did not respond, and I went on collecting other titles. I realized I had not picked up the message he was indirectly sending me. I had missed the opportunity to address some of the anger he was feeling and I was not tuned in to what was urgent to him at that moment. I was unable to set aside my own agenda. Had I picked up on his anger, I would have been able to recognize that his feelings were representative of much of what the group was feeling. Fortunately for the group (and for me), this anger would surface again in later groups and help break through the illusion of work that had formed.

In the second session, the members volunteered one another for jobs. In a some-what derisive manner, an older man named George volunteered Dana, one of the younger members, to be the editor. Dana was generally very quiet and reserved and seldom participated in other groups. I responded that I thought it was a great idea and asked Dana if he would consider accepting the position. He seemed pleased at this and accepted. Everyone applauded. At this point, Harold, another older man, said that, while he was in the army, he used to take a lot of pictures. I asked him if he wanted to be the photographer, and he agreed. The energy in the room seemed to increase, and everyone started volunteering for jobs. We decided to meet once a week as a group and to put the newsletter out once a month.

During the month, some of the members were very busy interviewing people and writing their stories. Others were not doing their jobs and were coming up with excuses for why they couldn't do them. I felt this was due to a lack of confidence in their abilities, so much of my work during this period focused on expressing my belief in their abilities to do the job. I began to recognize that a general theme was emerging on how disempowered the members were feeling.

During the fifth session, I noticed that many of the members were having difficulty concentrating and seemed completely disinterested in the group. I reached for what was happening. "What is going on today? Everyone seems to be having trouble focusing on the topic. You all look bored and tired." Dan responded, "We all just went out for a long walk, we are tired." Richard added, "They keep us too busy around here, all we do is go to groups. They never leave us alone." I asked if anyone else felt this way and if they wanted to spend a few minutes talking about this. Many members responded by agreeing that there were too many groups and they were feeling overwhelmed.

I tried to validate their feelings by saying that sometimes there were a lot of groups to attend, and then I asked if they had ever spoken to the staff and voiced their concerns. Jim, the member who had been so angry in the first session, responded by saying that it did no good, the staff didn't care what they wanted and they treated them all like children. I knew I had to be careful here. My natural inclination was to side with the group members. I had often been angered by the patronizing manner in which these men were treated. It would have been easy for me to have jumped on the bandwagon and started criticizing the hospital, but I knew that would not have been useful. I responded instead by reaching for his feelings, saying, "It must feel pretty frustrating to be treated in this way. After all, you're not children, you're grown men."

This opened the door for a lengthy discussion about how it felt to be a psychiatric patient and to lose so much control over one's life. I tried to bring the conversation back into focus by suggesting that the newsletter might be a forum the men could use in order to voice some of their concerns. Roland, a member whom I have always thought of as very ingratiating to the staff, eager and cooperative, fearful of making trouble and generally considered a "good" patient, said, "Oh no, we couldn't do that, they would never let us print it. Besides, it's not really so bad around here. The staff are all nice and they treat us well." Another member was made anxious by the interchange and completely changed the subject. Time was almost up, so I said that if the group wanted to, we could continue talking about this the next time we met.

The next session involved a field trip we had planned, and the session after that, the recreational therapist joined the group. Apparently, the news had gotten out about our discussion. I told the staff I was encouraging the members to write about things that were meaningful to them and that at times this might involve an expression of criticism toward the hospital. They joked about how I was getting the patients all riled up. I sensed some suspicion beneath the humor. I asked if they thought this was a bad thing. This brought the issue out to the surface and opened up the opportunity for me to speak with the staff about some of the feelings the patients were having.

During the next session we got back to the discussion and returned to the earlier topic. The members seemed distracted and uninterested. They were also having difficulties finishing the assignments they had volunteered for. I asked them what was going on. Jimmy, a member who attended only occasionally, responded, "How do you expect us to do anything? I can't write; look at my hands." He held up his hands, which were shaking visibly. "They keep us so medicated around here we can't even think straight." Jake agreed, "These doctors use us as guinea pigs. They try one medication after another on us. We are subjects in their experiments; they don't treat us like human beings." Roland began to get nervous. "Yes, but we need to take our medication, it helps us. I'm ready for my next shot. I get too agitated if I don't get my shot."

Jake responded, saying the medication didn't help him, that it had ruined his life. He spoke of how he was not able to have a relationship with women or to live a normal life. He said, "Any member in this room will tell you that the medicines make you impotent. How are you ever supposed to meet a girl or think about getting married?" Several of the men nodded their heads in agreement. I said that must be very difficult for them and asked if they had ever let the doctors know about the problems they had with the medications. Jake again responded, "They don't care. If you refuse to take the medications, they will just lock you up." He went on to tell of how he had been forcibly locked up in the hospital. Several other group members agreed, telling stories of how they had been locked in the seclusion room, beaten up by orderlies, or admitted to the hospital against their will. They said when they told someone, the doctors responded by saying it was just a symptom of their paranoia. Jake said that he was learning not to fight, that he was not a young man anymore. I empathized with the things that the group members had gone through and said it must be really difficult to always have someone questioning their reality. I then suggested that Jake might want to write about his experiences for the newsletter. I hoped to begin to help empower them and to show them a way to have their concerns heard. Jake expressed ambivalence about doing this. I said I could understand his reservations and said if he wanted to he could take some time and think about it or that he could do it anonymously. This all proved to be more than Roland could stand.

Under his breath, but loudly enough for everyone to hear, he said, "Communist!" I was taken aback by this expression of anger from Roland. I was also not sure whom he was talking to. Jake responded angrily, "What did you call me?" Roland looked in his direction and said, louder this time, "A communist. You're nothing but a communist. The doctors are just trying to help us. You're always going around trying to stir things up." Jake was very angry at this. A veteran considers this to be the worst kind of insult. Jake responded to Roland, "I'm no communist, and don't you call me that. I have a right to say what I feel." I was afraid the situation might escalate into violence, because Jake was extremely angry. (I also felt my maternal instincts surface.)

I interjected, "Roland, it seems as if you see the situation in one way and Jake sees it from a different perspective. But I don't think it is useful for us to call each other names." I had intended to try to create a culture in which discussions of such matters were allowed and also one in which members respected and listened to one another. But, in rushing to Jake's defense, I was sending a message that I didn't believe he could take care of himself and that he needed my protection. This was not a useful message to send to someone who already feels so oppressed. I might have done better if I had waited a little longer and allowed them to work things out themselves.

Roland apologized to Jake and said he was just a little "off" because he had not gotten his shot yet. Jake accepted this apology, and the conversation returned to a discussion of an article someone was writing for the newsletter. The session ended with me encouraging the members to consider writing about their hospital experiences for the newsletter.

Current Status of the Problem

Where the Problem Stands Now

I can safely say the newsletter has become firmly established as a part of the program. I've noticed more staff members becoming invested in its continuation. There has been discussion of who will take over the project after I am gone. The director of the program requested a copy of the newsletter to be sent with his semiannual report, and another staff member included it in a presentation she was giving about the program. I have witnessed some positive change, in that the system now relates in a different manner toward the veterans. I notice some staff now saying "members" or "veterans" instead of "patients." Several staff members have expressed surprise over the talent that the men are exhibiting. There is also less fear and suspicion about what kinds of things I am doing with the group. We are still working on the issue of censorship as I continue to advocate for as little as possible in order to make sure the newsletter remains within the patients' control.

The group is still working on how much they want to express themselves in the newsletter. Many of the members still feel very disempowered and alienated, but they have been receiving a lot of positive reinforcement from the hospital community, which has led to a tremendous boost in self-confidence and self-esteem. Some of the members of the newsletter group are working on submitting articles to a national journal that publishes works by disabled and hospitalized veterans. Others have expressed an interest in learning how to type so they can type the newsletter themselves. One member has decided to begin to study for his high school equivalency exam. This is truly an exciting process to watch.

Specific Next Steps

- I will continue to encourage the members to use the newsletter as a forum in which to voice their concerns.

- I will attempt to create a safe atmosphere within the group where members can feel free to discuss things that are truly meaningful to them.

- I will continue working with the larger system to sensitize it to some of the feelings, needs, and concerns of the veterans.

- I hope to continue making the newsletter a project the members feel they can have ownership of.

- I will continue to search for connections between the system and the group in order to help create more open systems and a healthier environment for the veterans.

- At every opportunity, I will endeavor to empower the individual members as well as the group as a whole.

- And lastly, I will continue to work on my skills as a group worker so I can "make more sophisticated mistakes" in the future.

It seems appropriate to conclude this last example of the chapter with some excerpts from the newspaper published by these veterans, the *War Memorial Gazette*. Their first issue did not directly deal with some of their concerns and feelings about the hospital and the staff; however, they did appear to employ indirect communications. For example, the comedy section of the first issue contained the following three jokes about psychiatrists.

Jokes by Ed

1. What's the difference between a neurotic, psychotic, and a psychiatrist? A neurotic builds castles in the clouds. A psychotic lives in them. A psychiatrist collects the rent for them.
2. How many psychiatrists does it take to change a light bulb? One, but the light bulb has to be willing to change.
3. This guy went to the psychiatrist and he is talking to the psychiatrist, and the psychiatrist says, "You're crazy!" And the guy says, "I want a second opinion." And the psychiatrist says, "OK, I think you're ugly too."

As the members' confidence grew, they began to be more direct, including columns about their concerns over the ward policies and procedures balanced with interviews that highlighted members of the staff. In their third issue, they included editorial and poetry pages, excerpts of which follow.

This newsletter is a project of the Community Support Program of this Veterans Administration Hospital. The opinions and views expressed within do not necessarily reflect those of the staff or administration of the Hospital.

Politicians

We as an individual should not form our opinions of a politician by their rhetoric and exposure by the media, but rather by their actual voting record, which should be publicly displayed. What is their background educationally, religiously, and what special interest groups support them physically and financially? This will determine their voting records and real selves. The news media should take more objective responsibility in this area.

Personal Philosophy

I'm a Vietnam combat vet. I've been in and out of the Veterans Hospital for many years for physical and mental problems. This doesn't mean I haven't got a good IQ or common sense.

On economics, it's about time we as Americans bought American products to put Americans to work. Our products are better, as good, or maybe not up to foreign products. Every individual makes our economy and jobs with their purchases.

On politics, it's about time we look at our representatives and the policies they put forward. Are they voting for money, people, and special interest groups or for the American people? Stop the political slander and get to the economic issues.

We have a beautiful system of checks and balances between the Congress, Presidency, and Supreme Court. We also have the right of petition if we disagree with what's going on. If we don't examine and vote, we stand a chance of losing this system.

Tom

Feeling Blue

When I'm out under the trees
I watch the flowers dance in the breeze
I feel the pain and sorrow that surround me
All I want is the sun to shine, the rain to fall
And no one to be left standing small.

Saying Good-Bye

For you there are always tears, the well is never dry
People live sadly, they must die
Think of a deep, deep sleep
Think of the trees swaying in the breeze
Think of a cool mountain stream you may see
Only in a dream.
To find the answer you must be keen
Just be sure life was not just a dream.

Teddy Bear

I wish I was your teddy bear
I would squeeze away your tears
I would squeeze away your sorrows
I would squeeze away your fears
I would hug you ever so tight
Tell you I love you so
And
Never
Never let you go.

The veterans published the *War Memorial Gazette* for over 5 years (and may still be publishing it). It has matured as a paper and has earned the respect and support of the staff. When the patients held a 5-year celebration of the inception of the paper, they invited the student who had helped them organize the paper, to thank her for her initiative and her faith in their ability. These excerpts serve as a tribute to the resilience and courage of clients and to the profound impact of one student who refused to give up on them or the system, her second client. It sends an important and appropriate message to our profession, reminding us of the roots of social work and the importance of the two-client concept.

Chapter Summary

The community social worker plays a specific role in working with task-focused community groups. Social work practice with community groups is called macro-practice, in contrast to micropractice, which is clinical practice. Macropractice can include direct as well as indirect social work activity. *Community* is here defined geographically and includes an institutional milieu. The concepts of group dynamics and the skills of working with groups introduced in earlier chapters focusing on micropractice also apply to work with community groups. Such work brings unique challenges because the second client often has much power and control over clients' lives.

Related Online Content and Activities

 Visit *The Skills of Helping* Book Companion Website at www.socialwork.wadsworth .com/Shulman06/ for learning tools such as glossary terms, InfoTrac College Edition keywords, links to related websites, and chapter practice quizzes.

The website for this chapter also features additional notes from the author.

CHAPTER SEVENTEEN

The Impact of the Agency, Ethics, Legislation, and Evaluation

I n this chapter we explore several factors that can profoundly affect practice. These include the agency culture, professional values and ethics, and legislative and legal issues. Although we have touched on many of these issues in previous chapters, here we examine each in greater detail. The final section centers on evaluation, a key process in determining the effects of our practice.

Agency Records, Referral Reports, and the Agency Culture

One worker reported a first session with a client who had a long history of contact with the agency. Before the worker could begin, the client, in a good-humored manner, said, "I bet you've read all about me." Many helping contacts involve clients who have had prior contact with the particular setting or with other professionals. The agency file system may contain detailed records on past experiences or a report from an **intake worker**, whose job it is to make the first contact with a client and conduct some form of assessment of suitability for services. Referrals from other professionals often include descriptions of the client, family, problems, and past history. Depending on how it is used, this prior information can be helpful or can become a obstacle to the work.

On the positive side, information about the client may help the worker develop the preliminary empathy needed to prepare for the first session. A review of past experiences with workers or a report of the intake conversation may reveal potential themes of concern to which the worker can be alert. Understanding the recent strains that have brought the client to the attention of the worker may help the worker develop a feel for the emotional state to be expected in early sessions. A summary of past experiences may also yield insight into the client's attitude toward helping professionals. If the records reveal that the going has been rough, the worker may want to plan how to change the client's stereotype of workers.

On the other hand, if the worker uses the information to develop a stereotype of the client, then the preparatory work can block the development of a working relationship. For example, say a worker begins a contact with a natural parent in a child welfare setting. If the worker believes that the client is defensive, resistant, hostile, and not open to help, then this mind-set may be the start of a self-fulfilling prophecy. Further, when one stereotype (the worker's) tries to deal with another stereotype (the client's), no real communication takes place. As one of my clients once described this problem, "It's like two ships passing in the night." In particular, the worker will miss seeing the potential resilience already demonstrated by the client's ability to survive in the face of adversity.

The agency culture often sets the stage for the new worker or student to develop a stereotypical view of a particular client or clients. A common example is what I call "the agency client." This is a family or client who has been with the agency for a long time, sometimes two or three generations, and who has developed a reputation for being "unworkable." These are the cases that students or new workers often receive. A common experience is for the new worker or student to mention this client to a colleague who exclaims, in amazement, "They gave you the Smith family!" Even before the first contact, the worker has been set up for a negative experience.

Sadly, agency cultures can foster stereotypes of a whole class of clients—a process that at its worst can be racist, sexist, ageist, homophobic, and so forth. In one of my studies, negative outcomes were associated with a worker's perception that Native families were more difficult to help than non-Native families. For example, there was a negative association with the Native family's perceptions of their workers' availability, their trust in their workers, and outcomes such as workers' helpfulness and Native children going into care (Shulman, 1991). These workers' perceptions may be rooted in the oppressive attitudes toward others we all must acknowledge within ourselves. When we experience difficulty in working with others who are different, our inherent racism, sexism, or homophobia may emerge as part of our efforts to explain our feelings of being ineffective.

Study findings also revealed positive practice outcomes related to workers' sensitivity to the impact of differences between the workers and their clients. A worker's cultural awareness and sensitivity also was associated with positive outcomes, as was the general attitude of the office involved. For example, the existence of cooperative rather than conflicted relationships between an office or region and the minority group's formal support system (such as Native court workers or homemakers, Native social workers, Native friendship centers) was associated with positive outcomes (such as fewer Native children going into care).

If most or all of the staff are members of the majority group (white, for example), then the chance of negative attitudes and stereotypes being maintained or heightened in an office increases. Agencies have begun to understand the importance of diversity in the management and frontline staff. Increasingly, affirmative action programs have been developed to address this issue.

In general, to avoid responding to clients as if they were stereotypes, workers need to remember that a client described in a report is constantly acting and reacting to systems, including the worker who wrote the report. One simply cannot know clients without understanding them in terms of this process. Their actions need to be viewed in relation to the actions of others.

I have found it interesting to sit in on case conferences where a client is being discussed. The helping professional will report on a home visit or a contact, describe the client in some detail, review the client's history, and then offer a diagnosis of the problem, a prognosis, and a proposal for treatment. If the worker reports that the client was defensive or hostile, this is discussed. Such a conference is following the medical paradigm described in Chapter 1. The discussion centers on assessing the client. If I suggest we shift from talking about the client as an entity to discussing the details of the interview between the worker and the client, the conversation changes dramatically. This represents a shift to what I described in Chapter 1 as the interactional model. I ask the worker to describe how the interview began, what was said to the client, and how the client responded. As the detailed description continues, the staff members begin to get a feeling for the reciprocal interaction between client and worker. The worker's and client's feelings are explored in the process; not surprisingly, the actions of the client often become quite explainable in relation to the worker's efforts. For example, the worker sensed the underlying resistance but did not respond by directly exploring it. Perhaps the worker read a previous report on the client and began the interview expecting trouble, thereby bringing it about. The worker's own feelings may have made empathy with the client's struggle difficult, thus closing off openings for work.

The result of such discussion, even when the worker was skillful in the first interview, is the emergence of a client who is more multidimensional than at first seemed. Workers can see ambivalence rather than just defensiveness. In addition to the anger, they can sense the client's underlying hurt, distrust, and bitterness that may have resulted from poor past experiences with professionals. What might have seemed like a hopeless case changes through this discussion to a difficult case with some important openings for work.

If workers using prior record material or referral material can keep in mind not only the tentativeness of the information but also the need to see the client in interaction rather than as a static entity, then this material can help them prepare for the first interview. As this interview begins, workers need to clear their minds of all of these facts, opinions, and even the workers' own tentative tuning-in guesses. The preparatory work has helped pave the way; now the workers will demonstrate skill in responding not to what was expected but to the actual productions of the client.

Values and Ethics in Social Work Practice

In addition to knowledge and a sense of professional function, specific values and ethics also guide the social worker's practice. In preparing to meet clients, a social worker needs to consider these areas, which will affect the process and content of practice in significant ways. Although preparing for every eventuality is impossible, familiarity with basic expectations of professional practice will alert a worker to potentially serious situations and possible missteps, thus encouraging consultation with colleagues or a supervisor.

In this section we focus, then, on issues related to values and ethics. These range from formal statements by agencies and other organizations to informal agreements concerning acceptable behavior on the social worker's part. In the section following, we continue by examining how laws and the legal system more sharply define ethical issues such as informed consent, confidentiality, and the duty to protect.

Values are defined in the *Social Work Dictionary* as "the customs, beliefs, standards of conduct, and principles considered desirable by a culture, a group of people, or an individual" (Barker, 2003, p. 453). The same dictionary defines **ethics** as "a system of moral principles and perceptions about right versus wrong and the resulting philosophy of conduct that is practiced by an individual, group, profession, or culture" (p. 147).

> Loewenberg and Dolgoff (1996) define professional ethics as a codification of the special obligations that arise out of a person's voluntary choice to become a professional, such as a social worker. Professional ethics clarify the ethical aspects of professional practice. Professional social work ethics are intended to help social work practitioners recognize the morally correct way of practice and to learn how to decide and act correctly with regard to the ethical aspects of any given professional situation. (p. 6)

The National Association of Social Workers (NASW) has developed a code of ethics that is defined as

> the explication of the values, rules, and principles of ethical conduct that apply to all social workers who are members of the National Association of Social Workers (NASW). The original code of ethics for social workers was implicit in the 1951 Standards for Professional Practice of the American Association of Social Workers (ASSW). NASW developed a formal code in 1960 and has since made subsequent revisions, the latest in 2002. (Barker, 2003, p. 286)

Links to the NASW Code of Ethics and the Code of Ethics of the Canadian Association of Social Workers (CASW) can be found in Appendix B of the companion web page for this text.

The drafters of the code recognized the difficulties involved when professionals attempt to make specific decisions based on general principles. They also introduced the notion of peer review and peer standards for judging ethical behavior.

In itself, this code does not represent a set of rules that will prescribe all the behaviors of social workers in all of the complexities of professional life. Rather, it offers general principles to guide conduct, as well as the judicious appraisal of conduct, in situations that have ethical implications. It provides the basis for making judgments about ethical actions before and after they occur. Frequently, the particular situation determines the ethical principles that apply and the manner of their application. In such cases, not only the particular ethical principles, but also the entire code and its spirit, are taken into consideration. One must judge specific applications of ethical principles in context. Ethical behavior in a given situation must satisfy not only the judgment of the individual social worker, but also the judgment of an unbiased jury of professional peers.

Historical Context

Reamer (1998) describes four stages in the evolution of the social work profession's ethical guidelines: (1) the morality period, (2) the values period, (3) the ethical theory and decision-making period, and (4) the ethical standards and risk management period (p. 488). Reamer describes the morality period as beginning in the late 19th century, when social work was inaugurated as a profession. At that point, concern centered on the morality of the client rather than the morality or ethics of the profession. This focused diminished in the early 20th century as the profession focused more on social issues and "cause" rather than "case." In the late 1940s and the early 1950s the profession's interest more fully shifted from the morality of the client to the morality, values, and ethics of the profession and its practitioners. The shift to the ethical theory and decision-making period, which occurred in the early 1980s, was influenced by a new field known as applied and professional ethics. Social work was at that time one of several professions interested in the application of values and ethics in day-to-day practice. Issues addressed included confidentiality, client self-determination, informed consent, and truth telling. Reamer identifies the most recent stage of development as marked by the ratification of the 1996 NASW code of ethics. This version of the code contains a comprehensive set of ethical standards and a mission statement for the profession, and it addresses the core values of the profession including service, social justice, the dignity and worth of the person, the importance of human relationships, integrity, and competence. The sections on standards deal with ethical responsibility to clients, to colleagues, in practice settings, as professionals, to the profession, and to society at large.

While respecting the importance and value of this version of the code, some have criticized its organizational approach and content. For example, Freud and Krug (2002), both of whom served for several years on the Massachusetts NASW ethics hotline, observe that the preamble contains an "idealistic" enumeration of values and question whether the code fulfills "its major purpose of guiding decision making and conduct when ethical issues arise . . . regardless of their professional functions, the settings in which they work, and the populations they serve" (pp. 476–477). The authors question the organization of the sections of the code, because they claim that the categories overlap and do not correspond to the "intuitive ways in which we encounter ethical dilemmas" (p. 477). They propose an alternative organization that would focus on boundary problems, self-interest versus client-interest problems, whistle-blowing problems, client versus larger society problems, and clashes between important values. Although the existing code addressed these issues, the authors suggest the current organization makes locating them difficult.

They also point to potentially conflicting advice such as allowing a social worker to terminate a client who is unable to pay for services while at the same time enjoining social workers to take reasonable steps to avoid abandoning clients in need.

Further, they cite conflicts that can emerge when social workers (and other professionals) practice "benevolent deception" (for example, providing services to illegal immigrants or ignoring a mother on welfare who earns additional income from a part-time job). The authors do acknowledge that the code recognizes limitations on the "rules" such as the impact of context. Freud and Krug conclude by recommending three central elements that should complement and inform use of the code for ethical decision making:

- Increased attention to one's moral intuitions and emotions
- Institutionalized opportunities for dialogue about ethical concerns
- Open acknowledgement of, and respect for, moral diversity within a shared body of basic values

Ethical Problems and Dilemmas

Of course, if all situations were clear and unambiguous, and if ethical codes were explicit enough to provide specific guidelines for all occasions (and all professionals could agree on these), then ethical practice would simply involve a learning process and the strict implementation of agreed-on standards of practice. In reality, however, it does not work that way. For example, Loewenberg and Dolgoff (1996) describe an important distinction between "ethical problems" and "ethical dilemmas":

> Ethical problems raise the question: What is the right thing to do in a given practice situation? How can a social worker avoid unethical behaviors in that situation? Ethical dilemmas occur in situations where the social worker must choose between two or more relevant, but contradictory, ethical directives, or when every alternative results in an undesirable outcome for one or more persons. (p. 8)

Loewenberg and Dolgoff (1996) also point out the difference between values and ethics. Ethics are deduced from values and must be in consonance with them. The difference between the two is that values are concerned with what is good and desirable, while ethics deals with what is right and correct (p. 21). An example of this distinction concerns everyone's general right to privacy, a value of American society. An ethical rule of the social work profession that this value generates is the idea of obtaining informed consent from clients. *Informed consent* is a broad concept that is defined in more detail later and applies to many circumstances. One specific example, however, is the requirement that a worker get permission from a client before taping or recording an interview or allowing observation by a third party. Informed consent, in this case, is the client's agreement to the recording or observation with full knowledge of the procedure involved. In short, then, ethics are descriptions of right and correct behavior through which we put our values into action.

The interplay among values, ethics, and practice is rarely simple and clear-cut. Workers often face an ethical dilemma in which several possible solutions are equally desirable or undesirable. Consider, for example, a case involving an **outreach program**—a program that attempts to bring services (such as homemaking services) directly to clients, usually in their own homes or neighborhoods. The social worker in this case is assisting an elderly man and his adult child as part of an elder care outreach program. A not-uncommon example of value conflicts may emerge when the client wants to remain in his home while his adult children want him to move to a nursing home for his own safety. The value systems of many parties and organizations may ultimately impinge on the worker's decision: the values of the elderly client, his family (the second client), the agency, the community, our society in general, the social work profession, and the individual social worker. If any of these are in conflict, which ethical rules will guide the worker?

For example, a generally accepted social work ethical principle is **self-determination**—the client's right to make her or his own choices, which seems to provide a clear direction. The worker must support the client's decision. What happens, however, if the client is so frail that his living independently may pose some danger to himself and to his neighbors? While the client adamantly insists that he can care for himself, the apartment desperately needs cleaning. The client mentions he is not feeling too well today because he sometimes forgets to take his medicine. He excuses himself in order to get his pills but opens the closet door instead of the door to the kitchen, appearing momentarily confused. His still-lit cigarette sits on the edge of the ashtray, close to falling off, the long ash suggesting it may have been forgotten. Old newspapers are strewn around the floor under the coffee table.

Add to the mix a worker whose elderly grandfather, living alone and unable to safely care for himself, accidentally set his house on fire by leaving a pot on a hot stove. The resulting fire almost killed the grandfather and posed a serious threat to the neighbors.

The client in this example values his independence, and the value system of the social work profession supports his right to make the decision. The agency also values outcomes that help elderly people remain at home. The funding for the agency may even depend on how many elderly people it can keep out of nursing homes. A recent memo from the agency director has encouraged staff to "keep the numbers up" as the agency prepares to renegotiate, with the health insurance provider, the contract on which its very existence depends.

The family members value the client's safety and their own peace of mind. The social worker's professional and personal value system, in part based on his or her own life experience, causes him to identify with the family. The community's value system, which may even be embodied in state legislation, may make the social worker a mandated reporter, required to report to the proper authorities if this elderly client is a potential threat to himself or others. The degree of seriousness of the danger is ambiguous in this case, and the regulations of the legislative act are somewhat unclear in providing specific guidelines. What ethical principles can guide this social worker's actions? What does the worker do when some of the ethical principles appear to conflict with the others?

Factors Affecting Ethical Decision Making

Some ethical issues are reasonably clear-cut, providing unambiguous guidelines that are universally agreed on. Take, for example, the injunction against a social worker engaging in sexual activity with a client. Given the power differential between the helper and the client, as well as the serious potential for long-range damage to the client, such activity is universally condemned. The National Association of Social Workers (NASW) *Code of Ethics* is very clear on this point:

> Social workers should under no circumstances engage in sexual activities or sexual contact with current clients, whether such contact is consensual or forced. (National Association of Social Workers, 1999, Section 1.09)

In some places, legislation has defined such unprofessional acts a crime, with violators subject to criminal penalties. Many ethical dilemmas, however, are less clear-cut and require careful thought and even consultation before action.

Loewenberg and Dolgoff (1996) identify several factors that can contribute to such moments of serious uncertainty. For example, in the illustration of the elderly client, we saw competing values (self-determination and the need to protect a client), multiple-client systems (the elderly client and the family), worker difficulty in maintaining objectivity (the impact of the worker's life experience), and ambiguity in the case (lack of clarity on the degree of danger to the client). By simply recognizing the factors contributing to the dilemma, the worker begins the processes of managing the problem rather than having the problem manage the worker.

Rather than naively operating under the assumption that social work practice is "value free," social workers must recognize that the very act of intervening in a situation is based on value assumptions. In an increasingly complex and changing society, with value systems constantly in flux, every social worker must be knowledgeable about current ethical dilemmas and must develop a methodology for analyzing value and ethical conflicts when they emerge. Many agencies and health settings have ethics committees in place to assist in this process.

For example, in the illustration of the elderly client, the social worker should have a forum either in supervision or in staff groups to raise this case for consultation. An atmosphere should exist in which a social worker can feel free to share honestly his or her own personal value conflicts in such a situation and thereby sort through the conflicting pressures.

Perhaps the agency should set up a committee to examine the specific criteria used to make decisions about the degree of danger required before a worker must implement the mandated reporter role. Would a checklist based on these criteria help to reduce the amount of ambiguity in such cases? Can the worker be helped to see a role in mediating the conflict between the client and his family so that their mutual concerns can be made clear to each other? Can the client and the family members be involved in a process of decision making in which they all feel their concerns are respected? The agency would not provide a simple answer to a complex problem, but rather would implement a process for recognizing and dealing with the complexity itself. In addition, the agency would take responsibility for actively assisting workers in dealing with these issues.

Given the complexity involved in trying to respond appropriately when ethical dilemmas emerge, Reamer (2000) proposes a social work ethics audit and a risk management strategy (p. 355). Pointing out that agencies routinely conduct financial audits, he suggests that an ethical audit might determine

> (1) the extent of social workers' familiarity with known ethics-related risks in practice settings, based on empirical trend data summarizing actual ethics complaints and lawsuits filed against social workers and summarizing ethics committee and court findings and dispositions; and (2) current agency procedures and protocols for handling ethical issues, dilemmas, and decisions. (p. 356)

Reamer (2000) further suggests that each topic, such as confidentiality procedures, can be assessed and assigned one of four risk categories:

> (1) no risk—current practices are acceptable and do not require modification; (2) minimal risk—current practices are reasonably adequate; minor modifications would be useful; (3) moderate risk—current practices are problematic;

modifications are necessary to minimize risks; and (4) high risk—current practices are seriously flawed; significant modifications are necessary to minimize risks. (p. 356)

He identifies the areas to be addressed in an audit as including client rights, confidentiality and privacy, informed consent, service delivery, boundary issues and conflicts of interest, documentation, defamation of character, supervision, training, consultation, referral, fraud, termination of services, and practitioner impairment (pp. 357–359).

Several texts have addressed in detail the issues introduced in this section and provide useful models for workers faced with an ethical dilemma. See, for example, Gambrill and Pruger (1997), Loewenberg and Dolgoff (1996), and Reamer (1990, 1998, 2000).

Values and Ethics in the Professional Literature

The professional literature offers efforts to provide moral and ethical direction for social workers. For example, the revised *Curriculum Policy Statement* of the Council on Social Work Education (2003) describes core values for the social work profession:

- Social workers' professional relationships are built on regard for individual worth and dignity and are furthered by mutual participation, acceptance, confidentiality, honesty, and responsible handling of conflict.

- Social workers respect people's rights to make independent decisions and to participate actively in the helping process.

- Social workers are committed to helping client systems obtain needed resources.

- Social workers strive to make social institutions more human and responsive to human needs.

- Social workers demonstrate respect for and acceptance of the unique characteristics of diverse populations.

- Social workers are responsible for their own ethical conduct and the quality of their practice; they should seek to attain continuous growth in the knowledge and skills of their profession.

Although the development of commonly accepted values for a profession is important, core values do not provide specific directions for actions in all situations. In the illustration of the elderly client, several of the values just listed may be in conflict. As pointed out by Loewenberg and Dolgoff (1996),

> There is a general consensus about social work values. For example, most professional social workers agree that client participation, self-determination, and confidentiality are among basic social work values. However, disagreements are likely to occur when it comes to implementing these generalized professional values. Social workers may differ about priorities, specific objectives, and the means necessary to put these generalized values into practice. Thus the value of "enhancing the dignity of life" may be used by one social worker to support a client's request for an abortion, while her social work colleague may call on the same generalized value to support her professional decision to try to persuade the client to go through a full-term pregnancy. (p. 20)

Guidelines for Practice in Family and Group Work

Although many of the ethical guidelines for practice with individuals apply to family or group work, the latter types of practice present unique ethical issues. For example, consider this variation on the confidentiality issue, introduced by the presence of other clients in group work, as raised in the *Ethical Guidelines for Group Counselors:*

- Members are made aware of the difficulties in enforcing and ensuring confidentiality in a group setting.
- The counselor provides examples of how confidentiality can nonmaliciously be broken to increase members' awareness and helps to lessen the likelihood that this breach of confidence will occur.
- Group counselors inform group members about potential consequences of intentionally breaching confidentiality. (American Association for Counseling and Development, 1989)

Although a group leader can make clear his or her position on confidentiality, the leader must also acknowledge that a "rule" of confidentiality cannot be imposed on group members. The group itself must discuss the issue and develop appropriate ground rules.

Researchers in the related field of group psychotherapy have also raised complex issues associated with disclosures in multiperson practice (Roback, Purdon, Ochoa, & Bloch, 1992). The authors conducted a multidisciplinary survey of 100 members of the American Group Psychotherapy Association. Thirty-six of the respondents were social workers. The survey described six hypothetical group therapy incidents that posed threats to the confidentiality of the group: (1) a group member has disclosed outside the group highly sensitive material about another group member, (2) a group member has disclosed current involvement in nonviolent criminal activity, (3) a moderately depressed outpatient group member has threatened physical harm to his ex-wife, (4) a moderately depressed inpatient group member has threatened physical harm to his ex-wife, (5) an adolescent group member has disclosed physical abuse that occurred for several years but is currently not present, and (6) an 8-year-old group member has disclosed an intention to run away from home, with no evidence of physical or sexual abuse (p. 172).

Each of these examples takes on special significance because the disclosures took place in the group context. For example, in those states and circumstances where the confidential patient-therapist communications are protected, is the protection voided because of the presence of third parties?

Respondents in the study answered three questions regarding each incident. These concerned the most appropriate context for dealing with the disclosure (group, individual, or both), with whom it should be discussed (therapist, group, or disclosing individual), who has primary decision-making responsibility for managing the situation, and what action the group leader should take.

Several of the study's findings provide insights into how group leaders would handle the ethical and practice issues associated with the six scenarios. For example, 80 percent of the group leaders indicated they would not contact authorities in response to a disclosure of involvement in nonviolent criminal activities; however, 53 percent would encourage the group member to do so. Open-ended responses indicated that the nature of the crime and the potential threat to others would modify their response. Arson, for example, is much more serious than shoplifting.

Almost all therapists (94 percent) reported that they would contact the authorities if confronted with an outpatient's threat to harm others, and 92 percent would do so in response to an inpatient's threat. An interesting related finding was that gender affected the context within which such threats would be handled, with male group leaders more likely to deal with them in group.

The same gender difference was found in the scenario in which a teenager disclosed prior physical abuse. Overall, 89 percent of the group leaders indicated that they would contact the authorities if confronted with such a disclosure. Approximately 50 percent of respondents would engage in each of the following four alternatives in response to a report of abuse that was no longer occurring:

(a) discuss and assess the legitimacy of the allegation with the group member; (b) discuss with the member in group his or her feelings about the abuse and abide by what, if anything, he or she wants to do; (c) explain to the group the therapist's responsibility to report this information to the proper agency and proceed to do so; and (d) discuss with the group members their feelings about the abuse and honor their chosen strategy for resolving the situation. (Roback et al., 1992, p. 178)

While the ethical issues and the guidelines for practice in situations where someone is at risk are clearer, and the social worker's responsibility as a mandated reporter removes much of the ambiguity in such a situation, the process can still be painful for all concerned. Consider the following example from a group of eight women who were survivors of childhood sexual abuse. It was a long-term open group and, while the group had continued for 2 years, this was the student group leader's first year. The student was a representative from the state child welfare agency, and a therapist from a local social service agency co-led the group. Here is part of the student's report:

Confidentiality is a particularly salient issue, because, while the group was voluntary for these women, the fact of my being an employee of the child welfare agency was concerning for them until they got to know me and became comfortable with me.

The week prior to this meeting was very emotional, as one of the women had talked about concerns about how her son behaved when he returned from a recent visit with his father. The description of his behavior and the things that he said pointed to the father having digitally penetrated the boy's anus after they had showered together. I reminded the group of my role as a mandated reporter, and stated that I would be filing a report alleging sexual abuse of the young boy by his father. I told the mother that I thought that it was clear to me that the fact that she brought it up in group was her way of trying to get help. I praised her courage and her concern for her son.

Eileen, the mother of the young boy, did express some concern that her exhusband, whom she was still emotionally attached to, was going to be mad at her. Mary, a young woman who was in the process of filing charges against her stepfather for her past sexual abuse as a child, expressed feeling empowered by what she saw as my immediate response to protect the child, because her mother had never believed her when she told her of the sexual abuse. After a short discussion, the group ended.

At the start of the next group meeting, there was a long silence of about 2 minutes. Several members were glancing at Eileen, and she was moving about in her seat in an agitated manner.

WORKER: Eileen, you appear to be upset. Is something going on for you?

EILEEN: This is very hard for me. I'm really pissed at you, and I'm having a hard time confronting you. I spoke with Alice (her individual therapist) about what you did last week, and she told me that I should tell you how I feel.

WORKER: You sound very angry. I would very much like to hear what you have to say. (There is about 30 seconds of silence.)

EILEEN: Well, I thought what we said in group was supposed to be confidential! You took what I said in group when I was upset last week, and then used it against me. How the hell am I supposed to ever trust you again?

WORKER: You feel I betrayed your trust by filing a report against Bobby and you feel that it is not safe in the group because it is not really confidential.

EILEEN: Damned straight! How can I trust you anymore? Bobby is blaming me. I know my own son. I know when he's exaggerating and when he's not.

MARY: (Angrily) Right! I'm sure that's the same excuse that our mothers used when we were abused.

WORKER: Eileen, I wonder what it means to you that I reported Bobby. Do you think that it means that I don't trust you to protect your son, or that I think that you are a bad mother? (Eileen starts to cry. As she sobs, others squirm about in their chairs. She looks up.) Yes, it means that I am no better than my mother!

In the worker's analysis of this incident, she describes how, even though she knew she was doing the right thing and that she had no choice, it was painful for her to hear the client's anger. The worker's skill was evident in her not falling into the trap of explaining and justifying her action but instead exploring the source of the member's distress. Because the worker had clearly described her role as a mandated reporter and had stated under what circumstances she would have to disclose confidential information (see Chapter 3 for a full discussion of contracting), she could be reasonably certain that the member knew she would take action. Many nonoffending parents, who were themselves sexually abused, report later that they wanted their social workers to intervene to protect their children because they were unable to do so themselves.

The Impact of Managed Care on Ethical Practice

New ethical dilemmas have arisen from a trend in health care. The significant cost of health care in the United States has led to an incredible growth in managed care as one major strategy to control health and mental health costs; this is done by monitoring what type of health care a patient will receive from a health care practitioner or from a health maintenance organization. The goal is to reduce costs by placing controls on health practitioners and by fostering competition among HMOs. Managed care plans attempt to reduce these costs through controlling the type of health practitioners used, limiting access to service, and prescribing the type and length of service to be provided. In Canada, the cutbacks in resources available to the universal provincial health programs have resulted in some of the same efforts to reduce costs and to manage care.

Loewenberg and Dolgoff (1996) address some of the ethical dilemmas facing social workers in this rapidly changing system. For example, the *Code of Ethics* requires the following: "The social worker should not participate in, condone, or be associated with dishonesty, fraud, deceit or misrepresentation" (NASW, 1997). Loewenberg and Dolgoff describe a case situation in which a client's symptoms could be defined either as psychiatric or associated with alcoholism and drugs, but the worker suspects the psychiatric assessment is not indicated. The dilemma is created by the third-party payer's rules, which would allow for more sessions if the diagnosis is psychiatric and less than is needed if the diagnosis is substance abuse. Should the social worker select the less likely diagnosis in order to assure that the client gets the needed number of sessions?

In another example provided by these authors, the *Code of Ethics* states, "The social worker should be alert to and resist the influences and pressures that interfere with the exercise of professional discretion and impartial judgment required for the performance of professional functions" (NASW, 1997). The authors then describe a scenario of a depressed college student who has been threatening suicide. The dilemma emerges when the claims reviewer for the third-party payer rejects hospitalization, citing recent research. The *Code of Ethics* holds the social worker responsible for ethical practice, and the legal system would hold the social worker responsible in the event the student did commit suicide (this general issue is discussed later in this chapter).

To complicate the scenario suggested by these authors, let us add a third-party payer or an HMO that takes the position that the social worker (or doctor) cannot inform the client that a recommended service is not being provided; thus, a "gag rule" is in effect. This would eliminate the option of empowering the client to fight for his or her own rights in the situation. Fortunately, abuse of this practice has led to legislation in several states to bar such rules. However, if the social worker is a private practitioner who depends on referrals from this third-party payer and whose participation in the panel of approved clinicians is coming up for review, the ethical issues are further heightened.

The profession is just starting to face some of the crucial debates associated with the rapid emergence of managed care and increased control over social work practice. Gordon and Klein (Gambrill & Pruger, 1997) debate whether social workers should even participate in for-profit managed care programs. Gordon argues that we should do so for several reasons, including the opportunity to influence the care provided. He draws on his own experience to support the ability to work ethically within a for-profit structure. Klein rejects this argument and suggests that working in a managed-care program would lead to damaging effects on the client-worker relationship, raise ethical issues because of competing economic pressures, and end up with workers justifying inadequate care with simplistic clinical reasoning (pp. 52–62).

Watt and Kallmann (1998) specifically address the issues involved in managing professional obligations within the constraints of managed care. They describe legal-ethical conflicts, such as confidentiality versus the requirement to report services to an employer. They also present legal-clinical conflicts. For example, under managed care, specific needed services may be limited to clients who have a specific diagnosis that may negatively label them and not be appropriate; this puts the social worker into the position of either denying the service or practicing a professional lie. The authors further point out that a decision in the legal-ethical area may impact on issues in the legal-clinical areas, and vice versa.

Clearly, the debate concerning these ethical issues and others has just begun. It mandates that the profession and every professional social worker attend to issues of social policy that will influence the core of their practice and profession. In the next section, we explore the impact of specific legislative acts and court decisions affecting social work practice.

The Impact of Legislation and the Court

In exploring the impact of laws and the court on social work practice, we need to discuss two interrelated factors that are increasingly affecting such practice. First is the trend toward licensing of the social work profession by state (U.S.) or provincial (Canadian) legislative bodies, and second is the growing body of case law (decisions of the courts) emerging from important legal decisions involving helping professionals. Both the legislation and the case law are more sharply defining the rights, duties, and obligations for agencies, host settings (such as hospitals), and social workers. These two forces have helped clarify social work practice guidelines and reduce professional vulnerability. The principles of practice emerging from most of these changes reveal that many of the regulations and directives codify sound practice concepts.

In this section, we examine several examples of the growing influence of the law on practice issues. Specifically, we discuss four topics: licensing, confidentiality and the client's right to privacy and privileged communications, informed consent, and the social worker's duty to protect a third party.

You might also want to refer to a series of papers, prepared by the Office of the General Counsel of the National Association of Social Workers, designed to provide information for social workers on topics of concern to the profession (Polowy, 1997). They cover topics including subpoenas, clinical notes, managed care contracts and antitrust issues, state mandated child abuse reporting requirements, protection of privacy, alternative dispute resolution, and expert witness issues.

Licensing and the Social Work Profession

Social work professional organizations have undertaken a major effort to lobby for legislation that would license and regulate the practice of social work. One impetus for this movement has been a concern for protecting the public through regulation of the quality of practice, even to the point of protecting the title "social worker." State or provincial legislation often defines different levels of educational requirements (e.g., BSW, MSW), and supervised practice experience required for different levels of licensing. Usually, passing a knowledge-based test is a prerequisite for licensing. Such legislation also calls for a professional to continue his or her education through certified programs of continuing education. Regulations associated with the legislation sometimes spell out the rights, duties, and obligations of a licensed professional. The legislation usually establishes a Board of Registration that defines and enforces a Code of Ethical Practice. Social workers need to become aware of and familiar with such legislation and the resulting codes.

Another powerful impetus for the licensing movement in the United States has been the acceptance of social work services for reimbursement by third-party payers such as health insurers. Both agencies and private practitioners increasingly depend on direct reimbursement or the ability of a client to obtain some portion of their fees from these third parties. Licensing and standards of practice are requirements for reimbursement eligibility.

Confidentiality and Privileged Communications

Confidentiality is the right of a client not to have private information shared with third parties. To see the influence of legislation on practice, let us examine how confidentiality and the client's right to privacy can be protected or limited. The Commonwealth of Massachusetts, for example, many years ago passed an act regulating social work practice. A licensing board was established to administer its provisions. Legislation amending that act in 1989 was designed to further protect communications between social workers and clients. These communications are held to be privileged, so that the social worker cannot disclose them without the client's permission, even in the course of legal proceedings. Social work–client privileged communications are thus in a similar category to the privileges associated with doctor-patient or lawyer-client communications, although the exceptions differ. The client's or patient's right to privileged communications strengthens the confidential nature of the professional relationship. When the client's right to privacy is protected, the client will tend to share private information more freely.

The statutory exceptions to privileged communications in Massachusetts arise in the following circumstances:

- A child custody and/or adoption suit
- When the client introduces her or his mental health as an issue in a court
- When it is necessary to commit a client to a hospital in the event of danger to the client or someone else
- When a social worker is conducting a court-ordered evaluation
- In a malpractice action brought by the client against the social worker
- After the death of the client
- In the case of a child abuse investigation or certain other state investigations

Exceptions are also found in other state regulations. For example, professionals are required to report suspicions of child and elder abuse or neglect, as illustrated in the example presented earlier in this chapter. While still leaving gray areas where professional judgment will come into play, regulations such as these provide helpful guidelines to workers and clients. For example, limits of confidentiality may be spelled out in the first interview with a client or at the first group session.

In any case, social workers must be aware of the rights and obligations that flow from legislation and case law. Consider the example of a social worker who is approached by a police investigator requesting information about the worker's client. The protections of confidentiality, and in some instances, privileged communications, mean the worker cannot be forced to disclose any information unless a clear exception exists or the client expressly consents. A social worker needs to be prepared to respond, for example, by stating, "I am not saying Mr. X is or is not my client; however, if he were my client, my communications with him would be confidential and protected, and I would not be able to share them with you."

Until a 1996 U.S. Supreme Court decision clarified the matter (*Jaffee v. Redmond*, 1996), the federal court system had held different views on whether communications between a social worker and a client were privileged. While communications with psychotherapists were privileged in all 50 states and the District of Columbia, the inclusion of clinical social workers remained in question. Alexander (1997) points out that in its 1996 decision, the Supreme Court recognized the "absoluteness of social workers' right to privileged communications; social workers can no longer be compelled to disclose confidential information in civil lawsuits filed in federal court" (p. 388). For example, if a licensed social worker is treating a child protective services worker by providing counseling to assist in overcoming grief related to the death of a child on a caseload, the counselor cannot be compelled to testify in federal court.

Alexander also points out that the absoluteness of privileged immunity does not carry over to nonfederal cases in state court systems. He describes one difficult situation in which a criminal defendant may request access to a sexual assault victim's records. Based on *Jaffee v. Redmond,* the privilege is absolute in a case occurring on federal property and tried in a federal court. In most states, however, if the defense meets certain standards, such as demonstrating the relevance of the information to the defense, the trial judge will review the records and decide if any information should be disclosed. Alexander (1997) emphasizes the importance of keeping these distinctions clear:

> On the whole, *Jaffee v. Redmond* recognizes and elevates the prestige of social work. The U.S. Supreme Court spoke positively of clinical social workers and stated that social workers are entitled to the same consideration in counseling that is given to psychologists and psychiatrists. However, social workers should keep in mind that Jaffee involves federal issues, and state laws do not provide absolute confidentiality to psychotherapists and differ in their exceptions for privileged communication. Thus, social work agencies should provide in-service training on the conditions of privileged communications in their states. (p. 390)

As pointed out by Alexander (1997), this absoluteness of privileged communications in federal cases can raise significant moral dilemmas for the social worker (p. 390). As recognized by the Court of Appeals and the Supreme Court in *Jaffee v. Redmond* (1996), the privilege is qualified and may not apply if "in the interest of justice, the evidentiary need for the disclosure of the contents of a patient's counseling sessions outweighs that patient's privacy interest." The Supreme Court itself, in a significant footnote in the *Jaffee* case, stated the following:

> Although it would be premature to speculate about most future developments in the federal psychotherapist privilege, we do not doubt that there are situations in which the privilege must give way, for example, if a serious threat of harm to the patient or to others can be averted only by means of a disclosure by the therapists.

More recently, the passage of the federal Health Insurance Patient Protection Act (HIPPA) in 2002 has further clarified and set limits on the ability of a social worker or other health professional to share confidential information and to whom such information can be shared. You have likely experienced these changes when visiting a doctor's office since the passage of this act. Patients now receive a description of their rights under HIPPA and must sign a release form that specifies what information can be released and to whom.

One immediate implication for students in social work programs is that case information presented in class or in papers needs to have all identifying information removed. That is, any information that would allow someone to know who the person was needs to be changed or eliminated. This includes obvious things like names and birth dates but may also contain other information that is so unique to the person that it will allow identification, including diagnosis, race/ethnicity, or gender. If diagnosis, race/ethnicity, or gender is directly related to the case presentation, students can include it if they are confident it will not allow identification.

All of the following are considered identifiers of the individual or of relatives, employers, or household members of the individual:

1. Names
2. All geographic subdivisions smaller than a State, including street address, city, county, precinct, zip code, and their equivalent geocodes, except for the initial three digits of a zip code if, according to the current publicly available data from the Bureau of the Census
3. All elements of dates (except year) for dates directly related to an individual, including birth date, admission date, discharge date, date of death; and all ages over 89 and all elements of dates (including year) indicative of such age, except that such ages and elements may be aggregated into a single category of age 90 or older
4. Telephone Numbers
5. Fax Numbers
6. Electronic Mail Addresses
7. Social Security Numbers
8. Medical Record Numbers
9. Health Plan Beneficiary Numbers
10. Account Numbers
11. Certificate/License Numbers
12. Vehicle Identifiers and Serial Numbers, including License Plate Numbers
13. Device Identifiers and Serial Numbers
14. Web Universal Resource Locators (URLs)
15. Internet Protocol (IP) Address Numbers
16. Biometric Identifiers, including Finger and Voice Prints
17. Full Face Photographic Images and any Comparable Images
18. Any other unique identifying number, characteristic, or code

Informed Consent

The requirement that the client provide informed consent to services offers another example of how legislation and the resulting codes of ethical practice influence a social worker's obligations. **Informed consent** is

> the client's granting of permission to the social worker and agency or other professional person to use specific intervention procedures, including diagnosis, treatment, follow up, and research. This permission must be based on full disclosure of the facts needed to make the decision intelligently. Informed consent must be based upon knowledge of the risks and alternatives. (Barker, 2003, p. 114)

Further guidance is available from the NASW's *Code of Ethics:*

> Social workers should provide services to clients only in the context of a professional relationship based, when appropriate, on valid informed consent. Social workers should use clear and understandable language to inform clients of the purposes of the services, risks related to the services, limits to services because of

the requirements of a third-party payer, relevant costs, reasonable alternatives, clients' right to refuse or withdraw consent, and the time frame covered by the consent. Social workers should provide clients with the opportunity to ask questions. (NASW, 1997, p. 2, Section 1.03a)

In Massachusetts, the code provides the following definition of *unethical or unprofessional conduct:*

Performing or attempting to perform ongoing social work services without the informed consent of the client, the client's legally authorized representative, or, in the case of an unemancipated minor client, the client's parent or legal guardian. (*Code of Ethical Practice,* 1991)

Generally, true informed consent contains the following five elements:

- The worker makes full disclosure of the nature and purposes of the service, including associated potential benefits and risks. The availability of alternatives must be explored.
- The client demonstrates an understanding of the information offered in the disclosure.
- The client must be competent to provide informed consent.
- The client's consent must be voluntary, with no coercion.
- The decision must be explicit and involve either consent to or refusal of services.

Although the guidelines for informed consent seem clear, one study (Lidz, 1984) identified several practical problems observed in an analysis of how informed consent actually works. For example, the study pointed out that the person responsible for obtaining informed consent was not always clearly identified. Informed consent was, in some cases, a "floating" responsibility. In addition, clients reported that family members often pressured them to act in a specific manner. Was consent under these circumstances really voluntary? Workers were not always trained to educate clients. A worker's perception of the client's intelligence and ability appeared to influence the disclosure process. Informed consent was often obtained after the caregiver had made an assessment and decision in favor of a specific intervention. Were other alternatives really considered? The authors also observed that a client's understanding appeared to occur over time rather than immediately. True informed consent might require revisiting the consent issue periodically as the client's understanding grows. The authors argue that it is important to review the informed consent procedures in every setting and to actively promote strategies to ensure that informed consent is real rather than illusionary.

The Duty to Warn

Another court decision has had a powerful impact on practice by defining the duties and obligations of a social worker in respect to her or his **duty to warn** (in some states, the "duty to protect") a third party if information shared by a client indicates the third party may be in danger. An important California decision, *Tarasoff v. Regents of the University of California* (1976), severely limited privileged communications under certain circumstances involving duty to warn.

In this case, a client of a therapist at the Berkeley University Clinic indicated murderous fantasies about his former girlfriend, Tatiana (Tanya) Tarasoff. The therapist became concerned and notified campus police, requesting that they have the client committed. After a brief confinement, the police, believing the client was rational, released him. No further steps were taken, on the orders of the therapist's superior. Neither Tarasoff nor her immediate family was notified. The family sued after the client followed through on his threats to kill Tarasoff. The court held that the therapist had been negligent in not notifying Tarasoff directly or in not taking other steps to prevent the attack. The court said the following:

> When a doctor or a psychotherapist, in the exercise of his professional skill and knowledge, determines, or should determine, that a warning is essential to avert danger arising from the medical or psychological condition of his patient, he incurs a legal obligation to give that warning.

This is another example where the evolving rules for professional behavior provide structure and clarity for the professional. In this case, if a client communicates a threat toward a specific person and either has the intent and ability to implement a violent act or has a history of such acts, the social worker is required to take appropriate actions. These may include warning the victim, calling the police, asking the client to accept voluntary hospitalization, or attempting to arrange an involuntary hospitalization. While helpful guidelines have emerged from legislation and the court decisions, the worker's judgment is still required.

Given the importance of understanding evolving legal requirements as they affect the obligations of the social worker, practitioners need to stay up-to-date with the law and its application to new sets of circumstances. Membership in a professional association, such as the National Association of Social Workers (NASW), can provide a means for keeping abreast. Consider, for example, an issue of the Massachusetts NASW Chapter's (1996) monthly newspaper, which provides advice on duty to warn:

> A clear case of duty to warn occurs when a client reports a clear intent to harm another and has the motivation, intention and means to fulfill this threat. It becomes incumbent on the clinician to report the client to both the police and the third party. A situation not involving weapons or arson, but where there is an explicit threat, would be the client who is HIV-positive, is aware of the risks of transmission, knows how to avoid such risks, but has no intention of doing so and wants to infect his partner(s). A more complicated case would be in the instance of an HIV-positive client who is not overtly threatening to harm a spouse or partner but is unwilling to disclose or take precautions against the risk of transmission. Although there may be no explicit oral threat, there may be an explicitly behavioral threat. Many states now have statutes requiring duty to warn in such instances. To date, however, Massachusetts does not require partner notification. The other side of the coin, however, is that the clinician, by not disclosing, runs the risk of suit should the partner at a later point become infected and learn that she/he had not been informed by either the infected client or the client's therapists. The therapist has a difficult decision here and should probably seek legal consultation on a case-by-case basis.

After reviewing the previous sections from the perspective of a student or any practicing social worker, it would not be surprising if, rather than feeling more prepared to meet a client, you might be having second thoughts about engaging in practice at all. Ethical issues, rules of professional conduct, and the still-evolving case law highlight the increasing clarity as well as the growing complexity of guidelines that affect practice. Understand that developing competency in practice takes time. The purpose of highlighting these issues was not to discourage you, but rather to sensitize you to be more alert to the signs of ethical dilemmas or legal questions. This awareness should encourage all workers to make use of supervisors, colleagues, agency procedural manuals, and other resources whenever such issues emerge. Thus, in a case-by-case manner, as the social worker raises her or his concerns about a client disclosure in an interview or group meeting, the worker will gradually learn when such a disclosure triggers the duty to warn or give an otherwise mandated report. This is an important part of the learning process, which in the long run will significantly strengthen a worker's competency and practice effectiveness.

Evaluation of Practice: Process and Outcomes

So far in this chapter, we have discussed how agency culture, values and ethics, and the law can affect social work practice. These represent forces that require the worker to carry certain responsibilities. Another such responsibility concerns evaluation. Agencywide research on effectiveness of service is becoming more common as managed care, federal and state funding agencies, and other forces are demanding greater accountability and evidence of effectiveness. The use of client satisfaction surveys can also provide any agency or setting with important information. Becoming a critical consumer of research is therefore essential for workers. This knowledge can help workers actively engage with the agency or other setting. In turn, this allows workers to help clients deal with the setting, as we saw in Chapter 15.

Social workers' responsibility regarding evaluation does not stop there. Ongoing evaluation of one's practice is an important element in social work. The ability to adapt intervention approaches and to work in a flexible and client-responsive manner depends on some form of feedback on how the process is going. Thought should be given to evaluation in the beginning phase of the engagement, when important baseline information may be available.

Two forms of evaluation that can be useful are process evaluation and outcome evaluation. In *process evaluation,* the social worker measures progress on factors such as developing a good working relationship that serves as a medium for helping clients achieve the outcomes. In group work practice, the process outcome might involve a mutual-aid support group creating a supportive culture in which to tackle difficult and taboo issues (such as a survivors' group dealing with disclosure issues). In another example, helping family members stop arguing and start listening to one another in order to address their problems and develop solutions would be a process outcome. The distinction between process and outcomes is artificial, because each of the examples just listed can also be considered an important outcome in its own right.

Outcome evaluation refers to the worker's efforts to assess how well the client is meeting the objectives of the work as defined in the mutually agreed-on contract, also known as the working agreement. For example, the client may have sought specific help in dealing with her or his family, coping with stress in the work environment, or maintaining abstinence from drugs or alcohol in the early recovery process. Most clients do not come to a social worker to develop a working relationship; they have other life-related concerns and goals in mind.

As noted, the distinction between process and outcome often blurs. For example, learning to speak to a social worker about a personal problem in one's life is both creating the conditions for effective work on the problems and also providing an opportunity to practice the skills required to speak to others who are important in the client's life. Developing trust in the social worker may be the first step in learning to risk, to be vulnerable, and to develop trust in other relationships. Note the addition of another false dichotomy to the list in this book: process versus outcome.

All too often social workers, or their agencies or funding sources, fail to recognize positive outcome points along the way. These may represent the most progress a client can make at a particular time. I remember a social worker in a residential setting for female teenage survivors of physical, emotional, or sexual abuse. She described one client to whom she had become close and who had seemed to be making progress. At the end of a year's work, in the spring, the teenager ran away. The worker informed me that this client was running from city to city across the United States. When I asked her how she knew this, the worker replied, "Because she calls me once a week, collect, to let me know she's all right!"

I maintain the staff had not failed with this client, and in fact, had taught the client that there could be adults who could care for her and not just exploit her. The client may not have been ready, at that time, to use all of the help the staff was prepared to provide. When she was ready, if ever, she would be able to build on the base they had provided. Unfortunately, the agency's evaluation model could not account for this point-in-process outcome and could only judge the work with this client as having failed.

Process Evaluation: The Record of Service

As you have seen, this book is filled with examples of a particular process outcome instrument called a record of service (Garfield & Irizary, 1971). Many of the process recording illustrations in this book have followed the basic structure of this instrument. Because this is such an important evaluation tool, I shall briefly review the overall structure here, relating it specifically to process evaluation.

In a record of service, after identifying the individual, family, group, community, or other system, and providing basic information (such as age, gender, race), the social worker identifies the process problem. For example, one worker's case recording reads as follows:

Description of the Problem

Every time we get close to talking about painful areas of her life, Jane takes off into a form of flight and changes the subject or denies any serious emotional impact. I often feel she is both asking me to explore these areas and, at exactly the same time, telling me how difficult that would be for her. She seems to be stuck in the beginning phase and is unable to make the transition to the middle phase of work.

The identification of the specific problem (in process terms) is followed by a section in which the worker describes, in brief detail, how the problem came to her or his attention:

How the Problem Came to the Attention of the Worker(s)

In the first few sessions Jane hinted about issues with her family that were difficult to talk about. In one session she angrily said: "I'm not too happy with my mother's current boyfriend. He gives me the creeps when he is around and I think both of them would just rather see me out of the house." When I asked her if anything specific had happened with the boyfriend, she switched to an example where he had sided with her mother on a discipline issue, which had made her angry. When I tried to get at the underlying hurt and rejection she might be feeling, she denied it. When I tried to get back to what made her feel "creepy," she changed the subject.

In the third part of this evaluation instrument, the worker examines and illustrates her interventions that are designed to effect a change in the state of the problem—in this case, the client's hesitancy about exploring painful emotions and disclosing details of her interaction with her mother's boyfriend. An example of one such intervention follows:

Summary of the Work

Third Session

I tried to indirectly let Jane know that I realized there were some issues that were hard for her to talk about. Near the end of the session, when I felt frustrated again about her mixed signals, I said, "I have worked with many girls just like you, and one of the things I have noted is that they are often afraid to share how much hurt they are carrying around inside. Sometimes it is easier to run from the pain or hide from it under a lot of anger. Sometimes people don't feel that anyone else really cares or could understand. Sometimes they are just afraid of opening the floodgates and that they will lose control, maybe even cry. I just want you to know that if you are feeling that way, I am prepared to hear what you have to say and I will try as best I can to understand." Jane just sat in silence, but I could tell she was taking in what I said.

Several excerpts such as this one helped the worker to examine her interventions and to consider their results. In the final section of the practice evaluation instrument, the worker takes stock of the current situation, referring back to the problem identified at the start of the record of service and then presenting specific next steps for intervention.

Current Status of the Problem

Where It Stands Now

Since the session when I told her about my other clients, Jane has been more forthcoming in our conversations. In the fourth session, when she told me of another confrontation with her mother and her mother's boyfriend, I reached past the anger for her feelings of rejection. Jane cried for the first time and talked about how upset she was and how she often cried herself to sleep at night, wishing her father were still alive, and desperately wanting her family to be back to the way it once was. While Jane seems more ready to work on her feelings of loss and rejection, she still only hints at what I suspect may be possible abuse or attempted abuse by the boyfriend. We are coming to the last few sessions and I feel I have to be more assertive in reaching for this issue.

Specific Next Steps

- I'm going to continue to reach for her losses and the associated pain, providing as much support as I can along the way.
- I'm going to be more direct and use the same method I used in session three, but this time, I'm going to address the issue of my client's having trouble disclosing issues like sexual abuse.
- I'm going to explore with her what would make it hard for her to share this aspect of her life with me, or anyone else, and what, if anything, I could do to make it easier. I'm prepared to discuss her fears of her mother's or the boyfriend's reactions, the legal consequences, etc.

- I'm going to make sure she feels in control of the process and that I am not forcing any disclosure.
- I'm going to remind her that we only have three sessions left.

In this example, Jane disclosed the following week that the boyfriend had been making sexual overtures toward her whenever her mother was not around. She discussed her concerns about raising the issue with her mother, who she was sure would not believe her. Jane said she was considering running away. The worker offered to help her to face the issue with the boyfriend and the mother and ended up intervening in the family situation.

There are also other instruments that can help a worker evaluate ongoing process and interaction with a client. By focusing on a specific problem, the worker can explore his or her own feelings about the issue and shape interventions to attempt to remove the obstacles to effective work.

Outcome Evaluation: The Single-System Research Design

One method of outcome evaluation that has been widely used in social work is called single-system research design (SSRD). Nugent (1991) defined this approach as consisting of "systematic, objective procedures for the study of the impact of an independent variable upon a specific individual subject. Thus, they are, in effect, systematic and objective procedures for carrying out case studies" (p. 5). In the simplest form of this approach, the practitioner-researcher might obtain data on a client's behaviors, attitudes, feelings, or other outcome measures at the start of the work (the A measurement). Specific treatment would be employed, during which the same outcome measures would be obtained (the B measurement). If all other extraneous variables could be controlled, then the changes in the B measurement would indicate the efficacy of the intervention. This would be termed a simple A-B single-case design. More-complex designs might obtain multiple measurements of the outcome variable before and after treatment (e.g., AAA-BBB) or even A-B-A-B single-case design that turns treatment "on" and "off."

In a bibliography of more than 250 citations of the use of SSRD by social work educators or practitioners, Thyer and Thyer describe the development, dissemination, and adoption of this approach as controversial (1992, p. 99). In part, the controversy centers on whether or not a conflict exists between a process designed to yield information about the efficacy of practice interventions (a research tool) and the demands of delivering the best clinical services, which the research agenda might negatively affect. Describing the debate in detail lies beyond the scope of this book. My focus is on the use of the method as a clinical tool for the practitioner interested in monitoring the effects of her or his interventions.

Berlin (1984) takes the same position. Regardless of the debate on SSRD as a research or practice tool, "it is possible to keep the obligations of practice central, systematically assess the extent of change in the client's problem, and become a more sensitive, knowledgeable, credible practitioner in the process" (p. 4).

In a description of a first interview with a client, Berlin's social worker implements most of the ideas outlined in the contracting discussion of Chapter 3:

> In the first interview, the worker encouraged Cynthia to say more about the bad time she had been having and to tell her story in her own way. The worker then gradually asked questions to identify more clearly the nature of Cynthia's despair and the situations, thoughts, and behavior that seemed to account for it.

In the next hour and a half, Cynthia and the worker put together a description of the problem that seemed right to Cynthia, was relatively specific, and by virtue of its credibility and logic, appeared to help her feel more "normal" and less out of control. They reached agreement on the target concerns, started to analyze the components of these concerns, began to speculate about contributing conditions, and set tentative goals—all in the context of trying to understand Cynthia's despair so she could find relief. By the end of the first interview, Cynthia felt somewhat reassured. The worker assigned specific tasks for Cynthia to carry out during the next week and asked her to fill out the Center for Epidemiological Study Depression (CES-D) Scale. (Radloff, 1977)

Berlin acknowledges several problems in the validity of this approach as a research design and also cautions against "bombarding" the client with instruments. As a tool for monitoring client progress, however (the instrument was completed at each session), it provided "objective" information to the social worker on the client's progress. The author also acknowledges the need for "flexibility" in design; for example, the model might change to an A-B-C analysis if psychotropic drugs were added at some point to the treatment plan.

As with most reports of SSRD, fully assessing the nature of the practice is difficult because it is summarized rather than reported verbatim or as a process recording. For example, we do not know if the social worker was using empathic skills in her responses; however, we might assume so from the sensitive description of the problem. Also, there is no mention of the working relationship as a key factor in the process, but again, I would assume it developed out of the clear contracting and the exploration work done by the worker. We could also debate whether the use of the depression inventory in the first session might enhance the practice or inhibit it. The author argues that it was not a major impediment. One could argue it provided the client as well as the worker with a clearer measure of the nature of the problem.

While reasonable people may differ on the relative importance of process or outcome evaluation, the impact that the use of formal data-gathering instruments may have on practice, the nature of the practice itself, the potential conflict between research and clinical goals, and so forth, most social workers would agree on the importance of developing both systematic methods for assessing what they do with each client and research that evaluates practice effectiveness with client populations. In this section, we have seen two illustrative approaches to this task. The position taken throughout this book is that we still have a great deal to learn about what works, with which clients, under what circumstances, and so on. Contributions that enhance our understanding should be gratefully accepted, no matter what their source.

The Scientist-Practitioner Model

While the psychology profession has mainly advocated the scientist-practitioner model, it is also seen as a paradigm for social workers. As mentioned, most social workers will not engage in major research studies of practice, though they may participate in studies conducted by others. Their job descriptions as well as the limits of their knowledge of research design, techniques, and statistical analysis make it highly unlikely that they could test practice theories and models on a large enough scale to obtain significant findings. The single-case designs just discussed are usually the most research that a practitioner can be expected to do. Given this reality, social workers essentially make use of empirical research as consumers and social work education programs usually focus on helping them to become more sophisticated in their ability to understand, evaluate, and implement research. In spite of this orientation and training, researchers and funding agencies face increasing frustration about the lack of *technology transfer,* that is, the ways in which research findings make their way into general practice.

Lampropoulos and colleagues (2002) address this issue in an effort to develop a "realistic version of the scientist-practitioner model" (p. 1242). They suggest that research-driven practice requires clinically meaningful research. Further, they propose that clinical research must keep the needs of the practitioner in the center of attention. Lueger (2002) agrees with this position, pointing out that the type of information that clinicians value should inform and give direction to research efforts. He identifies four approaches to conducting studies: research on technology transfer, quasi-experimental single-case designs, mental health services research, and case-focused patient profiling.

Another source of limitation on practitioner use of research findings may be found in the research itself. For example, Beutler, Moleiro, and Talebi (2002) point out that, in studies comparing practice models and theories, a considerable body of research indicates that all treatments produce similar effects. Practitioners who read that what approach they take does not matter will be less interested in empirical data. The authors suggest that identifying common and differential principles of change may be more productive.

Carter (2002) identifies three areas of divisiveness between science and practice: understanding of practitioner approaches to practice, definitions of scholarship, and the role of theory and diagnosis in practice. The first particularly applies to our discussion. Research efforts that are not based on an intimate understanding of practice will produce results that are not meaningful to the practitioner. In my own experience as an academic, researcher, and practitioner, I have found that my continuous involvement in practice, usually my leading at least one type of mutual-aid support group each year, has influenced my selection of research topics as well as my ability to make inferences from my data.

The ability to operationalize and measure independent (treatment) variables, moderating (intervening) variables, and dependant (outcome) variables is another factor that may limit the usefulness of empirical data for practitioners. For example, Gladis, Gosch, Dishuk, and Crits-Christoph (1999) point out that while "quality of life" has been increasingly used as an outcome measure for various treatments, the construct still lacks a good operational definition, uses subjective rather than objective criteria, and does not make a clear connection between quality of life measures and symptoms. The variables that are studied themselves may prove to be less than informative for the practitioner. For example, a major study that examined data from over 10,000 patients receiving psychotherapy looked at the association between the number of treatment sessions and clinically significant improvement (Lambert, Hansen, & Finch, 2001). This study, termed a "dose-response" examination, found that 50 percent of the patients required 21 sessions of treatment before they met the criteria for clinically significant improvement. This focus on the number of sessions does not clarify what actually happened in the detailed interaction between the therapists and the patients. Practitioners might be more interested in the relationships among interactional process, patient demographics, and number of sessions.

Finally, the manner in which the results of empirical research are transmitted to practitioners can also influence the use of these findings in practice. Research reports at conferences or in journals often describe their methodology more thoroughly than they describe direct and clear implications for the practitioner. While methodology, particularly limitations of a study, needs to be reported in order to evaluate the findings, a greater effort needs to be undertaken to help practitioners make direct connections to their work.

As we near the end of this book, we can see that social workers face many challenges in serving clients. Whether individuals, families, or groups, clients require workers to understand the many factors that affect practice and to acquire the skills that enable them to provide effective help. The measures of success depend largely on the worker's perspective. Throughout the book, we have focused on the interactional model. It is my hope that you find this approach helpful in developing your own practice framework.

Chapter Summary

Many factors profoundly affect social work and help define the worker's responsibilities. Agency records, referral reports, and agency culture can affect how a worker sees a client before the first meeting. Workers must take into account the effect of such information. Workers also face ethical dilemmas in serving clients. Guidelines concerning how to follow professional values come from many sources, including professional literature and organizations such as the NASW. Recent legal decisions have defined specific ways in which social workers must act. Finally, social workers are responsible for evaluating their own practice as well as understanding research evaluations of both process and outcomes.

Related Online Content and Activities

Visit *The Skills of Helping* Book Companion Website at www.socialwork.wadsworth.com/Shulman06/ for learning tools such as glossary terms, InfoTrac College Edition keywords, links to related websites, and chapter practice quizzes.

Glossary

act out To communicate thoughts and feelings through behavior, often in a disruptive manner.

active mistake A response by a worker than may be off target but, because it is an active rather than passive mistake (inaction), allows the worker to grow. Social workers are encouraged to make active rather than passive mistakes.

activity group A term usually applied to groups involved in a range of activities other than just conversation. *Program* is another term used to describe the activities implemented in such groups, such as the expressive arts (painting, dancing), games, folk singing, social parties, cooking, and so on.

"all-in-the-same-boat" phenomenon A mutual-aid process in which group members gain support from discovering that other group members have similar problems, concerns, feelings, and experiences.

ambivalence Mixed feelings about a problem, person, or issue. For example, a client may wish to finally deal with an issue, but because of the painful feelings associated with it, the client may also wish to deny that the problem exists.

anger over the ending A stage in the ending/transition phase whereby individuals, family members, or group members appear to be angry at the worker because of the ending of the relationship. This appears in direct or indirect forms.

authority theme Issues related to the relationship between the client (individual, family, or group) and the social worker.

basic assumption groups Bion's (1961) idea that group members appear to be acting as if their behavior were motivated by a shared basic assumption—other than the expressed group goal—about the purpose of the group.

beginning (or contracting) phase The engagement phase of work, during which the worker contracts with the client by clarifying the purpose of the engagement, by clarifying the role he or she will play, and by reaching for client feedback on the content of the work. Authority issues are also dealt with in this phase.

burnout A common problem in stressful practice situations in which the worker's emotional reactions lead to leaving the job or maladaptive behaviors such as overworking or closing off all emotional reactions.

caring One element of the construct "working relationship"; the client's sense that the worker is concerned about him or her and that the worker wishes to help with those concerns the client feels are important.

casework in the group A common pattern in which the group leader provides individual counseling to a client within a group setting. This contrasts with an effort to mobilize mutual aid for the client by involving the other members.

causal path analysis A form of statistical analysis that allows the researcher to create a model of a process that involves predictor variables having some impact on outcome variables. The analysis allows the researcher to determine the direction (path) of the influence and the strength (coefficient) of the influence. Thus, it is a useful tool for empirically based theory building.

check-in An exercise used in some groups at the start of the session, in which each member briefly shares what has happened to him or her during the preceding week.

checking for underlying ambivalence Exploring client ambivalence that may be hidden by an artificial agreement.

clarifying the worker's purpose and role Establishing the purpose of the contact, the various services offered by the agency or setting, and the specific ways in which the worker can help.

cleavage A process in a group in which the members split into distinct racial subgroups in response to a changing racial ratio. It can occur with an increase of the minority or "out" group members past the tipping point.

closed group A fixed-membership group in which the same people meet for a defined period of time. Members may drop out and new members may be added in the early sessions, but in general, the membership of the group remains constant.

cohesion The property of the group that describes the mutual attraction members feel for one another.

common ground The overlap or commonality between the specific services of the setting and the felt needs of the client.

confidentiality The right of a client not to have private information shared with third parties.

consensual validation The third subphase of the interdependence phase of group development (Bennis &

Shepard, 1956), in which the unconflicted members once again provide the leadership needed for the group to move to a new level of work characterized by honest communication among members.

containment The skill of refraining from responding immediately to a client's comment or question.

content The substance of the work, consisting of ideas, issues, problems, concerns, and so on that are part of the working contract.

contracting process A worker-initiated effort, usually in the beginning phase of the work, to establish the purpose of the contact, to explain the worker's role, to gain some sense of the client's issues (feedback), and to deal with issues of authority.

correlation A nondirectional measure of association between two variables, with the correlation r ranging from -1.0 to 1.0.

cost containment Efforts on the part of administrators to lower the cost of services. They are often introduced because of reduced funding by private and government agencies or third-party payers such as health insurance companies.

counterdependence-flight The second subphase of the dependency phase of group development, in which the leader attempts to take over the group and group members are in flight, exhibiting behaviors indicating fear of the leader's authority (Bennis & Shepard, 1956).

counterdependent member A member of the group who, during the counterdependence-flight subphase of group development, acts as if she or he is not dependent on the group leader and attempts to take over the group (Bennis & Shepard, 1956).

countertransference The complex of feelings of a worker toward a client.

culture for work An explicit or implied set of values, taboos, rules of interaction, and other concepts that are shared by the group members and that positively affect the group's ability to work at its tasks.

data gathering One of the functions of group activities; designed to help members obtain more information central to their tasks.

dealing with issues of authority The worker's efforts to clarify mutual expectations, confidentiality issues, and the authority theme.

demand for work The worker's confrontation of the client to work effectively on her or his tasks and to invest that work with energy and affect.

denial of the ending A stage in the ending/transition phase whereby individuals, families, or group members appear to ignore the imminent end of the sessions.

dependence phase The first phase of the group development, which is marked by group members' preoccupation with authority issues (Bennis & Shepard, 1956).

dependence-flight The first subphase of the dependency phase of group development, in which group members are in flight, exhibiting behaviors indicating dependence on the leaders (Bennis & Shepard, 1956).

dependent group One of Bion's (1961) basic assumption groups. The group appears to be meeting in order to be sustained by the leader rather than working on its purposes.

dependent member A member of a group who, during the dependence-flight subphase of group development, acts as if she or he is dependent on the group leader, wanting the leader to take control of the group (Bennis & Shepard, 1956).

detecting and challenging the obstacles to work Perceiving and then confronting directly the obstacles that impede the client's work.

developing a universal perspective A mutual-aid process in the group in which members begin to perceive universal issues, particularly in relation to oppression, thus allowing them to view their own problems in a more social context and with less personal blame.

deviant member The client who acts significantly differently from other clients in the system (such as the family or group) but may actually be sending an indirect signal of feelings and concerns on behalf of the other clients.

deviational allowance One of the functions of group activities; designed to create a flow of affect among members that builds up a positive relationship, allowing members to deviate from the accepted norms and raise concerns that might otherwise be taboo.

dialectical process A mutual-aid process in which group members confront each other's ideas in an effort to develop a synthesis for all group members.

direct macropractice Social work involving direct work with clients in pursuit of community goals and objectives.

discussing a taboo area A mutual-aid process in which one member enters a taboo area of discussion, thereby freeing other members to enter as well.

disenchantment-flight The second subphase of the interdependence phase of group development, in which the counterpersonals take over from the overpersonals in reaction to the growing intimacy (Bennis & Shepard, 1956).

displaying understanding of the client's feelings The skill of acknowledging to the client, through words or nonverbal means, that the worker has understood how the client feels after the affect has been expressed by the client (for example, the worker's response to crying).

division of labor The development of group structure in which the tasks to be performed are distributed among members in a formal or informal manner.

"doorknob" communication A client communication usually shared at the very end of a session (hand on the doorknob) or in the last sessions. This is one of the sessional ending and transition skills.

duty to warn The legal obligation by social workers and other professionals to warn a third party when they, in exercising their professional skill and knowledge, determine that a warning is essential to avert danger arising from the medical or psychological condition of their client.

dynamic interaction Interaction in which the parties involved affect each other reciprocally—that is, with the movements of one party affecting the other(s), moment by moment, in the interaction.

dynamic system A system in which the behavior of each participant in the system (for example, staff and clients) affects and is affected by the behaviors of all other members of the system.

elaborating Helping the client tell his or her story.

empathy Helping the client share the affective part of the message.

empirically based practice theory A research-based description of a social worker's valued outcomes and interventions, which are based on a set of underlying assumptions about human behavior and social organization and on a set of professional ethics and values.

empowerment process A process through which the social worker engages the client (individual, family, group, or community) in order to improve their circumstances.

enchantment-flight The first subphase of the interdependence phase of group development, in which good feelings abound and efforts are directed toward healing wounds (Bennis & Shepard, 1956).

ending and transition phase The termination phase of work, in which the worker prepares to end the relationship and to help the client review their work together as well as to prepare for transitions to new experiences.

entry One of the functions of group activities; designed as a way to enter an area of difficult discussion.

ethics A system of moral principles and perceptions about right versus wrong and the resulting philosophy of conduct that is practiced by an individual, group, profession, or culture (Barker, 2003, p. 147).

exploring client resistance Identifying and discussing, with the client, the meaning of the signals of a client's resistance.

external leader The social work group leader who derives his or her authority from external sources such as the sponsoring agency. This is in contrast to the internal leader, who is a member of the group.

facilitative confrontation Drawing on the fund of positive work with the client to use confrontation to make the work of the client easier.

family A natural living unit including all those persons who share identity with each other and are influenced by it in a circular exchange of emotions (Ackerman, 1958).

family facade A false front presented by the family in early contacts with the worker. The facade demonstrates how the family collaborates in hiding its problems from the social environment.

family secret An explicit or unspoken agreement in which all family members agree not to deal directly with a sensitive and taboo concern. Family violence, alcoholism, and sexual abuse are examples of family secrets often hidden behind a family facade.

family support (family counseling) A type of support that is usually short-term and designed to help families facing normative crises, such as the first child reaching the teen years, the birth of a new baby, or the loss of a job. The work centers on helping a relatively healthy family get through a difficult time, using the experience to strengthen rather than erode the family system.

farewell-party syndrome The tendency on the client's part, in the ending/transition phase, to avoid the pain of ending by planning some form of celebration. Also, the tendency to express only positive reactions about the experience, rather than being critical.

fear-of-groups syndrome The anxieties experienced by workers as they prepare to work with groups for the first time.

feeling-thinking-doing connection A process in which how we feel affects how we act and think, and how we act affects how we think and feel.

first offering An indirect communication from the client offering the worker a clue about the nature of the client's concerns. Often followed by a second (more direct) and even third or fourth offering designed to increase the signal's clarity.

flight-fight The natural tendency on the part of any organism to respond to a threat by either running from it (flight) or attacking it (fight). In human relationships, flight-fight usually (but not always) characterizes a maladaptive response to emotional pain that can lead to the avoidance of real work. Family violence is an example of fight, and drug and alcohol addictions are examples of flight.

flight-fight group One of Bion's (1961) basic assumption groups. When the work group gets close to painful feelings, the members sometimes unite in an instantaneous, unconscious process to form the flight-fight group, acting from the basic assumption that the group goal is to avoid the pain associated with the work group processes through flight (an immediate change of subject from the painful area) or fight (an argument developing in the group that moves from the emotional level to an intellectual one).

first decision The client's commitment to engage with the worker in a meaningful way and begin to develop a therapeutic alliance.

focused listening Concentrating on a specific part of the client's message.

function In social work, the specific part the professional plays in the helping process.

functional diffusion A loss of functional clarity that causes a worker to diffuse her or his activity and implement a role or roles inappropriate for the moment.

gatekeeper A group member who may intervene to distract the group each time the discussion approaches a painful subject.

generalist practice A social work practitioner whose knowledge and skills encompass a broad spectrum and who assesses problems and their solutions comprehensively (Barker, 2003).

generalizing Using specific instances to help the client identify general principles (such as the importance of being honest about one's feelings in different situations). This is one of the sessional ending and transition skills.

generic social work The social work orientation that emphasizes a common core of knowledge and skills associated with social service provision (Barker, 2003, p. 174).

grounded theory An approach to theory building, first described by Glaser and Strauss (1967) in the field of sociology, in which formal and informal observations from the field are used to develop constructs of the theory. Formal research is conducted to test propositions and to generate new ones.

group culture The norms, taboos, rules, and member roles that guide the generally accepted ways of acting within the group. In a group's early stage, the group members usually recreate a group culture representative of the larger community. This culture can be modified over time to become more conductive to effective work.

handles for work Concerns and problems, suggested by the worker in an opening or contracting statement, that offer possible areas of connection between the client's needs and the agency's services.

helping the client see life in new ways Skills designed to help clients modify their cognitions about themselves and their world (for example, reframing a situation in a more positive way).

holding to focus Asking the client to stay focused on one theme as opposed to jumping from issue to issue. It is one of the demand-for-work skills.

holistic theory A theoretical approach that includes a broad range of variables—personal, interactional, contextual, and time related—in describing social work practice.

hospice A residential setting for people who are in the final stage of a terminal illness.

human communications A complex process in which messages are encoded by a sender, transmitted through some medium (such as words or facial expressions), and received by the receiver, who must then decode the message. The response of the receiver involves encoding a new message and transmitting it, which keeps the cycle going.

human contact One of the functions of group activities; designed to focus on meeting a basic human need for social interaction.

identified patient (IP) The client in a family system who is identified as having the problem.

identifying process and content connections A skill set allowing the worker to see how the client uses the working relationship (process) as a medium for raising and working on issues central to the substantive issues under discussion (content).

identifying the next steps Helping the client use the current discussion to develop ideas about future actions. This is one of the sessional ending and transition skills.

identifying the stage of the ending process The skill of naming for the client the stage of the ending process for the purpose of helping the client to feel more in control of the endings. These stages are denial, indirect and direct expressions of anger, mourning, trying it on for size, and the farewell-party syndrome.

illusion of work A process in which the worker and the client engage in a conversation that is empty of real meaning and affect. It may be a form of passive resistance in which the client tries to please the worker by pretending to work.

indirect macropractice Activities of a social worker on behalf of a community, such as research or legislative report writing, that do not involve direct work with clients.

individual problem-solving A mutual-aid process through which group members help one member solve a particular problem, receiving help themselves while offering it to another.

informed consent "The client's granting of permission to the social worker and agency or other professional person to use specific intervention procedures, including diagnosis, treatment, follow up, and research. This permission must be based on full disclosure of the facts needed to make the decision intelligently. Informed consent must be based upon knowledge of the risks and alternatives" (Barker, 2003, p. 114).

intake worker Worker who usually makes the first contact with a client and conducts some form of assessment of suitability for services.

interactional model A model of practice that emphasizes the interactional nature of the helping process. The client in this model is viewed as a self-realizing, energy-producing person with certain tasks to perform, and the social worker as having a specific function to carry out. They engage each other as interdependent actors within an organic system that is best described as reciprocal, with each person affecting and being affected by the other moment to moment. The worker-client relationship is understood within the social context and is influenced by the impact of time.

interdependence phase The second phase of group development, which has to do with questions of intimacy—that is, and the group members' concerns about how close they wish to get to one another (Bennis & Shepard, 1956).

internal leader A member or members of the group who assume a leadership role in a situational or ongoing basis. This role needs to be confirmed by the other group members.

intimacy theme Concerns related to the interactions among the members of a group.

key worker A worker, usually in a residential setting, who has particular responsibility for providing continuity of service to a particular client.

listen first—talk later An approach used in work with information groups, in which the leader first listens to the group members' questions, issues, and concerns and then presents the required information.

looking for trouble when everything is going the worker's way The skill of exploring hidden ambivalence or a negative response when a client immediately responds positively to a difficult suggestion.

macropractice Social work with clients in the community.

mandated reporter A professional who is required by law to report if certain categories of clients (such as children and the elderly) are at risk (posing a threat to themselves or others or experiencing serious abuse or neglect).

mandatory client A client who is required to engage in services involuntarily, usually by an agency policy (as in preadoptive groups), a court (as in male batterers' groups), an employer (as in alcohol counseling) or a family member (as in support groups for spouses of addicts).

medical model The four-step process of organizing one's thinking about practice, commonly described as study, diagnosis, treatment, and evaluation. Also: sometimes used to describe a "pathology" model for diagnosing client problems.

micropractice Social work with individual clients, families, or support groups in a clinical setting.

microsociety A description of the small group as a special case of the larger individual-social interaction in society.

middle (or work) phase The phase of work in which the client and the worker focus on dealing with issues raised in the beginning phase or with new issues that have emerged since then.

mixed transactional model A way of seeing social work in terms of *transactions,* exchanges in which people give to and take from each other through different mediums of exchange, including words, facial and body expressions, touch, shared experiences of various kinds, and other forms of communication (often used simultaneously).

model A concrete, symbolic representation of an abstract phenomenon.

monitoring the group The skill of observing the second client—the group members—by watching for verbal and nonverbal clues as to their reactions while a member is speaking.

monitoring the individual The skill of observing individual group members, remaining alert to verbal and nonverbal clues signaled by each individual. This is an acquired skill. When this skill is integrated, a group leader can simultaneously monitor the group and each individual.

monopolizer A member of a group who talks a great deal and appears to monopolize the conversation. The monopolizer is usually described as someone who does not listen well to others.

moving from the general to the specific Helping a client share specific details about an issue first brought up on a more general level.

mourning period A stage in the ending process of a group, usually characterized by apathy and a general tone of sadness.

mutual demand A mutual-aid process in which group members offer each other help by making demands and setting expectations on personal behavior.

mutual support A mutual-aid process in which group members provide emotional support to one another.

near problems Legitimate issues raised by clients, early in the relationship, to establish trust before raising more difficult and often threatening issues.

nonverbal forms of communication The transmission of a communication without the use of words; for example, a posture or facial expression, where a client sits, getting up and leaving an interview, or an affectionate touch.

norms of behavior The rules of behavior generally accepted by a dominant group in society. These norms can be recreated within a social work group or other system. The existence of the norms is evident when the group members act as if the norms existed.

open-ended group A group in which new members can join at any point and ongoing members may leave at different times. For example, a ward group on a hospital may have new members join when admitted to the hospital and others leave when discharged.

opening statement The worker's statement, during the first contact, that attempts to identify the purpose of the encounter, the worker's role, and possible areas of connection with the felt needs of the client.

oppression psychology A theory of the impact of societal oppression on vulnerable populations.

organismic model A metaphor suggesting a capacity for growth and emergent behavior—that is, a process in which a system transcends itself and creates something new that is more than just the sum of its parts.

outreach process Process through which the social work service is brought to potential clients.

outreach program A program that attempts to bring services directly to clients, usually in their own homes or neighborhoods.

pairing group One of Bion's (1961) basic assumption groups, in which the group, often through a conversation between two members, avoids the pain of the work by discussing some future great event.

parallel process The way in which the process on one level (such as supervisor-worker) parallels the process on another level (such as worker-client).

partializing the client's concerns Helping the client deal with complex problems by breaking them down into their component parts and addressing the parts one at a time.

pointing out endings early The skill of reminding clients, far enough ahead of the last sessions to be helpful, that the working relationship is coming to a close. How early this is depends on the length of the working relationship, among other factors.

practitioner-researcher A social worker who is continuously involved in evaluating his or her own practice and developing generalizations from the practice experience.

preliminary (or preparatory) phase The phase of work prior to the worker engaging with the client. Usually used by the worker to develop a preliminary empathy about the client's issues and concerns.

process The interaction that takes place between the worker and the client during an interview, or between the client and another client, which characterizes the way of working versus the content of the work.

professional impact The activities of social workers designed to effect changes in (1) policies and services in their own agency and other agencies and institutions, as well as broader social policies that affect clients, and (2) the work culture that influences inter-staff relationships within their own agency and with other agencies and institutions.

pseudoeffectiveness Defined by Argyris (1954) as the ability of the organization to create the illusion of effective operation.

psychosocial history The client's story, taking into account personal, psychological, and social factors that may have some bearing on the current life situation. This is usually obtained during an intake interview or early history.

putting the client's feelings into words The skill of articulating the client's feelings, in response to tuning in or perceiving the client's indirect communications, prior to the client's direct expression of affect.

quasi-stationary social equilibrium A term used by Lewin (1951) to describe a stage in the change process at which a person is in balance with his or her social environment. This balance can be upset by external or internal forces, resulting in a state of disequilibrium that can lead to change and a new quasi-stationary equilibrium.

questioning In the elaboration process, the worker's requests for more information from the client regarding the client's problem, including who, what, where, when, and why.

quiet member A member of the group who remains noticeably silent over an extended period of time.

rapport One element of the construct "working relationship"; a general sense on the client's part that he or she gets along well with the worker.

reaching for feelings The empathic skill of asking the client to share the affective portion of the message.

reaching for the client's feedback Inviting a client to share his or her concerns related to the purpose of the contact and the agency service. This may be a simple question or a statement of specific illustrative examples of possible concerns (see *handles for work*).

reaching inside of silences The skill of exploring the meaning of a silence by putting the client's possible feelings into words (for instance, "Are you angry right now?").

recontracting The process in which the worker reopens the issues of contracting by providing a clearer statement of purpose or exploring the group members' resistance or lack of connection to the service.

record of service A written record that describes the client system, identifies the central problem area, describes and illustrates the practice over time, assesses the status of the problem after a period of work, and then identifies next worker interventions to continue the work.

reframing the problem The process, described by family theorists, as helping the family see a problem in a new way. One example of this would be helping the family move beyond viewing the family problem as concerning a single child (the identified patient) who may be serving as a family scapegoat.

regression analysis A statistical procedure for projecting the impact of predictor variables on outcome variables.

rehearsal (1) The process in which the client has an opportunity to practice a difficult next step in an informal role play, with the worker usually playing the role of the other person. This is one of the sessional ending and transition skills. (2) A mutual-aid process in which group members help one another by providing a forum in which members can try out ideas or skills. (3) One of the functions of group activities; designed to develop skills for specific life tasks.

resistance Behavior on the part of the client that appears to resist the worker's efforts to deal with the client's problems. Resistance may be open (active) or indirect (passive). It is usually a sign of the client's pain associated with the work.

resolution stage The stage of work in which a session is brought to some form of closure or resolution, which may include recognizing the lack of closure and determining next steps.

resolution-catharsis The third subphase of the dependency phase in group development, in which group leadership is assumed by members who are unconflicted (independent) (Bennis & Shepard, 1956). This "overthrow" of the worker leads to each member taking responsibility for the group: The worker is no longer seen as "magical," and the power struggles are replaced by work on shared goals.

role In the psychodynamic frame of reference, an "adaptational unit of personality in action" (Ackerman, 1958, p. 53).

scapegoat A member of the group attacked, verbally or physically, by other members who project onto the member their own negative feelings about themselves. The scapegoat role is often interactive in nature, with the scapegoat fulfilling a functional role in the group.

second decision The client's decision to continue engaging with the worker in the middle phase of work. This decision is made in the face of challenges such as dealing with painful issues and accepting personal responsibility for addressing issues.

self-determination The right of clients to make their own choices and decisions; an ethical principle in social work.

sessional contracting skills The skills usually employed at the start of a session to clarify the immediate work at hand. These include exploring client resistance, identifying process and content connections, and helping the client see life in new ways.

sessional ending and transition skills The skills designed to bring a session to a close and to make the connections between a single session and future work or issues in the life of the client. These include summarizing, generalizing, identifying the next steps, rehearsal, and identifying "doorknob" communications.

sessional tuning-in skills The skills designed to sensitize the worker, prior to each session, to the potential themes that may emerge during the work. These include tuning in to the client's sense of urgency, to the worker's own feelings, to the meaning of the client's struggle, to the worker's realities of time and stress, and to the worker's own life experiences.

sharing data A mutual-aid process in a group when members share accumulated knowledge, views, values, and so forth that can help others in the group.

sharing worker data Sharing facts, ideas, values, and beliefs that workers have accumulated from their own experiences and can make available to clients.

sharing worker's feelings The skill of appropriately sharing with the client the worker's own affect. These feelings should be shared in pursuit of professional purposes as the worker implements the professional function.

skill factor A set of closely related worker skills.

skills Specific behaviors on the part of the worker that are used in the implementation of the social work function.

societal taboos Commonly shared injunctions in our society that directly or indirectly inhibit our ability to talk about certain areas (such as sexual abuse, death and dying). More generally, *taboos* are social prohibitions that result from conventions or traditions. Norms and taboos are closely related, because a group norm may be one that upholds the tradition of making certain subjects taboo.

"strength-in-numbers" phenomenon The mutual-aid process in which group members are strengthened to take on difficult tasks (such as challenging agency policy) through the support of other group members.

structure and maintenance The work done by group members to develop, examine, and maintain in good working order their structure for work (roles, rules, culture, and so on).

structure for work The formal or informal rules, roles, communication patterns, rituals, and procedures developed by the group members to facilitate the work of the group.

summarizing Helping a client to identify the main themes of discussion during a session. This is one of the sessional ending and transition skills, to be employed at key moments, not necessarily in every session.

supporting clients in taboo areas Encouraging a client to discuss a sensitive or difficult area or concern (for example, sex, loss).

symbiotic assumption The assumption of a relationship between the individual and his or her nurturing group in which each needs the other for the life and growth of each, and each reaches out to the other with all the strength possible at a given moment.

symbiotic diffusion Obscuring of the mutual need between people and their social surroundings by the complexity of the situation, by divergent needs, or by the difficulties involved in communication.

systems or ecological approach A view of the client that takes into account his or her dynamic interaction with the social context.

systems work The set of activities in which social workers attempt to influence the systems and systems representatives (such as doctors, administrators, teachers) that are important to their clients.

taboo See *societal taboos.*

theoretical generalizations Testable propositions that receive repeated support from research.

third decision The decision clients make to deal with their most difficult issues as they approach the end of the working relationship.

tipping point The "saturation point" in the changing racial ratio of a group that leads majority group members to respond with anxiety and aggression toward the "out" group. Reaching the tipping point can generate such processes as cleavage and white flight.

triangulation A process in which one party attempts to gain the allegiance of a second party in the struggle with a third party (for example, the parents and the therapist versus the child; the mother and an older child versus the father) as a means of coping with anxiety.

trust An element of the construct "working relationship"; the client's perception that she or he can risk sharing thoughts, feelings, mistakes, and failures with the worker.

trying the ending on for size A stage in the ending/transition phase in which clients or group members operate independently of the worker or spend a great deal of time talking about new groups or new workers.

tuning in The skill of getting in touch with potential feelings and concerns that the client may bring to the helping encounter. For this to be done effectively, the worker has to actually experience the feelings, or an approximation, by using his or her own life experiences to recall similar emotions.

two-clients construct View of the social worker as always having two clients at any moment in time (for example, the individual and the family; the member and the group; the client and the system).

unconflicted member A member of the group who is independent and untroubled by authority.

values The customs, standards of conduct, and principles considered desirable by a culture, a group of people, or an individual (Barker, 2003, p. 453).

vulnerable client A client who is particularly exposed to the impact of oppression and stressful life events because of personal and/or social factors (such as lack of a strong social support system of family or friends; limited economic resources).

white flight The process of white members leaving a group when the racial composition ratio of the group changes, resulting in an increase in minority group members past the tipping point.

who owns the client? A maladaptive struggle in which helping professionals appear to fight over "ownership" of functional responsibility for a client.

work group The mental activity related to a group's task (Bion, 1961). When the work group is operating, one can see group members translating their thoughts and feelings into actions that are adaptive to reality.

worker data See *sharing worker data*.

working relationship A professional relationship between the client and worker that is the medium through which the social worker influences the client. A positive working relationship will be characterized by good rapport and a sense on the part of the client that he or she can trust the worker and that the worker cares for the client.

References

Ackerman, N. (1958). *Psychodynamics of family life* (3rd ed.). New York: Basic Books.

Addams, J. (1961). *Twenty years at Hull House*. New York: Signet.

Albert, J. (1994). Rethinking difference: A cognitive therapy group for chronic mental patients. *Social Work With Groups, 17,* 105–122.

Alexander, R., Jr. (1997). Social workers and privileged communication in the federal legal system. *Social Work, 42,* 387–391.

American Association for Counseling and Development. (1989). *Ethical guidelines for group counselors.* Alexandria, VA: American Association for Counseling and Development.

Amodeo, M., Wilson, S., & Cox, D. (1996). Mounting a community-based alcohol and drug abuse prevention effort in a multicultural urban setting: Challenges and lessons learned. *Journal of Primary Prevention, 16,* 165–185.

Argyris, C. (1964). *Integrating the individual and the organization.* New York: Wiley.

Barker, R. (2003). *The social work dictionary* (5th ed.). Silver Springs, MD: National Association of Social Workers.

Beasley, M., Thompson, T., & Davidson, J. (2003). Resilience in response to life stress: The effects of coping style and cognitive hardiness. *Personality and Individual Differences, 34,* 77–95.

Beck, A., Rush, A., Shaw, B., & Emery, G. (1979). *Cognitive theory of depression.* New York: Guilford Press.

Bell, N. W., & Vogel, E. F. (1960). The emotionally disturbed child as the family scapegoat. In N. W. Bell & E. F. Vogel (Eds.), *A modern introduction to the family* (pp. 382–397). New York: Free Press.

Bennis, W. G., & Shepard, H. A. (1956). A theory of group development. *Human Relations, 9,* 415–437.

Berlin, S. B. (1983). Cognitive-behavioral approaches. In A. Rosenblatt & D. Wald Fogel (Eds.), *Handbook of clinical social work* (pp. 1095–1119). San Francisco: Jossey-Bass.

Berlin, S. B. (1984). Single-case evaluation: Another version. *Social Work Research and Abstracts, 19*(1), 3–11.

Berlin, S. B., & Kravetz, D. (1981). Women as victims: A feminist social work perspective. *Social Work, 26,* 449.

Berman-Rossi, T., & Cohen, M. B. (1989). Group development and shared decision making working with homeless mentally ill women. In J. A. Lee (Ed.), *Group work with the poor and oppressed* (pp. 63–74). New York: Haworth Press.

Bernstein, S. (1965). *Explorations in group work.* Boston: Boston University School of Social Work.

Bernstein, S. (1970). *Further exploration in group work.* Boston: Boston University School of Social Work.

Beutler, L. E., Moleiro, C., & Talebi, H. (2002). How practitioners can systematically use empirical evidence in treatment selection. *Journal of Clinical Psychology, 58*(10), 1199–1212.

Bion, W. R. (1961). *Experience in groups.* New York: Basic Books.

Bowen, M. (1961). The family as a unit of study and treatment. *American Journal of Orthopsychiatry, 31,* 40–60.

Bowen, M. (1978). *Family therapy in clinical practice.* New York: Jason Aronson.

Boyle, D. P., & Springer, S. A. (2001). Toward a cultural competence measure for social work with specific populations. *Journal of Ethnic and Cultural Diversity in Social Work, 9,* 53–71.

Braeger, G., & Holloway, S. (1978). *Changing human service organizations: Politics and practice.* New York: Free Press.

Breton, M. (1988). The need for mutual-aid groups in a drop-in for homeless women: The sistering case. In J. A. Lee (Ed.), *Group work with the poor and oppressed* (pp. 47–60). New York: Haworth Press.

Bulhan, H. A. (1985). *Franz Fanon and the psychology of oppression.* New York: Plenum Press.

Butler, K. (1997, March/April). The anatomy of resilience. *Networker,* pp. 22–31.

Carter, J. A. (2002). Integrating science and practice: Reclaiming the science in practice. *Journal of Clinical Psychology, 58*(10), 1285–1290.

Castex, G. M. (1994). Providing services to Hispanic/Latino populations: Profiles in diversity. *Social Work, 39,* 288–296.

Christian, M. D., & Barbarin, O. A. (2001). Cultural resources and psychological adjustment of African American children: Effects of spirituality and racial attribution. *Journal of Black Psychology, 27,* 43–63.

Chung, R. C.-Y., & Bemak, F. (2002). The relationship of culture and empathy in cross-cultural counseling. *Journal of Counseling and Development, 80,* 154–159.

Clay, C., & Shulman, I. (1993). *Teaching about practice and diversity: Content and process in the classroom and the field* [videotape]. Produced and distributed by the Council on Social Work Education.

Code of ethical practice. (1991). Boston, MA: Board of Registration of Social Workers, 258 CMR-25.

Collins, B. G. (1994). Reconstructing codependency using self-in-relation theory: A feminist perspective. *Social Work, 38,* 470–476.

Congress, E. P. (1994). The use of culturagrams to assess and empower culturally diverse families. *Families in Society, 75,* 531–540.

Connell, J. P., Spencer, M. B., & Aber, J. L. (1994). Educational risk and resilience in African American youth: Context, self, action, and outcomes in school. *Child Development, 65,* 506.

Council on Social Work Education. (2003). *Curriculum policy statement.* New York: Author.

Cox, E. O. (2001). Community practice issues in the 21st century: Questions and challenges for empowerment-oriented practitioners. *Journal of Community Practice, 9,* 37–55.

Coyle, G. (1948). *Group work with American youth.* New York: Harper.

Daly, A., Jennings, J., Beckett, J. O., & Leashore, B. R. (1995). Effective coping strategies of African Americans. *Social Work, 40,* 240–248.

Davidson, K. W. (1985). Social work with cancer patients: Stresses and coping patterns. *Social work in health care, 10,* 73–82.

Davis, L. E. (1979). Racial composition of groups. *Social Work, 24,* 208–213.

Davis, L. E. (1981). Racial issues in the training of group workers. *Journal of Specialists in Group Work,* pp. 155–160.

Davis, L. E. (1984). *Ethnicity in social group work practice.* New York: Haworth Press.

Davis, L. E. (1999). *Working with African American males: A guide to practice.* Newbury Park, CA: Sage.

Davis, L. E., & Proctor, E. K. (1989). *Race, gender, and class: Guidelines for practice with individuals, families, and groups.* Englewood Cliffs, NJ: Prentice-Hall.

deShazer, S. (1988). *Clues: Investigating solutions in brief therapy.* New York: Norton.

deShazer, S., & Berg, R. (1992). Doing therapy: A post-structural revision. *Journal of Marital and Family Therapy, 18,* 71–81.

Devore, W., & Schlesinger, E. G. (1991). *Ethnic-sensitive social work practice* (3rd ed.). New York: Macmillan.

Devore, W., & Schlesinger, E. G. (1996). *Ethnic-sensitive social work practice* (4th ed.). New York: Macmillan.

DiClemente, C. C., Prochaska, J. O., Fairhurst, S. K., & Velicer, W. F. (1991). The process of smoking cessation: An analysis of precontemplation, contemplation, and preparation stages of change. *Journal of Consulting and Clinical Psychology, 59,* 191–204.

Douglas, T. (1995). *Scapegoats: Transferring blame.* New York: Routledge.

Egeland, B. R., Carlson, E., & Sroufe, L. A. (1993). Resilience as process. *Development and Psychopathology, 5,* 517–528.

Elkin, I., Parloff, M. B., Hadley, S. W., & Autry, J. H. (1985). NIMH treatment of Depression Collaborative Research Program: Background and research plan. *Archives of General Psychiatry, 42,* 305–316.

Fanon, F. (1968). *The wretched of the earth.* New York: Grove Press.

Fedele, N. (1994). *Relationships in groups: Connection, resonance, and paradox.* Wellesley, MA: Stone Center Working Papers.

Fischer, J. (1973). Is casework effective? A review. *Social Work, 18,* 5–20.

Flanders, N. A. (1970). *Analyzing teaching behaviors.* Reading, MA: Addison-Wesley.

Fonagy, P., Steele, M., Steele, H., & Higgitt, A. (1994). The Emanuel Miller Memorial Lecture 1992: The theory and practice of resilience. *Journal of Child Psychology and Psychiatry and Allied Disciplines, 35,* 231–257.

Freeman, D. S. (1981). *Techniques of family therapy.* New York: Jason Aronson.

Freud, S., & Krug, S. (2002, September–December). Beyond the code of ethics, part 1: Complexities of ethical decision making in social work practice. *Families in Society: The Journal of Contemporary Human Services,* pp. 474–482.

Galloway, V. A., & Brodsky, S. L. (2003). Caring less, doing more: The role of therapeutic detachment with volatile and unmotivated clients. *American Journal of Psychotherapy, 57,* 32–38.

Galper, J. (1967). Introduction to radical theory and practice in social work education: Social policy. *Journal of Education in Social Work, 12,* 3–9.

Gambrill, E., & Pruger, R. (1997). *Controversial issues in social work ethics, values, and obligations.* Boston: Allyn and Bacon.

Garfield, G. P., & Irizary, C. R. (1971). Recording the 'record of service': Describing social work practice. In W. Schwartz & S. Zalba (Eds.), *The practice of group work* (pp. 241–265). New York: Columbia Press.

Garland, J. A., Jones, H. E., & Kolodny, R. L. (1965). A model for stages of development in social work groups. In S. Bernstein (Ed.), *Explorations in group work* (pp. 17–71). Boston: Boston University School of Social Work.

Garland, J. A., & Kolodny, R. L. (1965). Characteristics and resolution of scapegoating. In S. Bernstein (Ed.), *Explorations in group work.* Boston: Boston University School of Social Work. (Published later under the same title by Boston: Charles River Books, 1976; Hebron, CT: Practitioner's Press, 1984).

Garmezy, N. (1991). Resilience and vulnerability to adverse developmental outcomes associated with poverty. *American Behavioral Scientist, 34,* 416–430.

Garmezy, N. (1993). Children in poverty: Resilience despite risk. *Psychiatry, 56,* 127–136.

Garmezy, N., Masten, A. S., & Tellegen, A. (1984). The study of stress and competence in children: A building block for developmental psychopathology. *Child Development, 55,* 98–111.

Garvin, C. (1969). Complementarity of role expectations in groups: The member-novice contact. In *Social work practice 1969* (pp. 127–145). New York: Columbia University Press.

Gary, L. E., & Leashore, B. R. (1982). High-risk status of black men. *Social Work, 27,* 54–58.

Germain, C. B., & Gitterman, A. (1996). *The life model of social work practice: Advances in theory and practice* (2nd ed.). New York: Columbia University Press.

Gilgun, J. F. (1996). Human development and adversity in ecological perspective, part 1: A conceptual framework. *Families in Society, 77,* 395–402.

Gilligan, C., Lyons, N. P., & Hammer, T. J. (1990). *Making connections: The relational worlds of adolescent girls at Emma Willard School.* Cambridge, MA: Harvard University Press.

Gladis, M. M., Gosch, E. A., Dishuk, N. M., & Crits-Christoph, P. (1999). Quality of life: Expanding the scope of clinical significance. *Journal of Consulting and Clinical Psychology, 67*(3), 320–331.

Glaser, B., & Strauss, A. (1967). *Grounded theory.* Chicago: Aldine.

Gutheil, I. A. (1992). Considering the physical environment: An essential component of good practice. *Social Work, 37*(5), 391–396.

Hacker, A. (1992). *Two nations: Black and white, separate, hostile, unequal.* New York: Scribner.

Hakansson, J., & Montgomery, H. (2002). The role of action in empathy from the perspective of the empathizer and the target. *Current Research in Social Psychology, 8,* 50–62. Retrieved from http://www.uiowa.edu/

Hakansson, J., & Montgomery, H. (2003). Empathy as an interpersonal phenomenon. *Journal of Social and Personal Relationships, 20,* 267–284.

Hardy, K. V., & Laszloffy, T. A. (1992). Training racially sensitive family therapists: Context, content, and contact. *Families in Society, 73*(6), 364–370.

Hare, P. A. (1962). *Handbook of small group research.* New York: Free Press.

Hearn, G. (1962). *The general systems approach to understanding groups.* New York: Society of Public Health Educators.

Hegel, G. W. F. (1966). *The phenomenology of mind.* London: Allen & Unwin.

Herrenkohl, E. C., Herrenkohl, R. C., & Egolf, B. (1994). Resilient early school-age children from maltreating homes: Outcomes in late adolescence. *American Journal of Orthopsychiatry, 64,* 301–309.

Heyman, D. (1971). A function for the social worker in anti-poverty programs. In W. Schwartz & S. Zalba (Eds.), *The practice of group work* (pp. 167–180). New York: Columbia University Press.

Holmes, M., & Lundy, C. (1990). Group work for abusive men: A profeminist response. *Canada's Mental Health, 38,* 12–17.

Horne, A. M., & Passmore, J. L. (1991). *Family counseling and therapy* (2nd ed.). Itasca, IL: Peacock.

Jaffee v. Redmond, 116 S.Ct. 1923 (1996). [Lexis, U. U. 3879]

Jordan, J. (1991). Empathy, mutuality, and therapeutic change: Clinical implications of a relational model. In *Women's growth in connections: Writings from the stone center.* New York: Guilford Press.

Jordan, J. (1993). *Challenges to connection.* Work in progress, No. 60. Wellesley, MA, Stone Center Working Paper Series.

Keith, D. V., & Whitaker, C. A. (1982). Experiential/symbolic family therapy. In A. M. Horne & M. M. Ohlsen (Eds.), *Family counseling and therapy.* Itasca, IL: Peacock.

Kirk, S. A., Siporin, M., & Kutchins, L. (1989). The prognosis for social work diagnosis. *Social Casework, 70,* 295–304.

Kobasa, S. C., & Pucetti, M. C. (1983). Personality and social resources in stress resistance. *Journal of Personality and Social Psychology, 45,* 839–850.

Kubler-Ross, E. (1969). *On death and dying.* New York: Macmillan.

Kuhn, T. H. (1962). *The structure of scientific revolution.* Chicago: University of Chicago Press.

Lambert, M. J., Hansen, N. B., & Finch, A. E. (2001). Patient-focused research: Using patient outcome data to enhance treatment effects. *Journal of Consulting and Clinical Psychology, 69*(2), 159–172.

Lampropoulos, G. K., Goldfried, M. R., Castonguay, L. G., Lambert, M. J., Stiles, W. B., & Nestoros, J. N. (2002). What kind of research can we realistically expect from the practitioner? *Journal of Clinical Psychology, 58*(10), 1241–1264.

Lee, J. A. (1994). *The empowerment approach to social work practice.* New York: Columbia University Press.

Lewin, K. (1935). *Field theory in social science: Selected theoretical papers.* New York: McGraw-Hill.

Lewin, K. (1951). *A dynamic theory of personality: Selected theoretical papers.* New York: McGraw-Hill.

Li, X., Stanton, B., Pack, R., Harris, C., Cottrell, L., & Burns, J. (2002). Risk and protective factors associated with gang involvement among urban African American adolescents. *Youth and Society, 34,* 172–194.

Lidz, C. (1984). *Informed consent.* New York: Guilford Press.

Loewenberg, F., & Dolgoff, R. (1996). *Ethical decisions for social work practice* (5th ed.). Itasca, IL: Peacock.

Lu, Y. E., Organista, K. C., Manzo, S. J., Wong, L. & Phung, J. (2001). Exploring dimensions of culturally sensitive clinical styles with Latinos. *Journal of Ethnic and Cultural Diversity in Social Work, 10,* 45–66.

Lueger, R. J. (2002). Practice-informed research and research-informed psychotherapy. *Journal of Clinical Psychology, 58*(10), 1265–1276.

Lum, D. (1996). *Social work practice and people of color: A process-stage approach* (3rd ed.). Pacific Grove, CA: Brooks/Cole.

Mailick, M. D. (1991). Re-assessing assessment in clinical social work practice. *Smith College Studies in Social Work, 62*(1), 3–19.

Massachusetts NASW Chapter. (1996). [monthly newspaper]

Masten, A. S. (2001). Ordinary magic: Resilience processes in development. *American Psychologist, 56,* 227–238.

McGloin, J., & Widom, C. S. (2001). Resilience among abused and neglected children grown up. *Development and Psychopathology, 13,* 1021–1038.

Mendez-Negrete, J. (2000). "Dime con quien andas": Notions of Chicano and Mexican-American families. *Families in Society: The Journal of Contemporary Human Services, 81,* 42–48.

Miller, J. B. (1987). *Toward a new psychology of women* (2nd ed.). Boston: Beacon Press.

Miller, J. B. (1988). *Connections, disconnections, and violations.* Wellesley, MA: Stone Center Working Papers.

Miller, J. B., & Stiver, I. P. (1991). *A relational framing of therapy.* Wellesley, MA: Stone Center Working Papers.

Miller, J. B., & Stiver, I. P. (1993). A relational approach to understanding women's lives and problems. *Psychiatric Annals, 23,* 424–431.

Miller, W. R., & Rollnick, S. (1991). *Motivational interviewing: Preparing people to change addictive behavior.* New York: Guilford Press.

Mills, C. W. (1959). *The sociological imagination.* New York: Oxford University Press.

Mizrahi, T. (2001). The status of community organizing in 2001: Community practice context, complexities, contradictions, and contributions. *Research on Social Work Practice, 11,* 176–189.

Mulroy, E. (1997). Building a neighborhood network: Interorganizational collaboration to prevent child abuse and neglect. *Social Work, 42,* 255–264.

Mulroy, E. A., & Shay, S. (1997). Nonprofit organizations and innovation: A model of neighborhood-based collaboration to prevent child maltreatment. *Social Work, 42,* 515–524.

Murray, C. (2003). Risk factors, protective factors, vulnerability, and resilience: A framework for understanding and supporting the adult transitions of youth with high-incidence disabilities. *Remedial and Special Education, 24,* 16–26.

Nartz, M., & Schoesch, D. (2000). Use of the Internet for community practice: A Delphi study. *Journal of Community Practice, 8,* 37–59.

National Association of Social Workers. (1996). *National Association of Social Workers code of ethics.* Washington, DC: NASW.

National Association of Social Workers. (1997). *National Association of Social Workers code of ethics.* Washington, DC: NASW. Accessed February 9, 2005, at http://www.socialworkers.org/pubs/codenew/code.asp.

National Association of Social Workers. (1999). *National Association of Social Workers code of ethics.* Washington, DC: NASW.

Nugent, W. R. (1991). An experimental and qualitative analysis of cognitive-behavioral intervention for anger. *Social Work Research and Abstracts, 27*(3): 3–8.

O'Brien, P. (1995). From surviving to thriving: The complex experience of living in public housing. *Affilia, 10,* 155–178.

Oei, T. P. S., & Shuttlewood, G. J. (1996). Specific and nonspecific factors in psychotherapy: A case of cognitive therapy for depression. *Clinical Psychology Review, 16,* 83–103.

Perlman, H. H. (1957). *Social casework: a problem-solving process.* Chicago: University of Chicago Press.

Pilsecker, C. (1979). Terminal cancer. *Social Work in Health Care, 4,* 237–264.

Polowy, C. I. (1997). *NASW law notes for social workers* [pamphlet].

Prochaska, J. O., & DiClemente, C. C. (1982). Transtheoretical therapy: Toward a more integrative model of change. *Psychotherapy: Theory, Research and Practice, 19,* 276–288.

Proctor, E. K., & Davis, L. E. (1994). The challenge of racial difference: Skills for clinical practice. *Social Work, 39,* 314–323.

Radloff, L. S. (1977). The CES-D scale: A self-report depression scale for research in the general population. *Applied Psychological Measurement, 1*(3), 385–401.

Rak, C. F., & Patterson, L. E. (1996). Promoting resilience in at-risk children. *Journal of Counseling and Development, 74,* 368–373.

Reamer, F. G. (1990). *Ethical dilemmas in social services* (2nd ed.). New York: Columbia University Press.

Reamer, F. G. (1998). The evolution of social work ethics. *Social Work, 43,* 488.

Reamer, F. G. (2000). The social work ethics audit: A risk-management strategy. *Social Work, 45,* 355–366.

Reed-Victor, E., & Stronge, J. (2002). Homeless students and resilience: Staff perspectives on individual and environmental factors. *Journal of Children and Poverty, 8,* 159–183.

Reid, W. J., & Shyne, A. W. (1969). *Brief and extended casework.* New York: Columbia University Press.

Reitzes, D., & Reitzes, D. (1986). Alinsky in the 1980's: Two contemporary Chicago community organizations. *Sociological Quarterly, 28,* 265–283.

Richards, M., Browne, C., & Broderick, A. (1994). Strategies for teaching clinical social work practice with Asians and Pacific Islanders. *Gerontology and Geriatric Education, 14*(3), 49–63.

Richmond, M. (1918). *Social diagnosis.* New York: Russell Sage Foundation.

Richters, J. E., & Martinez, P. E. (1993). Violent communities, family choices, and children's chances: An algorithm for improving the odds. *Development and Psychopathology, 5,* 609–627.

Roback, H. B., Purdon, S. E., Ochoa, E., & Bloch, F. (1992). Confidentiality dilemmas in group psychotherapy: Management strategies and utility of guidelines. *Small Group Research, 23,* 169–184.

Rodgers, K. B., & Rose, H. A. (2002). Risk and resilience factors among adolescents who experience marital transitions. *Journal of Marriage and Family, 64,* 1024–1037.

Rogers, C. R. (1961). *On becoming a person.* Boston: Houghton Mifflin.

Rogers, C. R. (1969). *Freedom to learn.* Columbus, OH: Merrill.

Rosenberg, M. (1978). *Logic of survey analysis.* New York: Basic Books.

Rothman, J. (1979). Three models of community organization practice: Their mixing and phasing. In F. M. Cox, J. L. Erlich, J. Rothman, & J. E. Tropman (Eds.), *Strategies of community organization* (pp. 25–45). Itasca, IL: Peacock.

Sands, R., & Nuccio, K. (1992). Post-modern feminist theory and social work. *Social Work, 37,* 489–494.

Satir, V. (1967). *Conjoint family therapy.* Palo Alto, CA: Science and Behavior Books.

Saulnier, C. F. (1996). *Feminist theories and social work: Approaches and applications.* New York: Haworth Press.

Saulnier, C. F. (2000). Incorporating feminist theory into social work practice: Group work examples. *Social Work With Groups, 23,* 5–29.

Scannapieco, M., & Jackson, S. (1996). Kinship care: The African American response to family preservation. *Social Work, 41,* 190–196.

Schaefer, D. S., & Pozzaglia, D. (1986). Living with a nightmare: Hispanic parents of children with cancer. In A. Gitterman & L. Shulman (Eds.), *Mutual aid groups and the life cycle.* Itasca, IL: Peacock.

Schiller, L. Y. (1993). *Stages of group development in women's groups: A relational model.* Paper presented at the 15th Annual Symposium of the Association for the Advancement of Social Work With Groups, New York.

Schwartz, W. (1961). The social worker in the group. In *New perspectives on services to groups: Theory, organization, and practice* (pp. 7–34). New York: National Association of Social Workers.

Schwartz, W. (1969). Private troubles and public issues: One social work job or two? In *The social welfare forum* (pp. 22–43). New York: Columbia University Press.

Schwartz, W. (1971). On the use of groups in social work practice. In W. Schwartz & S. Zalba (Eds.), *The practice of group work* (pp. 3–24). New York: Columbia University Press.

Shelley, M., Thrane, L., Shulman, S., Lang, E., Beisser, S., Larson, T., et al. (2004). *Social Service Computer Review, 22,* 2–14.

Shulman, L. (1967). Scapegoats, group workers, and the pre-emptive intervention. *Social Work, 12,* 43.

Shulman, L. (1970). Client, staff, and the social agency. In *Social work practice* (pp. 21–40). New York: Columbia University Press.

Shulman, L. (1971). Programs in group work: Another look. In W. Schwartz & S. Zalba (Eds.), *The practice of group work* (pp. 221–240). New York: Columbia University Press.

Shulman, L. (1978). A study of practice skills. *Social Work, 23,* 281.

Shulman, L. (1979a). *The skills of helping.* Montreal: Instructional Communications Centre, McGill University.

Shulman, L. (1979b). *A study of the helping process.* Vancouver: University of British Columbia, School of Social Work.

Shulman, L. (1980). Social work practice with foster parents. *Canadian Journal of Social Work Education, 6,* 71.

Shulman, L. (1981). *Identifying, measuring, and teaching helping skills.* New York: Council on Social Work Education and the Canadian Association of Schools of Social Work.

Shulman, L. (1982). *The skills of helping individuals and groups.* Itasca, IL: Peacock.

Shulman, L. (1984). *The skills of supervision and staff management.* Itasca, IL: Peacock.

Shulman, L. (1991). *Interactional social work practice: Toward an empirical theory.* Itasca, IL: Peacock.

Shulman, L. (1993a). *Interactional supervision.* Silver Springs, MD: National Association of Social Workers.

Shulman, L. (1993b). *Teaching the helping skills: A field instructor's guide.* Alexandria, VA: Council on Social Work Education.

Shulman, L., & Buchan, W. (1982). *The impact of the family physician's communication, relationship, and technical skills on patient compliance, satisfaction, reassurance, comprehension, and improvement.* Vancouver: University of British Columbia.

Shulman, L., & Clay, C. (1994). Teaching about practice and diversity: Content and process in the classroom and the field. Alexandria, VA: Council on Social Work Education.

Simmons, L. (2000). High stakes casinos and controversies. *Journal of Community Practice, 7*, 47–69.

Smalley, R. E. (1967). *Theory for social work practice.* New York: Columbia University Press.

Smith, A., & Siegal, R. (1985). Feminist therapy: Redefining power for the powerless. In *Handbook of feminist therapy: Women's issues in psychotherapy.* New York: Springer.

Soifer, S. (1998). A rural tenant organizing model: The case of TUFF Vermont. *Journal of Community Practice, 5,* 1–14.

Specht, H., & Courtney, M. E. (1993). *Unfaithful angels.* New York: Free Press.

Srebnik, D. S., & Saltzberg, E. A. (1994). Feminist cognitive-behavioral therapy for negative body image. *Women and Therapy, 15,* 117–133.

Stanton, A. H., & Schwartz, M. F. (1954). *Mental hospital: A study of institutional participation in psychiatric illness and treatment.* New York: Basic Books.

Staples, L. (1984). *Roots to power: A manual for grassroots organizing.* New York: Praeger.

Staudinger, U. M., Marsiske, M., & Baltes, P. B. (1993). Resilience and levels of reserve capacity in later adulthood: Perspectives from life-span theory. *Development and Psychopathology, 5,* 541–566.

Stern, S., & Smith, C. A. (1995). Family processes and delinquency. *Social Service Review,* 703–731.

Stevens, J. W. (1994). Adolescent development and adolescent pregnancy among late age African-American female adolescents. *Children and Adolescent Social Work Journal, 26*(6), 433–453.

Strean, H. (1978). *Clinical social work theory and practice.* New York: Free Press.

Swank, E., Asada, H., & Lott, J. (2002). Student acceptance of a multicultural education: Exploring the role of a social work curriculum, demographics, and symbolic racism. *Journal of Ethnic and Cultural Diversity in Social Work, 10,* 85–103.

Taft, J. (1933). Living and feeling. *Child Study, 10,* 100–112.

Taft, J. (1942). The relational function to process in social case work. In V. P. Robinson (Ed.), *Training for skill in social casework.* Philadelphia: University of Pennsylvania Press.

Taft, J. (1949). Time as the medium of the helping process. *Jewish Social Service Quarterly, 26,* 230–243.

Tarasoff v. Regents of the University of California, 551 P.2d 334 (1976).

Thayer, L. (1982). A person-centered approach to family therapy. In A. M. Horne & M. M. Ohlsen (Eds.), *Family counseling and therapy* (pp. 175–213). Itasca, IL: Peacock.

Thornton, S., & Garrett, K. (1995). Ethnography as a bridge to multicultural practice. *Journal of Social Work Education, 32*(1), 67–74.

Thyer, B. A. (1987). Contingency analysis: Toward a unified theory for social work practice. *Social Work, 32,* 150–157.

Thyer, B. A., & Thyer, K. B. (1992) Single-system research designs in social work practice. *Research on Social Work Practice, 2*(1), 99–116.

Tracy, E. M., & Whittaker, J. K. (1990). The social network map: Assessing social support in clinical practice. *Families in Society, 72*(8), 461–470.

Trimble, D. (1994). Confronting responsibility: Men who batter their wives. In A. Gitterman & L. Shulman (Eds.), *Mutual aid groups, vulnerable populations, and the life cycle* (2nd ed., pp. 257–263). New York: Columbia University Press.

Trimble, D. (2005). Uncovering kindness and respect: Men who have practiced violence in intimate relationships. In A. Gitterman & L. Shulman (Eds.), *Mutual aid groups, vulnerable populations, and the life cycle* (3rd ed., pp. 352–372). New York: Columbia University Press.

Truax, C. B. (1966). Therapist empathy, warmth, genuineness, and patient personality change in group psychotherapy: A comparison between interaction unit measures, time sample measures, and patient perception measures. *Journal of Clinical Psychology, 71,* 1–9.

Unger, D. G., & Wandersman, A. (1985). The importance of neighbors: The social, cognitive, and affective components of neighboring. *American Journal of Community Psychology, 13,* 139–169.

Vastola, J., Nierenberg, A., & Graham, E. H. (1994). The lost and found group: Group work and bereaved children. In A. Gitterman & L. Shulman (Eds.), *Mutual aid groups, vulnerable populations, and the life cycle* (2nd ed., pp. 81–96). New York: Columbia University Press.

Watt, J. W., & Kallmann, G. L. (1998). Managing professional obligations under managed care: A social work perspective. *Family and Community Health, 21,* 40–48.

Weaver, H. N., & White, B. J. (1997). The Native American family circle: Roots of resiliency. *Journal of Social Work, 2*(1), 67–79.

Weaver, H. N., & Wodarsky, J. S. (1995). Cultural issues in crisis intervention: Guidelines for culturally competent practice. *Family Therapy, 22*(3), 213–223.

Weick, A., & Vandiver, S. (1982). *Women, power, and change.* Silver Springs, MD: National Association of Social Workers.

Werner, E. E. (1989). Children of the garden. *Scientific American, 260,* 106–111.

Westbury, E., & Tutty, L. M. (1999). The efficacy of group treatment for survivors of childhood abuse. *Child Abuse and Neglect, 23,* 31–44.

Williams, E. E., & Ellison, F. (1996). Culturally informed social work practice with American Indian clients: Guidelines for non-Indian social workers. *Social Work, 41*(2), 147–151.

Wilson, G., & Ryland, G. (1949). *Social group work practice: The creative use of the social process.* Boston: Houghton Mifflin.

Wood, G. G., & Roche, S. E. (2001). Representing selves, reconstructing lives: Feminist group work with women survivors of male violence. *Social Work With Groups, 23,* 5–23.

Zachary, E. (2000). Grassroots leadership training: A case study of an effort to integrate theory and method. *Journal of Community Practice, 7,* 71–93.

Index of Case Examples

Name Index

Subject Index

American Indians
    culture and community impact in
        family counseling, 234–41
    Mashantucket Pequot Indians, 545
    oppression and alienation of, 32–3
    stereotypes of, 578
    suicide of teenager, 204–7
    working with, 107–9, 131
Anger
    confronting, 92, 141–2, 308–26,
        349, 488, 588, 598
    in the ending phase, 183–6, 454–6,
        464–8, 603
    hope in, 556
    and loss, 365–6
    of workers toward abusers, 163, 301
    See also Endings and transitions
        phase
Antipoverty action group, 548–51
Anti-Semitism, and scapegoating,
    476–7, 479
Apartheid, and oppression, 30
Apology, client, 91
Appointments
    client problems with, 90–1
    family caller and setting, 216
    permanent, 92–3
ARC (AIDS-related complex),
    65–6, 118
Argue, learning how to, 324
Articulating feelings. See Feelings
Arts and crafts group(s), for children,
    480–91
Assertiveness, developing skills in, 271
Assessment process
    in beginning phase, 6–9, 101–3
    and informed consent, 594
    instruments, 102–3, 253, 597–600
    three major determinants of, 102
    See also Record of Service
Assistance, clarifying possible forms
    of, 84–5
Attachment theory, 36
Attention Deficit Disorder (ADD),
    and family practice, 259–64
Audit, social work ethics, 584–5
Authority, 603
    and adoption process, 166–7
    and contract context, 55–6
    and culture, 445–6, 502
    dealing with theme of, 77, 90, 96–7,
        119, 158–60, 335, 604
    of Housing Authority, 560–1
    immigrant reactions to, 119–20
    impact on first group session, 100,
        329–35
    master-slave paradigm of, 12, 29–30
    mistake of trying to demonstrate,
        399–400
    and preadoption groups, 166–7
    taboos about feelings toward, 155
    and "who owns the client," 291
    See also Control

Authority theme
    dealing with the, 77, 90, 96–7, 119,
        158–60, 335, 604
    direct responses to, 71–2
    and gender, 163–4
    in group development, 419–25
    tuning in to, 58–60, 116
    and worker gender, 161
Automatic thoughts, 49, 170
Autoopressor, 8, 24, 29–30, 551

Baby at the group, 447
"Band-aid" work, 45
Bank employees, support for after
    robbery, 203
Barriers
    to communication, 280
    cultural differences as, 103–5
    types of differences as, 110
Basic assumption groups, 438,
    440, 603
Battered women. See Women
Batterers. See Male batterers' groups
Beginning (contracting) phase, 26,
    83–101, 603
    and contracting over time, 88–90
    culturally diverse practice and,
        103–10
    dynamics of new relationships and,
        78–83, 111
    first session, 599–600
    with resistant clients, 597
    See also Contracting process
Behavior
    activity groups for managing, 479
    of culturally diverse clients, 103–10
    See also specific groups; specific issues
Behavioral approach. See Cognitive-
    behavioral therapy
Behavior problems. See Acting out
    behavior; Children; Deviant
    group member
Best friend, death of a, 444
Big Brothers service, 241–2
Bilingual group members, 491–2
Board of Registration, 590
Bonds, affective neighborhood, 548
Boston Model, 47, 430
Boston University group types
    framework, 290–1
Boundary between individual
    problems and group work, 553
Boys
    activity group, 327–8
    in residential settings, 148,
        199–200, 369–70, 532–6
    sixth-grade, 327–9, 371
    underachieving, 371
    See also Adolescents; Children
Breast cancer support group, 430–5
Bribes from clients, 119–20
Buffering hypothesis, 35
Burnout, worker, 122, 603

Canada, 14, 104, 203, 250
Canadian Association of Social
    Workers (CASW), 580–1
Canadian Indians, 33, 104
    working with, 109, 500–2
Cancer. See Breast cancer support
    group; Living-with-cancer group
Capitulation stage, 33, 34
Caregivers
    adult children as, 303, 582–3
    foster parents and alternative, 248
    sibling, 373–4
    stressed, 62, 303
Caring element in working
    relationships, 62, 73, 139, 603
    and misconceptions, 15
    and reaching inside of silences, 131
    skills affecting, 151
Case conferences, 579–80
Case law, 591–2, 594–5
Case work, 18, 19
Caseworkers, 19
Casework while in group, 361, 603
Casino development opposition,
    544–5
Causal path analysis, 73, 73n1, 603
Center for Epidemiological Study
    Depression (CES-D) Scale, 600
Cerebral palsy, parents of children
    with, 335, 347
Ceremony and ritual, 107
Chair, the crying, 424
Challenge model, and risk factors, 35
Challenging obstacles to work, 155
Change
    assumption of strength for, 16–7,
        43–4
    between client sessions, 44
    in the control of the client, 332
    cycle of, 330–1
    demographic, 104
    divorce means, 485
    model of stages of, 330–1
    mutual support for, 275
    openness to, 159–60
    and plasticity, 40
    purposive community, 543
    resistance to, 330, 332–3, 520
    social, 18, 45
    systemic, 519–21
Chat messages, 547
Checking for underlying ambivalence,
    152–3, 603
Check-in rituals, 366–7, 603
Chicanos (Mexican Americans), 105
Child abuse, family, 373–4,
    537–8, 587–8
Child care for clients' children,
    448, 523
Child protective services worker,
    591–2
Children
    adopted, 166–7

Communication
  affective component of, 133
  among social workers, 291, 357–8
  with a quiet group member, 413–4
  behavior as, 366
  by clients, 509–13
  deviant behavior as, 394–401, 430
  doorknob, 26, 78, 116, 127, 175–6, 342, 604
  with dying client, 207–8
  in groups, 280, 281, 427–8
  impact of diversity on, 61–2
  indirect, 56–7, 319
  indirect cues as, 70–5
  with institutions and agencies, 499
  interdepartmental, 532–6
  metaphor as indirect, 57, 124
  between mother and adult daughter, 275–6
  nonverbal, 57
  obstacles to direct, 55–6, 280, 281
  patterned response, 136
  privileged, 590–3
  problems of interpersonal, 15–6, 377–80
  reaching for individual group member, 362–7
Community
  milieu as, 569–75
  and Native American family culture, 234–41
  neighborhood as, 36, 547–8
  social action in, 502–8, 525–8, 551–4, 554–62, 563–4
Community-based citizens' advisory board, 563–4
Community-based social work interventions, 544–5
Community organization
  around a specific issue, 544–5
  philosophy and models of, 543–7
Community practice
  rurally based, 545–6
  in the social work context, 541–2
  use of the Internet in, 546–7
Compensatory model, and risk factors, 35
Conditional model, and risk factors, 35
Conferences, case, 579–80
Confidentiality, 62, 225, 603
  definition of, 590
  dilemmas, hypothetical, 586–7
  and disclosure of client identity, 593
  and group work, 287–9, 298–9, 326, 373, 586–7
  guidelines, 355, 586
  legal aspects of, 590–1
  rules, 287–9, 298–9, 325, 326, 355, 373, 586–7
  See also Legislation
Confrontation
  of a quiet group member, 413
  facilitative, 605

and mutual aid, 271
  self, 94
  social pressure and advocacy and, 513–9
Confrontation-denial trap, 332–3
Connecticut, 545
Connection through disconnection paradox, 428–9
"Consciousness-raising" groups, women's, 273
Consent, informed, 81, 582, 606
Containment skill, 60, 126–7
Contemplation stage (risk-reward analysis), 331
Content
  of agency records and referrals, 577–9
  analysis, 51
  deepening a discussion of, 398–9
  defined, 160, 604
  expansions of, 90
  of group meeting, 290, 334
  process and, 160–4, 328, 368–9, 519
  synthesizing ending process and, 194–5
  topics for discussion, 334
Context of practice
  client-system interaction, 8, 578–9
  community social work, 541–2
  in contracting phase, 83–4
  See also Environment(s) of groups
Contracting, initial. See Beginning (contracting) phase
Contracting again. See Recontracting in groups
Contracting concept, 4, 60, 83
  use of term, 85
Contracting process, 76, 604
  ambiguity in, 327–8
  in children's groups, 327–8
  in couples group, 310
  documents, 85
  and ending process, 451
  examples of, 84–5
  in first sessions, 83–101, 334, 503, 599–600
  in group of 12-year-old boys, 327–8
  over time, 88–90, 296–8
  research findings on, 87–8
  with resistant clients, 90–101
  sessional, 123–6
  in single-session group, 475–6
  skills, 84
  variations in the, 86–7
  See also Client(s); Sessional contracting
Control
  by the client, 332
  in group development, 268, 333, 421
  over change, 332
  of worker-client sessions, 124–5

of worker emotions and feelings, 26, 67, 130
  See also Authority; Feelings
Coordination of services helping the client, 537–8
Coping questions, 44
Core values, social work profession, 585
Correlation, 125, 604
Cost containment, 284, 292, 604
Cottage life staff, institutional, 532–6
Council on Social Work Education, 585
Counseling. See Family support work (family counseling); Schools
Counterdependent member, 421, 604
Countertransference, 27, 122, 604
  authority theme and, 425
  in family counseling, 220
Couples' counseling, 22, 291–2
Couples' group
  communication about, 291–2
  composition and structure of, 293, 294, 296, 339
  continuing work in, 318–23, 363–5
  ending and transition phase of, 323–6
  expression of anger in, 440–1
  initial work in, 162–3, 308–18, 339, 343
  multigenerational communication in, 271, 293, 295
  sexual taboos in, 123, 314, 436, 441–3
Courts, and legislation impact on practice, 590–6
  See also Supreme Court; specific cases
Criminal activities, confidentiality or disclosure of, 586–7, 594–6
Criminal justice system setting of group work, 332–5, 444
Crisis theory, 513
Critical theory, 45
Cross-cultural practice, 61–2, 234–41, 296
  See also Cultural diversity; Race and racism
Crying
  by the client(s), 64, 137, 185, 242, 336, 424, 434, 462, 467–8, 503, 598
  in the first group session, 224, 335–7
  by the worker(s), 143, 185, 196, 208
  See also Emotions; Feelings
Cues, indirect, 57, 124
  responding directly to, 70–5
Culturegrams, 62, 102–3
Cultural diversity
  African Americans and, 74, 104
  awareness of, 103, 104–5, 235, 444–6

individual problem-solving and, 275–6
individual work versus work in, 291–2
interpreters in, 491–2
introductions in, 309
involuntary, 329–35
key variations in types of, 470–93
as mutual aid systems, 267, 299–300, 310, 331–2, 350, 371–81, 468
mutual demand and, 275
mutual support and, 17
open-ended, 289, 471–4
as organism, 416–8, 474
pairing, 440, 608
preparation for, 289
properties of, 417–8
purpose of, 287–9, 295, 297, 300–1, 310
quiet members in, 412–5
reaching for individual communication in, 291
reaching for work when obstacles threaten, 368–71
recontracting in, 306, 343–57, 608
referrals to, 300–1
rehearsal and, 271, 276–8
relational theory in, 428–30
as second client, 280–1, 310–1, 346, 383, 387, 417–618, 467–8, 563–4
selling the initiation of, 284–5, 303
sessional contracting in, 361–71
sessional endings and transitions in, 318–20, 452–4
setting of service, 289, 298
sharing data in, 270–1
single-session, 474–7
size of, 293–4
with specific client problems, 335–7
stereotypes of, 301
"strength-in-numbers" phenomenon in, 278–9, 288–9, 609
structure and timing of, 293–4, 296–8, 549–51
system problems created by, 287
task-focused, 548, 551–4
time factors in, 372–7
tipping point in, 295, 609
two-client theory and, 218–20, 353–7
type and structure of, 289–91
worker joining ongoing, 350–7
worker leaving ongoing, 452–4, 464–8
See also Group development phase
Group structural variables, research on, 296
Group work
preparing for, 283

resonance in, 428, 429
social work as, 18–9, 265
and staff dynamics, 283–4
Growth and education groups, 290
Guidance counselors. *See* Schools
Guilt feelings
of adult children, 277
of departing worker, 184–5
of parents, 96, 134, 138, 142, 273
of single parents, 233–4
the worker's, 64–5, 120, 142, 184

Haitians, 103
Handles for work, 85, 88, 606
Harvard Project on Women's Psychology and Girls' Development, 7
Health care system
cost-containment efforts, 169, 588
lack of universal, 12–3
Health insurance, 583, 590, 592
Health Insurance Patient Protection Act (HIPPA), 592
"Heart-soaring" sensation, worker's, 126
Helping process
based on medical paradigm, 73, 101–3
and group member problem-solving, 275–6
See also Mutual aid process
Helping the client see life in new ways, 116, 170–1, 606
Hidden agendas, 82
High-risk children, 36–7
See also Resilience theory; Risk factors
Hinting communication, 56
Hispanics. *See* Ethnicity
History. *See* Social work profession
HIV. *See* AIDS clients' groups
Holding to focus, 152, 606
Holidays, feelings about, 486–7
Holistic (empirically based) theory, 4, 606
Holocaust, group remembrance of, 476–7
Homes, group, 290
for the aged, 476–7, 525
leaving or loss of, 148, 194
Homework, resistance to, 371
Hong Kong, ethnicity and group culture of, 444–6
Hospice, 606
Hospitalization, involuntary, 595
Hospitals
complaining about staff of, 287–8
deviant units in, 497–8
emergency service workers and psychiatric department of, 522–5
environment of veterans in, 569–75

group formation in, 284–9
open-ended group on gynecological ward, 471–3
patient ward group in, 87, 337–8
professional impact on emergency room service in, 522–3, 536
psychiatric department in, 536
Hospital systems
helping individuals deal with, 169, 337–8, 448
mediation within, 508–13
Host settings. *See* Setting of service
Housing Authority, 560–1
Housing system
client advocacy in, 514–9
eviction issues, 568
public, 278, 518–9
and single parents, 513–9
welfare mothers and agency, 554–62
Hull House, 18
Human communications, 55, 606
Human contact, 478, 606
Humor, 108
gatekeeper use of, 402–3
nonhumiliating, 416
Hyperactive children, groups for parents of, 370–1, 380–1, 421–5, 437–40

Identification
of areas for future work, 166, 192–3
of major learning, 190–2
projective, 364
Identified patient (IP)
in families, 215, 218, 246, 606
in groups, 275
spouse as, 162, 312, 424
Identifiers of the client, confidential, 592–3
Identifying
the next steps, 173–4, 240–1, 606
process and content connections, 116, 160–4, 606
the stage of the ending process, 184, 284, 451, 606
Identity
cultural, 33–4
family, 105
mental patient, 49
parenthood and adult social, 106
positive racial, 37
and pregnancy, 106
school or home, 74
Illness
as family secret, 246–7
hospitalization and serious, 337–8
Illusion of agreement, 302
Illusion of work, 64, 94, 152, 178, 260, 330, 333, 426, 606
challenging, 153–4, 247
Immigrants
Asian men in Hong Kong groups, 444–6

Immigrants (*continued*)
European, 119–20, 218–9,
221–4, 229
Latino, 61–2, 103
Vietnamese women's group, 491–2
working with culturally
diverse, 103–4
See also Ethnicity
Immigration. *See* Cultural diversity;
specific groups
Immunity, absoluteness of
privileged, 592
Impotency treatments, 157
Independence
client's new, 188–9
father-son struggle and, 120, 121
of pregnant teens, 372–7
skills of, 116
Independent living skills, 344, 583
Indians. *See* American Indians;
Canadian Indians
Indirect communication, 104
in beginning phase, 56–7
disguising a call for help, 365
first offerings, 117, 123, 124, 605
metaphors used as, 57, 124
responding directly to, 70–5
Indirect cues, 70–5
Individual-group interaction,
367–8, 383
Individual problem-solving, 606
and group work, 275–6
Individual(s)
inner self of, 8, 23
quasi-stationary social equilibrium
of, 403, 513, 608
See also Client(s); Group member(s)
Individual-system interaction
breakdowns in, 498–9
first reactions to, 500–2
mediating the, 499–513
working with a school system,
502–8
Inequality in U.S. society, 543
Informational group session, 475–6
Informed consent, 81, 582,
593–4, 606
Inner-city elementary school group,
impact of family violence and,
443–4
Instructor's Guide to the Skills of Helping
(Shulman), 226
Insurance payments, third-party, 48,
169, 589
Intake worker, 578, 606
Integrated approach, *See also*
Substance abuse
Integration and differentiation
in a family, 217
and culture and community, 234–5
Intellectualizing
cognitive distortions and, 49, 170
not giving advice and, 349

by the teacher, 163
or tuning in, 65–6
by the worker, 96–7, 488
Intellectual tuning in, 134–5
Interaction, dynamic, 122
Interactional model, 606
assumptions in, 9–22
and client-system interaction, 4–9,
579–80
and group therapy, 265
practice theory, 3–4
and solution-focused practice,
42–4, 214
symbiotic assumption, 10–3, 52
and worker's realities of time and
stress, 121–2
See also Obstacles to work
Interactional Social Work Practice
Theory research. *See* Research
methodology
Interactional Supervision
(Shulman), 529
Interdepartmental communications in
a large system, 532–6
Interdisciplinary work, and "who
owns the client," 291, 508–13,
531–2, 610
Interethnic practice, 61–2, 102–5
Intergenerational contribution
within family, 36
work and, 217
Internal leader, 307, 315, 318,
319–20, 607
as ally or enemy, 399–401
citizens' action group, 548–9
Vietnamese women's group,
491–2
women's groups, 345
Internet
sharing data from, 270, 593
six primary tools of, 546–7
Interpreter in group, 491–2
Interrupting a group member, 420
Interstaff relationships, professional
impact on, 528–38
Intervention, strategies for, 232,
263–4, 357, 373–7, 392–3,
411–2, 440
See also Record of Service
Interview(s)
in beginning phase, 4–9, 599–600
client feelings about, 80
content analysis of, 51
fact-gathering, 78–80
first, 216–7, 599–600
in first family sessions, 221–5
and looking for trouble, 127
motivational, 330
phases of first, 216–7
potential group member initial,
301–4
question-and-answer format, 5–6
and service consensus, 284–9, 591

single-system research design,
599–600
SSD first, 599–600
in work phase, 114
See also Questioning
Intimacy stage
of group work, 369–70, 425–35
of Hong Kong group, 444–6
and the relational model, 428–30
Intimacy theme, 314, 369, 403, 607
Intraethnic practice, 61–2
Intropressor, self as, 8, 23
Involuntary groups, 329–35
client stages of change in, 331–2

Jaffee v. Redmond, 591–2
Jargon
professional, 82–3, 531
street, 199
See also Language
Jog Your Memory group, 303–4
Jokes about psychiatrists, 574

Key worker, 607
Kinship care, 41–2

"Labeling" trap, 332
Labor, division of, 548–50, 604
Language
appropriate for children, 87, 328
and culture, 199, 501, 515
and group membership, 296
informed consent, 593–4
professional jargon, 82–3, 531
silence for translating, 131, 501
vulgar, 328, 414
See also Ethnicity; Immigrants
Latinos. *See* Ethnic groups
Leadership of group
external and internal, 307
natural, 552
See also Coleadership in groups;
Group leaders
Leadership training, community, 544
Learning
about taboos from parents, 442
about taboos from peers, 111
identification of major, 190–2, 193
from mistakes, 27–8, 63, 97, 334
transfer of, 436
See also Training
Legal responsibilities, 590–6
and ethical conflicts, 587–9
federal versus state, 592
See also Mandated reporter
Legislation
and duty to warn, 594–6, 605
impact on practice, 590–6
and informed consent, 81, 582,
593–4, 606
Lesbians
daughter of, 184–5
survivors group including, 458–64

Monopolizer, 395, 476
  defined, 607
  parent of child with traumatic
    brain injury, 415–6
Morality and diversity, 582
Morality period of social work, 581
Mothers
  abused, 443–4
  and adult daughter issues, 275–6,
    341–2
  and agency housing, 554–62
  boyfriends of, 599
  family violence against, 443–4
  group of welfare, 554–62
  of hyperactive children, 370–1,
    380–1, 437–40
  overprotective, 172
  teenage, 373–7
  of underachieving boys, 371
  working, 270
  See also Single-parent family;
    Women
Motivational interviewing, 330
Mourning period
  endings and transitions phase,
    186–8, 607
  suicide, 205–7
  See also Death and dying
Moving from the general to the
    specific, 127–8, 237, 370–1,
    424–5, 607
Multigenerational issues, 13
  in couples' group, 271, 293, 295
  in family counseling, 217
Multiple clients. *See* Two-clients
    construct
Multiple sclerosis (MS)
  men's group, 452–4
  women's group, 335–7
Mutual aid
  in Hong Kong group, 444–6
  obstacles to, 279–80
  and problem-solving in groups,
    275–6, 331–2, 352–6, 377–80
  See also Group(s)
Mutual aid process
  dynamics of, 269–79, 468
  three major obstacles to,
    279–80, 281
  and ways of helping, 281
  in work phase sessions of groups,
    344–50, 371–2, 377–80
Mutual demand, 275, 607
Mutual support, 17, 274–5, 607

Narcotics Anonymous (NA), 275
National Association of Social
    Workers (NASW), 19, 583–4, 588,
    589, 590
  Code of Ethics, 81, 169, 580, 581,
    593–4
  Massachusetts chapter, 595
Nations, Native American, 109

Native Americans. *See* American
    Indians; Ethnicity
Native Canadians. *See* Canadian
    Indians
Near problems, 55, 82, 85, 310,
    318, 607
Negative behavior, and acting out in
    groups, 268
Negotiation. *See* Contracting process
Neighboring and neighbors
  as community, 547–69
  personal/emotional support
    from, 39
Networks
  intrafamilial and extrafamilial, 217
  map of informal social, 102, 547
  personal and neighborhood social,
    543, 547–8
"New at the job" question, 98
New relationships. *See* Beginning
    (contracting) phase
Newspaper
  story about client's problem, 517–8
  veterans group's, 574–5
"Noah's ark syndrome," 233
Nonverbal forms of communication,
    57, 607
Normal, being and feeling,
    509–13, 600
Normative crises, and family support
    work, 276
Norms of behavior, 607
  cultural differences in, 131
  group, 281, 417
  system, 520
  and taboos, 271–2, 417, 436
  See also Deviant group member
Not-in-my-backyard (NIMBY)
    scenario, 544–5
Number of sessions, 601
Numbers and dates, client
    identification, 593

Obstacles to work
  detecting and challenging, 155
  and group dynamics, 279–80, 281,
    368–71, 426
  pointing out, 154–60
  sessional, 115, 175–6
  and the worker-client relationship,
    14–5, 93, 110, 115
"Only game in town" problem, 546
Open-ended group, 289–91, 293, 334,
    523, 607
  hospital group on gynecological
    ward, 471–3
  new member in AIDS group, 473–4
  short-term, 339–43
Opening statements, 84–5, 86–7, 95,
    100, 332, 607
  and first meeting objectives, 307–8,
    335, 339, 343, 501
  tenants meeting, 552

Opinion versus fact, 167–8
Oppression
  defenses against, 7–8, 33–4
  gender, 163, 273, 344–50
  impact of, 200, 235, 501
  individual revolutions against, 63–4
  and inequality in U.S. society, 543
  institutional, 525
  and master-slave paradigm, 12,
    29–30
  and mental illness, 569
  roles of inner and outer self and,
    8, 23
  scapegoating and, 386
  six indicators of, 30–2
  triple, 8
  and women in shelter, 344–50
Oppression psychology, 8, 11–2,
    28–34, 607
Oppression theory, 551–2
Organismic model, 417–8, 474, 607
Organizing, community and group,
    541–2, 548–51
Outcome evaluation, 596–7
  Single-System Research Design for,
    599–600
  studies, 51
  See also Record of Service
Outpatient pain management clinic,
    430–5
Outpatient psychiatric group, 367–8
Outreach, for group membership,
    299–304, 475–6
Outreach process, 607
Outreach program, 582–3, 608
Overpersonal group members, 425
Overpoliteness, group member, 426

Pain
  of ending a relationship, 179, 180
  primitive response to, 381
  reaching for underlying, 64, 598
  social support when feeling, 257
  See also Feelings
Pairing group, 381, 440, 608
Paradoxes in group therapy, 428–9
Parallel process, 128, 135, 608
Paranoia, adaptive, 30
Paraplegics. *See* Rehabilitation
    institute
Parents
  angry, 120, 218–9, 221–4, 588
  of children with cerebral palsy,
    335, 347
  foster and biological, 251–3
  prospective, 98–9
  self-esteem of, 37
  sex talks with, 442
  teenage, 257–8
  of underachieving boys, 371
  visiting issues, 251–3
  See also Foster parents; Significant
    other(s); Single-parent family

Psychiatrist(s)
    interdisciplinary collaboration
        with, 531–2
    social worker and, 463, 508–13,
        514–5
Psychology, 600
Psychology of oppression. *See*
    Oppression psychology
Psychopathology
    alienation and, 32–3
    and social work, 41
Psychosocial history, 80, 608
Psychotherapy, 586, 591, 592,
    600, 601
    social work as, 48
Public housing, 278, 518–9,
    554–62, 568
    tenants' group in, 551–4
Public issues, professional impact and,
    518–9
Publicity for a problem, getting, 516–8
Puppets, children's use of, 483–4
Purpose. *See* Clarification
Putting the client's feelings into
    words, 58, 70–1, 73, 95–6, 115,
    138, 608
Putting words into the client's
    mouth, 132

Qualitative research methods, 51,
    131, 601
"Quality of life" outcome
    measure, 601
Quantitative research methods, 51,
    131, 601
Quasi-equilibrium, in residential
    system, 532–3
Quasi-stationary social equilibrium,
    513, 608
    of individual personality, 403
Question-and-answer format, 5–6
Questioning, 608
    of clients during interviewing,
        78–80, 599–600
    focusing on the client's strengths,
        43–4
    "New at the job?," 98
    single-system research design,
        599–600
    of the worker by the client,
        98–9, 306
Quiet group member, 302, 412–5, 608

Race and racism
    children's groups and, 454–5
    cross-racial practice and, 61–2, 74,
        107–10, 199–200, 205, 234–41,
        296, 500–2
    group membership and, 295–6
    and having to act white or black, 74
    and informality, 107
    institutionalized, 30, 501, 559
    mixed parentage and, 492

and the "only one" problem, 293
and oppression, 12, 28–9, 32–3,
    107–8, 458, 559
between school and parent, 508
"strength-in-numbers"
    phenomenon, 278, 288–9, 609
tipping point problem, 295
Tuskegee experiment and, 13
and white flight, 295, 610
See also Cultural diversity; People of
    color
Radical feminism, 45–8
Radicalization stage, 33, 34
Radical social work practice, 45
Rapport, 62, 608
Reaching
    for a negative attitude, 302
    for client feedback, 77, 85, 125, 608
    for feelings, 118, 136, 608
    for group response to an individual,
        367–8
    for individual communication in a
        group, 362–7
    for intermember negatives, 427–8
    for signs of life and strength,
        8, 17
    for the specifics, 127–8, 424–5
    for underlying message of deviant
        behavior, 396
    for underlying message of indirect
        communication, 57
    for underlying motivation for
        change, 74
    for underlying pain, 64
    for work when obstacles threaten,
        368–71
Reaching for client feedback, and
    handles for work, 85, 88, 606
Reaching inside of silences, 72, 73, 97,
    130–2, 552–3, 558, 608
    frequency of use of, 131–2
Reality
    cognitive, 529–30
    helping client see, 168–9
    of parenting, 347–8, 372–7, 398–9
Reassurance, efforts at, 137
Recapitulation and restitution
    groups, 290
Recommendations, institution
    change, 535
Recontracting in groups, 306,
    343–57, 608
    when worker joins ongoing group,
        350–7
    with worker's own group, 344–50
    See also Contracting process
Record of Service
    about the, 226, 608
    in adolescent group scapegoating,
        387–93
    adolescent peer leaders, 564–9
    in adult survivors of childhood
        sexual abuse group, 458–64

in breast cancer support group,
    430–5
in cancer patients and family
    members group, 406–12
childhood ADD and school, 259–64
in children's group with separated
    parents, 480–91
in family counseling, 226–32,
    259–64
in group counseling, 387–93
in group of parents with
    hyperactive children, 437–40
and milieu as veterans' community,
    569–75
with Native American family,
    235–41
pregnant teenagers group, 373–7
structure and process evaluation,
    597–9
task group for adolescent peer
    leaders, 564–9
of worker joining an ongoing
    group, 351–7
working with hospital psychiatrist,
    508–13
Record of Service examples, Strategies
    for Intervention, 232, 263–4,
    357, 373–7, 392–3, 411–2, 440
Record of Service recommendations,
    Specific Next Steps, 240–1,
    263–4, 377, 435, 490–1, 507,
    568–9, 573–4, 598–9
Records
    agency, 578–80
    patient release form, 592
    See also Confidentiality
Recovery
    dual-diagnosis group for persons
        with AIDS, 297–8
    group work with persons in, 270–1
Recreation, group. *See* Activity
    group(s)
Referral process, 283
    reports, 578–80
    workshop, 300–1
Reflection practice, 59
Reframing the problem, 116,
    170–1, 608
    in a family, 215–6, 217, 219, 224–5
    from personal to social
        perspective, 241
Regression analysis, 73, 608
Regulation, of social workers, 590–602
Rehabilitation institute
    paraplegic client in, 142–3
    professional impact in, 523–5
Rehearsal, 608
    in group work, 271, 276–8, 478
    of life tasks, 83
Reimbursement. *See* Funding
Rejection, fear of, 273, 302, 598
Relational model, in group work
    practice, 7–8, 428–30

categories of practice, 19–20
in community, 541–2
as community organization work, 18–9
function of the profession, 20–2
as group work, 18–9
history of, 17–22, 52, 499, 581–2
mediating individual-system interactions, 350–7, 499
method and basic tasks of, 121
the phases of, 25–6
practice observation, 97
professionalizing of, 18–9
psychotherapy and, 48, 600, 601
radical practice of, 603
risk categories, 584–5
solution-focused practice of, 42–4, 214
triangular model of, 21
the trinity of, 19
values and ethics, 580–9
See also Social change; *specific phases of social work*
Social worker(s)
beginning practice of, 269
beliefs of, 168
burnout, 122, 603
as caring and giving people, 424–5
clothing of, 110
cooperation with psychiatrists, 463, 508–13, 514–5
endings in ongoing groups, 452–4, 464–8
ethics and values of, 580–9
as external leader, 307
and feminist practice, 45–8, 213–4, 603
first reactions to a system by, 500–2
graduate students as, 532–6
as group coleaders, 357–9
group relationship to, 267
impact of, 64, 181
impact of vacation absence of, 454–5
intake function, 578, 606
integration of personal and professional selves of, 26–8
job termination and ending session, 183, 184–5, 201–3, 241–2, 464–8
joining ongoing groups, 350–7
licensing requirements for, 590
life experience of, 122, 499
limitations of, 423–4
looking for trouble when everything is going their way, 127, 286, 607
as mandated reporters, 62, 225, 329, 607
mediation of individual-system engagement by, 350–7, 499–513
morale of, 135, 529–31

new and previous, 71, 88, 97–8, 188–9, 224, 228–9, 231–2, 466–7, 578–90
opinions held by, 167–8, 529–31
as organizers, 548
as outsider to a group, 421–2
referrals strategizing with other, 300–1
reflective response by, 59–60
regulation of, 596–602
relationship with interpreter in group, 491–2
role in group, 267
skill profile of, 139
stereotypes of, 285
supervision of, 65, 122, 135, 528–9
support or motivation needs of, 538
as therapists, 48
third-force roles of, 554–62
time and stress, 121–2
the title of, 590
too many, 538–9
See also Professional impact
Social worker skills. *See* Skills
Social work for two clients. *See* Two-clients construct
Social working (as a verb), 505
Social work organizations, 19
Social work practice theory, 3–4, 51–2
and assessment models, 101–3
risk categories, 584–5
scientist-practitioner models of, 600–2
Social work profession
benefits of the, 122
core values, 585
the function of, 20–2, 499
history of, 17–22, 52, 499, 581–2
licensing and the, 590–1
managed care issues affecting, 169, 531, 588–9
need for, 16
roots of the, 18–20
See also Professionalism
Societal taboos. *See* Taboos
Socioeconomic factors, 14, 17, 273, 345–6
See also Poverty
Spontaneous informal group, 476–7
Spouse, dealing with former, 234
SSRD. *See* Single-System Research Design
Staff dynamics, 283
between agencies, 536–8
between departments, 534–6
and traumatic events, 203–7
Staff meetings
between group coleaders, 358
hospital, 287–9
interdepartmental, 532–6
and staff member territories, 533–6
Staff system
consensus on new service by, 284–9

diversity, 579
focusing on needs of, 206–7
impact of suicide on, 204–7
professional impact on interstaff relationships and, 528–38
resistance to group work, 284–7
work with the, 283–93
Stages
after parents and children separate, 339–40
identifying ending process, 184, 284, 451, 606
Stages of change model, 330–2
States, U.S.
confidentiality regulations in, 590–2
licensing in, 590
Statistical analysis, 51, 73
Stepparents
adolescents and, 226–32
couples group, 318–20
family conflict and, 226–32, 597–9
Native American family, 234–41
See also Family; *specific situations*
Stereotypes
of clients, 69, 80, 224, 578–9
of colleagues, 285, 288, 533–4, 537
of general population groups, 104, 301, 559
of oneself, 171
sex-role, 8
of social workers, 285
See also Race and racism
Stone Center, self-in-relation theory, 7, 47, 428–30
Strategies for Intervention. *See* Record of Service
Street self, adolescent, 568
Strength for change, assumption of, 16–7, 43–4
"Strength-in-numbers" phenomenon, 278, 288–9, 609
Strengths perspective, 43–4
Stress
and caseload, 121–2
in large organizations, 497–8, 536–7
Stressors
case-related, 412
environmental, 565–6
life, 36
Structure and maintenance, 293–9, 549–50, 609
citizens' antipoverty action group, 548–51
Structure for work, 609
developing a, 446–8
first meetings, 307–8, 549–50, 552–3, 599–600
for group of young recovering addicts, 446–8
open-ended group, 472
over time, 88–90, 296–8, 372–7

Timing
of agency change, 520
"fast food" social work, 254
of groups, 88–90, 293–4, 296–8,
474–7
Tipping point, in group, 295, 609
"Too many cooks" problem, 509,
537–8
Too many groups to attend, 571
Training, 163–4
for culturally sensitive practice,
77, 111
other peer leaders, 568
technique-centered, 136
See also Workshop(s)
Training groups (T-groups), 419, 425,
426, 530
Transactions, definition of, 478
Transference, and
countertransference, 27, 122,
220, 425, 604
Transgender clients, 274–5
Transition skills, 171–6, 189–98
Traps, confrontation of client, 332
Traumatic brain injury, parents of
children with, 415–6
Traumatic events
impact on social workers, 203–4
informal group dealing with, 476–7
Triangular model of social work, 21
Triangulation, 610
in a family, 216, 217
Trust, 62, 87, 427–8, 438–9,
468, 610
skills for developing, 151
Tuning in, 610
affective versus intellectual, 65–6,
133–6
to authority theme, 58–60
to client's sense of urgency, 81,
117–9, 123, 165–7, 398
to colleagues, 354
genuine, 59
to indirect communication, 57
levels of, 67–70
to meaning of client's struggle,
120–1, 509–13
objection to, 69
sessional skills in work phase, 114
by staff group about referrals,
300–1
synthesizing ending process and
content and, 194–5
to the worker's own feelings, 67,
119–20
to worker's own life
experiences, 122
and worker's realities of time and
stress, 121–2
See also Empathy
Tuskegee experiment, 13
Twelve-step groups, 275

Two-clients construct, 11, 20, 50, 610
child and parent, 56–7, 98,
218–20, 249
client and agency, 353–7
client and community, 541–2
client and group-as-a-whole,
417, 448
client and hospital, 508–13
client and the system, 497,
499–513, 538–9
in family counseling, 218–20
and foster parent(s), 248–51,
251–3
and individual-group interaction,
280–1, 310–1, 353–7, 383, 387,
417–618, 467–8, 563–4
multiple clients and, 582–3, 584
and triangular model, 21

Unconflicted group member, 421, 610
Understanding of client's feelings.
See Tuning in
Unemployment, 14
Unfinished business, reopening, 63
Unified social work practice
theory, 50
United Way campaigns, 19
Universal perspective, and group
work, 273–4, 604
Unprofessional or unethical
conduct, 594

Values
competing, 583, 584
definition of, 580, 610
of diverse ethnic groups, 103–5, 108
in professional literature, 585
of social work profession, 580–9
social work profession core, 585
Variable-focused study, 35
Variables, measuring treatment, 601
Veteran(s), ending work with, 204
Veterans, psychiatric patients ward,
569–75
Veterans Administration Hospital,
569–75
Vicarious relief, 429
Victim complex, 30, 378, 379
Victims, warning potential, 595
Videotaping
of client's dancing, 196, 197, 198
issue, 309
observation system, 97
of practice, 124–5, 148, 293
or tape recording of issues, 316–7,
526–8
Vietnamese immigrants, women's
group, 491–2
Violations as indicators
of oppression, 30
Violence
against siblings, 373–4

against women, 34, 443–4, 456–8
in boy's group, 328–9
in family, 136, 254–5, 443–4,
456–8, 537
impact of community, 38
impact on worker(s), 203
threats of, 586–8, 595
of young men in criminal justice
system, 444
Viral loads (counts), AIDS, 294
Visitation issues, foster child, 251–2
Volunteerism, Mexican American, 105
Vulnerability
of client(s), 8, 27, 235,
463–4, 610
risk factors, 35–6
Vulnerable populations
children, 36–7
group work for, 269, 273–4

Ward group
gynecological patients, 471–3
hospital patients, 87, 290
VA psychiatric, 569–74
War Memorial Gazette (veterans'
newspaper), 574–5
Warning, duty of, 594–6, 605
Appendix A research
supplement, 73n1
Web tools
community action, 546–7
and identifiers, 593
Welfare
and housing agency, 554–62
mothers' group, 554–62
Welfare Reform Act (1996), 13, 554
Welfare reform measures, 233, 498
Wheelchair patients, 452–3
"Which side are you on" issue, 224
White, having to act black or, 74
White flight, 295, 610
White social workers. *See* Cross-
cultural practice; Race
and racism
Who owns the client?, 291, 508–13,
531–2, 610
"Agency client," 578
and staff territories, 533–6
Women
assertiveness training for, 271
endings, 187–8
family violence against, 443–4
feminist practice and, 45–8,
213–4
initial interview, 5–6
as minority group, 12
oppression of, 163, 273, 344–50
resonance between, 429
in shelter, 344–50
single parents, 56–7, 233–4,
598–9
substance abusers, 90–4